About the Cover Image

***Portrait of a Young Woman*, pastel on paper, 18th century** The artist who created this painting, who may have been the Swiss portrait painter Jean-Etienne Liotard, has depicted the confident bearing and elegant dress of what appears to be a well-to-do free woman of color. During the eighteenth century a sizable population of free people of African or mixed descent emerged in European colonies in the Americas and in port cities in southern Europe. This woman is wearing a tignon, a type of head covering that women of African descent in the French Atlantic were required by sumptuary laws to wear. The purpose of tignon laws was to enforce racial boundaries, but the head covering became a fashion statement, especially, as here, when it was combined with an elegant muslin dress, lace collar, and jewelry. Jean-Etienne Liotard (1702–1789) (previously attr. to)/Saint Louis Art Museum, Missouri, USA/Bridgeman Images

VALUE EDITION

A History of Western Society

Thirteenth Edition

Volume 2: From the Age of Exploration to the Present

Merry E. Wiesner-Hanks
University of Wisconsin–Milwaukee

Clare Haru Crowston
University of Illinois at Urbana-Champaign

Joe Perry
Georgia State University

John P. McKay
University of Illinois at Urbana-Champaign

bedford/st.martin's
Macmillan Learning

Boston | New York

FOR BEDFORD/ST. MARTIN'S

Vice President, Editorial, Macmillan Learning Humanities: Edwin Hill
Senior Program Director for History: Michael Rosenberg
Senior Executive Program Manager for History: William J. Lombardo
History Marketing Manager: Melissa Rodriguez
Director of Content Development, Humanities: Jane Knetzger
Senior Developmental Editor: Heidi L. Hood
Senior Content Project Manager: Christina M. Horn
Assistant Content Project Manager: Natalie Jones
Senior Workflow Project Manager: Jennifer Wetzel
Production Coordinator: Brianna Lester
Advanced Media Project Manager: Sarah O'Connor Kepes
Media Editor: Mary Starowicz
Editorial Assistant: Carly Lewis
Editorial Services: Lumina Datamatics, Inc.
Composition: Lumina Datamatics, Inc.
Cartographer: Mapping Specialists, Ltd.
Text Permissions Manager: Kalina Ingham
Text Permissions Editor: Mark Schaefer
Executive Permissions Editor: Robin Fadool
Photo Researcher: Bruce Carson
Director of Design, Content Management: Diana Blume
Text Design: Lumina Datamatics, Inc.
Cover Design: William Boardman
Cover Image: Jean-Étienne Liotard (1702–1789) (previously attr. to)/Saint Louis Art Museum,
    Missouri, USA/Bridgeman Images
Printing and Binding: LSC Communications

Manufactured in the United States of America.
1 2 3 4 5 6   24 23 22 21 20 19

For information, write: Bedford/St. Martin's, 75 Arlington Street, Boston, MA 02116

ISBN 978-1-319-11241-7 (Combined Edition)
ISBN 978-1-319-11245-5 (Volume 1)
ISBN 978-1-319-11243-1 (Loose-leaf Edition, Volume 1)
ISBN 978-1-319-11246-2 (Volume 2)
ISBN 978-1-319-11244-8 (Loose-leaf Edition, Volume 2)

ACKNOWLEDGMENTS

*Acknowledgments and copyrights appear on the same page as the text and art selections they cover; these
acknowledgments and copyrights constitute an extension of the copyright page.*

Preface
Why This Book This Way

We are pleased to publish the Value Edition of *A History of Western Society*, Thirteenth Edition. The Value Edition provides our signature social and cultural approach to western history in a smaller, more affordable trim size. Featuring the full narrative of the parent text and select map, images, and pedagogical tools, the Value Edition continues to incorporate the latest and best scholarship in the field in an accessible, student-friendly matter.

A History of Western Society grew out of the initial three authors' desire to infuse new life into the study of Western Civilization. The three current authors, Merry E. Wiesner-Hanks, Clare Haru Crowston, and Joe Perry, who first used the book as students or teachers and took over full responsibilities with the eleventh edition, continue to incorporate the latest and best scholarship in the field and to give special attention to the history of daily life, which has long been a popular distinction of this text. All three of us regularly teach introductory history courses and thus bring insights into the text from the classroom, as well as from new secondary works and our own research in archives and libraries.

In this new thirteenth edition we have shortened and tightened the main chapter narratives to make the overall reading experience more manageable for students. We have also focused on ways to help students think about the big picture as they read. To help students look for and understand the most important points conveyed in each chapter, **section heading questions now drive the narrative** and replace traditional section titles.

The Story of *A History of Western Society*: Bringing the Past to Life for Students

When *A History of Western Society* was first conceptualized, social history was dramatically changing the ways we understood the past, and the original authors decided to create a book that would re-create the lives of ordinary people in appealing human terms, while also giving major economic, political, cultural, and intellectual developments the attention they unquestionably deserve. The current authors remain committed to advancing this vision for today's classroom, with a broader definition of social history that brings the original vision into the twenty-first century.

History as a discipline never stands still, and over the last several decades cultural history has joined social history as a source of dynamism. Because of its emphasis on the ways people made sense of their lives, *A History of Western Society* has always included a large amount of cultural history, ranging from foundational works of philosophy and literature to popular songs and stories. We have enhanced this focus on cultural history in recent editions in a way that highlights the interplay between men's and women's lived experiences and the ways men and women reflect on these experiences to create meaning. The joint social and cultural perspective requires — fortunately, in our opinion — the inclusion of objects as well as texts as important sources for studying history, which has allowed us to incorporate the growing emphasis on material culture in the work of many historians. We know that engaging students' interest in the past is often a challenge, but we also know that the text's hallmark approach — the emphasis on daily life and individual experience in its social and cultural dimensions — connects with students and makes the past vivid and accessible.

Chapters That Humanize the Past

Because students often have trouble engaging with the past, we seek to make it more approachable in human terms. One way we do this is by discussing social and cultural history, particularly in the acclaimed **"Life" chapters**, which emphasize daily life in a particular time period. The five chapters are Chapter 4: *Life* in the Hellenistic World, 338–30 B.C.E.; Chapter 10: *Life* in Villages and Cities of the High Middle Ages, 1000–1300; Chapter 18: *Life* in the Era of Expansion, 1650–1800; Chapter 22: *Life* in the Emerging Urban Society, 1840–1914; and Chapter 30: *Life* in an Age of Globalization, 1990 to the Present.

New Coverage and Updates to the Narrative

This edition is enhanced by the incorporation of a wealth of new scholarship and subject areas that immerse students in the dynamic and ongoing work of history. Revisions to the thirteenth edition include updated coverage of the domestication of plants and animals in Chapter 1; an expanded discussion of Kush and Assyria in Chapter 2; more analysis and attention to causation in sections on epics, warfare between city-states, gender, and philosophers in Chapter 3; and more analysis of Alexander the Great's legacy, Hellenistic commerce, mystery religions, and science in Chapter 4.

Chapters 5 and 6 have been substantially revised to reflect a wealth of recent scholarship. Chapter 5 now emphasizes that Rome's greatest achievement and basis for its success was its ability to incorporate conquered peoples as Roman citizens, an insight historians of Rome have increasingly stressed in the last several decades. Chapter 5 also devotes more attention to how the Roman army was organized and how conquered land was distributed. This chapter offers more analysis of the sources for Roman history; adds a discussion of aristocratic snobbery and attitudes toward "new men"; expands coverage of the patron-client system; de-emphasizes the role of Cato in the Third Punic War; presents an entirely new view of activity in the countryside in the late republic; broadens the analysis of patterns in Roman expansion and political challenges; provides new coverage of the Marian military reforms and the Catiline conspiracy; and supplies a revised discussion of the *populares* and *optimates*. Substantial changes in Chapter 6 reflect new scholarship as well. It emphasizes the continuing role of the Senate and other Roman elites in running the empire and adds more coverage of the auxiliary forces provided by Rome's allies, cultural blending in the provinces, and the diverse nature of early Christianity.

Chapter 8 offers revised coverage of Muslims in Europe as well as Carolingian royal politics. Coverage of the Black Death in Chapter 11 has been updated to reflect recent research, including exciting insights that have come from science. Chapter 14 contains more about Portuguese exploration and settlement; new discussion of the role of Islam in the Indian Ocean world; an updated account of the Spanish conquest; and revised coverage of European ideas about race.

Chapter 16 contains an updated discussion of Muslim and Arab scientific scholarship and of how patterns of education, trade, and patronage led the Scientific Revolution to take place in Europe rather elsewhere in the world. Chapter 17 includes information about important changes in financial systems and in thinking about governmental regulation of the economy, as well as an expanded section about Adam Smith and the emergence of the discipline of "political economy" in this period. Chapter 18 supplies new material on contraception methods in the eighteenth century and on attitudes toward miscarriage and abortion. Chapter 21 includes expanded coverage of Utopian socialism, Tories and Whigs, the Peterloo Massacre, and the Irish famine.

The reorganization of Chapters 22 and 23 made room for new and expanded coverage. Chapter 22 supplies a new and updated discussion of middle-class professionalization, an expanded discussion of the advent of the public health movement in London, and additional information about religion among the working classes. Chapter 23 includes more about the costs and benefits for ordinary people of the newly established responsive national states; new coverage of Florence Nightingale in the Crimean War; and new material and updated scholarship on Louis Napoleon and the Second Empire, the emergence of the British Liberal Party, Karl Lueger and anti-Semitism in Vienna, and pogroms in the Pale of Settlement.

A new section in Chapter 24 offers extended material about the immigrant experience in the United States. It also includes an expanded discussion of King Leopold's Congo Free State and updated material on British intervention in Egypt before World War I, Asian immigration and passport controls, the Berlin Conference, and German colonial war. Chapter 25 includes new material and updated scholarship on Wilhelm II's character, the First and Second Moroccan Crises, and Austro-Hungarian occupation of Serbia. Chapter 26 adds a new title and additional material to explain the changes associated with the consolidation of modernism and modernity in the decades around 1900. Chapter 30 includes updates and new information about populism, Russian interference in U.S. elections, the politics of Internet privacy, and American relations with the European Union under the Trump administration.

Helping Students Understand and Engage with the Narrative

We know firsthand and take seriously the challenges students face in understanding, retaining, and mastering so much material that is often unfamiliar. With the goal of making this the most student-centered edition yet, we have enhanced the text with new pedagogy and tools designed to prompt active reading and comprehension of the continuities and changes that are the driving forces of historical development. Our book now has a wealth of pedagogical aids that help students understand where they are going in their reading and where they have been. To focus students' reading, questions now drive the narrative. Not only does each chapter open with **a chapter preview that poses questions**, but **each major heading is now one of these questions**. These questions are repeated again in the **"Review & Explore" section** at the end of each chapter.

To help students understand the bigger picture, each chapter includes **"Looking Back, Looking Ahead" conclusions** that provide an insightful synthesis of the chapter's main developments, while connecting to events that students will encounter in the chapters to come. In this way students are introduced to history as an ongoing process of interrelated events. These conclusions are followed by **"Make Connections" questions** that prompt students to assess larger developments across chapters, thus allowing them to develop skills in evaluating change and continuity, making comparisons, and analyzing context and causation.

To help students prepare for exams, in addition to repeating the major section heading questions in **"Review the Main Ideas,"** each "Chapter Review" section includes an **"Identify Key Terms"** prompt, as well as a **"Chronology"** table that collects key dates from the chapter and helps students make connections among events. To promote clarity and comprehension, boldface **key terms** in the text are listed in the chapter review and collected in the **Glossary** at the end of the book. **Phonetic spellings** are located directly after terms that readers are likely to find hard to pronounce.

We are also proud of the text's high-quality art and map program, which has been thoroughly revised and features more than a hundred **contemporaneous illustrations** (30 percent new). As in earlier editions, all illustrations have been carefully selected to complement the text, and all include captions that inform students while encouraging them to read the text more deeply. High-quality **full-size maps** contextualize major developments in the narrative.

In addition, whenever an instructor assigns the **Achieve Read & Practice e-book** (which is free when bundled with the print book), students get an easy-to-use, affordable, and accessible e-book with full access to **LearningCurve**, an online adaptive learning tool that promotes mastery of the book's content and diagnoses students' trouble spots. With this adaptive quizzing, students accumulate points toward a target score as they go, giving the interaction a game-like feel. Feedback for incorrect responses explains why the answer is incorrect and directs students back to the text to review before they attempt to answer the question again. The end result is a better understanding of the key elements of the text. Instructors who actively assign LearningCurve report that their students come to class prepared for discussion and their students enjoy using it. In addition, LearningCurve's reporting feature allows instructors to quickly diagnose which concepts students are struggling with so they can adjust lectures and activities accordingly.

Helping Instructors Teach with Digital Resources

As noted, instructors who simply want an auto-graded tool that will ensure that students read the narrative before they come to class, mobile-ready and accessible **Achieve Read & Practice for *A History of Western Society*** offers an exceptionally easy-to-use and affordable option. This simple product pairs the Value Edition e-book—the two-color narrative-only text (no boxed features or sources and fewer visuals)—with the power of **LearningCurve** quizzing, all in a format that is mobile-friendly, allowing students to read and take quizzes on the reading on the device of their choosing.

For instructors who want an e-book with a full suite of primary sources and autograded assessments for the narrative and sources, *A History of Western Society* is offered in Macmillan Learning's premier learning platform, **LaunchPad**, an intuitive, interactive e-book and course space. Free when packaged with the print book or available at a low price when used on its own, LaunchPad grants students and teachers access to a wealth of online tools and resources built specifically for this text to enhance reading comprehension and promote in-depth study. LaunchPad's course space and interactive e-book are ready to use "as is," or they can be edited and customized with the instructor's own materials and assigned right away.

Developed with extensive feedback from history instructors and students, **LaunchPad for *A History of Western Society*** includes the complete narrative and special features of the comprehensive edition print book plus the companion reader, *Sources for Western Society*; and **LearningCurve**, an adaptive learning tool that is designed to get students to read before they come to class. With **source-based questions in the test bank and in LearningCurve**, instructors now have multiple ways to test students on their understanding of the narrative and sources.

This edition also includes **Guided Reading Exercises** that prompt students to be active readers of the chapter narrative and auto-graded **primary source quizzes** to test comprehension of written and visual sources. These features, plus **additional primary source documents, video sources and tools for making video assignments, map activities, flashcards, and customizable test banks**, make LaunchPad a great asset for any instructor who wants to enliven the history of Western Civilization for students.

These new directions have not changed the central mission of the book, which is to introduce students to the broad sweep of Western Civilization in a fresh yet balanced manner. Every edition has incorporated new research to keep the book up-to-date and respond to the changing needs of readers and instructors, and we have continued to do this in the thirteenth edition. As we have made these changes, large and small, we have sought to give students and teachers an integrated perspective so that they can pursue—on their own or in the classroom—the historical questions that they find particularly exciting and significant. To learn more about the benefits of LearningCurve and LaunchPad, see the "Versions and Supplements" section on page xi.

Acknowledgments

It is a pleasure to thank the instructors who read and critiqued the book in preparation for its revision:

Lisa Balabanlilar, *Rice University*; Peter Robert Dear, *Cornell University*; Fred M. Donner, *University of Chicago*; Alex d'Erizans, *Borough of Manhattan Community College*; Jacqueline deVries, *Augsburg University*; Arthur Eckstein, *University of Maryland*; Antonio Feros, *University of Pennsylvania*; Michelle Llyn Ferry, *Coastline Community College*; Jennifer L. Foray, *Purdue University*; Linda Frey, *University of Montana*; Peter Fritzsche, *University of Illinois at Urbana-Champaign*; Jane Hathaway, *Ohio State University*; Toby Huff, *Harvard University*; Robert L.

Janda, *Cameron University*; Julie Langford, *University of South Florida*; Leslie S. Leighton, *Georgia State University*; J. Michael Long, *Front Range Community College*; John F. Lyons, *Joliet Junior College*; Joseph Manning, *Yale University*; Tim Myers, *Butler County Community College*; Graham Oliver, *Brown University*; Gesche Peters, *Dawson College*; Julie M. Powell, *Ohio State University*; Sheila A. Redmond, *Algoma University*; Matthew Restall, *Pennsylvania State University*; William B. Robison, *Southeastern Louisiana University*; Annette Timm, *University of Calgary*; Sherry Hardin Turille, *Cape Fear Community College*; Luke Yarbrough, *St. Louis University*

It is also a pleasure to thank the many editors who have assisted us over the years, first at Houghton Mifflin and now at Bedford/St. Martin's (Macmillan Learning). At Bedford/St. Martin's these include senior development editor Heidi Hood, senior content project manager Christina Horn, assistant content project manager Natalie Jones, media editor Mary Starowicz, editorial assistant Carly Lewis, senior executive program manager William Lombardo, and senior program director Michael Rosenberg. Other key contributors were photo researcher Bruce Carson, text permissions researcher Mark Schaefer, copy editor Susan Zorn, proofreader Julie Kennedy, indexer Leoni McVey, and cover designer William Boardman.

Many of our colleagues at the University of Illinois, the University of Wisconsin–Milwaukee, and Georgia State University continue to provide information and stimulation, often without even knowing it. We thank them for it. We also thank the many students over the years with whom we have used earlier editions of this book. Their reactions and opinions helped shape the revisions to this edition, and we hope it remains worthy of the ultimate praise that they bestowed on it: that it's "not boring like most textbooks." Merry Wiesner-Hanks would, as always, also like to thank her husband, Neil, without whom work on this project would not be possible. Clare Haru Crowston thanks her husband, Ali, and her children, Lili, Reza, and Kian, who are a joyous reminder of the vitality of life that we try to showcase in this book. Joe Perry thanks his colleagues and students at Georgia State for their intellectual stimulation and is grateful to Joyce de Vries for her unstinting support and encouragement.

Each of us has benefited from the criticism of our coauthors, although each of us assumes responsibility for what he or she has written and revised. Merry Wiesner-Hanks takes responsibility for Chapters 1–13; Clare takes responsibility for Chapters 14–20; and Joe Perry takes responsibility for Chapters 21–30.

We'd especially like to thank the founding authors, John P. McKay, Bennett D. Hill, and John Buckler, for their enduring contributions and for their faith in each of us to carry on their legacy.

MERRY E. WIESNER-HANKS
CLARE HARU CROWSTON
JOE PERRY

Versions and Supplements

Adopters of *A History of Western Society* and their students have access to abundant print and digital resources and tools, the acclaimed *Bedford Series in History and Culture* volumes, and much more. Achieve Read & Practice supplies adaptive quizzing and our mobile, accessible Value Edition e-book in one easy-to-use, affordable product. The LaunchPad course space for *A History of Western Society* provides access to the comprehensive edition e-book with its wealth of primary sources and other features, along with assignment and assessment opportunities at the ready. See below for more information, visit the book's catalog site at macmillanlearning.com, or contact your local Bedford/St. Martin's representative.

Get the Right Version for Your Class

To accommodate different course lengths and course budgets, *A History of Western Society* is available in several different versions and formats to best suit your course needs. The comprehensive *A History of Western Society* includes a full-color art program and a robust set of features. *A History of Western Society*, Concise Edition, also provides the full narrative in full color, with a streamlined art and feature program, at a lower price. *A History of Western Society*, Value Edition, offers a trade-sized two-color option with the full narrative and selected art and maps at a steep discount. The Value Edition is also offered at the lowest price point in loose-leaf format, and all of these versions are available as e-books. To get the best values of all, package a new print book with Achieve Read & Practice or LaunchPad at no additional charge to get the best each format offers. Achieve Read & Practice users get a print version for easy portability with a mobile, interactive Value Edition e-book plus LearningCurve adaptive quizzing in one exceptionally affordable, easy-to-use product; LaunchPad users get a print version plus an interactive e-book of the full-feature text, including a multitude of primary sources and the companion reader, along with LearningCurve and loads of additional assignment and assessment options all in one course space.

- **Combined Edition** (Chapters 1–30): available in paperback, Concise Edition, Value Edition, loose-leaf, and e-book formats and in LaunchPad and Achieve Read & Practice
- **Volume 1, From Antiquity to the Enlightenment** (Chapters 1–16): available in paperback, Concise Edition, Value Edition, loose-leaf, and e-book formats and in LaunchPad and Achieve Read & Practice
- **Volume 2, From the Age of Exploration to the Present** (Chapters 14–30): available in paperback, Concise Edition, Value Edition, loose-leaf, and e-book formats and in LaunchPad and Achieve Read & Practice
- **Since 1300** (Chapters 11–30): available in paperback and e-book formats and in LaunchPad and Achieve Read & Practice

As noted below, any of these volumes can be packaged with additional titles for a discount. To get ISBNs for discount packages, visit **macmillanlearning.com** or contact your Bedford/St. Martin's representative.

Achie✓e READ & PRACTICE Assign Achieve Read & Practice So Your Students Can Read and Study Wherever They Go

Available for discount purchase on its own or for packaging with new survey books at no additional charge, Achieve Read & Practice is Bedford/St. Martin's most affordable digital solution for history courses. Intuitive and easy to use for students and instructors alike, Achieve Read & Practice is ready to use as is and can be assigned quickly. Achieve Read & Practice for *A History of Western Society* includes the Value Edition interactive e-book, LearningCurve adaptive quizzing, assignment tools, and a gradebook. Through the adaptive learning program of LearningCurve (see the full description ahead), students gain confidence and get into their reading before class. All this is built with an intuitive interface that can be read on mobile devices and is fully accessible, easily integrates with course management systems, and is available at a discounted price so anyone can use it. Instructors can set due dates for reading assignments and LearningCurve quizzes in just a few clicks, making it a simple and affordable way to engage students with the narrative and hold students accountable for course reading so they will come to class better prepared. For more information, visit **macmillanlearning.com/ReadandPractice**, or to arrange a demo, contact us at **historymktg@macmillan.com**.

LearningCurve macmillan learning Assign LearningCurve So Your Students Come to Class Prepared

Students using LaunchPad or Achieve Read & Practice receive access to Learning-Curve for *A History of Western Society*. Assigning LearningCurve in place of reading quizzes is easy for instructors, and the reporting features help instructors track overall class trends and spot topics that are giving students trouble so they can adjust their lectures and class activities. This online learning tool is popular with students because it was designed to help them rehearse content at their own pace in a nonthreatening, game-like environment. The feedback for wrong answers provides instructional coaching and sends students back to the book for review. Students answer as many questions as necessary to reach a target score, with repeated chances to revisit material they haven't mastered. When LearningCurve is assigned, students come to class better prepared.

LaunchPad macmillan learning Assign LaunchPad—an Assessment-Ready Interactive E-book with Sources and Course Space

Available for discount purchase on its own or for packaging with new survey books at no additional charge, LaunchPad is a breakthrough solution for history courses. Intuitive and easy to use for students and instructors alike, LaunchPad is ready to use as is and can be edited, customized with your own material, and assigned quickly.

LaunchPad for *A History of Western Society* includes Bedford/St. Martin's high-quality content all in one place, including the full interactive e-book and the companion reader *Sources for Western Society*, plus LearningCurve adaptive quizzing, guided reading activities designed to help students read actively for key concepts, auto-graded quizzes for each primary source, and chapter summative quizzes. Through a wealth of formative and summative assessments, including the adaptive learning program of LearningCurve (see the full description ahead), students gain confidence and get into their reading before class. These features, plus additional primary source documents, video sources and tools for making video assignments, map activities, flashcards, and customizable test banks, make LaunchPad an invaluable asset for any instructor.

LaunchPad easily integrates with course management systems, and with fast ways to build assignments, rearrange chapters, and add new pages, sections, or links, it lets teachers build the courses they want to teach and hold students accountable. For more information, visit launchpadworks.com, or to arrange a demo, contact us at historymktg@macmillan.com.

Tailor Your Text to Match Your Course with Bedford Select for History

Create the ideal textbook for your course with only the chapters you need. Starting from the Value Edition version of the text, you can delete and rearrange chapters, select chapters of primary sources from *Sources for Western Society* and add additional primary sources, curated skills tutorials, or your own original content to create just the book you're looking for. With Bedford Select, students pay only for material that will be assigned in the course, and nothing more. It is easy to build your customized textbook, without compromising the quality and affordability you've come to expect from Bedford/St. Martin's. For more information, talk to your Bedford/St. Martin's representative or visit macmillanlearning.com/bedfordselect.

▷ iClicker iClicker, Active Learning Simplified

iClicker offers simple, flexible tools to help you give students a voice and facilitate active learning in the classroom. Students can participate with the devices they already bring to class using our iClicker Reef mobile apps (which work with smartphones, tablets, or laptops) or iClicker remotes. iClicker Reef access cards can also be packaged with LaunchPad or your textbook at a significant savings for your students. To learn more, talk to your Macmillan Learning (Bedford/St. Martin's) representative or visit www.iclicker.com.

Take Advantage of Instructor Resources

Bedford/St. Martin's has developed a rich array of teaching resources for this book and for this course. They range from lecture and presentation materials and assessment tools to course management options. Most can be found in LaunchPad or can be downloaded or ordered at macmillanlearning.com.

Bedford Coursepack for Blackboard, Canvas, Brightspace by D2L, or Moodle. We can help you integrate our rich content into your course management system. Registered instructors can download coursepacks that include our popular free resources and book-specific content for *A History of Western Society*. Visit macmillanlearning.com to find your version or download your coursepack.

Instructor's Resource Manual. The instructor's manual offers both experienced and first-time instructors tools for presenting textbook material in engaging ways. It includes content learning objectives, annotated chapter outlines, and strategies for teaching with the textbook, plus suggestions on how to get the most out of Learning-Curve and a survival guide for first-time teaching assistants.

Guide to Changing Editions. Designed to facilitate an instructor's transition from the previous edition of *A History of Western Society* to this new edition, this guide presents an overview of major changes as well as of changes in each chapter.

Online Test Bank. The test bank includes a mix of fresh, carefully crafted multiple-choice, matching, short-answer, and essay questions for each chapter. Many of the multiple-choice questions feature a map, an image, or a primary source excerpt as the prompt. All questions appear in Microsoft Word format and in easy-to-use test bank software that allows instructors to add, edit, re-sequence, filter by question type or learning objective, and print questions and answers. Instructors can also export questions into a variety of course management systems.

The Bedford Lecture Kit: *Lecture Outlines, Maps, and Images.* Look good and save time with *The Bedford Lecture Kit*. These presentation materials include fully customizable multimedia presentations built around chapter outlines that are embedded with maps, figures, and images from the textbook and are supplemented by more detailed instructor notes on key points and concepts.

Print, Digital, and Custom Options for More Choice and Value

For information on free packages and discounts up to 50%, visit macmillanlearning .com, or contact your local Bedford/St. Martin's representative.

Sources for Western Society, *Thirteenth Edition.* This primary source collection — available in Volume 1, Volume 2, and Since 1300 versions — provides a revised selection of sources to accompany *A History of Western Society*, Thirteenth Edition. Each chapter features five or six written and visual sources by well-known figures and ordinary individuals alike. With over thirty new selections — including several new visual sources — and enhanced pedagogy throughout, this book gives students the tools to engage critically with canonical and lesser-known sources and prominent and ordinary voices. Each chapter includes a "Sources in Conversation" feature that presents differing views on key topics. This companion reader is an exceptional value for students and offers plenty of assignment options for instructors. Available free when packaged with the print text and included in the LaunchPad e-book with auto-graded quizzes for each source. Also available on its own as a downloadable e-book.

Bedford Select for History. Create the ideal textbook for your course with only the chapters you need. Starting from a Value Edition history text, you can rearrange chapters, delete unnecessary chapters, select chapters of primary sources from the companion reader and add primary source document projects from the Bedford Document Collections, or choose to improve your students' historical thinking skills with the Bedford Tutorials for History. In addition, you can add your own original content to create just the book you're looking for. With Bedford Select, students pay only for material that will be assigned in the course, and nothing more. Order your textbook every semester, or modify from one term to the next. It is easy to build your customized textbook, without compromising the quality and affordability you've come to expect from Bedford/St. Martin's.

Bedford Document Collections. These affordable, brief document projects provide 5 to 7 primary sources, an introduction, historical background, and other pedagogical features. Each curated project — designed for use in a single class period and written by a historian about a favorite topic — poses a historical question and guides students through analysis of the sources. Examples include: "Premodern Trade: Doing Business in the Land of Pepper," "The Spread of Christianity in the Sixteenth and Early Seventeenth Centuries," "Absolutism in Practice: Louis XIV, Versailles, and the Art of Personal Kingship," "Pirates and Empire in the Seventeenth-Century Atlantic World," and "Living through Perestroika: The Soviet Union in Upheaval, 1985–1991." These primary source projects are available in a low-cost, easy-to-use digital format or can be combined with other course materials in Bedford Select to create an affordable, personalized print product.

Bedford Tutorials for History. Designed to customize textbooks with resources relevant to individual courses, this collection of brief units, each 16 pages long and loaded with examples, guides students through basic skills such as using historical evidence effectively, working with primary sources, taking effective notes, avoiding plagiarism and citing sources, and more. Up to two tutorials can be added to a Bedford/St. Martin's history survey title at no additional charge, freeing you to spend your class time focusing on content and interpretation. For more information, visit macmillanlearning.com/historytutorials.

The Bedford Series in History and Culture. More than 100 titles in this highly praised series combine first-rate scholarship, historical narrative, and important primary documents for undergraduate courses. Each book is brief, inexpensive, and focused on a specific topic or period. Revisions of several popular titles, such as *Spartacus and the Slave Wars: A Brief History with Documents*, by Brent D. Shaw; *The Scientific Revolution: A Brief History with Documents*, by Margaret C. Jacob; THE COMMUNIST MANIFESTO *by Karl Marx and Frederick Engels with Related Documents*, edited by John E. Toews; *The Nuremberg War Crimes Trial, 1945–46: A Brief History with Documents*, by Michael R. Marrus, are now available. For a complete list of titles, visit macmillanlearning.com. Package discounts are available.

Rand McNally Atlas of World History. This collection of almost 70 full-color maps illustrates the eras and civilizations in world history from the emergence of human societies to the present. Free when packaged.

The Bedford Glossary for World History. This handy supplement for the survey course gives students historically contextualized definitions for hundreds of terms—from *abolitionism* to *Zoroastrianism*—that they will encounter in lectures, reading, and exams. Free when packaged.

Trade Books. Titles published by sister companies Hill and Wang; Farrar, Straus and Giroux; Henry Holt and Company; St. Martin's Press; Picador; and Palgrave Macmillan are available at a 50% discount when packaged with Bedford/St. Martin's textbooks. For more information, visit macmillanlearning.com/tradeup.

A Pocket Guide to Writing in History. Updated to reflect changes made in the 2017 *Chicago Manual of Style* revision, this portable and affordable reference tool by Mary Lynn Rampolla provides reading, writing, and research advice useful to students in all history courses. Concise yet comprehensive advice on approaching typical history assignments, developing critical reading skills, writing effective history papers, conducting research, using and documenting sources, and avoiding plagiarism—enhanced with practical tips and examples throughout—has made this slim reference a best seller. Package discounts are available.

A Student's Guide to History. This complete guide to success in any history course provides the practical help students need to be successful. In addition to introducing students to the nature of the discipline, author Jules Benjamin teaches a wide range of skills, from preparing for exams to approaching common writing assignments, and explains the research and documentation process with plentiful examples. Package discounts are available.

Brief Contents

Contents

CHAPTER 14

European Exploration and Conquest, 1450–1650   382

CHAPTER 20

CHAPTER 21

CHAPTER 22

Life in the Emerging Urban Society, 1840–1914 645

CHAPTER 23

The Age of Nationalism, 1850–1914 678

CHAPTER 24

The West and the World, 1815–1914   715

CHAPTER 25

War and Revolution, 1914–1919   748

CHAPTER 26

Opportunity and Crisis in the Age of Modernity, 1880–1940   784

CHAPTER 27

Dictatorships and the Second World War, 1919–1945   815

CHAPTER 28

Cold War Conflict and Consensus, 1945–1965   854

CHAPTER 29

Challenging the Postwar Order, 1960–1991   890

Maps, Figures, and Tables

Introduction
The Origins of Modern Western Society

The notion of "the West" has ancient origins. Greek civilization grew up in the shadow of earlier civilizations to the south and east of Greece, especially Egypt and Mesopotamia. Greeks defined themselves in relation to these more advanced cultures, which they lumped together as "the East." They passed this conceptualization on to the Romans, who in turn transmitted it to the peoples of western and northern Europe. When Europeans established overseas colonies in the late fifteenth century, they believed they were taking Western culture with them, even though many of its elements, such as Christianity, had originated in what Europeans by that point regarded as the East. Throughout history, the meaning of "the West" has shifted, but in every era it has meant more than a geographical location.

The Ancient World

The ancient world provided several cultural elements that the modern world has inherited. First came the traditions of the Hebrews, especially their religion, Judaism, with its belief in one god and in themselves as a chosen people. The Hebrews developed their religious ideas in books that were later brought together in the Hebrew Bible, which Christians term the Old Testament. Second, Greek architectural, philosophical, and scientific ideas have exercised a profound influence on Western thought. Third, Rome provided the Latin language, the instrument of verbal and written communication for more than a thousand years, and concepts of law and government that molded Western ideas of political organization. Finally, Christianity, the spiritual faith and ecclesiastical organization that derived from the life and teachings of a Jewish man, Jesus of Nazareth, also came to condition Western religious, social, and moral values and systems.

The Hebrews

The Hebrews were nomadic pastoralists who may have migrated into the Nile Delta from the east, seeking good land for their herds of sheep and goats. According to the Hebrew Bible, they were enslaved by the Egyptians but were led out of Egypt by a charismatic leader named Moses. The Hebrews settled in the area between the Mediterranean and the Jordan River known as Canaan. They were organized into tribes, each tribe consisting of numerous families who thought of themselves as all related to one another and having a common ancestor.

In Canaan, the nomadic Hebrews encountered a variety of other peoples, whom they both learned from and fought. The Bible reports that the inspired leader Saul established a monarchy over the twelve Hebrew tribes and that the kingdom grew under the leadership of King David. David's successor, Solomon (r. ca. 965–925 B.C.E.), launched a building program including cities, palaces, fortresses, roads, and a temple at Jerusalem, which became the symbol of Hebrew unity. This unity did not last long, however, as at Solomon's death his kingdom broke into two separate states, Israel and Judah.

In their migration, the Hebrews had come in contact with many peoples, such as the Mesopotamians and the Egyptians, who had many gods. The Hebrews came to believe in a single god, Yahweh, who had created all things and who took a strong personal interest in the individual. According to the Bible, Yahweh made a covenant with the Hebrews: if they worshipped Yahweh as their only god, he would consider them his chosen people and protect them from their enemies. This covenant was to prove a constant force in the Hebrews' religion, Judaism, a word taken from the kingdom of Judah.

Worship was embodied in a series of rules of behavior, the Ten Commandments, which Yahweh gave to Moses. These required certain kinds of religious observances and forbade the Hebrews to steal, lie, murder, or commit adultery, thus creating a system of ethical absolutes. From the Ten Commandments a complex system of rules of conduct was created and later written down as Hebrew law, beginning with the Torah—the first five books of the Hebrew Bible. Hebrew Scripture, a group of books written over many centuries, also contained history, hymns of praise, prophecy, traditions, advice, and other sorts of writings. Jews today revere these texts, as do many Christians, and Muslims respect them, all of which gives them particular importance.

The Greeks

The people of ancient Greece built on the traditions and ideas of earlier societies to develop a culture that fundamentally shaped Western civilization. Drawing on their day-to-day experiences as well as logic and empirical observation, the Greeks developed ways of understanding and explaining the world around them, which grew into modern philosophy and science. They also created new political forms, including the small independent city-state known as the *polis*. Scholars label the period dating from around 1100 B.C.E. to 323 B.C.E., in which the polis predominated, the Hellenic period. Two poleis were especially powerful: Sparta, which created a military state in which men remained in the army most of their lives, and Athens, which created a democracy in which male citizens had a direct voice.

Athens created a brilliant culture, with magnificent art and architecture whose grace and beauty still speak to people. In their comedies and tragedies, Athenians Aeschylus, Sophocles, and Euripides were the first playwrights to treat eternal problems of the human condition. Athens also experimented with the political system we call democracy. Greek democracy meant the rule of citizens, not "the people" as a whole, and citizenship was generally limited to free adult men whose parents were citizens. Women were citizens for religious and reproductive purposes, but their citizenship did not give them the right to participate in government. Slaves, resident foreigners, and free men who were not children of a citizen were not citizens and had no political voice. Thus ancient Greek democracy did not reflect the modern concept that all people are created equal, but it did permit male citizens to share in determining the diplomatic and military policies of the polis.

Classical Greece of the fifth and fourth centuries B.C.E. also witnessed an incredible flowering of philosophical ideas. Some Greeks began to question their old beliefs and myths, and sought rational rather than supernatural explanations for natural phenomena. They began an intellectual revolution with the idea that nature was predictable, creating what we now call philosophy and science. These ideas also emerged in medicine: Hippocrates, the most prominent physician and teacher of medicine of his time, sought natural explanations for diseases and natural means to treat them.

The Sophists, a group of thinkers in fifth-century-B.C.E. Athens, applied philosophical speculation to politics and language, questioning the beliefs and laws of the polis to understand their origin. They believed that excellence in both politics and language could be taught, and they provided lessons for the young men of Athens who wished to learn how to persuade others in the often-tumultuous Athenian democracy.

Socrates (ca. 470–399 B.C.E.), whose ideas are known only through the works of others, also applied philosophy to politics and to people. Because he posed questions rather than giving answers, it is difficult to say exactly what Socrates thought about many things, although he does seem to have felt that through knowledge people could approach the supreme good and thus find happiness. Most of what we know about Socrates comes from his student Plato (427–347 B.C.E.), who wrote dialogues in which Socrates asks questions and who also founded the Academy, a school dedicated to philosophy. Plato developed the theory that there are two worlds: the impermanent, changing world that we know through our senses, and the eternal, unchanging realm of "forms" that constitute the essence of true reality. According to Plato, true knowledge and the possibility of living a virtuous life come from contemplating ideal forms. Plato's student Aristotle (384–322 B.C.E.) also thought that true knowledge was possible, but he believed that such knowledge came from observation of the world, analysis of natural phenomena, and logical reasoning, not contemplation. He investigated the nature of government, ideas of matter and motion, outer space, ethics, and language and literature, among other subjects. Aristotle's ideas later profoundly shaped both Muslim and Western philosophy and theology.

Echoing the broader culture, Plato and Aristotle viewed philosophy as an exchange between men in which women had no part. The ideal for Athenian citizen women was a secluded life, although how far this ideal was actually a reality is impossible to know. Women in citizen families probably spent most of their time at home, leaving the house only to attend religious festivals and perhaps occasionally plays.

Greek political and intellectual advances took place against a background of constant warfare. The long and bitter struggle between the cities of Athens and Sparta called the Peloponnesian War (431–404 B.C.E.) ended in Athens's defeat. Shortly afterward, Sparta, Athens, and Thebes contested for hegemony in Greece, but no single state was strong enough to dominate the others. Taking advantage of the situation, Philip II (r. 359–336 B.C.E.) of Macedonia, a small kingdom encompassing part of modern Greece and other parts of the Balkans, defeated a combined Theban-Athenian army in 338 B.C.E. Unable to resolve their domestic quarrels, the Greeks lost their freedom to the Macedonian invader.

Philip was assassinated just two years after he had conquered Greece, and his throne was inherited by his son, Alexander. In twelve years, Alexander conquered an empire stretching from Macedonia across the Middle East into Asia as far as India. He established cities and military colonies in strategic spots as he advanced eastward, but he died at the age of thirty-two while planning his next campaign.

Alexander left behind an empire that quickly broke into smaller kingdoms, but more important, his death ushered in an era, the Hellenistic, in which Greek culture, the Greek language, and Greek thought spread widely, blending with local traditions. The Hellenistic period stretches from Alexander's death in 323 B.C.E. to the Roman conquest in 30 B.C.E. of the kingdom established in Egypt by Alexander's successors. Greek immigrants moved to the cities and colonies established by Alexander and his successors, spreading the Greek language, ideas, and traditions in a process scholars later called Hellenization. Local people who wanted to rise in wealth or status learned Greek. The economic and cultural connections of the Hellenistic world later proved valuable to the Romans, allowing them to trade products and ideas more easily over a broad area.

The mixing of peoples in the Hellenistic era influenced religion, philosophy, and science. The Hellenistic kings built temples to the old Greek gods and promoted rituals and ceremonies that honored them, but new deities, such as Tyche—the goddess and personification of luck, fate, chance, and fortune—also gained prominence. More people turned to mystery religions, which blended Greek and non-Greek elements and offered their adherents secret knowledge, unification with a deity, and sometimes life after death. Others turned to practical philosophies that provided advice on how to live a good life. These included Epicureanism, which advocated moderation to achieve a life of contentment, and Stoicism, which advocated living in accordance with nature. In the scholarly realm, Hellenistic thinkers made advances in mathematics, astronomy, and mechanical design. Additionally, physicians used observation and dissection to better understand the way the human body works.

Despite the new ideas, the Hellenistic period did not see widespread improvements in the way most people lived and worked. Cities flourished, but many people who lived in rural areas were actually worse off than they had been before, because of higher levels of rents and taxes. Technology was applied to military needs, but not to the production of food or other goods.

The Greek world was largely conquered by the Romans, and the various Hellenistic monarchies became part of the Roman Empire. In cultural terms the lines of conquest were reversed, however, as the Romans were tremendously influenced by Greek art, philosophy, and ideas, all of which have had a lasting impact on the modern world as well.

Rome: From Republic to Empire

The city of Rome, situated near the center of the boot-shaped peninsula of Italy, conquered all of Italy, then the western Mediterranean basin, and then areas in the east that had been part of Alexander's empire, creating an empire that at its largest stretched from England to Egypt and from Portugal to Persia. The Romans spread the Latin language throughout much of their empire, providing a common language for verbal and written communication for more than a thousand years. They also established concepts of law and government that molded Western legal systems, ideas of political organization, and administrative practices.

The city of Rome developed from small villages and was influenced by the Etruscans who lived to the north. Sometime in the sixth century B.C.E. a group of aristocrats revolted against the ruling king and established a republican form of government in which the main institution of power was the Senate, an assembly of aristocrats, rather than a single monarch. According to tradition, this happened in 509 B.C.E., so scholars customarily divide Roman history into two primary stages: the republic, from 509 to 27 B.C.E., in which Rome was ruled by the Senate; and the empire, from 27 B.C.E. to 476 C.E., in which Roman territories were ruled by an emperor.

In the years following the establishment of the republic, the Romans fought numerous wars with their neighbors on the Italian peninsula. Their superior military institutions, organization, and manpower allowed them to conquer or take into their influence most of Italy by about 265 B.C.E. Once they had conquered an area, the Romans built roads and often shared Roman citizenship, which made them different from other ancient peoples and was one of Rome's greatest achievements. Rome was thus a multiethnic society from the start, able to inspire loyalty to Rome in many different peoples.

Roman expansion continued. In a series of wars they conquered lands all around the Mediterranean, creating an overseas empire that brought them unheard-of power and wealth. First they defeated the Carthaginians in the Punic Wars, and then they turned east. Declaring the Mediterranean *mare nostrum*, "our sea," the Romans began to create a political and administrative machinery to hold the Mediterranean together under a mutually shared cultural and political system of provinces ruled by governors sent from Rome.

The Romans created several assemblies through which men elected high officials and passed ordinances. The most important of these was the Senate, a political assembly — initially only of hereditary aristocrats called patricians — that advised officials and handled government finances. The common people of Rome, known as plebeians, were initially excluded from holding offices or sitting in the Senate, but a long political and social struggle led to a broadening of the base of political power to include male plebeians. The basis of Roman society for both patricians and plebeians was the family, headed by the paterfamilias, who held authority over his wife, children, and servants. Households often included slaves, who also provided labor for fields and mines.

A lasting achievement of the Romans was their development of law. Roman civil law consisted of statutes, customs, and forms of procedure that regulated the lives of citizens. As the Romans came into more frequent contact with foreigners, Roman officials applied a broader "law of the peoples," to such matters as peace treaties, the treatment of prisoners of war, and the exchange of diplomats. All sides were to be treated the same regardless of their nationality. By the late republic, Roman jurists had widened this still further into the concept of natural law based in part on Stoic ideas they had learned from Greek thinkers. Natural law, according to these thinkers, is made up of rules that govern human behavior that come from applying reason rather than customs or traditions, and so apply to all societies. In reality, Roman officials generally interpreted the law to the advantage of Rome, of course, at least to the extent that the strength of Roman armies allowed them to enforce it. But Roman law came to be seen as one of the most important contributions Rome made to the development of Western civilization.

Law was not the only facet of Hellenistic Greek culture to influence the Romans. The Roman conquest of the Hellenistic East led to the wholesale confiscation of Greek sculpture and paintings to adorn Roman temples and homes. Greek literary and historical classics were translated into Latin; Greek philosophy was studied in the Roman schools; educated people learned Greek as well as Latin as a matter of course. Public baths based on the Greek model—with exercise rooms, swimming pools, and reading rooms—served not only as centers for recreation and exercise but also as centers of Roman public life.

The wars of conquest eventually created serious political problems for the Romans, which surfaced toward the end of the second century B.C.E. Ever-larger armies had to be recruited to defend Rome's larger territory, which cost more money and thus required higher taxes to support them. Roman generals, who commanded huge numbers of troops for long periods of time, acquired great power and ambition and were becoming too mighty for the Senate to control. The spoils of war seemed to many people to be unevenly distributed, with military contractors and those who collected taxes profiting greatly, while average soldiers gained little. Despite the losses due to foreign wars, the population of the countryside grew, and many people migrated to Rome in search of work and food. The city of Rome grew dramatically, and the landless poor in the city tended to back anyone who offered them better prospects than the Senate did. Rome divided into political factions, each of which named a supreme military commander, who led Roman troops against external enemies but also against each other. Civil war erupted.

Out of the violence and disorder emerged Julius Caesar (100–44 B.C.E.), a victorious general, shrewd politician, and highly popular figure. He took practical steps to end the civil war, such as expanding citizenship and sending large numbers of the urban poor to found colonies and spread Roman culture in Gaul, Spain, and North Africa. Fearful that Caesar's popularity and ambition would turn Rome into a monarchy, a group of aristocratic conspirators assassinated him in 44 B.C.E. Civil war was renewed. In 31 B.C.E. Caesar's grandnephew and adopted son Octavian defeated his rivals and became master of Rome. For his success, the Senate in 27 B.C.E. gave Octavian the name Augustus, meaning "revered one." Although the Senate did not mean this to be a decisive break, that date is generally used to mark the end of the Roman Republic and the start of the Roman Empire.

Augustus rebuilt effective government. Although he claimed that he was restoring the republic, he actually transformed the government into one in which all power was held by a single ruler, gradually taking over many of the offices and titles that traditionally had been held by separate people. One of these was the title *imperator*, often given to a general by his troops after a major victory, derived from the Latin word *imperium*, which means "power to command." *Imperator* is the origin of the English word "emperor," a word used to describe the rulers of Rome after Augustus, Augustus's title of imperator reflects the source of most of his power: his control and command of the army.

Augustus ended domestic turmoil and secured the provinces. He founded new colonies, mainly in the western Mediterranean basin, which promoted the spread of Greco-Roman culture and the Latin language to the West. Magistrates exercised authority in their regions as representatives of Rome. Augustus broke some of the barriers between Italy and the provinces by extending citizenship to many of the provincials who had supported him. Later emperors added more territory, and a system of Roman roads and sea-lanes united the empire, with trade connections extending to India and China. For two hundred years the Mediterranean world experienced a period of prosperity, order, and relative peace, which an eighteenth-century historian dubbed the *pax Romana*, although those the Romans conquered might not have agreed that Roman rule was so harmonious. The city of Rome grew to a huge size, and the emperor provided grain and bread at low prices to prevent social unrest. Emperors and other wealthy citizens also entertained the city's residents with gladiatorial contests, chariot racing, and other forms of popular entertainment.

The Spread of Christianity

According to the accounts of his life written down and preserved by his followers, during the reign of Augustus's successor Tiberius, a Jewish man, Jesus of Nazareth (ca. 3 B.C.E.–29 C.E.) began preaching and gathering followers in the Roman province of Judaea. He preached of a heavenly kingdom of eternal happiness in a life after death and of the importance of devotion to God and love of others. His teachings were based on Hebrew Scripture and reflected a conception of God and morality that came from Jewish tradition, but he deviated from traditional Jewish teachings in insisting that he taught in his own name, not simply in the name of Yahweh. He came to establish a spiritual kingdom, he said, not an earthly one, and he urged his followers and listeners to concentrate on the world to come, not on material goods or earthly relationships. His followers regarded him as the Messiah, the long-hoped-for anointed leader; the Greek translation of the Hebrew word *Messiah* is Christos, the origin of the English words *Christ* and *Christian*, which came to be used for his followers. The Roman official of Judaea, Pontius Pilate, feared that the popular agitation surrounding Jesus could lead to revolt against Rome and executed him. Jesus's followers maintained that he rose from the dead three days later.

Those followers might have remained a small Jewish sect but for the preaching of a Hellenized Jew, Paul of Tarsus (ca. 5–67 C.E.). Paul traveled widely and wrote letters of advice, many of which were copied and circulated, transforming Jesus's ideas into more specific moral teachings. Paul urged that Jews and non-Jews be accepted on an equal basis, and the earliest converts included men and women from all social classes. People were attracted to Christian teachings for a variety of reasons: it offered a message of divine forgiveness and eternal life, taught that every individual has a role to play in building the kingdom of God, and fostered a deep sense of community and identity in the often highly mobile Roman world.

Some Roman officials and emperors opposed Christianity and attempted to stamp it out, but most did not, and by the second century Christianity began to establish more permanent institutions, including a hierarchy of officials. It attracted more highly educated individuals, and modified teachings that seemed upsetting to Romans.

Late Antiquity

In the third century C.E. Roman prosperity and stability gave way to a period of domestic upheaval and foreign invasion. Rival generals backed by their troops contested the imperial throne in civil wars. Groups that the Romans labeled "barbarians," such as the Visigoths, Ostrogoths, and Gauls, migrated into and invaded the Roman Empire from the north and east. Civil war and invasions devastated towns and farms, and barbarians brought different social, political, and economic structures with them. Scholars have long seen this era as one of the great turning points in Western history, but during the past several decades, focus has shifted to continuities as well as changes, and what is now usually termed "late antiquity" has been recognized as a period of creativity and adaptation, not simply of decline and fall.

The emperors Diocletian (r. 284–305 c.e.) and Constantine (r. 306–337 c.e.) tried to halt the general disintegration by reorganizing the empire, expanding the state bureaucracy, building more defensive works, and imposing heavier taxes. For administrative purposes, Diocletian divided the empire into a western half and an eastern half, and Constantine established the new capital city of Constantinople in the East. The emperors ruling from Constantinople could not provide enough military assistance to repel invaders in the western half of the Roman Empire. In 476 a Germanic chieftain, Odoacer, deposed the Roman emperor in the West and did not take on the title of emperor, calling himself instead the king of Italy. This date thus marks the official end of the Roman Empire in the West. The Roman Empire in the East, later called the Byzantine Empire, would last for nearly another thousand years, however, and preserved and transmitted much of ancient Greco-Roman law, philosophy, and institutions.

The Christian Church was another agent of continuity in late antiquity. In 313 the emperor Constantine legalized Christianity, and in 380 the emperor Theodosius made it the official religion of the empire. Missionaries and church officials spread Christianity within and far beyond the borders of the Roman Empire, bringing with them the Latin language and institutions based on Roman models. Christian writers also played a powerful role in the conservation of Greco-Roman thought. They used Latin as their medium of communication, thereby preserving it. The Latin language remained the basic medium of communication among educated people in central and western Europe for the next thousand years; for almost two thousand years, Latin literature formed the core of all Western education. Writers such as Saint Augustine of Hippo (354–430) used Roman rhetoric and Roman history to defend Christian theology. In so doing, they assimilated classical culture into Christian teaching. As barbarians encountered Roman culture and became Christian, their own ways of doing things were also transformed.

The Middle Ages

Fifteenth-century scholars believed that they were living in a period of rebirth that had recaptured the spirit of ancient Greece and Rome. What separated their time from classical antiquity, in their opinion, was a long period of darkness to which a seventeenth-century professor gave the name "Middle Ages." In this conceptualization, Western history was divided into three periods — ancient, medieval, and modern — an organization that is still in use today. Recent scholars have demonstrated, however, that the thousand-year period between roughly the fifth and fourteenth centuries was not one of stagnation, but one of great changes in every realm of life: social, political, intellectual, economic, and religious. The men and women of the Middle Ages built on the cultural heritage of the Greco-Roman world and on the traditions of barbarian groups to create new ways of doing things.

The Early Middle Ages

The first several centuries in this new era (ca. 600–1000), conventionally known as the "early Middle Ages," was a time of disorder and destruction, but it also marked the creation of a new type of society and a cultural revival that influenced later intellectual and literary traditions. While agrarian life continued to dominate Europe, political and economic structures that would influence later European history began to form.

Several processes were responsible for the development of European culture. First, Europe became Christian. Missionaries traveled throughout Europe instructing Germanic, Celtic, and Slavic peoples in the basic tenets of the Christian faith. Seeking to gain more converts, the Christian Church incorporated pagan beliefs and holidays, creating new rituals and practices that were meaningful to people, and creating a sense of community through parish churches and the veneration of saints.

Second, as barbarian groups migrated into the Western Roman Empire, they often intermarried with the old Roman aristocracy. The elite class that emerged held the dominant political, social, and economic power in early—and later—medieval Europe. Barbarian customs and tradition, such as ideals of military prowess and bravery in battle, became part of the mental furniture of Europeans.

Third, in the seventh and eighth centuries, Muslim military conquests carried Islam, the religion inspired by the prophet Muhammad (ca. 571–632), from the Arab lands across North Africa, the Mediterranean basin, and Spain into southern France. Muslim scholars eventually translated many Greek texts. When, beginning in the ninth century, those texts were translated from Arabic into Latin, they came to play a role in the formation of European scientific and philosophical thought. The expansion of Islam profoundly affected the development of Western civilization as well as the history of Africa and Asia.

Monasticism, an ascetic form of Christian life first practiced in Egypt and characterized by isolation from the broader society, simplicity of living, and abstention from sexual activity, flourished and expanded in both the Byzantine East and the Latin West. Medieval people believed that the communities of monks and nuns provided an important service: prayer on behalf of the broader society. In a world lacking career opportunities, monasteries also offered education for the children of the upper classes. Men trained in monastery schools served royal and baronial governments as advisers, secretaries, diplomats, and treasurers; monks in the West also pioneered the clearing of wasteland and forestland.

One of the barbarian groups that settled within the Roman Empire and allied with the Romans was the Franks, and after the Roman Empire collapsed they expanded their holdings, basing some of their government on Roman principles. In the eighth century the dynamic warrior-king of the Franks, Charles the Great, or Charlemagne (r. 768–814), came to control most of central and western continental Europe except Muslim Spain, and western Europe achieved a degree of political unity. Charlemagne supported Christian missionary efforts and encouraged both classical and Christian scholarship. His coronation in 800 by the pope at Rome in a ceremony filled with Latin anthems represented a fusion of classical, Christian, and barbarian elements, as did Carolingian culture more generally.

In the ninth century Vikings, Muslims, and Magyars (early Hungarians), raided and migrated into Europe, leading to the collapse of centralized power. Charlemagne's empire was divided, and real authority passed into the hands of local strongmen.

Out of this vulnerable society, which was constantly threatened by outside invasions, a new political form involving mutual obligations, later called "feudalism," developed. Political authority was decentralized, with power spread among many lords, bishops, abbots, and other types of local rulers. The power of the local nobles in the feudal structure rested on landed estates worked by peasants in another system of mutual obligation termed "manorialism," in which the majority of peasants were serfs, required to stay on the land where they were born and pay obligations to a lord in labor and products.

The High and Later Middle Ages

By the beginning of the eleventh century, the European world showed distinct signs of recovery, vitality, and creativity. Over the next three centuries, a period called the High Middle Ages, that recovery and creativity manifested itself in every facet of culture—economic, social, political, intellectual, and artistic. A greater degree of peace paved the way for these achievements.

The Viking, Muslim, and Magyar invasions gradually ended. Warring knights supported ecclesiastical pressure against violence, and disorder declined. A warming climate, along with technological improvements such as water mills and horse-drawn plows, increased the available food supply. Most people remained serfs, living in simple houses in small villages, but a slow increase in population led to new areas being cultivated, and some serfs were able to buy their freedom.

Relative security and the increasing food supply allowed for the growth and development of towns in the High Middle Ages. Towns gained legal and political rights, merchant and craft guilds grew more powerful, and towns became centers of production as well as trading centers. In medieval social thinking, three classes existed: the clergy, who prayed; the nobility, who fought; and the peasantry, who tilled the land. The merchant class, engaging in manufacturing and trade, seeking freedom from the jurisdiction of feudal lords, and pursuing wealth with a fiercely competitive spirit, fit none of the standard categories. Townspeople represented a radical force for change. Trade brought in new ideas as well as merchandise, and towns developed into intellectual and cultural centers.

The growth of towns and cities went hand in hand with a revival of regional and international trade. For example, Italian merchants traveled to the regional fairs of France and Flanders to exchange silk from China and slaves from the Crimea for English woolens, French wines, and Flemish textiles. Merchants adopted new business techniques and a new attitude toward making money. They were eager to invest surplus capital to make more money. These developments added up to what scholars have termed a commercial revolution, a major turning point in the economic and social life of the West. The development of towns and commerce was to lay the foundations for Europe's transformation, centuries later, from a rural agricultural society into an urban industrial society—a change with global implications.

The High Middle Ages also saw the birth of the modern centralized state. The concept of the state had been one of Rome's great legacies to Western civilization, but for almost five hundred years after the disintegration of the Roman Empire in the West, political authority was weak. Charlemagne had far less control of what went on in his kingdom than Roman emperors had, and after the Carolingian Empire broke apart, political authority was completely decentralized, with power spread among many feudal lords. Beginning in the last half of the tenth century, however, feudal rulers started to develop new institutions of law and government that enabled them to assert their power over lesser lords and the general population. Centralized states slowly crystallized, first in France and England, and then in Spain and northern Europe. In Italy and Germany, however, strong independent local authorities predominated.

Medieval rulers required more officials, larger armies, and more money with which to pay for them. They developed financial bureaucracies, of which the most effective were those in England. They also sought to transform a hodgepodge of oral and written customs and rules into a uniform system of laws acceptable and applicable to all their peoples. In France, local laws and procedures were maintained, but the king also established a royal court that published laws and heard appeals. In England, the king's court regularized procedures, and the idea of a common law that applied to the whole country developed. Fiscal and legal measures enacted by King John led to opposition from the high nobles of England, who in 1215 forced him to sign the Magna Carta, agreeing to observe the law. English kings following John recognized this common law, a law that their judges applied throughout the country. Exercise of common law often involved juries of local people to answer questions of fact. The common law and jury systems of the Middle Ages have become integral features of Anglo-American jurisprudence. In the fourteenth century kings also summoned meetings of the leading classes in their kingdoms, and thus were born representative assemblies, most notably the English Parliament.

In their work of consolidation and centralization, kings increasingly used the knowledge of university-trained officials. Universities first emerged in western Europe in the twelfth century. Medieval universities were educational institutions for men that produced trained officials for the new bureaucratic states. The universities at Bologna in Italy and Montpellier in France, for example, were centers for the study of Roman law. Paris became the leading university for the study of philosophy and theology. Medieval Scholastics (philosophers and theologians) sought to harmonize Greek philosophy, especially the works of Aristotle, with Christian teaching. They wanted to use reason to deepen the understanding of what was believed on faith. At the University of Paris, Thomas Aquinas (1225–1274) wrote an important synthesis of Christian revelation and Aristotelian philosophy in his *Summa Theologica.* Medieval universities developed the basic structures familiar to modern students: colleges, universities, examinations, and degrees. Colleges and universities are another major legacy of the Middle Ages to the modern world.

At the same time that states developed, energetic popes built their power within the Western Christian Church and asserted their superiority over kings and emperors. A papal call to retake the holy city of Jerusalem led to nearly two centuries of warfare between Christians and Muslims. Christian warriors, clergy, and settlers moved out from western and central Europe in all directions, so that through conquest and colonization border regions were gradually incorporated into a more uniform European culture.

Most people in medieval Europe were Christian, and the village or city church was the center of community life, where people attended services, honored the saints, and experienced the sacraments. The village priest blessed the fields before the spring planting and the fall harvesting. In everyday life people engaged in rituals heavy with religious symbolism, and every life transition was marked by a ceremony with religious elements. Guilds of merchants sought the protection of patron saints and held elaborate public celebrations on the saints' feast days. Indeed, the veneration of saints—men and women whose lives contemporaries perceived as outstanding in holiness—and an increasingly sophisticated sacramental system became central features of popular religion. University lectures and meetings of parliaments began with prayers. Kings relied on the services of bishops and abbots in the work of the government. Gothic cathedrals, where people saw beautiful stained-glass windows and listened to complex music, manifested medieval people's deep Christian faith and their pride in their own cities.

The high level of energy and creativity that characterized the twelfth and thirteenth centuries could not be sustained indefinitely. In the fourteenth century every conceivable disaster struck western Europe. The climate turned colder and wetter, leading to poor harvests and widespread famine. People weakened by hunger were more susceptible to disease, and in the middle of the fourteenth century the bubonic plague (or Black Death) swept across the continent, taking a terrible toll on population. England and France became deadlocked in a long and bitter struggle known as the Hundred Years' War (1337–1453). War devastated the countryside, especially in France, leading to widespread discontent and peasant revolts. Workers in cities also revolted against dismal working conditions, and violent crime and ethnic tensions increased. Many urban residents were increasingly dissatisfied with the Christian Church and turned to heretical movements that challenged church power. Schism in the Catholic Church resulted in the simultaneous claim by two popes of jurisdiction. Yet, in spite of the pessimism and crises, important institutions and cultural forms, including representative assemblies and national literatures, emerged.

Early Modern Europe

While war gripped northern Europe, a new culture emerged in southern Europe. The fourteenth century witnessed the beginning of remarkable changes in many aspects of Italian intellectual, artistic, and cultural life. Artists and writers thought they were living in a new golden age, and in the sixteenth century this change was given the label we use today—the Renaissance, from the French version of a word meaning "rebirth." The term was first used by the artist and art historian Giorgio Vasari (1511–1574) to describe the art of "rare men of genius" such as his contemporary Michelangelo. Through their works, Vasari judged, the glory of the classical past had been reborn after centuries of darkness, or had perhaps even been surpassed. Vasari used the word *Renaissance* to describe painting, sculpture, and architecture, what he termed the "Major Arts." Gradually, however, *Renaissance* was used to refer to many aspects of life at this time, first in Italy and then in the rest of Europe. This new attitude had a slow diffusion out of Italy, with the result that the Renaissance happened at different times in different parts of Europe. Italian art of the fourteenth through the early sixteenth centuries is described as "Renaissance," as is English literature of the late sixteenth century (including Shakespeare).

About a century after Vasari coined the word *Renaissance*, scholars began to view the cultural and political changes of the Renaissance, along with the religious changes of the Reformation and the European voyages of exploration, as ushering in the "modern" world. Since then, some historians have chosen to view the Renaissance as a bridge between the medieval and modern eras, as it corresponded chronologically with the late medieval period and as there was much continuity along with the changes. Others have questioned whether the word *Renaissance* should be used at all to describe an era in which many social groups saw decline rather than advancement. These debates remind us that the labels *medieval, Renaissance,* and *modern* are intellectual constructs devised after the fact. They all contain value judgments, as do other chronological designations, such as the "golden age" of Athens and the "Roaring Twenties."

The Renaissance

In the commercial revival of the Middle Ages, ambitious merchants amassed great wealth, especially in the city-states of northern Italy. These city-states were communes in which all citizens shared power, but political instability often led to their transformation into city-states ruled by single individuals. As their riches and power grew, rulers and merchants displayed their wealth in great public buildings as well as magnificent courts—palaces where they lived and conducted business. Political rulers, popes, and powerful families hired writers, artists, musicians, and architects through the system of patronage, which allowed for a great outpouring of culture.

The Renaissance was characterized by self-conscious awareness among fourteenth- and fifteenth-century Italians—particularly scholars and writers known as humanists—that they were living in a new era. Key to this attitude was a serious interest in the Latin classics, a belief in individual potential, and a more secular attitude toward life. All of these are evident in the political theory developed in the Renaissance, particularly that of Machiavelli. Humanists opened schools to train boys and young men for active lives of public service, but had doubts about whether humanist education was appropriate for women. As humanism spread to northern Europe, religious concerns became more pronounced, and Christian humanists set out plans for the reform of church and society. Their ideas reached a much wider audience than did those of early humanists because of the development of the printing press with movable metal type, which revolutionized communication.

Interest in the classical past and in the individual also shaped Renaissance art in terms of style and subject matter. Painting became more naturalistic, and the individual portrait emerged as a distinct artistic genre. Wealthy merchants, cultured rulers, and powerful popes all hired painters, sculptors, and architects to design and ornament public and private buildings. Art in Italy became more secular and classical, while that in northern Europe retained a more religious tone. Artists began to understand themselves as having a special creative genius, though they continued to produce works on order for patrons, who often determined the content and form.

Social hierarchies in the Renaissance built on those of the Middle Ages, with the addition of new features that evolved into the modern social hierarchies of race, class, and gender. In the fifteenth century black slaves entered Europe in sizable numbers for the first time since the collapse of the Roman Empire, and Europeans fit them into changing understandings of ethnicity and race. The medieval hierarchy of orders based on function in society intermingled with a new hierarchy based on wealth, with new types of elites becoming more powerful. The Renaissance debate about women led many to discuss women's nature and proper role in society, a discussion sharpened by the presence of a number of ruling queens in this era.

Beginning in the fifteenth century rulers utilized aggressive methods to rebuild their governments. First in the regional states of Italy, then in the expanding monarchies of France, England, and Spain, rulers began the work of reducing violence, curbing unruly nobles, and establishing domestic order. They attempted to secure their borders and enhanced methods of raising revenue. The monarchs of western Europe emphasized royal majesty and royal sovereignty and insisted on the respect and loyalty of all subjects, including the nobility. In central Europe the Holy Roman emperors attempted to do the same, but they were not able to overcome the power of local interests to create a unified state.

The Reformation

Calls for reform of the Christian Church began very early in its history. When Christianity became the official religion of the Roman Empire in the fourth century, many believers thought that the church had abandoned its original mission, and they called for a return to a church that was not linked to the state. Throughout the Middle Ages, individuals and groups argued that the church had become too wealthy and powerful, and urged monasteries, convents, bishoprics, and the papacy to give up their property and focus on service to the poor. Some asserted that basic teachings of the church were not truly Christian and that changes were needed in theology as well as in institutional structures and practices. The Christian humanists of the late fifteenth and early sixteenth centuries urged reform, primarily through educational and social change. Throughout the centuries, men and women believed that the early Christian Church represented a golden age akin to the golden age of the classical past celebrated by Renaissance humanists.

Thus sixteenth-century cries for reformation were hardly new. What was new, however, was the breadth with which they were accepted and their ultimate impact. In 1500 there was one Christian Church in western Europe to which all Christians at least nominally belonged. Fifty years later there were many, a situation that continues today. Thus, along with the Renaissance, the Reformation is often seen as a key element in the creation of the "modern" world.

In 1517 Martin Luther (1483–1546), a priest and professor of theology at a small German university, launched an attack on clerical abuses. The Catholic Church in the early sixteenth century had serious problems, and many individuals and groups had long called for reform. This background of discontent helps explain why Martin Luther's ideas found such a ready audience. Luther and other Protestants developed a new understanding of Christian doctrine that emphasized faith, the power of God's grace, and the centrality of the Bible. Protestant ideas were attractive to educated people and urban residents, and they spread rapidly through preaching, hymns, and the printing press. By 1530 many parts of the Holy Roman Empire and Scandinavia had broken with the Catholic Church.

Some reformers developed more radical ideas about infant baptism, ownership of property, and the separation between church and state. Both Protestants and Catholics regarded these as dangerous, and radicals were banished or executed.

The German Peasants' War, in which Luther's ideas were linked to calls for social and economic reform, was similarly put down harshly. The Protestant reformers did not break with medieval ideas about the proper gender hierarchy, though they did elevate the status of marriage by denying the value of clerical celibacy and viewed orderly households as the key building blocks of society.

The progress of the Reformation was shaped by the political situation in the Holy Roman Empire. The Habsburg emperor, Charles V, ruled almost half of Europe along with Spain's overseas colonies. Within the empire his authority was limited, however, and local princes, nobles, and cities actually held the most power. This decentralization allowed the Reformation to spread. Charles remained firmly Catholic, and in the 1530s religious wars began in Germany. These were brought to an end with the Peace of Augsburg in 1555, which allowed rulers to choose whether their territory would be Catholic or Lutheran.

In England, the political issue of the royal succession triggered that country's break with Rome, and a Protestant Church was established. Protestant ideas also spread into France and eastern Europe. In all these areas, a second generation of reformers developed their own theology and plans for institutional change. The most important of the second-generation reformers was John Calvin, whose ideas would come to shape Christianity over a much wider area than did Luther's. The Roman Catholic Church responded slowly to the Protestant challenge, but by the 1530s the papacy was leading a movement for reform within the church instead of blocking it. Catholic doctrine was reaffirmed at the Council of Trent, and reform measures, such as the opening of seminaries for priests and a ban on holding multiple church offices, were introduced. New religious orders such as the Jesuits and the Ursulines spread Catholic ideas through teaching, and in the case of the Jesuits through missionary work.

Religious differences led to riots, civil wars, and international conflicts in the later sixteenth century. In France and the Netherlands, Calvinist Protestants and Catholics used violence against each other, and religious differences became mixed with political and economic grievances. Long civil wars resulted; one in the Netherlands became an international conflict. War ended in France with the Edict of Nantes in which Protestants were given some civil rights, and in the Netherlands with a division of the country into a Protestant north and a Catholic south. The era of religious wars was also the time of the most extensive witch persecutions in European history, as both Protestants and Catholics tried to rid their cities and states of people they regarded as linked to the Devil.

The Renaissance and the Reformation are often seen as two of the key elements in the creation of the "modern" world. The radical changes brought by the Reformation contained many aspects of continuity, however. Sixteenth-century reformers looked back to the early Christian Church for their inspiration, and many of their reforming ideas had been advocated for centuries. Most Protestant reformers worked with political leaders to make religious changes, just as early church officials had worked with Emperor Constantine and his successors as Christianity became the official religion of the Roman Empire in the fourth century. The spread of Christianity and the spread of Protestantism were accomplished not only by preaching, persuasion, and teaching, but also by force and violence. The Catholic Reformation was carried out by activist popes, a church council, and new religious orders, as earlier reforms of the church had been.

Just as they linked with earlier developments, the events of the Reformation were also closely connected with what is often seen as the third element in the "modern" world, discussed in the first chapter of this book: European exploration and conquest. Only a week after Martin Luther stood in front of Emperor Charles V at the Diet of Worms declaring his independence in matters of religion, Ferdinand Magellan, a Portuguese sea captain with Spanish ships, was killed in a group of islands off the coast of Southeast Asia. Charles V had provided the backing for Magellan's voyage, the first to circumnavigate the globe. Magellan viewed the spread of Christianity as one of the purposes of his trip, and later in the sixteenth century institutions created as part of the Catholic Reformation, including the Jesuit order and the Inquisition, would operate in European colonies overseas as well as in Europe itself. The islands where Magellan was killed were later named the Philippines, in honor of Charles's son Philip, who sent an ill-fated expedition, the Spanish Armada, against Protestant England. Philip's opponent Queen Elizabeth was similarly honored when English explorers named a huge chunk of territory in North America "Virginia" as a tribute to their "Virgin Queen." The desire for wealth and power was an important motivation in the European voyages and colonial ventures, but so was religious zeal.

14

European Exploration and Conquest

1450–1650

CHAPTER PREVIEW

- What was the Afro-Eurasian trading world before Columbus?

- How and why did Europeans undertake ambitious voyages of expansion?

- What was the impact of European conquest on the New World?

- How did Europe and the world change after Columbus?

- How did expansion change European attitudes and beliefs?

IN 1450 EUROPEANS WERE RELATIVELY MARGINAL PLAYERS in a centuries-old trading system that linked Africa, Asia, and Europe. In this vibrant cosmopolitan Afro-Eurasian trading world centered on the Indian Ocean, Arab, Persian, Turkish, Indian, African, Chinese, and European merchants and adventurers competed for trade in spices, silks, and other goods.

A century later, by 1550, the Portuguese search for better access to African gold and Asian trade goods had led to a new overseas empire and Spanish explorers had accidentally discovered the Western Hemisphere. Through violent conquest, the Iberian powers established large-scale colonies in the Americas, and northern European powers sought to establish colonies of their own. The era of European expansion had begun, creating new political systems and forms of economic exchange as well as cultural assimilation, conversion, and resistance. The Age of Discovery (1450–1650), as the time of these encounters is known, laid the foundations for the modern world.

What was the Afro-Eurasian trading world before Columbus?

Columbus did not sail west on a whim. To understand his and other Europeans' voyages of exploration, we must first understand late medieval trade networks. Historians now recognize that a type of world economy, known as the Afro-Eurasian trade world, linked the products, people, and ideas of Africa, Europe, and Asia during the Middle Ages. The West was not the dominant player before Columbus, and the voyages derived from a desire to gain direct access to the goods of overseas trade. European monarchs and explorers also wished to spread Christianity. Their projects for exploration and conquest received support from the papacy in Rome.

The Trade World of the Indian Ocean

Covering 20 percent of the earth's total ocean area, the Indian Ocean is the globe's third-largest waterway (after the Atlantic and Pacific). Moderate and predictable, monsoon winds blow from the northwest or northeast between November and January and from the south and southwest between April and August. These wind patterns enabled cross-oceanic travel and shaped its rhythms, creating a vibrant trade world in which goods, people, and ideas circulated among China, India, the Middle East, Southeast Asia, and Africa (Map 14.1). From the seventh through the fourteenth centuries, the volume and integration of Indian Ocean trade steadily increased, favored by two parallel movements: political unification and economic growth in China and the spread of Islam through much of the Indian Ocean world.

Merchants congregated in a series of cosmopolitan port cities strung around the Indian Ocean. Most of these cities had some form of autonomous self-government, and no one state or region dominated. Ethnic, religious, and family ties encouraged trust among traders and limited violence.

Located at the northeastern edge of the Indian Ocean trade world, China exercised a powerful economic and cultural influence. In addition to safeguarding the famous Silk Road overland trade routes through Central Asia and the Middle East, the Mongols also increased connections with Indian Ocean trade. The Venetian trader Marco Polo's tales of his travels from 1271 to 1295, including his encounter with the Great Khan, fueled Western fantasies about the exotic Orient. Polo vividly recounted the splendors of the khan's court and the city of Hangzhou, which he described as "the finest and noblest in the world" in which "the number and wealth of the merchants, and the amount of goods that passed through their hands, was so enormous that no man could form a just estimate thereof."[1]

After the Mongols fell to the Ming Dynasty in 1368, China entered a new period of economic expansion, population growth, and urbanization. China's huge cities hungered for luxury products of the Indian Ocean world, and its artisans produced goods highly prized in export markets, especially porcelain and silk. The Ming emperor dispatched Admiral Zheng He (JEHNG HUH) on a remarkable series of naval expeditions that traveled the oceanic web as far west as Egypt. From 1405 to 1433 each of his seven expeditions involved hundreds of ships and tens of thousands of men. In one voyage alone, Zheng He sailed more than 12,000 miles.[2]

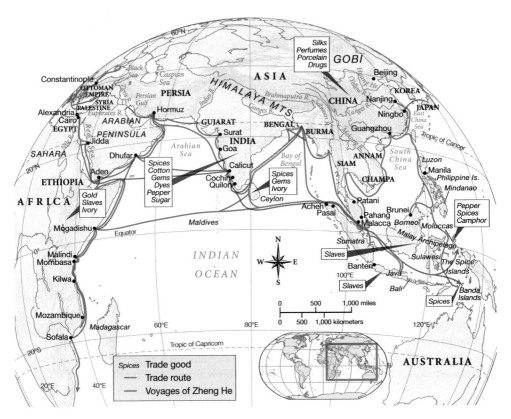

MAP 14.1   The Fifteenth-Century Afro-Eurasian Trading World
After a period of decline following the Black Death and the Mongol invasions, trade revived in the fifteenth century. Muslim merchants dominated trade, linking ports in East Africa and the Red Sea with those in India and the Malay Archipelago. Chinese admiral Zheng He's voyages (1405–1433) followed the most important Indian Ocean trade routes.

Although the ships brought back many wonders, such as giraffes and zebras, the purpose of the voyages was primarily diplomatic, to enhance China's prestige and seek tribute-paying alliances. After the deaths of Zheng He and the emperor, the voyages ceased, but Chinese overseas traders continued vigorous activity in the South China Sea and throughout the Indian Ocean.

India was the central hinge of Indian Ocean trade. Muslim Arab and Persian merchants who circumnavigated India on their way to trade in the South China Sea established trading posts along the southern coasts of east and west India. Cities such as Calicut and Quilon became thriving commercial centers. India was also an important contributor of goods to the world trading system. Most of the world's pepper was grown in India, and Indian cotton and silk textiles, mainly from the Gujarat region, were also highly prized.

Southeast Asia maintained an active trade with China across the South China Sea and with ports on the Coromandel Coast of southeast India. In the fifteenth century the strategically located port of Malacca became a great commercial entrepôt (AHN-truh-poh), a trading post to which goods were shipped for storage while awaiting redistribution. To Malacca came porcelains, silks, and camphor (used in the manufacture of many medications) from China; pepper, cloves, nutmeg, and raw materials such as sandalwood from the Moluccas; and textiles, copper weapons, incense, and dyes from India.

The Trading States of Africa

By 1450 Africa had a few large empires along with hundreds of smaller states. After the Mongol invasion of Baghdad in 1258, the Mamluk rulers of Egypt proclaimed a new Abbasid caliphate. Until its defeat by the Ottomans in 1517, the Mamluk empire was one of the most powerful on the continent. Its capital, Cairo, was a center of Islamic learning and religious authority as well as being a major hub for goods moving between the Indian Ocean trade world and the Mediterranean.

On the east coast of Africa, Swahili-speaking city-states engaged directly in the Indian Ocean trade, exchanging ivory, rhinoceros horn, tortoise shells, and slaves for textiles, spices, cowrie shells, porcelain, and other goods. Cities such as Kilwa, Malindi, Mogadishu, and Mombasa, dominated by Muslim merchants, were known for their prosperity and culture.

In the fifteenth century most of the gold that reached Europe came from the western part of the Sudan region in West Africa and from the Akan (AH-kahn) peoples living near present-day Ghana. Transported across the Sahara by Arab and African traders on camels, the gold was sold in the ports of North Africa. Other trading routes led to the Egyptian cities of Alexandria and Cairo, where the Venetians held commercial privileges.

Inland nations that sat astride the north-south caravan routes grew wealthy from this trade. In the mid-thirteenth century the kingdom of Mali emerged as an important player on the overland trade route, gaining prestige from its ruler Mansa Musa's fabulous pilgrimage to Mecca in 1324/25. Desire to gain direct access to African gold motivated the initial Portuguese voyages into northern and western Africa.

Gold was one important object of trade; slaves were another. Slavery was practiced in Africa, as it was virtually everywhere else in the world, long before the arrival of Europeans. Arab and East African merchants took West African slaves to the Mediterranean to be sold in European, Egyptian, and Middle Eastern markets and also brought eastern Europeans—a major element of European slavery—to West Africa as slaves. In addition, Indian and Arab merchants traded slaves in the coastal regions of East Africa.

The Middle East

From its capital in Baghdad, the Abbasid caliphate (750–1258) controlled an enormous region from Spain to the western borders of China, including the Red Sea and the Persian Gulf, the two major waterways linking the Indian Ocean trade world to the West. The political stability enshrined by the caliphate, along with the shared language, legal system, and culture of Islam, served to foster economic prosperity and commercial activity. During this period, Muslim Arab traders, who had spread through eastern Africa and western India in the early Middle Ages, reached even further across the trade routes of the Indian Ocean to obtain spices, porcelain, and other goods for the bustling cities of the caliphate.

After the Abbasids fell to Mongol invasions, two great rival Muslim empires, the Persian Safavids (sah-FAH-vidz) and the Turkish Ottomans, dominated the region and competed for control of east-west trade. Like Arabs, Persian merchants could be found in trading communities in India and throughout the Afro-Eurasian trade world. Persia was also a major producer and exporter of silk cloth.

Under Sultan Mohammed II (r. 1451–1481), the Ottomans captured Europe's largest city, Constantinople, in May 1453. The city became the capital of the Ottoman Empire. By the mid-sixteenth century the Ottomans had established control over the maritime trade in the eastern Mediterranean and their power extended into Europe as far west as Vienna. The extension of Ottoman control provided impetus for European traders to seek direct access to Eastern trade goods.

Genoese and Venetian Middlemen

In the late Middle Ages, the Italian city-states of Venice and Genoa controlled the European luxury trade with the East. In 1304 Venice established formal relations with the sultan of Mamluk Egypt, opening operations in Cairo, a major outlet for Asian trade goods brought through the Red Sea. Venetian merchants purchased goods such as spices, silks, and carpets in Cairo for re-export throughout Europe. Venetians funded these purchases through trade in European woolen cloth and metal goods, as well as through shipping and trade in firearms and slaves.

Venice's ancient rival was Genoa. In the wake of the Crusades, Genoa dominated the northern route to Asia through the Black Sea. Expansion in the thirteenth and fourteenth centuries took the Genoese as far as Persia and the Far East. In 1291 they sponsored an expedition into the Atlantic in search of India. The ships were lost, and their exact destination and motivations remain unknown. This voyage reveals the long roots of Genoese interest in Atlantic exploration.

In the fifteenth century, with Venice claiming victory in the spice trade, the Genoese shifted their focus from trade to finance and from the Black Sea to the western Mediterranean. When Spanish and Portuguese voyages began to explore the western Atlantic, Genoese merchants, navigators, and financiers provided their skills and capital to the Iberian monarchs, whose own subjects had less commercial experience. Genoese merchants would eventually help finance Spanish colonization of the New World.

A major element of Italian trade was slavery. Merchants purchased slaves, many of whom were fellow Christians, in the Balkans. The men were sold to Egypt for the sultan's army or sent to work as agricultural laborers in the Mediterranean. Young girls, who constituted the majority of the trade, were sold in western Mediterranean ports as servants and concubines. After the loss of the Black Sea—and thus the source of slaves—to the Ottomans, the Genoese sought new supplies of slaves in the West, taking the Guanches (indigenous peoples from the Canary Islands), Muslim prisoners, Jewish refugees from Spain, and by the early 1500s both sub-Saharan and Berber Africans. With the growth of Spanish colonies in the New World in the

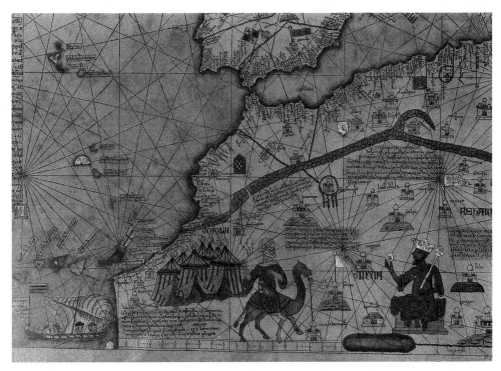

Detail from the *Catalan Atlas*, 1375 This detail from a medieval map depicts Mansa Musa (lower right), who ruled the powerful West African empire of Mali from 1312 to 1337. Musa's golden crown and scepter, and the gold ingot he holds in his hand, represent the empire's wealth. The map also depicts Catalan sailors heading from the Balearic Islands out to the Atlantic Ocean. (From *The Catalan Atlas*, 1375, by Abraham Cresques/Bibliothèque Nationale, Paris, France/Getty Images)

sixteenth century, Genoese and Venetian merchants would become important players in the transatlantic slave trade.

How and why did Europeans undertake ambitious voyages of expansion?

As we have seen, Europe was by no means isolated before the voyages of exploration and the "discovery" of the New World. Italian merchants traded actively in North Africa for gold and in eastern Mediterranean depots for Indian Ocean luxury goods, but trade through intermediaries was slow and expensive. In the first decades of the fifteenth century, new players entered the scene with novel technology, eager to spread Christianity and to obtain direct access to trade. First Portuguese and then Spanish expeditions undertook long-distance voyages that helped create the modern world, with tremendous consequences for their own continent and the rest of the planet.

Causes of European Expansion

European expansion had multiple causes. The first was economic. The Portuguese and Spanish, the first to undertake voyages of exploration, sought new sources of gold and silver as well as a direct route to the Asian trade in spices and other luxury goods. Financial incentives became even more important in the mid-fifteenth century as the revival of population after the Black Death increased demand and Ottoman control of eastern trade routes reduced the flow of trade.

Why were spices so desirable? Introduced into western Europe by the Crusaders in the twelfth century, pepper, ginger, mace, cinnamon, nutmeg, and cloves added flavor and variety to the monotonous European diet. Not only did spices serve as flavorings for food, but they were also used in anointing oil and as incense for religious rituals, and as perfumes, medicines, and dyes in daily life. Apart from their utility, the expense and exotic origins of spices meant that they were a high-status good, which European elites could use to demonstrate their social standing.

Religious fervor and the crusading spirit were another cause of expansion. From the eleventh through the thirteenth century, the Christian kingdoms of the Iberian Peninsula emerged through warfare against Muslim states, a process that became known as the *reconquista*. Portugal's expansion across the Mediterranean to North Africa in 1415 and Christopher Columbus's voyage in 1492 thus represented overseas extensions of the crusading spirit. Only seven months separated Isabella and Ferdinand's conquest of the emirate of Granada, the last remaining Muslim state on the Iberian Peninsula, and Columbus's departure across the Atlantic in 1492. As they conquered indigenous empires in the Americas, Iberians brought attitudes and administrative practices developed during the reconquista to the New World. **Conquistadors** (kohn-KEES-tuh-dorz) (Spanish for "conquerors") fully expected to be rewarded with land, titles, and power over conquered peoples, just as the leaders of the reconquista had been.

To gain authorization and financial support for their expeditions, explorers sought official sponsorship from the state. Competition among European monarchs for the prestige and profit of overseas exploration was thus another crucial factor in encouraging the steady stream of expeditions that began in the late fifteenth century.

Like other men of the Renaissance era, explorers demonstrated a genuine passion for expanding human knowledge. The European discoveries thus constituted one manifestation of Renaissance curiosity about the physical universe. The detailed journals many voyagers kept attest to their wonder and fascination with the new peoples and places they visited.

The small number of Europeans who could read provided a rapt audience for tales of fantastic places and unknown peoples. Cosmography, natural history, and geography aroused enormous interest among educated people in the fifteenth and sixteenth centuries. One of the most popular books of the time was the fourteenth-century text *The Travels of Sir John Mandeville*, which purported to be a firsthand account of the author's travels in the Middle East, India, and China.

Technology and the Rise of Exploration

The Portuguese were pioneers in seeking technological improvements in shipbuilding, weaponry, and navigation in order to undertake successful voyages of exploration and trade. Medieval European seagoing vessels consisted of single-masted sailing ships or narrow, open galleys propelled by oars, which were common in Mediterranean trade. Though adequate for short journeys that hugged the shore-line, such vessels were incapable of long-distance journeys or high-volume trade. In the fifteenth century, the Portuguese developed the **caravel**, a two- or three-masted sailing ship. Its multiple sails and sternpost rudder made the caravel a highly maneu-verable vessel that required fewer crewmen to operate. The Portuguese were also the first to fit their ships with cannon, which produced immense advantages for naval warfare and bombardment of port cities, both of which were to play a crucial role in their expansion into Asia.[3]

This period also saw great strides in cartography and navigational aids. Around 1410 Arab scholars reintroduced Europeans to **Ptolemy's** *Geography*. Written in the second century C.E., the work synthesized the geographical knowledge of the classical world. It represented a major improvement over medieval cartography by depicting the world as round and introducing the idea of latitude and longitude markings, but it also contained crucial errors. Unaware of the Americas, Ptolemy showed the world as much smaller than it is, so that Asia appeared not very much to the west of Europe.

Originating in China, the compass was brought to the West in the late Middle Ages. By using the compass to determine their direction and estimating their speed of travel over a set length of time, mariners could determine the course of a ship's voy-age, a system of navigation known as "dead reckoning." In the late fifteenth century Portuguese scholars devised a new technique of "celestial reckoning," which involved using the astrolabe, an instrument invented by the ancient Greeks to determine the position of the stars and other celestial bodies. Commissioned by Portuguese king John II, a group of astronomers in the 1480s showed that mariners could determine their latitude at sea by using a specially designed astrolabe to determine the altitude of the polestar or the sun, and by consulting tables of these bodies' movements. This was a crucial step forward in maritime navigational techniques.

Much of the new technology that Europeans used on their voyages originated in the East. Gunpowder, the compass, and the sternpost rudder were Chinese inven-tions. The triangular lateen sail, which allowed caravels to tack against the wind, was a product of the Indian Ocean trade world. Advances in navigational techniques and cartography, including the maritime astrolabe, drew on the rich tradition of Judeo-Arabic mathematical and astronomical learning in Iberia. In exploring new territories, European sailors thus called on techniques and knowledge developed over centuries in China, the Muslim world, and the Indian Ocean.

Despite technological improvements, life at sea meant danger, overcrowding, and hunger. For months at a time, 100 to 120 poorly paid crew members lived and worked in a space of 1,600 to 2,000 square feet. A lucky sailor would find enough space on deck to unroll his sleeping mat. Horses, cows, pigs, chickens, rats, and lice accompanied sailors on the voyages.

The Portuguese Overseas Empire

Established during the reconquista in the mid-thirteenth century, the kingdom of Portugal had a long Atlantic coastline that favored fishing and maritime trading. By the end of the thirteenth century Portuguese merchants were trading fish, salt, and wine to ports in northern England and the Mediterranean. Nature favored the Portuguese: winds blowing along their coast offered passage to Africa, its Atlantic islands, and, ultimately, Brazil. Once they had mastered the secret to sailing against the wind to return to Europe (by sailing further west to catch winds from the southwest), they were ideally poised to pioneer Atlantic exploration.

In the early phases of Portuguese exploration, Prince Henry (1394–1460), a younger son of the king, played a leading role. A nineteenth-century scholar dubbed Henry "the Navigator" because of his support for Portuguese voyages of discovery. Henry participated in Portugal's conquest of Ceuta, an Arab city in northern Morocco in 1415, an event that marked the beginning of European overseas expansion. In the 1420s, under Henry's direction, the Portuguese claimed sovereignty over islands in the Atlantic off the northwest coast of Africa, Madeira (ca. 1420) and the Azores (1427). In 1443 they founded their first African commercial settlement at Arguin in North Africa.

By the time of Henry's death in 1460, his support for exploration was vindicated—from the Portuguese point of view—by thriving sugar plantations on the Atlantic islands, the first arrival of enslaved Africans in Portugal, and new access to African gold. It was also authorized and legitimized by the Catholic Church. In 1454, Pope Nicholas V issued a bull reiterating the rights of the Portuguese crown to conquer and enslave non-Christians and recognizing Portuguese possession of territories in West Africa. Such papal proclamations legitimized Portuguese—and later Spanish—seizure of land and people in their own eyes, but of course it meant nothing to those suffering invasion and conquest.

The Portuguese next established fortified trading posts, called factories, on the gold-rich Guinea coast (Map 14.2). By 1500 Portugal controlled the flow of African gold to Europe. In contrast to the Spanish conquest of the Americas, the Portuguese did not seek to establish large settlements in West Africa or to control the political or cultural lives of those with whom they traded. Instead, they pursued easier and faster profits by inserting themselves into pre-existing trading systems. For the first century of their relations, African rulers were equal partners with the Portuguese, benefiting from their experienced armies and European vulnerability to tropical diseases.

The Portuguese then pushed farther south down the west coast of Africa. In 1487 Bartholomeu Dias rounded the Cape of Good Hope at the southern tip of Africa, but poor conditions forced him to turn back. A decade later Vasco da Gama succeeded in rounding the Cape while commanding a fleet of four ships in search of a sea route to India. With the help of an Arab guide, da Gama reached the port of Calicut in India in 1498. He returned to Lisbon loaded with spices and samples of Indian cloth, having proved the possibility of lucrative trade with the East via the Cape route. Thereafter, a Portuguese convoy set out for passage around the Cape every year in March or April.

Lisbon became the major entrance port for Asian goods into Europe, but this was not accomplished without a fight. Muslim-controlled port city-states had long controlled the rich trade of the Indian Ocean, and they did not surrender their dominance willingly. From 1500 to 1515 the Portuguese used a combination of bombardment and diplomatic treaties to establish trading forts at Goa, Malacca, Calicut, and Hormuz, thereby laying the foundation for a Portuguese trading empire in the

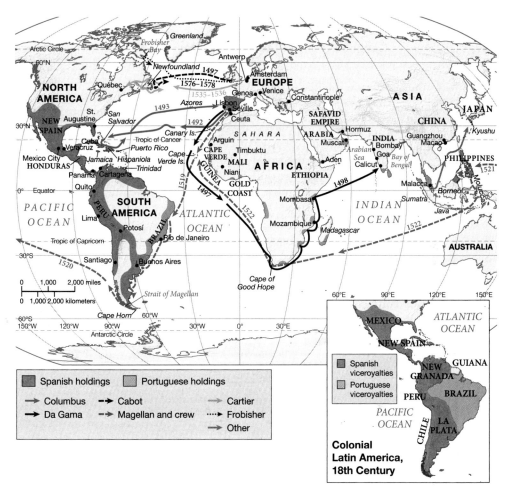

MAP 14.2   Overseas Exploration and Conquest in the Fifteenth and Sixteenth Centuries
The voyages of discovery marked a dramatic new phase in the centuries-old migrations of European peoples. This world map depicts the voyages of the most significant European explorers of this period, while the inset map shows Spanish and Portuguese colonies of the eighteenth century.

sixteenth and seventeenth centuries. The acquisition of port cities and their trade routes allowed Portugal to dominate trade in the Indian Ocean, but, as in Africa, the Portuguese did not seek to transform the lives and religious faith of peoples beyond their coastal holdings.

Inspired by the Portuguese, the Spanish had also begun to seek direct access to the wealth of Asian trade. Theirs was to be a second, entirely different, mode of colonization, leading to the conquest of existing empires, large-scale settlement, and the assimilation of a subjugated indigenous population.

Spain's Voyages to the Americas

Christopher Columbus was not the first to explore the Atlantic. Ninth-century Vikings established short-lived settlements in Newfoundland, and it is probable that others made the voyage, either on purpose or accidentally, carried by westward currents off the coast of Africa. In the late fifteenth century the achievements of Portugal's decades of exploration made the moment right for Christopher Columbus's attempt to find a westward route across the Atlantic to Asia.

Christopher Columbus, a native of Genoa, was an experienced seaman and navigator, with close ties to the world of Portuguese seafaring. He had worked as a mapmaker in Lisbon and spent time on Madeira, where his wife's father led the Portuguese colony. He was familiar with *portolans*—written descriptions of the courses along which ships sailed—and the use of the compass for dead reckoning. (He carried an astrolabe on his first voyage, but did not use it for navigation.) Columbus was also a deeply religious man. He had witnessed the Spanish conquest of Granada and shared fully in the religious and nationalistic fervor surrounding that event. Like the Spanish rulers and most Europeans of his age, Columbus understood Christianity as a missionary religion that should be carried to all places of the earth.

Given Portugal's leading role in Atlantic exploration and his personal connections, Columbus first appealed to the Portuguese rulers for support for a voyage to find a westward passage to the Indies in 1483. When they refused, he turned, unsuccessfully, to Ferdinand and Isabella in 1486 and then finally won the backing of the Spanish monarchy in 1492. Buoyed by the success of the reconquista and eager to earn profits from trade, the Spanish crown named Columbus viceroy over any territory he might discover and promised him one-tenth of the material rewards of the journey.

Columbus and his small fleet left Spain on August 3, 1492. Inspired by the stories of Mandeville and Marco Polo, Columbus dreamed of reaching the court of the Great Khan (not realizing that the Ming Dynasty had overthrown the Mongols in 1368). Based on Ptolemy's *Geography* and other texts, he expected to pass the islands of Japan and then land on the east coast of China.

On October 12, 1492, he landed in the Bahamas, which he christened San Salvador and claimed for the Spanish crown. In a letter submitted to Ferdinand and Isabella on his return to Spain, Columbus described the natives as handsome, peaceful, and primitive people whose body painting reminded him of that of the Canary Islands natives. Believing he was somewhere off the east coast of Japan, in what he considered the Indies, he called them "Indians," a name later applied to all inhabitants of the Americas. Columbus concluded that they would make good slaves and could easily be converted to Christianity.

Scholars have identified the inhabitants of the islands as the Taino people, who inhabited Hispaniola (modern-day Haiti and Dominican Republic) and other islands in the Caribbean. From San Salvador, Columbus sailed southwest, landing on Cuba on October 28. Deciding that he must be on the mainland near the coastal city of Quinsay (now Hangzhou), described by Marco Polo, he sent a small embassy inland with letters from Ferdinand and Isabella and instructions to locate the grand city. Although they found no large settlement or any evidence of a great kingdom, the sight of Taino people wearing gold ornaments on Hispaniola suggested that gold was available in the region. In January, confident that its source would soon be found, Columbus headed back to Spain to report on his discovery.[4]

On his second voyage in 1493, Columbus brought with him settlers for the new Spanish territories, along with agricultural seed and livestock. Columbus and his followers forcibly took control of the island of Hispaniola and enslaved its indigenous people. Columbus himself, however, had limited skills in governing. Revolt soon broke out against him and his brother on Hispaniola. A royal expedition sent to investigate his leadership returned the brothers to Spain in chains, and a royal governor assumed control of the colony.

Columbus was very much a man of his times. To the end of his life in 1506, he incorrectly believed that he had found small islands off the coast of Asia. He could not know that the scale of his discoveries would revolutionize world power and set in motion a new era of trade, conquest, and empire.

Spain "Discovers" the Pacific

The Florentine navigator Amerigo Vespucci (veh-SPOO-chee) (1454–1512) was one of the first to begin to perceive what Columbus had not. Writing about his discoveries on the coast of modern-day Venezuela, Vespucci stated: "Those new regions which we found and explored with the fleet . . . we may rightly call a New World." This letter, titled *Mundus Novus* (The New World), was the first document to describe America as a continent separate from Asia. In recognition of Amerigo's bold claim, a German mapmaker named the new continent for him in 1507.

As soon as Columbus returned from his first voyage, Isabella and Ferdinand sought to establish their claims to the new territories and forestall potential opposition from Portugal, which had previously dominated Atlantic exploration. Spanish-born Pope Alexander VI, to whom they appealed for support, proposed drawing an imaginary line down the Atlantic, giving Spain possession of all lands discovered to the west and Portugal everything to the east. The pope enjoined both powers to carry the Christian faith to these newly discovered lands and their peoples. The **Treaty of Tordesillas** (tor-duh-SEE-yuhs) negotiated between Spain and Portugal in 1494 retained the pope's idea, but moved the line further west as a concession to the Portuguese. This arbitrary division worked in Portugal's favor when in 1500 an expedition led by Pedro Álvares Cabral, en route to India, landed on the coast of Brazil, which Cabral claimed as Portuguese territory. (Because the line was also imagined to extend around the globe, it meant that the Philippine Islands would eventually end up in Spanish control.)

The search for profits determined the direction of Spanish exploration. Because its revenue from Hispaniola and other Caribbean islands was insignificant compared to the enormous riches that the Portuguese were reaping in Asia, Spain renewed the search for a western passage to Asia. In 1519 Charles I of Spain (who was also Holy Roman emperor Charles V) sent the Portuguese mariner Ferdinand Magellan (1480–1521) to find a sea route to the spices of Southeast Asia. Magellan sailed southwest across the Atlantic to Brazil, and after a long search along the coast he located the treacherous straits that now bear his name (see Map 14.2). The new ocean he sailed into after a rough passage through the straits seemed so calm that Magellan dubbed it the Pacific, from the Latin word for peaceful. His fleet sailed north up the west coast of South America and then headed west into the immense expanse of the Pacific in 1520 toward the Malay Archipelago, which includes modern-day Indonesia and other island nations.

Magellan's first impressions of the Pacific were terribly mistaken. Terrible storms, disease, starvation, and violence devastated the expedition. Magellan himself died in a skirmish in the Malay Archipelago, and only one of the five ships that began the expedition made it back to Spain. The ship returned home in 1522 with only 18 of the approximately 270 men who originally set out, having traveled from the east by way of the Indian Ocean, the Cape of Good Hope, and the Atlantic. The voyage—the first to circumnavigate the globe—had taken close to three years.

Despite the losses, this voyage revolutionized Europeans' understanding of the world by demonstrating the vastness of the Pacific. The earth was clearly much larger than Ptolemy's map had shown. Although the voyage made a small profit in spices, it also demonstrated that the westward passage to the Indies was too long and dangerous for commercial purposes. Spain's rulers soon abandoned the attempt to oust Portugal from the Eastern spice trade and concentrated on exploiting its New World territories.

Early Exploration by Northern European Powers

Shortly following Columbus's voyages, northern European nations entered the competition for a northwest passage to the Indies. In 1497 John Cabot, a Venetian merchant living in London, obtained support from English king Henry VII for such a voyage. Following a northern route that he believed would provide shorter passage to Asia, Cabot and his crew landed on Newfoundland. In subsequent years, Cabot made two additional voyages to explore the northeast coast of Canada. These forays did not reveal a passage to the Indies, and Cabot made no attempt to establish settlements in the coastal areas he explored.

News of the riches of Mexico and Peru later inspired the English to renew their efforts to find a westward passage, this time in the extreme north. Between 1576 and 1578 Martin Frobisher made three voyages in and around the Canadian bay that now bears his name. Frobisher brought a quantity of ore back to England with him, hoping he had found a new source of gold or silver, but it proved to be worthless.

The French crown also sponsored efforts to find a westward passage to Asia. Between 1534 and 1541 Frenchman Jacques Cartier made several voyages and explored the St. Lawrence River of Canada. His exploration of the St. Lawrence was halted at the great rapids west of the present-day island of Montreal; he named the rapids "La Chine" in the optimistic belief that China lay just beyond. When this hope proved vain, the French turned to a new source of profit within Canada itself: trade in beavers and other furs. As had the Portuguese in Asia, French traders bartered with local people, who maintained autonomous control of their trade goods.

French fishermen also competed with Portuguese and Spanish, and later English, ships for the teeming schools of cod they found in the Atlantic waters around Newfoundland, one of the richest fish stocks in the world. Fishing vessels salted the catch on board and brought it back to Europe, where a thriving market for fish was created by the Catholic prohibition on eating meat on Fridays and during Lent.

What was the impact of European conquest on the New World?

Before Columbus's arrival, the Americas were inhabited by thousands of groups of indigenous peoples with different languages and cultures. These groups ranged from hunter-gatherer tribes organized into tribal confederations to settled agriculturalists to large-scale empires containing bustling cities and towns. The best estimate is that the peoples of the Americas numbered between 35 and 50 million in 1492. Their lives were radically transformed by the arrival of Europeans.

The growing European presence in the New World transformed its land and its peoples forever. While Iberian powers conquered enormous territories in Central and South America, incorporating pre-existing peoples and empires, the northern European powers came later to colonization and established scattered settlements hugging the North American Atlantic coastline.

Conquest of the Aztec Empire

The first two decades after Columbus's arrival in the New World saw Spanish settlement of Hispaniola, Cuba, Puerto Rico, and other Caribbean islands. Based on rumors of a wealthy mainland civilization, the Spanish governor in Cuba sponsored expeditions to the Yucatán coast of the Gulf of Mexico, including one in 1519 under the command of Hernán Cortés (1485–1547), a minor Spanish nobleman who had spent fifteen years in the Caribbean as an imperial administrator. Alarmed by Cortés's ambition, the governor decided to withdraw his support, but Cortés quickly set sail before being removed from command. Cortés, accompanied by several hundred fellow conquistadors as well as Taino and African slaves, landed on the Mexican coast on April 21, 1519. His camp soon received visits by delegations from the Aztec emperor bearing gifts and news of their great emperor.

The **Aztec Empire** was formed in the early fifteenth century through an alliance of the Mexica people of Tenochtitlan (tay-nawch-teet-LAHN) with other city-states in the Valley of Mexico. Over the next decades, the empire expanded rapidly through conquest. At the time of the Spanish arrival, emperor Moctezuma II (r. 1502–1520) ruled an empire of several million inhabitants from the capital at Tenochtitlan, now Mexico City. The Aztec Empire had a highly developed culture with advanced mathematics, astronomy, and engineering, as well as oral poetry and written record keeping. Aztec society was highly hierarchical. A hereditary nobility dominated the army, the priesthood, and the state bureaucracy, and lived from tribute collected from conquered states and its own people. The Aztec state practiced constant warfare against neighboring peoples to secure captives for religious sacrifices and laborers for agricultural and building projects.

After arriving on the mainland, Cortés took steps to establish authority independent of Cuba and the Spanish governor. He formally declared the establishment of a new town called Vera Cruz, naming his leading followers as town councilors and himself as military commander. He then sent letters to the Spanish crown requesting authorization to conquer and govern new lands.

The brutal nature of the Aztec Empire provided an opening for Cortés to obtain local assistance, a necessity for conquistadors throughout the Americas given their small numbers and ignorance of local conditions. Within weeks of his arrival, Cortés acquired translators who provided vital information on the empire and its weaknesses. In September 1519, after initial hostilities in which many Spaniards died, Cortés formed an alliance with Tlaxcala (tlah-SKAH-lah), an independent city-state that had successfully resisted incorporation into the Aztec Empire.

In October a combined Spanish-Tlaxcalan force marched to the city of Cholula, which had recently switched loyalties from Tlaxcala to the Aztec Empire and massacred many thousands of inhabitants, including women and children. Impressed by this display of ruthless power, the other native kingdoms joined Cortés's alliance against Aztec rule. In November 1519, these combined forces marched on Tenochtitlan.

Historians have long debated Moctezuma's response to the arrival of the Spanish. Despite the fact that Cortés was allied with enemies of the empire, Moctezuma refrained from attacking the Spaniards and instead welcomed Cortés and approximately 250 Spanish followers into Tenochtitlan. Cortés later claimed that at this

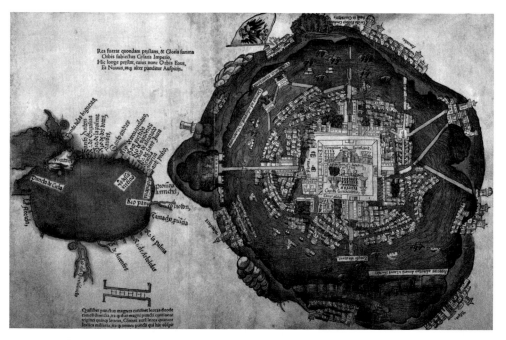

The Mexica Capital of Tenochtitlan This woodcut map was published in 1524 along with Cortés's letters describing the conquest of the Aztec Empire. As it shows, Tenochtitlan occupied an island and was laid out in concentric circles. The administrative and religious buildings were at the heart of the city, which was surrounded by residential quarters. Cortés himself marveled at the city in his letters: "The city is as large as Seville or Cordoba. . . . There are bridges, very large, strong, and well constructed, so that, over many, ten horsemen can ride abreast. . . . The city has many squares where markets are held. . . . There is one square . . . where there are daily more than sixty thousand souls, buying and selling. In the service and manners of its people, their fashion of living was almost the same as in Spain, with just as much harmony and order." (Newberry Library, Chicago, Illinois, USA/Bridgeman Images)

meeting the emperor, inspired by prophecies of the Spaniards' arrival, agreed to become a vassal of the Spanish king. Although impossible for historians to verify, Cortés and later Spanish colonists used this claim to legitimate violence against any who resisted their rule.

After spending more than seven months in the city, in an ambiguous position that combined the status of honored guests, occupiers, and detainees, the Spanish seized Moctezuma as a hostage. During the ensuing attacks and counterattacks, Moctezuma was killed. The city's population rose up against the Spaniards, who fled with heavy losses. In May 1521 the Spanish-Tlaxcalan alliance assaulted Tenochtitlan a second time with an army of approximately one thousand Spanish and seventy-five thousand native warriors.[5]

The fall of the Aztec capital in late summer 1521 was hard-won and greatly facilitated by the effects of smallpox, which had devastated the besieged population of the city. After establishing a new capital in the ruins of Tenochtitlan, Cortés and other conquistadors began the systematic conquest of Mexico. Major campaigns continued in Mesoamerica for at least two decades against ongoing resistance.

The Fall of the Incas

More surprising than the defeat of the Aztecs was the fall of the remote **Inca Empire**. Living in a settlement located more than 9,800 feet above sea level, the Incas were isolated from North American indigenous cultures and knew nothing of the Aztec Empire or its collapse. In 1438 the hereditary ruler of the Incas had himself crowned emperor and embarked on a successful campaign of conquest. At its greatest extent, the empire extended to the frontier of present-day Ecuador and Colombia in the north and to present-day Chile in the south, an area containing some 16 million people and 350,000 square miles.

Ruled from the capital city of Cuzco, the empire was divided into four major regions containing eighty provinces and twice as many districts. Officials at each level used an extensive network of roads to transmit information and orders back and forth through the empire. While the Aztecs used a system of glyphs for writing, the Incas had devised a complex system of colored and knotted cords, called *khipus*, for administrative bookkeeping. The empire also benefited from the use of llamas as pack animals (by contrast, no beasts of burden existed in Mesoamerica). The Incas integrated regions they conquered by spreading their religion and imposing their language, Quechua, as the official language of the empire.

By the time of the Spanish invasion, however, the Inca Empire had been weakened by a civil war over succession and an epidemic of disease, possibly smallpox, which may have spread through trade with groups in contact with Europeans. Francisco Pizarro (ca. 1475–1541), a conquistador of modest Spanish origins, landed on the northern coast of Peru on May 13, 1532, the very day the Inca leader Atahualpa (ah-tuh-WAHL-puh) won control of the empire after five years of fighting. As Pizarro advanced across the steep Andes toward Cuzco, the capital of the Inca Empire, Atahualpa was also heading there for his coronation.

Like Moctezuma in Mexico, Atahualpa was aware of the Spaniards' movements. He sent envoys to invite the Spanish to meet him in the provincial town of Cajamarca. His plan was to lure the Spanish into a trap, seize their horses and ablest men for his army, and execute the rest. With an army of some forty thousand men stationed nearby, Atahualpa felt he had little to fear. Instead, the Spaniards ambushed and captured him, collected an enormous ransom in gold, and then executed him in 1533 on trumped-up charges. The Spanish then marched on to Cuzco, profiting once again from internal conflicts to form alliances with local peoples. When Cuzco fell in 1533, the Spanish plundered the empire's wealth in gold and silver.

As with the Aztec Empire, the fall of the imperial capital did not end hostilities. Warfare between Spanish and Inca forces continued to the 1570s. During this period, civil war broke out among Spanish settlers vying for power.

For centuries students have wondered how it was possible for several hundred Spanish conquistadors to defeat powerful empires commanding large armies, vast wealth, and millions of inhabitants. This question is based on a mistaken understanding of the conquest as the rapid work of Spaniards acting alone, ideas that were spread in the aftermath by the conquistadors themselves. Instead, the defeat of the Aztec and Inca Empires was a long process enabled by divisions within the empires that produced political weakness and many skilled and motivated native allies who fought alongside the Spanish. Spanish steel swords, guns, horses, and dogs produced military advantages, but these tools of war were limited in number and effectiveness. Very few of the conquistadors were experienced soldiers. Perhaps the most important factor was the devastating impact of contagious diseases among the indigenous population, which swept through the Aztec and Inca Empires at the time of the conquest.

Portuguese Brazil

Unlike Mesoamerica or the Andes, the territory of Brazil contained no urban empires, but instead roughly 2.5 million nomadic and settled people divided into small tribes and many different language groups. In 1500 the Portuguese crown named Pedro Álvares Cabral commander of a fleet headed for the spice trade of the Indies. En route the fleet sailed far to the west, accidentally landing on the coast of Brazil, which Cabral claimed for Portugal under the terms of the Treaty of Tordesillas. The Portuguese soon undertook a profitable trade with local people in brazilwood, a valued source of red dye.

Portuguese settlers began arriving in the 1530s, with numbers rising after 1550. In the early years of settlement, the Portuguese brought sugarcane production to Brazil. They initially used enslaved indigenous laborers on sugar plantations, but the rapid decline in the indigenous population soon led to the use of forcibly transported Africans. In Brazil the Portuguese thus created a new form of colonization in the Americas: large plantations worked by enslaved people. This model would spread throughout the Caribbean along with sugar production in the seventeenth century.

Colonial Empires of England and France

For almost a century after the fall of the Aztec capital of Tenochtitlan, the Spanish and Portuguese dominated European overseas trade and colonization. In the early seventeenth century, however, northern European powers began to challenge the Iberian monopoly. They eventually succeeded in creating multisited overseas empires, consisting of settler colonies in North America, slave plantations in the Caribbean, and scattered trading posts in West Africa and Asia. Competition among European states for colonies was encouraged by mercantilist economic doctrine, which dictated that foreign trade was a zero-sum game in which one country's gains necessarily entailed another's losses.

Unlike the Iberian powers, whose royal governments financed exploration and directly ruled the colonies, England, France, and the Netherlands conducted the initial phase of colonization via chartered companies endowed with government monopolies over settlement and trade in a given area. These corporate bodies were granted extensive powers over faraway colonies, including exclusive rights to conduct trade, wage war, raise taxes, and administer justice.

The colony of Virginia, founded at Jamestown in 1607, initially struggled to grow sufficient food and faced hostility from the Powhatan Confederacy, a military alliance composed of around thirty Algonquian-speaking Native American tribes. Eventually it thrived by producing tobacco for a growing European market. Indentured servants obtained free passage to the colony in exchange for several years of work and the promise of greater opportunity for economic and social advancement than in England. In the 1670s English colonists from the Caribbean island of Barbados settled Carolina, where conditions were suitable for large rice plantations. During the late seventeenth century, following the Portuguese model in Brazil, enslaved Africans replaced indentured servants as laborers on tobacco and rice plantations, and a harsh racial divide was imposed.

Settlement on the coast of New England was undertaken for different reasons. There, radical Protestants sought to escape Anglican repression in England and begin new lives. The small and struggling outpost of Plymouth Colony (1620), founded by the Pilgrims who arrived on the *Mayflower*, was followed by Massachusetts Bay Colony (1630), which grew into a prosperous settlement. Because New England lacked the conditions for plantation agriculture, slavery was always a minor element of life there.

French navigator and explorer Samuel de Champlain founded the first permanent French settlement, at Quebec, in 1608. Ville-Marie, later named Montreal, was founded in 1642. Following the waterways of the St. Lawrence, the Great Lakes, and the Mississippi, the French ventured into much of modern-day Canada and at least thirty-five of the fifty states of the United States. French traders forged relations with the Huron Confederacy, a league of four indigenous nations that dominated a large region north of Lake Erie, as a means of gaining access to hunting grounds and trade routes for beaver and other animals. In 1682, French explorer René-Robert Cavelier LaSalle descended the Mississippi to the Gulf of Mexico, opening the way for French occupation of Louisiana.

Spanish expansion shared many similarities with that of other European powers, including the use of violence against indigenous populations and efforts toward Christian conversion, but there were important differences. Whereas the Spanish conquered indigenous empires, forcing large population groups to render tribute and enter state labor systems, English settlements merely hugged the Atlantic coastline and did not seek to incorporate the indigenous population. The English disinterest in full-scale conquest did not prevent conflict with native groups over land and resources, however. At Jamestown, for example, English expansion undermined prior cooperation with the Powhatan Confederacy; disease and warfare with the English led to drastic population losses among the Powhatans.

In the first decades of the seventeenth century, English and French naval captains also defied Spain's hold over the Caribbean Sea (see Map 14.2). The English seized control of Bermuda (1612), Barbados (1627), and a succession of other islands. The French took Cayenne (1604), St. Christophe (1625), Martinique and Guadeloupe (1635), and, finally, Saint-Domingue (1697) on the western half of Spanish-occupied Hispaniola. These islands acquired new importance after 1640, when the Portuguese brought sugar plantations to Brazil. Sugar and slaves quickly followed in the West Indies (see "Sugar and Slavery"), making the Caribbean plantations the most lucrative of all colonial possessions.

Northern European expansion also occurred in West Africa. In the seventeenth century France and England—along with Denmark and other northern European powers—established fortified trading posts in West Africa as bases for purchasing enslaved people and in India and the Indian Ocean as bases for purchasing spices and other luxury goods. Thus, by the end of the seventeenth century, a handful of European powers possessed overseas empires that truly spanned the globe.

Colonial Administration

In 1482, King John II of Portugal established a royal trading house in Lisbon to handle gold and other goods (including enslaved people) being extracted from Africa. After Portuguese trade expanded into the Indian Ocean spice trade, it was named the *Casa da India* (House of the Indies). Through the Casa, the Crown exercised a monopoly over the export of European goods and the import and distribution of spices and precious metals. It charged taxes on all other incoming goods. The Casa also established a viceroy in the Indian city of Goa to administer Portuguese trading posts and naval forces in Africa and Asia.

To secure the vast expanse of Brazil, in the 1530s the Portuguese implemented the system of captaincies, hereditary grants of land given to nobles and loyal officials who were to bear the costs of settling and administering their territories. The failure of this system led the Crown to bring the captaincies under state control by appointing royal governors to act as administrators. The captaincy of Bahia was the site of the capital, Salvador, home to the governor general and other royal officials.

Spain adopted a similar system for overseas trade. In 1503 the Spanish granted the port of Seville a monopoly over all traffic to the New World and established the *Casa de la Contratación* (House of Trade) to oversee economic matters. In 1524 Spain created the Royal and Supreme Council of the Indies, with authority over all colonial affairs, subject to approval by the king.

By the end of the sixteenth century the Spanish had successfully overcome most indigenous groups and expanded their territory throughout modern-day Mexico, the southwestern United States, and Central and South America (with the exception of Portuguese Brazil). In Mesoamerica and the Andes, the Spanish had taken over the cities and tribute systems of the Aztecs and the Incas, leaving in place well-established cities and towns, but redirecting tribute payments toward the Crown. Through laws and regulations, the Spanish crown strove to maintain two separate populations, a "Spanish Republic" and an "Indian Republic," with distinct rights and duties for each group.

The Spanish crown divided its New World possessions initially into two **viceroyalties**, or administrative divisions: New Spain, created in 1535, with its capital at Mexico City, and Peru, created in 1542, with its capital at Lima. In the eighteenth century two additional viceroyalties were added: New Granada, with Bogotá as its administrative center; and La Plata, with Buenos Aires as its capital (see Map 14.2).

Within each territory the viceroy, or imperial governor, exercised broad military and civil authority as the direct representative of Spain. The viceroy presided over the *audiencia* (ow-dee-EHN-see-ah), a board of twelve to fifteen judges that served as his advisory council and the highest judicial body. As in Spain, settlement in the Americas was centered on cities and towns. In each city, the municipal council, or *cabildo*, exercised local authority. Women were denied participation in public life, a familiar pattern from both European and precolonial indigenous society.

By the end of the seventeenth century the French crown had followed the Iberian example and imposed direct rule over its North American colonies. The king appointed military governors to rule alongside intendants, royal officials possessed of broad administrative and financial authority within their intendancies. In the mid-eighteenth century reform-minded Spanish king Charles III (r. 1759–1788) adopted the intendant system for the Spanish colonies.

England's colonies followed a distinctive path. Drawing on English traditions of representative government, its colonists established their own proudly autonomous assemblies to regulate local affairs. Wealthy merchants and landowners dominated the assemblies, yet common men had more say in politics than was the case in England.

How did Europe and the world change after Columbus?

The New and Old Worlds were brought into contact and forever changed by the European voyages of discovery and their aftermath. For the first time, a global economy emerged in the sixteenth and seventeenth centuries, and it forged new links among far-flung peoples, cultures, and societies. The ancient civilizations of Europe, Africa, the Americas, and Asia confronted each other in new and rapidly evolving ways. Those confrontations led to conquest, voluntary and forced migration, devastating population losses, and brutal exploitation. The exchange of goods and people between Europe and the New World brought highly destructive diseases to the Americas, but it also gave both the New and Old Worlds new crops that eventually altered consumption patterns across the globe.

Economic Exploitation of the Indigenous Population

From the first decades of settlement, the Spanish made use of the **encomienda system,** by which the Crown granted the conquerors the right to employ groups of Native Americans as laborers or to demand tribute from them in exchange for providing food and shelter. The encomiendas were also intended as a means to organize indigenous people for missionary work and Christian conversion. This system was first used in Hispaniola to work goldfields, then in Mexico for agricultural labor, and, when silver was discovered in the 1540s, for silver mining.

A 1512 Spanish law authorizing the use of encomiendas called for indigenous people to be treated fairly, but in practice the system led to terrible abuses, including overwork, beatings, and sexual violence. Spanish missionaries publicized these abuses, leading to debates in Spain about the nature and proper treatment of indigenous people (see "Religious Conversion" ahead in this chapter). King Charles I responded to complaints in 1542 with the New Laws, which set limits on the authority of encomienda holders, including their ability to transmit their privileges to heirs. The New Laws recognized indigenous people who accepted Christianity and Spanish rule as free subjects of the Spanish crown. According to these laws, they had voluntarily accepted to be vassals of the Spanish king and thereby gained personal liberty and the right to form their own communities.

The New Laws provoked a revolt in Peru among encomienda holders, and they were little enforced throughout Spanish territories. For example, although the laws forbade enslavement of indigenous people, the practice did not end completely. To respond to persistent abuses in the encomiendas and a growing shortage of indigenous workers, royal officials established a new government-run system of forced labor, called *repartimiento* in New Spain and *mita* in Peru. Administrators assigned a certain percentage of the inhabitants of native communities to labor for a set period each year in public works, mining, agriculture, and other tasks. Laborers received modest wages in exchange, which they could use to fulfill tribute obligations. In the seventeenth century, as land became a more important source of wealth than labor, elite settlers purchased *haciendas*, large tracts of farmland worked by dependent indigenous laborers and slaves.

Spanish systems for exploiting the labor of indigenous peoples were both a cause of and a response to the disastrous decline in their numbers that began soon after the arrival of Europeans. Some indigenous people died as a direct result of the violence of conquest and the disruption of agriculture and trade caused by warfare, but the most important cause of death was infectious disease. (See "The Columbian Exchange and Population Loss" ahead in this chapter.)

Colonial administrators responded to native population decline by forcibly combining dwindling indigenous communities into new settlements and imposing the rigors of the encomienda and the repartimiento. By the end of the sixteenth century the search for fresh sources of labor had given birth to the new tragedy of the transatlantic slave trade (see "Sugar and Slavery").

Society in the Colonies

Many factors helped shape life in European colonies, including geographical location, pre-existing indigenous cultures, patterns of settlement, and the policies and cultural values of the different nations that claimed them as empire. Throughout the New World, colonial settlements were hedged by immense borderlands where European power was weak and Europeans and non-Europeans interacted on a more equal basis.

Women played a crucial role in the emergence of colonial societies. The first explorers formed unions with native women, many of whom were enslaved, and relied on them as translators and guides and to form alliances with indigenous powers. As settlement developed, the character of each colony was influenced by the presence or absence of European women. Where women and children accompanied men, as in the Spanish mainland and British colonies, new settlements took on European languages, religion, and ways of life that have endured, with strong input from local cultures, to this day. Where European women did not accompany men, as on the west coast of Africa and most European outposts in Asia, local populations largely retained their own cultures, to which male Europeans acclimatized themselves.

Most women who crossed the Atlantic were captive Africans, constituting four-fifths of the female newcomers before 1800.[6] Wherever slavery existed, masters profited from their power to coerce sexual relations with enslaved women. One important difference among European colonies was in the status of children born from such unions. In some colonies, mostly those dominated by the Portuguese, Spanish, or French, substantial populations of free people of color descended from the freed children of such unions. In English colonies, masters were less likely to free children they fathered with female slaves. The mixing of indigenous peoples with Europeans and Africans created whole new populations and ethnicities and complex forms of identity (see "New Ideas About Race").

The Columbian Exchange and Population Loss

The migration of people to the New World led to an exchange of animals, plants, and diseases, a complex process known as the **Columbian exchange**.

Everywhere they settled, the Spanish and Portuguese brought and raised wheat with labor provided by the encomienda system. Grapes and olives brought over from Spain did well in parts of Peru and Chile. Perhaps the most significant introduction to the diet of Native Americans came via the meat and milk of the livestock that the early conquistadors brought with them, including cattle, sheep, and goats. The horse allowed for faster travel and easier transport of heavy loads.

In turn, Europeans returned home with many food crops that became central elements of their diet. Crops originating in the Americas included tomatoes, squash, pumpkins, peppers, and many varieties of beans, as well as tobacco. One of the most important of such crops was maize (corn). By the late seventeenth century maize had become a staple in Spain, Portugal, southern France, and Italy, and in the eighteenth century it became one of the chief foods of southeastern Europe and southern China. Even more valuable was the nutritious white potato, which slowly spread from west to east, contributing everywhere to a rise in population.

While the exchange of foods was a great benefit to both cultures, the introduction of European pathogens to the New World had a disastrous impact on the native population. In Europe, infectious diseases like smallpox, measles, and influenza—originally passed on from domestic animals living among the population—killed many people each year. Given the size of the population and the frequency of outbreaks, in most of Europe these diseases were experienced in childhood, and survivors carried immunity or resistance. Over centuries of dealing with these diseases, the European population had had time to adapt. Prior to contact with Europeans, indigenous peoples of the New World suffered from insect-borne diseases and some infectious ones, but their lack of domestic livestock spared them the host of highly infectious diseases known in the Old World. The arrival of Europeans spread these microbes among a completely unprepared population, and they fell victim in vast numbers.

Overall, the indigenous population declined by as much as 90 percent or more, but with important regional variations. In general, densely populated urban centers were worse hit than rural areas, and tropical, low-lying regions suffered more than

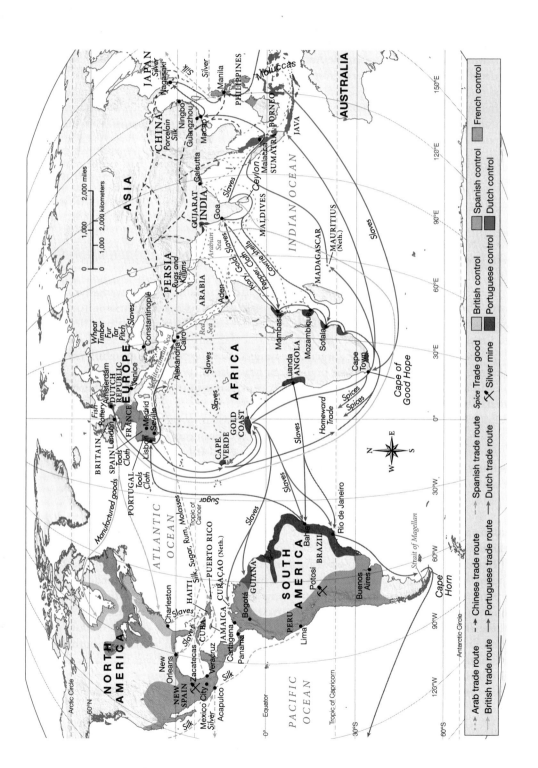

cooler, higher-altitude ones. The world after Columbus was thus marked by disease as well as by trade and colonization.

Sugar and Slavery

Throughout the Middle Ages slavery was deeply entrenched in the Mediterranean. The constant warfare of the reconquista had supplied captive Muslims for domestic slavery in Iberia, but the success of these wars meant that the number of captives had greatly dwindled by the mid-fifteenth century.

As Portuguese explorers began their voyages along the western coast of Africa, one of the first commodities they sought was enslaved human beings. In 1444 the first ship returned to Lisbon with a cargo of enslaved Africans. While the first slaves were simply seized by small raiding parties, Portuguese merchants soon found that it was easier to trade with local leaders, who were accustomed to dealing in captives acquired through warfare with neighboring powers. In 1483 the Portuguese established an alliance with the kingdom of Kongo. The royal family eventually converted to Christianity, and Portuguese merchants intermarried with Kongolese women, creating a permanent Afro-Portuguese community. From 1490 to 1530 Portuguese traders brought hundreds of enslaved Africans to Lisbon each year (Map 14.3) to work as domestic slaves.

In this stage of European expansion, the history of slavery became intertwined with the history of sugar. Originally sugar was an expensive luxury, but population increases and monetary expansion in the fifteenth century led to increasing demand. Native to the South Pacific, sugar was taken in ancient times to India, where farmers learned to preserve cane juice as granules that could be stored and shipped. From there, sugar crops traveled to China and the Mediterranean, where islands like Crete and Sicily had the warm and humid climate needed for growing sugarcane. When Genoese and other Italians colonized the Canary Islands and the Portuguese settled on the Madeira Islands, which possessed the requisite climate conditions, sugar plantations came to the Atlantic.

Sugar was a difficult and demanding crop to produce for profit. Seed-stems were planted by hand, thousands to the acre. When mature, the cane had to be harvested and processed rapidly to avoid spoiling. Moreover, sugar has a virtually constant growing season, meaning that there was no fallow period when workers could recuperate from the arduous labor. The invention of roller mills to crush the cane more efficiently meant that yields could be significantly augmented, but only if a sufficient labor force was found to supply the mills. Europeans solved the labor problem by forcing first native islanders and then enslaved Africans to provide the backbreaking work.

The transatlantic slave trade began in 1518 when Spanish king Charles I authorized traders to bring enslaved Africans to the Americas. The Portuguese brought the first slaves to Brazil around 1550; by 1600 four thousand were being imported

< **MAP 14.3 Seaborne Trading Empires in the Sixteenth and Seventeenth Centuries**
By the mid-seventeenth century trade linked all parts of the world except for Australia. Notice that trade in slaves was not confined to the Atlantic but involved almost all parts of the world.

Indians Working in a Spanish Sugar Mill Belgian engraver Theodor de Bry published many images of the European exploration and settlement of the New World. De Bry never crossed the Atlantic himself, instead drawing on images and stories from those who did. This image depicts the exploitation of indigenous people in a Spanish sugar mill. (ca. 1540 engraving by Theodore de Bry [1528–1598]/Bibliothèque Nationale, Paris, France/Snark/Art Resource, NY)

annually. After its founding in 1621, the Dutch West India Company transported thousands of Africans to Brazil and the Caribbean, mostly to work on sugar plantations. In the mid-seventeenth century the English got involved.

Before 1700, when slavers decided it was better business to improve conditions for the slaves, some 20 percent of captives died on the voyage across the Atlantic.[7] The most common cause of death was dysentery induced by poor-quality food and water, crowding, and lack of sanitation. Men were often kept in irons during the passage, while women and girls suffered sexual violence from sailors. On sugar plantations, death rates from the brutal pace of labor were extremely high, leading to demand for a constant stream of new shipments from Africa.

Spanish Silver and Its Economic Effects

In 1545, at an altitude of fifteen thousand feet, the Spanish discovered an extraordinary source of silver at Potosí (poh-toh-SEE) (in present-day Bolivia) in territory conquered from the Inca Empire. By 1550 Potosí yielded perhaps 60 percent of all the silver mined in the world. From Potosí and the mines at Zacatecas (za-kuh-TAY-kuhhs) and Guanajuato (gwah-nah-HWAH-toh) in Mexico, huge quantities of precious metals poured forth.

Mining became the most important industry in the colonies. Millions of indigenous laborers suffered brutal conditions and death in the silver mines. Demand for new sources of labor for the mines also contributed to the intensification of the African slave trade. Profits for the Spanish crown were immense. The Crown claimed the quinto, one-fifth of all precious metals mined in South America, which represented 25 percent of its total income. Between 1503 and 1650, 35 million pounds of silver and over 600,000 pounds of gold entered Seville's port.

Spain's immense profits from silver paid for the tremendous expansion of its empire and for the large armies that defended it. However, the easy flow of money also dampened economic innovation. It exacerbated the rising inflation Spain was already experiencing in the mid-sixteenth century, a period of growing population and stagnant production. Several times between 1557 and 1647, King Philip II and his successors wrote off the state debt, thereby undermining confidence in the government and damaging the economy. Only after 1600, when the population declined, did prices gradually stabilize.

Philip II paid his armies and foreign debts with silver bullion, and thus Spanish inflation was transmitted to the rest of Europe. Between 1560 and 1600 much of Europe experienced large price increases. Because money bought less, people who lived on fixed incomes, such as nobles, were badly hurt. Those who owed fixed sums of money, such as the middle class, prospered because in a time of rising prices, debts lessened in value each year. Food costs rose most sharply, and the poor fared worst of all.

In many ways, though, it was not Spain but China that controlled the world trade in silver. The Chinese demanded silver for their products and for the payment of imperial taxes. China was thus the main buyer of world silver, absorbing half the world's production. The silver market drove world trade, with New Spain and Japan being mainstays on the supply side and China dominating the demand side. The world trade in silver is one of the best examples of the new global economy that emerged in this period.

The Birth of the Global Economy

With the Europeans' discovery of the Americas and their exploration of the Pacific, the entire world was linked for the first time in history by seaborne trade. The opening of that trade brought into being three commercial empires: the Portuguese, the Spanish, and the Dutch.

The Portuguese were the first worldwide traders. In the sixteenth century they controlled the sea route to India (see Map 14.3). From their fortified bases at Goa on the Arabian Sea and at Malacca on the Malay Peninsula, ships carried goods to the Portuguese settlement at Macao, founded in 1557, in the South China Sea. From Macao Portuguese ships loaded with Chinese silks and porcelains sailed to the Japanese port of Nagasaki and the Philippines, where Chinese goods were exchanged for Spanish silver from New Spain. Throughout Asia the Portuguese traded in slaves, some of whom were brought all the way across the Pacific to Mexico. Returning to Portugal, they brought Asian spices that had been purchased with textiles produced

Goods from the Global Economy Spices from Southeast Asia were a driving force behind the new global economy and among the most treasured European luxury goods. They were used not only for cooking but also as medicines and health tonics. This fresco shows a fifteenth-century Italian pharmacist measuring out spices for a customer. After the discovery of the Americas, a wave of new items entered European markets, silver foremost among them. (Issogne Castle, Val d'Aosta, Italy/Alfredo Dagli Orti/Shutterstock)

in India and with gold and ivory from East Africa. From their colony in Brazil, they shipped sugar produced by enslaved Africans whom they had forcibly transported across the Atlantic.

Coming to empire a few decades later than the Portuguese, the Spanish were determined to claim their place in world trade. The Spanish Empire in the New World was basically a land empire, but across the Pacific the Spaniards built a seaborne empire centered at Manila in the Philippines. Established in 1571, the city of Manila served as a transpacific link between Spanish America and China. In Manila, Spanish traders used silver from American mines to purchase Chinese silk for European markets (see Map 14.3).

In the final years of the sixteenth century the Dutch challenged the Spanish and Portuguese Empires. During this period the Protestant Dutch were engaged in a long war of independence from their Spanish Catholic overlords. The joining of the Portuguese crown to Spain in 1580 meant that the Dutch had both strategic and commercial reasons to attack Portugal's commercial empire. In 1599 a Dutch fleet returned to Amsterdam carrying 600,000 pounds of pepper and 250,000 pounds of cloves and nutmeg. Those who had invested in the expedition received a 100 percent profit. The voyage led to the establishment in 1602 of the Dutch East India Company, founded with the stated intention of capturing the Asian spice trade from the Portuguese.

In return for assisting Indonesian princes in local conflicts and disputes with the Portuguese, the Dutch won broad commercial concessions and forged military alliances. With Indonesian assistance, they captured the strategically located fort of Malacca in 1641, gaining western access to the Malay Archipelago. Gradually, they acquired political domination over the archipelago itself. The Dutch were willing to use force more ruthlessly than the Portuguese and had superior organizational efficiency. These factors allowed them to expel the Portuguese from Sri Lanka in 1660 and henceforth control the immensely lucrative production and trade of spices. The company also established the colony of Cape Town on the southern tip of Africa as a provisioning point for its Asian fleets.

Not content with challenging the Portuguese in the Indian Ocean, the Dutch also aspired to a role in the Americas. Founded in 1621, during their war with Spain, the Dutch West India Company aggressively sought to open trade with North and South America and capture Spanish territories there. The company captured or destroyed hundreds of Spanish ships, seized the Spanish silver fleet in 1628, and captured portions of Brazil and the Caribbean. The Dutch also successfully interceded in the transatlantic slave trade, establishing a large number of trading stations on the west coast of Africa.

How did expansion change European attitudes and beliefs?

The age of overseas expansion heightened Europeans' contacts with the rest of the world. Religion was one of the most important arenas of cultural contact, as European missionaries aimed to spread Christianity throughout the territories they acquired, with mixed results. While Christianity was embraced in parts of the New World, it was met largely with suspicion in places such as China and Japan. However, the East-West contacts did lead to exchanges of influential cultural and scientific ideas.

These contacts also gave birth to new ideas about the inherent superiority or inferiority of different races, sparking vociferous debate about the status of Africans and indigenous peoples of the Americas. The essays of Michel de Montaigne epitomized a new spirit of skepticism and cultural relativism, while the plays of William Shakespeare reflected the efforts of one great writer to come to terms with the cultural complexity of his day.

Religious Conversion

Conversion to Christianity was one of the most important justifications for European expansion. Jesuit missionaries were active in Japan and China in the sixteenth and seventeenth centuries, until authorities banned their teachings. The first missionaries

Franciscan Monks Burning Indigenous Temples In the late sixteenth century, more than six decades after the fall of Tenochtitlan, Diego Muñoz Camargo, an educated *mestizo*, was chosen to draft a report on the province of Tlaxcala in response to a questionnaire issued by the king of Spain. Camargo produced a history of the Tlaxcala people — one of the first and most important Spanish allies against the Aztecs — starting from the time of conquest. An important theme of the text and its accompanying images was the efforts made by Franciscan missionaries to stamp out polytheistic indigenous religions in favor of Catholicism. This included, as shown here, burning temples, as well as destroying religious texts and punishing lapsed converts. (From "Historia de Tlaxcala" by Diego Munoz Camargo/Glasgow University Library, Scotland/Bridgeman Images)

to the New World accompanied Columbus on his second voyage, and more than 2,500 priests and friars of the Franciscan, Dominican, Jesuit, and other Catholic orders crossed the Atlantic in the following century. Later French explorers were also accompanied by missionaries who preached to the Native American tribes with whom the French traded. Protestants also led missionary efforts, but in much smaller numbers than Catholics. Colonial powers built convents, churches, and cathedrals for converted indigenous people and European settlers, and established religious courts to police correct beliefs and morals.

To stamp out old beliefs and encourage sincere conversions, colonial authorities destroyed shrines and objects of religious worship. They harshly persecuted men and women who continued to practice and participate in traditional spiritual rituals. They imposed European Christian norms of family life, especially monogamous marriage. While many resisted these efforts, over time a larger number accepted Christianity. It is estimated that missionaries had baptized between 4 and 9 million indigenous people in New Spain by the mid-1530s.[8]

Rather than a straightforward imposition of Christianity, conversion entailed a complex process of cultural exchange. Catholic friars were among the first Europeans to seek an understanding of native cultures and languages as part of their effort to render Christianity comprehensible to indigenous people. In Mexico they not only learned the Nahuatl language, but also taught it to non-Nahuatl-speaking groups to create a shared language for Christian teaching. In translating Christianity, missionaries, working in partnership with indigenous converts, adapted it to the symbols and ritual objects of pre-existing cultures and beliefs, thereby creating distinctive forms of Catholicism.

European Debates About Indigenous Peoples

Iberian exploitation of the native population of the Americas began from the moment of Columbus's arrival in 1492. Denunciations of this abuse by Catholic missionaries, however, quickly followed, inspiring vociferous debates both in Europe and in the colonies about the nature of indigenous peoples and how they should be treated. Bartolomé de Las Casas (1474–1566), a Dominican friar and former encomienda holder, was one of the earliest and most outspoken critics of the brutal treatment inflicted on indigenous peoples. He wrote:

> It was upon these gentle lambs [that] . . . the Spanish fell like ravening wolves upon the fold, or like tigers and savage lions who have not eaten meat for days. The pattern established at the outset has remained unchanged to this day, and the Spaniards still do nothing save tear the natives to shreds, murder them and inflict upon them untold misery, suffering and distress, tormenting, harrying and persecuting them mercilessly. . . .[9]

Mounting criticism in Spain led King Charles I to assemble a group of churchmen and lawyers to debate the issue in 1550 in the city of Valladolid. One side, led by Juan Ginés de Sepúlveda, argued that conquest and forcible conversion were both necessary and justified to save indigenous people from the horrors of human sacrifice, cannibalism, and idolatry. He described them as barbarians who belonged to a category of inferior beings identified by the ancient Greek philosopher Aristotle as naturally destined for slavery. Against these arguments, Las Casas and his supporters depicted indigenous people as rational and innocent children, who deserved protection and tutelage from more advanced civilizations. Although Las Casas was more sympathetic to indigenous people, both sides thus agreed on the superiority of European culture.

While the debate did not end exploitation of indigenous people, the Crown did use it to justify limiting the rights of settlers in favor of the Catholic Church and royal authorities and to increase legal protections for their communities. In 1573, Philip II issued detailed laws regulating how new towns should be formed and administered, and how Spanish settlers should interact with indigenous populations. The impact of these laws can still be seen in Mexico's colonial towns, which are laid out as grids around a central plaza.

New Ideas About Race

European conquest and settlement led to the emergence of new ideas about "race" as a form of biological difference among humans. In medieval Spain and Portugal, sharp distinctions were drawn between, on the one hand, supposedly "pure-blooded" Christians and, on the other hand, Jews and *conversos*, people of Jewish origins who had converted to Christianity. In the fifteenth century, Iberian rulers issued discriminatory laws against conversos as well as against Muslims and their descendants. Feeling that conversion could not erase the taint of heretical belief, they came to see Christian faith as a type of inherited identity that was passed through the blood.

The idea of "purity of blood" changed through experiences in the colonies. There the transatlantic slave trade initiated in the sixteenth century meant that the colonial population comprised people of European, indigenous, and African descent. Spanish colonizers came to believe that the indigenous people of the Americas were free from the taint of unbelief because they had never been exposed to Christianity. Accordingly, the ideology of "purity of blood" they brought from Iberia could more easily incorporate indigenous populations; by contrast, Africans—viewed as having refused the message of Christ that was preached in the Old World—were seen as impure, as much on the grounds of religious difference as physical characteristics.

Despite later efforts by colonial officials to segregate Europeans, Native Americans, and people of African descent, racial mixing began as soon as the first conquistadors arrived in the Americas. A complex system of racial classification, known as *castas* in Spanish America, emerged to describe different proportions of European, indigenous, and African parentage. Spanish concerns about religious purity were thus transformed in the colonial context into concerns about racial bloodlines, with "pure" Spanish blood occupying the summit of the racial hierarchy and indigenous and African descent ranked in descending order. These concerns put female chastity at the center of anxieties about racial mixing, heightening scrutiny of women's sexual activities.

All European colonies in the New World relied on racial distinctions drawn between Europeans and indigenous people and those of African descent, including later French and English settlements. With its immense slave-based plantation agriculture system, large indigenous population, and relatively low Portuguese immigration, Brazil developed a particularly complex racial and ethnic mosaic.

After 1700 the emergence of new methods of observing and describing nature led to the use of scientific frameworks to define race. Although it originally referred to a nation or an ethnic group, henceforth the term *race* would be used to describe supposedly biologically distinct groups of people, whose physical differences produced differences in culture, character, and intelligence. This occurred at the same time as a shift to defining gender differences as inherent in the biological differences between male and female bodies (see "Women and the Enlightenment" in Chapter 16). Science thus served to justify and naturalize existing inequalities between Europeans and non-Europeans and between men and women.

Michel de Montaigne and Cultural Curiosity

Decades of religious fanaticism and civil war led some Catholics and Protestants to doubt that any one faith contained absolute truth. Added to these doubts was the discovery of peoples in the New World who had radically different ways of life. These shocks helped produce ideas of skepticism and cultural relativism. Skepticism is a school of thought founded on doubt that total certainty or definitive knowledge is ever attainable. Cultural relativism suggests that one culture is not necessarily superior to another, just different. Both notions found expression in the work of Frenchman Michel de Montaigne (duh mahn-TAYN) (1533–1592).

Montaigne developed a new literary genre, the essay, to express his ideas. Intending his works to be accessible, he wrote in French rather than Latin and in an engaging conversational style. His essays were quickly translated into other European languages and became some of the most widely read texts of the early modern period. Montaigne's essay "Of Cannibals" reveals the impact of overseas discoveries on one thoughtful European. In contrast to the prevailing views of his day, he rejected the notion that one culture is superior to another. Speaking of native Brazilians, he wrote: "I find that there is nothing barbarous and savage in this nation [Brazil], . . . except, that everyone gives the title of barbarism to everything that is not according to his usage."[10]

In his own time, few would have agreed with Montaigne's challenge to ideas of European superiority or his even more radical questioning of the superiority of humans over animals. Nevertheless, his popular essays contributed to a basic shift in attitudes. "Wonder," he said, "is the foundation of all philosophy, research is the means of all learning, and ignorance is the end."[11] Montaigne thus inaugurated an era of doubt.

William Shakespeare and His Influence

In addition to the essay as a literary genre, the period fostered remarkable creativity in other branches of literature, which also reflected the impact of European expansion and changing ideas about race. England—especially in the latter part of Queen Elizabeth I's reign and in the first years of her successor, James I (r. 1603–1625)—witnessed remarkable developments in theater and poetry. The undisputed master of the period was the dramatist William Shakespeare. Born in 1564 to a successful glove manufacturer in Stratford-upon-Avon, his genius lay in the originality of his characterizations, the diversity of his plots, his understanding of human psychology, and his unsurpassed gift for language. Although he wrote sparkling comedies and stirring historical plays, his greatest masterpieces were his later tragedies, including *Hamlet*, *Othello*, and *Macbeth*, which explore an enormous range of human problems and are open to an almost infinite variety of interpretations.

Like Montaigne's essays, Shakespeare's work reveals the impact of the new discoveries and contacts of his day. The title character of *Othello* is described as a "Moor," a term that in Shakespeare's day referred to Muslims of North African origin, including those who had migrated to the Iberian Peninsula. It could also be applied, though, to natives of the Iberian Peninsula who converted to Islam or to non-Muslim Berbers in North Africa. To complicate things even more, references in the play to Othello as "black" in skin color have led many to believe that Shakespeare intended him to be a sub-Saharan African.

This confusion in the play aptly reflects the important links in this period between racial and religious classifications. In contrast to the prevailing view of Moors as inferior, a view echoed by the Venetian characters in the play, Shakespeare presents Othello as a complex human figure, capable of great courage and nobility, but flawed by jealousy and credulity.

The play also exposes women's suffering at the hands of the patriarchal family. In *Othello*, fathers treat unmarried daughters as property and husbands murder wives they suspect of infidelity. Revealing anxieties about racial purity and miscegenation, several characters assert that Othello's "blackness" has tainted his Venetian wife. The play thus shows how racial ideologies very similar to those developed in the Spanish Empire existed in Elizabethan England.

NOTES

1. Marco Polo, *The Book of Ser Marco Polo, the Venetian: Concerning the Kingdoms and Marvels of the East*, vol. 2, trans. and ed. Colonel Sir Henry Yule (London: John Murray, 1903), pp. 185–186.
2. Thomas Benjamin, *The Atlantic World: Europeans, Africans, Indians and Their Shared History, 1400–1900* (Cambridge: Cambridge University Press, 2009), p. 56.
3. John Law, "On the Methods of Long Distance Control: Vessels, Navigation, and the Portuguese Route to India," in *Power, Action and Belief: A New Sociology of Knowledge?* ed. John Law, Sociological Review Monograph 32 (London: Routledge & Kegan Paul, 1986), pp. 234–263.
4. Peter Hulme, *Colonial Encounters: Europe and the Native Caribbean, 1492–1797* (London: Methuen, 1986), pp. 22–31.
5. Benjamin, *The Atlantic World*, p. 141.
6. Geoffrey Vaughn Scammell, *The First Imperial Age: European Overseas Expansion, c. 1400–1715* (London: Routledge, 2002), p. 432.
7. Herbert S. Klein, "Profits and the Causes of Mortality," in *The Atlantic Slave Trade*, ed. David Northrup (Lexington, Mass.: D. C. Heath and Co., 1994), p. 116.
8. David Carrasco, *The Oxford Encyclopedia of Mesoamerican Cultures* (Oxford: Oxford University Press, 2001), p. 208.
9. Bartolomé de las Casas, *A Short Account of the Destruction of the Indies*, trans. Nigel Griffin (New York: Penguin, 2004), p. 11.
10. C. Cotton, trans., *The Essays of Michel de Montaigne* (New York: A. L. Burt, 1893), pp. 207, 210.
11. Cotton, *The Essays*, p. 523.

LOOKING BACK **LOOKING AHEAD**

In 1517 Martin Luther issued his "Ninety-five Theses," launching the Protestant Reformation; just five years later, Ferdinand Magellan's expedition sailed around the globe, shattering European notions of terrestrial geography. Within a few short years, old medieval certainties about Heaven and earth began to collapse. In the ensuing decades, Europeans struggled to come to terms with religious difference at home and the multitudes of new peoples and places they encountered abroad. While some Europeans were fascinated and inspired by this new diversity, much more often the result was hostility and violence. Europeans endured decades of civil war between Protestants and Catholics, and indigenous peoples suffered massive population losses as a result of European warfare, disease, and exploitation. Tragically, both Catholic and Protestant religious leaders condoned the African slave trade that brought suffering and death to millions of people as well as the conquest of Native American land and the subjugation of indigenous people.

Even as the voyages of discovery coincided with the fragmentation of European culture, they also played a role in longer-term processes of state centralization and consolidation. The new monarchies of the Renaissance produced stronger and wealthier governments capable of financing the huge expenses of exploration and colonization. Competition to gain overseas colonies became an integral part of

European politics. Spain's investment in conquest proved spectacularly profitable, and yet, as we will see in Chapter 15, the ultimate result was a weakening of its power. Over time the Netherlands, England, and France also reaped tremendous profits from colonial trade, which helped them build modernized, centralized states. The path from medieval Christendom to modern nation-states led through religious warfare and global encounter.

MAKE CONNECTIONS

Think about the larger developments and continuities within and across chapters.

1. Michel de Montaigne argued that people's assessments of what was "barbaric" merely drew on their own habits and customs; based on the earlier sections of this chapter, how widespread was this openness to cultural difference? Was he alone, or did others share this view?

2. To what extent did the European voyages of expansion and conquest inaugurate an era of global history? Is it correct to date the beginning of "globalization" from the late fifteenth century? Why or why not?

Chapter 14 Review

IDENTIFY KEY TERMS

Identify and explain the significance of each item below.

conquistadors (p. 388)

caravel (p. 389)

Ptolemy's *Geography* (p. 389)

Treaty of Tordesillas (p. 393)

Aztec Empire (p. 395)

Inca Empire (p. 397)

viceroyalties (p. 400)

encomienda system (p. 401)

Columbian exchange (p. 403)

REVIEW THE MAIN IDEAS

Answer the section heading questions from the chapter.

1. What was the Afro-Eurasian trading world before Columbus? (p. 383)

2. How and why did Europeans undertake ambitious voyages of expansion? (p. 387)

3. What was the impact of European conquest on the New World? (p. 395)

4. How did Europe and the world change after Columbus? (p. 401)

5. How did expansion change European attitudes and beliefs? (p. 409)

CHRONOLOGY

1271–1295	• Marco Polo travels to China
1443	• Portuguese establish first African trading post at Arguin
1492	• Columbus lands in the Americas
1498	• Vasco da Gama lands in Calicut, India
1510–1515	• Portuguese capture trading centers at Goa, Malacca, Calicut, and Hormuz
1518	• Spanish king authorizes slave trade to New World colonies
1519–1522	• Magellan's expedition circumnavigates the world
1521	• Fall of Tenochtitlan, leading to Spanish takeover of the Aztec Empire
1533	• Spanish execution of the Inca emperor
1602	• Dutch East India Company established

15

Absolutism and Constitutionalism

ca. 1589–1725

CHAPTER PREVIEW

- What made the seventeenth century an "age of crisis" and achievement?

- Why did France rise and Spain fall during the late seventeenth century?

- What explains the rise of absolutism in Prussia and Austria?

- What were the distinctive features of Russian and Ottoman absolutism?

- Why and how did the constitutional state triumph in the Dutch Republic and England?

THE SEVENTEENTH CENTURY was a period of crisis and transformation in Europe. Agricultural and manufacturing slumps led to food shortages and shrinking population rates. Religious and dynastic conflicts led to almost constant war, visiting violence and destruction on ordinary people and reshaping European states. To consolidate their authority and expand their territories, European rulers increased the size of their armies, imposed higher taxes, and implemented bureaucratic forms of government. By the end of the seventeenth century they had largely succeeded in restoring order and securing increased power for the state.

The growth of state power within Europe raised a series of questions for rulers and subjects: Who held supreme power? What made it legitimate? Conflicts over these questions led to rebellions and, in some areas, outright civil war. While absolutism emerged as the solution to these challenges in many European states, a small minority, most notably England and the Dutch Republic, adopted a different path, placing sovereignty in the hands of privileged groups rather than the Crown.

What made the seventeenth century an "age of crisis" and achievement?

Historians often refer to the seventeenth century as an "age of crisis" because Europe was challenged by population losses, economic decline, and social and political unrest. This was partially due to climate changes that reduced agricultural productivity, but it also resulted from bitter religious divides, war, and increased governmental pressures. Peasants and the urban poor were especially hard hit by the economic problems, and they frequently rioted against high food prices.

The atmosphere of crisis encouraged governments to take emergency measures to restore order, measures that they successfully turned into long-term reforms that strengthened the power of the state. These included a spectacular growth in army size as well as increased taxation, the expansion of government bureaucracies, and the acquisition of land or maritime empires. In the long run, European states proved increasingly able to impose their will on the populace. This period also saw the flourishing of art and music with the drama and emotional intensity of the baroque style.

The Social Order and Peasant Life

In the seventeenth century, society was organized in hierarchical levels. In much of Europe, the monarch occupied the summit and was celebrated as a semidivine being, chosen by God to embody the state. The clergy generally occupied the second level because of its sacred role in interceding with God and the saints on behalf of its flocks. Next came nobles, whose privileged status derived from their ancient bloodlines and centuries of leadership in battle. Many prosperous mercantile families constituted a second tier of nobles, having bought their way into the nobility through service to the rising monarchies of the fifteenth and sixteenth centuries. Those lower on the social scale, the peasants and artisans who constituted the vast majority of the population, were expected to show deference to their betters. This was the "Great Chain of Being" that linked God to his creation in a series of ranked social groups.

In addition to being rigidly hierarchical, European societies were patriarchal in nature, with men assuming authority over women as a God-given prerogative. The family thus represented a microcosm of the social order. The father ruled his family like a king ruled his domains. Religious and secular law commanded a man's wife, children, servants, and apprentices to defer to his will. Fathers were entitled to use physical violence, imprisonment, and other forceful measures to impose their authority. These powers were balanced by expectations that a good father would provide and care for his dependents.

In the seventeenth century most Europeans lived in the countryside. The hub of the rural world was the small peasant village centered on a church and a manor. In western Europe, a small number of peasants in each village owned enough land to feed themselves and possessed the livestock and plows necessary to work their land. These independent farmers were leaders of the peasant village. They employed the landless poor, rented out livestock and tools, and served as agents for the noble lord.

Below them were small landowners and tenant farmers who did not have enough land to be self-sufficient. These families sold their best produce on the market to earn cash for taxes, rent, and food. At the bottom were villagers who worked as dependent laborers and servants. In central and eastern Europe, the vast majority of peasants toiled as serfs for noble landowners and did not own land in their own right, while in the Ottoman Empire (the vast empire comprising modern-day Turkey, southeastern Europe, North Africa, and large portions of the Middle East) all land belonged to the sultan.

Economic Crisis and Popular Revolts

European rural society lived on the edge of subsistence. Because of crude agricultural technology and low crop yield, peasants were constantly threatened by scarcity and famine. In the seventeenth century a period of colder and wetter climate throughout Europe, dubbed a "little ice age" by historians, meant a shorter farming season with lower yields. A bad harvest created food shortages; a series of bad harvests could lead to famine. Recurrent famines significantly reduced the population of early modern Europe, through reduced fertility and increased susceptibility to disease, as well as outright starvation.

Industry also suffered. The output of woolen textiles, one of the most important European manufactures, declined sharply in the first half of the seventeenth century. Food prices were high, wages stagnated, and unemployment soared. This economic crisis was not universal: it struck various regions at different times and to different degrees. In the middle decades of the century, for example, Spain, France, Germany, and the British Isles all experienced great economic difficulties, but these years were the golden age of the Netherlands because of wealth derived from foreign trade.

The urban poor and peasants were the hardest hit. When the price of bread rose beyond their capacity to pay, they frequently expressed their anger by rioting. Women often led these actions, since their role as mothers gave them some impunity in authorities' eyes. Historians have used the term *moral economy* for this vision of a world in which community needs predominate over competition and profit.

During the middle years of the seventeenth century, harsh conditions transformed neighborhood bread riots into armed uprisings across much of Europe. Popular revolts were common in England, France, and throughout the Spanish Empire, particularly during the 1640s. At the same time that Spanish king Philip IV struggled to put down an uprising in Catalonia, the economic center of the realm, he faced revolt in Portugal and in Spanish-held territories in the northern Netherlands and Sicily. France suffered an uprising in the same period that won enthusiastic support from both nobles and peasants, while the English monarch was tried and executed by his subjects and Russia experienced an explosive rebellion.

Municipal and royal authorities struggled to overcome popular revolt. They feared that stern repressive measures, such as sending in troops to fire on crowds, would create martyrs and further inflame the situation, while full-scale occupation of a city would be very expensive and detract from military efforts elsewhere. The limitations of royal authority gave some leverage to rebels. To quell riots, royal edicts were sometimes suspended, prisoners released, and discussions initiated. By the beginning of the eighteenth century rulers had gained much greater control over

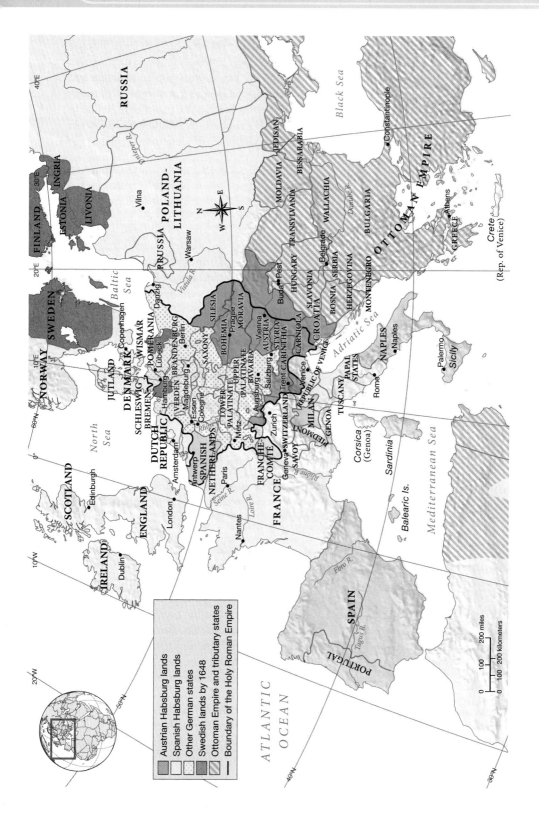

RUSSIA

FINLAND

INGRIA

ESTONIA

LIVONIA

Vilna

SWEDEN

NORWAY

RUSSIA

POLAND-
LITHUANIA

Warsaw

MOLDAVIA

BESSARABIA

WALLACHIA

TRANSYLVANIA

HUNGARY

Belgrade

SERBIA

BOSNIA

HERZEGOVINA

MONTENEGRO

BULGARIA

OTTOMAN EMPIRE

Constantinople

Black Sea

Athens

GREECE

Crete
(Rep. of Venice)

Baltic Sea

Danzig

Copenhagen

WISMAR

POMERANIA

BRANDENBURG

Berlin

Lübeck

SILESIA

Prague

MORAVIA

BOHEMIA

Buda Pest

SLAVONIA

CROATIA

CARNIOLA

CARINTHIA

STYRIA

AUSTRIA

Vienna

Salzburg

Trent

Venice

REPUBLIC OF VENICE

Adriatic Sea

DENMARK

JUTLAND

SCHLESWIG

BREMEN

VERDEN

Hamburg

Magdeburg

SAXONY

UPPER
PALATINATE

LOWER
PALATINATE

BAVARIA

Augsburg

Zurich

SWITZERLAND

Geneva

SAVOY

PIEDMONT

MILAN

GENOA

TUSCANY

PAPAL
STATES

Rome

NAPLES

Naples

Palermo

Sicily

North Sea

SCOTLAND

Edinburgh

ENGLAND

London

DUTCH
REPUBLIC

Amsterdam

Antwerp

SPANISH
NETHERLANDS

Essen

Cologne

Paris

FRANCHE-
COMTÉ

FRANCE

Nantes

IRELAND

Dublin

Metz

Corsica
(Genoa)

Sardinia

Balearic Is.

Mediterranean Sea

SPAIN

PORTUGAL

ATLANTIC
OCEAN

Rhine R.

Seine R.

Loire R.

Rhône R.

Ebro R.

Tagus R.

Vistula R.

Dnieper R.

Danube R.

N E W S

Austrian Habsburg lands
Spanish Habsburg lands
Other German states
Swedish lands by 1648
Ottoman Empire and tributary states
Boundary of the Holy Roman Empire

0   100   200 miles
0 100 200 kilometers

their populations as a result of various achievements in state-building (see "State-Building and the Growth of Armies" later in this chapter).

The Thirty Years' War

Harsh economic conditions were greatly exacerbated by the decades-long conflict known as the Thirty Years' War (1618–1648), a war that drew in almost every European state. The Holy Roman Empire was a confederation of hundreds of principalities, independent cities, duchies, and other polities loosely united under an elected emperor. The uneasy truce between Catholics and Protestants created by the Peace of Augsburg in 1555 (see "Religious Wars in Switzerland and Germany" in Chapter 13) deteriorated as the faiths of various areas shifted. Lutheran princes felt compelled to form the Protestant Union (1608), and Catholics retaliated with the Catholic League (1609). Each alliance was determined that the other should make no religious or territorial advance. Dynastic interests were also involved; the Spanish Habsburgs strongly supported the goals of their Austrian relatives, which was to preserve the unity of the empire and Catholicism within it.

The war began with a conflict in Bohemia (part of the present-day Czech Republic) between the Catholic League and the Protestant Union but soon spread through the Holy Roman Empire, drawing in combatants from across Europe. After a series of initial Catholic victories, the tide of the conflict turned because of the intervention of Sweden, under its king Gustavus Adolphus (r. 1594–1632), and then France, whose prime minister, Cardinal Richelieu (REESH-uh-lyuh), intervened on the side of the Protestants to undermine Habsburg power.

The 1648 **Peace of Westphalia** that ended the Thirty Years' War marked a turning point in European history. The treaties that established the peace not only ended conflicts fought over religious faith but also recognized the independent authority of more than three hundred German princes (Map 15.1), reconfirming the emperor's severely limited authority. The Augsburg agreement of 1555 became permanent, adding Calvinism to Catholicism and Lutheranism as legally permissible creeds. The United Provinces of the Netherlands, known as the Dutch Republic, won official freedom from Spain.

The Thirty Years' War was the most destructive event in central Europe prior to the world wars of the twentieth century. Perhaps one-third of urban residents and two-fifths of the rural population died, and agriculture and industry withered. Across Europe, states increased taxes to meet the cost of war, further increasing the suffering of a traumatized population.

< MAP 15.1   Europe After the Thirty Years' War
This map shows the political division of Europe after the Peace of Westphalia (1648) ended the war. France expanded its borders to the east and Sweden gained territory on the northern German coastline. The Dutch Republic formally won its independence after a long struggle against Spain, but Spain retained territory in the southern Netherlands and Italy.

State-Building and the Growth of Armies

In the context of warfare, economic crisis, and demographic decline, rulers took urgent measures to restore order and rebuild their states. Traditionally, historians have distinguished between the absolutist governments of France, Spain, central Europe, and Russia and the constitutionalist governments of England and the Dutch Republic. Whereas absolutist monarchs gathered all power under their personal control, English and Dutch rulers were obliged to respect laws passed by representative institutions. More recently, historians have emphasized commonalities among these powers. Despite their political differences, all these states shared common projects of protecting and expanding their frontiers, raising new taxes, consolidating central control, and competing for the new colonies opening up in the New and Old Worlds.

Rulers who wished to increase their authority encountered formidable obstacles, including poor communications, entrenched local power structures, and ethnic and linguistic diversity. Nonetheless, over the course of the seventeenth century both absolutist and constitutional governments achieved new levels of power and national unity. They did so by transforming emergency measures of wartime into permanent structures of government and by subduing privileged groups through the use of force and through economic and social incentives. Increased state authority could be seen in four areas in particular: greater taxation, growth in armed forces, larger and more efficient bureaucracies, and territorial expansion, both within Europe and overseas.

Over time, centralized power added up to something close to sovereignty. A state may be termed sovereign when it possesses a monopoly over the instruments of justice and the use of force within clearly defined boundaries. In a sovereign state, no system of courts, such as church tribunals, competes with state courts in the

Seventeenth-Century Artillery Mobile light artillery, consisting of bronze or iron cannon mounted on wheeled carriages, played a crucial role in seventeenth-century warfare. In contrast to earlier heavy artillery used in siege operations to breach fortifications, light artillery could be deployed to support troops during battle. This image is from an early seventeenth-century military manual. (Science History Images/Alamy)

dispensation of justice; and private armies, such as those of feudal lords, present no threat to central authority. While seventeenth-century states did not acquire total sovereignty, they made important strides toward that goal.

The driving force of seventeenth-century state-building was warfare. In medieval times, feudal lords had raised armies only for particular wars or campaigns; now monarchs began to recruit their own forces and maintain permanent standing armies. Instead of serving their own interests, army officers were required to be loyal and obedient to state officials. New techniques for training and deploying soldiers meant a rise in the professional standards of the army.

Along with professionalization came an explosive growth in army size. The French took the lead, with the army growing from roughly 125,000 men in the Thirty Years' War to 340,000 at the end of the seventeenth century.[1] Other European powers were quick to follow the French example. The rise of absolutism in central and eastern Europe led to a vast expansion in the size of armies. England followed a similar, albeit distinctive pattern. Instead of building a land army, the island nation focused on naval forces and eventually built the largest navy in the world.

Baroque Art and Music

State-building and the growth of armies were not the only achievements of the seventeenth century; the arts flourished as well. Rome and the revitalized Catholic Church of the late sixteenth century spurred the early development of the **baroque style** in art and music. The papacy and the Jesuits encouraged the growth of an intensely emotional, exuberant art. They wanted artists to appeal to the senses and thereby touch the souls and kindle the faith of ordinary churchgoers while proclaiming the power and confidence of the reformed Catholic Church. In addition to this underlying religious emotionalism, the baroque drew its sense of drama, motion, and ceaseless striving from the Catholic Reformation.

Taking definite shape in Italy after 1600, the baroque style in the visual arts developed with exceptional vigor in Catholic countries — in Spain and Latin America, Austria, southern Germany, and Poland. Yet baroque art was more than just "Catholic art" in the seventeenth century and the first half of the eighteenth. It had broad appeal, and Protestants accounted for some of the finest examples of baroque style, especially in music. The baroque style spread partly because its tension and bombast spoke to an agitated age that was experiencing great violence and controversy in politics and religion.

In painting, the baroque reached maturity early with Peter Paul Rubens (1577–1640), the most outstanding and most representative of baroque painters. Studying in his native Flanders and in Italy, where he was influenced by masters of the High Renaissance such as Michelangelo, Rubens developed his own rich, sensuous, colorful style, which was characterized by animated figures, melodramatic contrasts, and monumental size.

In music, the baroque style reached its culmination almost a century later in the dynamic, soaring lines of the endlessly inventive Johann Sebastian Bach (1685–1750). Organist and choirmaster of several Lutheran churches across Germany, Bach was equally at home writing secular concertos and sublime religious cantatas. Bach's organ music combined the baroque spirit of invention, tension, and emotion in an unforgettable striving toward the infinite. Unlike Rubens, Bach was not fully appreciated in his lifetime, but since the early nineteenth century his reputation has grown steadily.

Why did France rise and Spain fall during the late seventeenth century?

Kings in absolutist states asserted that, because they were chosen by God, they were responsible to God alone. They claimed exclusive, or absolute, power to make and enforce laws, denying any other institution or group the authority to check their power. In France the founder of the Bourbon monarchy, Henry IV, established foundations upon which his successors Louis XIII and Louis XIV built a stronger, more centralized French state. Louis XIV is often seen as the epitome of an "absolute" monarch, with his endless wars, increased taxes and economic regulation, and glorious palace at Versailles. In truth, his success relied on collaboration with nobles, and thus his example illustrates both the achievements and the compromises of absolutist rule.

As French power rose in the seventeenth century, the glory of Spain faded. Once the fabulous revenue from American silver declined, Spain's economic stagnation could no longer be disguised, and the country faltered under weak leadership.

The Foundations of French Absolutism

Louis XIV's absolutism had long roots. In 1589, his grandfather Henry IV (r. 1589–1610), the founder of the Bourbon dynasty, acquired a devastated country. Civil wars between Protestants and Catholics had wracked France since 1561. Poor harvests had reduced peasants to starvation, and commercial activity had declined drastically. Henri le Grand (Henry the Great), as the king was called, inaugurated a remarkable recovery by defusing religious tensions and rebuilding France's economy. He issued the Edict of Nantes in 1598, allowing Huguenots (French Protestants) the right to worship in 150 traditionally Protestant towns throughout France. He sharply lowered taxes and instead charged royal officials an annual fee to guarantee the right to pass their positions down to their heirs. He also improved the infrastructure of the country, building new roads and canals and repairing the ravages of years of civil war. Despite his efforts at peace, Henry was murdered in 1610 by a Catholic zealot.

Cardinal Richelieu (1585–1642) became first minister of the French crown on behalf of Henry's young son, Louis XIII (r. 1610–1643). Richelieu designed his domestic policies to strengthen royal control. He extended the use of intendants, commissioners for each of France's thirty-two districts who were appointed directly by the monarch and whose responsibilities included army recruitment, tax collection, and enforcement of royal law. As the intendants' power increased under Richelieu, so did the power of the centralized French state.

Richelieu also viewed France's Huguenots as potential rebels, and he laid seige to La Rochelle, a Protestant stronghold, to preserve control within France. Richelieu's anti-Protestant measures took second place, however, to his most important policy goal, which was to secure French pre-eminence in European power politics. This meant doing everything within his means to weaken the Habsburgs and prevent them from controlling territories that surrounded France. Consequently, Richelieu supported Habsburg enemies, including the Protestant nation of Sweden, during the Thirty Years' War.

Cardinal Jules Mazarin (1602–1661) succeeded Richelieu as chief minister for the next child-king, the four-year-old Louis XIV, who inherited the throne from his father in 1643. Along with the regent, Queen Mother Anne of Austria, Mazarin continued Richelieu's centralizing policies. However, his struggle to increase royal revenues to meet the costs of the Thirty Years' War led to the uprisings of 1648–1653 known as the **Fronde**. In Paris, magistrates of the Parlement of Paris, the nation's most important law court, were outraged by the Crown's autocratic measures. These so-called robe nobles (named for the robes they wore in court) encouraged violent protest by the common people. As rebellion spread outside Paris and to the sword nobles (the traditional warrior nobility), civil order broke down completely. In 1651, Anne's regency ended with the declaration of Louis as king in his own right. Much of the rebellion died away, and its leaders came to terms with the government.

The French people were desperate for peace and stability after the disorders of the Fronde and were willing to accept a strong monarch who could restore order. Louis pledged to be such a monarch, insisting that only his absolute authority stood between the French people and a renewed descent into chaos.

Louis XIV and Absolutism

In the reign of Louis XIV (r. 1643–1715), who was known as the "Sun King" in reference to his central role in the divine order, France overcame weakness and division to become the most powerful nation in western Europe. Louis based his authority on the divine right of kings: God had established kings as his rulers on earth, and they were answerable ultimately to him alone. However, Louis also recognized that kings could not simply do as they pleased. They had to obey God's laws and rule for the good of the people.

Louis worked very hard at the business of governing, refusing to delegate power to a first minister. He ruled his realm through several councils of state and insisted on taking a personal role in many of their decisions. Despite increasing financial problems, Louis never called a meeting of the Estates General, the traditional French representative assembly composed of the three estates of clergy, nobility, and commoners. The nobility, therefore, had no means of united expression or action. To further restrict nobles' political power, Louis chose his ministers from capable men of modest origins.

Although personally tolerant, Louis hated division within the realm and insisted that religious unity was essential to his royal dignity and to the security of the state. He thus pursued the policy of Protestant repression launched by Richelieu. In 1685 Louis revoked the Edict of Nantes. The new law ordered the Catholic baptism of Huguenots (French Calvinists), the destruction of Huguenot churches, the closing of schools, and the exile of Huguenot pastors who refused to renounce their faith. Around two hundred thousand Protestants, including some of the king's most highly skilled artisans, fled into exile.

Despite his claims to absolute authority, multiple constraints existed on Louis's power. As a representative of divine power, he was obliged to rule in a manner consistent with virtue and benevolence. He had to uphold the laws issued by his royal predecessors. He also relied on the collaboration of nobles, who maintained tremendous prestige and authority in their ancestral lands. Without their cooperation, it would have been impossible to extend his power throughout France or wage his many foreign wars. Louis's efforts to elicit noble cooperation led him to revolutionize court life at his spectacular palace at Versailles.

Life at Versailles

Through most of the seventeenth century the French court had no fixed home and instead followed the monarch to his numerous palaces and country residences. In 1682 Louis moved his court and government to the newly renovated palace at Versailles, a former hunting lodge. He then required all great nobles to spend at least part of the year in attendance on him there, so he could keep an eye on their activities. Because Louis controlled the distribution of state power and wealth, nobles had no choice but to obey and compete with each other for his favor at Versailles. The glorious palace, with its sumptuous interiors and extensive formal gardens, was

View of the Palace and Gardens of Versailles, 1668 Located ten miles southwest of Paris, Versailles began as a modest hunting lodge. Louis XIV spent decades enlarging and decorating the structure with the help of architect Louis Le Vau and gardener André Le Nôtre. In 1682, the new palace became the official residence of the Sun King and his court and an inspiration to absolutist palace builders across Europe. (Leemage/Corbis Historical/Getty Images)

a mirror to the world of French glory and was soon copied by would-be absolutist monarchs across Europe.

Louis further revolutionized court life by establishing an elaborate set of etiquette rituals to mark every moment of his day, from waking up and dressing in the morning to removing his clothing and retiring at night. Courtiers vied for the honor of participating in these ceremonies, with the highest in rank claiming the privilege of handing the king his shirt. These rituals may seem absurd, but they were far from trivial. The king controlled immense resources and privileges; access to him meant favored treatment for government offices, military and religious posts, state pensions, honorary titles, and a host of other benefits. Courtiers sought these rewards for themselves and their family members and followers. A system of patronage — in which a higher-ranked individual protected a lower-ranked one in return for loyalty and services — flowed from the court to the provinces. Through this mechanism Louis gained cooperation from powerful nobles.

Although they could not hold public offices or posts, women played a central role in the patronage system. At court the king's wife, mistresses, and other female relatives recommended individuals for honors, advocated policy decisions, and brokered alliances between factions. Noblewomen played a similar role, bringing their family connections to marriage to form powerful social networks.

Louis XIV was also an enthusiastic patron of the arts, commissioning many sculptures and paintings for Versailles as well as performances of dance and music. He also loved the stage, and in the plays of Molière and Racine his court witnessed the finest achievements in the history of French theater. Some of Molière's targets in this period were the aristocratic ladies who wrote many genres of literature and held receptions, called salons, in their Parisian mansions, where they engaged in witty and cultured discussions of poetry, art, theater, and the latest worldly events. Their refined conversational style led Molière and other observers to mock them as "*précieuses*" (PREH-see-ooz; literally "precious"), or affected and pretentious. Despite this mockery, the précieuses represented an important cultural force ruled by elite women.

With Versailles as the center of European politics, French culture grew in international prestige. French became the language of polite society and international diplomacy, gradually replacing Latin as the language of scholarship and learning. Royal courts across Europe spoke French, and the great aristocrats of Russia, Sweden, Germany, and elsewhere were often more fluent in French than in the tongues of their homelands. France inspired a cosmopolitan European culture in the late seventeenth century that looked to Versailles as its center.

Louis XIV's Wars

In pursuit of dynastic glory, Louis kept France at war for thirty-three of the fifty-four years of his personal rule. Under the leadership of François le Tellier, marquis de Louvois, Louis's secretary of state for war, France acquired a huge professional army that was employed by the French state rather than by private nobles. He standardized uniforms and weapons and devised a rational system of training and promotion. As in so many other matters, the French model influenced the rest of Europe.

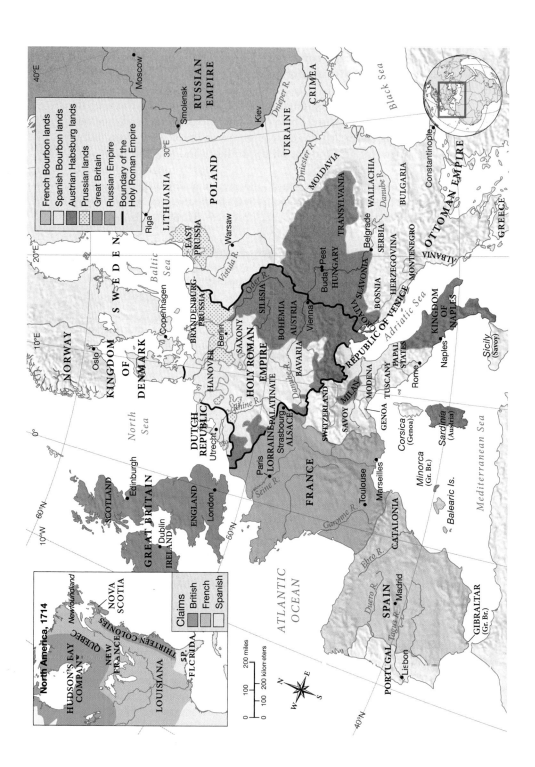

During this long period of warfare, Louis's goal was to expand France to what he considered its natural borders and to win glory for the Bourbon dynasty. The results were mixed. During the 1660s and 1670s, French armies managed to extend French borders to include important commercial centers in the Spanish Netherlands and Flanders as well as the entire province of Franche-Comté between 1667 and 1678, formerly held by Spain. In 1681 Louis seized the city of Strasbourg, and three years later he sent his armies into the province of Lorraine. At that moment the king seemed invincible, but in reality Louis had reached the limit of his expansion. The wars of the 1680s and 1690s brought no additional territories and strained French resources to the limit.

Louis's last war, the War of the Spanish Succession (1701–1713), was endured by a French people suffering from high taxes, crop failure, and widespread malnutrition and death.

This war was the result of Louis's unwillingness to abide by a previous agreement to divide Spanish possessions between France and the Holy Roman emperor upon the death of the childless Spanish king Charles II (r. 1665–1700). Instead, he succeeded in having his own grandson, Philip of Anjou, placed on the Spanish throne. (Louis's wife, Maria-Theresa, was Charles's sister.) In 1701 the English, Dutch, Austrians, and Prussians formed the Grand Alliance to prevent this expansion of Bourbon power.

War dragged on until 1713. The **Peace of Utrecht**, which ended the war, allowed Louis's grandson Philip to remain king of Spain on the understanding that the French and Spanish crowns would never be united. France surrendered Nova Scotia, Newfoundland, and the Hudson Bay territory to England, which also acquired Gibraltar, Minorca, and control of the African slave trade from Spain (Map 15.2).

The Peace of Utrecht marked the end of French expansion. Thirty-five years of war had given France the rights to all of Alsace and some commercial centers in the north. But at what price? At the time of Louis's death in 1715, an exhausted France hovered on the brink of bankruptcy.

The French Economic Policy of Mercantilism

France's ability to build armies and fight wars depended on a strong economy. Fortunately for Louis, his controller general, Jean-Baptiste Colbert (1619–1683), proved to be a financial genius. Colbert's central principle was that the wealth and

< MAP 15.2 **Europe After the Peace of Utrecht, 1715**
The series of treaties commonly called the Peace of Utrecht ended the War of the Spanish Succession and redrew the map of Europe. A French Bourbon king succeeded to the Spanish throne. France surrendered the Spanish Netherlands (later Belgium), then in French hands, to Austria, and recognized the Hohenzollern rulers of Prussia. Spain ceded Gibraltar to Great Britain, for which it has been a strategic naval station ever since. Spain also granted Britain the *asiento*, the contract for supplying African slaves to the Americas.

the economy of France should serve the state. To this end, from 1665 to his death in 1683, Colbert rigorously applied mercantilist policies to France.

Mercantilism was a collection of governmental policies for the regulation of economic activities by and for the state. It derived from the idea that a nation's international power is based on its wealth, specifically its supply of gold and silver. To accumulate wealth, a country always had to sell more goods abroad than it bought.

To increase exports, Colbert supported old industries and created new ones, focusing especially on textiles, which were the most important sector of manufacturing. He enacted new production regulations, created guilds to boost quality standards, and encouraged foreign craftsmen to immigrate to France. To encourage the purchase of French goods, he abolished many domestic tariffs and raised tariffs on foreign products. In 1664 Colbert founded the Company of the East Indies with (unfulfilled) hopes of competing with the Dutch for Asian trade.

Colbert also hoped to make Canada — rich in untapped minerals and some of the best agricultural land in the world — part of a vast French empire. He sent four thousand colonists to Quebec, whose capital had been founded in 1608 under Henry IV. Subsequently, the Jesuit Jacques Marquette and the merchant Louis Joliet sailed down the Mississippi River, which they named Colbert in honor of their sponsor (the name soon reverted to the original Native American one). Marquette and Joliet claimed possession of the land on both sides of the river as far south as present-day Arkansas. In 1684 French explorers continued down the Mississippi to its mouth and claimed vast territories for Louis XIV. The area was called, naturally, "Louisiana."

During Colbert's tenure as controller general, Louis was able to pursue his goals without massive tax increases and without creating a stream of new offices. The constant pressure of warfare after Colbert's death, however, undid many of his economic achievements.

The Decline of Absolutist Spain in the Seventeenth Century

At the beginning of the seventeenth century France's position appeared extremely weak. Struggling to recover from decades of religious civil war that had destroyed its infrastructure and economy, France could not dare to compete with Spain's empire or its powerful army. Yet by the end of the century their positions were reversed, and France had attained European dominance.

The discovery of silver at Potosí in 1545 had produced momentous wealth for Spain, allowing it to dominate Europe militarily (see "Spanish Silver and Its Economic Effects" in Chapter 14). Yet Spain had inherent weaknesses that the wealth of empire had hidden. When Philip IV took the throne in 1621, he inherited a vast and overstretched empire that combined different kingdoms with their own traditions and loyalties. Spanish silver had generated great wealth, but also dependency. While Creoles — people of European ancestry born in the colonies — undertook new industries and European nations targeted Spanish colonial trade, industry and finance in Spain itself did not develop.

Between 1610 and 1650 Spanish trade with the colonies in the New World fell 60 percent because of competition from local industries in the colonies and from Dutch and English traders. At the same time epidemic disease decimated the enslaved workforce in the South American silver mines. Moreover, the mines themselves started to run dry, and the quantity of metal produced steadily declined after 1620.

In Madrid, the expenses of war and imperial rule constantly exceeded income. Despite the efforts of Philip's able chief minister, Gaspar de Guzmán, Count-Duke of Olivares, it proved impossible to force the kingdoms of the empire to shoulder the cost of its defense. To meet mountainous state debt, the Crown repeatedly devalued the coinage and declared bankruptcy, which resulted in the collapse of national credit and steep inflation.

Spanish aristocrats, attempting to maintain an extravagant lifestyle they could no longer afford, increased the rents on their estates. High rents and heavy taxes in turn drove the peasants from the land, leading to a decline in agricultural productivity. In cities, wages and production stagnated. Steep inflation forced textile manufacturers out of business by increasing their production costs to the point where they could not compete in colonial and international markets.[2] Spain also ignored new scientific methods that might have improved agricultural or manufacturing techniques because they came from the heretical nations of Holland and England.

Spain's situation worsened with internal rebellions and military defeats during the Thirty Years' War and through the remainder of the seventeenth century. In 1640 Spain faced serious revolts in Catalonia and Portugal. In 1643 the French inflicted a crushing defeat on a Spanish army at Rocroi in what is now Belgium. The Peace of Westphalia, which ended the Thirty Years' War, compelled Spain to recognize the independence of the Dutch Republic, and another treaty in 1659 granted extensive territories to France. Finally, in 1688 the Spanish crown reluctantly recognized the independence of Portugal. With these losses, the era of Spanish dominance in Europe ended.

What explains the rise of absolutism in Prussia and Austria?

The rulers of central and eastern Europe also labored to build strong absolutist states in the seventeenth century. But they built on social and economic foundations far different from those in western Europe, namely, serfdom and the strong nobility who benefited from it. The constant warfare of the seventeenth century allowed monarchs to increase their power by building large armies, increasing taxation, and suppressing representative institutions. In exchange for their growing political authority, monarchs allowed nobles to remain as unchallenged masters of their peasants, a deal that appeased both king and nobility but left serfs at the mercy of the lords. The most successful states were Austria and Prussia, which witnessed the rise of absolutism between 1620 and 1740.

The Return of Serfdom

While economic and social hardship was common across Europe, important differences existed between east and west. In the west the demographic losses of the Black Death allowed peasants to escape from serfdom as they acquired enough land to feed themselves. In central and eastern Europe seventeenth-century peasants had largely lost their ability to own land independently. Their lords dealt with the labor short-ages caused by the Black Death by restricting the right of their peasants to move to take advantage of better opportunities elsewhere. In Prussian territories by 1500 the law required that runaway peasants be hunted down and returned to their lords. Moreover, lords steadily took more and more of their peasants' land and arbitrarily imposed heavier labor obligations.

The gradual erosion of the peasantry's economic position was bound up with manipulation of the legal system. The local lord was also the local prosecutor, judge, and jailer. There were no independent royal officials to provide justice or uphold the common law. The power of the lord reached far into serfs' everyday lives. Not only was their freedom of movement restricted, but they also required permission to marry or could be forced to marry. Lords could reallocate the lands worked by their serfs at will or sell serfs apart from their families.

Between 1500 and 1650 the consolidation of serfdom was accompanied by the growth of commercial agriculture, particularly in Poland and eastern Germany. As economic expansion and population growth resumed after 1500, lords increased the production of their estates by squeezing sizable surpluses out of the impoverished peasants. They then sold these surpluses to foreign merchants, who exported them to the growing cities of western Europe.

It was not only the peasants who suffered. With the approval of kings, landlords systematically undermined the medieval privileges of the towns and the power of the urban classes. Instead of selling products to local merchants, landlords sold directly to foreigners, bypassing local towns. Eastern towns also lost their medieval right of refuge and were compelled to return runaways to their lords. The population of the towns and the urban middle classes declined greatly.

The Austrian Habsburgs

Like all of central Europe, the Habsburgs emerged from the Thirty Years' War impov-erished and exhausted. Their efforts to destroy Protestantism in the German lands and to turn the weak Holy Roman Empire into a real state had failed. Although the Habsburgs remained the hereditary emperors, real power lay in the hands of a bewil-dering variety of separate political jurisdictions. Defeat in central Europe encour-aged the Habsburgs to turn away from a quest for imperial dominance and to focus inward and eastward in an attempt to unify their diverse holdings.

Habsburg victory over Bohemia during the Thirty Years' War was an important step in this direction. Ferdinand II (r. 1619–1637) drastically reduced the power of the Bohemian Estates, the largely Protestant representative assembly. He also confis-cated the landholdings of Protestant nobles and gave them to loyal Catholic nobles and to the foreign aristocratic mercenaries who led his armies. After 1650 a large portion of the Bohemian nobility was of recent origin and owed its success to the Habsburgs.

With the support of this new nobility, the Habsburgs established direct rule over Bohemia. Under their rule the condition of the enserfed peasantry worsened substantially: three days per week of unpaid labor became the norm. Protestantism was also stamped out. These changes were significant advances in creating absolutist rule in Bohemia.

Ferdinand III (r. 1637–1657) continued to build state power. He centralized the government in the empire's German-speaking provinces, which formed the core Habsburg holdings. For the first time, a permanent standing army was ready to put down any internal opposition. The Habsburg monarchy then turned east toward the plains of Hungary, which had been divided between the Ottomans and the Habsburgs in the early sixteenth century. Between 1683 and 1699 the Habsburgs pushed the Ottomans from most of Hungary and Transylvania. The recovery of all of the former kingdom of Hungary was completed in 1718.

The Hungarian nobility, despite its reduced strength, effectively thwarted the full development of Habsburg absolutism. Throughout the seventeenth century Hungarian nobles rose in revolt against attempts to impose absolute rule. They never triumphed decisively, but neither were they crushed the way the nobility in Bohemia had been in 1620. In 1703, with the Habsburgs bogged down in the War of the Spanish Succession, the Hungarians rose in one last patriotic rebellion under Prince Francis Rákóczy. The prince and his forces were eventually defeated, but the Habsburgs agreed to restore many of the traditional privileges of the aristocracy in return for Hungarian acceptance of hereditary Habsburg rule. Thus Hungary, unlike Austria and Bohemia, was never fully integrated into a centralized, absolute Habsburg state.

Despite checks on their ambitions in Hungary, the Habsburgs made significant achievements in state-building elsewhere by forging consensus with the church and the nobility. A sense of common identity and loyalty to the monarchy grew among elites in Habsburg lands, even to a certain extent in Hungary. German became the language of the state, and zealous Catholicism helped fuse a collective identity.

Vienna became the political and cultural center of the empire. By 1700 it was a thriving city with a population of one hundred thousand and its own version of Versailles, the royal palace of Schönbrunn.

Prussia in the Seventeenth Century

In the fifteenth and sixteenth centuries the Hohenzollern family had ruled parts of eastern Germany as the imperial electors of Brandenburg and the dukes of Prussia. The title of *elector* gave its holder the privilege of being one of only seven princes or archbishops entitled to elect the Holy Roman emperor, but the electors had little real power. When he came to power in 1640, the twenty-year-old Frederick William, later known as the "Great Elector," was determined to unify his three provinces and enlarge his holdings. These provinces were Brandenburg; Prussia, inherited in 1618; and scattered territories along the Rhine inherited in 1614 (Map 15.3). Each had its own estates. Although the estates had not met regularly during the chaotic Thirty Years' War, taxes could not be levied without their consent. The estates of Brandenburg and Prussia were dominated by the nobility and the landowning classes, known as the **Junkers**.

Frederick William profited from ongoing European war and the threat of invasion from Russia when he argued for the need for a permanent standing army. In 1660 he persuaded Junkers in the estates to accept taxation without consent in order to fund an army. They agreed to do so in exchange for reconfirmation of their own privileges, including authority over the serfs. Having won over the

MAP 15.3   The Growth of Austria and Brandenburg-Prussia to 1748
Austria expanded to the southwest into Hungary and Transylvania at the expense of the Ottoman Empire. It was unable to hold the rich German province of Silesia, however, which was conquered by Brandenburg-Prussia.

Junkers, the king crushed potential opposition to his power from the towns. One by one, Prussian cities were eliminated from the estates and subjected to new taxes on goods and services. Thereafter, the estates' power declined rapidly, for the Great Elector had both financial independence and superior force. During his reign, Frederick William tripled state revenue and expanded the army drastically. In 1688 a population of 1 million supported a peacetime standing army of 30,000. In 1701 the elector's son, Frederick I, received the elevated title of *king of Prussia* (instead of *elector*) as a reward for aiding the Holy Roman emperor in the War of the Spanish Succession.

The Consolidation of Prussian Absolutism

Frederick William I, "the Soldiers' King" (r. 1713–1740), completed his grandfather's work, eliminating the last traces of parliamentary estates and local self-government. It was he who truly established Prussian absolutism and transformed Prussia into a military state. Frederick William was intensely attached to military life. He always wore an army uniform, and he lived the highly disciplined life of the professional soldier. Years later he followed the family tradition by leaving his own written instructions to his son: "A formidable army and a war chest large enough to make this army mobile in times of need can create great respect for you in the world, so that you can speak a word like the other powers."[3]

Penny-pinching, ruthless, and hard-working, Frederick William achieved results. The king and his ministers built an exceptionally efficient bureaucracy to administer the country and foster economic development. Twelfth in Europe in population, Prussia had the fourth-largest army by 1740. The Prussian army was the best in Europe, astonishing foreign observers with its precision, skill, and discipline.

Nevertheless, Prussians paid a heavy and lasting price for the obsessions of their royal drillmaster. Army expansion was achieved in part through forced conscription, which was declared lifelong in 1713. Desperate draftees fled the country or injured themselves to avoid service. Finally, in 1733 Frederick William I ordered that all Prussian men undergo military training and serve as reservists in the army, allowing him to preserve both agricultural production and army size. To appease the Junkers, the king enlisted them to lead his growing army. The proud nobility thus commanded the peasantry in the army as well as on the estates.

With all men harnessed to the war machine, Prussian civil society became rigid and highly disciplined. As a Prussian minister later summed up, "To keep quiet is the first civic duty."[4] Thus the policies of Frederick William I, combined with harsh peasant bondage and Junker tyranny, laid the foundations for a highly militaristic country.

What were the distinctive features of Russian and Ottoman absolutism?

Russia occupied a unique position among Eurasian states. With borders straddling eastern Europe and northwestern Asia, its development into a strong imperial state drew on elements from both continents. Like the growth of the Muslim empires in Central and South Asia and the Ming Dynasty in China, the expansion of Russia was a result of the weakening of the great Mongol Empire. After declaring independence from the Mongols, the Russian tsars conquered a vast empire, extending through North Asia all the way to the Pacific Ocean. State-building and territorial expansion culminated during the reign of Peter the Great, who forcibly introduced elements of Western culture and society.

While Europeans debated, and continued to debate, whether or not Russia was a Western society, there was no question in their minds that the Ottomans were outsiders. Even absolutist rulers disdained Ottoman sultans as cruel and tyrannical despots. Despite stereotypes, however, the Ottoman Empire was in many ways more tolerant than its Western counterparts, providing protection and security to other religions while maintaining the Muslim faith. Flexibility and openness to other ideas and practices were sources of strength for the empire.

Mongol Rule in Russia and the Rise of Moscow

The two-hundred-year period of rule by the Mongol khan (king) set the stage for the rise of absolutist Russia. The Mongols, a group of nomadic tribes from present-day Mongolia, established an empire that, at its height, stretched from Korea to eastern Europe. In the thirteenth century the Mongols had conquered Kievan Rus, the medieval Slavic state that included most of present-day Ukraine, Belarus, and part of northwest Russia. The princes of the Grand Duchy of Moscow, a principality within Kievan Rus, became particularly adept at serving the Mongols. Eventually the Muscovite princes were able to destroy the other princes who were their rivals for power. Ivan III (r. 1462–1505), known as Ivan the Great, successfully expanded the principality of Moscow eastward toward the Baltic Sea and westward to the Ural Mountains and the Siberian frontier.

By 1480 Ivan III was strong enough to declare the autonomy of Moscow. To legitimize their new position, Ivan and his successors borrowed elements of Mongol rule. They forced weaker Slavic principalities to render tribute and borrowed Mongol institutions such as the tax system, postal routes, and census. Loyalty from the highest-ranking nobles, or **boyars**, helped the Muscovite princes consolidate their power.

Another source of legitimacy for Moscow was its claim to the political and religious legacy of the Byzantine Empire. After the fall of Constantinople to the Turks in 1453, the princes of Moscow saw themselves as the heirs of both the Byzantine caesars (or emperors) and the empire's Orthodox Christianity. The marriage of Ivan III to the daughter of the last Byzantine emperor further enhanced Moscow's assertion of imperial authority.

Building the Russian Empire

Developments in Russia took a chaotic turn with the reign of Ivan IV (r. 1533–1584), the famous "Ivan the Terrible," who ascended to the throne at age three. His mother died when he was eight, leaving Ivan to suffer insults and neglect from the boyars at court. At age sixteen Ivan pushed aside his advisers and crowned himself tsar.

After the sudden death of his wife, Ivan began a campaign of persecution against those he suspected of opposing him. He executed members of leading boyar families, along with their families, friends, servants, and peasants. To replace them, Ivan created a new service nobility, whose loyalty was guaranteed by their dependence on the state for land and titles.

As landlords demanded more from the serfs who survived the persecutions, growing numbers of peasants fled toward recently conquered territories to the east and south. There they joined free groups and warrior bands known as **Cossacks**. Ivan responded by tying peasants ever more firmly to the land. Simultaneously, so that he could tax them more heavily, he ordered that urban dwellers be bound to their towns and jobs. These restrictions checked the growth of the Russian middle classes and stood in sharp contrast to economic and social developments in western Europe.

Ivan's reign was successful in defeating the remnants of Mongol power and in laying the foundations for the huge, multiethnic Russian Empire. In the 1550s, strengthened by an alliance with Cossack bands, Ivan conquered the Muslim khanates of Kazan and Astrakhan and brought the fertile steppe region around the Volga River under Russian control. In the 1580s Cossacks fighting for the Russian state crossed the Ural Mountains and began the long conquest of Siberia. Because of the size of the new territories and their distance from Moscow, the Russian state did not initially seek to impose the Orthodox religion and maintained local elites in positions of honor and leadership, buying their loyalty with grants of land.

Following Ivan's death, Russia entered a chaotic period known as the "Time of Troubles" (1598–1613). While Ivan's relatives struggled for power, Cossacks and peasants rebelled against nobles and officials. This social explosion from below brought the nobles together. They crushed the Cossack rebellion and brought Ivan's sixteen-year-old grandnephew, Michael Romanov, to the throne (r. 1613–1645).

Despite the turbulence of the period, the Romanov tsars, like their Western counterparts, made several important achievements in territorial expansion and state-building. After a long war, Russia gained land to the west in Ukraine in 1667. By the end of the century, it had completed the conquest of Siberia (Map 15.4). This vast territorial expansion brought Russian power to the Sea of Okhotsk in the Pacific Ocean and was only checked by the powerful Qing Dynasty of China. As with the French in Canada, the basis of Russian wealth in Siberia was furs, which the state collected by forced annual tribute payments from local peoples. Profits from furs and other natural resources, especially mining in the eighteenth century, funded expansion of the Russian imperial bureaucracy and the army.

The growth of state power did nothing to improve the lot of the common people. In 1649 a new law code extended serfdom to all peasants in the realm, giving lords unrestricted rights over their serfs and establishing penalties for harboring runaways. The new code also removed the privileges that non-Russian elites had enjoyed within the empire and required conversion to Russian Orthodoxy. Henceforth, Moscow maintained strict control of trade and administration throughout the empire.

The peace imposed by harsh Russian rule was disrupted in 1670 by a failed rebellion led by the Cossack Stenka Razin, who attracted a great army of urban poor and peasants. The ease with which Moscow crushed the rebellion testifies to the success of the Russian state in unifying and consolidating its empire.

The Reforms of Peter the Great

Heir to the Romanovs, Peter the Great (r. 1682–1725) embarked on a tremendous campaign to accelerate and complete their efforts at state-building. Peter built on the service obligations of Ivan the Terrible and his successors and continued their tradition of territorial expansion. In particular, he was determined to gain access to the sea for his virtually landlocked state, by extending Russia's borders first to the Black Sea (controlled by the Ottomans) and then to the Baltic Sea (dominated by Sweden).

Peter moved toward the first goal by conquering the Ottoman fort of Azov near the Black Sea in 1696, and quickly built Russia's first navy base. In 1697 the tsar embarked on an eighteen-month tour of western European capitals. Peter was fascinated by foreign technology, and he hoped to forge an anti-Ottoman alliance to strengthen his claims on the Black Sea. Peter failed to secure a military alliance, but

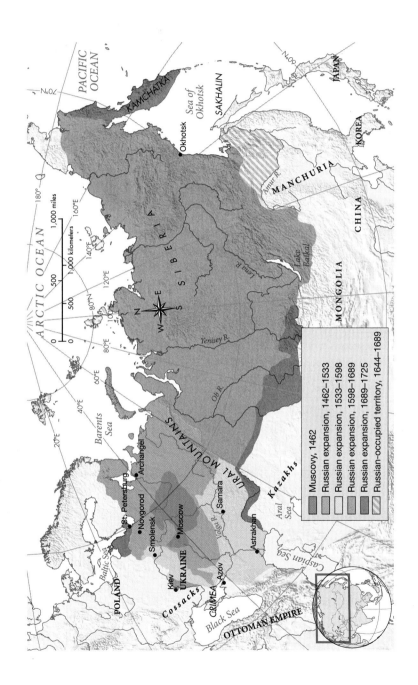

Peter the Great This compelling portrait by Grigory Musikiysky captures the strength and determination of the warrior-tsar in 1723, after more than three decades of personal rule. In his hand Peter holds the scepter, symbol of royal sovereignty, and across his breastplate is draped an ermine fur, a mark of honor. In the background are the battleships of Russia's new Baltic fleet and the famous St. Peter and St. Paul Fortress that Peter built in St. Petersburg. (State Hermitage Museum, St. Petersburg, Russia/Bridgeman Images)

he did learn his lessons from the growing power of the Dutch and the English. He also engaged more than a hundred foreign experts to return with him to Russia to help build the navy and improve Russian infrastructure.

To gain access to the Baltic Sea, Peter allied with Denmark and Poland to wage a sudden war of aggression against Sweden. Eighteen-year-old Charles XII of Sweden (1697–1718), however, surprised Peter. He defeated Denmark quickly in 1700 and then turned on Russia. His well-trained professional army attacked and routed unsuspecting Russians besieging the Swedish fortress of Narva on the Baltic coast. It was, for the Russians, a grim beginning to the long and brutal Great Northern War, which lasted from 1700 to 1721.

< MAP 15.4   The Expansion of Russia to 1725
This map shows the expansion of Russia from the mid-fifteenth century to 1725. Ivan IV "the Terrible" (r. 1533–1584) built on his predecessors' territorial gains by defeating remaining Mongol powers in southeastern Russia. During the seventeenth century, the Romanov dynasty extended Russian control across the vast territory of Siberia.

Peter responded to this defeat with new measures to increase state power, strengthen his military forces, and gain victory. He required all nobles to serve in the army or in the civil administration — for life. Peter also created schools of navigation and mathematics, medicine, engineering, and finance to produce skilled technicians and experts. He established an interlocking military-civilian bureaucracy with fourteen ranks, and he decreed that everyone had to start at the bottom and work toward the top. These measures gradually combined to make the army and government more powerful and efficient.

Peter also greatly increased the service requirements of commoners. In the wake of the Narva disaster, he established a regular standing army of more than two hundred thousand peasant-soldiers, drafted for life and commanded by noble officers. He added an additional hundred thousand men in special regiments of Cossacks and foreign mercenaries. To fund the army, taxes on peasants increased threefold during Peter's reign. Serfs were also arbitrarily assigned to work in the growing number of factories and mines that supplied the military.

In 1709 Peter's new war machine was able to crush the much smaller army of Sweden in Ukraine at Poltava, one of the most significant battles in Russian history. Russia's victory against Sweden was conclusive in 1721, and Estonia and present-day Latvia came under Russian rule for the first time. The cost was high: warfare consumed 80 to 85 percent of all revenues. But Russia became the dominant power in the Baltic and very much a great European power.

After his victory at Poltava, Peter channeled enormous resources into building a new Western-style capital on the Baltic to rival the great cities of Europe. Each summer, 25,000 to 40,000 peasants were sent to provide construction labor in St. Petersburg without pay. Many of these laborers died from hunger, sickness, and accidents. In order to populate his new capital, Peter ordered nobles to build costly palaces in St. Petersburg and to live in them most of the year. He also required merchants and artisans to settle and build in the new capital. The building of St. Petersburg was, in truth, an enormous direct tax levied on the wealthy, with the peasantry forced to do the work.

There were other important consequences of Peter's reign. For Peter, modernization meant westernization, and he encouraged the spread of Western culture along with technology and urban planning. Peter required nobles to shave their heavy beards and wear Western clothing, previously banned in Russia. He also ordered them to attend parties where young men and women would mix together and freely choose their own spouses. From these efforts a new elite class of Western-oriented Russians began to emerge.

Peter's reforms were unpopular with many Russians. For nobles, one of Peter's most detested reforms was the imposition of unigeniture — inheritance of land by one son alone — cutting daughters and other sons from family property. For peasants, the reign of the tsar saw a significant increase in the bonds of serfdom, and the gulf between the enserfed peasantry and the educated nobility increased. Despite the unpopularity of Peter's reforms, his modernizing and westernizing of Russia paved the way for it to move somewhat closer to the European mainstream in its thought and institutions during the Enlightenment, especially under Catherine the Great.

Entertainment at the Court of Ottoman Sultan Ahmet III Imitating the palace building of French monarchs, Sultan Ahmet III (r. 1703–1730) built a summer palace with extensive gardens, where he hosted extravagant parties featuring music, dancing, poetry recitations, and fine food. His courtiers quickly followed his example and built their own pleasure palaces nearby. ("A Dance for the Pleasure of Sultan Ahmet III" [1673–1736] from the "Surnama," 1720/Topkapi Palace Museum, Istanbul, Turkey/Bridgeman Images)

The Ottoman Empire

The Ottomans came out of Central Asia as conquering warriors, settled in Anatolia (present-day Turkey), and, at their peak in the mid-sixteenth century, ruled one of the most powerful empires in the world. Their possessions stretched from western Persia across North Africa and into the heart of central Europe (Map 15.5).

The Ottoman Empire was built on a unique model of state and society. Agricultural land was the personal hereditary property of the **sultan**, and peasants paid taxes to use the land. Thus there was an almost complete absence of private landed property and no hereditary nobility.

The Ottomans also employed a distinctive form of government administration. The top ranks of the bureaucracy were staffed by the sultan's slave corps. Because Muslim law prohibited enslaving other Muslims, the sultan's agents purchased slaves along the borders of the empire. Within the realm, the sultan levied a "tax" of one thousand to three thousand male children on the conquered Christian populations in the Balkans every year. These young slaves were raised in Turkey as Muslims and were trained as soldiers and government administrators. The most talented Ottoman slaves rose to the top of the bureaucracy, where they might acquire wealth and power. The less fortunate formed the core of the sultan's army, the **janissary corps**. These highly organized and efficient troops gave the Ottomans a formidable advantage in war with western Europeans. By 1683 service in the janissary corps had become so prestigious that the sultan ceased recruitment by force, and it became a volunteer army open to Christians and Muslims.

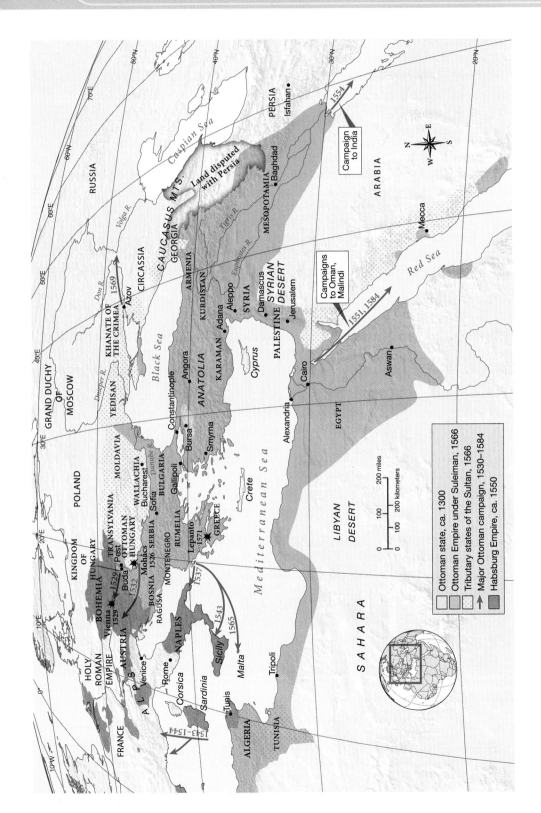

Campaign to India

Campaigns to Oman, Malindi

PERSIA
Isfahan

Baghdad
MESOPOTAMIA

ARABIA

Mecca

Red Sea

Land disputed with Persia

GEORGIA
ARMENIA
KURDISTAN
Aleppo
Adana
SYRIA
Damascus
Jerusalem
SYRIAN DESERT
PALESTINE

Cairo
EGYPT
Aswan

CAUCASUS MTS.

Caspian Sea

RUSSIA

Volga R.
Don R.

CIRCASSIA
KHANATE OF THE CREMEA
1569
Azov
YEDISAN

Black Sea

Constantinople
Bursa
Smyrna
Angora
ANATOLIA
KARAMAN
Cyprus

GRAND DUCHY OF MOSCOW

Dnieper R.

POLAND

MOLDAVIA
WALLACHIA
Bucharest
Danube R.
BULGARIA
Sofia
1526 SERBIA
RUMELIA
Gallipoli
MONTENEGRO
GREECE
Lepanto 1571

KINGDOM OF HUNGARY
TRANSYLVANIA
Pest
HUNGARY
Mohacs
Buda
1532
BOSNIA
RAGUSA

Vienna
1529
BOHEMIA
AUSTRIA
Venice
Rome
NAPLES
Corsica
Sardinia
Tunis

HOLY ROMAN EMPIRE
A L P S
FRANCE

1543-1544

ALGERIA
TUNISIA

Sicily
1543
Malta
1565
Tripoli

1537

Mediterranean Sea

Crete

Alexandria

LIBYAN DESERT

SAHARA

1551, 1584

1554

N
E
W
S

Ottoman state, ca. 1300
Ottoman Empire under Suleiman, 1566
Tributary states of the Sultan, 1566
Major Ottoman campaign, 1530–1584
Habsburg Empire, ca. 1550

0   100   200 miles
0   100   200 kilometers

The Ottomans divided their subjects into religious communities, and each *millet*, or "nation," enjoyed autonomous self-government under its religious leaders. The Ottoman Empire recognized Orthodox Christians, Jews, Armenian Christians, and Muslims as distinct millets. The **millet system** created a powerful bond between the Ottoman ruling class and religious leaders, who supported the sultan's rule in return for extensive authority over their own communities. Each millet collected taxes for the state, regulated collective behavior, and maintained law courts, schools, houses of worship, and hospitals for its people.

Istanbul (known outside the empire by its original name, Constantinople) was the capital of the empire. The "old palace" was for the sultan's female family members, who lived in isolation under the care of eunuchs, men who were castrated to prevent sexual relations with women. The newer Topkapi palace was where officials worked and young slaves were trained for future administrative or military careers. Sultans married women of the highest social standing, while keeping many concubines of low rank. To prevent the elite families into which they married from acquiring influence over the government, sultans had children only with their concubines and not with official wives. They also adopted a policy of allowing each concubine to produce only one male heir. At a young age, each son went to govern a province of the empire accompanied by his mother. These practices were intended to stabilize power and prevent a recurrence of the civil wars of the late fourteenth and early fifteenth centuries.

Sultan Suleiman undid these policies when he boldly married his concubine, a former slave of Polish origin named Hürrem, and had several children with her. Starting with Suleiman, imperial wives began to take on more power. Marriages were arranged between sultans' daughters and high-ranking servants, creating powerful new members of the imperial household. Over time, the sultan's exclusive authority waned in favor of a more bureaucratic administration.

Like European states, the Ottoman Empire suffered significant crises in the late sixteenth and early seventeenth centuries. Raised in the harem rather than taking on provincial governorships, the sultans who followed Suleiman were inexperienced and faced numerous political revolts. Ottoman finances suffered from the loss of international trade to the Portuguese and the Dutch, and the empire—like Spain—suffered from rising prices and a shrinking population. While the Bourbon monarchy was modernizing and enlarging the French army, the Ottomans failed to adopt new military technologies and training methods. As a result, the empire's military strength, long feared throughout Europe, declined, leading ultimately to the ceding of Hungary and Transylvania to the Austrian Habsburgs in 1699. The Ottoman state adapted to these challenges with some measure of success, but it did not recover the glory it held under Suleiman.

< MAP 15.5   **The Ottoman Empire at Its Height, 1566**
The Ottomans, like their great rivals the Habsburgs, rose to rule a vast dynastic empire encompassing many different peoples and ethnic groups. The army and the bureaucracy served to unite the disparate territories into a single state under an absolutist ruler.

Why and how did the constitutional state triumph in the Dutch Republic and England?

While France, Austria, Prussia, and Russia developed absolutist states, England and the Netherlands evolved toward **constitutionalism**, which is the limitation of government by law. Constitutionalism also implies a balance between the authority and power of the government, on the one hand, and the rights and liberties of the subjects, on the other. By definition, all constitutionalist governments have a constitution, be it written or unwritten.

Despite their common commitment to constitutional government, England and the Dutch Republic represented significantly different alternatives to absolute rule. After decades of civil war and an experiment with **republicanism**, the English opted for a constitutional monarchy in 1688. This settlement, which has endured to this day, retained a monarch as the titular head of government but vested sovereignty in an elected parliament. Upon gaining independence from Spain in 1648, the Dutch rejected monarchical rule and adopted a republican form of government in which elected estates held supreme power. Neither the English nor Dutch government was democratic by any standard, but to frustrated inhabitants of absolutist states they were shining examples of the restraint of arbitrary power and the rule of law.

Religious Divides and Civil War

In 1588 Queen Elizabeth I of England (r. 1558–1603) exercised very great personal power; by 1689 the English monarchy was severely circumscribed. A rare female monarch, Elizabeth was able to maintain control over her realm in part by refusing to marry and submit to a husband. She was immensely popular with her people but left no immediate heir to continue her legacy.

In 1603 Elizabeth's Scottish cousin James Stuart succeeded her as James I (r. 1603–1625). Like Louis XIV, James believed that a monarch had a divine right to his authority and is responsible only to God. James went so far as to lecture the House of Commons: "There are no privileges and immunities which can stand against a divinely appointed King." Such a view ran directly counter to English traditions that a person's property could not be taken away without due process of law. James I and his son Charles I (r. 1625–1649) considered such constraints intolerable and a threat to their divine-right prerogative. Consequently, bitter squabbles erupted between the Crown and the House of Commons. The expenses of England's intervention in the Thirty Years' War only exacerbated tensions. Charles I's response was to refuse to summon Parliament to convene from 1629 onward.

Religious issues also embittered relations between the king and the House of Commons. In the early seventeenth century many English people felt dissatisfied with the Church of England established by Henry VIII (r. 1509–1547). Calvinist **Puritans** wanted to take the Reformation further by "purifying" the Anglican Church of Roman Catholic elements, including crown-appointed bishops.

James I responded to such ideas by declaring, "No bishop, no king." His son and successor, Charles I, further antagonized religious sentiments by marrying a French Catholic princess and supporting the heavy-handed policies of the archbishop of Canterbury William Laud (1573–1645). Laud attempted to impose two new elements on church organization in Scotland: a new prayer book, modeled on the Anglican *Book of Common Prayer*, and bishoprics. Charles avoided addressing grievances against him by refusing to call Parliament into session from 1629 to 1640. Instead, he financed his government through extraordinary stopgap levies considered illegal by most English people. However, when Scottish Calvinists revolted against his religious policies, Charles was forced to summon Parliament to obtain funds for an army to put down the revolt. Angry with his behavior and sympathetic with the Scots' religious beliefs, in 1641 the House of Commons passed the Triennial Act, which compelled the king to summon Parliament every three years. The Commons also impeached Archbishop Laud and then threatened to abolish bishops. King Charles, fearful of a Scottish invasion, reluctantly accepted these measures. The next act in the conflict was precipitated by the outbreak of rebellion in Ireland, where English governors and landlords had long exploited the people. In 1641 the Catholic gentry of Ireland led an uprising in response to a feared invasion by English anti-Catholic forces.

Without an army, Charles I could neither come to terms with the Scots nor respond to the Irish rebellion. After a failed attempt to arrest parliamentary leaders, Charles left London for the north of England and began to raise an army. In response, Parliament formed its own army, the New Model Army, composed of the militia of the city of London and country squires with business connections.

The English Civil War (1642–1649) that erupted pitted the power of the king against that of the Parliament. After three years of fighting, Parliament's army defeated the king's forces at the Battles of Naseby and Langport in the summer of 1645. Charles refused to concede defeat, and both sides waited for a decisive event. This arrived in the form of the army under the leadership of Oliver Cromwell, a member of the House of Commons and a devout Puritan. In 1647 Cromwell's forces captured the king and dismissed anti-Cromwell members of the Parliament. In 1649 the remaining representatives, known as the "Rump Parliament," put Charles on trial for high treason. Charles was found guilty and beheaded on January 30, 1649, an act that sent shock waves around Europe.

The Puritan Protectorate

With the execution of Charles, kingship was abolished. The question remained of how the country would be governed. One answer was provided by philosopher Thomas Hobbes (1588–1679). Hobbes held a pessimistic view of human nature and believed that, left to themselves, humans would compete violently for power and wealth. The only solution, as he outlined in his 1651 treatise *Leviathan*, was a social contract in which all members of society placed themselves under the absolute rule of the sovereign, who would maintain peace and order. Hobbes imagined society as a human body in which the monarch served as head and individual subjects together made up the body. Just as the body cannot sever its own head, so Hobbes believed that society could not, having accepted the contract, rise up against its king.

Hobbes's longing for a benevolent absolute monarch was not widely shared in England. Instead, Oliver Cromwell and his supporters enshrined a commonwealth, or republican government, known as the **Protectorate**. Theoretically, legislative power rested in the surviving members of Parliament, and executive power was lodged in a council of state. In fact, the army controlled the government, and Oliver

Cromwell controlled the army. Though called the Protectorate, the rule of Cromwell (1653–1658) was a form of military dictatorship.

The fiction of republican government was maintained until 1655, when, after repeated disputes, Cromwell dismissed Parliament. Cromwell continued the standing army and proclaimed quasi-martial law. Reflecting Puritan ideas of morality, Cromwell's state forbade sports, closed the theaters, and rigorously censored the press.

On the issue of religion, Cromwell favored some degree of toleration, and all Christians except Roman Catholics held the right to practice their faiths. Cromwell had long associated Catholicism in Ireland with sedition and heresy, and he led an army there to reconquer the country in August 1649. One month later, his forces crushed a rebellion at Drogheda and massacred the garrison. After Cromwell's departure for England, atrocities worsened. The English banned Catholicism in Ireland, executed priests, and confiscated land from Catholics for English and Scottish settlers.

Cromwell adopted mercantilist policies similar to those of absolutist France. He enforced a Navigation Act (1651) requiring that English goods be transported on English ships. The act was a great boost to the development of an English merchant marine and brought about a short but successful war with the commercially threatened Dutch over trade with the Atlantic colonies. While mercantilist legislation ultimately benefited English commerce, for ordinary people the turmoil of foreign war only added to the harsh conditions of life induced by years of civil war. Cromwell also welcomed the immigration of Jews because of their experience in finance and trade, and they began to return to England four centuries after the expulsion of Jews by King Edward I in 1290.

The Protectorate collapsed when Cromwell died in 1658 and his ineffectual son succeeded him. Fed up with military rule, the English longed for a return to civilian government and, with it, common law and social stability. By 1660 they were ready to restore the monarchy.

The Restoration of the English Monarchy

The Restoration of 1660 brought to the throne Charles II (r. 1660–1685), eldest son of Charles I, who had been living on the continent. Both houses of Parliament were also restored, together with the established Anglican Church. The Restoration failed to resolve two serious problems, however. What was to be the attitude of the state toward Puritans, Catholics, and dissenters from the established church? And what was to be the relationship between the king and Parliament?

To answer the first question, Parliament enacted the **Test Act** of 1673 against those outside the Church of England, denying them the right to vote, hold public office, preach, teach, attend the universities, or even assemble for meetings. But these restrictions could not be enforced. When the Quaker William Penn held a meeting of his Friends and was arrested, the jury refused to convict him.

In politics, Charles II's initial determination to work well with Parliament did not last long. Finding that Parliament did not grant him an adequate income, Charles entered into a secret agreement with his cousin Louis XIV in 1679. The French king would give Charles £200,000 annually, and in return Charles would relax the laws against Catholics, gradually re-Catholicize England, and convert to Catholicism himself. When the details of this treaty leaked out, a great wave of anti-Catholic sentiment swept England.

The Family of Henry Chorley, Haberdasher of Preston, ca. 1680 This painting celebrates the Puritan family values of order, discipline, and self-restraint. The wife is surrounded by her young children, emphasizing her motherly duties, while her husband is flanked by their grown sons. Nevertheless, the woman's expression suggests she is a strong-minded partner to her husband, not meekly subservient. The couple probably worked side by side in the family business of selling men's clothing and accessories. (Harris Museum and Art Gallery, Preston, Lancashire, UK/Bridgeman Images)

When Charles died and his Catholic brother James became king, the worst English anti-Catholic fears were realized. In violation of the Test Act, James II (r. 1685–1688) appointed Roman Catholics to positions in the army, the universities, and local government. He also supported the opening of new Catholic churches and schools.

James's opponents, a powerful coalition of eminent persons in Parliament and the Church of England, bitterly resisted James's ambitions. They offered the English throne to James's heir, his Protestant daughter Mary, and her Dutch husband, Prince William of Orange. In December 1688 James II, his queen, and their infant son fled to France and became pensioners of Louis XIV. Early in 1689 William and Mary were crowned king and queen of England.

The English call the events of 1688 and 1689 the "Glorious Revolution" because they believe it replaced one king with another with barely any bloodshed. In truth, William's arrival sparked revolutionary riots and violence across the British Isles and in North American cities such as Boston and New York. Uprisings by supporters of James, known as Jacobites, occurred in 1689 in Scotland. In Ireland, the two sides waged outright war from 1689 to 1691. But William's victory at the Battle of the Boyne (1690) and the subsequent Treaty of Limerick (1691) sealed his accession to power.

Constitutional Monarchy

In England, the Glorious Revolution represented the final destruction of the idea of divine-right monarchy. The men who brought about the revolution framed their intentions in the Bill of Rights, which was formulated in direct response to Stuart absolutism. Law was to be made in Parliament; once made, it could not be suspended by the Crown. Parliament had to be called at least once every three years. The independence of the judiciary was established, and there was to be no standing army in peacetime. Protestants could possess arms, but the Catholic minority could not. A Catholic could not inherit the throne. Additional legislation granted freedom of worship to Protestant dissenters, but not to Catholics. William and Mary accepted these principles when they took the throne, and the House of Parliament passed the Bill of Rights in December 1689.

The Glorious Revolution and the concept of representative government found its best defense in political philosopher John Locke's *Two Treatises of Government* (1690). Locke (1632–1704) maintained that a government that oversteps its proper function — protecting the natural rights of life, liberty, and property — becomes a tyranny. Under a tyrannical government, the people have the natural right to rebellion.

Although the events of 1688 and 1689 brought England closer to Locke's ideal, they did not constitute a democratic revolution. The revolution placed sovereignty in Parliament, and Parliament represented the upper classes.

The Dutch Republic in the Seventeenth Century

In the late sixteenth century the seven northern provinces of the Netherlands fought for and won their independence from Spain. The independence of the Republic of the United Provinces of the Netherlands was recognized in 1648 in the treaty that ended the Thirty Years' War. In this period, often called the "golden age" of the Netherlands, Dutch ideas and attitudes played a profound role in shaping a new and modern worldview. At the same time, the United Provinces developed its own distinctive model of a constitutional state.

Rejecting the rule of a monarch, the Dutch established a republic, a state in which power rested in the hands of the people and was exercised through elected representatives. Other examples of republics in early modern Europe included the Swiss Confederation and several autonomous city-states of Italy and the Holy Roman Empire. Among the Dutch, an oligarchy of wealthy businessmen called regents handled domestic affairs in each province's Estates (assemblies). The provincial Estates held virtually all the power. A federal assembly, or States General, handled foreign affairs and war, but it did not possess sovereign authority. All issues had to be referred back to the local Estates for approval, and each of the seven provinces could veto any proposed legislation. Holland, the province with the largest navy and the most wealth, usually dominated the republic and the States General.

In each province, the Estates appointed an executive officer, known as the **stadholder**, who carried out ceremonial functions and was responsible for military defense. Although in theory the stadholder was freely chosen by the Estates and was answerable to them, in practice the strong and influential House of Orange usually held the office of stadholder in several of the seven provinces of the republic. Tensions persisted between supporters of the House of Orange and those of the staunchly republican Estates, who suspected that the princes of Orange harbored monarchical ambitions.

The political success of the Dutch rested on their phenomenal commercial prosperity. The Dutch originally came to dominate European shipping by putting profits from their original industry—herring fishing—into shipbuilding. They boasted the lowest shipping rates and largest merchant marine in Europe, which allowed them to undersell foreign competitors. In the seventeenth century global trade and commerce brought the Dutch the highest standard of living in Europe, perhaps in the world. Salaries were high, and all classes of society ate well. A scholar has described the Netherlands as "an island of plenty in a sea of want." Consequently, the Netherlands experienced very few of the food riots that characterized the rest of Europe.[5]

The moral and ethical bases of Dutch commercial wealth were thrift, social discipline, and religious toleration. Although there is scattered evidence of anti-Semitism, Jews enjoyed a level of acceptance and assimilation in business and general culture unique in early modern Europe. Anti-Catholic laws existed through the eighteenth century, but they were only partly enforced. In the Dutch Republic, toleration paid off: it attracted a great deal of foreign capital and investment. After Louis XIV revoked the Edict of Nantes, many Huguenots fled France for the Dutch Republic. They brought with them a high level of artisanal skill and business experience as well as a loathing for state repression that would inspire the political views of the Enlightenment (see "The Early Enlightenment" in Chapter 16).

NOTES

1. John A. Lynn, "Recalculating French Army Growth," in *The Military Revolution Debate: Readings on the Military Transformation of Early Modern Europe*, ed. Clifford J. Rogers (Boulder, Colo.: Westview Press, 1995), p. 125.
2. J. H. Elliott, *Imperial Spain, 1469–1716* (New York: Mentor Books, 1963), pp. 306–308.
3. Quoted in H. Rosenberg, *Bureaucracy, Aristocracy, and Autocracy: The Prussian Experience, 1660–1815* (Boston: Beacon Press, 1966), p. 43.
4. Quoted in Rosenberg, *Bureaucracy, Aristocracy, and Autocracy*, p. 40.
5. S. Schama, *The Embarrassment of Riches: An Interpretation of Dutch Culture in the Golden Age* (New York: Alfred A. Knopf, 1987), pp. 165–170; quotation is on p. 167.

LOOKING BACK **LOOKING AHEAD**

The seventeenth century represented a difficult passage between two centuries of dynamism and growth in Europe. On one side lay the sixteenth century's religious enthusiasm and strife, overseas discoveries, rising populations, and vigorous commerce. On the other side stretched the eighteenth century's renewed population growth, economic development, and cultural flourishing. The first half of the seventeenth century was marked by harsh climate conditions and violent conflict across Europe. Recurring crop failure, famine, and epidemic disease contributed to a stagnant economy and population loss. In the middle decades of the seventeenth century, the very survival of the European monarchies established in the Renaissance appeared in doubt.

With the re-establishment of order in the second half of the century, maintaining stability was of paramount importance to European rulers. While a few nations placed their trust in constitutionally limited governments, many more were ruled by monarchs proclaiming their absolute and God-given authority. Despite their political differences, most European states emerged from the period of crisis with shared achievements in state power, territorial expansion, and long-distance trade.

The eighteenth century was to see these power politics thrown into question by new Enlightenment aspirations for human society that derived from the inquisitive and self-confident spirit of the Scientific Revolution. These movements are explored in the next chapter. By the end of the eighteenth century demands for real popular sovereignty, colonial self-rule, and slave emancipation challenged the very bases of order so painfully achieved in the seventeenth century.

MAKE CONNECTIONS

Think about the larger developments and continuities within and across chapters.

1. This chapter has argued that, despite their political differences, rulers in absolutist and constitutionalist nations faced similar obstacles in the mid-seventeenth century and achieved many of the same goals. Based on the evidence presented here, do you agree with this argument? Why or why not?

2. Proponents of absolutism in western Europe believed that their form of monarchical rule was fundamentally different from and superior to what they saw as the "despotism" of Russia and the Ottoman Empire. What was the basis of this belief, and how accurate do you think it was?

3. What evidence does this chapter provide for the impact on European states of the discoveries and conquests discussed in Chapter 14?

Chapter 15 Review

IDENTIFY KEY TERMS

Identify and explain the significance of each item below.

Peace of Westphalia (p. 421)

baroque style (p. 423)

Fronde (p. 425)

Peace of Utrecht (p. 429)

mercantilism (p. 430)

Junkers (p. 433)

boyars (p. 436)

Cossacks (p. 436)

sultan (p. 441)

janissary corps (p. 441)

millet system (p. 443)

constitutionalism (p. 444)

republicanism (p. 444)

Puritans (p. 444)

Protectorate (p. 445)

Test Act (p. 446)

stadholder (p. 448)

REVIEW THE MAIN IDEAS

Answer the section heading questions from the chapter.

1. What made the seventeenth century an "age of crisis" and achievement? (p. 418)

2. Why did France rise and Spain fall during the late seventeenth century? (p. 424)

3. What explains the rise of absolutism in Prussia and Austria? (p. 431)

4. What were the distinctive features of Russian and Ottoman absolutism? (p. 435)

5. Why and how did the constitutional state triumph in the Dutch Republic and England? (p. 444)

CHRONOLOGY

ca. 1500–1650	• Consolidation of serfdom in eastern Europe
1533–1584	• Reign of Ivan the Terrible in Russia
1589–1610	• Reign of Henry IV in France
1598–1613	• Time of Troubles in Russia
1620–1740	• Growth of absolutism in Austria and Prussia
1642–1649	• English Civil War, which ends with execution of Charles I
1643–1715	• Reign of Louis XIV in France
1653–1658	• Military rule in England under Oliver Cromwell (the Protectorate)
1660	• Restoration of English monarchy under Charles II
1665–1683	• Jean-Baptiste Colbert applies mercantilism to France
1670–1671	• Cossack revolt led by Stenka Razin
ca. 1680–1750	• Construction of absolutist palaces
1682	• Louis XIV moves court to Versailles
1682–1725	• Reign of Peter the Great in Russia
1683–1699	• Habsburgs push the Ottoman Turks from Hungary
1685	• Edict of Nantes revoked in France
1688–1689	• Glorious Revolution in England
1701–1713	• War of the Spanish Succession

16

Toward a New Worldview

1540–1789

CHAPTER PREVIEW

- What revolutionary discoveries were made in the sixteenth and seventeenth centuries?

- What intellectual and social changes occurred as a result of the Scientific Revolution?

- How did the Enlightenment emerge, and what were major currents of Enlightenment thought?

- How did the Enlightenment change social ideas and practices?

- What impact did new ways of thinking have on politics?

IN THE SIXTEENTH AND SEVENTEENTH CENTURIES, new ways of understanding the natural world emerged. Those leading the changes saw themselves as philosophers and referred to their field of study as "natural philosophy." Whereas medieval scholars looked to authoritative texts like the Bible or the classics, early modern natural philosophers performed experiments and relied on increasingly complex mathematical calculations. The resulting conception of the universe and its laws remained in force until Albert Einstein's discoveries at the beginning of the twentieth century. Along with new discoveries in botany, zoology, chemistry, electricity, and other domains, these developments constituted a fundamental shift in the basic framework for understanding the natural world and the methods for examining it, known collectively as the "Scientific Revolution."

In the eighteenth century philosophers extended the use of reason from the study of nature to human society. They sought to bring the light of reason to bear on the darkness of prejudice, long-standing traditions, and general ignorance. Self-proclaimed members of an "Enlightenment" movement, they wished to bring the same progress to human affairs as their predecessors had brought to understanding of the natural world. While the Scientific Revolution ushered in modern science, the Enlightenment created concepts of human rights, equality, progress, universalism, and tolerance that still guide Western societies today. At the same time, some people used their new understanding of nature and reason to proclaim their own superiority, thus rationalizing attitudes now regarded as racist and sexist. These transformations in science and philosophy were encouraged by European overseas expansion, which challenged traditional ways of thinking by introducing an enormous variety of new peoples, plants, and animals.

What revolutionary discoveries were made in the sixteenth and seventeenth centuries?

Until the middle of the sixteenth century, Europeans relied on an understanding of motion and matter drawn from the ancient Greek philosopher Aristotle and adapted to Christian theology. The rise of the university, along with the intellectual vitality of the Renaissance and technological advancements, inspired European scholars to seek better explanations. From the work of Nicolaus Copernicus to the work of Isaac Newton, a revolutionary new understanding of the universe had emerged by the end of the seventeenth century. Collectively known as the "Scientific Revolution," the work of these scientists constituted significant milestones in the creation of modern science.

The major figures of the Scientific Revolution (ca. 1540–1700) were for the most part devout Christians who saw their work as heralding the glory of creation and who combined older traditions of magic, astrology, and alchemy with their pathbreaking experimentation. Their discoveries took place in a broader context of international trade, imperial expansion, and cultural exchange. Alongside developments in modern science and natural philosophy, the growth of natural history in this period is now recognized by historians as a major achievement of the Scientific Revolution.

Contributions from the Muslim World

In 1500 scientific activity flourished in many parts of the world. Between 750 and 950 Muslim, Christian, and Jewish scholars in the expanding Muslim world began translating the legacy of ancient Greek science and natural philosophy into Arabic, especially the works of Aristotle. The interaction of peoples and cultures across the vast Muslim world, facilitated by religious tolerance and the common scholarly language of Arabic, was highly favorable to advances in learning.

In a great period of cultural and intellectual flourishing from 1000 to 1500, Muslim scholars thrived in cultural centers such as Baghdad and Córdoba, the capital of Islamic Spain. They established the world's first institutions of higher learning, called *madrasas*, in Constantinople, Fez (Morocco), and Cairo, which were devoted to Islamic theology and law. In this fertile atmosphere, scholars surpassed the texts they had inherited in areas such as mathematics, physics, astronomy, and medicine. Arab and Persian mathematicians, for example, invented algebra, the concept of the algorithm, and decimal point notation. Arab astronomers built observatories to collect celestial observations, and an Egyptian scholar, Ibn al-Haytham (d. 1042), revolutionized optics by demonstrating mathematically that light travels in straight lines.

Given the scientific and philosophical knowledge possessed by Arab and Muslim scholars in the tenth and eleventh centuries, one might have expected that modern science would have emerged in the Muslim world first. However, the madrasas excluded study of the natural sciences, and Muslim scholars did not benefit from institutions dedicated to the creation and dissemination of scientific knowledge. This pattern of education was unlike that of the Europeans, who created independent institutions of higher education (universities) and then placed study of the Greek natural sciences at the center of the curriculum.

The growth of trade and the re-establishment of stronger monarchies in the High Middle Ages encouraged the circulation of ideas and the patronage of educational institutions in western Europe. As European scholars became aware of advances in knowledge made in Muslim territories, they traveled to Islamic territories in Iberia, Sicily, and the eastern Mediterranean to gain access to this knowledge. In the twelfth century, these scholars translated many Greek texts — including works of Aristotle, Ptolemy, Galen, and Euclid previously lost to the West — into Latin, along with the commentaries of Arab scholars. With the patronage of kings and religious institutions, groups of scholars created universities in which these translated works, especially those of the ancient Greek philosopher Aristotle, dominated the curriculum.

The intellectual and cultural movement known as the Renaissance provided a crucial foundation for the Scientific Revolution. The quest to restore the glories of the ancient past led to a new period of rediscovery of classical texts, including Ptolemy's *Geography*, which was translated into Latin around 1410. An encyclopedic treatise on botany by Theophrastus was rediscovered in the 1450s moldering on the shelves of the Vatican library. The fall of Constantinople to the Ottomans in 1453 resulted in a great influx of little-known Greek works, as Christian scholars fled to Italy with their precious texts.

In this period, western European universities established new professorships of mathematics, astronomy, and natural philosophy. The prestige of the new fields was low, especially of mathematics, which was reserved for practical problems such as accounting, surveying, and computing planetary tables, but not used to understand the functioning of the physical world itself. Nevertheless, these professorships eventually enabled the union of mathematics with natural philosophy that was to be a hallmark of the Scientific Revolution.

Scientific Thought to 1500

The term *science* as we use it today came into use only in the nineteenth century. For medieval scholars, philosophy was the path to true knowledge about the world, and its proofs consisted of the authority of ancients (as interpreted by Muslim and Christian theologians) and their techniques of logical argumentation. Questions about the physical nature of the universe and how it functioned belonged to a minor branch of philosophy, called **natural philosophy**. Drawing on scholarship in the Muslim world, natural philosophy was based primarily on the ideas of Aristotle, the great Greek philosopher of the fourth century B.C.E. Medieval theologians such as Thomas Aquinas brought Aristotelian philosophy into harmony with Christian doctrines. According to the Christianized view of Aristotle, a motionless earth stood at the center of the universe and was encompassed by ten separate concentric crystal spheres in which were embedded the moon, the sun, planets, and stars. Beyond the spheres was Heaven, with the throne of God and the souls of the saved. Angels kept the spheres moving in perfect circles.

Aristotle's views also dominated thinking about physics and motion on earth. Aristotle had distinguished between the world of the celestial spheres and that of the earth — the sublunar world. The spheres consisted of a perfect, incorruptible "quintessence," or fifth essence. The sublunar world, however, was made up of four imperfect, changeable elements: air, fire, water, and earth. Aristotle and his followers also believed that a uniform force moved an object at a constant speed and that the object would stop as soon as that force was removed.

Aristotle's cosmology made intellectual sense, but it could not account for the observed motions of the stars and planets and, in particular, provided no explanation for the apparent backward motion of the planets (which we now know occurs as the earth passes the slower-moving outer planets or is passed by the faster-moving inner ones). More than four centuries later the Greek scholar Ptolemy offered a theory for this phenomenon. According to Ptolemy, the planets moved in small circles, called epicycles, each of which moved in turn along a larger circle, or deferent. Ptolemaic astronomy was less elegant than Aristotle's neat nested circles and required complex calculations, but it provided a surprisingly accurate model for predicting planetary motion.

The work of Ptolemy also provided the basic foundation of knowledge about the earth. Rediscovered and translated from Arabic into Latin around 1410, his *Geography* presented crucial advances on medieval cartography by representing a round earth divided into 360 degrees with the major latitude marks. However, Ptolemy's map reflected the limits of ancient knowledge, showing only the continents of Europe, Africa, and Asia, with land covering three-quarters of the world.

These two frameworks reveal the strengths and limitations of European knowledge on the eve of the Scientific Revolution. Overcoming the authority of the ancients to develop a new understanding of the natural world, derived from precise techniques of observation and experimentation, was the Scientific Revolution's monumental achievement. Europeans were not the first to use experimental methods — of which there was a long tradition in the Muslim world and elsewhere — but they were the first to separate scientific knowledge decisively from philosophical and religious beliefs and to accord mathematics a fundamental role in understanding the natural world.

Model of the Ptolemaic System This seventeenth-century brass model was used to demonstrate the Ptolemaic astronomical system, with the earth at the center and the movement of the sun, stars, and planets around it. (Armillary sphere made by Adam Heroldt [fl. 1648]/Science Museum, London, UK/Bridgeman Images)

The Copernican Hypothesis

The first great departure from the medieval system was the work of the Polish cleric Nicolaus Copernicus (1473–1543). Copernicus studied astronomy, medicine, and church law at the famed universities of Bologna, Padua, and Ferrara before taking up a church position in East Prussia. Copernicus came to believe that Ptolemy's cumbersome rules detracted from the majesty of a perfect creator. He preferred an idea espoused by some ancient Greek scholars: that the sun, rather than the earth, was at the center of the universe. Without questioning the Aristotelian belief in crystal spheres or the idea that circular motion was divine, Copernicus theorized that the stars and planets, including the earth, revolved around a fixed sun. He laid out his hypothesis in an unpublished manuscript between 1510 and 1514, but, fearing the ridicule of other scholars, he did not publish *On the Revolutions of the Heavenly Spheres* until 1543, the year of his death.

The **Copernican hypothesis** had enormous scientific and religious implications, many of which the conservative Copernicus did not anticipate. First, it put the stars at rest, their apparent nightly movement simply a result of the earth's rotation. Thus it destroyed the main reason for believing in crystal spheres capable of moving the stars around the earth. Second, Copernicus's theory suggested a universe of staggering size. If in the course of a year the earth moved around the sun and yet the stars appeared to remain in the same place, then the universe was unthinkably large. Third, by using mathematics, instead of philosophy, to justify his theories, Copernicus challenged the traditional hierarchy of the disciplines. Finally, by characterizing the earth as just another planet, Copernicus destroyed the basic idea of Aristotelian physics—that the earthly sphere was quite different from the heavenly one. Where then were Heaven and the throne of God?

Religious leaders varied in their response to Copernicus's theories. A few Protestant scholars became avid Copernicans, while others accepted some elements of his criticism of Ptolemy but firmly rejected the notion that the earth moved, a doctrine that contradicted the literal reading of some passages of the Bible. Among Catholics, Copernicus's ideas drew little attention prior to 1600. Because the Catholic Church had never insisted on literal interpretations of the Bible, it did not officially declare the Copernican hypothesis false until provoked by the publications of Galileo Galilei in 1616 (see "Science and Religion" later in this chapter).

Other events were almost as influential in creating doubts about traditional astronomy. In 1572 a new star appeared and shone very brightly for almost two years. Actually a distant exploding star, it made an enormous impression on people and seemed to contradict the idea that the heavenly spheres were unchanging and therefore perfect. In 1577 a new comet suddenly moved through the sky, cutting a straight path across the supposedly impenetrable crystal spheres. It was time, as a sixteenth-century scientific writer put it, for "the radical renovation of astronomy."[1]

Brahe, Kepler, and Galileo: Proving Copernicus Right

One astronomer who partially agreed with the Copernican hypothesis was the Danish astronomer Tycho Brahe (TEE-koh BRAH-hee) (1546–1601). Brahe established himself as Europe's leading astronomer with his detailed observations of the new star that appeared in 1572. Impressed by his work, the king of Denmark provided funds for Brahe to build the most sophisticated observatory of his day. Upon the king's death, Brahe acquired a new patron in the Holy Roman emperor Rudolph II and built a new observatory in Prague.

For twenty years Brahe had observed the stars and planets with the aim of creating new and improved tables of planetary motions. He produced the most exact observations ever carried out with the naked eye, but his limited understanding of mathematics and his sudden death in 1601 prevented him from making much sense out of his mass of data. Part Ptolemaic, part Copernican, he believed that all the planets except the earth revolved around the sun and that the entire group of sun and planets revolved in turn around the earth-moon system.

It was Brahe's assistant, Johannes Kepler (1571–1630), who discovered what his observations revealed about planetary movements. Kepler carefully re-examined his predecessor's notations and came to believe that they could not be explained by Ptolemy's astronomy. Abandoning the notion of the circular paths of epicycles and deferents developed by Ptolemy to explain the retrograde motion of the planets—which even Copernicus had retained in part—Kepler developed three revolutionary laws of planetary motion. First, largely through observations of the planet Mars, he demonstrated that the orbits of the planets around the sun are elliptical rather than circular. Second, he demonstrated that the planets do not move at a uniform speed in their orbits. When a planet is close to the sun it moves more rapidly, and it slows as it moves farther away from the sun. Finally, Kepler's third law stated that the time a planet takes to make its complete orbit is precisely related to its distance from the sun.

Kepler's contribution was monumental. Whereas Copernicus had used mathematics to describe planetary movement, Kepler proved mathematically the precise relations of a sun-centered (solar) system. He thus united for the first time the theoretical cosmology of natural philosophy with mathematics. His work demolished the old system of Aristotle and Ptolemy, and with his third law he came close to formulating the idea of universal gravitation (see the next section). In 1627 he also published the *Rudolphine Tables*, named in honor of Emperor Rudolph and based on his observations and those of Tycho Brahe. The work consisted of a catalogue of more than one thousand stars as well as tables of the positions of the sun, moon, and planets. They were used by astronomers for many years.

While Kepler was unraveling planetary motion, a Florentine named Galileo Galilei (1564–1642) was challenging Aristotelian ideas about motion on earth. Galileo's fascination with mathematics led to a professorship during which he examined motion and mechanics in a new way. Galileo focused on deficiencies in Aristotle's theories of motion. He measured the movement of a rolling ball across a surface, repeating the action again and again to verify his results. In his famous acceleration experiment, he showed that a uniform force — in this case, gravity — produced a uniform acceleration. He also achieved new insight into the principle of inertia by hypothesizing that an object would continue in motion forever unless stopped by some external force. The **law of inertia** was formulated explicitly after Galileo's death by René Descartes (see "The Methods of Science: Bacon and Descartes" later in this chapter) and Pierre Gassendi. Galileo's work on mechanics proved Aristotelian physics wrong.

On hearing details about the invention of the telescope in Holland, Galileo made one for himself and trained it on the heavens. He quickly discovered that, far from being a perfect crystal sphere, the moon is cratered with mountains and valleys, just like the earth. He then discovered the first four moons of Jupiter, which clearly suggested that Jupiter could not possibly be embedded in an impenetrable crystal sphere as Aristotle and Ptolemy maintained. This discovery provided new evidence for the Copernican theory, in which Galileo already believed. He wrote in 1610 in *The Sidereal Messenger*: "By the aid of a telescope anyone may behold [the Milky Way] in a manner which so distinctly appeals to the senses that all the disputes which have tormented philosophers through so many ages are exploded by the irrefutable evidence of our eyes, and we are freed from wordy disputes upon the subject."[2]

A crucial corner in Western civilization had been turned. No longer should one rely on established authority. A new method of learning and investigating was being developed, one that proved useful in any field of inquiry. A historian investigating documents of the past, for example, is not so different from a Galileo studying stars and rolling balls.

Newton's Synthesis

By about 1640 the work of Brahe, Kepler, and Galileo had been largely accepted by the scientific community despite opposition from religious leaders. The old Aristotelian astronomy and physics were in ruins, and several fundamental breakthroughs had been made. But the new findings failed to explain what forces controlled the movement of the planets and objects on earth. That challenge was taken up by English scientist Isaac Newton (1642–1727), a genius who spectacularly united the experimental and theoretical-mathematical sides of modern science.

Newton was born into the lower English gentry, and he enrolled at Cambridge University in 1661. He arrived at some of his most basic ideas about physics in 1666 at age twenty-four but was unable to prove them mathematically. In 1684, after years of studying optics, Newton returned to mechanics for eighteen intensive months.

The result was his towering accomplishment, a single explanatory system that could integrate the astronomy of Copernicus, as corrected by Kepler's laws, with the physics of Galileo and his predecessors. Newton did this through a set of mathematical laws that explain motion and mechanics. These laws were published in 1687 in Newton's *Mathematical Principles of Natural Philosophy* (also known as the *Principia Mathematica*). Because of their complexity, it took scientists and engineers two hundred years to work out all their implications.

The key feature of the Newtonian synthesis was the **law of universal gravitation**. According to this law, every body in the universe attracts every other body in the universe in a precise mathematical relationship, whereby the force of attraction is proportional to the quantity of matter of the objects and inversely proportional to the square of the distance between them. The whole universe—from Kepler's elliptical orbits to Galileo's rolling balls—was unified in one majestic system. Newton's synthesis of mathematics with physics and astronomy established him as one of the most important figures in the history of science; it prevailed until Albert Einstein's formulation of the general theory of relativity in 1915. Yet, near the end of his life, he declared: "I do not know what I may appear to the world; but to myself I seem to have been only like a boy, playing on the seashore, and diverting myself, in now and then finding a smoother pebble or a prettier shell than ordinary, whilst the great ocean of truth lay all undiscovered before me."[3]

Natural History and Empire

At the same time that they made advances in astronomy and physics, Europeans embarked on the pursuit of knowledge about unknown geographical regions and the useful and valuable resources they contained. Because they were the first to acquire a large overseas empire, the Spanish pioneered these efforts. Following the conquest of the Aztec and Inca Empires (see "Conquest of the Aztec Empire" and "The Fall of the Incas" in Chapter 14), they sought to learn about and profit from their New World holdings. The Spanish crown sponsored many scientific expeditions to gather information and specimens, out of which emerged new discoveries that reshaped the fields of botany, zoology, cartography, and metallurgy, among others. These accomplishments have attracted less attention from historians in part because the strict policy of secrecy imposed on scientific discoveries by the Spanish crown limited the documents circulating about them.

Plants were a particular source of interest because they offered potential for tremendous profits in the form of spices, medicines, dyes, and cash crops. King Philip II of Spain sent his personal physician, Francisco Hernández, to New Spain for seven years in the 1560s. Hernández filled fifteen volumes with illustrations of three thousand plants previously unknown in Europe. He extensively interviewed local healers about the plants' medicinal properties, thereby benefiting from centuries of Mesoamerican botanical knowledge. In the seventeenth century, for example, the Spanish obtained a monopoly on the world's supply of cinchona bark, which comes from a tree native to the high altitudes of the Andes and was the first effective treatment for malaria.

Other countries followed the Spanish example as their global empires expanded, relying on both official expeditions and the private initiative of merchants, missionaries, and settlers. Royal botanical gardens served as living laboratories for cultivating valuable foreign plants. Over time, the stream of new information about plant and animal species overwhelmed existing intellectual frameworks. Carl Linnaeus (1707–1778) of Sweden sent his students on exploratory voyages around the world and, based on their observations and the specimens they collected, devised a formal system of naming and classifying living organisms still used today (with substantial revisions).

New encyclopedias of natural history popularized this knowledge with realistic drawings and descriptions emphasizing the usefulness of animals and plants. Audiences at home eagerly read the accounts of naturalists, who braved the heat, insects, and diseases of tropical jungles to bring home exotic animal, vegetable, and mineral specimens (along with captive indigenous human subjects). Audiences heard much less about the many local guides, translators, and practitioners of medicine and science who made these expeditions possible and who contributed a great deal of knowledge about the natural world.

Magic and Alchemy

Recent historical research on the Scientific Revolution has focused on the contribution of ideas and practices we no longer recognize as science, such as astrology and alchemy. For most of human history, interest in astronomy was inspired by the belief that the movement of heavenly bodies influenced events on earth. Many of the most celebrated astronomers also worked as astrologers. Used as a diagnostic tool in medicine, astrology formed a regular part of the curriculum of medical schools.

Centuries-old practices of magic and alchemy also remained important traditions for natural philosophers. Early modern practitioners of magic strove to understand and control hidden connections they perceived among different elements of the natural world, such as that between a magnet and iron. The idea that objects possessed hidden or "occult" qualities that allowed them to affect objects at a distance was a particularly important legacy of the magical tradition. Belief in occult qualities — or numerology or cosmic harmony — was not antithetical to belief in God. On the contrary, adherents believed that only a divine creator could infuse the universe with such meaningful mystery.

Johannes Kepler exemplifies the interaction among these different strands of interest. His duties as court mathematician included casting horoscopes for the royal family, and he guided his own life by astrological principles. He also wrote at length on cosmic harmonies and explained elliptical motion through ideas about the beautiful music created by the combined motion of the planets. Kepler's fictional account of travel to the moon, written partly to illustrate the idea of a non-earth-centered universe, caused controversy and may have contributed to the arrest and trial of his mother as a witch in 1620. Kepler also suffered because of his unorthodox brand of Lutheranism, which led to his condemnation by both Lutherans and Catholics.

Another example of the interweaving of ideas and beliefs is Sir Isaac Newton, who was both intensely religious and fascinated by alchemy, whose practitioners believed (among other things) that base metals could be turned into gold. Critics complained that his idea of universal gravitation was merely a restatement of old magical ideas about the innate sympathies between bodies; Newton himself believed that the attraction of gravity resulted from God's actions in the universe.

What intellectual and social changes occurred as a result of the Scientific Revolution?

The Scientific Revolution was not accomplished by a handful of brilliant individuals working alone. Advancements occurred in many fields—medicine, chemistry, and botany, among others—as scholars developed new methods to seek answers to long-standing problems. They did so in collaboration with skilled craftsmen who invented new instruments and helped conduct experiments. These results circulated in an intellectual community from which women were usually excluded.

The Methods of Science: Bacon and Descartes

One of the keys to the achievement of a new worldview in the seventeenth century was the development of better ways of obtaining knowledge. Two important thinkers, Francis Bacon (1561–1626) and René Descartes (day-KAHRT) (1596–1650), were influential in describing and advocating for improved scientific methods based, respectively, on empirical observation and on mathematical reasoning.

The English politician and writer Francis Bacon was the greatest early propagandist for the experimental method. Rejecting the Aristotelian and medieval method of using speculative reasoning to build general theories, Bacon called for a new approach to scientific inquiry based on direct observation, free from the preconceptions and prejudices of the past. The researcher who wants to learn more about leaves or rocks, for example, should not speculate about the subject but rather collect a multitude of specimens and then compare and analyze them to derive general principles. This technique of producing knowledge is known as inductive reasoning, which works from specific observations up to broader generalizations and theories. Bacon's work, and his prestige as lord chancellor under James I, led to the widespread adoption of what was called "experimental philosophy" in Britain after his death. In 1660 followers of Bacon created the Royal Society (still in existence), which met weekly to conduct experiments and discuss the latest findings of scholars across Europe.

On the continent, more speculative methods gained support. In 1619, as a twenty-three-year-old soldier serving in the Thirty Years' War, the French philosopher René Descartes experienced a life-changing intellectual vision. Descartes saw that there was a perfect correspondence between geometry and algebra and that geometrical spatial figures could be expressed as algebraic equations and vice versa. A major step forward in the history of mathematics, Descartes's discovery of analytic geometry provided scientists with an important new tool.

Descartes used mathematics to elaborate a new vision of the workings of the cosmos. Accepting Galileo's claim that all elements of the universe are composed of the same matter, Descartes began to investigate the basic nature of matter. Drawing on ancient Greek atomist philosophies, he developed the idea that matter was made up of "corpuscles" (tiny particles) that collided together in an endless series of motions, akin the workings of a machine. All occurrences in nature could be analyzed as matter in motion, and the total "quantity of motion" in the universe was constant. Descartes's mechanistic view of the universe depended on the idea that space was identical to matter and that empty space—a vacuum—was therefore impossible.

Although Descartes's hypothesis about the vacuum was proved wrong, his notion of a mechanistic universe intelligible through the physics of motion proved inspirational. Decades later, Newton rejected Descartes's idea of a full universe and several of his other ideas, but retained the notion of a mechanistic universe as a key element of his own system.

Descartes's greatest achievement was to develop his initial vision into a whole philosophy of knowledge and science. The Aristotelian cosmos was appealing in part because it corresponded with the evidence of the human senses. When experiments proved that sensory impressions could be wrong, Descartes decided it was necessary to doubt them and everything that could reasonably be doubted, and to then, as in geometry, use deductive reasoning from self-evident truths, which he called "first principles," to ascertain scientific laws.

Descartes's reasoning ultimately reduced all substances to "matter" and "mind" — that is, to the physical and the mental. The devout Descartes believed that God had endowed man with reason for a purpose and that rational speculation could provide a path to the truths of creation. His view of the world as consisting of these two fundamental entities is known as **Cartesian dualism**. Descartes's thought was highly influential in France and the Netherlands, but less so in England, where experimental philosophy won the day.

Both Bacon's inductive experimentalism and Descartes's deductive mathematical reasoning had flaws. Bacon's inability to appreciate the importance of mathematics and his obsession with practical results clearly showed the limitations of antitheoretical empiricism. Likewise, some of Descartes's positions demonstrated the inadequacy of rigid, dogmatic rationalism. For example, he believed that it was possible to deduce the whole science of medicine from first principles. Although insufficient on their own, Bacon's and Descartes's extreme approaches are combined in the modern scientific method, which began to crystallize in the late seventeenth century.

Medicine, the Body, and Chemistry

The Scientific Revolution, which began with the study of the cosmos, soon transformed the understanding of the microcosm of the human body. For many centuries the ancient Greek physician Galen's explanation of the body carried the same authority as Aristotle's account of the universe. According to Galen, the body contained four humors: blood, phlegm, black bile, and yellow bile. Illness was believed to result from an imbalance of humors, which is why doctors frequently prescribed bloodletting to expel excess blood.

Swiss physician and alchemist Paracelsus (1493–1541) was an early proponent of the experimental method in medicine and pioneered the use of chemicals to address what he saw as chemical, rather than humoral, imbalances. Another experimentalist, Flemish physician Andreas Vesalius (1514–1564), studied anatomy by dissecting human bodies, often those of executed criminals. In 1543, the same year Copernicus published *On the Revolutions*, Vesalius issued his masterpiece, *On the Structure of the Human Body*. Its two hundred precise drawings revolutionized the understanding of human anatomy, disproving Galen, just as Copernicus and his successors had disproved Aristotle and Ptolemy. The experimental approach also led English royal physician William Harvey (1578–1657) to discover the circulation of blood through the veins and arteries in 1628. Harvey was the first to explain that the heart worked like a pump and to explain the function of its muscles and valves.

Robert Boyle (1627–1691), a key figure in the victory of experimental methods in England, helped create the Royal Society in 1660. Among the first scientists to perform controlled experiments and publish details of them, he helped improve a number of scientific instruments. For example, he built and experimented with an air pump, which he used to investigate the properties of air and create a vacuum, thus disproving Descartes's belief that a vacuum could not exist in nature. Based on these experiments, he formulated a new law in 1662, now known as Boyle's law, that states that the pressure of a gas varies inversely with volume. Boyle also hypothesized that chemical substances were composed of tiny mechanical particles, out of which all other matter was formed.

Science and Religion

It is sometimes assumed that the relationship between science and religion is fundamentally hostile and that the pursuit of knowledge based on reason and proof is incompatible with faith. Yet during the Scientific Revolution most practitioners were devoutly religious and saw their work as contributing to the celebration of God's glory rather than undermining it. However, the concept of heliocentrism, which displaced the earth from the center of the universe, threatened the understanding of the place of mankind in creation as stated in Genesis. All religions derived from the Old Testament—Catholic, Protestant, Jewish, and Muslim—thus faced difficulties accepting the Copernican system. The leaders of the Catholic Church were initially less hostile than Protestant and Jewish religious leaders, but in the first decades of the sixteenth century the Catholic attitude changed. In 1616, alarmed by research findings by Galileo Galilei and other astronomers that undermined traditional astronomy, the Holy Office placed the works of Copernicus and his supporters on a list of books Catholics were forbidden to read. It also warned Galileo not to espouse heliocentrism or face the consequences.

Out of caution, Galileo silenced his views for several years, until 1623 saw the ascension of Pope Urban VIII, a man sympathetic to the new science. However, Galileo's 1632 *Dialogue on the Two Chief Systems of the World* went too far. Published in Italian and widely read, it openly lampooned the Aristotelian view and defended Copernicus. In 1633 the papal Inquisition placed Galileo on trial for heresy. Imprisoned and threatened with torture, the aging Galileo recanted, "renouncing and cursing" his Copernican errors.

Thereafter, the Catholic Church became more hostile to science, a change that helped account for the decline of science in Italy (but not in Catholic France, where there was no Inquisition and the papacy held less sway). At the same time, some Protestant countries, including the Netherlands, Denmark, and England, became quite "pro-science." This was especially true in countries without a strong religious authority capable of imposing religious orthodoxy on scientific questions.

Science and Society

The rise of modern science had many consequences. First, it created a new social group—the international scientific community. Members of this community were linked together by common interests and values as well as by scholarly journals and associations. The personal success of scientists and scholars depended on making new discoveries, and science became competitive. Second, as governments intervened to support and sometimes direct research, the new scientific community became closely tied to the state and its agendas. National academies of science were created under state sponsorship in London in 1660, Paris in 1666, Berlin in 1700, and later across Europe.

It was long believed that the Scientific Revolution had little relationship to practical concerns and the life of the masses until the late-eighteenth-century Industrial Revolution (see Chapter 20). More recently, historians have emphasized the importance of skilled craftsmen in the rise of science, particularly in the development of the experimental method. Many artisans developed a strong interest in emerging scientific ideas, and, in turn, the practice of science in the seventeenth century often relied on artisans' expertise in making instruments and conducting precise experiments.

Some things did not change in the Scientific Revolution. For example, scholars willing to challenge received ideas about the natural universe did not question the seemingly natural inequalities between the sexes. Instead, the emergence of professional science may have worsened them in some ways. When Renaissance courts served as centers of learning, talented noblewomen could find niches in study and research. But the rise of a scientific community raised new barriers for women because the universities and academies that furnished professional credentials refused them entry.

There were, however, a number of noteworthy exceptions. In Italy, universities and academies did offer posts to women. Across Europe, women worked as makers of wax anatomical models and as botanical and zoological illustrators, like Maria Sibylla Merian. They were also very much involved in informal scientific communities, attending salons (see "Women and the Enlightenment" later in this chapter), participating in scientific experiments, and writing learned treatises. Some female intellectuals became full-fledged members of the philosophical dialogue. In England, Margaret Cavendish, Anne Conway, and Mary Astell all contributed to debates about Descartes's mind-body dualism, among other issues. Descartes himself conducted an intellectual correspondence with the princess Elizabeth of Bohemia, of whom he stated: "I attach more weight to her judgment than to those messieurs the Doctors, who take for a rule of truth the opinions of Aristotle rather than the evidence of reason."[4]

How did the Enlightenment emerge, and what were major currents of Enlightenment thought?

The political, intellectual, and religious developments of the early modern period that gave rise to the Scientific Revolution further contributed to a series of debates about key issues in late-seventeenth- and eighteenth-century Europe and the wider world that came to be known as the **Enlightenment**. By shattering the unity of Western Christendom, the conflicts of the Reformation brought old religious certainties into question; the strong states that emerged to quell the disorder soon inspired questions about political sovereignty and its limits. Increased movement of peoples, goods, and ideas within and among the continents of Asia, Africa, Europe, and America offered examples of surprisingly different ways of life and patterns of thought. Finally, the tremendous achievements of the Scientific Revolution inspired intellectuals to believe that answers to all the questions being asked could be found through observation and critical thinking. Nothing was to be accepted on faith; everything was to be submitted to **rationalism**, a secular, critical way of thinking. It was believed that through such thinking progress could be made in human society as well as science.

The Early Enlightenment

Loosely united by certain key ideas, the European Enlightenment (ca. 1690–1789) was a broad intellectual and cultural movement that gained strength gradually and did not reach its maturity until about 1750. Its origins in the late seventeenth century lie in a combination of developments, including political opposition to absolutist rule; religious conflicts between Protestants and Catholics and within Protestantism; European contacts with other cultures; and the attempt to apply principles and practices from the Scientific Revolution to increase knowledge and improve living conditions in human society.

A key crucible for Enlightenment thought was the Dutch Republic, with its traditions of religious tolerance and republican rule. When Louis XIV demanded that all Protestants convert to Catholicism, around two hundred thousand French Protestants, or Huguenots, fled France, many destined for the Dutch Republic. From this haven of tolerance, Huguenots and their supporters began to publish tracts denouncing religious intolerance and suggesting that only a despotic monarch, not a legitimate ruler, would deny religious freedom. Their challenge to authority thus combined religious and political issues.

These dual concerns drove the career of one important early Enlightenment writer, Pierre Bayle (1647–1706), a Huguenot who took refuge in the Dutch Republic. Bayle critically examined the religious beliefs and persecutions of the past in his *Historical and Critical Dictionary* (1697). Demonstrating that human beliefs had been extremely varied and very often mistaken, he concluded that nothing can ever be known beyond all doubt, a view known as skepticism. His influential *Dictionary* was found in more private libraries of eighteenth-century France than any other book.

The Dutch Jewish philosopher Baruch Spinoza (1632–1677) was another key figure in the transition from the Scientific Revolution to the Enlightenment. Deeply inspired by advances in science — in particular by debates about Descartes's thought — Spinoza sought to apply natural philosophy to thinking about human society. He borrowed Descartes's emphasis on rationalism and his methods of deductive reasoning, but he rejected the French thinker's mind-body dualism. Instead, Spinoza came to espouse monism, the idea that mind and body were united in one substance and that God and nature were merely two names for the same thing. He envisioned a deterministic universe in which good and evil were merely relative values and human actions were shaped by outside circumstances, not free will. Spinoza was excommunicated by the Jewish community of Amsterdam for his controversial religious ideas, but he was heralded by his Enlightenment successors as a model of personal virtue and courageous intellectual autonomy.

The German philosopher and mathematician Gottfried Wilhelm von Leibniz (1646–1716), who had developed calculus independently of Isaac Newton, refuted both Cartesian dualism and Spinoza's monism. Instead, he adopted the idea of an infinite number of substances, or "monads," from which all matter is composed. His *Theodicy* (1710) declared that ours must be "the best of all possible worlds" because it was created by an omnipotent and benevolent God. Leibniz's optimism was later ridiculed by the French philosopher Voltaire in *Candide or Optimism* (1759).

Out of this period of intellectual turmoil came John Locke's *Essay Concerning Human Understanding* (1690), perhaps the most important text of the early Enlightenment. In this work Locke (1632–1704), a physician and member of the Royal Society, set forth a new theory about how human beings learn and form their ideas. Whereas Descartes based his deductive logic on the conviction that certain first principles, or innate ideas, are imbued in humans by God, Locke insisted that all ideas are derived from experience. The human mind at birth is like a blank tablet, or tabula rasa, on which understanding and beliefs are inscribed by experience. Human development is therefore determined by external forces, like education and social institutions, not innate characteristics. Locke's essay contributed to the theory of **sensationalism**, the idea that all human ideas and thoughts are produced as a result of sensory impressions.

Along with Newton's *Principia*, the *Essay Concerning Human Understanding* was one of the great intellectual inspirations of the Enlightenment. Locke's equally important contribution to political theory, *Two Treatises of Government* (1690), insisted on the sovereignty of the Parliament against the authority of the Crown (see "Constitutional Monarchy" in Chapter 15).

The Influence of the Philosophes

Divergences among the early thinkers of the Enlightenment show that, while they shared many of the same premises and questions, the answers they found differed widely. The spread of this spirit of inquiry owed a great deal to the work of the **philosophes** (fee-luh-ZAWFZ) (French for "philosopher"), a group of French intellectuals who proudly proclaimed that they were bringing the light of reason to their ignorant fellow humans.

In the mid-eighteenth century France became a hub of Enlightenment thought, for at least three reasons. First, French was the international language of the educated classes, and France was the wealthiest and most populous country in Europe. Second, the rising unpopularity of the French monarchy generated growing discontent and calls for reform among the educated elite. Third, the French philosophes made it their goal to reach a larger audience of elites, many of whom were joined together in a concept inherited from the Renaissance known as the Republic of Letters — an imagined transnational realm in which critical thinkers and writers participated.

To appeal to the public and get around the censors, the philosophes wrote novels and plays, histories and philosophies, and dictionaries and encyclopedias, all filled with satire and double meanings to spread their message. One of the greatest philosophes, the baron de Montesquieu (mahn-tuhs-KYOO) (1689–1755), pioneered this approach in *The Persian Letters*, published in 1721. This work consists of letters written by two fictional Persian travelers, who as outsiders see European customs in

Philosophes' Dinner Party This engraving depicts one of the famous dinners hosted by Voltaire at Ferney, the estate on the French-Swiss border where he spent the last twenty years of his life. A visit to the great philosophe (pictured in the center with arm raised) became a cherished pilgrimage for Enlightenment writers. (Engraving by Jean Huber [1721–1786]/Album/Art Resource, NY)

unique ways and thereby allow Montesquieu a vantage point for criticizing existing practices and beliefs.

Disturbed by the growth in absolutism under Louis XIV and inspired by the example of the physical sciences, Montesquieu set out to apply the critical method to the problem of government in *The Spirit of Laws* (1748). Arguing that forms of government were shaped by history and geography, Montesquieu identified three main types: monarchies, republics, and despotisms. A great admirer of the English parliamentary system, he argued for a separation of powers, with political power divided among different classes and legal estates holding unequal rights and privileges. Montesquieu was no democrat; he was apprehensive about the uneducated poor and did not question the sovereignty of the French monarchy. But he was concerned that absolutism in France was drifting into tyranny and believed that strengthening the influence of intermediary powers was the best way to prevent it. Decades later, his theory of separation of powers had a great impact on the constitutions of the young United States in 1789 and of France in 1791.

The most famous philosophe was François Marie Arouet, known by the pen name Voltaire (vohl-TAIR) (1694–1778). In his long career, Voltaire wrote more than seventy witty volumes, hobnobbed with royalty, and died a millionaire through shrewd speculations. His early career, however, was turbulent, and he was twice arrested for insulting noblemen. To avoid a prison term, Voltaire moved to England for three years, and there he came to share Montesquieu's enthusiasm for English liberties and institutions.

Returning to France, Voltaire met Gabrielle-Emilie Le Tonnelier de Breteuil, marquise du Châtelet (SHAH-tuh-lay) (1706–1749), a gifted noblewoman. Madame du Châtelet invited Voltaire to live in her country house at Cirey in Lorraine and became his long-time companion, under the eyes of her tolerant husband. Passionate about science, she studied physics and mathematics and published scientific articles and translations, including the first translation of Newton's *Principia* into French, still in use today. Excluded from the Royal Academy of Sciences because she was a woman, Madame du Châtelet had no doubt that women's limited role in science was due to their unequal education. Discussing what she would do if she were a ruler, she wrote, "I would reform an abuse which cuts off, so to speak, half the human race. I would make women participate in all the rights of humankind, and above all in those of the intellect."[5]

While living at Cirey, Voltaire wrote works praising England and popularizing English science. Yet, like almost all of the philosophes, Voltaire was a reformer, not a revolutionary, in politics. He pessimistically concluded that the best one could hope for in the way of government was a good monarch, since human beings "are very rarely worthy to govern themselves." Nor did Voltaire believe in social and economic equality. The only realizable equality, Voltaire thought, was that "by which the citizen only depends on the laws which protect the freedom of the feeble against the ambitions of the strong."[6]

Voltaire's philosophical and religious positions were much more radical. He believed in God, but he rejected Catholicism in favor of **deism**, belief in a distant noninterventionist deity. Drawing on mechanistic philosophy, he envisioned a universe in which God acted like a great clockmaker who built an orderly system and then stepped aside to let it run. Above all, Voltaire and most of the philosophes hated all forms of religious intolerance, which they believed led to fanaticism and cruelty.

The strength of the philosophes lay in their dedication and organization. Their greatest achievement was a group effort — the seventeen-volume *Encyclopedia: The Rational Dictionary of the Sciences, the Arts, and the Crafts*, edited by Denis Diderot (DEE-duh-roh) (1713–1784) and Jean le Rond d'Alembert (dah-luhm-BEHR) (1717–1783). Completed in 1766 despite opposition from the French state and the Catholic Church, the *Encyclopedia* contained seventy-two thousand articles by leading scientists, writers, skilled workers, and progressive priests. Science and the industrial arts were exalted, religion and immortality questioned. Intolerance, legal injustice, and out-of-date social institutions were openly criticized. The *Encyclopedia* also included many articles describing non-European cultures and societies, and it acknowledged Muslim scholars' contribution to Western science. Summing up the new worldview of the Enlightenment, the *Encyclopedia* was widely read, especially in less expensive reprint editions, and it was extremely influential.

After about 1770 a number of thinkers and writers began to attack the philosophes' faith in reason and progress. The most famous of these was Jean-Jacques Rousseau (1712–1778). The son of a poor Swiss watchmaker, Rousseau made his way into the Parisian Enlightenment through his brilliant intellect. Like other Enlightenment thinkers, he was passionately committed to individual freedom. Unlike them, however, he attacked rationalism and civilization as destroying, rather than liberating, the individual. Warm, spontaneous feeling, Rousseau believed, had to complement and correct cold intellect. Moreover, he asserted, the basic goodness of the individual and the unspoiled child had to be protected from the cruel refinements of civilization. Rousseau's ideals greatly influenced the early Romantic movement, which rebelled against the culture of the Enlightenment in the late eighteenth century.

Rousseau's contribution to political theory in *The Social Contract* (1762) was based on two fundamental concepts: the general will and popular sovereignty. According to Rousseau, the general will is sacred and absolute, reflecting the common interests of all the people, who have displaced the monarch as the holder of sovereign power (and thus exercise popular sovereignty). The general will is not necessarily the will of the majority, however. At times the general will may be the authentic, long-term needs of the people as correctly interpreted by a farsighted minority. Little noticed before the French Revolution, Rousseau's concept of the general will appealed greatly to democrats and nationalists after 1789.

Enlightenment Movements Across Europe

The Enlightenment was a movement of international dimensions, with thinkers traversing borders in a constant exchange of visits, letters, and printed materials. Voltaire alone wrote almost eighteen thousand letters to correspondents in France and across Europe. The Republic of Letters, as this international group of scholars and writers was called, was a truly cosmopolitan set of networks stretching from western Europe to its colonies in the Americas, to Russia and eastern Europe, and along the routes of trade and empire to Africa and Asia.

Within this broad international conversation, scholars have identified numerous regional and national particularities. Outside of France, many strains of Enlightenment — Protestant, Catholic, and Jewish — sought to reconcile reason with faith, rather than emphasizing the errors of religious fanaticism and intolerance. Some scholars point to a distinctive "Catholic Enlightenment" that aimed to renew and reform the church from within, looking to divine grace rather than human will as the source of progress.

The Scottish Enlightenment, which was centered in Edinburgh, was marked by an emphasis on common sense and scientific reasoning. After the Act of Union with England in 1707, Scotland was freed from political crisis to experience a vigorous period of intellectual growth. Advances in philosophy were also stimulated by the creation of the first public educational system in Europe.

A central figure in Edinburgh was David Hume (1711–1776), whose emphasis on civic morality and religious skepticism had a powerful impact at home and abroad. Hume strove to apply Newton's experimental methods to what he called the "science of man." Building on Locke's writings on learning, Hume argued that the human mind is really nothing but a bundle of impressions that originate only in sensory experiences and our habits of mentally joining these experiences together. Therefore, reason cannot tell us anything about questions that cannot be verified by sensory experience (in the form of controlled experiments or mathematics), such as the origin of the universe or the existence of God. Hume further argued, in opposition to Descartes, that reason alone could not supply moral principles and that they derived instead from emotions and desires, such as feelings of approval or shame.

Hume's rationalistic inquiry thus ended up undermining the Enlightenment's faith in the power of reason by emphasizing the superiority of the senses and the passions over reason in driving human thought and behavior.

Hume's emphasis on human experience, rather than abstract principle, had a formative influence on another major figure of the Scottish Enlightenment, Adam Smith (1723–1790). Smith argued that social interaction produced feelings of mutual sympathy that led people to behave in ethical ways, despite inherent tendencies toward self-interest. By observing others and witnessing their feelings, individuals imaginatively experienced such feelings and learned to act in ways that would elicit positive sentiments and avoid negative ones. Smith believed that the thriving commercial life of the eighteenth century was likely to produce civic virtue through the values of competition, fair play, and individual autonomy. In *An Inquiry into the Nature and Causes of the Wealth of Nations* (1776), Smith attacked the laws and regulations created by mercantilist governments that, he argued, prevented commerce from reaching its full capacity (see "Adam Smith and Economic Liberalism" in Chapter 17).

Inspired by philosophers of moral sentiments like Hume and Smith, as well as by physiological studies of the role of the nervous system in human perception, the celebration of sensibility became an important element of eighteenth-century culture. *Sensibility* referred to an acute sensitivity of the nerves and brains to outside stimuli, which produced strong emotional and physical reactions. Novels, plays, and other literary genres depicted moral and aesthetic sensibility as a particular characteristic of women and the upper classes. The proper relationship between reason and the emotions (or between *Sense and Sensibility*, as Jane Austen put it in the title of her 1811 novel) became a key question.

After 1760 Enlightenment ideas were hotly debated in the German-speaking states, often in dialogue with Christian theology. Immanuel Kant (1724–1804), a professor in East Prussia, was the greatest German philosopher of his day. Kant posed the question of the age when he published a pamphlet in 1784 titled *What Is Enlightenment?* He answered, "*Sapere Aude* [dare to know]! 'Have the courage to use your own understanding' is therefore the motto of enlightenment." He argued that if intellectuals were granted the freedom to exercise their reason publicly in print, enlightenment would almost surely follow. Kant was no revolutionary; he also insisted that in their private lives individuals must obey all laws, no matter how unreasonable, and should be punished for "impertinent" criticism. Like other Enlightenment figures in central and east-central Europe, Kant thus tried to reconcile absolute monarchical authority and religious faith with a critical public sphere.

Northern Europeans often regarded the Italian states as culturally backward, yet important developments in Enlightenment thought took place in the Italian peninsula. After achieving independence from Habsburg rule (1734), the kingdom of Naples entered a period of intellectual flourishing as reformers struggled to lift the heavy weight of church and noble power. In northern Italy a central figure was Cesare Beccaria (1738–1794), a nobleman educated at Jesuit schools and the University of Pavia. His *On Crimes and Punishments* (1764) was a passionate plea for reform of the penal system that decried the use of torture, arbitrary imprisonment, and capital punishment, and advocated the prevention of crime over the reliance on punishment. The text was quickly translated into French and English and made an impact throughout Europe and its colonies.

How did the Enlightenment change social ideas and practices?

Europeans' increased interactions with non-European peoples and cultures also helped produce the Enlightenment spirit. Enlightenment thinkers struggled to assess differences between Western and non-Western cultures, often adopting Eurocentric views, but sometimes expressing admiration for other cultures. These same thinkers focused a great deal of attention on other forms of cultural and social difference, developing new ideas about race, gender, and political power. Although new "scientific" ways of thinking often served to justify inequality, the Enlightenment did see a rise in religious tolerance, a particularly crucial issue for Europe's persecuted Jewish population. As literacy rates rose and print culture flourished, Enlightenment ideas spread in a new "public sphere" composed of coffeeshops, literary salons, lending libraries, and other social institutions.

Global Contacts

In the wake of the great discoveries of the fifteenth and sixteenth centuries, the rapidly growing travel literature taught Europeans that the peoples of China, India, Africa, and the Americas had very different beliefs and customs. Educated Europeans began to look at truth and morality in relative, rather than absolute, terms. If anything was possible, who could say what was right or wrong?

The powerful and advanced nations of Asia were obvious sources of comparison with the West. Seventeenth-century Jesuit missionaries brought knowledge to the West about Chinese history and culture. Leibniz corresponded with Jesuits stationed in China, coming to believe that Chinese ethics and political philosophy were superior but that Europeans had equaled China in science and technology; some scholars believe his concept of monads was influenced by Confucian teaching on the harmony between the cosmic order and human society.[7]

During the Enlightenment, European opinion on China was divided. Voltaire and some other philosophes revered China — without ever visiting or seriously studying it — as an ancient culture replete with wisdom and learning, ruled by benevolent absolutist monarchs. They enthusiastically embraced Confucianism as a natural religion in which universal moral truths were uncovered by reason. By contrast, Montesquieu and Diderot criticized China as a despotic land ruled by fear.

Attitudes toward Islam and the Muslim world were similarly mixed. As the Ottoman military threat receded at the end of the seventeenth century, some Enlightenment thinkers assessed Islam favorably. Some deists praised Islam as superior to Christianity and valued Judaism for its rationality, compassion, and tolerance. Others, including Spinoza, saw Islamic culture as superstitious and favorable to despotism. In most cases, writing about Islam and Muslim cultures served primarily as a means to reflect on Western values and practices. Thus Montesquieu's *Persian Letters* used the Persian harem as a symbol of despotic rule that he feared his own country was adopting. Voltaire's play about the life of the Prophet portrayed Muhammad as the epitome of the religious fanaticism the philosophes opposed.

One writer with considerable personal experience in a Muslim country was Lady Mary Wortley Montagu, wife of the English ambassador to the Ottoman Empire.

Portrait of Lady Mary Wortley Montagu Lady Mary Wortley Montagu accompanied her husband to the Ottoman Empire after he was named British ambassador to the empire. Her lively letters home, published after her death, question the supposedly inferior social status of Ottoman women compared to that of European women and other European assumptions about Ottoman society and culture. After her return home she publicized Ottoman practices of smallpox inoculation (as yet unknown in the West) and commissioned portraits of herself in Ottoman dress. (By George Knapton [1698–1778]/Private Collection/photo © Christie's Images/Bridgeman Images)

Her letters challenged prevailing ideas by depicting Turkish people as sympathetic and civilized. Montagu also disputed the notion that women were oppressed in Ottoman society.

Apart from debates about Asian and Muslim lands, the "discovery" of the New World and subsequent explorations in the Pacific Ocean also challenged existing norms and values in Europe. One popular idea, among Rousseau and others, was that indigenous peoples of the Americas were living examples of "natural man," who embodied the essential goodness of humanity uncorrupted by decadent society. Others depicted as utopian natural men were the Pacific Island societies explored by Captain James Cook and others from the 1770s on.

Enlightenment Debates About Race

As scientists developed taxonomies of plant and animal species in response to discoveries in the Americas, they also began to classify humans into hierarchically ordered "races" and to speculate on the origins of such races. In *The System of Nature* (1735), Swedish botanist Carl Linnaeus argued that nature was organized into a God-given hierarchy. The comte de Buffon (komt duh buh-FOHN) argued that humans originated with one species that then developed into distinct races due largely to climatic conditions. Although the notion of a single origin of human beings opened the door to arguments for equality, Buffon and others who espoused this idea maintained that white Europeans represented the human norm, while other groups had degenerated from this norm over time.

Enlightenment thinkers such as David Hume and Immanuel Kant helped popularize ideas about racial difference and inequality. In *Of Natural Characters* (1748), Hume wrote:

> I am apt to suspect the negroes and in general all other species of men (for there are four or five different kinds) to be naturally inferior to the whites. There never was a civilized nation of any other complexion than white, nor even any individual eminent amongst them, no arts, no sciences. . . . Such a uniform and constant difference could not happen, in so many countries and ages if nature had not made an original distinction between these breeds of men.[8]

Kant taught and wrote as much about anthropology and geography as he did about standard philosophical themes such as logic, metaphysics, and moral philosophy. He elaborated his views about race in *On the Different Races of Man* (1775), claiming that there were four human races, each of which had derived from an original race. The closest descendants of the original race, and the most superior, were the white inhabitants of northern Germany. (Scientists now know the human race originated in Africa.)

Using the word *race* to designate biologically distinct groups of humans, akin to distinct animal species, was new. Previously, Europeans had grouped other peoples into "nations" based on their historical, political, and cultural affiliations, rather than on supposedly innate physical differences. Unsurprisingly, when European thinkers drew up a hierarchical classification of human species, their own "race" was placed at the top. Europeans had long believed they were culturally superior to supposedly "barbaric" peoples in Africa and, since 1492, the New World. Now emerging ideas about racial difference taught them they were biologically superior as well. In turn, scientific racism helped legitimate and justify the tremendous growth of slavery that occurred during the eighteenth century. If one "race" of humans was fundamentally different and inferior, its members could be seen as particularly fit for enslavement and liable to benefit from tutelage by the superior race.

Racist ideas did not go unchallenged. The abbé Raynal's *History of the Two Indies* (1770) fiercely attacked slavery and the abuses of European colonization. *Encyclopedia* editor Denis Diderot adopted Montesquieu's technique of criticizing European attitudes through the voice of outsiders in "Supplement to Bougainville's Voyage," which contains an imaginary dialogue between Tahitian villagers and their European visitors. Scottish philosopher James Beattie (1735–1803) responded directly to claims of white superiority by pointing out that Europeans had started out as savage as nonwhites supposedly were and that many non-European peoples in the Americas, Asia, and Africa had achieved high levels of civilization. Former slaves, like Olaudah Equiano and Ottobah Cugoana, published eloquent memoirs testifying to the horrors of slavery and the innate equality of all humans. These challenges to racism, however, were in the minority. Many other Enlightenment voices supporting racial inequality—Thomas Jefferson among them—may be found.

Women and the Enlightenment

Dating back to the Renaissance *querelle des dames*, the debate over women's proper role in society and the nature of gender differences continued to fascinate Enlightenment thinkers. Some philosophes championed greater rights and expanded education for women, claiming that the position and treatment of women were the best indicators of a society's level of civilization and decency.[9] In *Persian Letters*, Montesquieu used the oppression of women in the harem, described in letters from the wives of Usbek, one of the Persian voyagers, as a potent symbol of the political tyranny he identified with the Persian Empire. At the end of the book, the rebellion of the harem against the cruel eunuchs Usbek left in charge serves to make Montesquieu's point that despotism must ultimately fail.

In the 1780s the marquis de Condorcet, a celebrated mathematician and contributor to the *Encyclopedia*, went so far as to urge that women should share equal rights with men. This was an extremely rare position. Most philosophes accepted that women were inferior to men intellectually as well as physically. They sought moderate reform at best, particularly in the arena of female education, and had no desire to upend men's traditional dominance over women.

From the first years of the Enlightenment, women writers made crucial contributions both to debates about women's rights and to the broader Enlightenment conversations. In 1694 Mary Astell published *A Serious Proposal to the Ladies*, which encouraged women to aspire to the life of the mind and proposed the creation of a college for women. Astell also harshly criticized the institution of marriage. Echoing arguments made against the absolute authority of kings during the Glorious Revolution (see "Constitutional Monarchy" in Chapter 15), she argued that husbands should not exercise absolute control over their wives in marriage. Yet Astell, like most female authors of the period, was careful to acknowledge women's God-given duties to be good wives and mothers.

The explosion of printed literature during the eighteenth century (see the next section) brought significant numbers of women writers into print, but they remained a small proportion of published authors. In the second half of the eighteenth century, women produced some 15 percent of published novels, the genre in which they enjoyed the greatest success. They constituted a much tinier proportion of nonfiction authors.[10]

If they remained marginal in the world of publishing, women played a much more active role in the informal dimensions of the Enlightenment: conversation, letter writing, travel, and patronage. A key element of their informal participation was as salon hostesses, or *salonnières* (sah-lahn-ee-EHRZ). **Salons** were weekly meetings held in wealthy households that brought together writers, aristocrats, financiers, and noteworthy foreigners for meals and witty discussions of the latest trends in literature, science, and philosophy. One prominent salonnière was Madame du Deffand, whose weekly Parisian salon included such guests as Montesquieu, d'Alembert, and Benjamin Franklin, then serving as the first U.S. ambassador to France. Invitations to salons were highly coveted; introductions to the rich and powerful could make the career of an ambitious writer, and, in turn, the social elite found amusement and cultural prestige in their ties to up-and-coming artists and men of letters.

Elite women also exercised great influence on artistic taste. Soft pastels, ornate interiors, sentimental portraits, and paintings featuring starry-eyed lovers protected by hovering cupids were all hallmarks of the style they favored. This style, known as **rococo** (ruh-KOH-koh), was popular throughout Europe from 1720 to 1780. It was particularly associated with the mistress of Louis XV, Madame de Pompadour, who used her position to commission paintings, furniture, and other luxury objects in the rococo style.

Women's prominent role as society hostesses and patrons of the arts and letters outraged some Enlightenment thinkers. According to Jean-Jacques Rousseau, women and men were radically different by nature and should play diametrically opposed roles in life. Destined by nature to assume the active role in sexual relations, men were naturally suited for the rough-and-tumble of politics and public life. Women's role was to attract male sexual desire in order to marry and create families and then to care for their homes and children in private. For Rousseau, wealthy Parisian women's love for attending social gatherings and pulling the strings of power was unnatural and had a corrupting effect on both politics and society. Some women eagerly accepted Rousseau's idealized view of their domestic role, but others—such as the English writer Mary Wollstonecraft—vigorously rejected his notion of women's limitations.

Rousseau's emphasis on the natural laws governing women echoed a wider shift in ideas about gender during this period, as doctors, scientists, and philosophers increasingly agreed that women's essential characteristics were determined by their sexual organs and reproductive functions. This turn to nature, rather than tradition or biblical scripture, as a means to understand human society had parallels in contemporary views on racial difference. Just as writers like Rousseau used women's allegedly "natural" passivity to argue for their subordinate role in society, so Kant and others used ideas about non-Europeans' "natural" inferiority to defend slavery and colonial domination. The new powers of science and reason were thus marshaled to imbue traditional stereotypes with the force of natural law. Scholars continue to debate the apparent paradox between Enlightenment thinkers' ideals of universalism, progress, and reason and their support for racial and gender inequality.

Urban Culture and Life in the Public Sphere

Enlightenment ideas did not float on thin air. A series of new institutions and practices encouraged the spread of enlightened ideas. From about 1700 to 1789, the production and consumption of books grew significantly and the types of books people read changed dramatically. For example, the proportion of religious and devotional books published in Paris declined after 1750; history and law held constant; the arts and sciences surged.

Reading more books on many more subjects, the educated public approached reading in a new way. The old style of reading in Europe had been centered on a core of sacred texts read aloud by the father to his assembled family. Now reading involved a broader field of books that constantly changed. Reading became individual and silent, and texts could be questioned.

For those who could not afford to purchase books, lending libraries offered access to the new ideas of the Enlightenment. Coffeehouses, which first appeared in the late seventeenth century, became meccas of philosophical discussion. In addition to these institutions, book clubs, debating societies, Masonic lodges (groups of Freemasons, a secret society based on egalitarian principles that accepted craftsmen and shopkeepers as well as middle-class men and nobles), salons, and newspapers all played roles in the creation of a new **public sphere** that celebrated open debate informed by critical reason. The public sphere was an idealized space where members of society came together as individuals to discuss issues relevant to the society, economics, and politics of the day.

What of the common people? Did they participate in the Enlightenment? Enlightenment philosophes did not direct their message to peasants or urban laborers. They believed that the masses had no time or talent for philosophical speculation and that elevating them would be a long and potentially dangerous process. Deluded by superstitions and driven by violent passions, the people, they thought, were like children in need of firm parental guidance. D'Alembert characteristically made a sharp distinction between "the truly enlightened public" and "the blind and noisy multitude."[11]

Despite these prejudices, the ideas of the philosophes did find an audience among some members of the common people. At a time of rising literacy, book prices were dropping, and many philosophical ideas were popularized in cheap pamphlets and through public reading. Although they were barred from salons and academies, ordinary people were not immune to the new ideas in circulation. Some of them made vital contributions to the debate, like Englishman Thomas Paine, born and apprenticed to a corset-maker, and author of *Common Sense*, a foundational text of the American Revolution.

What impact did new ways of thinking have on politics?

Enlightenment thinkers' insistence on questioning long-standing traditions and norms inevitably led to issues of power and politics. Most Enlightenment thinkers outside of Britain and the Netherlands, especially in central and eastern Europe, believed that political change could best come from above—from the ruler—rather than from below. Royal absolutism was a fact of life, and the monarchs of Europe's leading states clearly had no intention of giving up their great power. Therefore, the philosophes and their sympathizers realistically concluded that a benevolent absolutism offered the best opportunities for improving society.

Many government officials were interested in philosophical ideas. They were among the best-educated members of society, and their daily involvement in complex affairs of state made them naturally attracted to ideas for improving human society. Encouraged and instructed by these officials, some absolutist rulers tried to reform their governments in accordance with Enlightenment ideals—what historians have called the **enlightened absolutism** of the later eighteenth century. In both Catholic and Protestant lands, rulers typically fused Enlightenment principles with religion, drawing support for their innovations from reform-minded religious thinkers. The most influential of the new-style monarchs were in Prussia, Russia, and Austria, and their example illustrates both the achievements and the great limitations of enlightened absolutism. France experienced its own brand of enlightened absolutism in the contentious decades prior to the French Revolution.

Frederick the Great of Prussia

Frederick II (r. 1740–1786) of Prussia, commonly known as Frederick the Great, built masterfully on the work of his father, Frederick William I (see "The Consolidation of Prussian Absolutism" in Chapter 15). Although in his youth he embraced culture and literature rather than the militarism championed by his father, by the time he came to the throne Frederick was determined to use the splendid army he had inherited.

Therefore, when Maria Theresa inherited the Habsburg dominions upon the death of her father, Holy Roman emperor Charles VI, Frederick pounced. He invaded the rich province of Silesia (sigh-LEE-zhuh), which bordered the Prussian territory of Brandenburg, thereby defying solemn Prussian promises to respect the Pragmatic Sanction, a diplomatic agreement that had guaranteed Maria Theresa's succession. In 1742, as other powers vied for Habsburg lands in the European War of the Austrian Succession (1740–1748), Maria Theresa was forced to cede almost all of Silesia to Prussia. In one stroke Prussia had doubled its population to 6 million people and now stood as a major European power.

Though successful in 1742, Frederick had to fight against great odds to save Prussia from destruction after competition between Britain and France for colonial empire brought another great conflict in 1756. Maria Theresa, seeking to regain Silesia, formed an alliance with the leaders of France and Russia. The aim of the alliance during the resulting Seven Years' War (1756–1763) was to conquer Prussia and divide up its territory. Despite invasions from all sides, Frederick fought on. In the end he was unexpectedly saved when Peter III came to the Russian throne in 1762 and called off the attack against Frederick, whom he greatly admired.

The terrible struggle of the Seven Years' War tempered Frederick's interest in territorial expansion and brought him to consider how more humane policies for his subjects might also strengthen the state. He tolerantly allowed his subjects to believe as they wished in religious and philosophical matters. He promoted the advancement of knowledge, improving his country's schools and permitting scholars to publish their findings. Moreover, Frederick tried to improve the lives of his subjects more directly. As he wrote to his friend Voltaire in 1770, "[I have to] enlighten mind, cultivate morality, and make the people as happy as it suits human nature, and as the means at my disposal permit."[12]

The legal system and the bureaucracy were Frederick's primary tools. Prussia's laws were simplified, torture was abolished, and judges decided cases quickly and impartially. After the Seven Years' War ended in 1763, Frederick's government energetically promoted the reconstruction of agriculture and industry. Frederick himself set a good example. He worked hard and lived modestly, claiming that he was "only the first servant of the state." Thus Frederick justified monarchy in terms of practical results and said nothing of the divine right of kings.

Frederick's dedication to high-minded government went only so far, however. While he condemned serfdom in the abstract, he accepted it in practice and did not free the serfs on his own estates. He accepted and extended the privileges of the nobility, who remained the backbone of the army and the entire Prussian state.

In reforming Prussia's bureaucracy, Frederick drew on the principles of **cameralism**, the German science of public administration that emerged in the decades following the Thirty Years' War and came to occupy a central place in the university curriculum of the German lands. Cameralism held that monarchy was the best of all forms of government, that all elements of society should be placed at the service of the state, and that, in turn, the state should make use of its resources and authority to improve society. Predating the Enlightenment, cameralist interest in the public good was usually inspired by the needs of war. Cameralism shared with the Enlightenment an emphasis on rationality, progress, and utilitarianism.

Catherine the Great of Russia

Catherine the Great of Russia (r. 1762–1796) was one of the most remarkable rulers of her age, and the French philosophes adored her. Catherine was a German princess from Anhalt-Zerbst, a small principality sandwiched between Prussia and Saxony. Her father commanded a regiment of the Prussian army, but her mother was related to the Romanovs of Russia, and that proved to be Catherine's opening to power.

Catherine's Romanov connection made her a suitable bride at the age of fifteen for the heir to the Russian throne. It was a mismatch from the beginning, but her *Memoirs* made her ambitions clear: "I did not care about Peter, but I did care about the crown." When her husband, Peter III, came to power during the Seven Years' War, his decision to withdraw Russian troops from the coalition against Prussia alienated the army. Catherine profited from his unpopularity to form a conspiracy to depose

Catherine the Great and Denis Diderot Self-proclaimed adherent of Enlightenment ideals, Russian empress Catherine the Great enthusiastically corresponded with philosophes like Voltaire and Denis Diderot. When Diderot put his library on sale to raise much-needed funds, Catherine sent him the money but allowed him to keep his books. Historians have long debated the "enlightened despotism" represented by Catherine and other absolutist rulers. (Catherine: Based on a work by Alexander Roslin [1718–1793], [oil on canvas]/Museum of Art, Serpukhov, Russia/Bridgeman Images; Diderot: Heritage Images/Getty Images)

her husband. In 1762 Catherine's lover Gregory Orlov and his three brothers, all army officers, murdered Peter, and the German princess became empress of Russia.

Catherine had drunk deeply at the Enlightenment well. Never questioning that absolute monarchy was the best form of government, she set out to rule in an enlightened manner. She had three main goals. First, she worked hard to continue Peter the Great's effort to bring the culture of western Europe to Russia (see "The Reforms of Peter the Great" in Chapter 15). To do so, she imported Western architects, musicians, and intellectuals. She bought masterpieces of Western art and patronized the philosophes. An enthusiastic letter writer, she corresponded extensively with Voltaire and praised him as the "champion of the human race." When the French government banned the *Encyclopedia*, she offered to publish it in St. Petersburg, and she sent money to Diderot when he needed it. With these actions, Catherine won good press in the West for herself and for her country. Moreover, this intellectual ruler, who wrote plays and loved good talk, set the tone for the entire Russian nobility. Peter the Great westernized Russian armies, but it was Catherine who westernized the imagination of the Russian nobility.

Catherine's second goal was domestic reform, and she began her reign with sincere and ambitious projects. In 1767 she appointed a legislative commission to prepare a new law code. This project was never completed, but Catherine did restrict the practice of torture and allowed limited religious toleration. She also tried to improve education and strengthen local government. The philosophes applauded these measures and hoped more would follow.

Such was not the case. In 1773 a Cossack soldier named Emelian Pugachev sparked a gigantic uprising of serfs, very much as Stenka Razin had done a century earlier (see "Building the Russian Empire" in Chapter 15). Proclaiming himself the true tsar, Pugachev issued orders abolishing serfdom, taxes, and army service. Thousands joined his cause, slaughtering landlords and officials over a vast area of southwestern Russia. Pugachev's untrained forces eventually proved no match for Catherine's professional army. Betrayed by his own company, Pugachev was captured and brutally executed.

Pugachev's rebellion put an end to any intentions Catherine had about reforming the system and improving the lot of the peasantry. After 1775 Catherine gave the nobles absolute control of their serfs, and she extended serfdom into new areas, such as Ukraine. In 1785 she freed nobles from taxes and state service. Under Catherine the Russian nobility attained its most exalted position, and serfdom entered its most oppressive phase.

Catherine's third goal was territorial expansion, and in this respect she was extremely successful. Her armies subjugated the last descendants of the Mongols and the Crimean Tartars and began the conquest of the Caucasus (KAW-kuh-suhs), the region between the Black Sea and the Caspian Sea. Her greatest coup by far was the partition of Poland (Map 16.1). When, between 1768 and 1772, Catherine's armies scored unprecedented victories against the Ottomans and thereby threatened to disturb the balance of power between Russia and Austria in eastern Europe, Frederick of Prussia obligingly came forward with a deal. He proposed that the Ottomans be let off easily and that Prussia, Austria, and Russia each compensate itself by taking a gigantic slice of the weakly ruled Polish territory. Catherine jumped at the chance. The first partition of Poland took place in 1772. Subsequent partitions in 1793

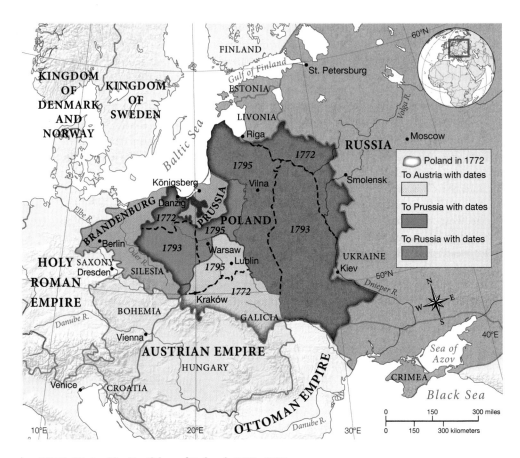

MAP 16.1 The Partition of Poland, 1772–1795
In 1772 war between Russia and Austria threatened over Russian gains from the Ottoman Empire. To satisfy desires for expansion without fighting, Prussia's Frederick the Great proposed that parts of Poland be divided among Austria, Prussia, and Russia. In 1793 and 1795 the three powers partitioned the remainder, and the republic of Poland ceased to exist.

and 1795 gave away the rest of Polish territory, and the ancient republic of Poland vanished from the map.

The Austrian Habsburgs

Another female monarch, Maria Theresa (r. 1740–1780) of Austria, set out to reform her nation, although traditional dynastic power politics was a more important motivation for her than were Enlightenment teachings. A devoutly Catholic mother and wife who inherited power from her father, Charles VI, Maria Theresa was a remarkable but old-fashioned absolutist. Her more radical son, Joseph II (r. 1780–1790), drew on Enlightenment ideals, earning the title of "revolutionary emperor."

Emerging from the long War of the Austrian Succession in 1748 with the serious loss of Silesia, Maria Theresa was determined to introduce reforms that would make the state stronger and more efficient. First, she initiated church reform, with measures aimed at limiting the papacy's influence, eliminating many religious holidays, and reducing the number of monasteries. Second, a whole series of administrative renovations strengthened the central bureaucracy, smoothed out some provincial differences, and revamped the tax system, taxing even the lands of nobles, previously exempt from taxation. Third, the government sought to improve the conditions of the agricultural population, cautiously reducing the power of lords over their hereditary serfs and their partially free peasant tenants.

Joseph II, coregent with his mother from 1765 onward and a strong supporter of change from above, implemented reform rapidly when he came to the throne in 1780. Most notably, Joseph abolished serfdom in 1781, and in 1789 he decreed that peasants could pay landlords in cash rather than through labor on their land. This measure was violently rejected not only by the nobility but also by the peasants it was intended to help, because they lacked the necessary cash. When a disillusioned Joseph died prematurely at forty-nine, the entire Habsburg empire was in turmoil. His brother Leopold II (r. 1790–1792) canceled Joseph's radical edicts in order to re-establish order. Peasants once again were required to do forced labor for their lords.

Despite differences in their policies, Joseph II and the other absolutists of the later eighteenth century combined old-fashioned state-building with the culture and critical thinking of the Enlightenment. In doing so, they succeeded in expanding the role of the state in the life of society. They perfected bureaucratic machines that were to prove surprisingly adaptive and enduring. Their failure to implement policies we would recognize as humane and enlightened—such as abolishing serfdom—probably reveal inherent limitations in Enlightenment thinking about equality and social justice, rather than deficiencies in their execution of Enlightenment programs. The fact that leading philosophes supported rather than criticized absolutist rulers' policies thus exposes the blind spots of the era.

Jewish Life and the Limits of Enlightened Absolutism

Perhaps the best example of the limitations of enlightened absolutism is the debates surrounding the emancipation of the Jews. Europe's small Jewish populations lived under highly discriminatory laws. For the most part, Jews were confined to tiny, overcrowded ghettos, were excluded by law from most professions, and could be ordered out of a kingdom at a moment's notice. Still, a very few did manage to succeed and to obtain the right of permanent settlement, usually by performing some special service for the state. Many rulers relied on Jewish bankers for loans to raise armies and run their kingdoms. Jewish merchants prospered in international trade because they could rely on contacts with colleagues in Jewish communities scattered across Europe.

In the eighteenth century an Enlightenment movement known as the **Haskalah** emerged from within the European Jewish community, led by the Prussian philosopher Moses Mendelssohn (1729–1786). Christian and Jewish Enlightenment philosophers, including Mendelssohn, began to advocate for freedom and civil rights for

European Jews. In an era of reason and progress, they argued, restrictions on religious grounds could not stand. The Haskalah accompanied a period of controversial social change within Jewish communities in which rabbinic controls loosened and interaction with Christians increased.

Arguments for tolerance won some ground. The British Parliament passed a law allowing naturalization of Jews in 1753, but it later repealed the law due to public opposition. The most progressive reforms took place under Austrian emperor Joseph II. Among his liberal edicts of the 1780s were measures intended to integrate Jews more fully into society, including eligibility for military service, admission to higher education and artisanal trades, and removal of requirements for special clothing or emblems. Welcomed by many Jews, these reforms raised fears among traditionalists about the possibility of assimilation into the general population.

Many monarchs rejected all ideas of emancipation. Although he permitted freedom of religion to his Christian subjects, Frederick the Great of Prussia firmly opposed any general emancipation for the Jews, as he did for the serfs. Catherine the Great, who acquired most of Poland's large Jewish population when she annexed part of that country in the late eighteenth century, similarly refused. In 1791 she established the Pale of Settlement, a territory including parts of modern-day Poland, Latvia, Lithuania, Ukraine, and Belarus, in which most Jews were required to live. Jewish habitation was restricted to the Pale until the Russian Revolution in 1917.

The first European state to remove all restrictions on the Jews was France during the French Revolution. Over the next hundred years, Jews gradually won full legal and civil rights throughout the rest of western Europe. Emancipation in eastern Europe took even longer and aroused more conflict and violence.

NOTES

1. Quoted in H. Butterfield, *The Origins of Modern Science* (New York: Macmillan, 1951), p. 47.
2. Quoted in Butterfield, *The Origins of Modern Science*, p. 120.
3. Quoted in John Freely, *Aladdin's Lamp: How Greek Science Came to Europe Through the Islamic World* (New York: Knopf, 2009), p. 225.
4. Quoted in Jacqueline Broad, *Women Philosophers of the Seventeenth Century* (Cambridge: Cambridge University Press, 2003), p. 17.
5. Quoted in L. Schiebinger, *The Mind Has No Sex? Women in the Origins of Modern Science* (Cambridge, Mass.: Harvard University Press, 1989), p. 64.
6. Quoted in G. L. Mosse et al., eds., *Europe in Review* (Chicago: Rand McNally, 1964), p. 156.
7. D. E. Mungello, *The Great Encounter of China and the West, 1500–1800*, 2d ed. (Lanham, Md.: Rowman & Littlefield, 2005), p. 98.
8. Quoted in Emmanuel Chukwudi Eze, ed., *Race and the Enlightenment: A Reader* (Oxford: Blackwell, 1997), p. 33.
9. See E. Fox-Genovese, "Women in the Enlightenment," in *Becoming Visible: Women in European History*, 2d ed., ed. R. Bridenthal, C. Koonz, and S. Stuard (Boston: Houghton Mifflin, 1987), esp. pp. 252–259, 263–265.
10. Aurora Wolfgang, *Gender and Voice in the French Novel, 1730–1782* (Aldershot, U.K.: Ashgate, 2004), p. 8.
11. Jean Le Rond d'Alembert, *Eloges lus dans les séances publiques de l'Académie française* (Paris, 1779), p. ix, quoted in Mona Ozouf, "'Public Opinion' at the End of the Old Regime," *The Journal of Modern History* 60, *Supplement: Rethinking French Politics in 1788* (September 1988): S9.
12. Cited in Giles McDonough, *Frederick the Great: A Life in Deed and Letters* (New York: St. Martin's Griffin, 2001), 341.

LOOKING BACK **LOOKING AHEAD**

Hailed as the origin of modern thought, the Scientific Revolution must also be seen as a product of its past and of the interaction between Europeans and non-Europeans. Medieval translations of ancient Greek texts from Arabic into Latin spurred the advance of scholarship in western Europe, giving rise to universities that produced and disseminated knowledge of the natural world. Natural philosophers following Copernicus pioneered new methods of observing and explaining nature while drawing on centuries-old traditions of Christian faith as well as astrology, alchemy, and magic. In expanding their knowledge about the natural world, Europeans drew on traditions of observation and practice among indigenous peoples of the New World.

The Enlightenment ideas of the eighteenth century were a similar blend of past and present, European and non-European; they could serve as much to bolster absolutist monarchical regimes as to inspire revolutionaries to fight for individual rights and liberties. Although the Enlightenment fostered critical thinking about everything from science to religion, the majority of Europeans, including many prominent thinkers, remained devout Christians. Enlightenment ideas were inspired by contact and exchange with non-Europeans in Asia, Africa, and the Americas.

The achievements of the Scientific Revolution and the Enlightenment are undeniable. Key Western values of rationalism, human rights, and open-mindedness were born from these movements. With their new notions of progress and social improvement, Europeans would embark on important revolutions in industry and politics in the centuries that followed. Nonetheless, others have seen a darker side. For these critics, the mastery over nature permitted by the Scientific Revolution now threatens to overwhelm the earth's fragile equilibrium, and the Enlightenment belief in the universal application of reason can lead to arrogance and intolerance of other people's spiritual, cultural, and political values. Such vivid debates about the legacy of these intellectual and scientific developments testify to their continuing importance in today's world.

MAKE CONNECTIONS

Think about the larger developments and continuities within and across chapters.

1. How did the era of European exploration and discovery (Chapter 14) affect the ideas of the scientists and philosophers discussed in this chapter? In what ways did contact with new peoples and places stimulate new forms of thought among Europeans?

2. What was the relationship between the Scientific Revolution and the Enlightenment? How did new ways of understanding the natural world influence thinking about human society?

3. Compare the policies and actions of seventeenth-century absolutist rulers (Chapter 15) with their "enlightened" descendants described in this chapter. How accurate is the term *enlightened absolutism*?

Chapter 16 Review

IDENTIFY KEY TERMS

Identify and explain the significance of each item below.

natural philosophy (p. 455)
Copernican hypothesis (p. 456)
law of inertia (p. 458)
law of universal gravitation (p. 459)
Cartesian dualism (p. 462)
Enlightenment (p. 464)
rationalism (p. 465)
sensationalism (p. 466)

philosophes (p. 466)
deism (p. 468)
salon (p. 474)
rococo (p. 474)
public sphere (p. 475)
enlightened absolutism (p. 476)
cameralism (p. 477)
Haskalah (p. 481)

REVIEW THE MAIN IDEAS

Answer the section heading questions from the chapter.

1. What revolutionary discoveries were made in the sixteenth and seventeenth centuries? (p. 453)
2. What intellectual and social changes occurred as a result of the Scientific Revolution? (p. 461)
3. How did the Enlightenment emerge, and what were major currents of Enlightenment thought? (p. 464)
4. How did the Enlightenment change social ideas and practices? (p. 471)
5. What impact did new ways of thinking have on politics? (p. 476)

CHRONOLOGY

ca. 1540–1700	• Scientific Revolution
ca. 1690–1789	• Enlightenment
ca. 1700–1789	• Growth of book publishing
1720–1780	• Rococo style in art and decoration
1740–1748	• War of the Austrian Succession
1740–1780	• Reign of the empress Maria Theresa of Austria
1740–1786	• Reign of Frederick the Great of Prussia
1751–1766	• Philosophes publish *Encyclopedia: The Rational Dictionary of the Sciences, the Arts, and the Crafts*
1756–1763	• Seven Years' War
1762–1796	• Reign of Catherine the Great of Russia
1780–1790	• Reign of Joseph II of Austria
1791	• Establishment of the Pale of Settlement

17

The Expansion of Europe

1650–1800

CHAPTER PREVIEW

- Why did European agriculture grow between 1650 and 1800?

- Why did the European population rise dramatically in the eighteenth century?

- How and why did rural industry intensify in the eighteenth century?

- What important changes occurred in economic thought and practice in the eighteenth century?

- What role did colonial markets play in Europe's development?

ABSOLUTISM AND ARISTOCRACY, a combination of raw power and elegant refinement, were a world apart from the common people of the eighteenth century. For most people, life remained a struggle with poverty and uncertainty, with the landlord and the tax collector. In 1700 peasants on the land and artisans in their shops lived little better than had their ancestors in the Middle Ages, primarily because European societies still could not produce very much as measured by modern standards. Despite the hard work of ordinary men, women, and children, there was seldom enough good food, warm clothing, and decent housing. The idea of progress, of substantial improvement in the lives of great numbers of people, was still the dream of only a small elite in fashionable salons.

Yet the economic basis of European life was beginning to change. In the course of the eighteenth century, the European economy emerged from the long crisis of the seventeenth century, responded to challenges, and began to expand once again. Population resumed its growth, while colonial empires were extended and developed. Some areas were more fortunate than others. The rising Atlantic powers—the Dutch Republic, France, and above all England—and their colonies led the way. The expansion of agriculture, industry, trade, and population marked the beginning of a surge comparable to that of the eleventh- and twelfth-century springtime of European civilization. But this time, broadly based expansion was not cut short by plague and famine. This time the response to new challenges led toward one of the most influential developments in human history, the Industrial Revolution, considered in Chapter 20.

Why did European agriculture grow between 1650 and 1800?

At the end of the seventeenth century the economy of Europe was agrarian. With the exception of the Dutch Republic and England, at least 80 percent of the people of western Europe drew their livelihoods from agriculture. In eastern Europe the percentage was considerably higher. Men and women were tied to the land, plowing fields and sowing seed, reaping harvests and storing grain. Yet even in a rich agricultural region such as the Po Valley in northern Italy, every bushel of wheat seed sown yielded on average only five or six bushels of grain at harvest. By modern standards, output was distressingly low.

In most regions of Europe, climatic conditions produced poor or disastrous harvests every eight or nine years. In famine years the number of deaths soared far above normal. A third of a village's population might disappear in a year or two. But new developments in agricultural technology and methods gradually brought an end to the ravages of hunger in western Europe.

The Legacy of the Open-Field System

Why, in the late seventeenth century, did many areas of Europe produce barely enough food to survive? The answer lies in patterns of farming inherited from the Middle Ages, which sustained fairly large numbers of people but did not produce material abundance. From the Middle Ages up to the seventeenth century, much of Europe was farmed through the open-field system. The land to be cultivated was divided into several large fields, which were in turn cut up into long, narrow strips. The fields were open, and the strips were not enclosed into small plots by fences or hedges. The whole peasant village followed the same pattern of plowing, sowing, and harvesting in accordance with long-standing traditions.

The ever-present problem was soil exhaustion. Wheat planted year after year in a field will deplete nitrogen in the soil. Since the supply of manure for fertilizer was limited, the only way for the land to recover was to lie fallow for a period of time. Clover and other annual grasses that sprang up in unplanted fields restored nutrients to the soil and also provided food for livestock. In the early Middle Ages a year of fallow was alternated with a year of cropping; then three-year rotations were intro-duced. On each strip of land, a year of wheat or rye was followed by a year of oats or beans and only then by a year of fallow. The three-year system was an important achievement because cash crops could be grown two years out of three, rather than only one year in two.

Traditional village rights reinforced communal patterns of farming. In addition to rotating field crops in a uniform way, villages maintained open meadows for hay and natural pasture. After the harvest villagers also pastured their animals on the wheat or rye stubble. In many places such pasturing followed a brief period, also established by tradition, for the gleaning of grain. In this process, poor women would go through the fields picking up the few single grains that had fallen to the ground in the course of the harvest. Many villages were surrounded by woodlands, also held in common, which provided essential firewood, building materials, and nutritional roots and berries.

The state and landlords continued to levy heavy taxes and high rents, thereby stripping peasants of much of their meager earnings. The level of exploitation var-ied. Generally speaking, the peasants of eastern Europe were worst off. As we saw in Chapter 15, they were serfs bound to their lords in hereditary service. In much of eastern Europe, working several days per week on the lord's land was not uncom-mon. Well into the nineteenth century, individual Russian serfs and serf families were regularly bought and sold.

Social conditions were better in western Europe, where peasants were generally free from serfdom. In France, western Germany, England, and the Low Countries (modern-day Belgium and the Netherlands), peasants could own land and could pass it on to their children. Even in these regions, however, life in the village was hard, and poverty was the reality for most people.

New Methods of Agriculture

The seventeenth century saw important gains in productivity in some regions that would slowly extend to the rest of Europe. By 1700 less than half of the popula-tion of Britain and the Dutch Republic worked in agriculture, producing enough to feed the remainder of the population. Many elements combined in this production growth, but the key was new ways of rotating crops that allowed farmers to forgo the unproductive fallow period altogether and maintain their land in continuous culti-vation. The secret to eliminating the fallow lay in deliberately alternating grain with crops that restored nutrients to the soil, such as peas and beans, root crops like tur-nips and potatoes, and clover and other grasses.

Clover was one of the most important crops, because it restores nitrogen directly to the soil through its roots. Other crops produced additional benefits. Potatoes and many types of beans came to Europe as part of the sixteenth-century Columbian exchange between the New and the Old Worlds (see "The Columbian Exchange and Population Loss" in Chapter 14). These crops were widely adopted, starting in Spain and Italy in the early seventeenth century, and spread across the continent by the end of the eighteenth century. Rich in nutrients, they provided a welcome supplement to the peasant's meager diet. With more fodder, hay, and root vegetables for the winter months, peasants and larger farmers could build up their herds of cattle and sheep. More animals meant more manure to fertilize and restore the soil. More animals also meant more meat and dairy products as well as more power to pull plows in the fields and bring carts to market.

Over time, crop rotation spread to other parts of Europe, and farmers developed increasingly specialized patterns of rotation to suit different kinds of soils. For example, in the late eighteenth century farmers in French Flanders near Lille alternated a number of grain, root, and hay crops in a given field on a ten-year schedule. Ongoing experimentation, fueled by developments in the Scientific Revolution, led to more methodical farming.

Advocates of the new crop rotations, who included an emerging group of experimental scientists, some government officials, and a few big landowners, believed that new methods were scarcely possible within the traditional framework of open fields and common rights. A farmer who wanted to experiment with new methods would have to get all the landholders in the village to agree to the plan. Advocates of improvement argued that innovating agriculturalists needed to enclose and consolidate their scattered holdings into compact, fenced-in fields in order to farm more effectively. In doing so, the innovators also needed to enclose the village's natural pastureland, or common, into individual shares. According to proponents of this movement, known as **enclosure**, the upheaval of village life was the necessary price of technical progress.

That price seemed too high to many rural people who had small, inadequate holdings or very little land at all. Traditional rights were precious to these poor peasants, who used commonly held pastureland to graze livestock, and marshlands or forest outside the village as a source for foraged goods. Thus, when the small landholders and the village poor could effectively oppose the enclosure of the open fields and the common lands, they did so. In many countries they found allies among the larger, predominantly noble landowners who were also wary of enclosure because it required large investments in purchasing and fencing land and thus posed risks for them as well.

The old system of unenclosed open fields and the new system of continuous rotation coexisted in Europe for a long time. Open fields could still be found in much of France and Germany as late as the nineteenth century because peasants there had successfully opposed eighteenth-century efforts to introduce the new techniques. Through the end of the eighteenth century, the new system of enclosure was extensively adopted only in the Low Countries and England.

The Leadership of the Low Countries and England

The seventeenth-century Dutch Republic, already the most advanced country in Europe in many areas of human endeavor (see "The Dutch Republic in the Seventeenth Century" in Chapter 15), pioneered advancements in agriculture. By the middle of the seventeenth century intensive farming was well established, and the innovations of enclosed fields, continuous rotation, heavy manuring, and a wide variety of crops were all present. Agriculture was highly specialized and commercialized, especially in the province of Holland.

One reason for early Dutch leadership in farming was that the area was one of the most densely populated in Europe. To feed themselves and provide employment, the Dutch were forced at an early date to seek maximum yields from their land and to increase the cultivated area through the steady draining of marshes and swamps. The pressure of population was connected with the second cause: the growth of towns and cities. Stimulated by commerce and overseas trade, Amsterdam grew from thirty thousand to two hundred thousand inhabitants in its golden seventeenth century. The growing urban population provided Dutch peasants with markets for all they could produce and allowed each region to specialize in what it did best. Thus the Dutch could develop their potential, and the Low Countries became, as one historian wrote, "the Mecca of foreign agricultural experts who came . . . to see Flemish agriculture with their own eyes, to write about it and to propagate its methods in their home lands."[1]

The English were among their best students. In the mid-seventeenth century English farmers borrowed the system of continuous crop rotation from the Dutch. They also drew on Dutch expertise in drainage and water control. Large parts of seventeenth-century Holland had once been sea and sea marsh, and the efforts of centuries had made the Dutch the world's leaders in drainage. In the first half of the seventeenth century, Dutch experts also helped to drain the extensive marshes, or fens, of wet and rainy England. The most famous of these Dutch engineers, Cornelius Vermuyden, directed one large drainage project in Yorkshire and another in Cambridgeshire. In the Cambridge fens, Vermuyden and his Dutch workers eventually reclaimed forty thousand acres, which were then farmed intensively in the Dutch manner. Swampy wilderness was converted into thousands of acres of some of the best land in England.

Based on the seventeenth-century achievements, English agriculture continued to progress during the eighteenth century, growing enough food to satisfy a rapidly growing population. Jethro Tull (1674–1741) was an important English innovator. A true son of the early Enlightenment, Tull adopted a critical attitude toward accepted ideas about farming and tried to develop better methods through empirical research. He was especially enthusiastic about using horses, rather than slower-moving oxen, for plowing. He also advocated sowing seed with drilling equipment rather than scattering it by hand. Drilling distributed seed in an even manner and at the proper depth. There were also improvements in livestock, inspired in part by the earlier successes of English country gentlemen in breeding ever-faster horses for the races and fox hunts that were their passions. Selective breeding of ordinary livestock was a marked improvement over the haphazard breeding of the past.

One of the most important—and bitterly contested—aspects of English agricultural development was the enclosure of open fields and commons. More than half the farmland in England was enclosed through private initiatives prior to 1700; Parliament completed this work in the eighteenth century. From the 1760s to 1815 a series of acts of Parliament enclosed most of the remaining common land. Arthur Young, another agricultural experimentalist, celebrated large-scale enclosure as a necessary means to achieve progress. Many of his contemporaries, as well as the historians that followed him, echoed that conviction. More recent research, however, has shown that regions that maintained open-field farming were still able to adopt crop

The Seed Drill The seed drill had a metal plow in front (depicted behind the horse's back feet) to dig channels in the earth and a container behind it that distributed seed evenly into the channels. The drill allowed farmers to plant seeds at consistent depths and in straight lines, a much more efficient system than the old method of simply scattering seed across the field. (Universal Images Group/Getty Images)

rotation and other innovations, suggesting that enclosures were not a prerequisite for increased production.

By eliminating common rights and greatly reducing the access of poor men and women to the land, the eighteenth-century enclosure movement marked the completion of two major historical developments in England — the rise of capitalist market-oriented estate agriculture and the emergence of a landless rural proletariat. By the early nineteenth century a tiny minority of wealthy English and Scottish landowners held most of the land and pursued profits aggressively, leasing their holdings through agents at competitive prices to middle-size farmers, who relied on landless laborers for their workforce. These landless laborers worked very long hours, usually following a dawn-to-dusk schedule six days a week all year long. Not only was the small landholder deprived of his land, but improvements in technology meant that fewer laborers were needed to work the large farms, and unemployment spread throughout the countryside. As one observer commented:

> It is no uncommon thing for four or five wealthy graziers to engross a large inclosed lordship, which was before in the hands of twenty or thirty farmers, and as many smaller tenants or proprietors. All these are thereby thrown out of their livings, and many other families, who were chiefly employed and supported by them, such as blacksmiths, carpenters, wheelwrights and other artificers and tradesmen, besides their own labourers and servants.[2]

In no other European country had this **proletarianization** — this transformation of large numbers of small peasant farmers into landless rural wage earners — gone so far. England's village poor found the cost of change heavy and unjust.

Why did the European population rise dramatically in the eighteenth century?

Another factor that affected the existing order of life and drove economic changes in the eighteenth century was the beginning of the population explosion. Explosive growth continued in Europe until the twentieth century, by which time it was affecting non-Western areas of the globe. In this section we examine the background and causes of the population growth; the following section considers how the challenge of more mouths to feed and more hands to employ affected the European economy.

Long-Standing Obstacles to Population Growth

Until 1700 the total population of Europe grew slowly much of the time, and it followed an irregular cyclical pattern (Figure 17.1). This cyclical pattern had a great influence on many aspects of social and economic life. The terrible ravages of the Black Death of 1348–1350 caused a sharp drop in population and food prices after 1350 and also created a labor shortage throughout Europe. Some economic historians calculate that for those common people in western Europe who managed to steer clear of warfare and power struggles within the ruling class, the later Middle Ages was an era of exceptional well-being.

But this well-being eroded in the course of the sixteenth century. The second great surge of population growth outstripped the growth of agricultural production after about 1500. There was less food per person, and food prices rose more rapidly than wages, a development intensified by the inflow of precious metals from the Americas and a general, if uneven, European price revolution. The result was a substantial decline in living standards throughout Europe. By 1600 the pressure of population on resources was severe in much of Europe, and widespread poverty was an undeniable reality.

For this reason, population growth slowed and stopped in seventeenth-century Europe. Births and deaths, fertility and mortality, were in a crude but effective balance. The population grew modestly in normal years at a rate of perhaps 0.5 to 1 percent, or enough to double the population in 70 to 140 years. This is, of course, a generalization encompassing many different patterns. In areas such as Russia and colonial New England, where there was a great deal of

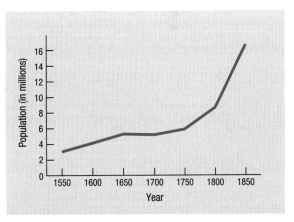

FIGURE 17.1   The Growth of Population in England, 1550–1850
England is a good example of both the uneven increase of European population before 1700 and the third great surge of growth that began in the eighteenth century.
(Source: Data from E. A. Wrigley et al., *English Population History from Family Reconstitution, 1580–1837* [Cambridge: Cambridge University Press, 1997], p. 614.)

frontier to be settled, the annual rate of natural increase, not counting immigration, might well have exceeded 1 percent. (The New England increase did not include Native Americans, whose numbers diminished sharply in the seventeenth century as a result of European diseases and, to a lesser extent, warfare.) In a country such as France, where the land had long been densely settled, the rate of increase might have been less than 0.5 percent.

Although a population growth of even 1 percent per year seems fairly modest, it will produce a very large increase over a long period: in three hundred years it will result in sixteen times as many people. Yet such significant increases did not occur in agrarian Europe. In certain abnormal years and tragic periods—the Black Death was only the most extreme example—many more people died than were born, and total population fell sharply, even catastrophically. A number of years of modest growth would then be necessary to make up for those who had died in an abnormal year. Such savage increases in deaths occurred periodically in the seventeenth century on a local and regional scale, and these demographic crises combined to check the growth of population until after 1700.

The grim reapers of demographic crisis were famine, epidemic disease, and war. Episodes of famine were inevitable in all eras of premodern Europe, given low crop yields and unpredictable climatic conditions. In the seventeenth century much of Europe experienced unusually cold and wet weather, which produced even more severe harvest failures and food shortages than usual. Contagious diseases, like typhus, smallpox, syphilis, and the ever-recurring bubonic plague, also continued to ravage Europe's population on a periodic basis and to inflict grievous losses on indigenous populations in European colonies, which are estimated to have reached their lowest numbers by the end of the seventeenth century. War was another scourge, and its indirect effects were even more harmful than the purposeful killing during military campaigns. Soldiers and camp followers passed all manner of contagious diseases throughout the countryside. Armies requisitioned scarce food supplies and disrupted the agricultural cycle while battles destroyed precious crops, livestock, and farmlands. The Thirty Years' War (1618–1648) witnessed all possible combinations of distress (see "The Thirty Years' War" in Chapter 15). The number of inhabitants in the German states alone declined by more than two-thirds in some large areas and by at least one-third almost everywhere else.

The New Pattern of the Eighteenth Century

In the eighteenth century the traditional demographic pattern of Europe was transformed. Growth took place unevenly, with Russia growing very quickly after 1700 and France much more slowly. Nonetheless, the explosion of population was a major phenomenon in all European countries. Europeans grew in numbers steadily from 1720 to 1789, with especially dramatic increases after about 1750 (Figure 17.2). Between 1700 and 1835 the population of Europe doubled in size.

What caused this population growth? In some areas, especially England, women had more babies than before because new opportunities for employment in rural industry (see "The Industrious Revolution" later in this chapter) allowed them to marry at an earlier age. But the basic cause of European population increase as a whole was a decline in mortality—fewer deaths.

One of the primary reasons behind this decline was the still-unexplained disappearance of the bubonic plague. Following the Black Death in the fourteenth century, plague had remained part of the European experience, striking again and again with savage force, particularly in towns. In 1720 a ship from Syria and the Levant brought the disease to Marseilles. As a contemporary account described it, "The Porters employ'd in unloading the Vessel, were immediately seiz'd with violent Pains in the Head . . . soon after they broke out in Blotches and Buboes, and died in three Days."[3] Plague quickly spread within and beyond Marseilles, killing up to one hundred thousand. By 1722 the epidemic had passed, and that was the last time plague fell on western and central Europe. Exactly why plague disappeared is unknown. Stricter measures of quarantine in Mediterranean ports and along the Austrian border with the Ottoman Empire helped by carefully isolating human carriers of plague. Chance and plain good luck were probably just as important.

Advances in medical knowledge did not contribute much to reducing the death rate in the eighteenth century. The most important advance in preventive medicine in this period was inoculation against smallpox, a dis-

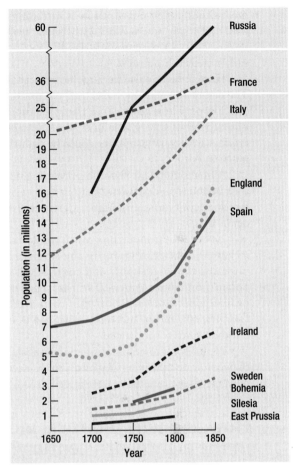

FIGURE 17.2   The Increase of Population in Europe, 1650–1850
Population grew across Europe in the eighteenth century, though the most dramatic increases occurred after 1750. Russia experienced the largest increase and emerged as Europe's most populous state, as natural increase was complemented by growth from territorial expansion.
(Source: Data from Massimo Livi Bacci, *The Population of Europe* [Wiley-Blackwell, 2000], p. 8.)

ease that killed approximately four hundred thousand people each year in Europe. Widely practiced in the Ottoman Empire, inoculation was popularized in England in the 1720s by the wife of the former English ambassador to the empire, but it did not spread to the rest of the continent for decades. Improvements in the water supply and sewage, which were frequently promoted by strong absolutist monarchies, did contribute to somewhat better public health and helped reduce such diseases as typhoid and typhus in urban areas of western Europe. Improvements in water supply and the drainage of swamps also reduced Europe's large insect population. Flies and mosquitoes played a major role in spreading diseases, especially those striking children and young adults. Thus early public health measures contributed to the decline in mortality that began with the disappearance of plague and continued into the early nineteenth century.

Human beings also became more successful in safeguarding the supply of food. The eighteenth century was a time of considerable canal and road building in western Europe. These advances in transportation, which were also among the more positive aspects of strong absolutist states, lessened the impact of local crop failure and famine. Emergency supplies could be brought in, and localized starvation became less frequent.

A final significant factor in preventing deaths in the eighteenth century was that wars became less destructive than in the previous century. Fewer people died in warfare and, even more important, there were fewer armies on the move to spread epidemic disease.

None of the population growth would have been possible if not for the advances in agricultural production in the seventeenth and eighteenth centuries, which increased the food supply and contributed nutritious new foods, particularly the potato from South America. In short, population grew in the eighteenth century primarily because years of higher-than-average death rates were less catastrophic. Famines, epidemics, and wars continued to occur and to affect population growth, but their severity moderated.

Population growth intensified the imbalance between the number of people and the economic opportunities available to them. Deprived of land by the enclosure movement, the rural poor were forced to look for new ways to make a living.

How and why did rural industry intensify in the eighteenth century?

The growth of population increased the number of rural workers with little or no land, and this in turn contributed to the development of industry in rural areas. The poor in the countryside increasingly needed to supplement their agricultural earnings with other types of work, and urban capitalists were eager to employ them, often at lower wages than urban workers received. **Cottage industry**, which consisted of manufacturing with hand tools in peasant cottages and work sheds, grew markedly in the eighteenth century and became a crucial feature of the European economy. The growth of rural industry led to far-reaching changes in daily life in the countryside.

The Putting-Out System

Cottage industry was often organized through the **putting-out system**. The two main participants in this system were the merchant capitalist and the rural worker. The merchant loaned, or "put out," raw materials to cottage workers, who processed the raw materials in their own homes and returned the finished products to the merchant. The relative importance of earnings from the land and from industry varied greatly for handicraft workers, although industrial wages usually became more important for a given family with time.

As industries grew in scale and complexity, production was often broken into many stages. For example, a merchant would provide raw wool to one group of workers for spinning into thread. He would then pass the thread to another group of workers to be bleached, to another for dyeing, and to another for weaving into cloth. The merchant paid outworkers by the piece and sold the finished product to regional, national, or international markets.

The putting-out system grew because it had competitive advantages. Underemployed labor was abundant, and poor peasants and landless laborers would work for low wages. Since production in the countryside was unregulated, workers and merchants could change procedures and experiment as they saw fit. Because workers did not need to meet rigid guild standards, cottage industry became capable of producing many kinds of goods. Textiles; all manner of knives, forks, and housewares; buttons and gloves; and clocks could be produced quite satisfactorily in the countryside. Although luxury goods for the rich, such as exquisite tapestries and fine porcelain, demanded special training, close supervision, and centralized workshops, the limited skills of rural industry were sufficient for everyday articles.

Rural manufacturing did not spread across Europe at an even rate. It developed most successfully in England, particularly for the spinning and weaving of woolen cloth. By 1500 half of England's textiles were being produced in the countryside. By 1700 English industry was generally more rural than urban and heavily reliant on the putting-out system. Most continental countries, with the exception of Flanders and the Dutch Republic, developed rural industry more slowly. The latter part of the eighteenth century witnessed a remarkable expansion of rural industry in certain densely populated regions of continental Europe. This was in contrast to metal production, which usually occurred in areas of less dense population (Map 17.1).

The Lives of Rural Textile Workers

Until the nineteenth century the industry that employed the most people in Europe was textiles. The making of linen, woolen, and eventually cotton cloth was the typical activity of cottage workers engaged in the putting-out system. A look inside the cottage of the English weaver illustrates a way of life as well as an economic system. The rural worker lived in a small cottage with tiny windows and little space. The cottage was often a single room that served as workshop, kitchen, and bedroom. There were only a few pieces of furniture, of which the weaver's loom was by far the largest and most important. That loom changed somewhat in the early eighteenth century when John Kay's invention of the flying shuttle enabled the weaver to throw the shuttle back and forth between the threads with one hand. Aside from that improvement, however, the loom was as it had been for much of history and as it would remain until the arrival of mechanized looms in the first decades of the nineteenth century.

Handloom weaving was a family enterprise. All members of the family helped in the work, so that "every person from seven to eighty (who retained their sight and who could move their hands) could earn their bread," as one eighteenth-century English observer put it.[4] Operating the loom was usually considered a man's job, reserved for the male head of the family. Women and children worked at auxiliary tasks; they prepared the warp (vertical) threads and mounted them on the loom,

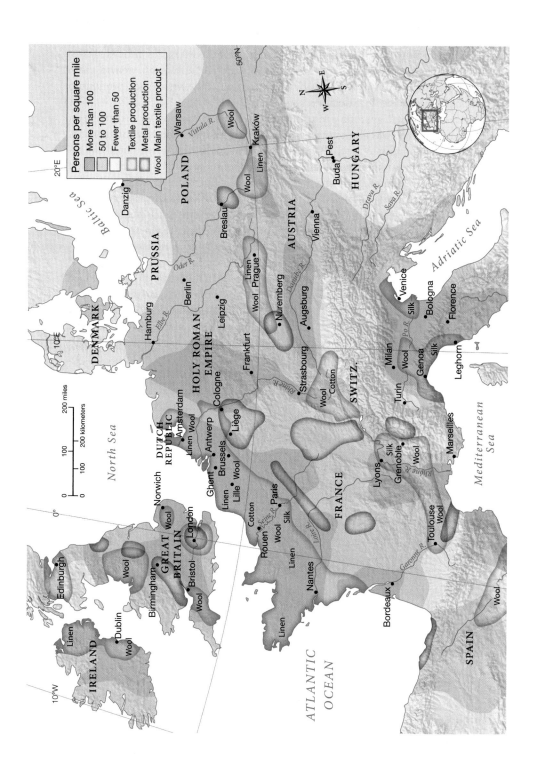

Persons per square mile
- More than 100
- 50 to 100
- Fewer than 50
- Textile production
- Metal production
- Wool Main textile product

wound threads on bobbins for the weft (horizontal) threads, and sometimes operated the warp frame while the father passed the shuttle.

The work of four or five spinners was needed to keep one weaver steadily employed. Since the weaver's family usually could not produce enough thread, merchants hired the wives and daughters of agricultural workers, who took on spinning work in their spare time. In England, many widows and single women also became spinners or "spinsters," so many in fact that the word became a synonym for an unmarried woman. In parts of Germany, spinning employed whole families and was not reserved for women.

Relations between workers and employers were often marked by sharp conflict. There were constant disputes over the weights of materials and the quality of finished work. Merchants accused workers of stealing raw materials, and weavers complained that merchants delivered underweight bales. Suspicion abounded.

Conditions were particularly hard for female workers. While men could earn decent wages through long hours of arduous labor, women's wages were usually much lower because they were not considered the family's primary wage earner. In England's Yorkshire wool industry, a male wool comber earned a good wage of 12 shillings or more a week, while a female spinner could hope for only 3½ shillings.[5] A single or widowed spinner faced a desperate struggle with poverty. Any period of illness or unemployment could spell disaster for her and any children she might have.

From the merchant capitalist's point of view, the problem was not low wages but maintaining control over the labor force. Cottage workers were scattered across the countryside, and their work depended on the agricultural calendar. In spring and late summer planting and haymaking occupied all hands in the rural village, leading to shortages in the supply of thread. Merchants bitterly resented their lack of control over rural labor because their own livelihood depended on their ability to meet orders on time. They accused workers—especially female spinners—of laziness, drunkenness, and immorality. If workers failed to produce enough thread, they reasoned, it must be because their wages were too high and they had little incentive to work.

Merchants thus insisted on maintaining the lowest possible wages to force the "idle" poor into productive labor. They also lobbied for, and obtained, new police powers over workers. Imprisonment and public whipping became common punishments for pilfering small amounts of yarn or cloth. For poor workers, their right to hold on to the bits and pieces left over in the production process was akin to the traditional peasant right of gleaning in common lands. With progress came the loss of traditional safeguards for the poor.

< MAP 17.1   Industry and Population in Eighteenth-Century Europe
The growth of cottage manufacturing in rural areas helped country people increase their income and contributed to population growth. The putting-out system began in England, and much of the work was in the textile industry. Cottage industry was also strong in the Low Countries—modern-day Belgium and the Netherlands.

The Industrious Revolution

One scholar has used the term **industrious revolution** to summarize the social and economic changes taking place in northwestern Europe in the late seventeenth and early eighteenth centuries.[6] This occurred as households reduced leisure time, stepped up the pace of work, and, most important, redirected the labor of women and children away from the production of goods for household consumption and toward wage work. In the countryside the spread of cottage industry can be seen as one manifestation of the industrious revolution, while in the cities there was a rise in female employment outside the home. By working harder and increasing the number of wageworkers, rural and urban households could purchase more goods, even in a time of stagnant or falling wages.

The effect of these changes is still debated. While some scholars lament the encroachment of longer work hours and stricter discipline on traditional family life, others insist that poor families made decisions based on their own self-interests. With more finished goods becoming available at lower prices, households sought cash income to participate in an emerging consumer economy.

The role of women and girls in this new economy is particularly controversial. When women entered the labor market, they almost always worked at menial, tedious jobs for very low wages. Yet when women earned their own wages, they also seem to have exercised more independence in marriage choices and household decision making. Most of their scant earnings went for household necessities, items of food and clothing they could no longer produce now that they worked full-time, but sometimes a few shillings were left for a ribbon or a new pair of stockings. Women's use of their surplus income thus helped spur the rapid growth of the textile industries in which they labored so hard.

These new sources and patterns of labor established important foundations for the Industrial Revolution of the late eighteenth and nineteenth centuries (see Chapter 20). They created households in which all members worked for wages rather than in a family business and in which consumption relied on market-produced rather than homemade goods. It was not until the mid-nineteenth century, with rising industrial wages, that a new model emerged in which the male "breadwinner" was expected to earn enough to support the whole family and women and children were relegated back to the domestic sphere. With women estimated to compose more than 40 percent of the global workforce, today's world is experiencing a second industrious revolution in a similar climate of stagnant wages and increased demand for consumer goods.[7]

What important changes occurred in economic thought and practice in the eighteenth century?

Late-seventeenth- and eighteenth-century Europe also experienced revolutionary developments in finance and economic thought. Up to the mid-eighteenth century, governments heavily controlled the circulation of grain and the price of bread, fearing the social turmoil and political instability that would arise from food shortages. In urban areas, the **guild system** dominated production of artisanal goods, providing their masters with economic privileges as well as a proud social identity.

In the second half of the eighteenth century, political economy emerged as a new mode of thought influenced by the Enlightenment. Economic thinkers, like Adam Smith, attacked government regulations as a hindrance to innovation and competition, developing a doctrine known as economic liberalism (see "Adam Smith and Economic Liberalism" later in the chapter).

Economic Regulation and the Guilds

Given the precariousness of survival for most people, European governments believed that it was essential to regulate economic production and exchange. They feared that shortages of bread could lead to social turmoil and political upheaval, as they did many times in the hard conditions of the seventeenth century (see "Economic Crisis and Popular Revolts" in Chapter 15). Moreover, mercantilist doctrine dictated that maintaining a trade surplus was crucial to obtain the funds necessary to build a strong state. Thus rulers believed they must impose strict production standards on industry and control access to trade to ensure that craftsmen and manufacturers produced goods of high quality, especially for export markets.

Based on these ideas, the guild system, which had originated during the economic boom of the Middle Ages, reached its peak in most of Europe in the seventeenth and eighteenth centuries. During this period, the number of urban guilds increased dramatically in cities and towns across Europe. Authorities granted each guild a detailed set of privileges, including exclusive rights to produce and sell certain goods, access to restricted markets in raw materials, and the rights to train apprentices, hire workers, and open shops. Guilds also served social and religious functions, providing a locus of sociability and group identity to the middling classes of European cities.

To ensure there was enough work to go around, guilds restricted their membership to men who were Christians, had several years of work experience, paid membership fees, and successfully completed a masterpiece. Masters' sons enjoyed automatic access to their fathers' guilds, while outsiders — including Jews and Protestants in Catholic countries — were barred from entering. Most urban men and women worked in non-guild trades as domestic servants, manual laborers, and vendors of food, used clothing, and other goods.

While most were hostile to women, a small number of guilds did accept women. Most involved needlework and textile production, occupations that were considered appropriate for women. In 1675 seamstresses gained a new all-female guild in Paris, and soon seamstresses joined tailors' guilds in parts of France, England, and the Dutch Republic. By the mid-eighteenth century male masters began to hire more female workers, often in defiance of their own guild statutes.

The Financial Revolution

Changes in overseas trade and rural industry, combined with the militaristic ambitions of European rulers, helped bring about crucial changes in economic life. In the early seventeenth century, Dutch prosperity in agriculture and overseas trade encouraged the development of new financial innovations, including short-term bonds for public credit and a maritime insurance industry. The Bank of Amsterdam (founded in 1609) issued paper money and traded bills of exchange, which facilitated merchant ventures at home and abroad. Dutch financial methods came to England when William of Orange and his wife Mary Stuart took control of the English throne in the Glorious Revolution (see "The Restoration of the English Monarchy" in Chapter 15). The Bank of England was founded in 1694 as a government-chartered joint stock company, and William used the bank as a source of credit to pursue war against the French. In subsequent decades, hundreds of new private banks were created in London and across the country to provide credit to private individuals. These innovations laid the foundations of modern banking and finance systems, a development described by historians as a "financial revolution."

Another element of this revolution was the emergence of financial speculation, enabled by the creation of stock exchanges in Amsterdam, London, and other European capitals. Speculative bubbles occurred in the Netherlands as early as the 1630s based on trading in tulip bulbs. In 1720, both England and France experienced catastrophic financial crises caused by the collapse of shares in colonial trading companies. The shock of this experience dissuaded the French from creating a national bank until the reign of Napoleon (see Chapter 20).

Adam Smith and Economic Liberalism

At the same time that cottage industry began to infringe on the livelihoods of urban artisans and new financial institutions encouraged the circulation of credit, philosophers and administrators began to develop new ways of thinking about economic production and exchange. The notion of the "economy" as a discrete entity, subject to natural laws that could be discovered by rational thought, constituted an important element of Enlightenment thought. The first university positions devoted to "political economy," as the formal study of production and exchange came to be called, were established in the 1760s. In France, the Physiocrats, a distinctive group of economic thinkers, established the first large-scale explanation of the economy, what we now call a "macro-economic" model, based on land as the sole source of economic value.

Many economic thinkers in this period came to believe that the economy could best function when unimpeded by government laws. They attacked tariffs and other forms of government regulation and ridiculed guilds as outmoded and exclusionary institutions that obstructed technical innovation and progress. One of the best-known critics of government regulation of trade and industry was Adam Smith (1723–1790), a leading figure of the Scottish Enlightenment (see "Enlightenment Movements Across Europe" in Chapter 16). Smith developed the general idea of freedom of enterprise and established the basis for modern economics in his groundbreaking work *Inquiry into the Nature and Causes of the Wealth of Nations* (1776). Smith criticized guilds for their stifling restrictions, a critique he extended to all state monopolies and privileged companies. Far preferable, in his view, was free competition, which would protect consumers from price gouging and give all citizens an equal right to do what they did best. Smith advocated a more highly developed "division of labor" that entailed separating craft production into individual tasks to increase workers' speed and efficiency.

In keeping with his fear of political oppression and with the "system of natural liberty" that he championed, Smith argued that government should limit itself to "only three duties": it should provide a defense against foreign invasion, maintain civil order with courts and police protection, and sponsor certain indispensable public works and institutions that could never adequately profit private investors. He believed that the pursuit of self-interest in a competitive market would be sufficient to improve the living conditions of citizens, a view that quickly emerged as the classic argument for **economic liberalism**.

However, Smith did not advocate unbridled capitalism. Unlike many disgruntled merchant capitalists, he applauded the modest rise in real wages of British workers in the eighteenth century, stating: "No society can surely be flourishing and happy, of which the far greater part of the members are poor and miserable." Smith also acknowledged that employers were "always and everywhere in a sort of tacit, but constant and uniform combination, not to raise the wages of labor above their actual rate" and sometimes entered "into particular combinations to sink the wages even below this rate." While he celebrated the rise in productivity allowed by the division of labor, he also acknowledged its demoralizing effects on workers and called for government intervention to raise workers' living standards.[8]

Many educated people in France, including Physiocrats and some government officials, shared Smith's ideas. In 1774, the reform-minded economics minister Anne-Robert-Jacques Turgot issued a law in the name of Louis XV, ordering the grain trade to be freed from state regulation. Two years later, another edict abolished all French guilds. Vociferous popular protest against these measures led to Turgot's disgrace shortly afterward and the cancellation of his reforms. But the legislators of the French Revolution (see "The Thermidorian Reaction and the Directory" in Chapter 19) returned to a liberal economic agenda in 1789. The National Assembly definitively abolished guilds in 1791. Other European countries followed suit more slowly, with guilds surviving in central Europe and Italy into the second half of the nineteenth century. By the middle of the nineteenth century economic liberalism was championed by most European governments and elites.

What role did colonial markets play in Europe's development?

In addition to agricultural improvement, population pressure, and a growing cottage industry, the expansion of Europe in the eighteenth century was characterized by the increase of world trade. Adam Smith declared that "the discovery of America and that of a passage to the East Indies by the Cape of Good Hope, are the two greatest and most important events recorded in the history of mankind."[9] In the eighteenth century Spain and Portugal revitalized their empires and began drawing more wealth from renewed colonial development. Yet once again the countries of northwestern Europe — the Dutch Republic, France, and above all Great Britain — benefited most.

The Atlantic economy that these countries developed from 1650 to 1790 would prove crucial in the building of a global economy. Great Britain, which was formed in 1707 by the union of England and Scotland into a single kingdom, gradually became the leading maritime power. Thus the British played the critical role in building a fairly unified Atlantic economy that provided remarkable opportunities for them and their colonists. They also competed ruthlessly with France and the Netherlands for trade and territory in the Americas and Asia.

Mercantilism and Colonial Competition

Britain's commercial leadership had its origins in mercantilist doctrine. Eventually eliciting criticism from Enlightenment thinker Adam Smith and other proponents of free trade in the late eighteenth century, European mercantilism was a system of economic regulations aimed at increasing the power of the state. As practiced by a leading figure such as Colbert under Louis XIV, mercantilism aimed particularly at creating a favorable balance of foreign trade in order to increase a country's stock of gold. A country's gold holdings served as an all-important treasure chest that could be opened periodically to pay for war in a violent age.

The desire to increase both military power and private wealth led England's rulers to impose the mercantile system of the **Navigation Acts**. Oliver Cromwell established the first of these laws in 1651, and the restored monarchy of Charles II extended them in 1660 and 1663. The acts required that most goods imported from Europe into England and Scotland (Great Britain after 1707) be carried on British-owned ships with British crews or on ships of the country producing the articles. Moreover, these laws gave British merchants and shipowners a virtual monopoly on trade with British colonies. The colonists were required to ship their products on British (or American) ships and to buy almost all European goods from Britain. It was believed that these economic regulations would eliminate foreign competition, thereby helping British merchants and workers as well as colonial plantation owners and farmers. It was hoped, too, that the emerging British Empire would develop a shipping industry with a large number of experienced seamen who could serve during wartime in the Royal Navy.

The Navigation Acts were a form of economic warfare. Their initial target was the Dutch, who were far ahead of the English in shipping and foreign trade in the mid-seventeenth century (see "The Dutch Republic in the Seventeenth Century" in Chapter 15). In conjunction with three Anglo-Dutch wars between 1652 and 1674, the Navigation Acts seriously damaged Dutch shipping and commerce. The British seized the thriving Dutch colony of New Amsterdam in 1664 and renamed it New York. By the late seventeenth century the Dutch Republic was falling behind England in shipping, trade, and colonies.

Thereafter France stood clearly as England's most serious rival in the competition for overseas empire. Rich in natural resources, with a population three or four times that of England, and allied with Spain, continental Europe's leading military power was already building a powerful fleet and a worldwide system of rigidly monopolized colonial trade. Thus from 1701 to 1763 Britain and France were locked in a series of wars to decide, in part, which nation would become the leading maritime power and claim the profits of Europe's overseas expansion (Map 17.2).

The first round was the War of the Spanish Succession (see "Louis XIV's Wars" in Chapter 15), which started in 1701 when Louis XIV accepted the Spanish crown willed to his grandson. Besides upsetting the continental balance of power, a union of France and Spain threatened to encircle and destroy the British colonies in North America (see Map 17.2). Defeated by a great coalition of states after twelve years of

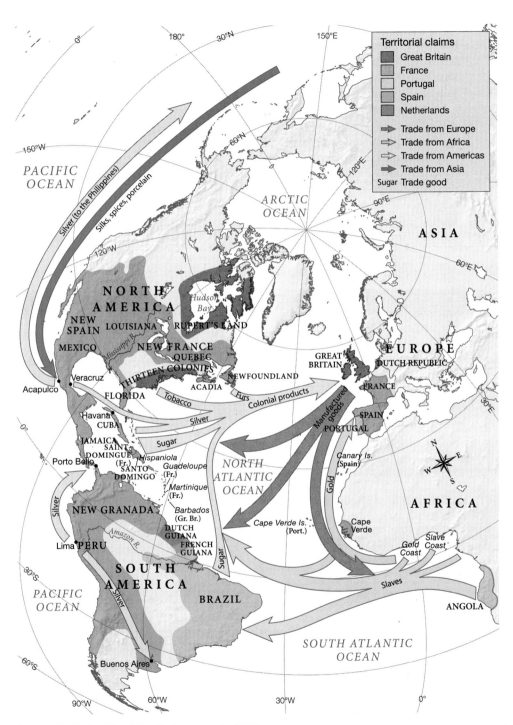

MAP 17.2   The Atlantic Economy in 1701

The growth of trade encouraged both economic development and military conflict in the Atlantic basin. Four continents were linked together by the exchange of goods and people.

fighting, Louis XIV was forced in the Peace of Utrecht (YOO-trehkt) in 1713 to cede his North American holdings in Newfoundland, Nova Scotia, and the Hudson Bay territory to Britain. Spain was compelled to give Britain control of its West African slave trade — the so-called *asiento* (ah-SYEHN-toh) — and to let Britain send one ship of merchandise into the Spanish colonies annually.

Conflict continued among the European powers over both domestic and colonial affairs. The War of the Austrian Succession (1740–1748), which started when Frederick the Great of Prussia seized Silesia from Austria's Maria Theresa (see "Frederick the Great of Prussia" in Chapter 16), gradually became a world war that included Anglo-French conflicts in India and North America. The war ended with no change in the territorial situation in North America. This inconclusive standoff helped set the stage for the Seven Years' War (1756–1763; see Chapter 19). In central Europe, France aided Austria's Maria Theresa in her quest to win back Silesia from the Prussians, who had formed an alliance with England. In North America, French

Siege of the French Fortress of Louisbourg in 1745 In the eighteenth century, European wars were increasingly waged in overseas theaters. The so-called War of the Austrian Succession (1740–1748) saw hostilities between France and England in North America, including a British assault on the French fort of Louisbourg (Cape Breton Island) in 1745. French-English rivalry in North America culminated in the Seven Years' War (1756–1763), which led to the loss of most French territory, with the exception of France's Caribbean holdings. (Private Collection/Peter Newark American Pictures/Bridgeman Images)

and British settlers engaged in territorial skirmishes that eventually resulted in an all-out war that drew in Native American allies on both sides of the conflict (see Map 19.1). By 1763 Prussia had held off the Austrians, and British victory on all colonial fronts was ratified in the **Treaty of Paris**. British naval power, built in large part on the rapid growth of the British shipping industry after the passage of the Navigation Acts, had triumphed decisively: Britain had realized its goal of monopolizing a vast trading and colonial empire.

The Atlantic Economy

As the volume of transatlantic trade increased, the regions bordering the ocean were increasingly drawn into an integrated economic system. Commercial exchange in the Atlantic has often been referred to as the "triangle trade," designating a three-way transport of goods: European commodities, like guns and textiles, to Africa; enslaved Africans to the colonies; and colonial goods, such as cotton, tobacco, and sugar, back to Europe (see Map 17.2).

Over the course of the eighteenth century, the economies of European nations bordering the Atlantic Ocean, especially England, relied more and more on colonial exports. In England, sales to the mainland colonies of North America and the West Indian sugar islands — with an important assist from West Africa and Latin America — soared from £500,000 to £4 million (Figure 17.3). Exports to England's colonies in Ireland and India also rose substantially from 1700 to 1800. By 1800 sales to European countries — England's traditional trading partners — represented only one-third of exports, down from two-thirds a century earlier.

England also benefited from importing colonial products. Colonial monopolies allowed the English to obtain a steady supply of such goods at beneficial prices and to re-export them to other nations at high profits. Moreover, many colonial goods, like sugar and tobacco, required processing before consumption and thus contributed new manufacturing jobs in England. In the eighteenth century, stimulated by trade and empire building, England's capital city, London, grew into the West's largest and richest city. Thus the

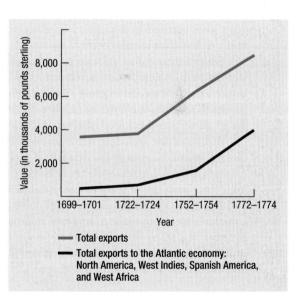

FIGURE 17.3 Exports of English Manufactured Goods, 1700–1774
While trade between England and Europe stagnated after 1700, English exports to Africa and the Americas boomed and greatly stimulated English economic development.
(Source: Data from R. Davis, "English Foreign Trade, 1700–1774," *Economic History Review*, 2d ser., 15 [1962]: 302–303.)

mercantilist system of foreign trade achieved remarkable success for England, and by the 1770s the country stood on the threshold of the epoch-making changes that would become known as the Industrial Revolution (see Chapter 20). This was also the period when Adam Smith and other political economists began to criticize mercantilism and argue for free trade as a means to increase prosperity for all people and nations.

Although they lost many possessions to the English in the Seven Years' War, the French still profited enormously from colonial trade. The colonies of Saint-Domingue (modern-day Haiti), Martinique, and Guadeloupe remained in French hands and provided immense fortunes in plantation agriculture and slave trading during the second half of the eighteenth century. By 1789 the population of Saint-Domingue included five hundred thousand slaves whose labor had allowed the colony to become the world's leading producer of coffee and sugar and the most profitable plantation colony in the New World.[10] The wealth generated from colonial trade fostered the confidence of the merchant classes in Paris, Bordeaux, and other large cities, and merchants soon joined other elite groups clamoring for political reforms.

The third major player in the Atlantic economy, Spain, also saw its colonial fortunes improve during the eighteenth century. Not only did it gain Louisiana from France in 1763, but its influence expanded westward all the way to northern California through the efforts of Spanish missionaries and ranchers. Its mercantilist goals were boosted by a recovery in silver production, which had dropped significantly in the seventeenth century.

Silver mining also stimulated food production for the mining camps, and wealthy Spanish landowners developed a system of **debt peonage** to keep indigenous workers on their estates to grow food for this market. Under this system, which was similar to serfdom, a planter or rancher would keep workers in perpetual debt bondage by advancing them food, shelter, and a little money.

Although the "triangle trade" model highlights some of the most important flows of commerce across the Atlantic, it significantly oversimplifies the picture. For example, a brisk intercolonial trade also existed, with the Caribbean slave colonies importing food in the form of fish, flour, and livestock from the northern colonies and rice from the south, in exchange for sugar and slaves (see Map 17.2). Many colonial traders also violated imperial monopolies to trade with the most profitable partners, regardless of nationality. Moreover, the Atlantic economy was inextricably linked to trade with the Indian and Pacific Oceans (see "Trade and Empire in Asia and the Pacific" at the end of this chapter).

The Transatlantic Slave Trade

At the core of the transatlantic world were the misery and profit of the **transatlantic slave trade**. The forced migration of millions of Africans was a key element in the Atlantic system and western European economic expansion throughout the eighteenth century. The brutal practice intensified dramatically after 1700 and especially after 1750 with the growth of trade and demand for slave-produced goods like sugar and cotton. According to the most authoritative source, European traders purchased and shipped 6.5 million enslaved Africans across the Atlantic between 1701 and 1800 — more

The Transatlantic Slave Trade This engraving from 1814 shows traders leading a group of slaves to the West African coast, where they will board ships to cross the Atlantic. Many slaves died en route or arrived greatly weakened and ill. (Bibliothèque de l'Arsenal, Paris, France/Archives Charmet/Bridgeman Images)

than half of the estimated total of 12.5 million Africans transported between 1450 and 1900, of whom 15 percent died in procurement and transit.[11]

The rise of plantation agriculture was responsible for the tremendous growth of the slave trade. Among all European colonies, the plantations of Portuguese Brazil received by far the largest number of enslaved Africans over the entire period of the slave trade — 45 percent of the total. Another 45 percent were divided among the many Caribbean colonies. The colonies of mainland North America took only 3 percent of slaves arriving from Africa, a little under four hundred thousand, relying mostly on natural growth of the enslaved population.

Eighteenth-century intensification of the slave trade resulted in fundamental changes in its organization. After 1700, as Britain became the undisputed leader in shipping enslaved people across the Atlantic, European governments and ship captains cut back on fighting among themselves and concentrated on commerce. They generally adopted the shore method of trading, which was less expensive than maintaining fortified trading posts. Under this system, European ships sent boats ashore to trade with African dealers or invited dealers to bring traders and the enslaved out to their ships. This method allowed ships to move easily along the coast from market to market and to depart more quickly for the Americas.

Some African merchants and rulers who controlled exports profited from the greater demand for slaves. With their newfound wealth, they gained access to European and colonial goods, including firearms. But generally such economic returns did not spread very far, and the negative consequences of the expanding slave trade predominated. Wars among African states to obtain salable captives increased, and leaders used profits to purchase more arms than textiles and consumer goods. While the populations of Europe and Asia grew substantially in the eighteenth century, the population of Africa stagnated or possibly declined. As one contemporary critic observed:

> I do not know if coffee and sugar are essential to the happiness of Europe, but I know that these two products have accounted for the unhappiness of two great regions of the world: America has been depopulated so as to have land on which to plant them; Africa has been depopulated so as to have the people to cultivate them.[12]

Most Europeans did not personally witness the horrors of the slave trade between Africa and the Americas, and until the early part of the eighteenth century they considered the African slave trade a legitimate business. But as details of the plight of enslaved people became known, a campaign to abolish slavery developed in Britain. In the late 1780s the abolition campaign grew into a mass movement of public opinion, the first in British history. British women were prominent in this movement, denouncing the immorality of human bondage and stressing the cruel and sadistic treatment of enslaved women and families. These attacks put the defenders of slavery on the defensive. In 1807 Parliament abolished the British slave trade, although slavery continued in British colonies and the Americas for decades.

Identities and Communities of the Atlantic World

As contacts between the Atlantic coasts of the Americas, Africa, and Europe became more frequent, and as European settlements grew into well-established colonies, new identities and communities emerged. The term *Creole* referred to people of Spanish ancestry born in the Americas. Wealthy Creoles and their counterparts throughout the Atlantic colonies prided themselves on following European ways of life. In addition to their lavish plantation estates, they maintained townhouses in colonial cities built on the European model, with theaters, central squares, churches, and coffeehouses. They purchased luxury goods made in Europe, and their children were often sent to be educated in the home country.

Over time, however, the colonial elite came to feel that their circumstances gave them different interests and characteristics from those of their home population. As one observer explained, "A turn of mind peculiar to the planter, occasioned by a physical difference of constitution, climate, customs, and education, tends . . . to repress the remains of his former attachment to his native soil."[13] Colonial elites became "Americanized" by adopting native foods, like chocolate and potatoes, and sought relief from tropical disease in native remedies. Creole traders and planters, along with their counterparts in English colonies, increasingly resented the regulations and taxes imposed by colonial bureaucrats. Such resentment would eventually lead to revolution against colonial powers (see Chapter 19).

Not all Europeans in the colonies were wealthy; indeed, many arrived as indentured servants and had to labor for several years before acquiring freedom. Numerous poor or middling whites worked as clerks, shopkeepers, craftsmen, and, in North America, farmers and laborers. With the exception of British North America, white Europeans made up a minority of the population; they were outnumbered in Spanish America by indigenous peoples and in the Caribbean and Brazil by the growing numbers of enslaved people of African descent. Since European migrants were disproportionately male, much of the population of the Atlantic world descended from unions—often forced—of European men and indigenous or African women. Colonial attempts to identify and control racial categories greatly influenced developing Enlightenment thought on racial difference (see "Enlightenment Debates About Race" in Chapter 16).

Mixed-race populations sometimes rose to the colonial elite. The Spanish conquistadors often consolidated their power through marriage to the daughters of local rulers, and their descendants were among the most powerful inhabitants of Spanish America. In the Spanish and French Caribbean, as in Brazil, many masters acknowledged and freed their mixed-race children, leading to sizable populations of free people of color. Advantaged by their fathers, some became wealthy land and slave owners in their own right. In the second half of the eighteenth century, the prosperity of some free people of color brought a backlash from the white population of Saint-Domingue in the form of new race laws prohibiting nonwhites from marrying whites and forcing them to adopt distinctive attire.

British colonies followed a distinctive pattern. There, whole families, rather than individual men, migrated, resulting in a rapid increase in the white population. This development was favored by British colonial law, which forbade marriage between English men and women and Africans or Native Americans. In the British colonies of the Caribbean and the southern mainland, masters tended to leave their mixed-race progeny in slavery rather than freeing them, maintaining a stark discrepancy between free whites and enslaved people of color.[14] The identities inspired by the Atlantic world were equally complex. In some ways, the colonial encounter helped create new and more fixed forms of identity. Inhabitants of distinct regions of European nations came to see themselves as "Spanish" or "English" when they crossed the Atlantic; similarly, their colonial governments imposed the identity of "Indian" and "African" on peoples with vastly different linguistic, cultural, and political origins. The result was the creation of new Creole communities that melded cultural and social elements of various groups of origin with the new European cultures.

The status of mixed-race people, known as mestizos in Spanish America and métis in New France, was ambiguous. Spanish administrators applied purity of blood (*limpieza de sangre*) laws—originally used to exclude Jews and Muslims during the *reconquista* (Christian reconquest of Spain)—to indigenous and African peoples.[15] Some mixed-race people sought to enter Creole society and obtain its many official and unofficial privileges by passing as white. Over time, where they existed in any number, mestizos and free people of color established their own communities and social hierarchies based on wealth, family connections, occupation, and skin color.

Converting indigenous people to Christianity was a key ambition for all European powers in the New World. Galvanized by the Protestant Reformation and the perceived need to protect and spread Catholicism, Catholic powers actively sponsored missionary efforts. Jesuits, Franciscans, Dominicans, and other religious orders established missions throughout Spanish, Portuguese, and French colonies (see "Religious Conversion" in Chapter 14). In Central and South America, large-scale conversion forged enduring Catholic cultures in Portuguese and Spanish colonies. Conversion efforts in North America were less effective because indigenous settlements were more scattered and native people were less integrated into colonial communities. On the whole, Protestants were less active as missionaries in this period, although some dissenters, like Moravians, Quakers, and Methodists, did seek converts among indigenous and enslaved people.

The practice of slavery reveals important limitations on efforts to spread Christianity. Slave owners often refused to baptize their slaves, fearing that enslaved people would use their Christian status to claim additional rights. In some areas, particularly among the mostly African-born slaves of the Caribbean, elements of African religious belief and practice endured, often incorporated with Christian traditions.

Restricted from owning land and holding many occupations in Europe, Jews were eager participants in the new Atlantic economy and established a network of mercantile communities along its trade routes. As in the Old World, Jews in European colonies faced discrimination; for example, restrictions existed on the number of slaves they could own in Barbados in the early eighteenth century.[16] Jews were considered to be white Europeans and thus ineligible to be slaves, but they did not enjoy equal status with Christians. The status of Jews adds one more element to the complexity of Atlantic identities.

The Atlantic Enlightenment

Enlightenment ideas thrived in the colonies, although with as much diversity and disagreement as in Europe (see Chapter 16). The colonies of British North America were deeply influenced by the Scottish Enlightenment, with its emphasis on pragmatic approaches to the problems of life. Following the Scottish model, leaders in the colonies adopted a moderate, "commonsense" version of the Enlightenment that emphasized self-improvement and ethical conduct. In most cases, this version of the Enlightenment was perfectly compatible with religion and was chiefly spread through the growing colleges and universities of the colonies, which remained church-based institutions.

Some thinkers went even further in their admiration for Enlightenment ideas. Benjamin Franklin's writings and political career provide an outstanding example of the combination of the pragmatism and economic interests of the Scottish Enlightenment with the constitutional theories of John Locke, Jean-Jacques Rousseau, and the baron de Montesquieu. Franklin was privately a lifelong deist, meaning that he believed in God but not in organized religion. Nonetheless, he continued to attend church and respect religious proprieties, a cautious pattern followed by fellow deist Thomas Jefferson and other leading thinkers of the American Enlightenment.

Northern Enlightenment thinkers often depicted Spain and its American colonies as the epitome of the superstition and barbarity they contested. The Catholic Church strictly controlled the publication of books on the Iberian Peninsula and in Spanish America. Nonetheless, the Bourbon dynasty that took power in Spain in the early eighteenth century followed its own course of enlightened absolutism, just like its counterparts in the rest of Europe (see "What impact did new ways of thinking have on politics?" in Chapter 16). Under King Carlos III (r. 1759–1788) and his son Carlos IV (r. 1788–1808), Spanish administrators attempted to strengthen colonial rule by posting a standing army in the colonies and increasing royal monopolies and taxes to pay for it. They also ordered officials to gather more accurate information about the colonies as a basis for improving the government. Enlightened administrators debated the status of indigenous peoples and whether it would be better for these peoples (and for the prosperity of Spanish America) if they maintained their distinct legal status or were integrated into Spanish society.

Educated Creoles were well aware of the new currents of thought, and the universities, newspapers, and salons of Spanish America produced their own reform ideas. The establishment of a mining school in Mexico City in 1792, the first in the Spanish colonies, illuminates the practical achievements of reformers. As in other European colonies, one effect of Enlightenment thought was to encourage Creoles to criticize the policies of the mother country and aspire toward greater autonomy.

Trade and Empire in Asia and the Pacific

As the Atlantic economy took shape, Europeans continued to vie for dominance in the Asian trade. Between 1500 and 1600 the Portuguese had become major players in the Indian Ocean trading world, eliminating Venice as Europe's chief supplier of spices and other Asian luxury goods. The Portuguese dominated but did not fundamentally alter the age-old pattern of Indian Ocean trade, which involved merchants from many areas as more or less autonomous players. This situation changed radically with the intervention of the Dutch and then the English.

Formed in 1602, the Dutch East India Company had taken control of the Portuguese spice trade in the Indian Ocean, with the port of Batavia (Jakarta) in Java as its center of operations. Within a few decades the Dutch had expelled the Portuguese from Ceylon and other East Indian islands. Unlike the Portuguese, the Dutch transformed the Indian Ocean trading world. Whereas East Indian states and peoples maintained independence under the Portuguese, who treated them as autonomous business partners, the Dutch established outright control and reduced them to dependents.

After these successes, the Dutch hold in Asia faltered in the eighteenth century because the company failed to diversify to meet changing consumption patterns. Spices continued to compose much of its shipping, despite their declining importance in the European diet, probably due to changing fashions in food and luxury consumption. Fierce competition from its main rival, the English East India Company (established 1600), also severely undercut Dutch trade.

Colonel James Tod of the East India Company Traveling by Elephant Through Rajasthan, India By the end of the eighteenth century agents of the British East India Company exercised growing military and political authority in India, in addition to monopolizing Britain's lucrative economic trade with the subcontinent. (Victoria & Albert Museum, London, UK/Bridgeman Images)

Britain initially struggled for a foothold in Asia. With the Dutch monopolizing maritime trade in the Indian Ocean, the British sought to establish trading relations with rulers on the subcontinent of India, the source of lucrative trade in silks, textiles, and pepper. Throughout the seventeenth century the English East India Company relied on trade concessions from the powerful Mughal emperor, who granted only piecemeal access to the subcontinent. Finally, in 1716 the Mughals conceded empire-wide trading privileges. As Mughal power waned, British East India Company agents increasingly intervened in local affairs and made alliances or waged war against Indian princes.

Britain's great rival for influence in India was France. During the War of the Austrian Succession, British and French forces in India supported opposing rulers in local power struggles. In 1757 East India Company forces under Robert Clive conquered the rich northeastern province of Bengal at the Battle of Plassey. French-English rivalry was finally resolved by the Treaty of Paris, which granted all of France's possessions in India to the British with the exception of Pondicherry, an Indian Ocean port city. With the elimination of their rival, British ascendancy in India accelerated. In 1765 the Mughal ruler granted the East India Company *diwani*, the right to civil administration and tax collection, in Bengal and neighboring provinces.

By the early nineteenth century the company had overcome vigorous Indian resistance to gain economic and political dominance of much of the subcontinent; direct administration by the British government replaced East India Company rule after a large-scale rebellion in 1857.

The late eighteenth century also witnessed the beginning of British settlement of the continent of Australia. The continent was first sighted by Europeans in the early seventeenth century, and thereafter parts of the coast were charted by European ships. Captain James Cook, who charted much of the Pacific Ocean for the first time, claimed the east coast of Australia for England in 1770, naming it New South Wales. The first colony was established there in the late 1780s, relying on the labor of convicted prisoners forcibly transported from Britain. Settlement of the western portion of the continent followed in the 1790s. The first colonies struggled for survival and, after an initial period of friendly relations, soon aroused the hostility and resistance of Aboriginal peoples. Cook himself was killed by islanders in Hawaii in 1779.

The rising economic and political power of Europeans in this period drew on the connections they established between the Asian and Atlantic trade worlds. An outstanding example is the trade in cowrie shells. These seashells, originating in the Maldive Islands in the Indian Ocean, were used as a form of currency in West Africa. European traders obtained them in Asia and packed them alongside porcelains, spices, and silks for the journey home. The cowries were then brought from European ports to the West African coast to be traded for slaves. Indian textiles were also prized in Africa and played a similar role in exchange. Thus the trade of the Atlantic was inseparable from Asian commerce, and Europeans were increasingly found dominating commerce in both worlds.

NOTES

1. B. H. Slicher van Bath, *The Agrarian History of Western Europe, A.D. 500–1850* (New York: St. Martin's Press, 1963), p. 240.
2. Quoted in Paul Mantoux, *The Industrial Revolution in the Eighteenth Century: An Outline of the Beginnings of the Modern Factory System* (1961; Abingdon, U.K.: Routledge, 2005), p. 175.
3. Thomas Salmon, *Modern History: Or the Present State of All Nations* (London, 1730), p. 406.
4. Quoted in I. Pinchbeck, *Women Workers and the Industrial Revolution, 1750–1850* (1930; Abingdon, U.K.: Frank Cass, 1977), p. 113.
5. Richard J. Soderlund, "'Intended as a Terror to the Idle and Profligate': Embezzlement and the Origins of Policing in the Yorkshire Worsted Industry, c. 1750–1777," *Journal of Social History* 31 (Spring 1998): 658.
6. Jan de Vries, *The Industrious Revolution: Consumer Behavior and the Household Economy, 1650 to the Present* (Cambridge: Cambridge University Press, 2008).
7. Jan de Vries, "The Industrial Revolution and the Industrious Revolution," *The Journal of Economic History* 54, no. 2 (June 1994): 249–270; discusses the industrious revolution of the second half of the twentieth century.
8. R. Heilbroner, *The Essential Adam Smith* (New York: W. W. Norton, 1986), p. 196.
9. S. Pollard and C. Holmes, eds., *Documents of European Economic History*, vol. 1: *The Process of Industrialization, 1750–1870* (New York: St. Martin's Press, 1968), p. 281.
10. Laurent Dubois and John D. Garrigus, *Slave Revolution in the Caribbean, 1789–1904* (New York: Palgrave, 2006), p. 8.
11. Figures obtained from Voyages: The Trans-Atlantic Slave Trade Database, http://www.slavevoyages.org/assessment/estimates (accessed January 17, 2016).

12. Quoted in Thomas Benjamin, *The Atlantic World: Europeans, Africans, Indians and Their Shared History, 1400–1900* (Cambridge: Cambridge University Press, 2009), p. 211.
13. Pierre Marie François Paget, *Travels Round the World in the Years 1767, 1768, 1769, 1770, 1771*, vol. 1 (London, 1793), p. 262.
14. Orlando Patterson, *Slavery and Social Death* (Cambridge, Mass.: Harvard University Press, 1982), p. 255.
15. Tamar Herzog, "Identities and Processes of Identification in the Atlantic World," in *The Oxford Handbook of the Atlantic World, 1450–1850*, ed. Nicholas Canny and Philip Morgan (Oxford: Oxford University Press, 2011), pp. 480–491.
16. Erik R. Seeman, "Jews in the Early Modern Atlantic: Crossing Boundaries, Keeping Faith," in *The Atlantic in Global History, 1500–2000*, ed. Jorge Cañizares-Esguerra and Erik R. Seeman (Upper Saddle River, N.J.: Pearson Prentice Hall, 2007), p. 43.

LOOKING BACK **LOOKING AHEAD**

By the turn of the eighteenth century, western Europe had begun to shake off the effects of a century of famine, disease, warfare, economic depression, and demographic stagnation. The eighteenth century witnessed a breakthrough in agricultural production that, along with improved infrastructure and the retreat of epidemic disease, contributed to a substantial increase in population. One crucial catalyst for agricultural innovation was the Scientific Revolution, which provided new tools of empirical observation and experimentation. The Enlightenment as well, with its emphasis on progress and public welfare, convinced government officials, scientists, and informed landowners to seek better solutions to old problems. By the end of the century, industry and trade had also attracted enlightened commentators who advocated free markets and less government control. Modern ideas of political economy thus constitute one more legacy of the Enlightenment, but—like the Enlightenment itself—they drew criticism from nineteenth- and twentieth-century thinkers.

As the era of European exploration and conquest gave way to colonial empire building, the eighteenth century witnessed increased consolidation of global markets and bitter competition among Europeans for the spoils of empire. From its slow inception in the mid-fifteenth century, the African slave trade reached appalling heights in the second half of the eighteenth century. The eighteenth-century Atlantic world thus tied the shores of Europe, the Americas, and Africa in a web of commercial and human exchange that also had strong ties with the Pacific and the Indian Oceans.

The new dynamics of the eighteenth century prepared the way for world-shaking changes. Population growth and rural industry began to undermine long-standing traditions of daily life in western Europe. The transformed families of the industrious revolution developed not only new habits of work, but also a new sense of confidence in their abilities. By the 1770s England was approaching an economic transformation fully as significant as the great political upheaval destined to develop shortly in neighboring France. In the same period, the first wave of resistance to European domination rose up in the colonies. The great revolutions of the late eighteenth century would change the world forever.

MAKE CONNECTIONS

Think about the larger developments and continuities within and across chapters.

1. How did agriculture, industry, and population affect each other in the eighteenth century? How and why did developments in one area affect the other areas?

2. Compare the economic and social situation of western Europe in the mid-eighteenth century with that of the seventeenth century (Chapter 15). What were the achievements of the eighteenth century, and what factors allowed for such progress to be made?

3. The eighteenth century was the period of the European Enlightenment, which celebrated tolerance and human liberty (Chapter 16). Paradoxically, it was also the era of a tremendous increase in slavery, which brought suffering and death to millions. How can you explain this paradox?

Chapter 17 Review

IDENTIFY KEY TERMS

Identify and explain the significance of each item below.

enclosure (p. 488)

proletarianization (p. 490)

cottage industry (p. 494)

putting-out system (p. 494)

industrious revolution (p. 498)

guild system (p. 498)

economic liberalism (p. 501)

Navigation Acts (p. 502)

Treaty of Paris (p. 505)

debt peonage (p. 506)

transatlantic slave trade (p. 506)

REVIEW THE MAIN IDEAS

Answer the section heading questions from the chapter.

1. Why did European agriculture grow between 1650 and 1800? (p. 486)

2. Why did the European population rise dramatically in the eighteenth century? (p. 491)

3. How and why did rural industry intensify in the eighteenth century? (p. 494)

4. What important changes occurred in economic thought and practice in the eighteenth century? (p. 498)

5. What role did colonial markets play in Europe's development? (p. 501)

CHRONOLOGY

1600–1850	• Growth in agriculture, pioneered by the Dutch Republic and England
1651–1663	• British Navigation Acts
1652–1674	• Anglo-Dutch wars
1700–1790	• Height of transatlantic slave trade; expansion of rural industry in Europe
1701–1763	• British and French mercantilist wars of empire
1720–1722	• Last outbreak of bubonic plague in Europe
1720–1789	• Growth of European population
1756–1763	• Seven Years' War
1760–1815	• Height of parliamentary enclosure in England
1763	• Treaty of Paris; France cedes its possessions in India and North America
1770	• James Cook claims the east coast of Australia for England
1776	• Adam Smith publishes *An Inquiry into the Nature and Causes of the Wealth of Nations*
1807	• British slave trade abolished

18

Life in the Era of Expansion

1650–1800

CHAPTER PREVIEW

- How did marriage and family life change in the eighteenth century?

- What was life like for children, and how did attitudes toward childhood evolve?

- How did increasing literacy and new patterns of consumption affect people's lives?

- What role did religion play in eighteenth-century society?

- How did the practice of medicine evolve in the eighteenth century?

THE DISCUSSION OF AGRICULTURE AND INDUSTRY in the last chapter showed the common people at work, straining to make ends meet within the larger context of population growth, economic expansion, and ferocious competition at home and overseas. This chapter shows how that world of work was embedded in a rich complex of family organization, community practices, everyday experiences, and collective attitudes. As with the economy, traditional habits of daily life changed considerably over the eighteenth century. Change was particularly dramatic in the growing cities of northwestern Europe, where traditional social controls were undermined by the anonymity and increased social interaction of the urban setting.

Historians have studied many aspects of popular life, including marriage patterns and family size, childhood and education, nutrition, health care, and religious worship. While common people left few written records, imaginative research has resulted in major findings and much

greater knowledge. It is now possible to follow the common people into their homes, workshops, churches, and taverns and to ask, "What were the everyday experiences and attitudes of ordinary people, and how did they change over the eighteenth century?"

How did marriage and family life change in the eighteenth century?

The family is an institution that has evolved and changed throughout history, assuming different forms in different times and places. The eighteenth century was an important moment of change in family life, as patterns of marriage shifted and individuals adapted and conformed to the new and changing realities of the family unit.

Late Marriage and Nuclear Families

The three-generation extended family was a rarity in western and central Europe. When young European couples married, they normally established their own households and lived apart from their parents, much like the nuclear families (a family group consisting of parents and their children with no other relatives) common in the United States today. If a three-generation household came into existence, it was usually because a widowed parent moved into the home of a married child.

Most people did not marry young in the seventeenth and eighteenth centuries. The average person married many years after reaching adulthood and many more after beginning to work. Studies of western Europe in the seventeenth and eighteenth centuries show that both men and women married for the first time at an average age of twenty-five to twenty-seven. Furthermore, 10 to 20 percent of men and women in western Europe never married at all. Matters were different in eastern Europe, where the multigeneration household was the norm, marriage occurred around age twenty, and permanent celibacy was much less common.

Why did young people in western Europe delay marriage? The main reason was that couples normally did not marry until they could start an independent household and support themselves and future children. Peasants often needed to wait until their father's death to inherit land and marry. In the towns, men and women worked to accumulate enough savings to start a small business and establish their own home.

Laws and tradition also discouraged early marriage. In some areas couples needed permission from the local lord or landowner in order to marry. Poor couples had particular difficulty securing the approval of local officials, who believed that freedom to marry for the lower classes would result in more landless paupers, more abandoned children, and more money for welfare. Village elders often agreed.

The custom of late marriage combined with the nuclear family household distinguished western European society from other areas of the world. Historians have argued that this late-marriage pattern was responsible for at least part of the economic advantage western Europeans acquired relative to other world regions. Late marriage joined a mature man and a mature woman — two adults who had already accumulated social and economic capital and could transmit self-reliance and skills to the next generation. The relative closeness in age between husband and wife favored a greater degree of gender equality than existed in areas where older men married much younger women.

Work Away from Home

Many young people worked within their families until they could start their own households. Boys plowed and wove; girls spun and tended the cows. In cities and towns, teenaged boys were apprenticed to learn a trade. If a boy were lucky and had connections, he might eventually be admitted to a guild and establish his economic independence. Many poor families could not afford apprenticeships for their sons. Without craft skills, these youths drifted from one tough job to another: wage laborer on a new road, carrier of water, or domestic servant.

Many adolescent girls also left their families to work. The range of opportunities open to them was more limited, however. Apprenticeship was sometimes available with mistresses in traditionally female occupations like seamstress, linen draper, or midwife. With the growth in production of finished goods for the emerging consumer economy during the eighteenth century, demand rose for skilled female labor, and a wider range of jobs became available for women. Nevertheless, women still continued to earn much lower wages for their work than men.

Service in another family's household was by far the most common job for girls, and even middle-class families often sent their daughters into service. The legions of young servant girls worked hard but had little independence. Constantly under the eye of her mistress, the servant girl had many tasks—cleaning, shopping, cooking, and child care. Often the work was endless, for there were few laws to limit exploitation. Court records are full of servant girls' complaints of physical mistreatment by their mistresses. There were many like the fifteen-year-old English girl in the early eighteenth century who told the judge that her mistress had not only called her "very opprobrious names, as Bitch, Whore and the like," but also "beat her without provocation and beyond measure."[1]

In theory, domestic service offered a girl security in a new family. But in practice, she was often the easy prey of a lecherous master or his sons or friends. If the girl became pregnant, she could be thrown out in disgrace and her family might refuse to take her back. Forced to make their own way, these girls had no choice but to turn to a harsh life of prostitution and petty thievery. "What are we?" exclaimed a bitter Parisian prostitute. "Most of us are unfortunate women, without origins, without education, servants and maids for the most part."[2] Adult women who remained in service, at least in large towns and cities, could gain more autonomy and distressed their employers by changing jobs frequently.

Contraception and Community Controls

Ten years between puberty and marriage was a long time for sexually mature young people to wait. Many unmarried couples satisfied their sexual desires with fondling and petting. Others went further and engaged in premarital intercourse. Those who did so risked pregnancy and the stigma of illegitimate birth.

Sexually active men and women sought to control when and with whom they had children. They drew on a variety of methods, some more effective than others. Washing after intercourse, wearing amulets, and burying the afterbirth from a previous birth were among the folk methods that we now know were useless in preventing pregnancy. Condoms, made from sheep intestines, became available in the mid-seventeenth century, replacing uncomfortable earlier versions made from cloth. They were expensive and mainly used by aristocratic libertines and prostitutes. Apart from abstinence, the most common and somewhat effective method of contraception was coitus interruptus—withdrawal by the male before ejaculation. This method appears to have been widespread in Europe by the end of the eighteenth century.

Women also sought to end unwanted pregnancies through a variety of means, including physical exertion and bleedings, magical spells, and consumption of herbs known to induce miscarriage. Using such methods to produce early-term miscarriage was often considered legitimate across Protestant, Catholic, and Muslim regions as a means to restore the "normal" flow of menstrual blood; however, they were often unsuccessful. The term *abortion* usually only applied to the termination of pregnancies past the fourth month, when the fetus was developed enough to move perceptibly in the womb. Such abortions were capital crimes in most parts of Europe.

Despite the lack of reliable contraception, premarital sex did not result in a large proportion of illegitimate births in most parts of Europe until 1750. Where collective control over sexual behavior among youths failed, community pressure to marry often prevailed. A comparison of marriage and birth dates of seven representative parishes in seventeenth-century England shows that around 20 percent of children

Young Serving Girl Increased migration to urban areas in the eighteenth century contributed to a loosening of traditional morals and soaring illegitimacy rates. Young women who worked as servants or shopgirls could not be supervised as closely as those who lived at home. The themes of seduction, fallen virtue, and familial conflict were popular in eighteenth-century art. (*The Beautiful Kitchen Maid*, by François Boucher [1703–1770], [oil on canvas]/Musée Cognacq-Jay, Paris, France/Bridgeman Images)

must have been conceived before the couple was married, but only 2 percent were born out of wedlock.[3] Figures for the French village of Auffay in Normandy in the eighteenth century were remarkably similar.

The combination of low rates of illegitimate birth with large numbers of pregnant brides reflects the powerful **community controls** of the traditional village, particularly the open-field village, with its pattern of cooperation and common action. An unwed mother with an illegitimate child was viewed as a grave threat to the economic, social, and moral stability of the community. Irate parents, anxious village elders, indignant priests, and stern landlords all combined to pressure young people who wavered about marriage in the face of unexpected pregnancies. In the countryside these controls meant that premarital sex was not entered into lightly and that it was generally limited to those contemplating marriage.

The concerns of the village and the family weighed heavily on couples' lives after marriage as well. Whereas uninvolved individuals today often try to stay out of the domestic disputes of their neighbors, peasant communities gave such affairs loud and unfavorable publicity either at the time or during the carnival season (see "Leisure and Recreation" later in this chapter). Relying on degrading public rituals, known as **charivari**, the young men of the village would typically gang up on their victim and force him or her to sit astride a donkey facing backward and holding up the donkey's tail. They would parade the overly brutal spouse-beater or the adulterous couple around the village, loudly proclaiming the offenders' misdeeds. The donkey ride and other colorful humiliations, ranging from rotten vegetables splattered on the doorstep to obscene and insulting midnight serenades, were common punishments throughout much of Europe. They epitomized the community's effort to police personal behavior and maintain moral standards.

New Patterns of Marriage and Illegitimacy

In the second half of the eighteenth century, long-standing patterns of marriage and illegitimacy shifted dramatically. One important change was an increased ability for young people to make decisions about marriage for themselves, rather than following the interests of their families. This change occurred because social and economic transformations made it harder for families and communities to supervise their behavior. More youths in the countryside worked for their own wages as agricultural laborers, rather than on a family farm, and their economic autonomy translated into increased freedom of action. Moreover, many youths joined the flood of migrants to the cities, either with their families or in search of work on their own. Urban life provided young people with more social contacts and less social control.

A less positive outcome of loosening social control was an **illegitimacy explosion**, concentrated in England, France, Germany, and Scandinavia. In Frankfurt, Germany, for example, births out of wedlock rose steadily from about 2 percent of all births in the early eighteenth century to a peak of about 25 percent around 1850. In Bordeaux, France, 36 percent of all babies were being born out of wedlock by 1840. Given the meager economic opportunities open to single mothers, their circumstances were desperate.

Why did the number of illegitimate births skyrocket? One reason was a rise in sexual activity among young people. The loosened social controls that gave young people more choice in marriage also provided them with more opportunities to yield to sexual desire. As in previous generations, many of the young couples who engaged in sexual activity intended to marry. In one medium-size French city in 1787–1788, the great majority of unwed mothers stated that sexual intimacy had followed promises of marriage. Their sisters in rural Normandy frequently reported that they had been "seduced in anticipation of marriage."[4]

The problem for young women who became pregnant was that fewer men followed through on their promises. The second half of the eighteenth century witnessed sharply rising prices for food, homes, and other necessities of life. Many soldiers, day laborers, and male servants were no doubt sincere in their proposals, but their lives were insecure, and they hesitated to take on the burden of a wife and child.

The romantic yet practical dreams and aspirations of young people were thus frustrated by low wages, inequality, and changing economic and social conditions. Old patterns of marriage and family were breaking down. Only in the late nineteenth century would more stable patterns reappear.

Sex on the Margins of Society

Not all sex acts took place between men and women hopeful of marriage. Prostitution offered both single and married men an outlet for sexual desire. After a long period of relative tolerance, prostitutes encountered increasingly harsh and repressive laws in the sixteenth and early seventeenth centuries as officials across Europe closed licensed brothels and declared prostitution illegal.

Despite this repression, prostitution continued to flourish in the eighteenth century. Most prostitutes were working women who turned to the sex trade when confronted with paltry wages and unemployment. Such women did not become social pariahs, but retained ties with the communities of laboring poor to which they belonged. If caught by the police, however, they were liable to imprisonment or banishment. Venereal disease was also a constant threat. Prostitutes were subjected to humiliating police examinations for disease, although medical treatments were at best rudimentary. Farther up the social scale were courtesans whose wealthy protectors provided apartments, servants, fashionable clothing, and cash allowances. After a brilliant but brief career, an aging courtesan faced with the loss of her wealthy client could descend once more to streetwalking.

Relations between individuals of the same sex attracted even more condemnation than did prostitution, since they defied the Bible's limitation of sex to the purposes of procreation. Male same-sex relations, described as "sodomy" or "buggery," were prohibited by law in most European states, under pain of death. Such laws, however, were enforced unevenly, most strictly in Spain and far less so in the Scandinavian countries and Russia.[5]

Protected by their status, nobles and royals sometimes openly indulged their same-sex desires, which were accepted as long as they married and produced legitimate heirs. It was common knowledge that King James I, sponsor of the first translation of the Bible into English, had male lovers, but these relationships were tolerated because they did not prevent him from having seven children with his wife, Anne of Denmark. The duchess of Orléans, sister-in-law of French king Louis XIV, complained in her letters about her husband's male lovers, one of whom was appointed tutor to the couple's son. She also repeated rumors about the homosexual inclinations of King William of England, hero of the Glorious Revolution (see "The Restoration of the English Monarchy" in Chapter 15).

In the late seventeenth century male homosexual subcultures began to emerge in Paris, Amsterdam, and London, with their own slang, meeting places, and styles of dress. Unlike men who took both wives and male lovers, these groups included men exclusively oriented toward other men. In London, they called themselves "mollies," a term originally applied to prostitutes, and some began to wear women's clothing and adopt effeminate behavior. A new self-identity began to form among homosexual men: a belief that their same-sex desire made them fundamentally different from other men. As a character in one late-eighteenth-century fiction declared, he was in "a category of men different from the other, a class Nature has created in order to diminish or minimize propagation."[6]

Same-sex relations existed among women as well, but they attracted less attention and condemnation than those among men. Some women were prosecuted for "unnatural" relations; others attempted to escape the narrow confines imposed on them by dressing as men. Cross-dressing women occasionally snuck into the armed forces, such as Ulrika Elenora Stålhammar, who served as a man in the Swedish army for thirteen years and married a woman. After confessing her transgressions, she was sentenced to a lenient one-month imprisonment.[7] The beginnings of a distinctive lesbian subculture appeared in London and other large cities at the end of the eighteenth century.

What was life like for children, and how did attitudes toward childhood evolve?

On the whole, western European women married late but then began bearing children rapidly. If a woman married before she was thirty, and if both she and her husband lived to fifty, she would most likely give birth to six or more children. Infant mortality varied across Europe, but it was very high by modern standards, and many women died in childbirth due to limited medical knowledge and technology.

For those children who did survive, Enlightenment ideals that emerged in the latter half of the century stressed the importance of parental nurturing. The new worldview also led to an increase in elementary schools throughout Europe. Despite the efforts of enlightened absolutists and religious institutions, however, formal education reached only a minority of ordinary children.

Child Care and Nursing

Newborns entered a dangerous world. They were vulnerable to infectious diseases, and many babies died of dehydration brought about by bad bouts of ordinary diarrhea. Of those who survived infancy, many more died in childhood. Even in a rich family, little could be done for an ailing child. Childbirth was also dangerous. Women who bore six children faced a cumulative risk of dying in childbirth of 5 to 10 percent, a thousand times as great as the risk in Europe today.[8] They died from blood loss and shock during delivery and from infections caused by unsanitary conditions. The joy of pregnancy was thus shadowed by fear of loss of the mother or her child.

In the countryside, women of the lower classes generally breast-fed their infants for two years or more. Although not a foolproof means of birth control, breast-feeding decreases the likelihood of pregnancy by delaying the resumption of ovulation. By nursing their babies, women spaced their children two or three years apart. Nursing also saved lives: breast-fed infants received precious immunity-producing substances and were more likely to survive than those who were fed other food.

Areas where babies were not breast-fed — typically in northern France, Scandinavia, and central and eastern Europe — experienced the highest infant mortality rates. In these areas, many people believed that breast-feeding was bad for a woman's health or appearance. Across Europe, women of the aristocracy and upper middle class seldom nursed their own children because they found breast-feeding undignified and it interfered with their social responsibilities. The alternatives to breast-feeding were feeding babies cow's or goat's milk or paying lactating women to provide their milk.

Wealthy women hired live-in wet nurses to suckle their babies (which usually meant sending the nurse's own infant away to be nursed by someone else). Working women in the cities also relied on the cheaper services of wet nurses in the countryside because they needed to earn a living. In the eighteenth century rural **wet-nursing** was a widespread business, conducted within the framework of the putting-out system. The traffic was in babies rather than in yarn or cloth, and two or three years often passed before the wet-nurse worker in the countryside finished her task.

Wet-nursing was particularly common in northern France. Toward the end of the century, roughly twenty thousand babies were born in Paris each year. Almost half were placed with rural wet nurses through a government-supervised distribution network; 20 to 25 percent were placed in the homes of Parisian nurses personally selected by their parents; and another 20 to 25 percent were abandoned to foundling hospitals, which would send them to wet nurses in the countryside. The remainder (perhaps 10 percent) were nursed at home by their mothers or live-in nurses.[9]

Reliance on wet nurses raised levels of infant mortality because of the dangers of travel, the lack of supervision of conditions in wet nurses' homes, and the need to share milk between a wet nurse's own baby and the one or more babies she was hired to feed. A study of mortality rates in mid-eighteenth-century France shows that 25 percent of babies died before their first birthday, and another 30 percent before age ten.[10] In England, where more mothers nursed, only some 30 percent of children did not reach their tenth birthday.

Within each country and across Europe, tremendous regional variation existed. Mortality rates were higher in overcrowded and dirty cities; in low-lying, marshy regions; and during summer months when rural women were busy in agricultural work and had less time to tend to infants. The corollary of high infant mortality was high fertility. Women who did not breast-feed their babies or whose children died in infancy became pregnant more quickly and bore more children. Thus, on balance, the number of children who survived to adulthood tended to be the same across Europe, with higher births balancing the greater loss of life in areas that relied on wet-nursing.

In the second half of the eighteenth century, critics mounted a harsh attack against wet-nursing. Enlightenment thinkers proclaimed that wet-nursing was preventing European society from reaching its full potential. They were convinced, incorrectly, that the population was declining (in fact it was rising, but they lacked accurate population data) and blamed this decline on women's failure to nurture their children properly. Some also railed against practices of contraception and masturbation, which they believed were robbing their nations of potential children. Despite these complaints, many women continued to rely on wet nurses for convenience or from necessity.

Foundlings and Infanticide

The young woman who could not provide for an unwanted child had few choices, especially if she had no prospect of marriage. In desperation, some women, particularly in the countryside, hid unwanted pregnancies, delivered in secret, and smothered their newborn infants. The punishment for infanticide was death. Yet across Europe, convictions for infanticide dropped in the second half of the eighteenth century, perhaps due to growing social awareness of the crushing pressures caused by unwanted pregnancies.

Another sign of this awareness was the spread of homes for abandoned children. Homes for abandoned children first took hold in Italy, Spain, and Portugal in the sixteenth century, spreading to France in 1670 and the rest of Europe thereafter. By the end of the eighteenth century, European foundling hospitals were admitting annually about one hundred thousand abandoned children, nearly all of them infants. One-third of all babies born in Paris in the 1770s were immediately abandoned to foundling homes. There appears to have been no differentiation by sex in the numbers of children sent to foundling hospitals. Many of the children were the offspring of single women, the result of the illegitimacy explosion of the second half of the eighteenth century. But fully one-third of all the foundlings were abandoned by married couples too poor to feed another child.[11]

At their best, foundling homes were a good example of Christian charity and social concern in an age of great poverty and inequality. They provided the rudiments of an education and sought to place the children in apprenticeship or domestic service once they reached an appropriate age. Yet the foundling system was no panacea. Even in the best of these institutions, 50 percent of the babies normally died within a year. In the worst, fully 90 percent did not survive, falling victim to infectious disease, malnutrition, and neglect.[12] Because raising foundling children was a significant financial burden, many small towns and even some major cities sent babies to hospitals in large cities, like Paris and London, which had the policy of accepting all children.

Attitudes Toward Children

Parents were well aware of the dangers of infancy and childhood. The great eighteenth-century English historian Edward Gibbon (1737–1794) wrote, with some exaggeration, that "the death of a new born child before that of its parents may seem unnatural but it is a strictly probable event, since of any given number the greater part are extinguished before the ninth year, before they possess the faculties of the mind and the body." Gibbon's father named all his boys Edward after himself, hoping that at least one of them would survive to carry his name. His prudence was not misplaced. Edward the future historian and eldest survived. Five brothers and sisters who followed him all died in infancy.

Emotional prudence could lead to emotional distance. The French essayist Michel de Montaigne, who lost five of his six daughters in infancy, wrote, "I cannot abide that passion for caressing new-born children, which have neither mental activities nor recognizable bodily shape by which to make themselves loveable and I have never willingly suffered them to be fed in my presence."[13] In contrast to this harsh picture, however, historians have drawn ample evidence from diaries, letters, and family portraits that parents of all social classes cherished their children and experienced great emotional distress when they died. This was equally true of mothers and fathers and of attitudes toward sons and daughters. The English poet Ben Jonson wrote movingly in "On My First Son" of the death of his six-year-old son Benjamin, which occurred during a London plague outbreak in 1603:

> Farewell, thou child of my right hand, and joy;
> My sin was too much hope of thee, loved boy.
> Seven years thou wert lent to me, and I thee pay,
> Exacted by thy fate, on the just day.

Parental love was often expressed through harsh discipline. The axiom "Spare the rod and spoil the child" seems to have been coined in the mid-seventeenth century. Susannah Wesley (1669–1742), mother of John Wesley, the founder of Methodism (see "Protestant Revival" later in this chapter), agreed. According to her, the first task of a parent toward her children was "to conquer the will, and bring them to an obedient temper." She reported that her babies were "taught to fear the rod, and to cry softly; by which means they escaped the abundance of correction they might otherwise have had, and that most odious noise of the crying of children was rarely heard in the house."[14] They were beaten for lying, stealing, disobeying, and quarreling, and forbidden from playing with other children. Susannah's methods of disciplining her children were probably extreme even in her own day, but they do reflect a broad consensus that children were born with an innately sinful will that parents must overcome.

The Enlightenment produced an enthusiastic new discourse about childhood and child rearing. Starting around 1760 critics called for greater tenderness toward children and proposed imaginative new teaching methods. In addition to supporting foundling homes and urging women to nurse their babies, these new voices ridiculed the practices of swaddling babies and dressing children in miniature versions of adult clothing. They called instead for children to wear comfortable garments allowing freedom of movement. Rather than emphasizing original sin, these enlightened voices celebrated the child as an innocent product of nature. Since they viewed nature as inherently positive, Enlightenment educators advocated safeguarding and developing children's innate qualities rather than thwarting and suppressing them. Accordingly, they believed the best hopes for a new society lay in a radical reform of child-rearing techniques.

One of the century's most influential works on child rearing was Jean-Jacques Rousseau's *Emile, or On Education* (1762), inspired in part, Rousseau claimed, by remorse for the abandonment of his own children. In *Emile*, Rousseau argued that boys' education should include plenty of fresh air and exercise and that boys should be taught practical craft skills in addition to book learning. Reacting to what he perceived as the vanity and frivolity of upper-class Parisian women, Rousseau insisted that girls' education focus on their future domestic responsibilities. For Rousseau, women's "nature" destined them solely for a life of marriage and child rearing. The sentimental ideas of Rousseau and other reformers were enthusiastically adopted by elite women, some of whom began to nurse their own children.

The Spread of Elementary Schools

The availability of education outside the home gradually increased over the early modern period. The wealthy led the way in the sixteenth century with special colleges, often run by Jesuits in Catholic areas. Schools charged specifically with educating children of the common people began to appear in the second half of the seventeenth century. They taught six- to twelve-year-old children basic literacy, religion, and perhaps some arithmetic for the boys and needlework for the girls. The number of such schools expanded in the eighteenth century, although they were never sufficient to educate the majority of the population.

Religion played an important role in the spread of education. From the middle of the seventeenth century, Presbyterian Scotland was convinced that the path to salvation lay in careful study of the Scriptures, and it established an effective network of parish schools for rich and poor alike. The first proponents of universal education, in Prussia, were inspired by the Protestant idea that every believer should be able to read the Bible and by the new idea of raising a population capable of effectively serving the state. As early as 1717 Prussia made attendance at elementary schools compulsory for boys and girls in areas where schools existed.[15] More Protestant German states followed suit in the eighteenth century.

Catholic states pursued their own programs of popular education. In the 1660s France began setting up charity schools to teach poor children their catechism and prayers as well as reading and writing. These were run by parish priests or by new educational teaching orders. One of the most famous orders was Jean-Baptiste de la Salle's Brothers of the Christian Schools. Founded in 1684, the schools had thirty-five thousand students across France by the 1780s. Enthusiasm for popular education was even greater in the Habsburg empire. Inspired by the expansion of schools in rival Protestant German states, Maria Theresa issued her own compulsory education edict in 1774, imposing five hours of school, five days a week, for all children aged six to twelve.[16] Across Europe some elementary education was becoming a reality, and schools became increasingly significant in the life of the child.

How did increasing literacy and new patterns of consumption affect people's lives?

Because of the new efforts in education, basic literacy expanded among the popular classes, whose reading habits centered primarily on religious material, but who also began to incorporate more practical and entertaining literature. In addition to reading, people of all classes enjoyed a range of leisure activities, including storytelling, fairs, festivals, and sports.

One of the most important developments in European society in the eighteenth century was the emergence of a fledgling consumer culture. Much of the expansion took place among the upper and upper-middle classes, but a boom in cheap reproductions of luxury items also opened doors for people of modest means. From food to ribbons and from coal stoves to umbrellas, the material worlds of city dwellers grew richer and more diverse. This "consumer revolution," as it has been called, created new expectations for comfort, hygiene, and self-expression, thus dramatically changing European daily life in the eighteenth century.

Popular Literature

The surge in childhood education in the eighteenth century led to a remarkable growth in literacy between 1600 and 1800. Whereas in 1600 only one male in six was barely literate in France and Scotland, and one in four in England, by 1800 almost nine out of ten Scottish males, two out of three French males (Map 18.1), and more than half of English males were literate. In all three countries, most of the gains occurred in the eighteenth century. Women were also increasingly literate, although they lagged behind men.

The growth in literacy promoted growth in reading, and historians have carefully examined what the common people read. While the Bible remained the overwhelming favorite, especially in Protestant countries, short pamphlets known as chapbooks were the staple of popular literature. Printed on the cheapest paper, many chapbooks featured Bible stories, prayers, and the lives of saints and exemplary Christians. This pious literature gave believers moral teachings and a faith that helped them endure their daily struggles.

Entertaining, often humorous stories formed a second element of popular literature. Fairy tales, romances, true crime stories, and fantastic adventures were some of the delights that filled the peddler's pack as he approached a village. These tales presented a world of danger and magic, of supernatural powers, fairy godmothers, and evil trolls that provided a temporary escape from harsh everyday reality. They also contained nuggets of ancient folk wisdom, counseling prudence in a world full of danger and injustice, where wolves dress like grandmothers and eat Little Red Riding Hoods.

Finally, some popular literature was highly practical, dealing with rural crafts, household repairs, useful plants, and similar matters. Much

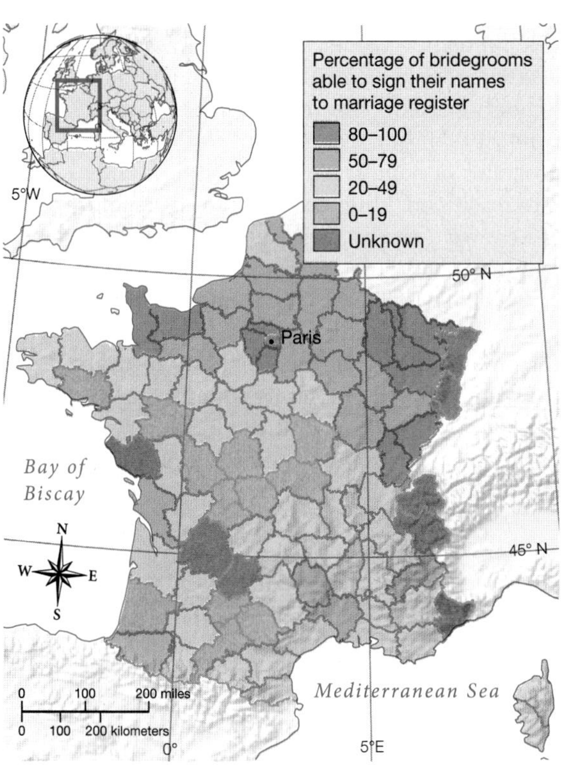
Percentage of bridegrooms able to sign their names to marriage register
80–100
50–79
20–49
0–19
Unknown
5°W
50° N
Paris
Bay of Biscay
N
W
E
S
45° N
0
100
200 miles
0
100
200 kilometers
0°
Mediterranean Sea
5°E

MAP 18.1 Literacy in France, ca. 1789
Literacy rates increased but still varied widely between and within states in eighteenth-century Europe.

lore was stored in almanacs, where calendars listing secular, religious, and astrological events were mixed with agricultural schedules, arcane facts, and jokes. The almanac was highly appreciated even by many in the comfortable classes. In this way, elites shared some elements of a common culture with the masses.

While it is safe to say that the vast majority of ordinary people did not read the great works of the Enlightenment, they were not cut off entirely from the new ideas. Urban working people were exposed to Enlightenment thought through the news and gossip that spread across city streets, workshops, markets, and taverns. They also had access to cheap pamphlets that helped translate Enlightenment critiques into ordinary language. Servants, who usually came from rural areas and traveled home periodically, were well situated to transmit ideas from educated employers to the village.

Leisure and Recreation

Despite the spread of literacy, the culture of the village remained largely oral rather than written. In the cold, dark winter months, peasant families gathered around the fireplace to sing, tell stories, do craftwork, and keep warm. In some parts of Europe, women would gather together in someone's cottage to chat, sew, spin, and laugh. Sometimes a few young men would be invited so that the daughters (and mothers) could size up potential suitors in a supervised atmosphere. A favorite recreation of men was drinking and talking with buddies in public places, and it was a sorry village that had no tavern. In addition to old favorites such as beer and wine, the common people turned with gusto to cheap and potent hard liquor, which fell in price because of improved techniques for distilling grain in the eighteenth century.

Towns and cities offered a wider range of amusements, including public parks, theaters, and lending libraries. Urban fairs featured prepared foods, acrobats, and conjuring acts. Leisure activities were another form of consumption marked by growing commercialization. For example, commercial, profit-making spectator sports emerged in this period, including horse races, boxing matches, and bullfights. Modern sports heroes, such as brain-bashing heavyweight champions and haughty bullfighting matadors, made their appearance on the historical scene.

Blood sports, such as bullbaiting and cockfighting, also remained popular with the masses. In bullbaiting, the bull, usually staked on a chain in the courtyard of an inn, was attacked by ferocious dogs for the amusement of the innkeeper's clients. Eventually the maimed and tortured animal was slaughtered by a butcher and sold as meat. In cockfighting, two roosters, carefully trained by their owners and armed with razor-sharp steel spurs, slashed and clawed each other in a small ring until the victor won — and the loser died. An added attraction of cockfighting was that the screaming spectators could bet on the lightning-fast combat.

Popular recreation merged with religious celebration in a variety of festivals and processions throughout the year. The most striking display of these religiously inspired events was **carnival**, a time of reveling and excess in Catholic Europe, especially in Mediterranean countries. Carnival preceded Lent — the forty days of fasting and penitence before Easter — and for a few exceptional days in February or March, a wild release of drinking, masquerading, and dancing reigned. Moreover, a combination of plays, processions, and raucous spectacles turned the established order upside down. Peasants dressed as nobles and men as women, and rich masters

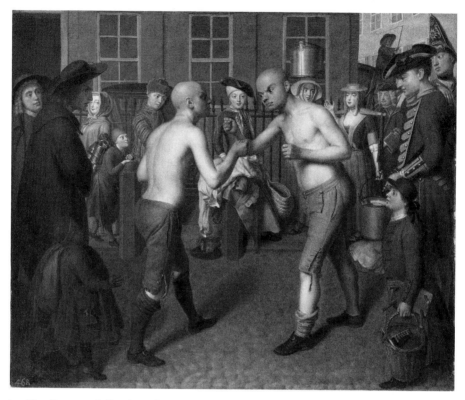

The Commercialization of Sports Sports events became popular commercial spectacles during the eighteenth century. In this early-eighteenth-century painting, two men spar in a boxing match staged in London for the entertainment of the gathered crowd. (bpk Bildagentur/ Gemaeldegalerie Alte Meiser, Museumslandschaft Hessen Kassel, Germany/Art Resource, NY)

waited on their servants at the table. This annual holiday gave people a much-appreciated chance to release their pent-up frustrations and aggressions before life returned to the usual pattern of hierarchy and hard work.

The rowdy pastimes of the populace attracted criticism from clerical and lay elites in the second half of the eighteenth century. In 1772 the Spanish Crown banned dragons and giants from the Corpus Christi parade, and the vibrant carnival of Venice was outlawed under Napoleon's rule in 1797. In the same period English newspapers publicly denounced boxing, gambling, blood sports, and other uncouth activities; one described bullbaiting in 1791 as "a disgrace to a civilized people."[17] However, historians have tended to overstate claims for a "culture war" between elites and the populace in the eighteenth century. Certainly, many wealthy and educated Europeans continued to enjoy the folktales of the chapbooks and they shared the love of gambling, theater, and sport. Moreover, both peasants and patricians—even most enlightened thinkers—shared a deep religiosity. In turn, as we have seen, common people were by no means cut off from the new currents of thought. Thus cultural elements continued to be shared across social divides.

New Foods and Appetites

At the beginning of the eighteenth century, ordinary men and women depended on grain as fully as they had in the past. Bread was quite literally the staff of life. Peasants in the Beauvais region of France ate two pounds of bread a day, washing it down with water, wine, or beer. Their dark bread was made from roughly ground wheat and rye—the standard flour of the common people. Even peasants normally needed to buy some grain for food, and, in full accord with landless laborers and urban workers, they believed in the moral economy and the **just price**. That is, they believed that prices should be "fair," protecting both consumers and producers, and that just prices should be imposed by government decree if necessary. When prices rose above this level, they often took action in the form of bread riots.

The rural poor also ate a quantity of vegetables. Peas and beans were probably the most common. Grown as field crops in much of Europe since the Middle Ages, they were eaten fresh in late spring and summer. Dried, they became the basic ingredients in the soups and stews of the long winter months. In most regions other vegetables appeared on the tables of the poor in season, primarily cabbages, carrots, and wild greens. Fruit was mostly limited to the summer months. Too precious to drink, milk was used to make cheese and butter, which peasants sold in the market to earn cash for taxes and land rents.

The common people of Europe ate less meat in 1700 than in 1500 because their general standard of living had declined and meat was more expensive. Moreover, harsh laws in most European countries reserved the right to hunt and eat game, such as rabbits, deer, and partridges, to nobles and large landowners. Few laws were more bitterly resented—or more frequently broken—by ordinary people than those governing hunting.

The diet of small traders and artisans—the people of the towns and cities—was less monotonous than that of the peasantry. Bustling markets provided a substantial variety of meats, vegetables, and fruits, although bread and beans still formed the bulk of such families' diets. Not surprisingly, the diet of the rich was quite different from that of the poor. The upper classes were rapacious carnivores, and a truly elegant dinner consisted of an abundance of rich meat and fish dishes laced with piquant sauces and complemented with sweets, cheeses, and wine in great quantities. During such dinners, it was common to spend five or more hours at table, eating and drinking and enjoying the witty banter of polite society.

Patterns of food consumption changed markedly as the century progressed. Because of a growth of market-oriented gardening, a greater variety of vegetables appeared in towns and cities. This was particularly the case in the Low Countries and England, which pioneered new methods of farming. Introduced into Europe from the Americas—along with corn, squash, tomatoes, and many other useful plants—the humble potato provided an excellent new food source. Containing a good supply of carbohydrates, calories, and vitamins A and C, the potato offset the lack of vitamins in the poor person's winter and early-spring diet, and it provided a much higher caloric yield than grain for a given piece of land. After initial resistance, the potato became an important dietary supplement in much of Europe by the end of the century.

The most remarkable dietary change in the eighteenth century was in the consumption of commodities imported from abroad. Originally expensive and rare

Café Society Italian merchants introduced coffee to Europe around 1600, and the first European coffee shop opened in Venice in 1645, soon followed by ones in Oxford, England, in 1650, London in 1652, and Paris in 1672. Open to all social classes, they provided a new public space for urban Europeans to learn about and debate the issues of the day. Within a few years, each political party, philosophical sect, scientific society, and literary circle had its own coffeehouse. (Heritage Images/ London Metropolitan Archives [City of London]/ akg-images)

luxury items, goods like tea, sugar, coffee, chocolate, and tobacco became staples for people of all social classes. With the exception of tea — which originated in China — most of the new consumables were produced in European colonies in the Americas. In many cases, the labor of enslaved peoples enabled the expansion in production and drop in prices that allowed such items to spread to the masses.

Part of the motivation for consuming colonial products was a desire to emulate the luxurious lifestyles of the elite that people witnessed as domestic servants and in public spaces. In addition, the quickened pace of work in the eighteenth century created new needs for stimulants among working people. Whereas the gentry took tea as a leisurely and genteel ritual, the lower classes drank tea or coffee at work to fight monotony and fatigue. With the widespread adoption of these products (which turned out to be mildly to extremely addictive), working people in Europe became increasingly dependent on faraway colonial economies and enslaved labor. Their understanding of daily necessities and how to procure those necessities shifted definitively, linking them to global trade networks they could not comprehend or control.

Toward a Consumer Society

Along with foodstuffs, all manner of other goods increased in variety and number in the eighteenth century. This proliferation led to a growth in consumption and new attitudes toward consumer goods so wide-ranging that some historians have referred to an eighteenth-century **consumer revolution**.[18] The result of this revolution was the birth of a new type of society in which people derived their self-identity as much from their consuming practices as from their working lives and place in the production process. As people gained the opportunity to pick and choose among a wide variety of consumer goods, new notions of individuality and self-expression developed. A shopgirl could stand out from her peers by her choice of a striped jacket, a colored parasol, or simply a new ribbon for her hair. The full emergence of a consumer society did not take place until much later, but its roots lie in the eighteenth century.

Increased demand for consumer goods was not merely an innate response to increased supply. Eighteenth-century merchants cleverly pioneered new techniques to incite demand: they initiated marketing campaigns, opened fancy boutiques with large windows, and advertised the patronage of royal princes and princesses. By diversifying their product lines and greatly accelerating the turnover of styles, they seized the reins of fashion from the courtiers who had earlier controlled it. Instead of setting new styles, duchesses and marquises now bowed to the dictates of fashion merchants. Fashion also extended beyond court circles to influence many more items and social groups.

Clothing was one of the chief indicators of the growth of consumerism. Shrewd entrepreneurs made fashionable clothing seem more desirable, while legions of women entering the textile and needle trades made it ever cheaper. As a result, eighteenth-century western Europe witnessed a dramatic rise in the consumption of clothing, particularly in large cities. Colonial economies again played an important role in lowering the cost of materials, such as cotton cloth and vegetable dyes, largely due to the unpaid toil of enslaved Africans. Cheaper copies of elite styles made it possible for working people to aspire to follow fashion for the first time.

Elite onlookers were sometimes shocked by the sight of lower-class people in stylish outfits. In 1784 Mrs. Fanny Cradock described encountering her milkman during an evening stroll "dressed in a fashionable suit, with an embroidered waist-coat, silk knee-breeches and lace cuffs."[19] The spread of fashion challenged the traditional social order of Europe by blurring the boundaries between social groups and making it harder to distinguish between noble and commoner on the bustling city streets.

Mrs. Cradock's milkman notwithstanding, women took the lead in the spread of fashion. Parisian women significantly out-consumed men, acquiring larger and more expensive wardrobes than those of their husbands, brothers, and fathers. This was true across the social spectrum; in ribbons, shoes, gloves, and lace, European working women reaped in the consumer revolution what they had sown in the industrious revolution (see "The Industrious Revolution" in Chapter 17). There were also new gender distinctions in dress. Previously, noblemen had vied with noblewomen in the magnificence of their apparel; by the end of the eighteenth century men had renounced brilliant colors and voluptuous fabrics to don early versions of the plain dark suit that remains standard male formal wear in the West. This was one more aspect of the increasingly rigid boundaries drawn between appropriate male and female behavior.

Changes in outward appearances were reflected in inner spaces, as new attitudes about privacy, individualism, and intimate life also emerged. In 1700 the cramped home of a modest family consisted of a few rooms, each of which had multiple functions. The same room was used for sleeping, receiving friends, and working. In the eighteenth century rents rose sharply, making it impossible to gain more space, but families began attributing specific functions to specific rooms. They also began to partition space within the home to provide small niches in which individuals could seek privacy.

New levels of comfort and convenience accompanied this trend toward more individualized ways of life. In 1700 a meal might be served in a common dish, with each person dipping his or her spoon into the pot. By the end of the eighteenth century even humble households contained a much greater variety of cutlery and dishes, making it possible for each person to eat from his or her own plate. More books and prints, which also proliferated at lower prices, decorated the shelves and walls. Improvements in glassmaking provided more transparent glass, which allowed daylight to penetrate into gloomy rooms. Cold and smoky hearths were increasingly replaced by more efficient and cleaner coal stoves, which also eliminated the back-ache of cooking over an open fire. Rooms were warmer, better lit, more comfortable, and more personalized, and the spread of street lighting made it safer to travel in cities at night.

Standards of bodily and public hygiene also improved. Public bathhouses, popular across Europe in the Middle Ages, had gradually closed in the early modern period due to concerns over sexual promiscuity and infectious disease. Many Europeans came to fear that immersing the body in hot water would allow harmful elements to enter the skin. Carefully watched by his physician, Louis XIII of France took his first bath at age seven, while James I of England refused to wash more than his hands. Personal cleanliness consisted of wearing fresh linen and using perfume to mask odors, both expensive practices that bespoke wealth and social status. From the mid-eighteenth century on, enlightened doctors revised their views and began to urge more frequent bathing. Spa towns, like Bath, England, became popular sites for the wealthy to see each other and be seen. Officials also took measures to improve the cleaning of city streets in which trash, human soil, and animal carcasses were often left to rot.

The scope of the new consumer economy should not be exaggerated. These developments were concentrated in large cities in northwestern Europe and North America. Even in these centers the elite benefited the most from new modes of life. This was not yet the society of mass consumption that emerged toward the end of the nineteenth century with the full expansion of the Industrial Revolution. The eighteenth century did, however, lay the foundations for one of the most distinctive features of modern Western life: societies based on the consumption of goods and services obtained through the market in which individuals form their identities and self-worth through the goods they consume.

What role did religion play in eighteenth-century society?

Though the critical spirit of the Enlightenment made great inroads in the eighteenth century, the majority of ordinary men and women, especially those in rural areas, retained strong religious faith. The church promised salvation, and it gave comfort in the face of sorrow and death. Religion also remained strong because it was embedded in local traditions and everyday social experience.

Yet the popular religion of village Europe was also enmeshed in a larger world of church hierarchies and state power. These powerful outside forces sought to regulate religious life at the local level. Their efforts created tensions that helped set the scene for vigorous religious revivals in Protestant Germany and England as well as in Catholic France.

Church Hierarchy

In the eighteenth century religious faith not only endured, but grew more fervent in many parts of Europe. The local parish church remained the focal point of religious devotion and community cohesion. Congregants gossiped and swapped stories after services, and neighbors came together in church for baptisms, marriages, and funerals. Priests and parsons kept the community records of births, deaths, and marriages; distributed charity; and provided primary education to the common people. Thus the parish church was woven into the very fabric of community life.

While the parish church remained central to the community, it was also subject to greater control from the state. In Protestant areas, princes and monarchs headed the official church, and they regulated their "territorial churches" strictly, selecting personnel and imposing detailed rules. Clergy of the official church dominated education, and followers of other faiths suffered religious and civil discrimination. By the eighteenth century the radical ideas of the Reformation had resulted in another version of church bureaucracy.

Catholic monarchs in this period also took greater control of religious matters in their kingdoms, weakening papal authority. In both Spain and Portugal, the Catholic Church was closely associated with the state, a legacy of the long internal reconquista and sixteenth-century imperial conquests overseas. In the eighteenth century the Spanish Crown took firm control of ecclesiastical appointments. Papal proclamations could not even be read in Spanish churches without prior approval from the government. In Portugal, religious enthusiasm led to a burst of new churches and monasteries in the early eighteenth century.

France went even further in establishing a national Catholic Church, known as the Gallican Church. Louis XIV's expulsion of Protestants in 1685 was accompanied by an insistence on the king's prerogative to choose and control bishops and issue laws regarding church affairs. Catholicism gained new ground in the Holy Roman Empire with the conversion of a number of Protestant princes and successful missionary work by Catholic orders among the populace. While it could not eradicate Protestantism altogether, the Habsburg monarchy successfully consolidated Catholicism as a pillar of its political control.

The Jesuit order played a key role in fostering the Catholic faith, providing extraordinary teachers, missionaries, and agents of the papacy. In many Catholic countries they exercised tremendous political influence, holding high government positions and educating the nobility in their colleges. By playing politics so effectively, however, the Jesuits elicited a broad coalition of enemies. Bitter controversies led Louis XV to order the Jesuits out of France in 1763 and to confiscate their property. France and Spain then pressured Rome to dissolve the Jesuits completely. In 1773 a reluctant pope caved in, although the order was revived after the French Revolution.

The Jesuit order was not the only Christian group to come under attack in the middle of the eighteenth century. The dominance of the larger Catholic Church and established Protestant churches was also challenged, both by enlightened reformers from above and by the faithful from below. Influenced by Enlightenment ideals, some Catholic rulers believed that the clergy in monasteries and convents should make a more practical contribution to social and religious life. Austria, a leader in controlling the church and promoting primary education, showed how far the process could go. Maria Theresa began by sharply restricting entry into what she termed "unproductive" orders. In his Edict on Idle Institutions, her successor, Joseph II, abolished contemplative orders, henceforth permitting only orders that were engaged in teaching, nursing, or other practical work. The state expropriated the dissolved monasteries and convents and used their wealth to create more parishes throughout Austria. This edict had a disproportionate effect on women because most of their orders were cloistered from the outside world and thus were not seen as "useful." Joseph II also issued edicts of religious tolerance, including for Jews, making Austria one of the first European states to lift centuries-old restrictions on its Jewish population.

Protestant Revival

By the late seventeenth century the vast transformations of the Protestant Reformation were complete and had been widely adopted in most Protestant churches. Medieval practices of idolatry, saint worship, and pageantry were abolished; stained-glass windows were smashed and murals whitewashed. Yet many official Protestant churches had settled into a smug complacency. This, along with the growth of state power and bureaucracy in local parishes, threatened to eclipse one of the Reformation's main goals — to bring all believers closer to God.

In the Reformation heartland, one concerned German minister wrote that the Lutheran Church "had become paralyzed in forms of dead doctrinal conformity" and badly needed a return to its original inspiration.[20] His voice was one of many that prepared and then guided a Protestant revival that succeeded because it answered the intense but increasingly unsatisfied needs of common people.

The Protestant revival began in Germany in the late seventeenth century. It was known as **Pietism** (PIGH-uh-tih-zum), and three aspects helped explain its powerful appeal. First, Pietism called for a warm, emotional religion that everyone could experience. Enthusiasm — in prayer, in worship, in preaching, in life itself — was the key concept. "Just as a drunkard becomes full of wine, so must the congregation become filled with spirit," declared one exuberant writer.[21]

Second, Pietism reasserted the earlier radical stress on the priesthood of all believers, thereby reducing the gulf between official clergy and Lutheran laity. Bible reading and study were enthusiastically extended to all classes, and this provided a powerful spur for popular literacy as well as individual religious development. Pietists were largely responsible for the educational reforms implemented by Prussia in the early eighteenth century. Third and finally, Pietists believed in the practical power of Christian rebirth in everyday affairs. Reborn Christians were expected to lead good, moral lives and to come from all social classes.

Pietism soon spread through the German-speaking lands and to Scandinavia. It also had a major impact on John Wesley (1703–1791), who served as the catalyst for popular religious revival in England. Wesley came from a long line of ministers, and when he went to Oxford University to prepare for the clergy, he mapped a fanatically earnest "scheme of religion." After becoming a teaching fellow at Oxford, Wesley organized a Holy Club for similarly minded students, who were soon known contemptuously as **Methodists** because they were so methodical in their devotion. Yet like the young Martin Luther, Wesley remained intensely troubled about his own salvation even after his ordination as an Anglican priest in 1728.

Wesley's anxieties related to grave problems of the faith in England. The government used the Church of England to provide favorites with high-paying jobs. Both church and state officials failed to respond to the spiritual needs of the people, and services and sermons had settled into an uninspiring routine. Moreover, Enlightenment skepticism was making inroads among the educated classes, and deism — a belief in God but not in organized religion — was becoming popular. Some bishops and church leaders seemed to believe that doctrines such as the virgin birth were little more than elegant superstitions.

Wesley's inner search in the 1730s was deeply affected by his encounter with Moravian Pietists, whom he first met on a ship as he traveled across the Atlantic to take up a position in Savannah, Georgia. The small Moravian community in Georgia impressed him as a productive, peaceful, and pious world, reflecting the values of the first apostles. After returning to London, following a disastrous failed engagement and the disappointment of his hopes to convert Native Americans, he sought spiritual counseling from a Pietist minister from Germany. Their conversations prepared Wesley for a mystical, emotional "conversion" in 1738. He described this critical turning point in his *Journal*:

> In the evening I went to a [Christian] society in Aldersgate Street where one was reading Luther's preface to the Epistle to the Romans. About a quarter before nine, while he was describing the change which God works in the heart through faith in Christ, I felt my heart strangely warmed. I felt I did trust in Christ, Christ alone for salvation; and an assurance was given me that he had taken away my sins, even mine, and saved me from the law of sin and death.[22]

Wesley's emotional experience resolved his intellectual doubts about the possibility of his own salvation. Moreover, he was convinced that any person, no matter how poor or uneducated, might have a similarly heartfelt conversion and gain the same blessed assurance. He took the good news to the people, traveling some 225,000 miles by horseback and preaching more than forty thousand sermons between 1750 and 1790. Since existing churches were often overcrowded and the church-state establishment was hostile, Wesley preached in open fields. People came in large numbers. Of critical importance was Wesley's rejection of Calvinist predestination — the doctrine of salvation granted to only a select few. Instead, he preached that all men and women who earnestly sought salvation might be saved. It was a message of hope and joy, of free will and universal salvation.

Wesley's ministry used lay preachers to reach new converts, formed Methodist cells, and eventually resulted in a new denomination. And just as Wesley had been inspired by the Pietist revival in Germany, so evangelicals in the Church of England and the old dissenting groups now followed Wesley's example of preaching to all people, giving impetus to an even broader awakening among the lower classes. Thus in Protestant countries religion continued to be a vital force in the lives of the people.

Catholic Piety

Religion also flourished in Catholic Europe around 1700, but there were important differences from Protestant practice. First, the visual contrast was striking; baroque art still lavished rich and emotionally exhilarating figures and images on Catholic churches, whereas most Protestant churches had removed their art during the Reformation. Moreover, people in Catholic Europe on the whole participated more actively in formal worship than did Protestants. More than 95 percent of the population probably attended church for Easter communion, the climax of the religious year.

The tremendous popular strength of religion in Catholic countries can in part be explained by the church's integral role in community life and popular culture. Thus, although Catholics reluctantly confessed their sins to priests, they enthusiastically came together in religious festivals to celebrate the passage of the liturgical year. In addition to the great processional days—such as Palm Sunday, the joyful re-enactment of Jesus's triumphal entry into Jerusalem—each parish had its own saints' days, processions, and pilgrimages. Led by its priest, a congregation might march around the village or across the countryside to a local shrine. Millions of Catholic men and women also joined religious associations, known as confraternities, where they participated in prayer and religious services and collected funds for poor relief and members' funerals. The Reformation had largely eliminated such activities in Protestant areas.

Catholicism had its own version of the Pietist revivals that shook Protestant Europe in the form of **Jansenism**. It originated with Cornelius Jansen (1585–1638), bishop of Ypres in the Spanish Netherlands, who called for a return to the austere early Christianity of Saint Augustine. In contrast to the worldly Jesuits, Jansen emphasized the heavy weight of original sin and accepted the doctrine of predestination. Although outlawed by papal and royal edicts as Calvinist heresy, Jansenism attracted Catholic followers eager for religious renewal, particularly among the French. Many members of France's urban elite, especially judicial nobles and some parish priests, became known for their Jansenist piety and spiritual devotion. Such stern religious values encouraged the judiciary's increasing opposition to the French monarchy in the second half of the eighteenth century.

Among the urban poor, a different strain of Jansenism took hold. Prayer meetings brought men and women together in ecstatic worship, and some participants fell into convulsions and spoke in tongues. The police of Paris posted spies to report on such gatherings and conducted mass raids and arrests.

Marginal Beliefs and Practices

In the countryside, many peasants continued to hold religious beliefs that were marginal to the Christian faith altogether, often of obscure or even pagan origin. On the Feast of Saint Anthony, for example, priests were expected to bless salt and bread for farm animals to protect them from disease. Catholics believed that saints' relics could

The Repression of Jansenism In 1710, the French royal government ordered the destruction of the convent of Port-Royal des Champs and the expulsion of the nuns living there, accusing the convent of being a hotbed of Jansenist subversion. Despite royal oppression, Jansenism—a movement within Catholicism emphasizing human sinfulness that was condemned by the papacy—continued to thrive in France among educated elites and the common people. (Tallandier/Bridgeman Images)

bring fortune or attract lovers, and there were healing springs for many ailments. In 1796 the Lutheran villagers of Beutelsbach in southern Germany incurred the ire of local officials when they buried a live bull at a crossroads to ward off an epidemic of hoof-and-mouth disease.[23] The ordinary person combined strong Christian faith with a wealth of time-honored superstitions.

Inspired initially by the fervor of the Reformation era, then by the critical rationalism of the Enlightenment, religious and secular authorities sought increasingly to "purify" popular spirituality. Thus one parish priest in France lashed out at his parishioners, claiming that they were "more superstitious than devout . . . and sometimes appear as baptized idolators."[24] French priests particularly denounced the "various remnants of paganism" found in popular bonfire ceremonies during Lent, in which young men, "yelling and screaming like madmen," tried to jump over the bonfires in order to help the crops grow and to protect themselves from illness. One priest saw rational Christians regressing into pagan animals—"the triumph of Hell and the shame of Christianity."[25]

The severity of the attack on popular belief varied widely by country and region. Where authorities pursued purification vigorously, as in Austria under Joseph II, pious peasants saw only an incomprehensible attack on age-old faith and drew back in anger. It was in this era of rationalism and disdain for superstition that the persecution of witches slowly came to an end across Europe. Common people in the countryside continued to fear the Devil and his helpers, but the elite increasingly dismissed such fears and refused to prosecute suspected witches. The last witch was executed in England in 1682, the same year France prohibited witchcraft trials. By the late eighteenth century the witchcraft hunts had ended across Europe.

How did the practice of medicine evolve in the eighteenth century?

Although significant breakthroughs in medical science would not come until the middle and late nineteenth century, the Enlightenment's optimism and its focus on improving human life through understanding of the laws of nature produced a great deal of research and experimentation in the eighteenth century. Medical practitioners greatly increased in number, although their techniques did not differ much from those of previous generations. Care of the sick in this era was the domain of several competing groups: traditional healers, apothecaries (pharmacists), physicians, surgeons, and midwives. From the Middle Ages through the seventeenth century, both men and women were medical practitioners. However, since women were generally denied admission to medical colleges and lacked the diplomas necessary to practice, the range of medical activities open to them was restricted. In the eighteenth century women's traditional roles as midwives and healers eroded even further.

Faith Healing and General Practice

In the course of the eighteenth century, traditional healers remained active, drawing on centuries of folk knowledge about the curative properties of roots, herbs, and other plants. Faith healing also remained popular, especially in the countryside. Faith healers and their patients believed that evil spirits caused illness by lodging in people and that the proper treatment was to exorcise, or drive out, the offending devil. Religious and secular officials did their best to stamp out such practices, but with little success.

In the larger towns and cities, apothecaries sold a vast number of herbs, drugs, and patent medicines for every conceivable "temperament and distemper." By the eighteenth century many of these medicines were derived from imported plants. The Asian spices prized since medieval times often had medicinal uses; from the sixteenth century onward, the Portuguese and then the Dutch dominated the Indian Ocean trade in these spices. As Europeans expanded to the New World, they brought a keen interest in potentially effective and highly profitable medicinal plants. Botanists accompanied European administrators and explorers to the Americas, where they profited from the healing traditions of indigenous peoples and, in the plantation societies of the Caribbean, enslaved Africans. They returned to Europe with a host of medicinal plants such as ipecacuanha, sarsaparilla, opium, and cinchona, the first effective treatment for fever. Over the course of the seventeenth century, imports of medicinal plants boomed. By the late eighteenth century, England was importing annually £100,000 worth of drugs, compared to only £1,000 or £2,000 in 1600.[26]

Like all varieties of medical practitioners, apothecaries advertised their wares, their high-class customers, and their miraculous cures in newspapers and commercial circulars. Medicine, like food and fashionable clothing, thus joined the era's new and loosely regulated commercial culture.

Physicians, who were invariably men, were apprenticed in their teens to practicing physicians for several years of on-the-job training. This training was then rounded out with hospital work or some university courses. Seen as gentlemen who did not labor with their hands, many physicians diagnosed and treated patients by correspondence or through oral dialogue, without conducting a physical examination.

Because their training was expensive, physicians came mainly from prosperous families and usually concentrated on urban patients from similar social backgrounds. Nevertheless, even poor people spent hard-won resources to seek treatment for their loved ones.

Physicians in the eighteenth century were increasingly willing to experiment with new methods, but time-honored practices lay heavily on them. They laid great stress on purging, and bloodletting was still considered a medical cure-all. It was the way "bad blood," the cause of illness, was removed and the balance of humors necessary for good health was restored.

Improvements in Surgery

Long considered to be craftsmen comparable to butchers and barbers, surgeons began studying anatomy seriously and improved their art in the eighteenth century. With endless opportunities to practice, army surgeons on gory battlefields led the way. They learned that the life of a soldier with an extensive wound, such as a shattered leg or arm, could perhaps be saved if the surgeon could apply a flat surface above the wound that could be cauterized with fire. Thus, if a soldier had a broken limb and the bone stuck out, the surgeon amputated so that the remaining stump could be cauterized and the likelihood of death reduced.

The eighteenth-century surgeon (and patient) labored in the face of incredible difficulties. Almost all operations were performed without painkillers, for the anesthesia of the day was hard to control and too dangerous for general use. Many patients died from the agony and shock of such operations. Surgery was also performed in utterly unsanitary conditions, for there was no knowledge of bacteriology and the nature of infection. The simplest wound treated by a surgeon could fester and lead to death.

Midwifery

Midwives continued to deliver the overwhelming majority of babies throughout the eighteenth century. Trained initially by another woman practitioner—and regulated by a guild in many cities—the midwife primarily assisted in labor and delivering babies. She also ministered to small children and treated female problems, such as irregular menstrual cycles, breast-feeding difficulties, infertility, and venereal disease.

The midwife orchestrated labor and birth in a woman's world, where friends and relatives assisted the pregnant woman in the familiar surroundings of her own home. The male surgeon (and the husband) rarely entered this female world, because most births, then as now, were normal and spontaneous. After the invention of forceps became publicized in 1734, surgeon-physicians used their monopoly over this and other instruments to seek lucrative new business. Attacking midwives as ignorant and dangerous, they sought to undermine faith in midwives and persuaded growing numbers of wealthy women of the superiority of their services. Despite criticism, it appears that midwives generally lost no more babies than did male doctors, who were still summoned to treat non-elite women only when life-threatening situations required surgery.

Women also continued to perform almost all nursing. Female religious orders ran many hospitals, and at-home nursing was almost exclusively the province of women.

Thus, although they were excluded from the growing ranks of formally trained and authorized practitioners, women continued to perform the bulk of informal medical care. Nursing as a secular profession did not emerge until the nineteenth century.

The Conquest of Smallpox

Experimentation and the intensified search for solutions to human problems led to some real advances in medicine after 1750. The eighteenth century's greatest medical triumph was the eradication of smallpox. With the progressive decline of bubonic plague, smallpox became the most terrible of the infectious diseases, and it is estimated that 60 million Europeans died of it in the eighteenth century.

The first step in the conquest of this killer in Europe came in the early eighteenth century. An English aristocrat whose beauty had been marred by the pox, Lady Mary Wortley Montagu, learned about the long-established practice of smallpox inoculation in the Muslim lands of western Asia while her husband was serving as British ambassador to the Ottoman Empire. She had her own son successfully inoculated with the pus from a smallpox victim and was instrumental in spreading the practice in England after her return in 1722. But inoculation was risky and was widely condemned because about one person in fifty died from it. In addition, people who had been inoculated were infectious and often spread the disease.

While the practice of inoculation with the smallpox virus was refined over the century, the crucial breakthrough was made by Edward Jenner (1749–1823), a talented country doctor. His starting point was the countryside belief that dairymaids who had contracted cowpox did not get smallpox. Cowpox produces sores that resemble those of smallpox, but the disease is mild and is not contagious.

For eighteen years Jenner practiced a kind of Baconian science, carefully collecting data. Finally, in 1796 he performed his first vaccination on a young boy using matter taken from a milkmaid with cowpox. After performing more successful vaccinations, Jenner published his findings in 1798. The new method of treatment spread rapidly, and smallpox soon declined to the point of disappearance in Europe and then throughout the world.

NOTES

1. Quoted in J. M. Beattie, "The Criminality of Women in Eighteenth-Century England," *Journal of Social History* 8 (Summer 1975): 86.
2. Quoted in R. Cobb, *The Police and the People: French Popular Protest, 1789–1820* (Oxford: Clarendon Press, 1970), p. 238.
3. Peter Laslett, *Family Life and Illicit Love: Essays in Historical Sociology* (Cambridge: Cambridge University Press, 1977).
4. G. Gullickson, *Spinners and Weavers of Auffay: Rural Industry and the Sexual Division of Labor in a French Village, 1750–1850* (Cambridge: Cambridge University Press, 1986), p. 186.
5. Louis Crompton, *Homosexuality and Civilization* (Cambridge, Mass.: Belknap Press, 2003), p. 321.
6. D. S. Neff, "Bitches, Mollies, and Tommies: Byron, Masculinity and the History of Sexualities," *Journal of the History of Sexuality* 11, no. 3 (July 2002): 404.
7. George E. Haggerty, ed., *Encyclopedia of Gay Histories and Cultures* (New York: Garland Publishing, 2000), pp. 1311–1312.
8. Pier Paolo Viazzo, "Mortality, Fertility, and Family," in *Family Life in Early Modern Times, 1500–1789*, ed. David I. Kertzer and Marzio Barbagli (New Haven, Conn.: Yale University Press, 2001), p. 180.
9. George Sussman, *Selling Mother's Milk: The Wet-Nursing Business in France, 1715–1914* (Urbana: University of Illinois Press, 1982), p. 22.

10. Yves Blayo, "La Mortalité en France de 1740 à 1820," *Population*, special issue 30 (1975): 135.

11. Viazzo, "Mortality, Fertility, and Family," pp. 176–178.

12. Alysa Levene, "The Estimation of Mortality at the London Foundling Hospital, 1741–99," *Population Studies* 59, no. 1 (2005): 87–97.

13. Quoted in Robert Woods, "Did Montaigne Love His Children? Demography and the Hypothesis of Parental Indifference," *Journal of Interdisciplinary History* 33, no. 3 (2003): 421.

14. Quoted in Gay Ochiltree and Don Edgar, *The Changing Face of Childhood* (Melbourne: Institute of Family Studies, 1981), p. 11.

15. James Van Horn Melton, *Absolutism and the Eighteenth-Century Origins of Compulsory Schooling in Prussia and Austria* (Cambridge: Cambridge University Press, 2003), p. 46.

16. James Van Horn Melton, "The Theresian School Reform of 1774," in *Early Modern Europe*, ed. James B. Collins and Karen L. Taylor (Oxford: Blackwell, 2006).

17. Jeremy Black, *The English Press in the Eighteenth Century* (Philadelphia: University of Pennsylvania Press, 1987), p. 262.

18. Neil McKendrik, John Brewer, and J. H. Plumb, *The Birth of a Consumer Society: The Commercialization of Eighteenth-Century England* (Bloomington: Indiana University Press, 1982).

19. Quoted in Cissie Fairchilds, "The Production and Marketing of Populuxe Goods in Eighteenth-Century Paris," in *Consumption and the World of Goods*, ed. John Brewer and Roy Porter (London: Routledge, 1993), p. 228.

20. Quoted in K. Pinson, *Pietism as a Factor in the Rise of German Nationalism* (New York: Columbia University Press, 1934), p. 13.

21. Pinson, *Pietism as a Factor*, pp. 43–44.

22. Quoted in S. Andrews, *Methodism and Society* (London: Longmans, Green, 1970), p. 327.

23. David Sabean, *The Power in the Blood: Popular Culture and Village Discourse in Early Modern Germany* (Cambridge: Cambridge University Press, 1984), p. 174.

24. Quoted in I. Woloch, *Eighteenth-Century Europe: Tradition and Progress, 1715–1789* (New York: W. W. Norton, 1982), p. 292.

25. Quoted in T. Tackett, *Priest and Parish in Eighteenth-Century France* (Princeton, N.J.: Princeton University Press, 1977), p. 214.

26. Patrick Wallis, "Exotic Drugs and English Medicine: England's Drug Trade, c. 1550–c. 1800," *Social History of Medicine* 2, no. 1 (2012): 26.

LOOKING BACK **LOOKING AHEAD**

The fundamental patterns of life in early modern Europe remained very much the same up to the eighteenth century. The vast majority of people lived in the countryside and followed age-old rhythms of seasonal labor in the fields and farmyard. Community ties were close in small villages, where the struggle to prevail over harsh conditions called on all hands to work together and to pray together. The daily life of a peasant in 1700 would have been familiar to his ancestors in the fifteenth century. Indeed, the three orders of society enshrined in the medieval social hierarchy—clergy, nobility, peasantry—were binding legal categories in France up to 1789.

And yet, the economic changes inaugurated in the late seventeenth century—intensive agriculture, cottage industry, the industrious revolution, and colonial expansion—contributed to the profound social and cultural transformation of daily life in eighteenth-century Europe. Men and women of the laboring classes, especially in the cities, experienced change in many facets of their daily lives: in loosened community controls over sex and marriage, rising literacy rates, new goods and new forms of self-expression, and a wave of religious piety that challenged traditional orthodoxies. Lay and secular elites attacked some forms of popular life, but considerable overlap continued between popular and elite culture.

Economic, social, and cultural change would culminate in the late eighteenth century with the outbreak of revolution in the Americas and Europe. Initially led by the elite, political upheavals relied on the enthusiastic participation of the poor and their desire for greater inclusion in the life of the nation. Such movements also encountered resistance from the common people when revolutionaries trampled on their religious faith. For many observers, contemporaries and historians alike, the transformations of the eighteenth century constituted a fulcrum between the old world of hierarchy and tradition and the modern world with its claims to equality and freedom.

MAKE CONNECTIONS

Think about the larger developments and continuities within and across chapters.

1. How did the expansion of agriculture and trade (Chapter 17) contribute to changes in daily life in the eighteenth century?

2. What were the main areas of improvement in the lives of the common people in the eighteenth century, and what aspects of life remained unchanged or even deteriorated?

3. How did Enlightenment thought (Chapter 16) affect education, child care, medicine, and religion in the eighteenth century?

Chapter 18 Review

IDENTIFY KEY TERMS

Identify and explain the significance of each item below.

community controls (p. 521)
charivari (p. 521)
illegitimacy explosion (p. 521)
wet-nursing (p. 524)
blood sports (p. 529)
carnival (p. 529)

just price (p. 531)
consumer revolution (p. 532)
Pietism (p. 536)
Methodists (p. 537)
Jansenism (p. 538)

REVIEW THE MAIN IDEAS

Answer the section heading questions from the chapter.

1. How did marriage and family life change in the eighteenth century? (p. 518)

2. What was life like for children, and how did attitudes toward childhood evolve? (p. 523)

3. How did increasing literacy and new patterns of consumption affect people's lives? (p. 527)

4. What role did religion play in eighteenth-century society? (p. 534)

5. How did the practice of medicine evolve in the eighteenth century? (p. 540)

CHRONOLOGY

1684	• Jean-Baptiste de la Salle founds Brothers of the Christian Schools
1717	• Elementary school attendance mandatory in Prussia
1750–1790	• John Wesley preaches revival in England
1750–1850	• Illegitimacy explosion
1757	• Madame du Coudray publishes *Manual on the Art of Childbirth*
1762	• Jean-Jacques Rousseau advocates more attentive child care in *Emile*
1763	• Louis XV orders Jesuits out of France
1774	• Elementary school attendance mandatory in Austria
1796	• Edward Jenner performs first smallpox vaccination

19

Revolutions in Politics

1775–1815

CHAPTER PREVIEW

- What were the factors behind the revolutions of the late eighteenth century?

- Why and how did American colonists forge a new, independent nation?

- How did the events of 1789 result in a constitutional monarchy in France?

- Why and how did the French Revolution take a radical turn?

- How did Napoleon Bonaparte create a French empire, and why did it fail?

- How did slave revolt on colonial Saint-Domingue lead to the independent nation of Haiti?

A GREAT WAVE OF REVOLUTION rocked both sides of the Atlantic Ocean in the last decades of the eighteenth century. With trade goods, individuals, and ideas circulating in ever-greater numbers across the Atlantic Ocean, debates and events in one locale soon influenced those in another. Changing social realities challenged the old order of life, and Enlightenment ideals of freedom and equality flourished, leading reformers in many places to demand fundamental changes in politics and government. At the same time, wars fought for dominance of the Atlantic economy left European states weakened by crushing debts, making them vulnerable to calls for reform.

The revolutionary era began in North America in 1775, and the United States of America won freedom from Britain in 1783. Then in 1789, France, the most populous country in western Europe and a center of culture and intellectual life, became the leading revolutionary nation. It established first a constitutional monarchy, then a radical republic, and finally a new European empire under Napoleon that would last until 1815. Inspired both by the ideals of the Revolution on the continent and by their own experiences and desires, enslaved people in the French colony of Saint-Domingue rose up in 1791. Their rebellion would eventually lead to the creation of the new independent nation of Haiti in 1804. In Europe and its colonies abroad, the age of modern politics was born.

What were the factors behind the revolutions of the late eighteenth century?

The origins of the late-eighteenth-century revolutions in British North America, France, and Haiti were complex. No one cause lay behind them, nor was revolution inevitable or certain of success. However, a set of shared factors helped set the stage for revolt. Among them were fundamental social and economic changes and political crises that eroded state authority. Another significant cause of revolutionary fervor was the impact of political ideas derived from the Enlightenment. Even though most Enlightenment writers were cautious about political reform, their confidence in reason and progress helped inspire a new generation to fight for greater freedom from repressive governments. Perhaps most important, financial crises generated by the expenses of imperial warfare brought European states to their knees and allowed abstract discussions of reform to become pressing realities.

Social Change

Eighteenth-century European society was legally divided into groups with special privileges, such as the nobility and the clergy, and groups with special burdens, such as the peasantry. Nobles were the largest landowners, possessing one-quarter of the agricultural land of France, while constituting less than 2 percent of the population. In many parts of Europe, nobles enjoyed exemption from direct taxation as well as exclusive rights to hunt game, bear swords, and use gold thread in their clothing. Various middle-class groups—professionals, merchants, and guild masters—enjoyed privileges that allowed them to monopolize all sorts of economic activity. Poor peasants and urban laborers, who constituted the vast majority of the population, bore the brunt of taxation and were excluded from the world of privilege.

Traditional prerogatives persisted in societies undergoing dramatic and destabilizing change. Europe's population rose rapidly after 1750, and its cities and towns swelled in size. Inflation kept pace with population growth, making it ever more difficult to find affordable food and living space. One way the poor kept up, and even managed to participate in the new consumer revolution (see "How did increasing literacy and new patterns of consumption affect people's lives?" in Chapter 18), was by working harder and for longer hours. More women and children entered the paid labor force, challenging the traditional hierarchies and customs of village life.

Economic growth created new inequalities between rich and poor. While the poor struggled with rising prices, investors grew rich from the spread of rural manufacture and overseas trade, including the trade in enslaved Africans and in the products of slave labor. Old distinctions between landed aristocracy and city merchants began to fade as enterprising nobles put money into trade and rising middle-class bureaucrats and merchants purchased landed estates and noble titles. Marriages between proud nobles and wealthy, educated commoners (called the *bourgeoisie* [boor-ZHWAH-zee] in France) served both groups' interests, and a mixed elite began to take shape. In the context of these changes, ancient privileges seemed to pose an intolerable burden to many observers.

Another social change involved the racial regimes established in European colonies to legitimize and protect slavery. By the late eighteenth century European law accepted that only Africans and people of African descent were subject to slavery. Even free people of color—a term for nonslaves of African or mixed African-European descent—were subject to special laws restricting the property they could own, whom they could marry, and what clothes they could wear. Racial privilege conferred a new dimension of entitlement on European settlers in the colonies, and they used extremely brutal methods to enforce it. The contradiction between slavery and the Enlightenment ideals of liberty and equality was all too evident to enslaved and free people of color.

Growing Demands for Liberty and Equality

In addition to destabilizing social changes, the ideals of liberty and equality helped fuel revolutions in the Atlantic world. The call for liberty was first of all a call for individual human rights. Supporters of the cause of individual liberty (who became known as "liberals" in the early nineteenth century) demanded freedom to worship according to the dictates of their consciences, an end to censorship, and freedom from arbitrary laws and from judges who simply obeyed orders from the government. The Declaration of the Rights of Man and of the Citizen, issued at the beginning of the French Revolution, proclaimed that "liberty consists in being able to do anything that does not harm another person." In the context of the monarchical and absolutist forms of government then dominating Europe, this was a truly radical idea.

The call for liberty was also a call for a new kind of government. Reformers believed that the people had sovereignty—that is, that the people alone had the authority to make laws limiting an individual's freedom of action. In practice, this system of government meant choosing legislators who represented the people and were accountable to them. Monarchs might retain their thrones, but their rule should be constrained by the will of the people.

Equality was a more ambiguous idea. Eighteenth-century liberals argued that, in theory, all citizens should have identical rights and liberties and that the nobility had no right to special privileges based on birth. However, they accepted a number of distinctions. First, most eighteenth-century liberals were men of their times, and they generally believed that equality between men and women was neither practical nor desirable. Women played an important political role in the revolutionary movements at several points, but the men who wrote constitutions for the new republics limited formal political rights—the right to vote, to run for office, and to participate in government—to men. Second, few questioned the superiority of people of European descent over those of indigenous or African origin. Even those who believed that the slave trade was unjust and should be abolished, such as Thomas Jefferson, usually felt that emancipation was so dangerous that it must be undertaken slowly and gradually, if at all.

Third, liberals never believed that everyone should be equal economically. Great differences in fortune between rich and poor were perfectly acceptable. The essential point was that every free white male should have a legally equal chance at economic gain. However limited they appear to modern eyes, these demands for liberty and equality were revolutionary in the eighteenth-century context.

The two most important Enlightenment references for late-eighteenth-century liberals were John Locke and the baron de Montesquieu (see Chapter 16). Locke maintained that England's long political tradition rested on "the rights of Englishmen" and on representative government through Parliament. He argued that if a government oversteps its proper function of protecting the natural rights of life, liberty, and private property, it becomes a tyranny. Montesquieu was also inspired by English constitutional history and the Glorious Revolution of 1688–1689, which placed sovereignty in Parliament. He, too, believed that powerful "intermediary groups"—such as the judicial nobility of which he was a proud member—offered the best defense of liberty against despotism.

The belief that representative institutions could defend their liberty and interests appealed powerfully to the educated middle classes. Yet liberal ideas about individual rights and political freedom also appealed to members of the hereditary nobility, at least in western Europe and as formulated by Montesquieu. Representative government did not mean democracy, which liberal thinkers tended to equate with mob rule. Rather, they envisioned voting for representatives as being restricted to men who owned property—those with "a stake in society." The blurring of practical distinctions between landed aristocrats and wealthy commoners meant that there was no clear-cut opposition between nobles and non-nobles on political issues.

Revolutions thus began with aspirations for equality and liberty among the social elite. Soon, however, dissenting voices emerged as some revolutionaries became frustrated with the limitations of liberal notions of equality and liberty and clamored for a fuller realization of these concepts. Depending on location, their demands included universal male suffrage, political rights for women and free people of color, the emancipation of slaves, and government regulations to reduce economic inequality. The age of revolution was thus marked by bitter conflicts over how far reform should go and to whom it should apply.

The Seven Years' War

The roots of revolutionary ideas could be found in Enlightenment texts, but it was by no means inevitable that such ideas would result in revolution. Instead, events—political, economic, and military—created crises that opened the door for the development of radical thought and action. One of the most important was the global conflict known as the Seven Years' War (1756–1763).

The war's battlefields stretched from central Europe to India, West Africa, the Philippines, and North America (where the conflict was known as the French and

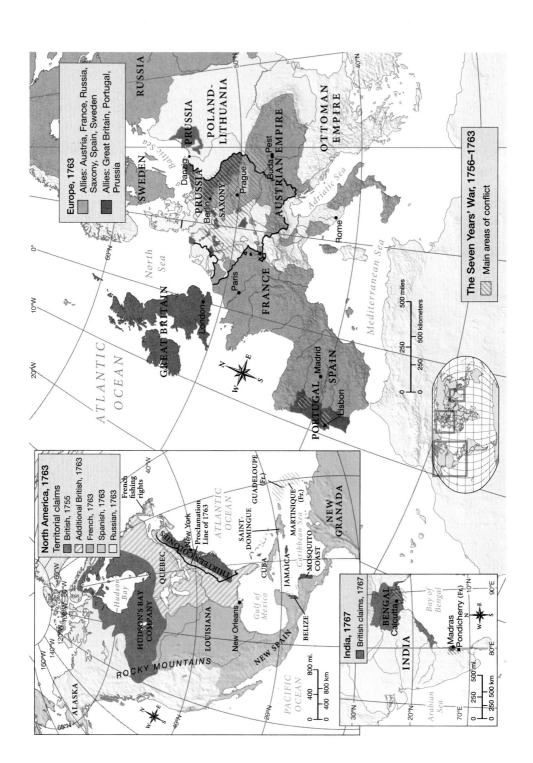

Europe, 1763

Allies: Austria, France, Russia, Saxony, Spain, Sweden

Allies: Great Britain, Portugal, Prussia

RUSSIA

SWEDEN

PRUSSIA

POLAND-LITHUANIA

Danzig

PRUSSIA

Berlin

SAXONY

Prague

Buda Pest

AUSTRIAN EMPIRE

OTTOMAN EMPIRE

Adriatic Sea

Rome

Paris

FRANCE

Mediterranean Sea

PORTUGAL

Madrid

SPAIN

Lisbon

North Sea

GREAT BRITAIN

London

ATLANTIC OCEAN

The Seven Years' War, 1756–1763

Main areas of conflict

500 miles

250

0

500 kilometers

250

0

North America, 1763

Territorial claims

British, 1755

Additional British, 1763

French, 1763

Spanish, 1763

Russian, 1763

French fishing rights

Proclamation Line of 1763

New York

THIRTEEN COLONIES

QUEBEC

ATLANTIC OCEAN

GUADELOUPE (Fr.)

SAINT-DOMINGUE

MARTINIQUE (Fr.)

CUBA

JAMAICA

Caribbean Sea

MOSQUITO COAST

NEW GRANADA

HUDSON'S BAY COMPANY

Hudson Bay

LOUISIANA

New Orleans

Gulf of Mexico

BELIZE

NEW SPAIN

ROCKY MOUNTAINS

ALASKA

PACIFIC OCEAN

800 mi.

400

0

800 km

400

India, 1767

British claims, 1767

BENGAL

Calcutta

Bay of Bengal

Madras

Pondicherry (Fr.)

INDIA

Arabian Sea

500 mi.

250

0

500 km

250

Indian War), pitting a new alliance of England and Prussia against the French, Austrians, and, later, Spanish. The origins of war in Europe lay in conflicts left unresolved at the end of the War of the Austrian Succession in 1748 (see "Frederick the Great of Prussia" in Chapter 16), during which Prussia seized the Austrian territory of Silesia. In central Europe, Austria's Maria Theresa vowed to win back Silesia and to crush Prussia, thereby re-establishing the Habsburgs' traditional leadership in German affairs. By the end of the Seven Years' War, Austria had almost succeeded, but Prussia survived with its boundaries intact.

Inconclusive in Europe, the Seven Years' War was the decisive round in the Franco-British competition for colonial empire. In North America, hostilities resulted from unresolved tensions regarding the border between the French and British colonies. The population of New France was centered in Quebec and along the St. Lawrence River, but French soldiers and Canadian fur traders had also built forts and trading posts along the Great Lakes, through the Ohio country, and down the Mississippi to New Orleans. Allied with Native American nations, the French built more forts in 1753 in what is now western Pennsylvania to protect their claims. The following year a Virginia force attacked a small group of French soldiers; thus war began in North America prior to the formal outbreak of hostilities between France and Britain on the European continent.

Although the inhabitants of New France were greatly outnumbered—Canada counted 55,000 inhabitants, compared to 1.2 million in the thirteen English colonies—French forces achieved major victories until 1758. Both sides relied on the participation of Native American groups with whom they had long-standing trading contacts and actively sought new indigenous allies during the conflict. The tide of the conflict turned when the British diverted resources from the war in Europe, using superior sea power to destroy France's fleet and choke its commerce around the world. In 1759 the British laid siege to Quebec for four long months, finally defeating the French in a battle that sealed the nation's fate in North America.

British victory on all colonial fronts was ratified in the 1763 Treaty of Paris. Canada and all French territory east of the Mississippi River passed to Britain, and France ceded Louisiana to Spain as compensation for Spain's loss of Florida to Britain. France also gave up most of its holdings in India, opening the way to British dominance on the subcontinent (Map 19.1).

By 1763 Britain had realized its goal of monopolizing a vast trading and colonial empire, but at a tremendous cost in war debt. France emerged from the conflict humiliated and broke, but with its profitable Caribbean colonies intact. In the aftermath of war, both British and French governments had to raise taxes to repay loans, raising a storm of protest that led to demands for fundamental reform. Since

< MAP 19.1 The Seven Years' War in Europe, North America, and India, 1756–1763
As a result of the war, France lost its vast territories in North America and India. In an effort to avoid costly conflicts with Native Americans living in the newly conquered territory, the British government in 1763 prohibited colonists from settling west of the Appalachian Mountains. One of the few remaining French colonies in the Americas, Saint-Domingue (on the island of Hispaniola) was the most profitable plantation colony in the New World.

the Caribbean colony of Saint-Domingue remained French, political turmoil in France would directly affect its population. The seeds of revolutionary conflict in the Atlantic world were thus sown.

Why and how did American colonists forge a new, independent nation?

Increased taxes and increased government control were crucial factors behind colonial protests in the New World, where the era of liberal political revolution began. After revolting against their home country, the thirteen mainland colonies of British North America succeeded in establishing a new unified government. Participants in the revolution believed they were demanding only the traditional rights of English men and women. Those traditional rights were liberal rights, and in the American context they had strong democratic and popular overtones. Yet in challenging and recasting authority in the colonies, the revolution did not resolve the question of social and political equality, which continued to elude enslaved people, women, free people of color, and indigenous people.

The Origins of the Revolution

The high cost of the Seven Years' War doubled the British national debt. Anticipating further expenses to defend the half a billion acres in new territory granted by the Treaty of Paris, the government in London imposed bold new administrative measures. Breaking with a tradition of loose colonial oversight, the British announced that they would maintain a large army in North America and tax the colonies directly. In 1765 Parliament passed the Stamp Act, which levied taxes on a long list of commercial and legal documents, diplomas, newspapers, almanacs, and playing cards. A stamp glued to each article indicated that the tax had been paid.

These measures seemed perfectly reasonable to the British, for a much heavier stamp tax already existed in Britain, and proceeds from the tax were to fund the defense of the colonies. Nonetheless, the colonists vigorously protested the Stamp Act by rioting and by boycotting British goods. Thus Parliament reluctantly repealed it.

Another area of contention was settlement of the new territory acquired by the Treaty of Paris. At the end of the Seven Years' War, land-squeezed settlers quickly moved west across the Appalachian Mountains into the Ohio Valley, sparking conflict with the Ottawa and other indigenous groups already present in the region as well as remaining French settlers. To prevent costly wars in distant territory, the British government in 1763 issued a royal proclamation prohibiting colonists to settle west of the Appalachian Mountains. The so-called Proclamation Line did little to stem land speculation and the flow of migrants, but it did exacerbate suspicion and tensions between Britain and its colony.

These disputes raised important political questions. To what extent could the British government reassert its power while limiting the authority of elected colonial bodies? Who had the right to make laws for Americans? The British government replied that Americans were represented in Parliament, albeit indirectly (like most British people), and that Parliament ruled throughout the empire. Many Americans felt otherwise. In the words of John Adams, a major proponent of colonial independence, "A Parliament of Great Britain can have no more rights to tax the colonies than a Parliament of Paris." Thus British colonial administration and parliamentary supremacy came to appear as unacceptable threats to existing American liberties.

Americans' resistance to these threats was fed by the great degree of independence they had long enjoyed. In British North America, unlike in England and Europe, no powerful established church existed, and religious freedom was taken for granted. Colonial assemblies made the important laws, which were seldom overturned by the British government. Also, the right to vote was much more widespread than in England. In many parts of colonial Massachusetts, for example, as many as 95 percent of adult males could vote.

Moreover, greater political equality was matched by greater social and economic equality, at least for the free white population. No hereditary nobility exercised privileges over peasants and other social groups. Instead, independent farmers dominated colonial society. This was particularly true in the northern colonies, where the revolution originated.

In 1773 disputes over taxes and representation flared up again. Under the Tea Act of that year, the British government permitted the financially struggling East India Company to ship tea from China directly to its agents in the colonies, rather than through London middlemen, who sold to independent merchants in the colonies. Thus the company secured a profitable monopoly on the tea trade, and colonial merchants were excluded. The price on tea was actually lowered for colonists, but the act generated a great deal of opposition because of its impact on local merchants.

In protest, Boston men disguised as Native Americans staged a raucous protest (later called the "Tea Party") by boarding East India Company ships and throwing tea from them into the harbor. The British responded with the so-called Coercive Acts of 1774, which closed the port of Boston, curtailed local elections, and expanded the royal governor's power. County conventions in Massachusetts urged that the acts be "rejected as the attempts of a wicked administration to enslave America." Other colonial assemblies joined in the denunciations. In September 1774 the First Continental Congress — consisting of colonial delegates who sought at first to peacefully resolve conflicts with Britain — met in Philadelphia. The more radical members of this assembly argued successfully against concessions to the English Crown. The British Parliament also rejected compromise, and in April 1775 fighting between colonial and British troops began at Lexington and Concord.

Independence from Britain

As fighting spread, the colonists moved slowly toward open calls for independence. The uncompromising attitude of the British government and its use of German mercenaries did much to dissolve loyalties to the home country and to unite the separate colonies. *Common Sense* (1775), a brilliant attack by the recently arrived English radical Thomas Paine (1737–1809), also mobilized public opinion in favor of independence.

On July 4, 1776, the Second Continental Congress adopted the Declaration of Independence. Written by Thomas Jefferson and others, this document boldly listed the tyrannical acts committed by George III (r. 1760–1820) and confidently proclaimed the natural rights of mankind and the sovereignty of the American states. The Declaration of Independence in effect universalized the traditional rights of English people and made them the individual rights of all men. It stated that "all Men are created equal, that they are endowed by their Creator with certain unalienable Rights, that among these are Life, Liberty, and the Pursuit of Happiness." The purpose of the state was to protect these individual rights, not the interests of privileged groups. No other American political document has ever caused such excitement, either at home or abroad.

After the Declaration of Independence, the conflict often took the form of a civil war pitting patriots against Loyalists, those who maintained an allegiance to the Crown. The Loyalists, who numbered up to 20 percent of the total white population, tended to be wealthy and politically moderate. They were small in number in New England and Virginia, but more common in the Deep South and on the western frontier. British commanders also recruited Loyalists among enslaved people by promising freedom to any slave who left his master to fight for the mother country.

Many wealthy patriots—such as John Hancock and George Washington—willingly allied themselves with farmers and artisans in a broad coalition. This coalition harassed the Loyalists and confiscated their property to help pay for the war, causing 60,000 to 80,000 of them to flee, mostly to Canada. The broad social base of the revolutionaries tended to make the revolution democratic. State governments extended the right to vote to many more men, including free African American men in many cases, but not to women.

On the international scene, the French wanted revenge against the British for the humiliating defeats of the Seven Years' War. Thus they sympathized with the rebels and supplied guns and gunpowder from the beginning of the conflict. By 1777 French volunteers were arriving in Virginia, and a dashing young nobleman, the marquis de Lafayette (1757–1834), quickly became one of the most trusted generals of George Washington, who was commanding American troops. In 1778 the French government offered a formal alliance to the American ambassador in Paris, Benjamin Franklin, and in 1779 and 1780 the Spanish and Dutch declared war on Britain. Catherine the Great of Russia helped organize the League of Armed Neutrality to protect neutral shipping rights and succeeded in hampering Britain's naval power.

Thus by 1780 Britain was engaged in a war against most of Europe as well as the thirteen colonies. In these circumstances, and in the face of severe reverses in India, in the West Indies, and at Yorktown in Virginia, a new British government decided to cut its losses and end the war. American officials in Paris were receptive to negotiating a deal with England alone, for they feared that France wanted a treaty that would bottle up the new nation east of the Appalachian Mountains and give British holdings west of the Appalachians to France's ally, Spain. Thus the American negotiators deserted their French allies and accepted the extraordinarily favorable terms Britain offered.

Under the Treaty of Paris of 1783, Britain recognized the independence of the thirteen colonies and ceded all its territory between the Allegheny Mountains and the Mississippi River to the Americans. Out of the bitter rivalries of the Old World, the Americans snatched dominion over a vast territory.

Framing the Constitution

The liberal program of the American Revolution was consolidated by the federal Constitution, the Bill of Rights, and the creation of a national republic. Assembling in Philadelphia in the summer of 1787, the delegates to the Constitutional Convention were determined to end the period of economic depression, social uncertainty, and leadership under a weak central government that had followed independence. The delegates thus decided to grant the federal, or central, government important powers: regulation of domestic and foreign trade, the right to tax, and the means to enforce its laws.

Strong rule would be placed squarely in the context of representative self-government. Senators and congressmen would be the lawmaking delegates of the voters, and the president of the republic would be an elected official. The central government would operate in Montesquieu's framework of checks and balances, under which authority was distributed across three different branches—the executive, legislative, and judicial branches—to prevent one interest from gaining too much power. The power of the federal government would in turn be checked by that of the individual states.

When the results of the Constitutional Convention were presented to the states for ratification, a great public debate began. The opponents of the proposed Constitution—the Antifederalists—charged that the framers of the new document had taken too much power from the individual states and made the federal government too strong. Moreover, many Antifederalists feared for the individual freedoms for which they had fought. To overcome these objections, the Federalists promised to spell out these basic freedoms as soon as the new Constitution was adopted. The result was the first ten amendments to the Constitution, which the first Congress passed shortly after it met in New York in March 1789. These amendments, ratified in 1791, formed an effective Bill of Rights to safeguard the individual. Most of them—trial by jury, due process of law, the right to assemble, freedom from unreasonable search—had their origins in English law and the English Bill of Rights of 1689. Other rights—the freedoms of speech, the press, and religion—reflected natural-law theory and the strong value colonists had placed on independence from the start.

Limitations of Liberty and Equality

The American Constitution and the Bill of Rights exemplified the strengths and the limits of what came to be called classical liberalism. Liberty meant individual freedoms and political safeguards. Liberty also meant representative government, but it did not mean democracy, with its principle of one person, one vote. Equality meant equality before the law, not equality of political participation or wealth. It did not mean equal rights for slaves, indigenous peoples, or women.

A vigorous abolitionist movement during the 1780s led to the passage of emancipation laws in all northern states, but slavery remained prevalent in the South, and discord between pro- and antislavery delegates roiled the Constitutional Convention of 1787. The result was a compromise stipulating that an enslaved person would count as three-fifths of a person in tallying population numbers for taxation and proportional representation in the House of Representatives. This solution levied higher taxes on the South, but it also guaranteed slaveholding states greater representation in Congress, which they used to oppose emancipation. Congress did ban slavery in federal territory in 1789, then the export of slaves from any state, and finally, in 1808, the import of slaves to any state.

The new republic also failed to protect the Native American nations whose lands fell within or alongside the territory ceded by Britain at the Treaty of Paris. The 1787 Constitution promised protection to Native Americans and guaranteed that their land would not be taken without consent. Nonetheless, the federal government forced them to concede their land for meager returns; state governments and the rapidly expanding population paid even less heed to the Constitution and often simply seized Native American land for new settlements.

Although lacking the voting rights enjoyed by so many of their husbands and fathers in the relatively democratic colonial assemblies, women played a vital role in the American Revolution. As household provisioners, women were essential participants in boycotts of British goods, like tea, which squeezed profits from British merchants and fostered the revolutionary spirit. After the outbreak of war, women raised funds for the Continental Army and took care of homesteads, workshops, and other businesses when their men went off to fight. Yet despite Abigail Adams's plea to her husband, John Adams, that the framers of the Declaration of Independence should "remember the ladies," women did not receive the right to vote in the new Constitution, an omission confirmed by a clause added in 1844.

How did the events of 1789 result in a constitutional monarchy in France?

No country felt the consequences of the American Revolution more deeply than France. Hundreds of French officers served in America and were inspired by the experience. The most famous of these, the marquis de Lafayette, left home as a proud young aristocrat determined to fight France's traditional foe, England. He returned with a love of liberty and firm republican convictions. French intellectuals engaged in passionate analysis of the federal Constitution as well as the constitutions of the various states of the new United States. The American Revolution undeniably fueled dissatisfaction with the old monarchical order in France. Yet the French Revolution did not mirror the American example. It was more radical and more complex, more influential and more controversial, more loved and more hated. For Europeans and most of the rest of the world, it was the great revolution of the eighteenth century, the revolution that opened the modern era in politics.

Breakdown of the Old Order

As did the American Revolution, the French Revolution had its immediate origins in the government's financial difficulties. The ministers of King Louis XV (r. 1715–1774) sought to raise taxes to meet the expenses of the War of the Austrian Succession and the Seven Years' War and to make nobles pay direct taxes for the first time. These efforts were thwarted by the high courts, known as the parlement. The noble judges of the parlements resented the Crown's threat to their exemption from taxation and decried the government's actions as a form of royal despotism.

When renewed efforts to reform the tax system similarly failed in 1776, the government was forced to finance its enormous expenditures during the American war with borrowed money. As a result, the national debt soared. Fully 50 percent of France's annual budget went to interest payments on the ever-increasing debt. By 1786 the nation was on the verge of bankruptcy.

Financial crisis struck a monarchy whose royal authority was badly tarnished. Louis XV had scandalized the country with a series of mistresses of low social origins. To make things worse, he refused to take communion because his adultery placed him in a state of sin. The king was being stripped of the sacred aura of God's anointed on earth (a process called desacralization) and was being reinvented in the popular imagination as a degenerate. Maneuverings among political factions at court further distracted the king and prevented decisive action from his government.

Despite the progressive desacralization of the monarchy, Louis XV would probably have prevailed had he lived longer, but he died in 1774. The new king, Louis XVI (r. 1774–1792), was a shy twenty-year-old with good intentions. Taking the throne, he is reported to have said, "What I should like most is to be loved."[1] The eager-to-please monarch Louis waffled on political reform and the economy and proved unable to quell the rising storm of opposition.

The Formation of the National Assembly

Spurred by a depressed economy and falling tax receipts, Louis XVI's minister of finance revived old proposals to impose a general tax on all landed property as well as to form provincial assemblies to help administer the tax, and he convinced the king to call an assembly of notables in 1787 to gain support for the idea. The assembled notables, mainly aristocrats and high-ranking clergy, declared that such sweeping tax changes required the approval of the **Estates General**, the representative body of all three estates, which had not met since 1614.

Facing imminent bankruptcy, the king tried to reassert his authority. He dismissed the notables and established new taxes by decree. The judges of the Parlement of Paris promptly declared the royal initiative null and void. When the king tried to exile the judges, a tremendous wave of protest swept the country. Frightened investors refused to advance more loans to the state. Finally in July 1788, a beaten Louis XVI bowed to public opinion and called for the Estates General. Absolute monarchy was collapsing.

As its name indicates, the Estates General was a legislative body with representatives from the three orders, or **estates**, of society: the clergy, the nobility, and everyone else. Following centuries-old tradition, each estate met separately to elect delegates, first at a local and then at a regional level. Results of the elections reveal the mind-set of each estate on the eve of the Revolution. The local assemblies of the clergy, representing the first estate, elected mostly parish priests rather than church leaders, demonstrating their dissatisfaction with the church hierarchy. The nobility, or second estate, voted in a majority of conservatives, primarily from the provinces, where nobles were less wealthy, more devout, and more numerous. Nonetheless, fully one-third of noble representatives were liberals committed to major changes. Commoners of the third estate, who constituted over 95 percent of the population, elected primarily lawyers and government officials to represent them, with few delegates representing business and the poor.

The petitions for change drafted by the assemblies showed a surprising degree of consensus about the key issues confronting the realm. In all three estates, voices

The Awakening of the Third Estate This cartoon from July 1789 represents the third estate as a common man throwing off his chains and rising up against his oppression, as the first estate (the clergy) and the second estate (the nobility) look on in fear. (Musée de la Ville de Paris, Musée Carnavalet, Paris, France/Bridgeman Images)

spoke in favor of replacing absolutism with a constitutional monarchy in which laws and taxes would require the consent of the Estates General in regular meetings. There was also a strong feeling that individual liberties would have to be guaranteed by law and that economic regulations should be loosened.

On May 5, 1789, the twelve hundred delegates of the three estates gathered in Versailles for the opening session of the Estates General. Despite widespread hopes for serious reform, the Estates General quickly deadlocked over voting procedures. Controversy had begun during the electoral process itself, when the government confirmed that, following precedent, each estate should meet and vote separately. This meant that the two privileged estates could always outvote the third.

During the lead-up to the Estates General, critics had demanded a single assembly dominated by the third estate. In his famous pamphlet *What Is the Third Estate?* Emmanuel Joseph Sieyès (himself a member of the first estate) argued that the nobility was a tiny, overprivileged minority and that the third estate constituted the true strength of the French nation.

The issue came to a crisis in June 1789 when delegates of the third estate refused to meet until the king ordered the clergy and nobility to sit with them in a single body. On June 17 the third estate, which had been joined by a few parish priests, voted to call itself the **National Assembly**. On June 20, excluded from their hall because of "repairs," the delegates moved to a large indoor tennis court where they swore the famous Tennis Court Oath, pledging not to disband until they had been recognized as a national assembly and had written a new constitution.

The king's response was disastrously ambivalent. Although he made conciliatory gestures in favor of the Assembly's demands, he called an army of eighteen thousand troops toward the capital to bring the delegates under control, and on July 11 he dismissed his finance minister and other liberal ministers. It appeared that the monarchy was prepared to use violence to restore its control.

Popular Uprising and the Rights of Man

While delegates at Versailles were pressing for political rights, economic hardship gripped the common people. Conditions were already tough because of the government's disastrous financial situation. Then a poor grain harvest in 1788 caused the price of bread to soar, and inflation spread quickly through the economy. As a result, demand for manufactured goods collapsed, and many artisans and small traders lost work. In Paris perhaps 150,000 of the city's 600,000 people were unemployed by July 1789.

Against this background of poverty and political crisis, the people of Paris entered decisively onto the revolutionary stage. They believed that, to survive, they should have steady work and enough bread at fair prices. They also feared that the dismissal of the king's liberal finance minister would put them at the mercy of aristocratic landowners and grain speculators. At the beginning of July, knowledge spread of the massing of troops near Paris. On July 14, 1789, several hundred people stormed the Bastille (ba-STEEL), a royal prison, to obtain weapons for the city's defense. Faced with popular violence, Louis soon announced the reinstatement of his finance minister and the withdrawal of troops from Paris. The National Assembly was free to continue its work.

Just as the laboring poor of Paris had decisively intervened in the Revolution, the struggling French peasantry also took matters into their own hands. Peasants bore the brunt of state taxation, church tithes, and noble privileges. Since most did not own enough land to be self-sufficient, they were hard-hit by the rising price of bread. In the summer of 1789, throughout France peasants began to rise in insurrection against their lords, ransacking manor houses and burning feudal documents that recorded their obligations. In some areas peasants reoccupied common lands enclosed by landowners and seized forests. Fear of the retaliation from the state and noble landowners against these actions—called the **Great Fear** by contemporaries—seized the rural poor and fanned the flames of rebellion.

Faced with chaos, the National Assembly responded to the swell of popular uprising with a surprise maneuver on the night of August 4, 1789. By a decree of the Assembly, all the old noble privileges—peasant serfdom where it still existed, exclusive hunting rights, fees for having legal cases judged in the lord's court, the right to make peasants work on the roads, and a host of other dues—were abolished along with the tithes paid to the church. On August 27, 1789, the Assembly further issued the Declaration of the Rights of Man and of the Citizen. This clarion call of the liberal revolutionary ideal guaranteed equality before the law, representative government for a sovereign people, and individual freedom. It was quickly disseminated throughout France and the rest of Europe and around the world.

The National Assembly's declaration had little practical effect for the poor and hungry people of France. The economic crisis worsened after the fall of the Bastille, as aristocrats fled the country and the luxury market collapsed. Foreign markets also shrank, and unemployment among the urban working classes grew. In addition, women—the traditional managers of food and resources in poor homes—could no longer look to the church, which had been stripped of its tithes, for aid.

On October 5 some seven thousand women marched the twelve miles from Paris to Versailles to demand action. This great crowd, "armed with scythes, sticks and pikes," invaded the National Assembly. Interrupting a delegate's speech, an old woman defiantly shouted into the debate, "Who's that talking down there? Make the chatterbox shut up. That's not the point: the point is that we want bread."[2] The women invaded the royal apartments, killed some of the royal bodyguards, and searched for

The Women of Paris March to Versailles   On October 5, 1789, thousands of poor Parisian women marched to Versailles to protest the price of bread. For the common people, the king was the baker of last resort, responsible for feeding his people during times of scarcity. The image of a set of scales one woman holds aloft (along with a loaf of bread stuck on the tip of her pike) symbolizes the crowd's desire for justice and for bread to be sold at the same price per pound as it always had been. The women forced the royal family to return with them to live in Paris, rather than remain isolated from their subjects at court. (DEA Picture Library/Gianni Dagli Orti/ Getty Images)

the queen, Marie Antoinette, who was widely despised for her frivolous and supposedly immoral behavior. It seems likely that only the intervention of Lafayette and the National Guard saved the royal family. But the crowd demanded that the king live closer to his people in Paris, and that seemed the only way to calm the disorder.

A Constitutional Monarchy and Its Challenges

The next two years, until September 1791, saw the consolidation of the liberal revolution. In June 1790 the National Assembly abolished the nobility, and in July the king swore to uphold the as-yet-unwritten constitution, effectively enshrining a constitutional monarchy. The king remained the head of state, but all lawmaking power now resided in the National Assembly, elected by French males who possessed a set amount of property, comprising roughly half the male population. The constitution passed in September 1791 was the first in French history. It legalized divorce and broadened women's rights to inherit property and to obtain financial support for illegitimate children from fathers, but excluded women from political office and voting.

This decision was attacked by a small number of men and women who believed that the rights of man should be extended to all French citizens. Politically active women wrote pamphlets, formed clubs, and petitioned the Assembly on behalf of women's right to participate in the life of the nation. Olympe de Gouges (1748–1793), a self-taught writer and woman of the people, protested the evils of slavery as well as the injustices done to women. In September 1791 she published her *Declaration of the Rights of Woman*, which echoed its famous predecessor, the Declaration of the Rights of Man and of the Citizen, proclaiming, "Woman is born free and remains equal to man in rights." De Gouges's position found little sympathy among leaders of the Revolution, however.

In addition to ruling on women's rights, the National Assembly replaced the complicated patchwork of historic provinces with eighty-three departments of approximately equal size, a move toward more rational and systematic methods of administration. In the name of economic liberty, the deputies prohibited guilds and workers' associations and abolished internal customs fees. Thus the National Assembly applied the spirit of the Enlightenment in a thorough reform of France's laws and institutions.

The National Assembly also imposed a radical reorganization on religious life. The Assembly granted religious freedom to the small minority of French Protestants and Jews. In November 1789 it nationalized the property of the Catholic Church and abolished monasteries. The government used all former church property as collateral to guarantee a new paper currency, the assignats (A-sihg-nat), and then sold the property in an attempt to put the state's finances on a solid footing.

Imbued with the rationalism and skepticism of the eighteenth-century Enlightenment, many delegates distrusted popular piety and "superstitious religion." Thus in July 1790, with the Civil Constitution of the Clergy, they established a national church with priests chosen by voters. The National Assembly then forced the Catholic clergy to take an oath of loyalty to the new government. The pope formally condemned this measure, and only half the priests of France swore the oath. Many sincere Christians, especially those in the countryside, were appalled by these changes in the religious order.

Why and how did the French Revolution take a radical turn?

When Louis XVI accepted the National Assembly's constitution in September 1791, a young provincial lawyer and delegate named Maximilien Robespierre (1758–1794) concluded that "the Revolution is over." Robespierre was right in the sense that the most constructive and lasting reforms were in place. Yet he was wrong in suggesting that turmoil had ended, for a much more radical stage lay ahead, one that would bring war with foreign powers, the declaration of terror at home, and a transformation in France's government.

The International Response

The outbreak of revolution in France produced great excitement and a sharp division of opinion in Europe and the United States. On the one hand, liberals and radicals saw a mighty triumph of liberty over despotism. On the other hand, conservative leaders such as British statesman Edmund Burke (1729–1797) were intensely troubled. In 1790 Burke published *Reflections on the Revolution in France*, one of the great expressions of European conservatism. He derided abstract principles of "liberty" and "rights" and insisted on the importance of inherited traditions and privileges as a bastion of social stability.

One passionate rebuttal came from a young writer in London, Mary Wollstonecraft (1759–1797). Incensed by Burke's book, Wollstonecraft (WOOL-stuhn-kraft) wrote a blistering attack, *A Vindication of the Rights of Man* (1790). Two years later, she published her masterpiece, *A Vindication of the Rights of Woman* (1792). Like de Gouges in France, Wollstonecraft demanded equal rights for women. She also advocated coeducation out of the belief that it would make women better wives and mothers, good citizens, and economically independent. Considered very radical for the time, the book became a founding text of later feminist movements.

The kings and nobles of continental Europe, who had at first welcomed the revolution in France as weakening a competing power, now feared its impact. In June 1791 the royal family was arrested after a failed attempt to escape France. To supporters of the Revolution, the attempted flight was proof that the king was treacherously seeking foreign support for an invasion of France. To the monarchs of Austria and Prussia, the arrest of a crowned monarch was an unacceptable outrage. Two months later they issued the Declaration of Pillnitz, proclaiming their willingness to intervene in France to restore Louis XVI's rule if necessary.

But the crowned heads of Europe misjudged the situation. The new French representative body, called the Legislative Assembly, had new delegates and a different character. Although the delegates were still prosperous, well-educated middle-class men, they were younger and less cautious than their predecessors. Since the National Assembly had declared sitting deputies ineligible for re-election, none of them had previously served as national representatives. Many of them belonged to the political **Jacobin Club**, one of the many political clubs that had formed to debate the political issues of the day.

Jacobins and other deputies reacted with patriotic fury to the Declaration of Pillnitz. In a speech to the Assembly, one deputy declared that if the kings of Europe were attempting to incite war against France, then "we will incite a war of people against kings. . . . Ten million Frenchmen, kindled by the fire of liberty, armed with the sword, with reason, with eloquence would be able to change the face of the world and make the tyrants tremble on their thrones."[3] In April 1792 France declared war on Francis II of Austria, the Habsburg monarch.

France's crusade against tyranny went poorly at first. Prussia joined Austria against the French forces, who broke and fled at their first military encounter with this First Coalition of antirevolutionary foreign powers. On behalf of the Crowns of Austria and Prussia, the duke of Brunswick, commander of the coalition armies, issued a declaration threatening to destroy Paris if harm came to the royal family. The Legislative Assembly declared the country in danger, and volunteers rallied to the capital. The Brunswick manifesto heightened suspicions of treason on the part of the French king and queen. On August 10, 1792, a revolutionary crowd attacked the royal palace at the Tuileries (TWEE-luh-reez), while the royal family fled to the Legislative Assembly. Rather than offering refuge, the Assembly suspended the king from all his functions, imprisoned him, and called for a constitutional assembly to be elected by universal male suffrage.

The Second Revolution and the New Republic

The fall of the monarchy marked a radicalization of the Revolution, a phase that historians often call the **second revolution**. Louis's imprisonment was followed by the September Massacres. Fearing invasion by the Prussians and riled up by rumors that counter-revolutionaries would aid the invaders, angry crowds stormed the prisons and killed jailed priests and aristocrats. In late September 1792 the new, popularly elected National Convention, which replaced the Legislative Assembly, proclaimed France a republic, a nation in which the people, instead of a monarch, held sovereign power.

As with the Legislative Assembly, many members of the new National Convention belonged to the Jacobin Club of Paris. But the Jacobins themselves were increasingly divided into two bitterly opposed groups — the **Girondists** (juh-RAHN-dihsts) and **the Mountain**, led by Robespierre and another young lawyer, Georges Jacques Danton.

This division emerged clearly after the National Convention overwhelmingly convicted Louis XVI of treason. The Girondists accepted his guilt but did not wish to put the king to death. By a narrow majority, the Mountain carried the day, and Louis was executed on January 21, 1793, by guillotine, which the French had recently perfected. Marie Antoinette suffered the same fate later that year. But both the Girondists and the Mountain were determined to continue the "war against tyranny." The Prussians had been stopped at the Battle of Valmy on September 20, 1792, one day before the republic was proclaimed. French armies then invaded Savoy and captured Nice, moved into the German Rhineland, and by November 1792 were occupying the entire Austrian Netherlands (modern Belgium).

Everywhere they went, French armies of occupation chased princes, abolished feudalism, and found support among some peasants and middle-class people. But French armies also lived off the land, requisitioning food and supplies and plundering local treasures. The liberators therefore looked increasingly like foreign invaders. Meanwhile, international tensions mounted. In February 1793 the National Convention, at war with Austria and Prussia, declared war on Britain, the Dutch Republic, and Spain as well. Republican France was now at war with almost all of Europe.

Groups within France added to the turmoil. Peasants in western France revolted against being drafted into the army, with the Vendée region of Brittany emerging as the epicenter of revolt. Devout Catholics, royalists, and foreign agents encouraged their rebellion, and the counter-revolutionaries recruited veritable armies to fight for their cause.

In March 1793 the National Convention was locked in a life-and-death political struggle between members of the Mountain and the more moderate Girondists. With the middle-class delegates so bitterly divided, the people of Paris once again emerged as the decisive political factor. The laboring poor and the petty traders were often known as the **sans-culottes** because their men wore trousers instead of the knee breeches of the aristocracy and the solid middle class. They demanded radical political action to defend the Revolution. The Mountain, sensing an opportunity to outmaneuver the Girondists, joined with sans-culottes activists to engineer a popular uprising. On June 2, 1793, armed sans-culottes invaded the Convention and forced its deputies to arrest twenty-nine Girondist deputies for treason. All power passed to the Mountain.

The Convention also formed the Committee of Public Safety in April 1793 to deal with threats from within and outside France. The Committee, led by Robespierre, held dictatorial power and was allowed to use whatever force necessary to defend the Revolution. Moderates in leading provincial cities revolted against the committee's power and demanded a decentralized government. Counter-revolutionary forces in the Vendée won significant victories, and the republic's armies were driven back on all fronts. By July 1793 only the areas around Paris and on the eastern frontier were firmly held by the central government. Defeat seemed imminent.

Total War and the Terror

A year later, in July 1794, the central government had reasserted control over the provinces, and the Austrian Netherlands and the Rhineland were once again in French hands. This remarkable change of fortune was due to the revolutionary government's success in harnessing the explosive forces of a planned economy, revolutionary terror, and modern nationalism in a total war effort.

Robespierre and the Committee of Public Safety advanced on several fronts in 1793 and 1794, seeking to impose republican unity across the nation. First, they collaborated with the sans-culottes, who continued pressing the common people's case for fair prices and a moral economic order. Thus in September 1793 Robespierre and his coworkers established a planned economy with egalitarian social overtones. Rather than let supply and demand determine prices, the government set maximum prices for key products. Though the state was too weak to enforce all its price regulations, it did fix the price of bread in Paris at levels the poor could afford.

The people were also put to work producing arms, munitions, uniforms, boots, saddles, and other necessary supplies for the war effort. The government told craftsmen what to produce, nationalized many small workshops, and requisitioned raw materials and grain. These reforms amounted to an emergency form of socialism, which thoroughly frightened Europe's propertied classes and greatly influenced the subsequent development of socialist ideology.

The Execution of Robespierre After overseeing the Terror, during which thousands of men and women accused of being enemies of the Revolution faced speedy trial and execution, it was Maximilien Robespierre's turn to face the guillotine on 9 Thermidor Year II (July 28, 1794). (Musée de la Ville de Paris, Musée Carnavalet, Paris, France/Bridgeman Images)

Second, while radical economic measures furnished the poor with bread and the armies with supplies, the **Reign of Terror** (1793–1794) enforced compliance with republican beliefs and practices. The Constitution of 1793, which had been completed in June 1793 and approved by a national referendum, was indefinitely suspended in favor of a "revolutionary government." Special courts responsible only to Robespierre's Committee of Public Safety tried "enemies of the nation" for political crimes. Some forty thousand French men and women were executed or died in prison, and around three hundred thousand were arrested, making the Reign of Terror one of the most controversial phases of the Revolution. Presented as a necessary measure to save the republic, the Terror was a weapon directed against all suspected of opposing the revolutionary government.

In their efforts to impose unity, the Jacobins also took actions to suppress women's participation in political debate, which they perceived as disorderly and a distraction from women's proper place in the home. On October 30, 1793, the National Convention declared that "the clubs and popular societies of women, under whatever denomination are prohibited." Among those convicted of sedition was writer Olympe de Gouges, who was sent to the guillotine in November 1793.

The third element of the Committee's program was to bring about a cultural revolution that would transform former royal subjects into republican citizens. The government sponsored revolutionary art and songs as well as a new series of secular festivals to celebrate republican virtue and patriotism. It also attempted to rationalize

French daily life by adopting the decimal system for weights and measures and a new calendar based on ten-day weeks. Another important element of this cultural revolution was the campaign of de-Christianization, which aimed to eliminate Catholic symbols and beliefs. Fearful of the hostility aroused in rural France, however, Robespierre called for a halt to de-Christianization measures in mid-1794.

The final element in the program of the Committee of Public Safety was its appeal to a new sense of national identity and patriotism. With a common language and a common tradition newly reinforced by the revolutionary ideals of popular sovereignty and democracy, many French people developed an intense emotional commitment to the defense of the nation, and they saw the war against foreign opponents as a life-and-death struggle between good and evil. This was the birth of modern nationalism, which would have a profound effect on subsequent European history.

The all-out mobilization of French resources under the Terror combined with the fervor of nationalism to create an awesome fighting machine. A decree of August 1793 imposed the draft on all unmarried young men, and by January 1794 French armed forces outnumbered those of their enemies almost four to one.[4] Well trained, well equipped, and constantly indoctrinated, the enormous armies of the republic were led by young, impetuous generals who often had risen from the ranks and who personified the opportunities the Revolution offered gifted sons of the people. By spring 1794 French armies were victorious on all fronts and domestic revolt was largely suppressed. The republic was saved.

The Thermidorian Reaction and the Directory

The success of French armies led the Committee of Public Safety to relax the emergency economic controls, but the Committee extended the political Reign of Terror. In March 1794 the revolutionary tribunal sentenced many of its critics to death. Two weeks later Robespierre sent long-standing collaborators whom he believed had turned against him, including Danton, to the guillotine. In June 1794 a new law removed defendants' right of legal counsel and criminalized criticism of the Revolution.

A group of radicals and moderates in the Convention, knowing that they might be next, organized a conspiracy. They howled down Robespierre when he tried to speak to the National Convention on July 27, 1794—a date known as 9 Thermidor according to France's newly adopted republican calendar. The next day it was Robespierre's turn to be guillotined.

As Robespierre's closest supporters followed their leader to the guillotine, the respectable middle-class lawyers and professionals who had led the liberal Revolution of 1789 reasserted their authority. This period of **Thermidorian reaction**, as it was called, hearkened back to the ideals of the early Revolution; the new leaders of government proclaimed an end to the revolutionary expediency of the Terror and the return of representative government, the rule of law, and liberal economic policies. In 1795 the National Convention abolished many economic controls, let prices rise sharply, and severely restricted the local political organizations through which the sans-culottes exerted their strength.

In the same year, members of the National Convention wrote a new constitution to guarantee their economic position and political supremacy. As in previous elections, the mass of the population could vote only for electors who would in turn elect the legislators, but the new constitution greatly reduced the number of men eligible to become electors by instating a substantial property requirement. It also inaugurated a bicameral legislative system for the first time in the Revolution, with a Council of 500 serving as the lower house that initiated legislation and a Council of Elders (composed of about 250 members aged forty years or older) acting as the upper house that approved new laws. To prevent a new Robespierre from monopolizing power, the constitution granted executive power to a five-man body, called the Directory.

The Directory continued to support French military expansion abroad. War was no longer so much a crusade as a response to economic problems. Large, victorious French armies reduced unemployment at home. However, the French people quickly grew weary of the corruption and ineffectiveness that characterized the Directory. The trauma of years of military and political violence had alienated the public, and the Directory's heavy-handed and opportunistic policies did not reverse the situation. This general dissatisfaction revealed itself clearly in the national elections of 1797, which returned a large number of conservative and even monarchist deputies who favored peace at almost any price. Two years later Napoleon Bonaparte ended the Directory in a coup d'état (koo day-TAH; violent overthrow of government by a small number of people) and substituted a strong dictatorship for a weak one.

How did Napoleon Bonaparte create a French empire, and why did it fail?

For almost fifteen years, from 1799 to 1814, France was in the hands of a keen-minded military dictator of exceptional ability. One of history's most fascinating leaders, Napoleon Bonaparte (1769–1821) realized that he needed to put an end to civil strife in France in order to create unity and consolidate his rule. And he did. But Napoleon saw himself as a man of destiny, and the glory of war and the dream of universal empire proved irresistible. For years he triumphed from victory to victory, but in the end he was destroyed by a mighty coalition united in fear of his restless ambition.

Napoleon's Rule of France

Born in Corsica into an impoverished noble family in 1769, Napoleon left home and became a lieutenant in the French artillery in 1785. Converted to the revolutionary cause and rising rapidly in the republican army, Napoleon gained command of French forces in Italy and won brilliant victories there in 1796 and 1797. His next campaign, in Egypt, was a failure, but Napoleon returned to France before the fiasco was generally known, and his reputation remained intact. French aggression in Egypt and elsewhere provoked the British to organize a new alliance in 1798, the Second Coalition that also included Austria and Russia.

Napoleon soon learned that prominent members of the legislature were plotting against the Directory. The plotters' dissatisfaction stemmed not so much from the Directory's dictatorial rule as from the fact that it was an ineffective dictatorship. Ten years of upheaval and uncertainty had made firm rule much more appealing than liberty and popular politics to these disillusioned revolutionaries. The abbé Sieyès personified this evolution in thinking. In 1789 he had written that the nobility was grossly overprivileged and that the entire people should rule the French nation. Now Sieyès's motto was "Confidence from below, authority from above."

The flamboyant thirty-year-old Napoleon, nationally revered for his military exploits, was an ideal figure of authority. On November 9, 1799, Napoleon and his conspirators ousted the Directors, and the following day soldiers disbanded the legislature at bayonet point. Napoleon was named first consul of the republic, and a new constitution consolidating his position was overwhelmingly approved by a nationwide vote in December 1799. Republican appearances were maintained, but Napoleon became the real ruler of France.

Napoleon worked to maintain order and end civil strife by appeasing powerful groups in France, offering them favors in return for loyal service. Napoleon's bargain with the middle class was codified in the Civil Code of March 1804, also known as the **Napoleonic Code**, which reasserted two of the fundamental principles of the Revolution of 1789: equality of all male citizens before the law, and security of wealth and private property. Napoleon and the leading bankers of Paris established the privately owned Bank of France in 1800, which served the interests of both the state and the financial oligarchy. Napoleon won over peasants by defending the gains in land and status they had won during the Revolution.

At the same time, Napoleon consolidated his rule by recruiting disillusioned revolutionaries to form a network of ministers, prefects, and centrally appointed mayors. Nor were members of the old nobility slighted. In 1800 and again in 1802 Napoleon granted amnesty to one hundred thousand émigrés on the condition that they return to France and take a loyalty oath. Members of this returning elite soon occupied many high posts in the expanding centralized state. Napoleon also created a new imperial nobility to reward his most talented generals and officials.

Furthermore, Napoleon sought to restore the Catholic Church in France so that it could serve as a bulwark of social stability. After arduous negotiations, Napoleon and Pope Pius VII (pontificate 1800–1823) signed the Concordat (kuhn-KOHR-dat) of 1801. The pope obtained the right for French Catholics to practice their religion freely, but Napoleon's government now nominated bishops, paid the clergy, and exerted great influence over the church.

The domestic reforms of Napoleon's early years were his greatest achievement. Much of his legal and administrative reorganization has survived in France to this day, but order and unity had a price: authoritarian rule. Women lost many of the gains they had made in the 1790s. Under the Napoleonic Code, women became dependents of either their fathers or their husbands, and they could not make contracts or have bank accounts in their own names. Napoleon and his advisers aimed at re-establishing a family monarchy, where the power of the husband and father was as absolute over the wife and the children as that of Napoleon was over his subjects. He also curtailed free speech and freedom of the press and manipulated voting in the occasional elections. After 1810 political suspects were held in state prisons, as they had been during the Terror.

Napoleon's Expansion in Europe

Napoleon was above all a great military man. After coming to power in 1799, he sent peace feelers to Austria and Great Britain, the dominant members of the Second Coalition. When these overtures were rejected, Napoleon's armies decisively defeated the Austrians. In the Treaty of Lunéville (1801), Austria accepted the loss of almost all

Portrait of Napoleon Bonaparte (1769–1821) on the Imperial Throne Napoleon Bonaparte was crowned as emperor of France on December 2, 1804, at a spectacular ceremony in Notre-Dame Cathedral in Paris. As shown in this portrait by Jean-Auguste-Dominique Ingres, Napoleon wore crimson velvet robes decorated with golden bees, the emblem he chose to replace the fleur-de-lis, the traditional symbol of the French monarchy. To proclaim his legitimacy as emperor, he wears a laurel crown (as did ancient Roman emperors) and holds in his left hand a sceptre topped with a statue of Charlemagne and in his right the rod of justice. A sword inspired by the one carried by Charlemagne stands on his right side. (Photo Josse/Leemage/Getty Images)

its Italian possessions, and German territory on the west bank of the Rhine was incorporated into France. The British agreed to the Treaty of Amiens in 1802, allowing France to control the former Dutch Republic (known as the Batavian Republic since 1795), the Austrian Netherlands, the west bank of the Rhine, and most of the Italian peninsula. The Treaty of Amiens was a diplomatic triumph for Napoleon, and peace with honor and profit increased his popularity at home.

In 1802 Napoleon was secure but still driven to expand his power. Aggressively redrawing the map of German-speaking lands so as to weaken Austria and encourage the secondary states of southwestern Germany to side with France, Napoleon tried to restrict British trade with all of Europe. He then plotted to attack Great Britain, but his Mediterranean fleet was destroyed by Lord Nelson at the Battle of Trafalgar on October 21, 1805. Invasion of England was henceforth impossible. Renewed fighting had its advantages, however, for the first consul used the wartime atmosphere to have himself proclaimed emperor in late 1804.

Austria, Russia, and Sweden joined with Britain to form the Third Coalition against France shortly before the Battle of Trafalgar. Actions such as Napoleon's assumption of the Italian Crown had convinced both Alexander I of Russia and Francis II of Austria that Napoleon was a threat to the European balance of power. Yet they were no match for Napoleon, who scored a brilliant victory over them at the Battle of Austerlitz in December 1805. Alexander I decided to pull back, and Austria accepted large territorial losses in return for peace as the Third Coalition collapsed.

Napoleon then reorganized the German states to his liking. In 1806 he abolished many of the tiny German states as well as the ancient Holy Roman Empire and established by decree the German Confederation of the Rhine, a union of fifteen German states minus Austria, Prussia, and Saxony. Naming himself "protector" of the confederation, Napoleon firmly controlled western Germany.

Napoleon's intervention in German affairs alarmed the Prussians, who mobilized their armies after more than a decade of peace with France. Napoleon attacked and won two more brilliant victories in October 1806 at Jena and Auerstädt, where the Prussians were outnumbered two to one. The war with Prussia, now joined by Russia, continued into the following spring. After Napoleon's larger armies won another victory, Alexander I of Russia was ready to negotiate the peace. In the subsequent treaties of Tilsit in 1807, Prussia lost half of its population, while Russia accepted Napoleon's reorganization of western and central Europe and promised to enforce Napoleon's economic blockade against British goods.

The Grand Empire and Its End

Increasingly, Napoleon saw himself as the emperor of Europe, not just of France. The so-called **Grand Empire** he built had three parts. The core, or first part, was an ever-expanding France, which by 1810 included today's Belgium and the Netherlands, parts of northern Italy, and German territories on the west bank of the Rhine. The second part consisted of a number of dependent satellite kingdoms, on the thrones of which Napoleon placed members of his large family. The third part comprised the independent but allied states of Austria, Prussia, and Russia. After 1806 Napoleon expected both satellites and allies to support his **Continental System**, a blockade in which no ship coming from Britain or her colonies could dock at a port controlled by the French. It was intended to halt all trade between Britain and continental Europe, thereby destroying the British economy and its military force.

The impact of the Grand Empire on the peoples of Europe was considerable. In the areas incorporated into France and in the satellites (Map 19.2), Napoleon followed revolutionary principles by abolishing feudal dues and serfdom, to the benefit of the peasants and middle class. Yet Napoleon had to put the prosperity and special interests of France first in order to safeguard his power base. Levying heavy taxes in money and men for his armies, he came to be regarded more as a conquering tyrant than as an enlightened liberator. Thus French rule sparked patriotic upheavals and encouraged the growth of reactive nationalism, for individuals in different lands learned to identify emotionally with their own embattled national families as the French had done earlier.

The first great revolt occurred in Spain. In 1808 Napoleon deposed Spanish king Ferdinand VII and placed his own brother Joseph on the throne. However, a coalition of Catholics, monarchists, and patriots rebelled against Napoleon's attempts to make Spain a French satellite. French armies occupied Madrid, but the foes of

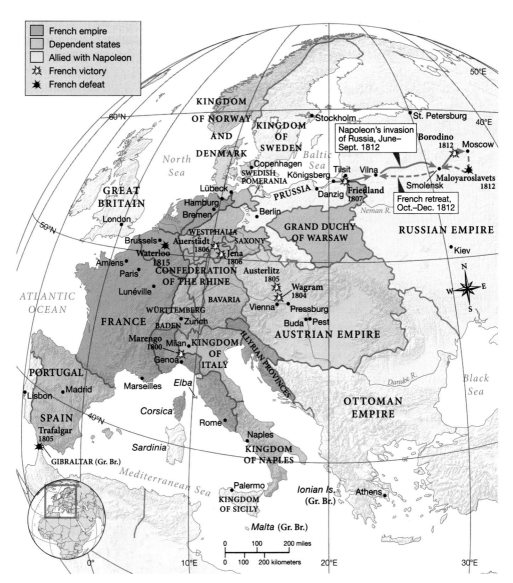

MAP 19.2   Napoleonic Europe in 1812
At the height of the Grand Empire in 1810, Napoleon had conquered or allied with every major European power except Britain. But in 1812, angered by Russian repudiation of his ban on trade with Britain, Napoleon invaded Russia with disastrous results. Compare this map with Map 15.2 (page 428), which shows the division of Europe in 1715.

Napoleon fled to the hills and waged uncompromising guerrilla warfare. Spain was a clear warning: resistance to French imperialism was growing.

Yet Napoleon pushed on. In 1810, when the Grand Empire was at its height, Britain still remained at war with France, helping the guerrillas in Spain and Portugal. The Continental System was a failure. Instead of harming Britain, the system provoked the British to set up a counter-blockade, which created hard times in France. Perhaps looking for a scapegoat, Napoleon turned on Alexander I of Russia, who had opened Russian ports to British goods in December 1810.

Napoleon's invasion of Russia began in June 1812 with a force that eventually numbered 600,000, probably the largest force yet assembled in a single army. Only one-third of this army was French, however; nationals of all the satellites and allies were drafted into the operation. Originally planning to winter in the Russian city of Smolensk, Napoleon recklessly pressed on toward Moscow. The great Battle of Borodino that followed was a draw. Alexander ordered the evacuation of Moscow, which the Russians then burned in part, and he refused to negotiate. Finally, after five weeks in the scorched and abandoned city, Napoleon ordered a retreat, one of the greatest military disasters in history. The Russian army, the Russian winter, and starvation cut Napoleon's army to pieces. When the frozen remnants staggered into Poland and Prussia in December, 370,000 men had died and another 200,000 had been taken prisoner.[5]

Leaving his troops to their fate, Napoleon raced to Paris to raise yet another army. Possibly he might still have saved his throne if he had been willing to accept a France reduced to its historical size—the proposal offered by Austria's foreign minister, Prince Klemens von Metternich. But Napoleon refused. Austria and Prussia deserted Napoleon and joined Russia and Great Britain in the Treaty of Chaumont in March 1814, by which the four powers formed the Quadruple Alliance to defeat the French emperor.

All across Europe patriots called for a "war of liberation" against Napoleon's oppression. Less than a month later, on April 4, 1814, a defeated Napoleon abdicated his throne. After this unconditional abdication, the victorious allies granted Napoleon the island of Elba off the coast of Italy as his own tiny state. Napoleon was allowed to keep his imperial title, and France was required to pay him a yearly income of 2 million francs.

The allies also agreed to the restoration of the Bourbon dynasty under Louis XVIII (r. 1814–1824) and promised to treat France with leniency in a peace settlement. The new monarch sought support among the people by issuing the Constitutional Charter, which accepted many of France's revolutionary changes and guaranteed civil liberties.

Yet Louis XVIII lacked the magnetism of Napoleon. Hearing of political unrest in France and diplomatic tensions in Vienna, Napoleon staged a daring escape from Elba in February 1815 and marched on Paris with a small band of followers. French officers and soldiers who had fought so long for their emperor responded to the call. Louis XVIII fled, and once more Napoleon took command. But Napoleon's gamble was a desperate long shot, for the allies were united against him. At the end of a frantic period known as the Hundred Days, they crushed his forces at Waterloo on June 18, 1815, and imprisoned him on the rocky island of St. Helena, off the western coast of Africa. Louis XVIII returned to the throne, and the allies dealt more harshly with the French. As for Napoleon, he took revenge by writing his memoirs, nurturing the myth that he had been Europe's revolutionary liberator, a romantic hero whose lofty work had been undone by oppressive reactionaries.

How did slave revolt on colonial Saint-Domingue lead to the independent nation of Haiti?

The events that led to the creation of the independent nation of Haiti constitute the third, and perhaps most extraordinary, chapter of the revolutionary era in the late eighteenth century. Prior to 1789 Saint-Domingue, the French colony that was to become Haiti, reaped huge profits through a ruthless system of slave-based plantation agriculture. News of revolution in France lit a powder keg of contradictory aspirations among white planters, free people of color, and slaves. While revolutionary authorities debated how far to extend the rights of man on Saint-Domingue, first free people of color and then enslaved people took matters into their own hands, rising up to demand their rights. They succeeded, despite invasion by the British and Spanish and Napoleon Bonaparte's bid to reimpose French control. In 1804 Haiti became the only nation in history to claim its freedom through slave revolt.

Revolutionary Aspirations in Saint-Domingue

On the eve of the French Revolution, Saint-Domingue — the most profitable of all Caribbean colonies — was even more rife with social tensions than France itself. The colony, which occupied the western third of the island of Hispaniola, was inhabited by a variety of social groups who resented and mistrusted one another. The European population included French colonial officials, wealthy plantation owners and merchants, and poor artisans and clerks. Individuals of French or European descent born in the colonies were called "Creoles," and over time they had developed their own interests, at times distinct from those of metropolitan France. Vastly outnumbering the white population were the colony's five hundred thousand enslaved people alongside a sizable population of some forty thousand free people of African and mixed African and European descent. Members of this last group referred to themselves as free people of color.

Legal and economic conditions on Saint-Domingue vastly favored the white population. Most of the island's enslaved population performed grueling toil in the island's sugar plantations. The highly outnumbered planters used extremely brutal methods, such as beating, maiming, and executing slaves, to maintain their control. The 1685 Code Noir (Black Code) that legally regulated slavery was intended to provide minimal standards of humane treatment, but its tenets were rarely enforced. Masters calculated that they could earn more by working slaves ruthlessly and purchasing new ones when they died, than by providing the food, rest, and medical care needed to allow the enslaved population to reproduce naturally. This meant that a constant inflow of newly enslaved people from Africa was necessary to work the plantations. Some slaves found freedom from this brutality by escaping into the mountains to join groups of fugitive slaves, known as "maroons."

Slaveholders on Saint-Domingue granted formal freedom to a small number of their slaves, mostly their own mixed-race children, thereby contributing to one of the largest populations of free people of color in any slaveholding colony. The Code Noir had originally granted free people of color the same legal status as whites: they could own property, live where they wished, and pursue any education or career they desired. From the 1760s on, however, the rising prosperity and visibility of this group provoked resentment from the white population. In response, colonial administrators began rescinding the rights of free people of color, and by the time of the French Revolution myriad aspects of their lives were subject to discriminatory laws.

The political and intellectual turmoil of the 1780s, with its growing rhetoric of liberty, equality, and fraternity, raised new challenges and possibilities for each of Saint-Domingue's social groups. For enslaved people, who constituted approximately 90 percent of the population, news of abolitionist movements in France led to hopes that the mother country might grant them freedom. Free people of color looked to reforms in Paris as a means of gaining political enfranchisement and reasserting equal status with whites. The Creole elite, however, was determined to protect its way of life, including slaveholding. They looked to revolutionary ideals of representative government for the chance to gain control of their own affairs, as had the American colonists before them.

The National Assembly frustrated the hopes of all these groups. Cowed by colonial representatives who claimed that support for free people of color would result in slave insurrection and independence, the Assembly refused to extend French constitutional safeguards to the colonies. After dealing this blow to the aspirations of slaves and free people of color, the Assembly also reaffirmed French monopolies over colonial trade, thereby angering Creole planters as well.

In July 1790 Vincent Ogé (aw-ZHAY) (ca. 1750–1791), a free man of color, returned to Saint-Domingue from Paris determined to win rights for his people. He raised an army of several hundred and sent letters to the new Provincial Assembly of Saint-Domingue demanding political rights for all free citizens. When Ogé's demands were refused, he and his followers turned to armed insurrection. After initial victories, his army was defeated, and Ogé was tortured and executed by colonial officials. Revolutionary leaders in Paris were more sympathetic to Ogé's cause. In May 1791, responding to what it perceived as partly justified grievances, the National Assembly granted political rights to free people of color born to two free parents who possessed sufficient property. When news of this legislation arrived in Saint-Domingue, the colonial governor refused to enact it. Violence then erupted between groups of whites and free people of color in parts of the colony.

The Outbreak of Revolt

Just as the sans-culottes helped push forward more radical reforms in France, decisive action from below brought about the second stage of revolution in Saint-Domingue. In August 1791 slaves, who had witnessed the confrontation between whites and free people of color for over a year, took events into their own hands. Groups of slaves held a series of nighttime meetings to plan a mass insurrection. In doing so, they drew on their own considerable military experience; the majority of slaves had been born in Africa, and many had served in the civil wars of the kingdom of Kongo and other conflicts before being taken into slavery.[6] They also drew on a long tradition of slave resistance prior to 1791, which had ranged from work slowdowns, to running away, to taking part in African-derived religious rituals and dances known as *vodou* (or voodoo). According to some sources, the August 1791 pact to take up arms was sealed by such a voodoo ritual.[7]

Revolts began on a few plantations on the night of August 22. Within a few days the uprising had swept much of the northern plain, creating a slave army estimated at around 2,000 individuals. By August 27 it was described by one observer as "10,000 strong, divided into 3 armies, of whom 700 or 800 are on horseback, and tolerably well-armed."[8] During the next month enslaved combatants attacked and destroyed hundreds of sugar and coffee plantations.

On April 4, 1792, as war loomed with the European states, the National Assembly issued a decree extending full citizenship rights to free people of color, including the right to vote. As in France, voting rights and the ability to hold public office applied to men only. The Assembly hoped this measure would win the loyalty of free people of color and their aid in defeating the slave rebellion.

Warfare in Europe soon spread to Saint-Domingue (Map 19.3). Since the beginning of the slave insurrection, the Spanish colony of Santo Domingo, on the eastern side of the island of Hispaniola, had supported rebel slaves. In early 1793 the Spanish began to bring slave leaders and their soldiers into the Spanish army. Toussaint L'Ouverture (TOO-sahn LOO-vair-toor) (1743–1803), a freed slave who had joined

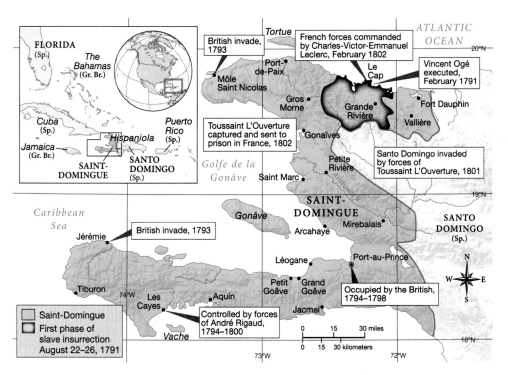

MAP 19.3 The War of Haitian Independence, 1791–1804
Neighbored by the Spanish colony of Santo Domingo, Saint-Domingue was the most profitable European colony in the Caribbean. In 1770 the French transferred the capital from Le Cap to Port-au-Prince. Slave revolts erupted in the north near Le Cap in 1791. Port-au-Prince became the capital of the newly independent Haiti in 1804.

the revolt, was named a Spanish officer. In September the British navy blockaded the colony, and invading British troops captured French territory on the island. For the Spanish and British, revolutionary chaos provided a tempting opportunity to capture a profitable colony.

Desperate for forces to oppose France's enemies, commissioners sent by the newly elected National Convention promised freedom to slaves who fought for France. By October 1793 they had abolished slavery throughout the colony. On February 4, 1794, the Convention ratified the abolition of slavery and extended it to all French territories. In some ways this act merely acknowledged the achievements already won by the slave insurrection itself.

The tide of battle began to turn when Toussaint L'Ouverture switched sides, bringing his military and political skills, along with four thousand well-trained soldiers, to support the French war effort. By 1796 the French had regained control of the colony, and L'Ouverture had emerged as a key military leader. In May 1796 he was named commander of the western province of Saint-Domingue (see Map 19.3). The increasingly conservative nature of the French government during the Thermidorian reaction, however, threatened to undo the gains made by former slaves and free people of color.

The War of Haitian Independence

With Toussaint L'Ouverture acting increasingly as an independent ruler of the western province of Saint-Domingue, another general, André Rigaud (1761–1811), set up his own government in the southern peninsula. Tensions mounted between L'Ouverture and Rigaud. While L'Ouverture was a freed slave of African descent, Rigaud belonged to the free colored elite. This elite resented the growing power of former slaves like L'Ouverture, who in turn accused them of adopting the prejudices of white colonizers. Civil war broke out between the two sides in 1799, when L'Ouverture's forces, led by his lieutenant, Jean Jacques Dessalines (1758–1806), invaded the south. Victory over Rigaud in 1800 gave L'Ouverture control of the entire colony.

This victory was soon challenged by Napoleon, who had his own plans for reestablishing slavery and using the profits as a basis for expanding French power. Napoleon ordered his brother-in-law, General Charles-Victor-Emmanuel Leclerc (1772–1802), to lead an expedition to the island to crush the new regime. In 1802 Leclerc landed in Saint-Domingue and ordered the arrest of Toussaint L'Ouverture. The rebel leader, along with his family, was deported to France, where he died in 1803.

It was left to L'Ouverture's lieutenant, Jean Jacques Dessalines, to unite the resistance, and he led it to a crushing victory over French forces. On January 1, 1804, Dessalines formally declared the independence of Saint-Domingue and the creation of the new sovereign nation of Haiti, the name used by the pre-Columbian inhabitants of the island. The Haitian constitution was ratified in 1805.

Haiti, the second independent state in the Americas and the first in Latin America, was born from the first successful large-scale slave revolt in history. This event spread shock and fear through slaveholding societies in the Caribbean and the United States, bringing to life their worst nightmares of the utter reversal of their power and privilege. Fearing the spread of rebellion to the United States, President Thomas Jefferson refused to recognize Haiti as an independent nation. The liberal proponents of the American Revolution thus chose to protect slavery at the expense of revolutionary ideals of universal human rights. The French government imposed crushing indemnity charges on Haiti to recompense the loss of French property, dealing a harsh blow to the fledgling nation's economy.

Yet Haitian independence had fundamental repercussions for world history, helping spread the idea that liberty, equality, and fraternity must apply to all people. The next phase of Atlantic revolution soon opened in the Spanish American colonies.

NOTES

1. Quoted in G. Wright, *France in Modern Times*, 4th ed. (New York: W. W. Norton, 1987), p. 34.
2. G. Pernoud and S. Flaisser, eds., *The French Revolution* (Greenwich, Conn.: Fawcett, 1960), p. 61.
3. Quoted in L. Gershoy, *The Era of the French Revolution, 1789–1799* (New York: Van Nostrand, 1957), p. 150.
4. T. Blanning, *The French Revolutionary Wars, 1787–1802* (London: Arnold, 1996), pp. 116–128.
5. D. Sutherland, *France, 1789–1815: Revolution and Counterrevolution* (New York: Oxford University Press, 1986), p. 420.
6. John K. Thornton, "'I Am the Subject of the King of Congo': African Political Ideology and the Haitian Revolution," *Journal of World History* 4, no. 2 (Fall 1993): 181–214.
7. Laurent Dubois, *Avengers of the New World: The Story of the Haitian Revolution* (Cambridge, Mass.: Belknap Press, 2004), pp. 43–45, 99–100.
8. Quoted in Dubois, *Avengers of the New World*, p. 97.

LOOKING BACK **LOOKING AHEAD**

A great revolutionary wave swept both sides of the Atlantic Ocean in the late eighteenth century. The revolutions in British North America, France, and Haiti were individual and unique, but they had common origins and consequences for Western and, indeed, world history. The eighteenth century had witnessed monumental social and economic changes, as population grew, urbanization spread, and literacy increased. Enlightenment ideals, especially those of John Locke and the baron de Montesquieu, influenced all orders of society, and reformers increasingly championed limiting monarchical authority in the name of popular sovereignty.

The Atlantic world was the essential context for this age of revolutions. The movement of peoples, commodities, and ideas across the Atlantic Ocean in the eighteenth century created a world of common debates, conflicts, and aspirations. Moreover, the high stakes of colonial empire heightened competition among European states, leading to a series of wars that generated crushing costs for overburdened treasuries. For both the British in their North American colonies and the French at home, the desperate need for new taxes weakened government authority and opened the door to revolution. In turn, the ideals of the French Revolution inspired slaves and free people of color in Saint-Domingue, thus opening the promise of liberty, equality, and fraternity to people of all races.

The chain reaction did not end with the birth of an independent Haiti in 1804. On the European continent throughout the nineteenth and early twentieth centuries, periodic convulsions occurred as successive generations struggled over political rights first proclaimed by the generation of 1789. Meanwhile, as dramatic political events unfolded, a parallel economic revolution was gathering steam. This was the Industrial Revolution, originating around 1780 and accelerating through the end of the eighteenth century (see Chapter 20). After 1815 the twin forces of industrialization and democratization would combine to transform Europe and the world.

MAKE CONNECTIONS

Think about the larger developments and continuities within and across chapters.

1. What were major differences and similarities among the American, French, and Haitian Revolutions?
2. How did the increased circulation of goods, people, and ideas across the Atlantic in the eighteenth century (Chapter 17) contribute to the outbreak of revolution on both sides of the ocean?
3. To what extent would you characterize the revolutions discussed in this chapter as Enlightenment movements (Chapter 16)?

Chapter 19 Review

IDENTIFY KEY TERMS

Identify and explain the significance of each item below.

Estates General (p. 557)
estates (p. 557)
National Assembly (p. 558)
Great Fear (p. 559)
Jacobin Club (p. 562)
second revolution (p. 563)
Girondists (p. 563)

the Mountain (p. 563)
sans-culottes (p. 564)
Reign of Terror (p. 565)
Thermidorian reaction (p. 566)
Napoleonic Code (p. 568)
Grand Empire (p. 570)
Continental System (p. 570)

REVIEW THE MAIN IDEAS

Answer the section heading questions from the chapter.

1. What were the factors behind the revolutions of the late eighteenth century? (p. 547)
2. Why and how did American colonists forge a new, independent nation? (p. 552)
3. How did the events of 1789 result in a constitutional monarchy in France? (p. 556)
4. Why and how did the French Revolution take a radical turn? (p. 562)
5. How did Napoleon Bonaparte create a French empire, and why did it fail? (p. 567)
6. How did slave revolt on colonial Saint-Domingue lead to the independent nation of Haiti? (p. 573)

CHRONOLOGY

1775–1783	• American Revolution
1776	• Thomas Paine publishes *Common Sense*
1786–1789	• Height of French monarchy's financial crisis
1789	• Ratification of U.S. Constitution; storming of the Bastille; feudalism abolished in France
1789–1799	• French Revolution
1790	• Burke publishes *Reflections on the Revolution in France*
1791	• Slave insurrection in Saint-Domingue
1792	• Wollstonecraft publishes *A Vindication of the Rights of Woman*
1793	• Execution of Louis XVI
1793–1794	• Robespierre's Reign of Terror
1794	• Robespierre deposed and executed; France abolishes slavery in all territories
1794–1799	• Thermidorian reaction
1799–1815	• Napoleonic era
1804	• Haitian republic declares independence
1812	• Napoleon invades Russia
1814–1815	• Napoleon defeated and exiled

20

The Revolution in Energy and Industry

ca. 1780–1850

CHAPTER PREVIEW

- Why and how did the Industrial Revolution emerge in Britain?

- How did countries outside Britain respond to the challenge of industrialization?

- How did work and daily life evolve during the Industrial Revolution?

- What were the social consequences of industrialization?

WHILE REVOLUTIONS IN FRANCE AND ACROSS THE ATLANTIC were opening a new political era, another revolution was beginning to transform economic and social life. The Industrial Revolution took off around 1780 in Great Britain and soon began to influence continental Europe and the United States. Non-European nations began to industrialize after 1860.

Industrialization profoundly modified much of human experience. It changed patterns of work and daily life, transformed the social class structure and the way people thought about class, and eventually altered the international balance of political power. Quite possibly only the development of agriculture during Neolithic times had a comparable impact and significance.

What was revolutionary about the Industrial Revolution was not its pace or that it represented a sharp break with the previous period. On the contrary, the Industrial Revolution built on earlier developments, and the rate of progress was slow. What was remarkable about the Industrial

Revolution was that it inaugurated a period of sustained economic and demographic growth that has continued to the present day. Although it took time, the Industrial Revolution eventually helped ordinary people in the West gain a higher standard of living as the widespread poverty of preindustrial Europe gradually receded.

Such fundamental transitions did not occur overnight. National wealth rose much more quickly than improvements in the European standard of living until about 1850. This was because, even in Britain, only a few key industries experienced a technological revolution. Many more industries continued to use old methods. In addition, wage increases were modest until the mid-nineteenth century, and the gradual withdrawal of children and married women from paid work meant that the household as a whole earned the same or less.

Why and how did the Industrial Revolution emerge in Britain?

The Industrial Revolution began in Great Britain, the nation created in 1707 by the formal union of Scotland, Wales, and England. The transformation in industry was something new in history, and it was unplanned. With no models to copy and no idea of what to expect, Britain pioneered not only in industrial technology but also in social relations and urban living. Just as France was a trailblazer in political change, Britain was the leader in economic development, and it must therefore command special attention.

Why Britain?

Perhaps the most important debate in economic history focuses on why the Industrial Revolution originated in western Europe, and Britain in particular, rather than in other parts of the world, such as Asia. Historians continue to debate this issue, but the best answer seems to be that Britain possessed a unique set of possibilities and constraints — abundant coal deposits, high wages, a relatively peaceful and centralized government, well-developed financial systems, an innovative culture, highly skilled craftsmen, and a strong position in empire and global trade — that spurred its people to adopt a capital-intensive, machine-powered system of production. The long-term economic advantages of this system were not immediately apparent, and its adoption by the British was more a matter of circumstance than a planned strategy.

Thus a number of factors came together over the long term to give rise to the Industrial Revolution in Britain. The Scientific Revolution and the Enlightenment fostered a new worldview that embraced progress and the role of research and experimentation in understanding and mastering the natural world. Britain's intellectual culture extended across many institutions: scientific societies, universities, museums, and workers' associations. The institutions constituted a network for the public sharing of knowledge, including the work of scientists and technicians from other countries. The British Royal Society of Arts, for example, sponsored prizes for innovations in machinery and agriculture and played a pivotal part in the circulation of "useful knowledge."

In the economic realm, the seventeenth-century expansion of rural industry produced a surplus of English woolen cloth. Exported throughout Europe, English cloth brought commercial profits and high wages to the detriment of traditional producers in Flanders and Italy. By the eighteenth century the expanding Atlantic economy and trade with India and China were also serving Britain well. The mercantilist colonial empire Britain aggressively built, augmented by a strong position in Latin America and in the transatlantic slave trade, provided raw materials like cotton and a growing market for British manufactured goods. Strong demand for British manufacturing meant that British workers earned high wages compared to the rest of Europe and that capital was available for investment in new industrial development.

Agriculture also played an important role in bringing about the Industrial Revolution in Britain. English farmers were second only to the Dutch in productivity in 1700, and they were continually adopting new methods of farming. The result, especially before 1760, was a period of bountiful crops and low food prices. Because of increasing efficiency, landowners were able to produce more food with a smaller workforce. The enclosure movement had deprived many small landowners of their land, leaving the landless poor to work as hired agricultural laborers or in cottage industry. By the 1760s, on the eve of the Industrial Revolution, less than 40 percent of Britain's population worked in agriculture (as compared to 60 percent in 1700), while fully one-third worked in the manufacturing sectors, weaving textiles and producing other craft goods.

Abundant food and high wages in turn meant that many English families no longer had to spend almost everything they earned just to buy bread. Thus the family could spend more on manufactured goods—a razor for the man or a shawl for the woman. They could also pay to send their children to school. Britain's populace enjoyed high levels of literacy and numeracy (knowledge of mathematics) compared to the rest of Europe. Moreover, in the eighteenth century the members of the average British family were redirecting their labor away from unpaid work for household consumption and toward work for wages that they could spend on goods, a trend reflecting the increasing commercialization of the entire European economy.

Britain also benefited from rich natural resources and a well-developed infrastructure. In an age when it was much cheaper to ship goods by water than by land, no part of England was more than fifty miles from navigable water. Beginning in the 1770s a canal-building boom enhanced this advantage. Rivers and canals provided easy movement of England's and Wales's enormous deposits of iron and coal, resources that would be critical raw materials in Europe's early industrial age. The abundance of coal combined with high wages in manufacturing placed Britain in a unique position among European nations: its manufacturers had strong incentives to develop technologies to draw on the power of coal to increase workmen's productivity. In parts of the world with lower wages, such as India and China, the costs of mechanization at first outweighed potential gains in productivity.

A final factor favoring British industrialization was the heavy hand of the British state and its policies, especially in the formative decades of industrial change. Despite its rhetoric in favor of "liberty," Britain's parliamentary system taxed its population aggressively. The British state collected twice as much per capita as the supposedly "absolutist" French monarchy and spent the money on a navy to protect imperial commerce and on an army that could be used to quell uprisings by disgruntled workers. Starting with the Navigation Acts under Oliver Cromwell (see "The Puritan Protectorate" in Chapter 15), the British state also adopted aggressive tariffs, or duties, on imported goods to protect its industries.

All these factors combined to initiate the **Industrial Revolution**, a term first coined by contemporaries in 1799 to describe the burst of major inventions and technical changes under way. This technical revolution contributed to an impressive quickening in the annual rate of industrial growth in Britain. Whereas industry had grown at only 0.7 percent between 1700 and 1760 (before the Industrial Revolution), it grew at almost 3 percent between 1801 and 1831 (when industrial transformation was in full swing).[1]

Technological Innovations and Early Factories

The pressure to produce more goods for a growing market and to reduce the labor costs of manufacturing was directly related to the first decisive breakthrough of the Industrial Revolution: the creation of the world's first machine-powered factories in the British cotton textile industry. Technological innovations in the manufacture of cotton cloth led to a new system of production and social relationships. This was not the first time in European history that large numbers of people were systematically put to work in a single locale; the military arsenals of late medieval Venice are one example of a much older form of "factory." The crucial innovation in Britain was the introduction of machine power into the factory and the organization of labor around the functioning of highly productive machines.

The putting-out system that developed in the seventeenth-century textile industry involved a merchant who loaned, or "put out," raw materials to cottage workers who processed the raw materials in their own homes and returned the finished products to the merchant. There was always a serious imbalance in textile production based on cottage industry: the work of four or five spinners was needed to keep one weaver steadily employed. Cloth weavers constantly had to find more thread and more spinners. During the eighteenth century the putting-out system grew across Europe, but most extensively in Britain. There, pressured by growing demand, the system's limitations began to outweigh its advantages around 1760.

Many a tinkering worker knew that a better spinning wheel promised rich rewards. It proved hard to spin the traditional raw materials—wool and flax—with improved machines, but cotton was different. Cotton textiles had first been imported into Britain from India by the East India Company as a rare and delicate luxury for the upper classes. In the eighteenth century, as the transatlantic slave trade reached its peak, a lively market for cotton cloth emerged in West Africa, where the English and other Europeans traded it for human captives. By 1760 a tiny domestic cotton industry had emerged in northern England, but it could not compete with cloth produced in India and other parts of Asia. At this time, Indian cotton textiles dominated the world market because of their workers' mastery over design and dyeing techniques, easy access to raw materials, and relatively low wages.

International competition thus drove English entrepreneurs to invent new technologies to bring down labor costs.

After many experiments over a generation, a gifted carpenter and jack-of-all-trades, James Hargreaves, invented his cotton-spinning jenny about 1765. At almost the same moment, a barber-turned-manufacturer named Richard Arkwright invented (or possibly pirated) another kind of spinning machine, the water frame. These breakthroughs produced an explosion in the infant cotton textile industry in the 1780s, when it was increasing the value of its output at an unprecedented rate of about 13 percent each year. In 1793, Eli Whitney's invention of the cotton gin, a machine for separating cotton fibers from seeds, vastly increased the productivity of cotton fields in the United States, leading to an expansion of slavery and an influx of raw materials for British manufacturers. In the 1790s, the new machines were producing ten times as much cotton yarn as had been made in 1770.

Hargreaves's **spinning jenny** was simple, inexpensive, and powered by hand. In early models from six to twenty-four spindles were mounted on a sliding carriage, and each spindle spun a fine, slender thread. The machines were usually worked by women, who moved the carriage back and forth with one hand and turned a wheel

Woman Working a Spinning Jenny The loose cotton strands on the slanted bobbins shown in this illustration of Hargreaves's spinning jenny passed up to the sliding carriage and then on to the spindles in back for fine spinning. The worker, almost always a woman, regulated the sliding carriage with one hand, and with the other she turned the crank on the wheel to supply power. By 1783 one woman could spin by hand a hundred threads at a time. (© Mary Evans Picture Library/The Image Works)

to supply power with the other. Now it was the male weaver who could not keep up with the vastly more efficient female spinner.

Arkwright's spinning frame employed a different principle, using a series of rollers to stretch the yarn. It quickly acquired a capacity of several hundred spindles and demanded much more power than a single operator could provide. A solution was found in waterpower. The **water frame** required large specialized mills located beside rivers in factories that employed as many as one thousand workers. The water frame did not completely replace cottage industry, however, for it could spin only a coarse, strong thread, which was then put out for respinning on hand-operated cottage jennies. Around 1780 a hybrid machine—called a mule—invented by Samuel Crompton proved capable of spinning very fine and strong thread in large quantities. Gradually, all cotton spinning was concentrated in large-scale water-powered factories.

These revolutionary developments in the textile industry allowed British manufacturers to compete successfully in international markets in both fine and coarse cotton thread. At first, the machines were too expensive to build and did not provide enough savings in labor to be adopted in continental Europe or elsewhere. Where wages were low and investment capital was scarce, there was little point in adopting mechanized production until significant increases in the machines' productivity, and a drop in the cost of manufacturing them, occurred in the first decades of the nineteenth century.[2]

Families using cotton in cottage industry were freed from their constant search for adequate yarn from scattered part-time spinners, since all the thread needed could be spun in the cottage on the jenny or obtained from a nearby factory. The income of weavers, now hard-pressed to keep up with the spinners, rose markedly until about 1792. They were among the highest-earning workers in England. As a result, large numbers of agricultural laborers became handloom weavers, while mechanics and capitalists sought to invent a power loom to save on labor costs. This Edmund Cartwright achieved in 1785. But the power looms of the factories worked poorly at first and did not replace handlooms until the 1820s.

The creation of the world's first machine-powered factories in the British cotton textile industry in the 1770s and 1780s, which grew out of the putting-out system of cottage production, was a major historical development. Both symbolically and substantially, the big new cotton mills marked the beginning of the Industrial Revolution in Britain. By 1831 the largely mechanized cotton textile industry accounted for fully 22 percent of the country's entire industrial production. British cotton textiles cost half as much as Indian ones even though labor costs were many times higher.

The Steam Engine Breakthrough

Human beings have long used their toolmaking abilities to construct machines that convert one form of energy into another for their own benefit. In the medieval period, Europeans began to adopt water mills to grind their grain and windmills to pump water and drain swamps. More efficient use of water and wind in the sixteenth and seventeenth centuries enabled them to accomplish more. Nevertheless, even into the eighteenth century Europe, like other areas of the world, continued to rely mainly on wood for energy, and human beings and animals continued to perform most work. This dependence meant that Europe and the rest of the world remained poor in energy and power.

By the eighteenth century wood was in ever-shorter supply in Britain. Processed wood (charcoal) was the fuel that was mixed with iron ore in the blast furnace to produce pig iron, crude iron molded into ingots called "pigs" that could be processed into steel, cast iron, or wrought iron. The iron industry's appetite for wood was enormous, and by 1740 the British iron industry was stagnating due to the depleted supply of fuel. Vast forests enabled Russia in the eighteenth century to become the world's leading producer of iron, much of which was exported to Britain. As wood became ever more scarce, the British looked to coal (combustible rock composed of fossilized organic matter) as an alternative. They had first used coal in the late Middle Ages as a source of heat. By 1640 most homes in London were heated with coal, and it was also used in industry to provide heat for making beer, glass, soap, and other products. The breakthrough came when industrialists began to use coal to produce mechanical energy and to power machinery.

To produce more coal, mines had to be dug deeper and deeper and, as a result, were constantly filling with water. Mechanical pumps, usually powered by animals walking in circles at the surface, had to be installed. But animal power was expensive and bothersome. In an attempt to overcome these disadvantages, Thomas Savery in 1698 and Thomas Newcomen in 1705 invented the first primitive **steam engines**. Both engines burned coal to produce steam, which was then used to operate a pump. Although both models were extremely inefficient, by the early 1770s many of the Savery engines and hundreds of the Newcomen engines were operating successfully in English and Scottish mines.

In 1763 a gifted young Scot named James Watt (1736–1819) was drawn to a critical study of the steam engine. Watt was employed at the time by the University of Glasgow as a skilled craftsman making scientific instruments. Scotland's Enlightenment emphasis on practicality and social progress had caused its universities to become pioneers in technical education. In 1763 Watt was called on to repair a Newcomen engine being used in a physics course. After a series of observations, Watt saw that the Newcomen engine's waste of energy could be reduced by adding a separate condenser. This splendid invention, patented in 1769, greatly increased the efficiency of the steam engine.

To invent something is one thing; to make it a practical success is quite another. Watt needed skilled workers, precision parts, and capital, and the relatively advanced nature of the British economy proved essential. A partnership in 1775 with Matthew Boulton, a wealthy English industrialist, provided Watt with adequate capital and exceptional skills in salesmanship. Among Britain's highly skilled locksmiths, tin-smiths, and millwrights, Watt found mechanics who could install, regulate, and repair his sophisticated engines. This support allowed him to create an effective vacuum in the condenser and regulate a complex engine. In more than twenty years of constant effort, Watt made many further improvements. By the late 1780s the firm of Boulton and Watt had made the steam engine a practical and commercial success in Britain.

The coal-burning steam engine of Watt and his followers was the Industrial Revolution's most fundamental advance in technology. For the first time, inventors and engineers could devise and implement all kinds of power equipment to aid people in their work. The steam-power plant began to replace waterpower in cotton-spinning factories during the 1780s, contributing to that industry's phenomenal rise. Steam also gradually took the place of waterpower in flour mills, in the malt mills used in breweries, in the flint mills supplying the pottery industry, and in the mills exported by Britain to the West Indies to crush sugarcane.

The British iron industry was radically transformed. Originally, the smoke and fumes resulting from coal burning meant that coal could not be substituted for charcoal in smelting iron. Starting around 1710, ironmakers began to use coke — a smokeless and hot-burning fuel produced by heating coal to rid it of water and other impurities — to smelt pig iron. After 1770 the adoption of steam-driven bellows in blast furnaces allowed for great increases in the quantity of pig iron produced by British ironmakers.

In the 1780s Henry Cort developed the coke-fired puddling furnace, which allowed for brittle pig iron to be refined into malleable wrought iron. Strong, skilled ironworkers — the puddlers — "cooked" molten pig iron in a great vat, raking off globs of refined iron for further processing. Cort also developed steam-powered rolling mills, which quickly and efficiently pressed the molten iron into bars, further purifying them in the process. These technical innovations fostered a great boom in the British iron industry. In 1740 annual British iron production was only 17,000 tons. With the spread of coke smelting and the impact of Cort's inventions, production had reached 250,000 tons by 1806. In 1844 Britain produced 3 million tons of iron. Once expensive, iron became the cheap, basic, indispensable building block of the British economy, used to manufacture railway tracks, textile machines, bridges, iron frames for factories and warehouses, weapons, pipes, gears, and steam engines themselves, among other goods.

Steam-Powered Transportation

The coal industry had long used plank roads and rails to move coal wagons within mines and at the surface. Rails reduced friction and allowed a horse or a human being to pull a much heavier load. Thus, once a rail capable of supporting a heavy locomotive was developed in 1816, all sorts of experiments with steam engines on rails went forward.

The first steam locomotive was built by Richard Trevithick after much experimentation. George Stephenson acquired glory for his locomotive named ***Rocket***, which sped down the track of the just-completed Liverpool and Manchester Railway at a maximum speed of 35 miles per hour, without a load, in 1829. The line from Liverpool to Manchester was the first modern railroad, using steam-powered locomotives to carry customers to the new industrial cities. It was a financial as well as a technical success, and many private companies quickly began to build more rail lines. Within twenty years they had completed the main trunk lines of Great Britain (Map 20.1). Other countries were quick to follow, with the first steam-powered trains operating in the United States in the 1830s and in Brazil, Chile, Argentina, and the British colonies of Canada, Australia, and India in the 1850s.

The arrival of the railroad had many significant consequences. It dramatically reduced the cost and uncertainty of shipping freight over land. Previously, markets had tended to be small and local; as the barrier of high transportation costs was lowered,

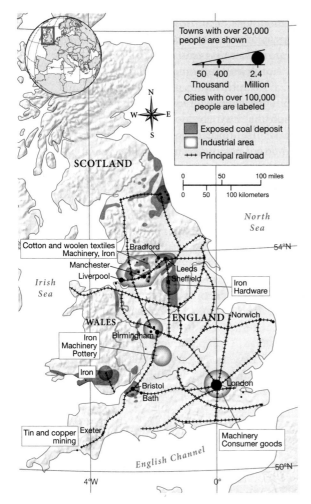

Towns with over 20,000 people are shown

50   400   2.4
Thousand   Million
Cities with over 100,000 people are labeled

▨ Exposed coal deposit
▢ Industrial area
•••• Principal railroad

0   50   100 miles
0   50   100 kilometers

North Sea

54°N

Irish Sea

Cotton and woolen textiles Machinery, Iron — Bradford

Manchester
Liverpool
Leeds
Sheffield

Iron Hardware

SCOTLAND

WALES   ENGLAND   Norwich

Iron Machinery Pottery — Birmingham

Iron

Bristol
Bath

London

Tin and copper mining — Exeter

Machinery Consumer goods

English Channel

50°N

4°W   0°

MAP 20.1   The Industrial Revolution in Great Britain, ca. 1850
Industry concentrated in the rapidly growing cities of the north and the center of England, where rich coal and iron deposits were close to one another.

markets became larger and even nationwide. Larger markets encouraged manufacturers to build larger factories with more sophisticated machinery in a growing number of industries. Such factories could make goods more cheaply and gradually subjected most cottage workers and many urban artisans to severe competitive pressures. In all countries, the construction of railroads created a strong demand for unskilled labor and contributed to the growth of a class of urban workers.

The steam engine also transformed water travel. French engineers completed the first steamships in the 1770s, and the first commercial steamships came into use in North America several decades later. The *Clermont* began to travel the waters of the Hudson River in New York State in 1807, shortly followed by ships belonging to brewer John Molson on the St. Lawrence River. The steamship brought the advantages of the railroad — speed, reliability, efficiency — to water travel.

Industry and Population

In 1851 Great Britain celebrated the new era of industrial technology and its role as a world economic leader through an industrial fair in London called the Great Exhibition. Sponsored by the British royal family and situated in the newly built **Crystal Palace**, the fair drew more than 6 million visitors from all over Europe who marveled at the gigantic new exhibition hall set in the middle of a large, centrally located park. The building was made entirely of glass and iron, both of which were now cheap and abundant.

Britain's claim to be the "workshop of the world" was no idle boast, for it produced two-thirds of the world's coal and more than half of all iron and cotton cloth. More generally, in 1860 Britain produced a remarkable 20 percent of the entire world's output of industrial goods, whereas it had produced only about 2 percent of the total in 1750.[3] As the British economy significantly increased its production

Environmental Impact of Industrialization Flames from a coke-fired blast furnace light up the night sky in the village of Coalbrookdale, an early center of the English iron ore smelting industry. With smoke billowing from the furnace and broken machinery scattered in the foreground, this painting highlights the environmental degradation that accompanied industrialization. (WHA/World History Archive/akg-images)

of manufactured goods, the gross national product (GNP) rose roughly fourfold at constant prices between 1780 and 1851. At the same time, the population of Britain boomed, growing from about 9 million in 1780 to almost 21 million in 1851. Thus growing numbers consumed much of the increase in total production.

Rapid population growth in Britain was key to industrial development. More people meant a more mobile labor force, with many young workers in need of employment and ready to go where the jobs were. The dramatic increase in population, in turn, was only sustained through advances in production in agriculture and industry. Based on the lessons of history, many contemporaries feared that the rapid growth in population would inevitably lead to disaster. In his *Essay on the Principle of Population* (1798), Thomas Malthus (1766–1834) examined the dynamics of human populations. He argued:

> There are few states in which there is not a constant effort in the population to increase beyond the means of subsistence. This constant effort as constantly tends to subject the lower classes of society to distress, and to prevent any great permanent melioration of these conditions.[4]

Given the limited resources available, Malthus concluded that the only hope of warding off such "positive checks" to population growth as famine and disease was "prudential restraint." That is, young men and women had to limit the growth of

Interior View of the Crystal Palace Built for the Great Exhibition of 1851, the Crystal Palace was a spectacular achievement in engineering, prefabricated from 300,000 sheets of glass. With almost 15,000 exhibitors, the event constituted the first international industrial exhibition, showcasing manufactured products from Britain, its empire, and the rest of the world. Later, the building was disassembled and moved to another site in London, where it stood until destroyed by fire in 1936. (Engraved by William Simpson [1823–1899]/London Metropolitan Archives [City of London]/Bridgeman Images)

population by marrying late in life. But Malthus was not optimistic about this possibility. The powerful attraction of the sexes, he feared, would cause most people to marry early and have many children.

Economist David Ricardo (1772–1823) spelled out the pessimistic implications of Malthus's thought. Ricardo's depressing **iron law of wages** posited that over an extended period of time, because of the pressure of population growth, wages would always sink to subsistence level. That is, wages would be just high enough to keep workers from starving.

Malthus, Ricardo, and their followers were proved wrong by the second half of the nineteenth century, largely because industrialization improved productivity beyond what they could imagine. However, until the 1820s, or even the 1840s, contemporary observers might reasonably have concluded that the economy and the total population were racing neck and neck, with the outcome very much in doubt. There was another problem as well. Perhaps workers, farmers, and ordinary people did not get their rightful share of the new wealth. Perhaps only the rich got richer, while the poor got poorer or made no progress. We will turn to this great issue after situating the process of industrialization in its European and global context (see "Living Standards for the Working Class" later in this chapter).

How did countries outside Britain respond to the challenge of industrialization?

As new technologies and a new organization of labor began to revolutionize production in Britain, other countries took notice and began to emulate its example. With the end of the Napoleonic Wars, the nations of the European continent quickly adopted British inventions and achieved their own pattern of technological innovation and economic growth. By the last decades of the nineteenth century, western European countries as well as the United States and Japan had industrialized their economies to a considerable, albeit variable, degree.

Industrialization in other parts of the world proceeded more gradually, with uneven jerks and national and regional variations. Scholars are still struggling to explain these variations as well as the dramatic gap that emerged for the first time in history between Western and non-Western levels of economic production. These questions are especially important because they may offer valuable lessons for poor countries that today are seeking to improve their material condition through industrialization and economic development. The latest findings on the nineteenth-century experience are encouraging. They suggest that there were alternative paths to the industrial world and that there was and is no need to follow a rigid, predetermined British model.

National and International Variations

Comparative data on industrial production in different countries over time help give us an overview of what happened. One set of data, the work of a Swiss scholar, compares the level of industrialization on a per capita basis in several countries from 1750 to 1913. These data are far from perfect, but they reflect basic trends and are presented in Table 20.1 for closer study.

Table 20.1 presents a comparison of how much industrial product was produced, on average, for each person in a given country in a given year. All the numbers are expressed in terms of a single index number of 100, which equals the per capita level of industrial goods in Great Britain in 1900. Every number in the table is thus a percentage of the 1900 level in Britain and is directly comparable with other numbers. The countries are listed in roughly the order that they began to use large-scale, power-driven technology.

What does this overview tell us? First, one sees in the first column that in 1750 all countries were fairly close together, including non-Western nations such as China and India. Both China and India had been extremely important players in early modern world trade; both were sophisticated, technologically advanced, and economically powerful up to 1800. However, the column headed 1800 shows that Britain had opened up a noticeable lead over all countries by 1800, and that gap progressively widened as the Industrial Revolution accelerated through 1830 and reached full maturity by 1860.

TABLE 20.1	PER CAPITA LEVELS OF INDUSTRIALIZATION, 1750–1913						
	1750	1800	1830	1860	1880	1900	1913
Great Britain	10	16	25	64	87	100	115
Belgium	9	10	14	28	43	56	88
United States	4	9	14	21	38	69	126
France	9	9	12	20	28	39	59
Germany	8	8	9	15	25	52	85
Austria-Hungary	7	7	8	11	15	23	32
Italy	8	8	8	10	12	17	26
Russia	6	6	7	8	10	15	20
China	8	6	6	4	4	3	3
India	7	6	6	3	2	1	2

Note: All entries are based on an index value of 100, equal to the per capita level of industrialization in Great Britain in 1900. Data for Great Britain includes Ireland, England, Wales, and Scotland.
Source: P. Bairoch, "International Industrialization Levels from 1750 to 1980," *Journal of European Economic History* 11 (Spring 1982): 294, U.S. Journals at Cambridge University Press.

Second, the table shows that Western countries began to emulate the British model successfully over the course of the nineteenth century, with significant variations in the timing and in the extent of industrialization. Belgium, achieving independence from the Netherlands in 1831 and rich in iron and coal, led in adopting Britain's new technology, and it experienced a great surge between 1830 and 1860. France developed factory production more gradually and did not experience "revolutionary" growth in overall industrial output.

Slow but steady growth in France was overshadowed by the spectacular rise of the German lands and the United States after 1860 in what has been termed the "Second Industrial Revolution." In general, eastern and southern Europe began the process of modern industrialization later than northwestern and central Europe. Nevertheless, these regions made real progress in the late nineteenth century, as growth after 1880 in Austria-Hungary, Italy, and Russia suggests. This meant that all European states as well as the United States managed to raise per capita industrial levels in the nineteenth century.

These increases stood in stark contrast to the decreases that occurred at the same time in many non-Western countries, most notably in China and India, as Table 20.1 shows. European countries industrialized to a greater or lesser extent even as most of the non-Western world stagnated. Japan, which is not included in this table, stands out as an exceptional area of non-Western industrial growth in the second half of the nineteenth century. After the forced opening of the country to the West in the 1850s, Japanese entrepreneurs began to adopt Western technology and manufacturing methods, resulting in a production boom by the late nineteenth century. Different rates of wealth- and power-creating industrial development, which heightened disparities within Europe, also greatly magnified existing inequalities between Europe and the rest of the world.

Industrialization in Continental Europe

Throughout Europe the eighteenth century was an era of agricultural improvement, population increase, expanding foreign trade, and growing cottage industry. Thus, when the pace of British industry began to accelerate in the 1780s, continental businesses began to emulate the new methods. British industry enjoyed clear superiority, but the European continent was close behind. During the period of the revolutionary and Napoleonic wars, from 1793 to 1815, however, western Europe experienced tremendous political and social upheaval that temporarily halted economic development. With the return of peace in 1815, western European countries again began to play catch-up.

They faced significant challenges. In the newly mechanized industries, British goods were being produced very efficiently, and these goods had come to dominate world markets. In addition, British technology had become so advanced that few engineers or skilled technicians outside England understood it. Moreover, the technology of steam power had grown much more expensive. It involved large investments in the iron and coal industries and, after 1830, in railroads. Continental business people had difficulty amassing the large sums of money the new methods demanded, and laborers bitterly resisted the move to working in factories. All these factors slowed the spread of machine-powered industry (Map 20.2).

Nevertheless, western European nations possessed a number of advantages that helped them respond to these challenges. First, most had rich traditions of putting-out enterprise, merchant capitalists, and skilled urban artisans. These assets gave their firms the ability to adapt and survive in the face of new market conditions. Second, continental capitalists did not need to develop their own advanced technology. Instead, they could simply "borrow" the new methods developed in Great Britain. European countries also had a third asset that many non-Western areas lacked in the nineteenth century: they had strong, independent governments that did not fall under foreign political control. These governments would use the power of the state to promote industry and catch up with Britain.

Most continental businesses adopted factory technology slowly, and handicraft methods lived on. Indeed, for a time continental industrialization usually brought substantial but uneven expansion of handicraft industry in both rural and urban areas. Artisan production of luxury items grew in France as the rising income of the international middle class created increased foreign demand for silk scarves, embroidered needlework, perfumes, and fine wines. Focusing on artisanal luxury production made sense for French entrepreneurs given their long history of dominance in that sector. Rather than being a "backward" refusal to modernize, it represented a sound strategic choice that allowed the French to capitalize on their know-how and international reputation for high-quality goods.

Agents of Industrialization

Western European success in adopting British methods took place despite the best efforts of the British to prevent it. The British realized the great value of their technical discoveries and tried to keep their secrets to themselves. Until 1825 it was illegal

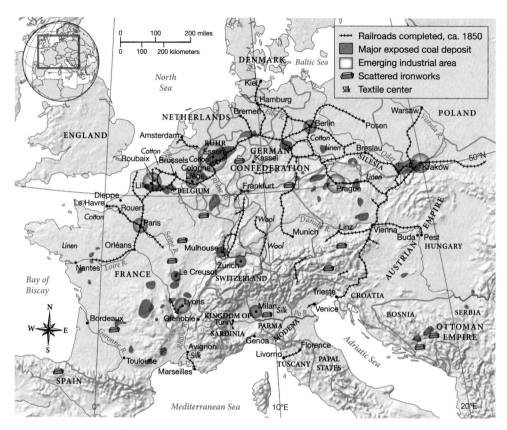

MAP 20.2   Continental Industrialization, ca. 1850

Although continental countries were beginning to make progress by 1850, they still lagged far behind Great Britain. For example, continental railroad building was still in an early stage, whereas the British rail system was essentially complete (see Map 20.1). Coal played a critical role in nineteenth-century industrialization, both as a power source for steam engines and as a raw material for making iron and steel.

for artisans and skilled mechanics to leave Britain; until 1843 the export of textile machinery and other equipment was forbidden. Many talented, ambitious workers, however, slipped out of the country illegally and introduced the new methods abroad.

One such man was William Cockerill, a Lancashire carpenter. He and his sons began building cotton-spinning equipment in French-occupied Belgium in 1799. In 1817 the most famous son, John Cockerill, built a large industrial enterprise in Liège in southern Belgium, which produced machinery, steam engines, and then railway locomotives. He also established modern ironworks and coal mines. Cockerill's plants in the Liège area became a center for the gathering and transmitting of industrial information across Europe. Many skilled British workers came to work for Cockerill, and some went on to found their own companies throughout Europe.

Thus British technicians and skilled workers were a powerful force in the spread of early industrialization. A second agent of industrialization consisted of talented entrepreneurs such as Fritz Harkort (1793–1880), a pioneer in the German machinery industry. Serving in England as a Prussian army officer during the Napoleonic Wars, Harkort was impressed with what he saw. He set up shop building steam engines in the Ruhr Valley, on the western border with France. In spite of problems obtaining skilled workers and machinery, Harkort succeeded in building and selling engines. However, his ambitious efforts also resulted in large financial losses for himself and his partners. His career illustrates both the great efforts of a few important business leaders to duplicate the British achievement and the difficulty of the task.

National governments played an even more important role in supporting industrialization in continental Europe than in Britain. **Tariff protection** was one such support, and it proved to be important. The French, for example, responded to a flood of cheap British goods in 1815 after the Napoleonic Wars by laying high taxes on imported goods. Customs agreements emerged among some German states starting in 1818, and in 1834 a number of states signed a treaty creating a customs union, or *Zollverein*. The treaty allowed goods to move between member states without tariffs, while erecting a single uniform tariff against other nations.

After 1815 continental governments also bore the cost of building roads, canals, and railroads to improve transportation. Belgium led the way in the 1830s and 1840s. Built rapidly as a unified network, Belgium's state-owned railroads stimulated the development of heavy industry and made the country an early industrial leader. In France, the state shouldered all the expense of acquiring and laying roadbed, including bridges and tunnels. In short, governments helped pay for railroads, the all-important leading sector in continental industrialization.

Finally, banks also played a larger and more creative role on the continent than in Britain. Previously, almost all banks in Europe had been private. Because of the possibility of unlimited financial loss, the partners of private banks tended to be conservative and were content to deal with a few rich clients and a few big merchants. They generally avoided industrial investment as being too risky.

In the 1830s two important Belgian banks pioneered in a new direction. They received permission from the growth-oriented government to establish themselves as corporations enjoying limited liability. That is, if the bank went bankrupt, stockholders could now lose only their original investments in the bank's common stock, and they could not be forced by the courts to pay for any additional losses out of other property they owned. Limited liability helped these Belgian banks attract investors. They mobilized impressive resources for investment in big companies, became industrial banks, and successfully promoted industrial development.

Similar corporate banks became important in France and the German lands in the 1850s and 1860s. Usually working in collaboration with governments, corporate banks established and developed many railroads and many companies working in heavy industry, which were also increasingly organized as limited liability corporations.

The combined efforts of governments, skilled workers, entrepreneurs, and industrial banks meshed successfully after 1850 and the financial crash of 1873. In Belgium, France, and the German states, key indicators of modern industrial development—such as railway mileage, iron and coal production, and steam engine capacity—increased at average annual rates of 5 to 10 percent. As a result, rail networks were completed in western and much of central Europe, and the leading continental countries mastered the industrial technologies that had first been developed by the British. In the early 1870s Britain was still Europe's most industrial nation, but a select handful of nations had closed the gap.

The Global Picture

The Industrial Revolution did not have a transformative impact beyond Europe prior to the 1860s, with the exception of the United States and Japan, both early adopters of British practices. In many countries, national governments and pioneering entrepreneurs did make efforts to adopt the technologies and methods of production that had proved so successful in Britain, but they fell short of transitioning to an industrial economy. For example, in Russia the imperial government brought steamships to the Volga River and a railroad to the capital, St. Petersburg, in the first decades of the nineteenth century. By midcentury ambitious entrepreneurs had established steam-powered cotton factories using imported British machines. However, these advances did not lead to overall industrialization of the country, most of whose people remained mired in rural servitude. Instead, Russia confirmed its role as provider of raw materials, especially timber and grain, to the hungry West.

Egypt, a territory of the Ottoman Empire, similarly began an ambitious program of modernization after a reform-minded viceroy took power in 1805. This program included the use of imported British technology and experts in textile manufacture and other industries. These industries, however, could not compete with lower-priced European imports. Like Russia, Egypt fell back on agricultural exports to European markets, like sugar and cotton.

Such examples of faltering efforts at industrialization could be found in many other regions of the Middle East, Asia, and Latin America. Where European governments maintained direct or indirect political control, they aggressively acted to monopolize colonial markets as sources of raw materials and as consumers for their own products, rather than encouraging the spread of industrialization. Such regions could not respond to low-cost imports by raising tariffs, as the United States and western European nations had done, because they were controlled by imperial powers that did not allow them to do so. In India, for example, which was a British colony, millions of poor textile workers lost their livelihood and experienced dire poverty because they could not compete with industrially produced British cottons. The British charged stiff import duties on Indian cottons entering the kingdom, but prohibited the Indians from doing the same to British imports. As a British trade encyclopedia boasted in 1844:

> The British manufacturer brings the cotton of India from a distance of 12,000 miles, commits it to his spinning jennies and power-looms, carries back their products to the East, making them again to travel 12,000 miles; and in spite of the loss of time, and of the enormous expense incurred by this voyage of 24,000 miles, the cotton manufactured by his machinery becomes less costly than the cotton of India spun and woven by the hand near the field that produced it.[5]

Latin American economies were disrupted by the early-nineteenth-century wars of independence. As these countries' economies recovered in the mid-nineteenth century, they increasingly adopted steam power for sugar and coffee processing and for transportation. Like elsewhere, this technology first supported increased agricultural production for export and only later drove domestic industrial production. As in India, the arrival of cheap British cottons destroyed the pre-existing textile industry that had employed many people.

The rise of industrialization in Britain, western Europe, and the United States thus caused other regions of the world to become increasingly economically dependent. Instead of industrializing, many territories underwent a process of deindustrialization due to formal and informal European imperialism and economic competition. In turn, relative economic weakness made them vulnerable to the new wave of imperialism undertaken by industrialized nations in the second half of the nineteenth century (see Chapter 24).

As for China, it did not adopt mechanized production until the end of the nineteenth century, but continued as a market-based, commercial society with a massive rural sector and industrial production based on traditional methods. Some regions of China experienced slow economic growth, while others were stagnant. In the 1860s and 1870s, when Japan was successfully adopting industrial methods, the Chinese government showed similar interest in Western technology and science. However, China faced widespread uprisings in the mid-nineteenth century, which drained attention and resources to the military. With China now poised to surpass the United States in global economic production, scholars wonder whether the ascension of Europe and the West from 1800 on was merely a brief interruption in a much longer pattern of Asian dominance.

How did work and daily life evolve during the Industrial Revolution?

Having first emerged in the British countryside in the late eighteenth century, factories and industrial labor began migrating to cities by the early nineteenth century. As factories moved from rural to urban areas, their workforce evolved as well, from pauper children to families to men and women uprooted from their traditional rural communities. Many women, especially young single women and poor women, continued to work, but married women began to limit their participation in the workforce when possible. For some people, the Industrial Revolution brought improvements, but living and working conditions for the poor stagnated or even deteriorated until around 1850, especially in overcrowded industrial cities.

Work in Early Factories

The first factories of the Industrial Revolution were cotton mills, which began functioning in the 1770s along fast-running rivers and streams and were often located in sparsely populated areas. Cottage workers, accustomed to the putting-out system, were reluctant to work in the new factories even when they received relatively good wages. In a factory, workers had to keep up with the machine and follow its relentless tempo. Moreover, they had to show up every day, on time, and work long, monotonous hours under the constant supervision of demanding overseers, and they were punished systematically if they broke the work rules. For example, if a worker was late to work, or accidentally spoiled material, the employer deducted fines from the weekly pay. Employers frequently beat children and adolescents for their infractions.

Cottage workers were not used to that way of life. All members of the family worked hard and long, but in spurts, setting their own pace. They could interrupt their work when they wished. Women and children could break up their long hours of spinning with other tasks. On Saturday afternoon the head of the family delivered the week's work to the merchant manufacturer and got paid. Saturday night was a time of relaxation and drinking, especially for the men.

Also, early factories resembled English poorhouses, where destitute people went to live at public expense. Some poorhouses were industrial prisons, where the inmates had to work in order to receive food and lodging. The similarity between large brick factories and large stone poorhouses increased the cottage workers' fear of factories and their hatred of factory discipline. It was cottage workers' reluctance to work in factories that prompted early cotton mill owners to turn to pauper children. Mill owners contracted with local officials to take on large numbers of such children as "apprentices," boys and girls as young as five or six years of age who had no say in the matter.

Housed, fed, and locked up nightly in factory dormitories, the young workers labored thirteen or fourteen hours a day for little or no pay and for periods up to fourteen years. Harsh physical punishment maintained brutal discipline. Attitudes began to change in the last decade of the eighteenth century, as middle-class reformers publicized the brutal toil imposed on society's most vulnerable members.

Working Families and Children

By the 1790s the early pattern had begun to change. The use of pauper apprentices was in decline, and in 1802 it was forbidden by Parliament. Many more textile factories were being built, mainly in urban areas, where they could use steam power rather than waterpower and attract a workforce more easily than in the countryside. People came from near and far to work in the cities, as factory workers and as porters, builders, and domestic servants. Collectively, these wage laborers came to be known as the "working class," a term first used in the late 1830s.

In some cases, workers accommodated to the system by carrying over familiar working traditions. Some came to the mills and the mines in the family units in which they had labored on farms and in the putting-out system. The mill or mine owner bargained with the head of the family and paid him or her for the efforts of the whole family. In the cotton mills, children worked for their mothers or fathers, collecting scraps and "piecing" broken threads together. In the mines, children sorted coal and worked the ventilation equipment. Their mothers hauled coal in the tunnels below the surface, while their fathers hewed with pick and shovel at the face of the seam.

Ties of kinship were particularly important for newcomers, who often traveled great distances to find work. Many urban workers in Great Britain migrated from Ireland, either on a seasonal or a permanent basis. They were forced out of rural Ireland by population growth and deteriorating economic conditions from 1817 on, and their numbers increased dramatically in the desperate years of the potato famine, from 1845 to 1851 (see "Ireland and the Great Famine" in Chapter 21). As early as

1824 most of the workers in the Glasgow cotton mills were Irish; in 1851 one-sixth of the population of Liverpool was Irish. Like many other immigrant groups held together by ethnic and religious ties, the Irish worked together, formed their own neighborhoods, and preserved their cultural traditions.

In the early decades of the nineteenth century, however, technical changes made it less and less likely that workers could continue to labor in family groups. As control and discipline passed into the hands of impersonal managers and overseers, adult workers began to protest against inhuman conditions on behalf of their children. Some enlightened employers and social reformers in Parliament argued that more humane standards were necessary, and they used widely circulated parliamentary reports to influence public opinion. For example, Robert Owen (1771–1858), a successful manufacturer in Scotland, testified in 1816 before an investigating committee on the basis of his experience. He argued that employing children under ten years of age as factory workers was "injurious to the children, and not beneficial to the proprietors."[6] Workers also provided graphic testimony at such hearings as reformers pressed Parliament to pass corrective laws. These efforts resulted in a series of British **Factory Acts** from 1802 to 1833 that progressively limited the workday of child laborers and set minimum hygiene and safety requirements. The Factory Act of 1833 installed a system of full-time professional inspectors to enforce the provisions of previous acts. Children between ages nine and thirteen could work a maximum of eight hours per day, not including two hours for education. Teenagers aged fourteen to eighteen could work up to twelve hours, while those under nine were banned from employment. The Factory Acts constituted significant progress in preventing the exploitation of children. One unintended drawback of restrictions on child labor, however, was that they broke the pattern of whole families working together in the factory because efficiency required standardized shifts for all workers. After 1833 the number of children employed in industry declined rapidly.

The New Sexual Division of Labor

With the restriction of child labor and the collapse of the family work pattern in the 1830s came a new sexual division of labor. By 1850 the man was emerging as the family's primary wage earner, while the married woman found only limited job opportunities. Generally denied good jobs at high wages in the growing urban economy, wives were expected to concentrate on their duties at home.

This new pattern of **separate spheres** had several aspects. First, all studies agree that married women from the working classes were much less likely to work full-time for wages outside the house after the first child arrived, although they often earned small amounts doing putting-out handicrafts at home and taking in boarders. Second, when married women did work for wages outside the house, they usually came from the poorest families, where the husbands were poorly paid, sick, unemployed, or missing. Third, these poor married or widowed women were joined by legions of young unmarried women, who worked full-time but only in certain jobs, of which textile factory work, laundering, and domestic service were particularly important. Fourth, all women were generally confined to low-paying, dead-end jobs. Evolving gradually, but largely in place by 1850, the new sexual division of labor constituted a major development in the history of women and of the family.

Several factors combined to create this new sexual division of labor. First, the new and unfamiliar discipline of the clock and the machine was especially hard on married women of the laboring classes. Relentless factory discipline conflicted with child care in a way that labor on the farm or in the cottage had not. A woman operating earsplitting spinning machinery could mind a child of seven or eight working beside her (until such work was outlawed), but she could no longer pace herself through pregnancy or breast-feed her baby on the job. Thus a working-class woman had strong incentives to stay home, if she could afford it. Caring for babies was a less important factor in areas of continental Europe, such as northern France and Scandinavia, where women relied on paid wet nurses instead of breast-feeding their babies (see "Child Care and Nursing" in Chapter 18).

Second, running a household in conditions of urban poverty was an extremely demanding job in its own right. There were no supermarkets or public transportation. Shopping, washing clothes, and feeding the family constituted a never-ending challenge. Taking on a brutal job outside the house — a "second shift" — had limited appeal for the average married woman from the working class. Thus many women might well have accepted the emerging division of labor as the best available strategy for family survival in the industrializing society.[7]

Third, to a large degree the young, generally unmarried women who did work for wages outside the home were segregated from men and confined to certain "women's jobs" because the new sexual division of labor replicated long-standing patterns of gender segregation and inequality. In the preindustrial economy, a small sector of the labor market had always been defined as "women's work," especially tasks involving needlework, spinning, food preparation, child care, and nursing. This traditional sexual division of labor took on new overtones, however, in response to the factory system. Previously, at least in theory, young people worked under a watchful parental eye. The growth of factories and mines brought unheard-of opportunities for girls and boys to mix on the job, free of familial supervision. Such opportunities led to more unplanned pregnancies and fueled the illegitimacy explosion that had begun in the late eighteenth century and that gathered force until at least 1850. Thus segregation of jobs by gender was partly an effort by older people to control the sexuality of working-class youths.

Investigations into the British coal industry before 1842 provide a graphic example of this concern. The middle-class men leading the inquiry professed horror at the sight of girls and women working without shirts, which was a common practice because of the heat, and they quickly assumed the prevalence of licentious sex with the male miners, who also wore very little clothing. In fact, many girls and married women worked for related males in a family unit that provided considerable protection and restraint. Yet many witnesses from the working class also believed that the mines were inappropriate and dangerous places for women and girls. Some miners stressed particularly the danger of sexual aggression for girls working past puberty. As one explained, "I consider it a scandal for girls to work in the pits. Till they are 12 or 14 they may work very well but after that it's an abomination. . . . The work of the pit does not hurt them, it is the effect on their morals that I complain of."[8] The **Mines Act of 1842** prohibited underground work for all women and girls as well as for boys under ten.

Some women who had to support themselves protested against being excluded from coal mining, which paid higher wages than most other jobs open to working-class women. But provided they were part of families that could manage

Child Labor in Coal Mines Public sentiment against child labor in coal mines was provoked by the publication of dramatic images of the harsh working conditions children endured. The Mines Act of 1842 prohibited the employment underground of women and girls and of boys under the age of ten. (akg-images)

economically, the girls and the women who had worked underground were generally pleased with the law. In explaining her satisfaction in 1844, one mother of four provided real insight into why many married working women accepted the emerging sexual division of labor:

> While working in the pit I was worth to my [miner] husband seven shillings a week, out of which we had to pay 2½ shillings to a woman for looking after the younger children. I used to take them to her house at 4 o'clock in the morning, out of their own beds, to put them into hers. Then there was one shilling a week for washing; besides, there was mending to pay for, and other things. The house was not guided. The other children broke things; they did not go to school when they were sent; they would be playing about, and get ill-used by other children, and their clothes torn. Then when I came home in the evening, everything was to do after the day's labor, and I was so tired I had no heart for it; no fire lit, nothing cooked, no water fetched, the house dirty, and nothing comfortable for my husband. It is all far better now, and I wouldn't go down again.[9]

A final factor encouraging working-class women to withdraw from paid labor was the domestic ideals emanating from middle-class women, who had largely embraced the "separate spheres" ideology. Middle-class reformers published tracts and formed societies to urge poor women to devote more care and attention to their homes and families.

Living Standards for the Working Class

Despite the best efforts of hard-working men and women, living conditions for the industrialized poor were often abysmal. Although the evidence is complex and sometimes contradictory, most historians of the Industrial Revolution now agree that overall living standards for the working class did not rise substantially until the 1840s. British wages were always high compared to those in the rest of Europe, but the stresses of war with France from 1792 to 1815 led to a decline in the average British worker's real wages and standard of living. These difficult war years, with high unemployment and inflation, lent a grim color to the new industrial system. Factory wages began to rise after 1815, but these gains were modest and were offset by a decline in the labor of children and married women, meaning that many households had less total income than before. Moreover, many people still worked outside the factories as cottage workers or rural laborers, and in those sectors wages declined. Thus the increase in the productivity of industry did not lead to an increase in the purchasing power of the British working classes. Only after 1830, and especially after the mid-1840s, did real wages rise substantially, so that the average worker earned roughly 30 percent more in real terms in 1850 than in 1770.[10]

Up to that point, the demands of labor in the new industries probably outweighed their benefits as far as working people were concerned. Many landless poor people in the late eighteenth century were self-employed cottage workers living in close-knit rural communities; with industrialization they worked longer and harder at jobs that were often more grueling and more dangerous. In England nonagricultural workers labored about 250 days per year in 1760 as compared to 300 days per year in 1830, while the normal workday remained an exhausting eleven hours throughout the entire period. In 1760 nonagricultural workers still observed many religious and public holidays by not working, and many workers took Monday off. These days of leisure and relaxation declined rapidly after 1760, and by 1830 nonagricultural workers had joined landless agricultural laborers in toiling six rather than five days a week.[11]

As the factories moved to urban areas, workers followed them in large numbers, leading to an explosion in the size of cities, especially in the north of England. Life in the new industrial cities, such as Manchester and Glasgow, was grim. Migrants to the booming cities found expensive, hastily constructed, overcrowded apartments and inadequate sanitary systems. Infant mortality, disease, malnutrition, and accidents took such a high toll in human life that average life expectancy was only around twenty-five to twenty-seven years, some fifteen years less than the national average.[12] Perhaps the most shocking evidence of the impact of the Industrial Revolution on living standards is the finding that child mortality levels rose in the first half of the nineteenth century, especially in industrial areas.

Another way to consider the workers' standard of living is to look at the goods they purchased. Such evidence is somewhat contradictory, but generally suggestive of stagnant or declining living standards until the middle of the nineteenth century. One important area of improvement was in the consumption of cotton goods, which became much cheaper and could be enjoyed by all classes. Now millions of poor people could afford to wear cotton slips and underpants as well as cotton dresses and shirts. However, in other areas, food in particular, the modest growth in factory wages was not enough to compensate for rising prices.

From the mid-1840s onward, matters improved considerably as wages made substantial gains and the prices of many goods dropped. A greater variety of foods became available, including the first canned goods. Some of the most important advances were in medicine. Smallpox vaccination became routine, and surgeons began to use anesthesia in the late 1840s. By 1850 trains had revolutionized transportation for the masses, while the telegraph made instant communication possible for the first time in human history. In addition, gaslights greatly expanded the possibilities of nighttime activity. Gas lighting is one of the most important examples of a direct relationship between the scientific advances of the eighteenth century — in this case, chemistry — and the development of new technologies of the Industrial Revolution.

More difficult to measure than real wages or life expectancy was the impact of the Industrial Revolution on community and social values. As young men and women migrated away from their villages to seek employment in urban factories, many close-knit rural communities were destroyed. Village social and cultural traditions disappeared without new generations to carry them on. Although many young people formed new friendships and appreciated the freedoms of urban life, they also suffered from the loneliness of life in the anonymous city. The loss of skills and work autonomy, along with the loss of community, must be included in the assessment of the Industrial Revolution's effect on the living conditions of workers.

What were the social consequences of industrialization?

In Great Britain, industrial development led to the creation of new social groups and intensified long-standing conflicts between capital and labor. A new class of factory owners and industrial capitalists arose. These men and women and their families strengthened the wealth and size of the middle class, which had previously been made up mainly of merchants and professional people. The demands of modern industry regularly brought the interests of the middle-class industrialists into conflict with those of the people who worked for them — the working class. As observers took notice of these changes, they raised new questions about how industrialization affected social relationships. Meanwhile, enslaved labor in European colonies contributed to the industrialization process in multiple ways (see "The Impact of Slavery" at the end of this chapter).

The New Class of Factory Owners

Early industrialists operated in a highly competitive economic system. As the careers of James Watt and Fritz Harkort illustrate, there were countless production problems, and success and large profits were by no means certain. Manufacturers therefore waged a constant battle to cut their production costs and stay afloat. Much of the profit had to go back into the business for new and better machinery.

Most early industrialists drew upon their families and friends for labor and capital, but they came from a variety of backgrounds. Many, such as Harkort, were from well-established families with rich networks of contacts and support. Others, such as Watt and Cockerill, were of modest means, especially in the early days. Artisans and skilled workers of exceptional ability had unparalleled opportunities. Members of ethnic and religious groups who had been discriminated against jumped at the new chances and often helped each other. Scots, Quakers, and other Protestant dissenters were tremendously important in Britain; Protestants and Jews dominated banking in Catholic France.

As factories and firms grew larger, opportunities declined, at least in well-developed industries. It became considerably harder for a gifted but poor young mechanic to start a small enterprise and end up as a wealthy manufacturer. Formal education became more important for young men as a means of success and advancement, but studies at the advanced level were expensive. In Britain by 1830 and in France and Germany by 1860, leading industrialists were more likely to have inherited their well-established enterprises, and they were financially much more secure than their struggling parents had been. They also had a greater sense of class-consciousness; they were fully aware that ongoing industrial development had widened the gap between themselves and their workers.

Just like working-class women, the wives and daughters of successful businessmen found fewer opportunities for active participation in Europe's increasingly complex business world. Rather than contributing as vital partners in a family-owned enterprise, as so many middle-class women had done, these women were increasingly valued for their ladylike gentility. By 1850 some influential women writers and most businessmen assumed that middle-class wives and daughters should avoid work in offices and factories. Rather, a middle-class lady was expected to concentrate on her proper role as wife and mother, preferably in an elegant residential area far removed from ruthless commerce and the volatile working class.

Responses to Industrialization

From the beginning, the British Industrial Revolution had its critics. Among the first were the Romantic poets. William Blake (1757–1827) called the early factories "satanic mills" and protested against the hard life of the London poor. William Wordsworth (1770–1850) lamented the destruction of the rural way of life and the pollution of the land and water. Some handicraft workers — notably the **Luddites**, members of a secret textile workers organization who attacked factories in northern England in 1811 and later — smashed the new machines, which they believed were putting them out of work. Doctors and reformers wrote of problems in the factories and new towns, while Malthus and Ricardo concluded that workers would earn only enough to stay alive.

This pessimistic view was accepted and reinforced by Friedrich Engels (1820–1895), the future revolutionary and colleague of Karl Marx (see Chapter 21). After studying conditions in northern England, this young son of a wealthy Prussian cotton manufacturer published in 1844 *The Condition of the Working Class in England,* a blistering indictment of the capitalist classes. "At the bar of world opinion," he wrote, "I charge the English middle classes with mass murder, wholesale robbery, and all the other crimes in the calendar." The new poverty of industrial workers was worse than the old poverty of cottage workers and agricultural laborers, according to Engels. The culprit was industrial capitalism, with its relentless competition and constant technical change. Engels's extremely influential charge of capitalist exploitation and increasing worker poverty was embellished by Marx and later socialists (see "The Birth of Marxist Socialism" in Chapter 21).

Analysis of industrial capitalism, often combined with reflections on the French Revolution, led to the development of a new overarching interpretation—a new paradigm—regarding social relationships. Briefly, this paradigm argued that individuals were members of separate classes based on their relationship to the means of production, that is, the machines and factories that dominated the new economy. As owners of expensive industrial machinery and as dependent laborers in their factories, the two main groups of society had separate and conflicting interests. Accordingly, the comfortable, well-educated "public" of the eighteenth century came increasingly to be defined as the middle class ("middle" because they were beneath the small group of aristocracy at the top of society who claimed to be above industrial activity), and the "people" gradually began to perceive themselves as composing a modern working class. And if the new class interpretation was more of a simplification than a fundamental truth for some critics, it appealed to many because it seemed to explain the dramatic social changes wrought by industrialization. Therefore, conflicting classes existed, in part, because many individuals came to believe they existed and developed an awareness that they belonged to a particular social class—what Karl Marx called **class-consciousness**.

Meanwhile, other observers believed that conditions were improving for the working people. In his 1835 study of the cotton industry, Andrew Ure (yoo-RAY) wrote that conditions in most factories were not harsh and were even quite good. Edwin Chadwick, a government official well acquainted with the problems of the working population, concluded that the "whole mass of the laboring community" was increasingly able "to buy more of the necessities and minor luxuries of life."[13] Nevertheless, those who thought—correctly—that conditions were getting worse for working people were probably in the majority.

The Early British Labor Movement

Not everyone worked in large factories and coal mines during the Industrial Revolution. In 1850 more British people still worked on farms than in any other single occupation, although rural communities were suffering from outward migration. The second-largest occupation was domestic service, with more than 1 million household servants, 90 percent of whom were women. Thus many old, familiar jobs outside industry lived on and provided alternatives to industrial labor.

Within industry itself, the pattern of artisans working with hand tools in small shops remained unchanged in many trades, even as others were revolutionized by technological change. For example, the British iron industry was completely dominated by large-scale capitalist firms by 1850. Many large ironworks had more than one thousand people on their payrolls. Yet the firms that fashioned iron into small metal goods, such as tools, tableware, and toys, employed on average fewer than ten wage workers who used handicraft skills. The survival of small workshops gave many workers an alternative to factory employment.

Working-class solidarity and class-consciousness developed both in small workshops and in large factories. In the northern factory districts, anticapitalist sentiments were frequent by the 1820s. Commenting in 1825 on a strike in the woollen center of Bradford and the support it had gathered from other regions, one newspaper claimed with pride that "it is all the workers of England against a few masters of Bradford."[14] Even in trades that did not undergo mechanization, unemployment and stagnant wages contributed to class awareness.

Such sentiments ran contrary to the liberal tenets of economic freedom championed by eighteenth-century thinkers like Adam Smith (see "Adam Smith and Economic Liberalism" in Chapter 17). Liberal economic principles were embraced by statesmen and middle-class business owners in the late eighteenth century and continued to gather strength in the early nineteenth century. In 1799 Parliament passed the **Combination Acts**, which outlawed unions and strikes. In 1813 and 1814 Parliament repealed an old law regulating the wages of artisans and the conditions of apprenticeship. As a result of these and other measures, certain skilled artisan workers, such as bootmakers and high-quality tailors, found aggressive capitalists ignoring traditional work rules and trying to flood their trades with unorganized women workers and children to beat down wages.

The capitalist attack on artisan guilds and work rules was bitterly resented by many craftworkers, who subsequently played an important part in Great Britain and in other countries in gradually building a modern labor movement. The Combination Acts were widely disregarded by workers. Printers, papermakers, carpenters, tailors, and other such craftsmen continued to take collective action, and societies of skilled factory workers also organized unions in defiance of the law. Unions sought to control the number of skilled workers, to limit apprenticeship to members' own children, and to bargain with owners over wages.

They were not afraid to strike; there was, for example, a general strike of adult cotton spinners in Manchester in 1810. In the face of widespread union activity, Parliament repealed the Combination Acts in 1824, and unions were tolerated, though not fully accepted, after 1825. The next stage in the development of the British trade-union movement was the attempt to create a single large national union. This effort was led not so much by working people as by social reformers such as Robert Owen. Owen, a self-made cotton manufacturer, had pioneered in industrial relations by combining strict discipline with paternalistic concern for the health, safety, and hours of his workers. After 1815 he experimented with cooperative and socialist communities, including one at New Harmony, Indiana. Then in 1834 Owen was involved in the organization of one of the largest and most visionary of the early national unions, the Grand National Consolidated Trades Union. When Owen's and other ambitious labor organizing schemes collapsed, the British labor movement moved once again after 1851 in the direction of craft unions. The most famous of these was the Amalgamated Society of Engineers, which represented skilled machinists. These unions won real benefits for members by fairly conservative means and thus became an accepted part of the industrial scene.

British workers also engaged in direct political activity in defense of their interests. After the collapse of Owen's national trade union, many working people went into the Chartist movement, which sought political democracy. The key Chartist demand — that all men be given the right to vote — became the great hope of millions of common people. Workers were also active in campaigns to limit the workday in factories to ten hours and to permit duty-free importation of wheat into Great Britain to secure cheap bread. Thus working people developed a sense of their own identity and played an active role in shaping the new industrial system. They were neither helpless victims nor passive beneficiaries.

The Impact of Slavery

Another mass labor force of the Industrial Revolution was composed of the millions of enslaved men, women, and children who toiled in European colonies in the Caribbean and in North and South America. Historians have long debated the extent to which revenue from slavery contributed to Britain's achievements in the Industrial Revolution.

Most now agree that profits from colonial plantations and slave trading were a small portion of British national income in the eighteenth century and were probably more often invested in land than in industry. Nevertheless, the impact of slavery on Britain's economy was much broader than its direct profits alone. In the mid-eighteenth century the need for items to exchange for colonial cotton, sugar, tobacco, and slaves stimulated demand for British manufactured goods in the Caribbean, North America, and West Africa. Britain's dominance in the slave trade also led to the development of finance and credit institutions that helped early industrialists obtain capital for their businesses. Investments in canals, roads, and railroads made possible by profits from colonial trade provided the necessary infrastructure to move raw materials and products of the factory system.

The British Parliament abolished the slave trade in 1807 and freed all slaves in British territories in 1833, but by 1850 most of the cotton processed by British mills was supplied by the labor of enslaved people in the southern United States. Thus the Industrial Revolution was deeply entangled with the Atlantic world and the misery of slavery.

NOTES

1. Nicholas Crafts, "Productivity Growth During the British Industrial Revolution: Revisionism Revisited" (September 2014), Working Paper, Department of Economics, University of Warwick.
2. Robert C. Allen, *The British Industrial Revolution in Global Perspective* (Cambridge: Cambridge University Press, 2009), pp. 1–2.
3. P. Bairoch, "International Industrialization Levels from 1750 to 1980," *Journal of European Economic History* 11 (Spring 1982): 269–333.
4. Quoted in J. Bowditch and C. Ramsland, eds., *Voices of the Industrial Revolution* (Ann Arbor: University of Michigan Press, 1961), p. 55, from the fourth edition of Thomas Malthus, *Essay on the Principle of Population* (1807).
5. Quoted in Emma Griffin, *A Short History of the British Industrial Revolution* (Basingstoke, U.K.: Palgrave Macmillan, 2010), p. 126.
6. Quoted in E. R. Pike, *"Hard Times": Human Documents of the Industrial Revolution* (New York: Praeger, 1966), p. 109.

7. See especially J. Brenner and M. Rama, "Rethinking Women's Oppression," *New Left Review* 144 (March–April 1984): 33–71, and sources cited there.

8. J. Humphries, " . . . 'The Most Free from Objection' . . . The Sexual Division of Labor and Women's Work in Nineteenth-Century England," *Journal of Economic History* 47 (December 1987): 941; Pike, *"Hard Times,"* p. 266.

9. Quoted in Pike, *"Hard Times,"* p. 208.

10. Joel Mokyr, *The Enlightened Economy: An Economic History of Britain, 1700–1850* (New Haven, Conn.: Yale University Press, 2009), pp. 460–461.

11. Hans-Joachim Voth, *Time and Work in England, 1750–1830* (Oxford: Oxford University Press, 2000), pp. 118–133, 268–270.

12. Mokyr, *The Enlightened Economy*, p. 455.

13. Quoted in W. A. Hayek, ed., *Capitalism and the Historians* (Chicago: University of Chicago Press, 1954), p. 126.

14. Quoted in D. Geary, ed., *Labour and Socialist Movements in Europe Before 1914* (Oxford: Berg, 1989), p. 29.

LOOKING BACK **LOOKING AHEAD**

The Industrial Revolution was a long process of economic innovation and growth originating in Britain around 1780 and spreading to the European continent after 1815. The development of manufacturing machines powered first by water and then by steam allowed for a tremendous growth in productivity, which enabled Britain to assume the lead in the world's production of industrial goods. Industrialization fundamentally changed the social landscape of European countries, creating a new elite of wealthy manufacturers and a vast working class of urban wage laborers whose living conditions remained grim until the mid-nineteenth century.

One popular idea in the 1830s, first developed by a French economist, was that Britain's late-eighteenth-century "industrial revolution" paralleled the political events in France during the French Revolution. One revolution was economic, while the other was political; the first was ongoing and successful, while the second had failed and come to a definite end in 1815, when Europe's conservative monarchs defeated Napoleon and restored the French kings of the Old Regime.

In fact, in 1815 the French Revolution, like the Industrial Revolution, was an unfinished work-in-progress. Just as Britain was still in the midst of its economic transformation and the states of northwestern Europe had only begun industrialization, so too after 1815 were the political conflicts and ideologies of revolutionary France still very much alive. The French Revolution had opened the era of modern political life not just in France but also across Europe. It had brought into existence many of the political ideologies that would interact with the social and economic forces of industrialization to refashion Europe and create a new urban society. Moreover, in 1815 the unfinished French Revolution carried the very real possibility of renewed political upheaval. This possibility, which conservatives feared and radicals longed for, would become dramatic reality in first briefly in 1830 and then again in 1848, when political revolutions swept across Europe like a whirlwind.

MAKE CONNECTIONS

Think about the larger developments and continuities within and across chapters.

1. Why did Great Britain take the lead in industrialization, and when and how were other countries able to adopt the new techniques and organization of production?

2. How did the achievements in agriculture and rural industry of the late seventeenth and eighteenth centuries (Chapter 17) pave the way for the Industrial Revolution of the late eighteenth century?

3. How would you compare the legacy of the political revolutions of the late eighteenth century (Chapter 19) with that of the Industrial Revolution? Which seems to you to have created the most important changes, and why?

Chapter 20 Review

IDENTIFY KEY TERMS

Identify and explain the significance of each item below.

Industrial Revolution (p. 583)	tariff protection (p. 595)
spinning jenny (p. 584)	Factory Acts (p. 599)
water frame (p. 585)	separate spheres (p. 599)
steam engines (p. 586)	Mines Act of 1842 (p. 600)
Rocket (p. 587)	Luddites (p. 604)
Crystal Palace (p. 588)	class-consciousness (p. 605)
iron law of wages (p. 590)	Combination Acts (p. 606)

REVIEW THE MAIN IDEAS

Answer the section heading questions from the chapter.

1. Why and how did the Industrial Revolution emerge in Britain? (p. 581)

2. How did countries outside Britain respond to the challenge of industrialization? (p. 591)

3. How did work and daily life evolve during the Industrial Revolution? (p. 597)

4. What were the social consequences of industrialization? (p. 603)

CHRONOLOGY

ca. 1765	• Hargreaves invents spinning jenny; Arkwright creates water frame
1769	• Watt patents modern steam engine
ca. 1780–1850	• Industrial Revolution; population boom in Britain
1799	• Combination Acts passed in England
1802–1833	• Series of Factory Acts passed by British government to limit the workday of child laborers and set minimum hygiene and safety requirements
1805	• Egypt begins process of modernization
1810	• Strike of Manchester cotton spinners
ca. 1815	• Western European countries seek to adopt British industrial methods
1824	• Combination Acts repealed
1829	• Stephenson's *Rocket,* an early locomotive
1830s	• Industrial banks in Belgium
1834	• *Zollverein* erected among most German states
1842	• Mines Act passed in Britain
1844	• Engels, *The Condition of the Working Class in England*
1850s	• Japan begins to adopt Western technologies; industrial gap widens between the West and the rest of the world
1851	• Great Exhibition held at Crystal Palace in London
1860s	• Germany and the United States begin to rapidly industrialize

21

Ideologies and Upheavals

1815–1850

CHAPTER PREVIEW

- How was peace restored and maintained after the Napoleonic Wars?

- What new ideologies emerged to challenge conservatism?

- What were the characteristics of the Romantic movement?

- How did reforms and revolutions challenge conservatism after 1815?

- What were the main causes and consequences of the revolutions of 1848?

THE MOMENTOUS ECONOMIC AND POLITICAL TRANSFORMATION of modern times that began in the late eighteenth century with the "unfinished" revolutions—the Industrial Revolution in England and the political revolution in France—would play out with unpredictable consequences in the first half of the nineteenth century. Attempts to halt the spread of the progressive forces associated with the French Revolution led first to a reassertion of conservative political control in continental Europe. Following the leadership of Austrian foreign minister Klemens von Metternich, the aristocratic leaders of the Great Powers sought to stamp out the spread of liberal and democratic reforms.

The political and cultural innovations made possible by the unfinished revolutions, however, proved difficult to contain. In politics, powerful new ideologies—liberalism, nationalism, and socialism—emerged to oppose Metternich's revitalized conservatism. In literature, art, and music, Romanticism—an intellectual and artistic movement that challenged the certainties of the Enlightenment and fed the growth of popular nationalism—captured the intensity of the era. A successful revolution in Greece, liberal reform in Great Britain, and popular unrest in France gave voice to ordinary people's desire for political and social change. All these movements helped launch the great wave of revolutions that swept across Europe in 1848, and the dramatic results would have a lasting impact on politics and political culture across Western society.

How was peace restored and maintained after the Napoleonic Wars?

The eventual eruption of revolutionary political forces in 1848 was by no means pre-dictable at the end of the Napoleonic era. Quite the contrary. After finally defeating Napoleon, the conservative, aristocratic monarchies of Russia, Prussia, Austria, and Great Britain—known as the Quadruple Alliance—reaffirmed their determination to hold France in line. Even before Napoleon's final defeat, the allies had agreed to fashion a general peace accord in 1814 at the Congress of Vienna, where they faced a great challenge: how could they construct a lasting settlement that would not sow the seeds of another war? By carefully managing the balance of power, redrawing the boundar-ies of formerly French-held territories, and embracing conservative restoration, they brokered an agreement that contributed to fifty years of peace in Europe (Map 21.1).

The European Balance of Power

Leading representatives of the Quadruple Alliance (plus a representative of the restored Bourbon monarch of France)—including Tsar Alexander I of Russia, King Friedrich Wilhelm III of Prussia, Emperor Franz II of Austria, and their foreign min-isters—met to fashion the peace at the **Congress of Vienna** from September 1814 to June 1815. A host of delegates from the smaller European states also attended the conference and offered minor assistance.

Such a face-to-face meeting of kings and emperors was very rare. Professional ambassadors and court representatives typically conducted state-to-state negotiations; now leaders engaged, for one of the first times, in what we would today call "summit diplomacy." Beyond formal discussions, congress participants enjoyed festivities asso-ciated with aristocratic court culture, including formal receptions, military parades and reviews, sumptuous dinner parties, fancy ballroom dances, fireworks displays, opera, and theater. Visits to Vienna's vibrant salons offered further opportunities to socialize, discuss current affairs, and make informal deals that could be confirmed at the conference table. All the while, newspapers, pamphlets, periodicals, and satiric cartoons kept readers across Europe up-to-date on social events and the latest polit-ical developments. The conference thus marked an important transitional moment in Western history. The salon society and public sphere of the seventeenth-century Enlightenment (see "How did the Enlightenment emerge, and what were the major currents of Enlightenment thought?" in Chapter 16) gradually shifted toward nineteenth-century cultures of publicity and public opinion informed by more modern mass-media campaigns.[1]

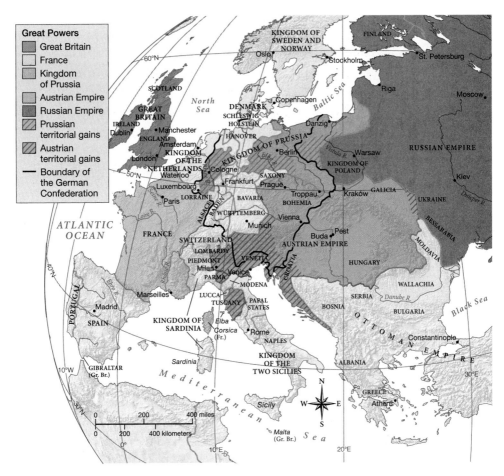

MAP 21.1   Europe in 1815
In 1815 Europe contained many different states, but after the defeat of Napoleon international politics was dominated by the five Great Powers: Russia, Prussia, Austria, Great Britain, and France. (The number rises to six if one includes the Ottoman Empire.) At the Congress of Vienna, the Great Powers redrew the map of Europe.

The allied powers were concerned first with the defeated enemy, France. Motivated by self-interest and traditional ideas about the balance of power, they practiced moderation toward the former foe. To Klemens von Metternich (MEH-tuhr-nihk) and Robert Castlereagh (KA-suhl-ray), the foreign ministers of Austria and Great Britain, the balance of power meant an international equilibrium of political and military forces that would discourage aggression by any combination of states or, worse, the domination of Europe by any single state. Their French negotiating partner, the skillful and cynical diplomat Charles Talleyrand, concurred.

The allies offered France lenient terms after Napoleon's abdication. They agreed to restore the Bourbon king to the French throne. The first Treaty of Paris, signed before the conference (and before Napoleon escaped from Elba and attacked the

Congress of Vienna The Congress of Vienna was renowned for its intense diplomatic deal making, resulting in the Treaty of Vienna, the last page of which was signed and sealed in 1815 by the representatives of the various European states attending the conference. The congress won notoriety for its ostentatious parades, parties, and dance balls. The painting here portrays a mounted group of European royalty, led by the Prussian emperor and the Russian tsar, in a flamboyant parade designed to celebrate Napoleon's defeat the year before. Onlookers toast the victorious monarchs. The display of flags, weapons, and heraldic emblems symbolizes the unity of Europe's Great Powers, while the long tables in the background suggest the extent of the festivities. Such images were widely distributed to engender popular support for the conservative program. (*The Celebration at the Prater in the Presence of the Reigning Monarchs*, colored lithograph by Franz Wolf [1795–1859]/Collection of the Palaces Artstetten and Luberegg/akg-images)

Bourbon regime), gave France the boundaries it had possessed in 1792, which were larger than those of 1789. In addition, France did not have to pay war reparations. Thus the victorious powers avoided provoking a spirit of victimization and desire for revenge in the defeated country.

The Quadruple Alliance combined leniency with strong defensive measures designed to raise barriers against the possibility of renewed French aggression. Belgium and Holland—incorporated into the French empire under Napoleon—were united under an enlarged and independent "Kingdom of the Netherlands" capable of opposing French expansion to the north. The German-speaking lands on France's eastern border, also taken by Napoleon, were returned to Prussia. As a famous German anthem put it, the expanded Prussia would now stand as the "watch on the Rhine" against French attack. In addition, the allies reorganized the German-speaking territories of central Europe. A new German Confederation, a loose association of German-speaking states based on Napoleon's reorganization of the territory dominated by Prussia and Austria, replaced the roughly three hundred principalities, free cities, and dynastic states of the Holy Roman Empire with just thirty-eight German states (see Map 21.1).

Austria, Britain, Prussia, and Russia used the balance of power to settle their own potentially dangerous disputes. The victors generally agreed that they should receive territory for their victory over the French. Great Britain had already won colonies and strategic outposts during the long wars. Austria gave up territories in Belgium and southern Germany but expanded greatly elsewhere, taking the rich provinces of Venetia and Lombardy in northern Italy as well as former Polish possessions and new lands on the eastern coast of the Adriatic.

Russian and Prussian claims for territorial expansion were more contentious. When Russia had pushed Napoleon out of central Europe, its armies had expanded Russian control over Polish territories. Tsar Alexander I wished to make Russian rule permanent. But when France, Austria, and Great Britain all argued for limits on Russian gains, the tsar ceded territories back to Prussia and accepted a smaller Polish kingdom. Prussian claims on the state of Saxony, a wealthy kingdom in the German Confederation, were particularly divisive. The Saxon king had supported Napoleon to the bitter end; now Wilhelm III wanted to incorporate Saxony into Prussia. Under pressure, he agreed to partition the state, leaving an independent Saxony in place, a change that posed no real threat to its Great Power neighbors but soothed their fears of Prussian expansionism. These territorial changes and compromises fell very much within the framework of balance-of-power ideology.

Unfortunately for France, in February 1815 Napoleon suddenly escaped from his "comic kingdom" on the island of Elba and briefly reignited his wars of expansion for a brief time (see "The Grand Empire and Its End" in Chapter 19). Yet the second Treaty of Paris, concluded in November 1815 after Napoleon's final defeat at Waterloo, was still relatively moderate toward France. The elderly Louis XVIII was restored to his throne for a second time. France lost only a little territory, had to pay an indemnity of 700 million francs, and was required to support a large army of occupation for five years. The rest of the settlement concluded at the Congress of Vienna was left intact. The members of the Quadruple Alliance, however, did agree to meet periodically to discuss their common interests and to consider appropriate measures for the maintenance of peace in Europe. This agreement marked the beginning of the European "Congress System," which lasted long into the nineteenth century and settled many international crises peacefully through international conferences or "congresses" and balance-of-power diplomacy.

Metternich and Conservatism

The political ideals of conservatism, often associated with Austrian foreign minister Prince Klemens von Metternich (1773–1859), dominated Great Power discussions at the Congress of Vienna. Metternich's determined defense of the monarchical status quo made him a villain in the eyes of most progressive, liberal thinkers of the nineteenth century. Yet rather than denounce his politics, we can try to understand the general conservatism he represented. Metternich was an internationally oriented aristocrat who made a brilliant diplomatic career. Austrian foreign minister from 1809 to 1848, his conservatism derived from his pessimistic view of human nature, which he believed was ever prone to error, excess, and self-serving behavior. The disruptive events of the French Revolution and the Napoleonic Wars confirmed these views, and Metternich's conservatism would emerge as a powerful new political ideology, an attempt to manage the many crises of the revolutionary age.

Metternich firmly believed that liberalism, as embodied in revolutionary America and France, bore the responsibility for the untold bloodshed and suffering caused by twenty-five years of war. Like Edmund Burke and other conservatives, Metternich blamed liberal middle-class revolutionaries for stirring up the lower classes. Authoritarian, aristocratic government, he concluded, was necessary to protect society from the baser elements of human behavior, which were easily released in a democratic system. Organized religion was another pillar of strong government. Metternich despised the anticlericalism of the Enlightenment and the French Revolution and maintained that Christian morality was a vital bulwark against radical change.

Born into the landed nobility, Metternich defended his elite class and its rights and privileges with a clear conscience. The church and nobility were among Europe's most ancient and valuable institutions, and conservatives regarded tradition as the basic foundation of human society. The threat of liberalism appeared doubly dangerous to Metternich because it generally went with aspirations for national independence. Liberals believed that each people, each national group, had a right to establish its own independent government and fulfill its own destiny; this system threatened to revolutionize central Europe and destroy the Austrian Empire.

After centuries of war, royal intermarriage, and territorial expansion, the vast Austrian Empire of the Habsburgs included many regions and peoples (Map 21.2). The numerous kingdoms, duchies, and principalities under Habsburg rule included the lands of the Austrian Crown, the Kingdom of Hungary, the Kingdom of Bohemia, and the Kingdom of Lombardy-Venetia. Noble houses in these territories maintained some control, but ultimate authority rested with the Habsburg emperor. The peoples of the Austrian Empire spoke at least eleven different languages and observed vastly different customs; an astonishing variety of different ethnic groups mingled in the same provinces and the same villages. They included about 8 million Germans, almost one-fourth of the population. Some 5.5 million Magyars (Hungarians), 5 million Italians, 4 million Czechs, and 2 million Poles lived alongside each other in the imperial state, as did smaller groups of Slovenes, Croats, Serbs, Romanians, Jews, and Armenians.[2] The various Slavic groups, together with the Italians and the Romanians, lived in widely scattered regions, yet they outnumbered the politically dominant Germans and Hungarians.

The multiethnic empire Metternich served had strengths and weaknesses. A large population and vast territories gave the empire economic and military clout, but its potentially dissatisfied ethnicities and nationalities undermined political unity. Under these circumstances, Metternich and the Habsburg dynasty had to oppose liberalism and nationalism — if Austria was to remain intact and powerful, it could hardly accommodate ideologies that demanded national independence.

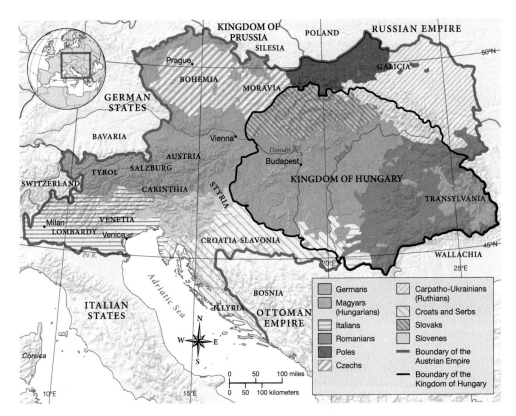

MAP 21.2   Peoples of the Habsburg Monarchy, 1815
The old dynastic state ruled by the Habsburg monarchy was a patchwork of nationalities and ethnic groups, in which territorial borders barely reflected the diversity of where different peoples actually lived. Note especially the widely scattered pockets of Germans and Hungarians. How do you think this ethnic diversity might have led to the rise of national independence movements in the Austrian Empire?

On the Austrian Empire's borders, the Russian Empire and, to a lesser extent, the Ottoman Empire supported and echoed Metternich's efforts to hold back liberalism and nationalism. Bitter enemies, the far-flung Russian and Ottoman Empires were both absolutist states with powerful armies and long traditions of expansion and conquest. Because of those conquests, both were also multinational empires with many peoples, languages, and religions, but most of the ruling elite came from the dominant ethnic group — the Orthodox Christian Russians of central and northern Russia and the Muslim Ottoman Turks of Anatolia (much of modern Turkey). After 1815 both of these multinational absolutist states worked to preserve their respective traditional conservative orders. Only after 1840 did each in turn experience a profound crisis and embark on a program of fundamental reform and modernization, as we shall see in Chapter 23.

Repressing the Revolutionary Spirit

Conservative political ideologies had important practical consequences. Under Metternich's leadership, Austria, Prussia, and Russia embarked on a decades-long crusade against the liberties and civil rights associated with the French and American Revolutions. The first step was the formation in September 1815 of the **Holy Alliance** by Austria, Prussia, and Russia. First proposed by Russia's Alexander I, the alliance worked to repress reformist and revolutionary movements and stifle desires for national independence across Europe.

The conservative restoration first brought its collective power to bear in Austria, Prussia, and the entire German Confederation — the German-speaking lands of central Europe. The states in the German Confederation retained independence, and though ambassadors from each met in the Confederation Diet, or assembly, it had little real political power. When liberal reformers and university students began to protest for the national unification of the German states, the Austrian and Prussian leadership used the diet to issue and enforce the infamous **Karlsbad Decrees** in 1819. These decrees required the German states to outlaw liberal political organizations, police their universities and newspapers, and establish a permanent committee with spies and informers to clamp down on liberal or radical reformers.

The conservative policies of Metternich and the Holy Alliance limited reform not only in central Europe but also in Spain and the Italian peninsula. In 1820 revolutionaries successfully forced the kings of Spain and the southern Italian Kingdom of the Two Sicilies to establish constitutional monarchies, with press freedoms, universal male suffrage, and other liberal reforms. Metternich was horrified; revolution was rising once again. Calling a conference at Troppau in Austria, he and Alexander I proclaimed the principle of active intervention to maintain all autocratic regimes whenever they were threatened. Austrian forces then marched into Naples in 1821 and restored the autocratic power of Ferdinand I in the Two Sicilies. A French invasion of Spain in 1823 likewise returned power to the king there.

The forces of reaction squelched reform in Russia as well, in the Decembrist Revolt of 1825. In St. Petersburg in December that year, a group of about three thousand army officers inspired by liberal ideals staged a protest against the new tsar, Nicholas I. Troops loyal to Nicholas I surrounded and assaulted the group with gunfire, cavalry, and cannon, leaving some sixty men dead; the surviving leaders were publicly hanged, and the rest sent to exile in Siberia. Through censorship, military might, secret police, imprisonment, and execution, conservative regimes in central Europe used the powers of the state to repress liberal reform wherever possible.

Limits to Conservative Power and Revolution in South America

Metternich liked to call himself "the chief Minister of Police in Europe,"[3] and under his leadership the Holy Alliance sought to slow or halt liberal political reform. Metternich's system proved quite effective in central Europe, at least until 1848, but the monarchists failed to stop dynastic change in France in 1830 or to prevent Belgium from winning independence from the Netherlands in 1831. Yet the most dramatic challenge to conservative power occurred not in Europe, but overseas in South America.

In the 1820s South American elites broke away from the Spanish Crown and established a number of new republics based at first on liberal Enlightenment ideals.

Simón Bolívar's Triumph in Caracas The military and political expertise of General Simón Bolívar, the South American George Washington, helped liberate Venezuela, Ecuador, Colombia, and other states from Spanish rule in the first decades of the 1800s. Here he leads a triumphal parade through Caracas, Venezuela. Bolívar's vision of a united South America fell apart by 1830, leading the disillusioned general to famously remark that trying to unite the region through revolutionary means was like "plowing the sea." (akg-images/Newscom)

The leaders of the revolutions were primarily wealthy Creoles, direct descendants of Spanish parents born in the Americas. The well-established and powerful Creoles — only about 5 percent of the population — resented the political and economic control of an even smaller elite minority of *peninsulares*, people born in Spain who lived in and ruled the colonies. The vast majority of the population, composed of "mestizos" and "mulattos" (people of ethnically mixed heritage), enslaved and freed Africans, and native indigenous peoples, languished at the bottom of the social pyramid.

By the late 1700s the Creoles had begun to question Spanish policy and even the necessity of further colonial rule. The spark for revolt came during the Napoleonic Wars, when the French occupation of Spain in 1808 weakened the power of the autocratic Spanish Crown and the Napoleonic rhetoric of rights inspired revolutionaries. Yet the Creoles hesitated, worried that open revolt might upend the social pyramid or even lead to a slave revolution as in Haiti (see "How did slave revolt on colonial Saint-Domingue lead to the independent nation of Haiti?" in Chapter 19).

The South American revolutions thus began from below, with spontaneous uprisings by subordinated peoples of color. Creole leaders quickly took control of a struggle that would be more prolonged and violent than the American Revolution, with outcomes less clear. In the north, the competent general Simón Bolívar — the Latin American equivalent of George Washington — defeated Spanish forces and established a short-lived "Gran Colombia," which lasted from 1819 to 1830. Bolívar, the "people's liberator," dreamed of establishing a federation of South American states, modeled on the United States. To the south, José de San Martín, a liberal-minded military commander, successfully threw off Spanish control by 1825.

Dreams of South American federation and unity proved difficult to realize. By 1830 the large northern state established by Bolívar had fractured, and by 1840 the borders of the new nations looked much like the map of Latin America today. Most of the new states initially received liberal constitutions, but these were difficult to implement in lands where the vast majority of people had no experience with constitutional rule and women and the great underclass of non-Creoles were not allowed to vote. Experiments with liberal constitutions soon gave way to a new political system controlled by *caudillos* (cow-DEE-yohs), or strongmen, sometimes labeled warlords. Often Creoles, the caudillos ruled limited territories on the basis of military strength, family patronage, and populist politics. The South American revolutions had failed to establish lasting constitutional republics, but they did demonstrate the revolutionary potential of liberal ideals and the limits on conservative control.

What new ideologies emerged to challenge conservatism?

In the years following the peace settlement of 1815, intellectuals and social observers sought to harness the radical ideas of the revolutionary age to new political movements. Many rejected conservatism, with its stress on tradition, a hereditary monarchy, a privileged landowning aristocracy, and an official state church. Often inspired by liberties championed during the French Revolution, radical thinkers developed alternative ideologies and tried to convince people to follow them. In so doing, they helped articulate the basic political ideals that continue to shape Western society today.

Liberalism and the Middle Class

The principal ideas of **liberalism**—liberty and legal equality—were by no means defeated in 1815. First realized successfully in the American Revolution and then achieved in part in the French Revolution, liberalism demanded representative government as opposed to autocratic monarchy, and equality before the law for all as opposed to separate classes with separate legal rights. Liberty also meant specific individual freedoms: freedom of the press, freedom of speech, freedom of assembly, freedom of worship, and freedom from arbitrary arrest. Such ideas are still the guiding beliefs in modern democratic states, but in Europe in 1815 only France with Louis XVIII's Constitutional Charter and Great Britain with its Parliament had realized any of the liberal program. Even in those countries, liberalism had only begun to succeed.

Although conservatives still saw liberalism as a profound threat, it had gained a group of powerful adherents: the new upper classes made wealthy through growing industrialization and global commerce. This group promoted the liberal economic doctrine of **laissez faire** (lay-say FEHR), which called for free trade (including relaxation of import/export duties), unrestricted private enterprise, and no government interference in the economy.

As we saw in Chapter 17, Adam Smith posited the idea of economic liberalism and free-market capitalism in 1776 in opposition to mercantilism and its attempt to regulate trade. Smith argued that freely competitive private enterprise would give all citizens a fair and equal opportunity to do what they did best and would result in greater income for everyone, not just the rich. (Smith's form of liberalism is often called "classical liberalism" in the United States, to distinguish it sharply from modern American liberalism, which generally favors government intervention to address social inequality and regulate the economy.)

In the first half of the nineteenth century, liberal political ideals became closely associated with narrow class interests. Starting in the 1820s in Britain, business elites enthusiastically embraced laissez-faire policies because they proved immensely profitable, and they used liberal ideas to defend their right to do as they wished in their factories. Labor unions were outlawed because, these elites argued, unions restricted free competition and the individual's "right to work." Early nineteenth-century liberals favored representative government, but they generally wanted property qualifications attached to the right to vote. In practice, this meant limiting the vote to very small numbers of the well-to-do. Workers, peasants, and women, as well as middle-class shopkeepers, clerks, and artisans, did not own the necessary property and thus could not participate in the political process.

As liberalism became increasingly identified with upper-class business interests, some opponents of conservatism felt that liberalism did not go nearly far enough. Inspired by memories of the French Revolution, this group embraced republicanism: an expanded liberal ideology that endorsed universal democratic voting rights, at least for males, and radical equality for all. Republicans were more willing than most liberals to endorse violent upheaval to achieve goals. In addition, republicans might advocate government action to create jobs, redistribute income, and level social differences. As the results of the revolutions of 1830 and 1848 suggest, liberals and radical republicans could join forces against conservatives only up to a point.

The Growing Appeal of Nationalism

Nationalism was another radical idea that gained popularity after 1815. The power of nationalism was revealed by the success of the French armies in the revolutionary and Napoleonic wars, when soldiers inspired by patriotic loyalty to the French nation achieved victory after victory. Early nationalists found inspiration in the vision of a people united by a common language, a common history and culture, and a common territory. In German-speaking central Europe, defeat by Napoleon's armies had made the vision of a national people united in defense of their "fatherland" particularly attractive.

In the early nineteenth century such national unity was more a dream than a reality for most ethnic groups or nationalities. Local dialects abounded, even in relatively cohesive countries like France, where peasants from nearby villages often failed to understand each other. Moreover, a variety of ethnic groups shared the territory of most states, not just the Austrian, Russian, and Ottoman Empires discussed earlier. During the nineteenth century, nationalism nonetheless gathered force as a political philosophy. Advancing literacy rates, new mass-circulation newspapers, larger state bureaucracies, compulsory education, and conscription armies all created a common culture that encouraged ordinary people to take pride in their national heritage.

Recognizing the power of the "national idea," European nationalists—generally educated, middle-class liberals and intellectuals—sought to turn the cultural unity that they desired into political reality. They believed that every nation, like every citizen, had the right to exist in freedom and to develop its unique character and spirit, and they hoped to make the territory of each people coincide with well-defined borders in an independent nation-state.

This political goal made nationalism explosive, particularly in central and eastern Europe, where different peoples overlapped and intermingled. As discussed, the Austrian, Russian, and Ottoman central states refused to allow national minorities independence. This suppression fomented widespread discontent among nationalists who wanted freedom from oppressive imperial rule. In the many different principalities of the Italian peninsula and the German Confederation, to the contrary, nationalists yearned for unification across what they saw as divisive and obsolete state borders. Whether they sought independence or unification, before 1850 nationalist movements were fresh, idealistic, and progressive, if not revolutionary.

In recent years historians have tried to understand why the nationalist vision, which typically fit poorly with existing conditions and promised much upheaval, was so successful in the long run. Of fundamental importance in the rise of nationalism was the development of a complex industrial and urban society, which required more sophisticated forms of communication between individuals and groups.[4] The need for improved communication promoted the use of a standardized national language in many areas, creating at least a superficial cultural unity as a standard tongue spread through mass education and the emergence of the popular press. When a minority population was large and concentrated, the nationalist campaign for a standardized language often led the minority group to push for a separate nation-state.

Scholars generally argue that nations are recent creations, the product of a new, self-conscious nationalist ideology. Thus nation-states emerged in the nineteenth century as "imagined communities" that sought to bind millions of strangers together around the abstract concept of an all-embracing national identity. This meant bringing citizens together with emotionally charged symbols and ceremonies, such as independence holidays and patriotic parades. On these occasions the imagined nation of equals might celebrate its most hallowed traditions, which were often relatively recent inventions.[5]

Between 1815 and 1850 most people who believed in nationalism also believed in either liberalism or radical republicanism. They typically shared a deep belief in the creativity and nobility of "the people." Liberals and especially republicans, for example, saw the people as the ultimate source of all government. Yet nationally minded liberals and republicans agreed that the benefits of self-government would be possible only if individuals were bonded together by common traditions that transcended local interests and even class differences. Thus in the early nineteenth century the liberty of the individual and the love of a free nation overlapped greatly.

Despite some confidence that a world system based on independent nation-states would promote global harmony, early nationalists eagerly emphasized the differences between peoples and developed a strong sense of "us" versus "them." To this "us-them" outlook, nationalists could all too easily add two highly volatile ingredients: a sense of mission and a sense of national superiority. As Europe entered an age of increased global interaction, these ideas would lead to conflict, as powerful nation-states backed by patriotic citizens competed with each other on the international stage.

The Foundations of Modern Socialism

More radical than liberalism, republicanism, or nationalism was **socialism**. Early socialist thinkers were a diverse group with wide-ranging ideas. Yet they shared a sense that the political revolution in France, the growth of industrialization in Britain, and the rise of laissez faire had created a profound spiritual and moral crisis. Modern capitalism, they believed, fomented a selfish individualism that encouraged inequality and split the community into isolated fragments. Society urgently required fundamental change to re-establish a sense of community.

Early socialists felt an intense desire to help the poor, and they preached that the rich and the poor should be more nearly equal economically. They believed that private property should be strictly regulated by the government, or abolished outright and replaced by state or community ownership. Economic planning, greater social equality, and state regulation of property were the key ideas of early socialism—and have remained central to all socialism since.

One influential group of early socialist advocates became known as the "utopian socialists" because their grand schemes for social improvement ultimately proved unworkable. The Frenchmen Count Henri de Saint-Simon (san-see-MOHN) (1760–1825) and Charles Fourier (FAWR-ee-ay) (1772–1837), as well as the British industrialist Robert Owen, all founded movements intended to establish model communities that would usher in a new age of happiness and equality.

Saint-Simon's "positivism" optimistically proclaimed the tremendous possibilities of industrial development: "The golden age of the human species," he wrote, "is before us!"[6] The key to progress was proper social organization that required the "parasites"—the court, the aristocracy, lawyers, and churchmen—to give way to the "doers"—highly trained scientists, engineers, and industrialists. These doers would abolish poverty and war by leading society through a process he called "industrialization," based on scientific principles. Government administrators would carefully plan the economy and guide it forward by establishing investment banks and undertaking vast public works projects that promised employment for all. Saint-Simon also stressed in highly moralistic terms that every social institution ought to have as its main goal human brotherhood and improved conditions for the poor.

Charles Fourier, a follower of Saint-Simon, likewise condemned the inequality and poverty he saw at the base of contemporary capitalism and called for a society based on cooperation rather than rampant individualism. To heal social ills, Fourier called for the construction of mathematically precise, self-sufficient communities called "phalanxes," each made up of 1,620 people. In the phalanx, all property was owned by the community and used for the common good. Fourier was also an early proponent of the total emancipation of women. According to Fourier, under capitalism young single women were shamelessly "sold" to their future husbands for dowries and other financial considerations. Therefore, he called for the abolition of marriage and for sexual freedom and free unions based only on love. The great British utopian Robert Owen, an early promoter of labor unions, likewise envisaged a society organized into socialistic industrial-agricultural communities. Saint-Simon, Fourier, and Owen all had followers who tried to put their ideas into practice. Though these attempts had mostly collapsed by the 1850s, utopian socialist ideas remained an inspiration for future reformers and revolutionaries.

Some socialist thinkers embraced the even more radical ideas of anarchism. In his 1840 pamphlet *What Is Property?* Pierre-Joseph Proudhon (1809–1865), a self-educated printer, famously argued that "property is theft!" Property, he claimed, was profit that was stolen from the worker, the source of all wealth. Distrustful of all authority and political systems, Proudhon believed that states should be abolished and that society should be organized in loose associations of working people.

Other early socialists, like Louis Blanc (1811–1882), a sharp-eyed, intelligent journalist, focused on more practical reforms. In his *Organization of Work* (1839), he urged workers to agitate for universal voting rights and take control of the state peacefully. Blanc believed that the government should provide aid to the sick and elderly and set up publicly funded workshops and factories to guarantee full employment. The right to work had to become as sacred as any other right. Karl Marx would later adopt Blanc's guiding principle "From each according to his abilities, to each according to his needs" in his own synthesis of socialist thought.

As industrialization advanced in European cities, working people began to embrace the socialist message. This happened first in France, where workers cherished the memory of the radical phase of the French Revolution and became violently opposed to laissez-faire laws that denied their right to organize in guilds and unions. Developing a sense of class in the process of their protests, workers favored collective action and government intervention in economic life. Thus the aspirations of workers and radical theorists reinforced each other, and a genuine socialist movement emerged in Paris in the 1830s and 1840s.

The Birth of Marxist Socialism

In the 1840s France was the center of socialism, but in the following decades the German intellectual Karl Marx (1818–1883) would weave the diffuse strands of socialist thought into a distinctly modern ideology. Marxist socialism — or **Marxism** — would have a lasting impact on political thought and practice.

The son of a Jewish lawyer who had converted to Lutheranism, the young Marx was a brilliant student. After earning a Ph.D. in philosophy at Humboldt University in Berlin in 1841, he turned to journalism, and his critical articles about the plight of the laboring poor caught the attention of the Prussian police. Forced to flee Prussia in 1843, Marx traveled around Europe, promoting socialism and avoiding the authorities. He lived a modest, middle-class life with his wife, Jenny, and their children, often relying on his friend and colleague Friedrich Engels for financial support. After the revolutions of 1848, Marx settled in London, where he spent the rest of his life as an advocate of working-class revolution. *Capital*, his magnum opus, appeared in 1867.

Marx was a dedicated scholar, and his work united sociology, economics, philosophy, and history in an impressive synthesis. From Scottish and English political economists like Adam Smith and David Ricardo, Marx learned to apply social-scientific analysis to economic problems, though he pushed these liberal ideas in radical directions. Influenced by the utopian socialists, Marx championed ideals of social equality and community. He criticized his socialist predecessors, however, for their fanciful utopian schemes, claiming that his version of "scientific" socialism was rooted in historic law, and therefore realistic. Deeply influenced by the German philosopher Georg Hegel (1770–1831), Marx came to believe that history had patterns and purpose and moved forward in stages toward an ultimate goal.

Karl Marx and His Family Active in the revolutions of 1848, Marx fled Germany and eventually settled in London, where he wrote *Capital*, the weighty exposition of his socialist theories. Despite his advocacy of radical revolution, Marx and his wife, Jenny, pictured here with two of their daughters, lived a respectable though modest middle-class life. Standing on the left is Friedrich Engels, an accomplished writer and political theorist who was Marx's long-time friend, financial supporter, and intellectual collaborator. (© Mary Evans/ Marx Memorial Library/The Image Works)

Bringing these ideas together, Marx argued that class struggle over economic wealth was the great engine of human history. In his view, one class had always exploited the other, and with the advent of modern industry, society was split more clearly than ever before: between the **bourgeoisie** (boor-ZHWAH-zee), or the upper class, and the **proletariat**, the working class. The bourgeoisie, a tiny minority, owned factories, land, and farms (what Marx called the means of production) and grew rich by exploiting the labor of workers. Over time, Marx argued, the proletariat would grow ever larger and ever poorer, and their increasing alienation would lead them to develop a sense of revolutionary class-consciousness. Then, just as the bourgeoisie had triumphed over the feudal aristocracy in the French Revolution, the proletariat would overthrow the bourgeoisie in a violent revolutionary cataclysm. The result would be the end of class struggle and the arrival of communism, a system of radical equality.

Fascinated by the rapid expansion of modern capitalism, Marx based his revolutionary program on an insightful yet critical analysis of economic history. Under feudalism, he wrote, labor had been organized according to long-term contracts of rights and privileges. Under capitalism, to the contrary, labor was a commodity like any other, bought and sold for wages in the free market. The goods workers produced were always worth more than what those workers were paid, and the difference — "surplus value," in Marx's terms — was pocketed by the bourgeoisie in the form of profit.

According to Marx, capitalism was immensely productive but highly exploitative. In a never-ending search for profit, the bourgeoisie would squeeze workers dry and then expand across the globe, until all parts of the world were trapped in capitalist relations of production. Contemporary ideals, such as free trade, private property, and even marriage and Christian morality, were myths that masked and legitimized class exploitation. To many people, Marx's argument that the contradictions inherent in this unequal system would eventually be overcome in a working-class revolution appeared to be the irrefutable capstone of a brilliant interpretation of historical trends.

When Marx and Engels published *The Communist Manifesto* on the eve of the revolutions of 1848, their opening claim that "a spectre is haunting Europe — the spectre of Communism" was highly exaggerated. The Communist movement was in its infancy. Scattered groups of socialists, anarchists, and labor leaders were hardly united around Marxist ideas. But by the time Marx died in 1883, Marxist socialism had profoundly reshaped left-wing radicalism in ways that would inspire revolutionaries around the world for the next one hundred years.

What were the characteristics of the Romantic movement?

Intellectuals in the early nineteenth century transformed political ideas, and they also embraced radical changes in literature and the arts. Followers of the new Romantic movement (or Romanticism) revolted against the emphasis on rationality, order, and restraint that characterized the Enlightenment and the controlled style of classicism. Forerunners appeared from about 1750 on, but the movement crystallized fully in the 1790s, primarily in England and Germany. Romanticism gained strength and swept across Europe until the 1840s, when it gradually gave way to Realism.

The Tenets of Romanticism

Although **Romanticism** was characterized by intellectual diversity, common parameters stand out. Artists inspired by Romanticism repudiated the emphasis on reason associated with well-known Enlightenment philosophes like Voltaire or Montesquieu (see "The Influence of the Philosophes" in Chapter 16). Romantics championed instead emotional exuberance, unrestrained imagination, and spontaneity in both art and personal life.

Where Enlightenment thinkers applied the scientific method to social issues and cast rosy predictions for future progress, Romantics valued intuition and nostalgia for the past. Where Enlightenment thinkers embraced secularization, Romantics sought the inspiration of religious ecstasy. Where Enlightenment thinkers valued public life and civic affairs, Romantics delved into the supernatural and turned inward, pondering the awesome power of love and desire, and hatred and despair, all found in the hidden recesses of the self. As the Austrian composer Franz Schubert exclaimed in 1824: "Oh imagination, thou supreme jewel of mankind, thou inexhaustible source from which artists and scholars drink! Oh, rest with us — despite the fact that thou art recognized only by a few — so as to preserve us from that so-called Enlightenment, that ugly skeleton without flesh or blood!"[7]

Nowhere was the break with Enlightenment classicism more apparent than in Romanticism's general conception of nature. Classicists were not particularly interested in the natural world. The Romantics, in contrast, were enchanted by stormy seas, untouched forests, and icy arctic wastelands. Nature could be awesome and tempestuous, a source of beauty or spiritual inspiration. Most Romantics saw the growth of modern industry as an ugly, brutal attack on their beloved nature and on venerable traditions. They sought escape—in the unspoiled Lake District of northern England, in exotic North Africa, in an imaginary and idealized Middle Ages.

The study of history became a Romantic obsession. History held the key to a universe now perceived to be organic and dynamic, not mechanical and static, as Enlightenment thinkers had believed. Historical novels like Sir Walter Scott's *Ivanhoe* (1820), a passionate romance set in twelfth-century England, found eager readers among the literate middle classes. Professional historians influenced by Romanticism, such as Jules Michelet, went beyond the standard accounts of great men or famous battles. Michelet's many books on the history of France encouraged the French people to search the past for their special national destiny.

Romanticism was a lifestyle as well as an intellectual movement. Many early nineteenth-century Romantics lived lives of tremendous emotional intensity. Obsessive love affairs, duels to the death, madness, strange illnesses, and suicide were not uncommon. Romantic artists typically led bohemian lives, wearing their hair long and uncombed in preference to donning powdered wigs, and rejecting the manners and morals of refined society. Romantics believed that the full development of one's unique human potential was the supreme purpose in life.

Romantic Literature

Romanticism found its distinctive voice in poetry, as the Enlightenment had in prose. Though Romantic poetry had important forerunners in the German "Storm and Stress" movement of the 1770s and 1780s, its first great poets were English: William Blake, William Wordsworth, Samuel Taylor Coleridge, and Sir Walter Scott were all active by 1800, followed shortly by Lord Byron, Percy Bysshe Shelley, and John Keats.

A towering leader of English Romanticism, William Wordsworth was deeply influenced by Rousseau and the liberal spirit of the early French Revolution. Wordsworth settled in the rural Lake District of England with his sister, Dorothy, and Samuel Taylor Coleridge (1772–1834). In 1798 Wordsworth and Coleridge published their *Lyrical Ballads*, which abandoned flowery classical conventions for the language of ordinary speech and endowed simple subjects with the loftiest majesty. Wordsworth believed that all natural things were sacred, and his poetry often expressed a mystical appreciation of nature:

> To every natural form, rock, fruit or flower
> Even the loose stones that cover the high-way
> I gave a moral life, I saw them feel,
> Or link'd them to some feeling: the great mass
> Lay bedded in a quickening soul, and all
> That I beheld, respired with inward meaning.[8]

Here Wordsworth expressed his love of nature in commonplace forms that a variety of readers could appreciate. The short stanza well illustrates his famous conception of poetry as the "spontaneous overflow of powerful feeling [which] takes its origin from emotion recollected in tranquility."[9]

Literature and lifestyle came together in the experience of the writers, friends, and lovers who gathered around Percy Shelley and Lord Byron in the years after the Napoleonic Wars. Self-styled bohemians who lived life for poetic experience, the circle included Mary Shelley, who eventually married the Romantic poet Percy Shelley. On vacation with Percy, Lord Byron, and others in Switzerland in 1816, Mary Shelley wrote *Frankenstein*, one of the best-known Romantic works, a genre-bending novel that tells the tragic story of a scientist who is able to invent a living, almost-human creature.

In France under Napoleon, classicism remained strong and at first inhibited the growth of Romanticism. Between 1820 and 1850, however, the Romantic impulse broke through in the poetry and prose of Alphonse de Lamartine, Victor Hugo, and George Sand (pseudonym of the woman writer Amandine-Aurore-Lucile Dudevant). Of these, Victor Hugo (1802–1885) achieved the most renown with novels that exemplified the Romantic fascination with fantastic characters, exotic historical settings, and extreme emotions. The hero of Hugo's famous *The Hunchback of Notre Dame* (1831) is the great cathedral's deformed bell-ringer, a "human gargoyle" overlooking the teeming life of fifteenth-century Paris. Renouncing his early conservatism, Hugo equated freedom in literature with liberty in politics and society. His political evolution was thus exactly the opposite of Wordsworth's, in whom youthful radicalism gave way to middle-aged caution. Thus Romanticism was compatible with many political beliefs.

In central and eastern Europe, literary Romanticism and early nationalism often reinforced one another. Well-educated Romantics championed their own people's histories, cultures, and unique greatness. Like modern anthropologists, they studied peasant life and transcribed the folk songs, tales, and proverbs that the cosmopolitan Enlightenment had disdained. The brothers Jacob and Wilhelm Grimm were particularly successful at rescuing German folktales from oblivion. Determined to preserve what Wilhelm called "a world of magic" in a time of rapid social change, the Grimms viewed folktales as a reservoir of "long neglected treasures" that testified to the deep roots of the German national character. Wilhelm's assumption that folktales persisted "only in places where there is a warm openness to poetry or where there are imaginations not yet deformed by the perversities of modern life" voiced the typical Romantic idealization of past times.[10] In the Slavic lands, Romantics converted spoken peasant languages into modern written languages, building regional national identities. In the vast Austrian, Russian, and Ottoman Empires, with their many ethnic minorities, the combination of Romanticism and nationalism was particularly potent. Ethnic groups dreaming of independence could find revolutionary inspiration in Romantic visions of a historic national destiny.

Romanticism in Art and Music

Romantic concerns with nature, history, and the imagination extended well beyond literature, into the realms of art and music. France's Eugène Delacroix (deh-luh-KWAH) (1798–1863), one of Romanticism's great artists, painted dramatic, colorful scenes that stirred the emotions. Delacroix was fascinated with remote and exotic subjects, whether lion hunts in Morocco or languishing, sensuous women in a sultan's harem. The famous German painter Casper David Friedrich (1774–1840) preferred somber landscapes of ruined churches or remote arctic shipwrecks, which captured the divine presence in natural forces.

In England the Romantic painters Joseph M. W. Turner (1775–1851) and John Constable (1776–1837) were fascinated by nature, but their interpretations of it contrasted sharply, aptly symbolizing the tremendous emotional range of the Romantic movement. Turner depicted nature's power and terror; wild storms and sinking ships were favorite subjects. Constable painted gentle Wordsworthian landscapes in which human beings lived peacefully with their environment, the comforting countryside of unspoiled rural England.

Musicians and composers likewise explored the Romantic sensibility. Abandoning well-defined musical structures, the great Romantic composers used a wide range of forms to create profound musical landscapes that evoked powerful emotions. They transformed the small classical orchestra, tripling its size by adding wind instruments, percussion, and more brass and strings. The crashing chords evoking the surge of the masses in Chopin's *Revolutionary Etude* and the bottomless despair of the funeral march in Beethoven's Third Symphony—such were the modern orchestra's musical paintings that plumbed the depths of human feeling.

This range and intensity gave music and musicians much greater prestige and publicity than in the past. Music no longer simply complemented a church service or helped a nobleman digest his dinner. It became a sublime end in itself, most perfectly realizing the endless yearning of the soul. The great virtuoso who could transport the listener to ecstasy and hysteria—such as pianist Franz Liszt (1811–1886)—became a cultural hero, a "rock star" of the classical age.

The most famous and prolific of Romantic composers, Ludwig van Beethoven (1770–1827), used contrasting themes and tones to produce dramatic conflict and inspiring resolutions. As one contemporary admirer wrote, "Beethoven's music sets in motion the lever of fear, of awe, of horror, of suffering, and awakens just that infinite longing which is the essence of Romanticism."[11] His own life embodied these emotional extremes, as he struggled to accept the loss of hearing that began at the peak of his fame. In true Romantic fashion he declared, "I will take fate by the throat; it will not bend me completely to its will."[12] Beethoven continued to pour out immortal music, although his last years were silent, spent in total deafness.

How did reforms and revolutions challenge conservatism after 1815?

While the Romantics enacted a revolution in the arts, liberal, national, and socialist forces battered against the conservative restoration of 1815. Political change could result from gradual and peaceful reform or from violent insurrection, but everywhere it took the determination of ordinary people standing up to the prerogatives of the powerful. Between 1815 and 1848 three important countries—Greece, Great Britain, and France—experienced variations on this basic theme.

National Liberation in Greece

Though conservative statesmen had maintained the autocratic status quo despite revolts in Spain and the Two Sicilies, a national revolution succeeded in Greece in the 1820s. Since the fifteenth century the Greeks had lived under the domination of the Ottoman Turks. In spite of centuries of foreign rule, the Greeks had survived as a people, united by their language and the Greek Orthodox religion, and they were inspired by nationalist ideas of self-determination. This rising national movement led to the formation of secret societies and then to open revolt in 1821, led by Alexander Ypsilanti (ihp-suh-LAN-tee), a Greek patriot and a general in the Russian army.

At first, the Great Powers, particularly Metternich, opposed the revolution and refused to back Ypsilanti, primarily because they sought a stable Ottoman Empire as a bulwark against Russian interests in southeast Europe. Yet the Greek cause had powerful defenders. Educated Europeans and Americans cherished the culture of classical Greece; Russians admired the piety of their Orthodox brethren. Writers and artists, moved by the Romantic impulse, responded enthusiastically to the Greek national struggle. The English Romantic poet Lord Byron even joined the Greek revolutionaries to fight (as he wrote in a famous poem) "that Greece might yet be free."

The Greeks, though often quarreling among themselves, battled the Ottomans while hoping for the support of European governments. In 1827 Britain, France, and Russia yielded to popular demands at home and directed Ottoman leaders to accept an armistice. When they refused, the navies of these three powers trapped the Ottoman fleet at Navarino. Russia then declared another of its periodic wars of expansion against the Ottomans. This led to the establishment of a Russian protectorate over much of present-day Romania, which had also been under Ottoman rule. Great Britain, France, and Russia finally declared Greece independent in 1830 and installed a German prince as king of the new country in 1832. Despite this imposed regime, which left the Greek people restive, they had won their independence in a heroic war of liberation against a foreign empire.

Liberal Reform in Great Britain

Pressure from below also reshaped politics in Great Britain, but through a process of gradual reform rather than revolution. Eighteenth-century Britain had been remarkably stable. The landowning aristocracy dominated society, but that class was neither closed nor rigidly defined. Successful business and professional people could buy land and become gentlefolk, while the common people enjoyed limited civil rights. Yet the constitutional monarchy was hardly democratic. With only about 8 percent of the population allowed to vote, the British Parliament, easily manipulated by the king, remained in the hands of the upper classes. The two main political parties—the Tories, which later evolved into the modern British Conservative Party, and the slightly more liberal Whigs—were both led by titled aristocrats, leaving ordinary folk little opportunity to use the formal political process to advance reform. Indeed, government policies consistently supported the aristocracy and the new industrial capitalists at the expense of the laboring classes, while workers fought back with grassroots organizing and public protest.

By the 1780s there was growing interest in some kind of political reform, yet the radical aspects of the French Revolution threw the British aristocracy into a panic for a generation, making it extremely hostile to any attempts to change the status quo. In 1815 open conflict emerged when the aristocracy rammed far-reaching changes in the **Corn Laws** through Parliament. Britain had been unable to import inexpensive grain from eastern Europe during the war years, leading to high prices and large profits for the landed aristocracy. With the war over, grain (which

Delacroix, *Massacre at Chios*, 1824 This moving masterpiece by Romantic artist Eugène Delacroix portrays an Ottoman massacre of ethnic Greeks on the island of Chios during the struggle for national independence in Greece. The Greek revolt won the enthusiastic support of European liberals, nationalists, and Romantics, and this massive oil painting (about 13 feet by 11 feet) portrays the Ottomans as cruel and violent oppressors holding back the course of history. (Musée du Louvre, Paris, France/Bridgeman Images)

the British generically called "corn") could be imported again, allowing the price of wheat and bread to go down and benefiting almost everyone—except aristocratic landlords. The new Corn Laws placed high tariffs (or fees) on imported grain. Its cost rose to improbable levels, ensuring artificially high bread prices for working people and handsome revenues for aristocrats. Seldom has a class legislated more selfishly for its own narrow economic advantage or done more to promote a class-based view of political action.

The change in the Corn Laws, coming as it did at a time of postwar economic distress, triggered protests and demonstrations by urban laborers, who enjoyed the support of radical intellectuals. In 1817 the Tory government, controlled completely by the landed aristocracy, responded by temporarily suspending the traditional rights of peaceable assembly and habeas corpus, which gives a person under arrest the right to a trial. Two years later, in August 1819, at least 60,000 lower-class citizens gathered at Saint Peter's Fields in Manchester to demand parliamentary reform. Eighteen demonstrators were killed and over 600 wounded by a savage government cavalry assault. Nicknamed the **Peterloo Massacre**, in scornful reference to the British victory at Waterloo, this incident demonstrated the government's determination to repress dissenters. Parliament then passed the infamous Six Acts, which placed controls on a heavily taxed press and practically eliminated all mass meetings.

Strengthened by ongoing industrial development, emerging manufacturing and commercial groups insisted on a place in the framework of political power and social prestige for their new wealth, alongside the "landed wealth" (based on long-term land ownership) of the aristocracy. They called for many kinds of liberal reform: changes in town government, organization of a new police force, more rights for Catholics and dissenters, and reform of the Poor Laws to provide aid to some low-paid workers. In the 1820s a more secure Tory government moved in the direction of better urban administration, greater economic liberalism, civil equality for Catholics, and limited imports of foreign grain. These actions encouraged the middle classes to press on for reform of Parliament so they could have a larger say in government.

The Whig Party, though led like the Tories by elite aristocrats, had by tradition been more responsive to middle-class commercial and manufacturing interests. After a series of setbacks, the Whigs' **Reform Bill of 1832** was propelled into law by a mighty surge of popular support. The bill moved British politics in a democratic direction and allowed the House of Commons to emerge as the all-important legislative body, at the expense of the aristocrat-dominated House of Lords. The new industrial areas of the country gained representation in the Commons, and many old "rotten boroughs" — electoral districts that had very few voters and that the landed aristocracy had bought and sold — were eliminated. The number of voters increased by about 50 percent, to include about 12 percent of adult men in Britain and Ireland. Comfortable middle-class groups in the urban population, as well as some substantial farmers who leased their land, received the vote. Thus the conflicts building in Great Britain were successfully — though only temporarily — resolved. Continued peaceful reform within the system appeared difficult but not impossible.

The "People's Charter" of 1838 and the Chartist movement it inspired pressed British elites for yet more radical reform. Dismayed by the economic distress of the working class in the 1830s and 1840s, the Chartists demanded universal male (but not female) suffrage. They saw complete political democracy and rule by the common people as the means to a good and just society. Hundreds of thousands of people signed gigantic petitions calling on Parliament to grant all men the right to vote, first in 1839, again in 1842, and yet again in 1848. Parliament rejected all three petitions. In the short run, the working poor failed with their Chartist demands, but they learned a valuable lesson in mass politics.

While calling for universal male suffrage, many working-class people joined with middle-class manufacturers in the Anti–Corn Law League, founded in Manchester in 1839. Mass participation made possible a popular crusade led by liberal intellectuals and politicians, who argued that lower food prices and more jobs in industry depended on repeal of the Corn Laws. Much of the working class agreed. When Ireland's potato crop failed in 1845 and famine prices for food seemed likely in England, Tory prime minister Robert Peel joined with the Whigs and a minority of his own party to repeal the Corn Laws in 1846 and allow free imports of grain. England escaped famine. Thereafter the liberal doctrine of free trade became almost sacred dogma in Great Britain.

The following year, the Tories passed a bill designed to help the working classes, but in a different way. The Ten Hours Act of 1847 limited the workday for women and young people in factories to ten hours. In competition with the middle class for the support of the working class, Tory legislators continued to support legislation regulating factory conditions. This competition between a still-powerful aristocracy and a strong middle class was a crucial factor in Great Britain's peaceful political evolution. The working classes could make temporary alliances with either competitor to better their own conditions.

Ireland and the Great Famine

The people of Ireland did not benefit from the political competition in England. In the mid-nineteenth century, Ireland was an agricultural nation, and the great majority of the rural population (outside of the northern counties of Ulster, which were partly Presbyterian) were Irish Catholics. They typically rented their land from a tiny minority of Church of England Protestant landowners, who often resided in England. Using a middleman system, these absentee landlords leased land for short periods only, set rents at will, and easily evicted their tenants. In short, landlords used their power to grab as much profit as possible.

Irish peasants, trapped in an exploitative tenant system, lived in abominable conditions. Hundreds of shocking contemporary accounts described hopeless poverty. A compassionate French traveler wrote that Ireland was "pure misery, naked and hungry. . . . I saw the American Indian in his forests and the black slave in his chains, and I believed that I was seeing the most extreme form of human misery; but that was before I knew the lot of poor Ireland."[13]

Despite the terrible conditions, population growth sped upward, part of Europe's general upward trend begun in the early eighteenth century (see "The New Pattern of the Eighteenth Century" in Chapter 17). Between 1780 and 1840 the Irish population doubled from 4 million to 8 million. Extensive cultivation of the humble potato was largely responsible for this rapid rise. A single acre of land planted with the nutritious potato could feed a family of six for a year, and the hardy tuber thrived on Ireland's boggy wastelands. About one-half of the Irish population subsisted almost exclusively on potatoes, supplemented perhaps with a bit of grain or milk and little else. Needing only a potato patch to survive, the rural poor married early. To be sure, a young couple faced a life of extreme poverty, yet the decision to marry and have large families made sense. A couple could manage rural poverty better than someone living alone, and children meant extra hands in the fields.

As population and potato dependency grew, however, conditions became more precarious. From 1820 onward, deficiencies and diseases in the potato crop occurred with disturbing frequency. Then in 1845 and 1846, and again in 1848 and 1851, the potato crop failed in Ireland. Blight attacked the young plants, and leaves and tubers rotted. Unmitigated disaster — the **Great Famine** — followed, as already impoverished peasants experienced widespread sickness and starvation.

The British government reacted slowly. Its rigid commitment to free-trade ideology meant that relief efforts were avoided lest they interfere with the sacrosanct free market or contribute to Irish "indolence." Though the British did eventually provide aid, their relief efforts were tragically inadequate. Moreover, the government continued to collect taxes, landlords demanded their rents, and tenants who could not pay were evicted and their homes destroyed. Famine or no, foreign landowners continued to dominate the Irish people and their economy.

The Great Famine shattered the pattern of Irish population growth. Fully 1 million emigrants fled the famine between 1845 and 1851, mostly to the United States and Canada, and up to 1.5 million people died. The elderly and the very young were hardest hit. Alone among the countries of Europe, Ireland experienced a declining population in the second half of the nineteenth century, as it became a land of continuous out-migration, early death, late marriage, and widespread celibacy.

The Great Famine intensified anti-British feeling and promoted Irish nationalism, for the bitter memory of starvation, exile, and British inaction burned deeply into the popular consciousness. Patriots of the later nineteenth and early twentieth centuries would call on powerful collective emotions in their campaigns for land reform, home rule, and, eventually, Irish independence.

The Revolution of 1830 in France

Like Greece and the British Isles, France experienced dramatic political change in the first half of the nineteenth century, and the French experience especially illustrates the disruptive potential of popular liberal politics. The Constitutional Charter granted by Louis XVIII in the Bourbon restoration of 1814 was a limited liberal constitution. The charter protected economic and social gains made by sections of the middle class and the peasantry in the French Revolution, permitted some intellectual and artistic freedom, and created a parliament with upper and lower houses. Immediately after Napoleon's abortive Hundred Days, the moderate, worldly king refused to bow to the wishes of die-hard aristocrats who wanted to sweep away all the revolutionary changes. Instead, Louis appointed as his ministers moderate royalists, who sought and obtained the support of a majority of the representatives elected to the lower Chamber of Deputies between 1816 and Louis's death in 1824.

Louis XVIII's charter was liberal but hardly democratic. Only about 100,000 of the wealthiest males out of a total population of 30 million had the right to vote for the deputies who, with the king and his ministers, made the laws of the nation. Nonetheless, the "notable people" who did vote came from very different backgrounds. There were wealthy businessmen, war profiteers, successful professionals, ex-revolutionaries, large landowners from the old aristocracy and the middle class, Bourbons, and Bonapartists. The old aristocracy, with its pre-1789 mentality, was a minority within the voting population.

Louis's conservative successor, Charles X (r. 1824–1830), a true reactionary, wanted to re-establish the old order in France. Increasingly blocked by the opposition of the deputies, Charles's government turned in 1830 to military adventure in an effort to rally French nationalism and gain popular support. A long-standing economic and diplomatic dispute with Muslim Algeria, a vassal state of the Ottoman Empire, provided the opportunity.

In June 1830 a French force of thirty-seven thousand crossed the Mediterranean, landed to the west of Algiers, and took the capital city in three short weeks. Victory seemed complete, but in 1831 Algerians in the interior revolted and waged a fearsome war that lasted until 1847, when French armies finally subdued the country. The conquest of Algeria marked the rebirth of French imperial expansion, and the colonial government encouraged French, Spanish, and Italian immigrants to move to Algeria and settle on large tracts of land expropriated from the region's Muslim inhabitants.

Emboldened by the initial good news from Algeria, Charles repudiated the Constitutional Charter in an attempted coup in July 1830. He censored the press and issued decrees stripping much of the wealthy middle class of its voting rights. The immediate reaction, encouraged by liberal lawyers, journalists, and middle-class businessmen, was an insurrection in the capital. Printers, other artisans, and small traders fired up by popular republicanism rioted in the streets of Paris, and three days of vicious street fighting brought down the government. Charles fled. Then the upper middle class, which had fomented the revolt, abandoned the more radical workers and skillfully seated Charles's cousin, Louis Philippe, duke of Orléans, on the vacant throne.

Events in Paris reverberated across Europe. In the Netherlands, Belgian Catholics revolted against the Dutch king and established the independent kingdom of Belgium. In Switzerland, regional liberal assemblies forced cantonal governments to amend their constitutions, leading to two decades of political conflict. And in partitioned Poland, an armed nationalist rebellion against the tsarist government was crushed by the Russian Imperial Army.

Despite the abdication of Charles X, in France the political situation remained more or less unchanged. The new king, Louis Philippe (r. 1830–1848), accepted the Constitutional Charter of 1814 and adopted the red, white, and blue flag of the French Revolution. Beyond these symbolic actions, however, popular demands for thorough reform went unanswered. The upper middle class had effected a change in dynasty that maintained the status quo and the narrowly liberal institutions of 1815. Republicans, democrats, social reformers, and the poor of Paris were bitterly disappointed. They had made a revolution, but it seemed for naught.

What were the main causes and consequences of the revolutions of 1848?

In the late 1840s Europe entered a period of tense economic and political crisis. Bad harvests across the continent caused widespread distress. Uneven industrial development failed to provide jobs or raise incomes and boosted the popularity of the radical ideologies that emerged in the wake of the French Revolution. As a result, limited revolts broke out across Europe: a rebellion in the northern part of Austria in 1846, a civil war in Switzerland in 1847, and an uprising in Naples, Italy, in January 1848.

Full-scale revolution broke out in France in February 1848, and its shock waves rippled across the continent. Only the most developed countries — Great Britain, Belgium, and the Netherlands — and the least developed — the Ottoman and Russian Empires — escaped untouched. Elsewhere governments toppled, as monarchs and ministers bowed or fled. National independence, democratic constitutions, and social reform: the lofty aspirations of a generation of liberal reformers seemed at hand. Yet in the end, the revolutions failed.

A Democratic Republic in France

By the late 1840s revolution in Europe was almost universally expected, but it took events in Paris — once again — to turn expectations into realities. For eighteen years Louis Philippe's reign, labeled the "bourgeois monarchy" because it served the selfish interests of France's wealthy elites, had been characterized by stubborn inaction and complacency. Corrupt politicians refused to approve social legislation or consider electoral reform. Frustrated desires for change, high-level financial scandals, and a general sense of stagnation dovetailed with a severe depression that began with crop failures in 1846 to 1847. The government did little to prevent the agrarian crisis from dragging down the entire economy.

The government's failures united a diverse group of opponents against the king. Bourgeois merchants, opposition deputies, and liberal intellectuals shared a sense of outrage with middle-class shopkeepers, skilled artisans, and unskilled working people. Widespread discontent eventually touched off a popular revolt in Paris. On the night of February 22, 1848, workers joined by some students began tearing up cobblestones and building barricades. Armed with guns and dug in behind their makeshift fortresses, the workers and students demanded a new government. On February 24 the National Guard broke ranks and joined the revolutionaries. Louis Philippe refused to call in the army and abdicated in favor of his grandson. But the common people in arms would tolerate no more monarchy. This refusal led to the proclamation of a provisional republic, headed by a ten-man executive committee and certified by cries of approval from the revolutionary crowd.

The revolutionaries immediately set about drafting a democratic, republican constitution for France's Second Republic. Building such a republic meant giving the right to vote to every adult male, and this was quickly done. Bold decrees issued by the provisional republican government expressed sympathy for revolutionary freedoms by calling for liberty, fraternity, and equality. The revolutionary government guaranteed workplace reforms, freed all slaves in French colonies, and abolished the death penalty.

Yet there were profound differences within the revolutionary coalition. On the one hand, the moderate liberal republicans of the middle class viewed universal male suffrage as the ultimate concession to dangerous popular forces, and they strongly opposed any further social measures. On the other hand, radical republicans, influenced by a generation of utopian socialists and appalled by the poverty and misery of the urban poor, were committed to some kind of socialism. Hard-pressed urban artisans, who hated the unrestrained competition of cutthroat capitalism, advocated a combination of strong craft unions and worker-owned businesses.

Worsening depression and rising unemployment brought these conflicting goals to the fore in 1848. Socialist journalist Louis Blanc and Alexandre Martin — the first member of the industrial working class to enter the French government — represented the republican socialists in the provisional government. Blanc and Martin pressed for official recognition of a socialist right to work. Blanc urged the creation of the permanent government-sponsored cooperative workshops he had advocated in *The Organization of Work*. Such workshops would be an alternative to capitalist employment and a decisive step toward a new, noncompetitive social order.

The moderate republicans, willing to provide only temporary relief, wanted no such thing. The resulting compromise set up National Workshops — soon to become little more than a vast program of pick-and-shovel public works — and established a special commission under Blanc to "study the question." This satisfied no one. The National Workshops were, however, better than nothing. An army of desperate poor from the French provinces and even from foreign countries streamed into Paris to sign up for the workshops. As the economic crisis worsened, the number enrolled in the workshops soared from 10,000 in March to 120,000 by June, and another 80,000 tried unsuccessfully to join.

While the Paris workshops grew, the French people went to the election polls in late April. The result was a bitter loss for the republicans. Voting in most cases for the first time, the people of France elected to the new 900-person Constituent Assembly 500 monarchists and conservatives, only about 270 moderate republicans, and just 80 radicals or socialists.

One of the moderate republicans elected to the assembly was the author of *Democracy in America*, Alexis de Tocqueville (1805–1859), who had predicted the overthrow of Louis Philippe's government. He explained the election results by observing that the socialist movement in Paris aroused the fierce hostility of France's peasants as well as the middle and upper classes. The French peasants owned land, and according to Tocqueville, "private property had become with all those who owned it a sort of bond of fraternity."[14] Tocqueville saw that a majority of the members of the new Constituent Assembly was firmly committed to centrist moderation and strongly opposed to the socialists and their artisan allies, a view he shared.

This clash of ideologies — between moderate liberalism and radical social-ism — became a clash of classes and arms after the elections. The new government's executive committee dropped Blanc and thereafter included no representative of the Parisian working class. Fearing that their socialist hopes were about to be dashed, artisans and unskilled workers invaded the Constituent Assembly on May 15 and tried to proclaim a new revolutionary state. The government used the mid-dle-class National Guard to squelch this uprising. As the workshops continued to fill and grow more radical, the fearful but powerful propertied classes in the Assembly took the offensive. On June 22 the government dissolved the workshops in Paris, giving the workers the choice of joining the army or going to workshops in the provinces.

A spontaneous and violent uprising followed. Frustrated in their thwarted attempt to create a socialist society, masses of desperate people were now losing even their life-sustaining relief. Barricades sprang up again in the narrow streets of Paris, and a terrible class war began. Working people fought with the courage of utter desperation, but this time the government had the army and the support of peasant France. After three terrible "June Days" of street fighting and the death or injury of more than ten thousand people, the republican army under General Louis Cavaignac stood triumphant in a sea of working-class blood and hatred.

The revolution in France thus ended in spectacular failure. The February coa-lition of the middle and working classes had in four short months become locked in mortal combat. In place of a generous democratic republic, the Constituent Assembly completed a constitution featuring a strong executive. This allowed Louis Napoleon, nephew of Napoleon Bonaparte, to win a landslide victory in the election of December 1848. The appeal of his famous name as well as the desire of the prop-ertied classes for order at any cost had led to what would become a semi-authoritarian regime (see "Napoleon III's Second Empire" in Chapter 23).

Revolution and Reaction in the Austrian Empire

Throughout central Europe, the first news of the upheaval in France evoked feverish excitement and then popular revolution, lending credence to Metternich's
famous quip "When France sneezes, all Europe catches cold." Across the Austrian
Empire and the German Confederation, liberals demanded written constitutions,
representative government, and greater civil liberties from authoritarian regimes
(Map 21.3). When governments hesitated, popular revolts broke out. Urban workers and students served as the shock troops, but they were allied with middle-class
liberals and peasants seeking land reforms. In the face of this united front, monarchs made quick concessions. The revolutionary coalition, having secured great

MAP 21.3 The Revolutions of 1848
In February and March 1848 revolutions broke out in the European heartlands: France, the Austrian
Empire, and the German Confederation. In contrast, relative stability reigned in Great Britain,
Belgium, the Netherlands, and the Russian and Ottoman Empires. Why did some regions descend
into revolution, and not others? Can a study of geography help explain the difference?

and easy victories, then broke down as it had in France. The traditional forces—the monarchy, the aristocracy, the regular army—recovered their nerve, reasserted their authority, and revoked many, though not all, of the reforms. Reaction was everywhere victorious.

The revolution in the Austrian Empire began in Hungary in March 1848, when nationalistic Hungarians demanded national autonomy, full civil liberties, and universal suffrage. Anti-imperial insurrection broke out in the northern Italian territories of Lombardy-Venetia the same month, and Austrian forces retreated after five days of street fighting. As the monarchy in Vienna hesitated, radicalized Viennese students and workers took to the streets of the imperial capital and raised barricades in defiance of the government. Meanwhile, peasant disturbances broke out across the empire. The Habsburg emperor Ferdinand I (r. 1835–1848) capitulated and promised reforms and a liberal constitution. When Metternich refused to compromise, the aging conservative was forced to resign and fled to London. The old absolutist order seemed to be collapsing with unbelievable rapidity.

Yet the revolutionary coalition lacked stability. When the monarchy abolished serfdom, with its degrading forced labor and feudal services, the newly free peasants lost interest in the political and social questions agitating the cities. Meanwhile, the coalition of urban revolutionaries were increasingly divided along class lines, over the issue of socialist workshops and universal voting rights for men.

Conflicting national aspirations further weakened and ultimately destroyed the revolutionary coalition. In March the Hungarian revolutionary leaders pushed through an extremely liberal, almost democratic, constitution for the Kingdom of Hungary. But the Hungarian revolutionaries also sought to transform the mosaic of provinces and peoples in their territories into a unified, centralized Hungarian nation. The minority groups that formed half of the population—the Croats, Serbs, and Romanians—rejected such unification (see Map 21.2). Each group felt entitled to political autonomy and cultural independence. In a similar way, Czech nationalists based in Prague and other parts of Bohemia came into conflict with German nationalists living in the same region. Thus desires for national autonomy within the Austrian Empire enabled the monarchy to maintain power by playing off one ethnic group against the other.

Finally, conservative aristocratic forces rallied under the leadership of the archduchess Sophia, a Bavarian princess married to the Habsburg emperor's brother. Deeply ashamed of the emperor's collapse before a "mess of students," she insisted that Ferdinand I, who had no heir, abdicate in favor of her son, Franz Joseph.[15] Powerful nobles organized around Sophia in a secret conspiracy to reverse and crush the revolution.

The first conservative breakthrough came when the army bombarded Prague and savagely crushed a working-class revolt there on June 17, 1848. By August the Austrians had crushed the Italian insurrection. At the end of October, the well-equipped, predominantly peasant troops of the regular Austrian army bombarded the student and working-class radicals dug in behind barricades in Vienna with heavy artillery. They retook the city at the cost of more than four thousand casualties. The determination of the Austrian aristocracy and the loyalty of its army sealed the triumph of reaction and the defeat of revolution.

When Franz Joseph (r. 1848–1916) was crowned emperor of Austria immediately after his eighteenth birthday in December 1848, only the Hungarians had yet to be brought under control. Another determined conservative, Nicholas I of Russia (r. 1825–1855), obligingly lent his iron hand. On June 6, 1849, 130,000 Russian troops poured into Hungary and subdued the country after bitter fighting. For a number of years, the Habsburgs ruled the Kingdom of Hungary as a conquered territory.

Prussia, the German Confederation, and the Frankfurt National Parliament

After Austria, Prussia was the largest and most influential kingdom in the German Confederation. Since the Napoleonic Wars, liberal German reformers had sought to transform absolutist Prussia into a constitutional monarchy, hoping it would then lead the thirty-eight states of the German Confederation into a unified nation-state. The agitation that followed the fall of Louis Philippe, on top of several years of crop failure and economic crises, encouraged liberals to press their demands. In March 1848 excited crowds in urban centers across the German Confederation called for liberal reforms and a national parliament, and many regional rulers quickly gave in to their demands.

When artisans and factory workers rioted in Berlin, the capital of Prussia, and joined temporarily with the middle-class liberals in the struggle against the monarchy, the autocratic yet compassionate Prussian king, Friedrich Wilhelm IV (r. 1840–1861), vacillated and then caved in. On March 21 he promised to grant Prussia a liberal constitution and to merge Prussia into a new national German state.

But urban workers wanted much more — and the Prussian aristocracy wanted much less — than the moderate constitutional liberalism conceded by the king. The workers issued a series of democratic and vaguely socialist demands that troubled their middle-class allies. An elected Prussian Constituent Assembly met in Berlin to write a constitution for the Prussian state, and a conservative clique gathered around the king to urge counter-revolution.

At the same time, elections were held across the German Confederation for a national parliament, which convened to write a federal constitution that would lead to national unification. When they met in Frankfurt that May, the state officials, lawyers, professors, and businessmen elected to parliament represented the interests of the social elite. Their calls for constitutional monarchy, free speech, religious tolerance, and abolition of aristocratic privilege were typical of moderate national liberalism. The deputies essentially ignored calls for more radical action from industrial workers, peasants, republicans, and socialists.

In October 1848 the Frankfurt parliament turned to the question of national unification and borders. At first, the deputies proposed unification around a **Greater Germany** that would include the German-speaking lands of the Austrian Empire in a national state — but not non-German territories in Italy and central Europe. This proposal foundered on Austrian determination to maintain its empire, and some parliamentarians advocated the development of a Lesser Germany that would unify Prussia and other German states without Austria. Even as the deputies debated Germany's future in the autumn of 1848, the forces of counter-revolution pushed back reformists and revolutionaries in Prussia and the other German states.

Despite Austrian intransigence, in March 1849 the national parliament finally completed its draft of a liberal constitution and requested Friedrich Wilhelm IV of Prussia to serve as emperor of a "lesser" German national state (minus Austria). By early 1849, however, reaction had rolled back liberal reforms across the German Confederation. Prussian troops had already crushed popular movements across the German Confederation, and Friedrich Wilhelm had reasserted his royal authority and disbanded the Prussian Constituent Assembly. He contemptuously refused to accept the "crown from the gutter" offered by the parliament in Frankfurt. Bogged down by their preoccupation with nationalist issues, the reluctant revolutionaries in Frankfurt had waited too long and acted too timidly. By May 1849 all but the most radical deputies had resigned from the parliament, and in June Prussian troops forcibly dissolved what remained of the assembly.

Friedrich Wilhelm in fact wanted to be emperor of a unified Germany, but only on his own authoritarian terms. With the liberal threat successfully squelched, he tried to get the small monarchies of Germany to elect him emperor. Austria balked. Supported by Russia, the Austrians forced Prussia to renounce all schemes of unification in late 1850. The German Confederation was re-established in 1851, and a decade of reaction followed. In an echo of the Karlsbad Decrees, state security forces monitored universities, civic organizations, and the press throughout the confederation. Former revolutionaries fled into exile, and German liberals gave up demands for national unification. In the various German states, reactionary monarchs, aided by ever-growing state bureaucracies, granted their subjects conservative constitutions and weak parliaments that maintained aristocratic control. Attempts to unite the Germans — first in a liberal national state and then in a conservative Prussian empire — had failed completely.

NOTES

1. See B. E. Vick, *The Congress of Vienna: Power and Politics After Napoleon* (Cambridge, Mass.: Harvard University Press, 2014), pp. 11–14.
2. A. Sked, *The Decline and Fall of the Habsburg Empire, 1815–1918* (London: Longman, 1989), pp. 1–2.
3. Quoted in D. Blackbourn, *The Long Nineteenth Century: A History of Germany, 1780–1918* (New York: Oxford University Press, 1998), p. 122.
4. E. Gellner, *Nations and Nationalism* (Oxford: Basil Blackwell, 1983), especially pp. 19–39.
5. This paragraph draws on the influential views of B. Anderson, *Imagined Communities: Reflections on the Origins and Spread of Nationalism*, rev. ed. (London: Verso, 1991), and E. J. Hobsbawm and T. Ranger, eds., *The Invention of Tradition* (Cambridge: Cambridge University Press, 1983).
6. Quoted in F. E. Manuel and F. P. Manuel, *Utopian Thought in the Western World* (Cambridge, Mass.: Harvard University Press, 1979), p. 589.
7. Quoted in H. G. Schenk, *The Mind of the European Romantics* (New York: Oxford University Press, 1979), p. 5.
8. Quoted in Schenk, p. 169.
9. Quoted in O. Frey, *Emotions Recollected in Tranquility — Wordsworth's Concept of Poetry in "I Wandered Lonely as a Cloud"* (Munich: GRIN Verlag, 2008), p. 5.
10. Quoted in Maria Tartar, ed., *The Annotated Brothers Grimm*, bicentennial ed. (New York: Norton, 2012), pp. 436, 443.

11. Quoted in A. Comini, *The Changing Image of Beethoven: A Study in Mythmaking* (Santa Fe, N.M.: Sunstone Press, 2008), p. 79.

12. Quoted in F. B. Artz, *From the Renaissance to Romanticism: Trends in Style in Art, Literature, and Music, 1300–1830* (Chicago: University of Chicago Press, 1962), pp. 276, 278.

13. Quoted in G. O'Brien, *The Economic History of Ireland from the Union to the Famine* (London: Longmans, Green, 1921), pp. 23–24.

14. A. de Tocqueville, *Recollections* (New York: Columbia University Press, 1949), p. 94.

15. W. L. Langer, *Political and Social Upheaval, 1832–1852* (New York: Harper & Row, 1969), p. 361.

LOOKING BACK **LOOKING AHEAD**

Viewed from a broad historical perspective, Europe's economic and social foundations in 1750 remained agricultural and rural. Although Enlightenment thought was beginning to question the status quo, authoritarian absolutism dominated political life. One hundred years later, the unfinished effects of the Industrial and French Revolutions had brought fundamental changes to the social fabric of daily life and politics across Europe. The liberal ideals of representative government and legal equality realized briefly in revolutionary France inspired intellectuals and social reformers, who adopted ideologies of liberalism, nationalism, Romanticism, and socialism to challenge the conservative order. The uneven spread of industrial technologies and factory organization into developed areas across Europe spurred the growth of an urban working class but did little to raise the living standards of most workers, peasants, and artisans. Living on the edge of subsistence, the laboring poor in rural and urban areas alike remained subject to economic misfortune, mass unemployment, and food shortages, and they turned repeatedly to protest, riots, and violent insurrection in pursuit of economic and political rights.

In 1848 the poor joined middle- and upper-class reformers in a great wave of revolution that forced conservative monarchs across the continent to grant liberal and national concessions — at least for a moment. Divisions in the revolutionary coalition and the power of the autocratic state forced back the wave of reform, and the revolutions ended in failure. Conservative monarchies revived, nationalist movements collapsed, and hopes for German unification withered. Yet protest on the barricades and debate in liberal parliaments had given a generation a wealth of experience with new forms of participatory politics, and the ideologies associated with the French Revolution would continue to invigorate reformers and revolutionaries after 1850. Nationalism, with its commitment to the imagined community of a great national family and the nation-state, would become a dominant political force, particularly as European empires extended their reach after 1875. At the same time, as agriculture and rural life gradually declined in economic importance, the spread of industrialization would raise living standards, sustain a growing urban society, and reshape family and class relationships. Diverse, complicated, and fascinating, pockets of this new urban society already existed in 1850. By 1900 it dominated northwestern Europe and was making steady inroads to the east and south.

MAKE CONNECTIONS

Think about the larger developments and continuities within and across chapters.

1. How did the spread of radical ideas and the movements for reform and revolution explored in this chapter draw on the "unfinished" political and industrial revolutions (Chapters 19 and 20) of the late eighteenth century? Why did the conservative policies put in place by Metternich and the leaders of the Holy Alliance fail to halt the spread of such ideas?

2. Why did the ideas of the Romantic movement so easily support reformist and radical political ideas, including liberalism, republicanism, and nationalism? What does this reveal about the general connections between art and politics?

3. The years between 1815 and 1850 witnessed the invention of a number of new political ideologies. To what extent do the ideas advanced by conservatives, liberals, nationalists, and socialists in the first half of the nineteenth century continue to shape our political debates?

Chapter 21 Review

IDENTIFY KEY TERMS

Identify and explain the significance of each item below.

Congress of Vienna (p. 612)	bourgeoisie (p. 625)
Holy Alliance (p. 618)	proletariat (p. 625)
Karlsbad Decrees (p. 618)	Romanticism (p. 626)
liberalism (p. 620)	Corn Laws (p. 630)
laissez faire (p. 620)	Peterloo Massacre (p. 631)
nationalism (p. 621)	Reform Bill of 1832 (p. 632)
socialism (p. 623)	Great Famine (p. 633)
Marxism (p. 624)	Greater Germany (p. 640)

REVIEW THE MAIN IDEAS

Answer the section heading questions from the chapter.

1. How was peace restored and maintained after the Napoleonic Wars? (p. 612)
2. What new ideologies emerged to challenge conservatism? (p. 620)
3. What were the characteristics of the Romantic movement? (p. 626)
4. How did reforms and revolutions challenge conservatism after 1815? (p. 629)
5. What were the main causes and consequences of the revolutions of 1848? (p. 635)

CHRONOLOGY

1790s–1848	• Romantic movement in literature and the arts
1809–1848	• Metternich serves as Austrian foreign minister
1810–1829	• Revolutions in South America throw off Spanish rule
1814–1815	• Congress of Vienna
1815	• Revision of Corn Laws in Great Britain; Holy Alliance formed
June 18, 1815	• Napoleon defeated at the Battle of Waterloo
1818	• Mary Shelley publishes *Frankenstein*
1819	• Karlsbad Decrees issued by German Confederation
1820	• Congress of Troppau proclaims the principle of intervention to maintain autocratic regimes
1821	• Austria crushes a liberal revolution in Naples and restores the Sicilian autocracy
1823	• French armies restore the Spanish Crown
1825	• Decembrist Uprising crushed by Russian tsar
1830	• Greece wins independence from Ottomans
1830	• France invades Algeria
1830	• French king Charles X repudiates the Constitutional Charter; insurrection and collapse of the government follow
1830	• Louis Philippe succeeds to the French throne and maintains a narrowly liberal regime
1832	• Reform Bill in Britain
1839	• Socialist Louis Blanc publishes *The Organization of Work*
1845–1851	• Great Famine in Ireland
1848	• Revolutions in France, Austria, and Prussia; Marx and Engels publish *The Communist Manifesto*

22

Life in the Emerging Urban Society

1840–1914

CHAPTER PREVIEW

- What were the main changes in urban life in the nineteenth century?

- How did class and gender reinforce social difference in the nineteenth century?

- How did urbanization affect family life and gender roles?

- What were the most important changes in science and culture?

WHEN LONDONERS GATHERED IN 1860 at the Grand Fete in the Crystal Palace, they enjoyed the pleasures of an established urban society that would have been unthinkable just sixty years earlier. Across the nineteenth century, as industrialization expanded exponentially, Europeans left their farms and country villages to find work in the ever-growing towns and cities. By 1900, in much of developed northwestern Europe, more than half the population lived in urban settings. On Europe's periphery—in Poland, Russia, and central Europe; in southern Italy and Spain; in Greece and the Balkan lands to the southeast—urbanization and industrialization moved more slowly. Nonetheless, rural-to-urban migration spread across Europe and continued into the twentieth century.

Despite the happy faces in the London crowd at the palace, the emerging urban society brought costs as well as benefits. Although living standards rose in the nineteenth century, wages and living conditions varied greatly, and many city dwellers were still poor. Advances in public health and urban planning brought some relief to the squalid working-class slums, yet vast differences in income, education, and occupation still divided people into socially stratified groups. Major changes in family life and gender roles accompanied this diversified class system. Dramatic breakthroughs in chemistry, medicine, and electrical engineering further transformed urban society after 1880, and a new generation of artists, writers, and professional social scientists worked to understand and portray the changes wrought by urbanization.

What were the main changes in urban life in the nineteenth century?

Since the Middle Ages, European cities had been centers of government, culture, and large-scale commerce. They had also been congested, dirty, and unhealthy. Beginning in the early nineteenth century, the Industrial Revolution took these unfortunate realities of urban life to unprecedented levels. Rapid city growth worsened long-standing overcrowding, pollution, and unhealthy living conditions. Taming the city posed a major challenge. Only the full-scale efforts of government leaders, city planners, reformers, scientists, and civic-minded citizens would eventually ameliorate the ferocious savagery of the industrial metropolis.

Industry and the Growth of Cities

The main causes of the poor quality of urban life—dense overcrowding, pervasive poverty, and lack of medical knowledge—had existed for centuries. Because the typical city had always been a "walking city," with no public transportation, great masses of people needed to live in close proximity to shops, markets, and workplaces. Packed together almost as tightly as possible, people in cities suffered and died from the spread of infectious disease in far greater numbers than their rural counterparts. In the larger towns, more people died each year than were born, on average, and urban populations maintained their numbers only because newcomers continually arrived from rural areas.

The Industrial Revolution exacerbated these deplorable conditions. The steam engine freed industrialists from dependence on the energy of fast-flowing streams and rivers, so that by 1800 there was every incentive to build new factories in urban areas, which had many advantages. Cities had better transportation facilities than the countryside and thus better supplies of coal and raw materials. Cities had many hands wanting work, for they drew people like a magnet, and as a result concentrated the demand for manufactured goods. And it was a great advantage for a producer to have other factories nearby to supply the business's needs and buy its products. Therefore, as industry grew, already overcrowded and unhealthy cities expanded rapidly.

Great Britain, the first country to go through the early stages of the Industrial Revolution, faced the challenges of a changing urban environment early on. In the 1820s and 1830s the populations of a number of British cities increased by 40 to 70 percent each decade. The number of people living in cities of 20,000 or more in England and Wales jumped from 1.5 million in 1801 to 6.3 million in 1851 and reached 15.6 million in 1891. Such cities accounted for 17 percent of the total English population in 1801, 35 percent as early as 1851, and fully 54 percent in 1891. Other countries duplicated the English pattern as they industrialized (Map 22.1). And as we will see in Chapter 24, rapid growth drew migrants from the countryside and across national borders, leaving ever-larger European cities centers of ethnic and religious diversity.

Except on the outskirts, early-nineteenth-century cities in Britain used every scrap of available land. Parks and open areas were almost nonexistent. Developers erected buildings on the smallest possible lots in order to pack the maximum number of people into a given space. Narrow houses were built attached to one another in long rows. These row houses had neither front nor back yards, and only a narrow alley in

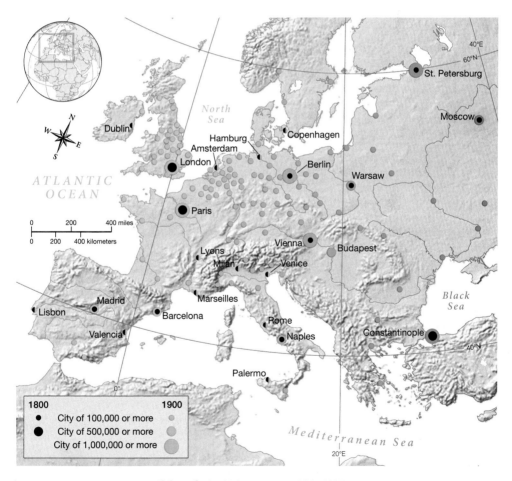

MAP 22.1 **European Cities of 100,000 or More, 1800–1900**
There were more large cities in Great Britain in 1900 than in all of Europe in 1800.

back separated one row from the next. Other buildings were built around courtyards completely enclosed on all four sides. Many people lived in tiny apartments or small, overcrowded cellars or attics; entire families often shared a single room.

These highly concentrated urban populations lived in extremely unsanitary and unhealthy conditions. The sad state of urban sewage systems in London and elsewhere epitomized the problem. Before the mid-nineteenth century, human waste was typically deposited in chamber pots and tossed into the street with a warning shout, where rainwater carried it through open canals into local rivers. In densely populated urban areas, open drains and sewers flowed alongside or down the middle of unpaved streets. Waste was often collected through latrines in cesspools, underground pits located beneath living quarters. Cesspool cleaners, or "nightsoilmen," periodically emptied the pits, carting waste to designated dumpsites where it might be turned into fertilizer.

The rapid growth of cities across the nineteenth century overwhelmed these methods of sewage disposal. In an ironic twist, the popularization of a sanitation improvement—the flush toilet—spelled disaster for the cesspool. With each flush, a large volume of water accompanied a small amount of waste, rapidly filling cesspools with liquid. Cesspool pits then leaked, spilling untreated sewage into waterways. As one historian put it, by the 1840s the better-off classes had come to the "shocking realization that millions of English men, women, and children were living in shit."[1] The results—unbearably odorous—were also deadly. Water polluted with the bacteria that cause cholera and typhoid seeped into drinking supplies, causing mass epidemics across Europe.

London, the largest city in the world at the time, was a perfect example. As the population more than tripled from about 1.3 million in 1825 to 4.2 million in 1875, the sewage problem became catastrophic. Cesspools overflowed, and flush toilets installed in new buildings drained directly into the River Thames, the main source of drinking water for London residents. Over twenty thousand died in the cholera epidemics of 1832 and 1849, and another eleven thousand perished of the same disease in 1854. Outbreaks of cholera also swept across Europe and the globe with stunning frequency in the nineteenth century, killing hundreds of thousands. So many died in Poland that the word *cholera* became an obscene term, still used today as a curse word. As late as 1892, over 8,500 people died of the disease in the German port city of Hamburg.

The environmental costs of rapid urbanization and industrialization were enormous as well, and London again is a good example. Black soot from coal-fired factories and train engines fouled city air. Throughout the nineteenth century the city experienced frequent and severe fogs that could bring economic activity to a complete halt. By 1850 the River Thames, which courses through London, was so polluted that it was essentially biologically dead.

Who or what bore responsibility for these awful conditions? The crucial factors included the tremendous pressure of more people and the total absence of public transportation. People simply had to jam themselves together to get to shops and factories on foot. In addition, government in Great Britain, both local and national, only slowly established sanitary facilities and adequate building codes. Finally, most people knew little about germs and basic hygiene. Ordinary folk rarely washed and took dirt for granted, habits that encouraged the spread of infectious disease.

The Advent of the Public Health Movement

Around the middle of the nineteenth century, people's fatalistic acceptance of their overcrowded, unsanitary surroundings began to give way to a growing interest in reform and improvement. Events in London were again exemplary. British reformers such as Edwin Chadwick, John Snow, and Joseph Bazalgette engaged in a process of collaborative problem solving that fed the beginnings of the British public health movement. Chadwick, one of the commissioners charged with the administration of relief to paupers under Britain's revised Poor Law of 1834, emerged as a powerful voice for reform. Chadwick found inspiration in the ideas of radical philosopher Jeremy Bentham (1748–1832), whose approach to social issues, called **utilitarianism**, had taught that public problems ought to be dealt with on a rational, scientific basis to advance the "greatest good for the greatest number." Applying these principles, Chadwick soon became convinced that disease and death actually caused poverty, because a sick worker was an unemployed worker and orphaned children were poor children. Most important, Chadwick believed that government could help prevent disease by cleaning up the urban environment.

Chadwick collected detailed reports from local Poor Law officials on the "sanitary conditions of the laboring population" and published his hard-hitting findings in 1842. Early reformers, including Chadwick, were seriously handicapped by their adherence to the prevailing miasmatic theory of disease — the belief that people contracted disease when they inhaled the bad odors of decay and putrefying excrement. Nonetheless, the mass of widely publicized evidence gathered in his report suggested that disease was related to filthy environmental conditions, which were in turn caused largely by lack of drainage, sewers, and garbage collection. In 1848, with the public health cause strengthened by a cholera epidemic that raged across Britain, Chadwick's report became the basis of Great Britain's first public health law, which created a national health board and gave cities broad authority to build modern sanitation systems.

The English physician John Snow encouraged further reform. Snow had doubts about the miasma theory, which were confirmed in his famous study of the 1854 Broad Street cholera outbreak that killed over six hundred people in central London. After interviewing local residents, Snow determined that the initial victims had been exposed to a drinking water pump built next to an aging cesspool and that the disease had spread from this point. Although he was unaware of germ theory (see "The Bacterial Revolution" ahead), Snow did correctly identify putrid water as the cause and called on urban authorities to take action.

The work of these and other early public health reformers remained controversial; many scientists clung to the miasma theory, and the London city government moved only haltingly to implement reforms. The famous **"Great Stink"** of the summer of 1858, when fumes from the River Thames closed Parliament and threatened to shut down the city, underscored the urgent need for change.

In response, between 1858 and 1865 the London Metropolitan Board of Works, led by engineer Joseph Bazalgette, built a massive network of new sewers. Bazalgette and his construction crews enclosed open waste canals and drained private toilets into underground channels that combined flows of rainwater and human waste. London's massive interception sewers now emptied sewage into irrigation fields and

Urban Poverty In late-nineteenth-century Rome, poor Italians still lived in ramshackle, unrenovated apartments dating back to the medieval era, as portrayed in this watercolor (circa 1883) by Ettore Roesler Franz. For the families that lived there, the unsanitary street out front served as a space for work and recreation. (By Ettore Roesler Franz [1845–1907]/Gabinetto Comunale delle Stampe, Rome, Italy/De Agostini Picture Library/Bridgeman Images)

treatment plants rather than directly into the Thames. Inspired by London's example, urban engineers across Europe and North America built their own sewers and treatment plants, which limited the dumping of raw waste into local rivers, lakes, or seas.

The public health movement won dedicated supporters in the United States, France, and Germany from the 1850s on. Governments accepted at least limited responsibility for the health of all citizens, and their programs broke decisively with the age-old fatalism of urban populations. By the 1860s and 1870s European cities were making real progress toward adequate water supplies and sewer systems. Though factories and coal stoves continued to pump black smoke into the air and pollution remained a serious problem, city dwellers started to reap the reward of better health, and death rates began to decline (Figure 22.1).

The Bacterial Revolution

Improved sanitation in cities promoted a better quality of life and some improvements in health care, but effective control of communicable disease required a great leap forward in medical knowledge and biological theory. Although keen observation by doctors and public health officials pinpointed the role of filth and bad drinking water in the transmission of disease, thus weakening the miasmatic idea, they had little idea of how the process actually made people sick.

The breakthrough arrived when the French chemist Louis Pasteur developed the **germ theory** of disease, which finally convinced city officials to institute thorough public sanitation programs. Pasteur (pas-TUHR) (1822–1895), who began studying fermentation for brewers in 1854, used a microscope to develop a simple test that brewers could use to monitor the fermentation process and avoid spoilage. He found that fermentation depended on the growth of living organisms and that the activity of these organisms could be suppressed by heating the beverage — a process that came to be called pasteurization, which he first implemented in the early 1860s. The breathtaking implication of this discovery was that specific diseases were caused by specific living organisms — germs — and that those organisms could be controlled.

By 1870 the work of Pasteur and others had demonstrated the general connection between germs and disease. When, in the

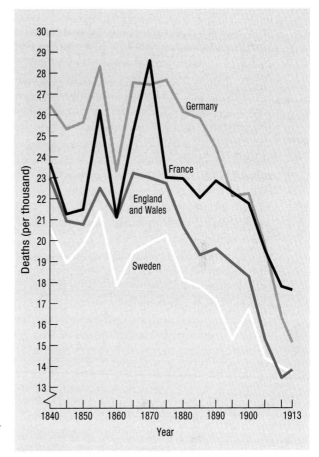

FIGURE 22.1 **The Decline of Death Rates in England and Wales, Germany, France, and Sweden, 1840–1913**
A rising standard of living, improvements in public health, and better medical knowledge all contributed to the dramatic decline of death rates in the nineteenth century.

middle of the 1870s, German country doctor Robert Koch (kawkh) and his coworkers developed pure cultures of harmful bacteria and described their life cycles, the dam broke. Over the next twenty years, researchers — mainly Germans — identified the organisms responsible for disease after disease. These discoveries led to the development of effective vaccines, though some infections resisted treatment until scientists developed antibiotics in the middle of the next century.

Acceptance of germ theory brought about dramatic improvements in the deadly environment of hospitals and operating rooms. In 1865, when Pasteur showed that the air was full of bacteria, English surgeon Joseph Lister (1827–1912) immediately grasped the connection between aerial bacteria and the problem of wound infection. He reasoned that a chemical disinfectant applied to a wound dressing would "destroy the life of the floating particles" (or germs). Lister's antiseptic principle worked wonders. In the 1880s German surgeons developed the more sophisticated practice of sterilizing not only the wound but also everything—hands, instruments, clothing—that entered the operating room. The simple practice of washing hands before birthing procedures saved the lives of countless mothers.

The professionalization of public health and the spread of Western medical knowledge around the world went hand in hand, in a process that often (but not always) overlapped with colonialism and Christian missions. By the close of the nineteenth century, medicine had become a key tool of Protestant missionary methods, as well as a means through which Western nations like Britain could demonstrate interest in and care for their colonial subjects. Providing much of the energy for these trends were the growing ranks of educated women who sought career and service opportunities abroad. As medical education opened for women in both England and India, medical work provided British women with fulfilling careers and social networks of like-minded individuals.

The bacterial revolution and the public health movement saved millions of lives, particularly after about 1880. Mortality rates began to decline dramatically in European countries (see Figure 22.1) as the awful death sentences of the past—cholera, diphtheria, typhoid, typhus, yellow fever—became vanishing diseases. City dwellers in Europe especially benefited from these developments. By 1910 a great silent revolution had occurred: the death rates for people of all ages in Western urban areas were generally no greater than those for people in rural areas, and sometimes they were lower.

Improvements in Urban Planning

More effective planning was also an important key to unlocking a better quality of urban life. France took the lead during the rule of Napoleon III (r. 1848–1870), who used government action to promote the welfare of his subjects. Napoleon III believed that rebuilding much of Paris would provide employment, improve living conditions, limit the outbreak of cholera epidemics—and testify to the power and glory of his empire. He hired Baron Georges Haussmann (HOWS-muhn) (1809–1884), an aggressive, impatient Alsatian, to modernize the city. An authoritarian manager and capable city planner, Haussmann bulldozed both buildings and opposition. In twenty years Paris was completely transformed (Map 22.2).

The Paris of 1850 was a labyrinth of narrow, dark streets, the results of desperate overcrowding and a lack of effective planning. More than one-third of the city's 1 million inhabitants lived in a central district not twice the size of New York's Central Park. Residents faced terrible conditions and extremely high death rates. The entire metropolis had few open spaces and only two public parks.

For two decades Haussmann and his fellow planners proceeded on many fronts. With a bold energy that often shocked their contemporaries, they razed old buildings in order to cut broad, straight, tree-lined boulevards through the center of the city as well as in new quarters rising on the outskirts (see Map 22.2). These boulevards, designed in part to prevent the easy construction and defense of barricades by revolutionary crowds, permitted traffic to flow freely and afforded impressive vistas. Their creation demolished some of the worst slums. New streets stimulated

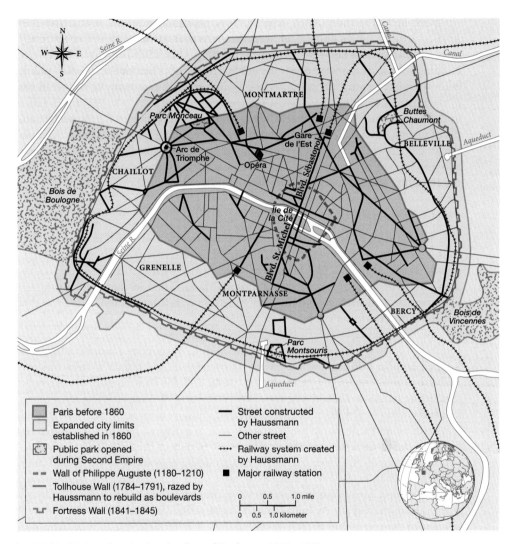

MAP 22.2   The Modernization of Paris, ca. 1850–1870
The addition of broad boulevards, large parks, and grand train stations transformed Paris. The cutting of the new north-south axis—known as the Boulevard Saint-Michel—was one of Haussmann's most controversial projects. His plan razed much of Paris's medieval core and filled the Île de la Cité with massive government buildings. Note the addition of new streets and light rail systems (the basis of the current Parisian subway system, the "metro") that encircle the city core, emblematic of the public transportation revolution that enhanced living conditions in nineteenth-century European cities.

the construction of better housing, especially for the middle classes. Planners created small neighborhood parks and open spaces throughout the city and developed two very large parks suitable for all kinds of holiday activities—one on the affluent west side and one on the poor east side. The city improved its sewers, and a system of aqueducts more than doubled the city's supply of clean, fresh water.

Rebuilding Paris stimulated urban reform throughout Europe, particularly after 1870. Aided by the technological breakthroughs that made improved urban planning and living possible — structural engineering, the use of iron and steel in city buildings, the arrival of electricity, the establishment of urban police forces — public authorities in city after city mounted a coordinated attack on many of the problems of the urban environment.

Urban planners in cities such as Vienna and Cologne followed the Parisian example of tearing down old walled fortifications and replacing them with broad, circular boulevards on which they erected office buildings, town halls, theaters, opera houses, and museums. These ring roads and the new boulevards that radiated outward from the city center eased movement and encouraged urban expansion (see Map 22.2).

Public Transportation

The development of mass public transportation often accompanied urban planning. In the 1870s many European cities authorized private companies to operate horse-drawn streetcars, which had been developed in the United States, to carry riders along the growing number of major thoroughfares. Then in the 1890s European countries adopted another revolutionary American transit innovation, a streetcar that ran along iron tracks on the power of electricity.

Electric streetcars were cheaper, faster, more dependable, cleaner, and more comfortable than their horse-drawn counterparts. Workers, shoppers, and schoolchildren hopped on board during the workweek. On weekends and holidays, streetcars carried urban dwellers on happy outings to parks and the countryside, to racetracks and music halls. In 1886 the horse-drawn streetcars of Austria-Hungary, France, Germany, and Great Britain carried about 900 million riders per year. By 1910 electric streetcar systems in those four countries were carrying 6.7 billion riders annually.[2]

Mass transit encouraged the development of decent housing. The new boulevards and horse-drawn streetcars facilitated a middle-class move to better and more spacious housing in the 1860s and 1870s; after 1890 electric streetcars meant people of even modest means could access new, improved housing. Though still densely populated, cities expanded and became less congested. In England in 1901, only 9 percent of the urban population was overcrowded in terms of the official definition of more than two persons per room. On the continent, many city governments in the early twentieth century built electric streetcar and light rail systems to provide transportation for the growing number of workers who lived in the new public and private housing developments built beyond the city limits. Suburban commuting was born.

How did class and gender reinforce social difference in the nineteenth century?

In the *Communist Manifesto*, Karl Marx predicted that modern capitalist society would be split into "two great hostile camps": the wealthy, powerful bourgeoisie and the impoverished, miserable proletariat. Like Marx, historians see modern class society as a product of the nineteenth century, which built on, but also transformed, earlier social distinctions based on orders and estates. But society did not split into two sharply defined opposing classes, as Marx predicted. To the contrary, as the quality of urban life improved across Europe, the class structure became more complex and diverse. The gap between rich and poor remained enormous, but there were numerous gradations between the extremes. And all along these social hierarchies, gender differences between men and women had a major impact on the way class status was lived and perceived.

The Distribution of Income

By 1850 at the latest, real wages—that is, wages received by workers adjusted for changes in the prices they paid—were rising for the mass of the population, and they continued to do so until 1914. The real wages of British male workers, for example, almost doubled between 1850 and 1906. Similar increases occurred in continental countries as industrial development quickened after 1850. This represented a major step forward in the centuries-old battle against poverty, reinforcing efforts to improve many aspects of human existence. At the same time, as women (and children) entered the industrial workforce, a lasting income gap emerged. Women worked in less desirable, poorly paid jobs, rarely held supervisory positions, and received less pay than men even when they did the same work.

Greater economic rewards for the average person hardly eliminated hardship and poverty, nor did it shrink the gaps between the rich and the poor. The aristocracy—with imposing wealth, unrivaled social prestige, and substantial political influence—retained its position at the very top of the social ladder, followed closely by a new rich elite, composed mainly of the most successful business families from banking, industry, and large-scale commerce. In fact, the prominent families of the commercial elite tended to marry into the old aristocracy, to form a new upper class of at most 5 percent of the population.

Much of the aristocracy welcomed this development. Having experienced a sharp decline in its relative income in the course of industrialization, the landed aristocracy eagerly allied with big business and was often delighted to trade titles, country homes, and snobbish elegance for good, hard cash. Some of the best bargains were made through marriages to American heiresses. Wealthy aristocrats also increasingly exploited their agricultural and mineral resources as if they were business people.

Income inequality was closely linked to social status. In almost every advanced country around 1900, the richest 5 percent of all households in the population received about a third of all national income, and the richest 20 percent of households received from 50 to 60 percent of it. As a result, the lower 80 percent received only 40 to 50 percent of all income—far less per household than the two richest groups. Moreover, the bottom 30 percent of all households received 10 percent or less of all income. To understand the full significance of these statistics, one must realize that the middle classes were much smaller than they are today. Across the nineteenth century they accounted for less than 20 percent of the population.

Class differences were also "gendered"; that is, being a man or a woman had a significant impact on earnings and employment. In wealthy families, women rarely had to seek paid work. As the nineteenth century progressed, women in the middle classes fought for and increasingly found work in professions such as teaching, social work, and nursing. Poorer women took a variety of jobs, ranging from factory labor to domestic service; single poor women were generally at the bottom of all income earners.

The great gap between rich and poor endured, in part, because industrial and urban development made society more diverse and classes less unified. There developed an almost unlimited range of jobs, skills, and earnings; one group or subclass blended into another in a complex, confusing hierarchy. Between the tiny elite of the very rich and the sizable mass of the dreadfully poor lived a range of subclasses, each filled with individuals struggling to rise or at least to hold their own in the social order. In this atmosphere of competition and hierarchy, neither the "middle class" nor the "working class" actually acted as a single unified force. It makes more sense to speak of the "middle classes" and "working classes."

The People and Occupations of the Middle Classes

By the beginning of the twentieth century, the variations within the urban middle classes were striking. Below the top tier whose riches were based on land and title, the larger, much less wealthy, and increasingly diversified middle classes engaged in occupations requiring mental, rather than physical, skill. This group engaged in a wide range of occupations.

As industry and technology expanded, a number of skilled trades and occupations underwent a process historians call **professionalization**. Attorneys, university professors, architects, chemists, accountants, and surveyors, to name only a few, established criteria for training and certification, including advanced degrees, and banded together in organizations to promote and defend their interests. The new professions were almost entirely dominated by men, and their specialized knowledge — and professional credentials — bolstered their wages and social standing. Professionalization furthermore limited the ability of amateurs and outsiders, and in most cases women who mostly lacked access to higher education, from working in the field. Engineering and medicine, for example, emerged as full-fledged professions with considerable power, prestige, and privilege. Dentistry was taken out of the hands of working-class barbers and placed in the hands of highly trained (and middle-class) professionals. As governments grew and provided more services, and very large corporations (such as railroads or arms manufacturers) controlled ever-larger numbers of human and physical resources, middle-class male professionals also found jobs as managers in large public and private institutions.

Industrialization expanded and diversified the lower middle class as well, and opportunities grew for women as well as men in the service sector — the proliferating jobs in commerce, government, and business that were neither strictly agricultural nor industrial. The number of independent, property-owning male shopkeepers and small business people grew, as did the number of white-collar employees — a mixed group of traveling salesmen, bookkeepers, store managers, and clerks who staffed the offices and branch stores of large corporations. Women took jobs as shop assistants, department store sales staff, and low-level typists and clerical workers in fast-growing businesses.

Both male and female white-collar employees owned little property and often earned no more than better-paid skilled or semiskilled workers. Yet white-collar workers were fiercely committed to the middle-class ideal of upward social mobility.

The business clothes and the soft clean hands that accompanied low-level retail and managerial work became important status symbols that set this group above those who earned a living through manual labor. For women, white-collar positions offered a way to earn both money and independence outside the home, loosening former restrictions on employment and social mobility.

Many middle-class women accepted the ideologies of "separate spheres" (see "Separate Spheres and the Importance of Homemaking" later in this chapter) and preferred to expend their energies shaping a comfortable home life, but some struggled to break into the world of professional training and employment. In the second half of the nineteenth century they made important although limited gains. One avenue women used to break into the world of professional training and employment was charity and social work: privileged women increasingly found volunteer and paid work in public poor houses, prisons, schools, and hospitals, where their supposedly "natural" inclinations for motherly nurturing might help alleviate the plight of the poor.

Women also sought access to higher education. With the great expansion of public education and health systems, many entered teaching or nursing schools, and women came to predominate in these low-paid professions. By 1911 in England, for example, 77,000 women worked as nurses and 183,298 women were employed as teachers, about 73 percent of the total.[3] Nursing and teaching, like social work, were considered appropriate for women's "natural" talents.

The battle to enter new, modern universities and earn professional degrees was more difficult, but by 1900 most major European universities had accepted at least a handful of female students. Women such as the Polish-French scientist Marie Curie, whose pathbreaking work on radioactivity earned a Nobel Prize, or the German physician Franziska Tibertius, who opened a clinic for women factory workers in Berlin, made pioneering inroads into professions previously reserved for men.

The People and Occupations of the Working Classes

At the beginning of the twentieth century, about four out of five people belonged to the working classes — that is, people whose livelihoods depended primarily on physical labor and who did not employ domestic servants. Many of them were still small landowning peasants and hired farm hands, especially in eastern Europe. In western and central Europe, however, the typical worker had left the land. By 1900 less than 8 percent of the people in Great Britain worked in agriculture, and in rapidly industrializing Germany only 25 percent were employed in agriculture and forestry. Even in less industrialized France, under 50 percent of the population worked the land.

Urban workers were as heterogeneous as the middle classes. Economic development and increased specialization expanded the traditional range of working-class skills, earnings, and experiences. Meanwhile, the sharp distinction between highly skilled artisans and unskilled manual workers gradually broke down. To be sure, highly skilled printers and masons as well as unskilled dockworkers and common laborers continued to exist. But between these extremes there appeared ever more semiskilled groups, including trained factory workers. Skilled, semiskilled, and unskilled workers developed divergent lifestyles and cultural values, and unlike the homemakers in middle-class families, many working-class women had to find paid employment to keep their families afloat, furthering the great diversity at the lower levels of society. These differences contributed to a keen sense of social status and hierarchy within the working classes, undermining the class unity predicted by Marx.

Highly skilled male workers—about 15 percent of the working classes—were later termed the **labor aristocracy**. They earned only about two-thirds of the income of the bottom ranks of the servant-keeping classes, but that was fully double the earnings of unskilled workers. The most "aristocratic" of these highly skilled workers were construction bosses and factory foremen, who had risen from the ranks and were fiercely proud of their achievement. The labor aristocracy also included members of the traditional highly skilled handicraft trades that had not been mechanized or placed in factories, like cabinetmakers, jewelers, and printers.

While the labor aristocracy enjoyed its exalted position, maintaining that status was by no means certain. Gradually, as factory production eliminated more and more crafts, lower-paid, semiskilled factory workers replaced many skilled artisans. Traditional wood-carvers and watchmakers virtually disappeared, for example, as the making of furniture and timepieces now took place in factories. At the same time, industrialization opened new opportunities for new kinds of highly skilled workers, such as shipbuilders and railway locomotive engineers. Thus the labor elite remained in a state of flux, as individuals and whole crafts moved up and down the social scale.

To maintain their precarious standing, the upper working class adopted distinctive values and straitlaced, almost puritanical behavior. Like the middle classes, the labor aristocracy believed firmly in middle-class morality and economic improvement. They saved money regularly, worried about their children's education, and valued good housing. Wives seldom sought employment outside the home. They practiced self-discipline and stern morality and generally frowned on heavy drinking and sexual permissiveness, believing that they set a model for the rest of the working classes. As one German skilled worker somberly warned, "The path to the brothel leads through the tavern" and from there to drastic decline or total ruin.[4]

Below the labor aristocracy stood the enormously complex world of hard work, composed of both semiskilled and unskilled workers, men and women. Established male construction workers—carpenters, bricklayers, pipe fitters—stood near the top of the semiskilled hierarchy, often flirting with (or sliding back from) the labor elite. A large number of the semiskilled were factory workers, who earned highly variable but relatively good wages. These workers included substantial numbers of unmarried women, who began to play an increasingly important role in the industrial labor force.

Below the semiskilled workers, a larger group of unskilled workers included day laborers, mostly men, such as longshoremen, wagon-driving teamsters, and "helpers" of all kinds. Many of these people had real skills and performed valuable services, but they were unorganized and divided, united only by the common fate of meager earnings and poor living conditions. The same lack of unity characterized male and female street vendors and market people—these self-employed members of the lower working classes competed savagely with each other and with established shopkeepers of the lower middle class.

Working-class women labored in factories and as street vendors, but by far the largest number of unskilled women worked as domestic servants, whose numbers grew steadily in the nineteenth century. In Great Britain, for example, one out of every seven employed persons in 1911 was a domestic servant. The great majority were women; indeed, one out of every three girls in Britain between the ages of fifteen and twenty worked as a domestic servant. Throughout Europe, many female domestics in the cities were recent migrants from rural areas. As in earlier times, domestic service meant hard work at low pay with limited personal independence and the danger of sexual exploitation. For the full-time general maid in a lower-middle-class family, an unending routine of babysitting, shopping, cooking, and cleaning defined a lengthy working day. In the wealthiest households, the serving girl was at the bottom of a rigid hierarchy of status-conscious butlers and housekeepers.

Nonetheless, domestic service had real attractions for young women from rural areas who had few specialized skills. Marriage prospects were better, or at least more varied, in the city than back home. And though wages were low, they were higher and more regular than in hard agricultural work—which was being replaced by mechanization, at any rate. Finally, as one London observer noted, young girls and other migrants from the countryside were drawn to the city by "the contagion of numbers, the sense of something going on, the theaters and the music halls, the brightly lighted streets and busy crowds—all, in short, that makes the difference between the Mile End fair on a Saturday night, and a dark and muddy country lane, with no glimmer of gas and with nothing to do."[5]

Some young domestics made the successful transition to working-class wife and mother. Yet with an unskilled or unemployed husband, a growing family, and limited household income, many working-class wives had to join the broad ranks of working women in the **sweated industries**. These industries expanded rapidly after 1850 and resembled the old putting-out and cottage industries of earlier times. The women normally worked at home and were paid by the piece, not by the hour. They and their young children who helped them earned pitiful wages and lacked any job security. Women decorated dishes or embroidered linens, took in laundry for washing and ironing, or made clothing, especially after the advent of the sewing machine. An army of poor women, usually working at home, accounted for many of the inexpensive ready-made clothes displayed on department store racks and in tiny shops.

Prostitution

In the late nineteenth century prostitution was legal in much of Europe, offering another means of employment for lower-class women hard pressed to find better paying jobs in domestic service or factories. In Italy, France, Great Britain, and much of Germany, the state licensed brothels and registered individual prostitutes, and they were a ubiquitous public presence. In Paris, 155,000 women were registered as prostitutes between 1871 and 1903, and 750,000 others were suspected of prostitution in the same years. In Berlin, in 1909 alone, the authorities registered over 40,000 prostitutes. The totals are probably low, since most women in the sex trade tried to avoid government regulation.

In streets, dance halls, and pubs across Europe, working-class women used prostitution as a source of second income or as a way to weather a period of joblessness, in a working environment with few other options. Their clients were generally lower-class men, soldiers, and sailors, though middle- and upper-class men looking to "sow wild oats" also paid for sexual encounters. In some places, particularly Germany, visits to prostitutes were rites of passage formalized in the culture of student fraternities. Prostitution offered women some measure of financial independence, but the work was dangerous. Violence and rape, police harassment, and venereal disease were commonplace hazards.

Prostitutes clearly transgressed middle-class ideals of feminine respectability, but among the working classes prostitution was tolerated as more or less acceptable work of a temporary nature. Like domestic service, prostitution was a stage of life, not permanent employment. After working as prostitutes in their youth, many women went on to marry and build homes and families.

As middle-class family values became increasingly prominent after the 1860s, prostitution generated great concern among social reformers. The prostitute—immoral, lascivious, and unhealthy in middle-class eyes—served as the dark mirror image of the respectable middle-class woman. Authorities blamed prostitutes for spreading crime and disease, particularly syphilis. Before the discovery of penicillin, syphilis was indeed a widespread and terrifying affliction. Its painful symptoms led to physical and mental disorder and often death. Medical treatment was expensive, painful, and slow. It required access to regular health care and was, for the most part, ineffective.

As general concerns with public health gained recognition, state and city authorities across Europe subjected prostitutes to increased surveillance. Under the British Contagious Diseases Acts, in force between 1864 and 1886, special plainclothes policemen required women identified as "common prostitutes" to undergo biweekly medical exams. If they showed signs of venereal disease, they were interned in a "lock hospital" and forced to undergo treatment; when the outward signs of disease went away, they were released.

The Contagious Diseases Acts were controversial from the start. A determined middle-class feminist campaign against the policy, led by feminist Josephine Butler and the Ladies National Association, loudly proclaimed that the acts physically abused poor women, violated their constitutional rights, and legitimized male vice. Under pressure, Parliament repealed the laws in 1886. Yet heavy-handed government regulation had devastated the informality of working-class prostitution. Now branded as "registered girls," prostitutes experienced new forms of public humiliation. Having been registered made it difficult to return to respectable employment, and the trade was increasingly controlled by male pimps rather than by the women themselves. Prostitution had never been safe, but it had been more or less accepted, at least among the working classes. Prostitutes were now stigmatized as social and sexual outsiders.

The Leisure Pursuits of the Working Classes

Notwithstanding hard physical labor and lack of wealth, the urban working classes sought fun and recreation, and they found both. Across Europe, drinking remained the favorite leisure-time activity of working-class men. For many middle-class moralists, as well as moralizing historians since, love of drink was the curse of the modern age—a sign of social dislocation and popular suffering. One English slum dweller recalled that "drunkenness was by far the commonest cause of dispute and misery in working class homes. On account of it one saw many a decent family drift down through poverty into total want."[6]

Generally, however, heavy problem drinking declined in the late nineteenth century as it became less socially acceptable. This decline reflected in part the moral leadership of the labor aristocracy. Drinking also became more publicly acceptable. Cafés and pubs became increasingly bright, friendly places. Working-class political activities, both moderate and radical, were also concentrated in taverns and pubs. Moreover, social drinking in public places by married couples and sweethearts became an accepted and widespread practice for the first time. This greater participation by women undoubtedly helped civilize the world of drink and hard liquor.

The two other leisure-time passions of working-class culture were sports and music halls. "Cruel sports," such as bullbaiting and cockfighting, still popular in the middle of the century, had greatly declined throughout Europe by the 1880s. Commercialized spectator sports filled their place; horse racing and soccer were the

Rat Catching Although antivivisectionist reform groups successfully pressured city and state authorities to ban many forms of cruelty to animals, the sport of "ratting" continued to attract working- and middle-class crowds in England well into the nineteenth century. In this 1852 painting, an all-male crowd at the Blue Anchor Tavern on the outskirts of London lays bets on Tine, a trained Manchester terrier, as he tries to kill two hundred rats in a single hour. Because they saw rats as verminous pests that brought filth and disease into Europe's rapidly growing cities, the authorities tolerated rat killing for sport, a pastime that was a throwback to the inhumane bullbaiting and cockfighting popular in the early modern era (see "Leisure and Recreation" in Chapter 18). (Museum of London, UK/Bridgeman Images)

most popular. Working people gambled on sports events, and a desire to decipher racing forms provided a powerful incentive toward literacy. Music halls and vaudeville theaters were enormously popular throughout Europe. In 1900 London had more than fifty such halls and theaters. Music hall audiences included men and women, which may account for the fact that drunkenness, premarital sex, marital difficulties, and mothers-in-law were all favorite themes of broad jokes and bittersweet songs.

Faith and Religion

In more serious moments, religion continued to provide working people with solace and meaning. The eighteenth-century vitality of popular religion in Catholic countries and the Protestant rejuvenation exemplified by German Pietism and English Methodism (see "What role did religion play in eighteenth-century society?" in Chapter 18) carried over into the nineteenth century. Indeed, many historians see the early nineteenth century as an age of religious revival. The second half of the century likewise saw an upswing in popular faith, embodied in the new religions and institutions that emerged: Theosophy, Seventh-Day Adventism, spiritualism, Christian Science, the Salvation Army. Religious revivals were a working-class sensation, and many grew attached to the fervid Marian devotions, in which prayers called on Jesus's mother Mary to intercede with God on behalf of the believer. In addition, the first mosques were being built in Britain and western Europe, and Jewish migration from eastern Europe was fast diversifying established Jewish populations.

Yet historians also recognize that by the last few decades of the nineteenth century, both church attendance and church donations had declined in most European countries, particularly in big cities. And it seems clear that this decline was greater for the urban working classes than for their rural counterparts or for the middle classes.

Why did working-class church attendance decline? On one hand, the construction of churches failed to keep up with the rapid growth of the urban population, especially in new working-class neighborhoods. On the other, throughout the nineteenth century workers saw Catholic and Protestant churches as conservative institutions that defended status quo politics, hierarchical social order, and middle-class morality. Socialist political parties, in particular, attacked organized religion as a pillar of bourgeois society; as the working classes became more politically conscious, they tended to see established churches as allied with their political opponents. In addition, religion underwent a process historians call "feminization": in the working and middle classes alike, women were more pious and attended service more regularly than men. Urban workingmen in particular developed vaguely antichurch attitudes, even though they might remain neutral or positive toward God and religion itself.

The pattern was different in the United States, where most nineteenth-century churches also preached social conservatism. But because church and state had always been separate and because a host of denominations and even different religions competed for members, working people identified churches much less with the political and social status quo. Instead, individual churches in the United States were often closely identified with an ethnic group rather than a social class, and churches thrived, in part, as a means of asserting ethnic identity. This same process occurred in Europe if the church or synagogue had never been linked to the state and served as a focus for ethnic cohesion. Irish Catholic churches in Protestant Britain,

Catholic churches in partitioned Polish lands, and Jewish synagogues in Russia were prominent examples.

How did urbanization affect family life and gender roles?

Buffeted by the results of industrialization and urbanization, the nineteenth-century middle classes invented a distinctive middle-class lifestyle that set them off from peasants, workers, and the aristocracy. New ideas about marriage, family, homemaking, and child rearing would have a profound impact on family life in the century to come. Leading a middle-class lifestyle was prohibitively expensive for workers and peasants, and middle-class family values at first had little relevance for their lives. Yet as the nineteenth century drew to a close, the middle-class lifestyle increasingly became the norm for all classes.

Lifestyles of the Middle Classes

Despite growing occupational diversity and conflicting interests, lifestyle preferences loosely united the European middle classes. Shared tastes for food, housing, clothes, and behavior helped define the middle classes as a group apart from the average worker, who could hardly afford such delicacies. The employment of at least one full-time maid to cook and clean was the clearest sign that a family had crossed the cultural divide separating the working classes from the "servant-keeping classes." The greater a family's income, the greater the number of servants it employed.

Unlike the working classes, the middle classes had the money to eat well, and they spent a substantial portion of their household budget on food and entertainment. They consumed meat in abundance: a well-off family might spend 10 percent of its annual income on meat and fully 25 percent on food and drink. The dinner party—a favored social occasion—boosted spending.

Well fed and well served, the middle classes were also well housed by 1900. And, just as the aristocracy had long divided the year between palatial country estates and lavish townhouses during "the season," so the upper middle class purchased country homes or built beach houses for weekend and summer use.

The middle classes paid great attention to outward appearances, especially their clothes. The factory, the sewing machine, and the department store had all helped reduce the cost and expand the variety of clothing. Private coaches and carriages, expensive items in the city, further testified to rising social status. Middle-class families could devote more time to "culture" and leisure pursuits than less wealthy or well-established families could, including books, music, and travel. The long Realist novel, the heroic operas of Wagner and Verdi, the diligent striving of the dutiful daughter at the piano, and the packaged tour to a foreign country were all sources of middle-class pleasure.

In addition to their material tastes, the middle classes generally agreed upon a strict code of manners and morality. They stressed hard work, self-discipline, and personal achievement. Reformers denounced drunkenness and gambling as vices and celebrated sexual purity and fidelity as virtues, especially for women. A stern sense of Christian morals, preached tirelessly by religious leaders, educators, and politicians, reaffirmed these values. Those who fell into vice, crime, or poverty were held responsible for their own circumstances. The middle-class individual was supposed to know right from wrong and act accordingly.

Middle-Class Marriage and Courtship Rituals

Rather than marry for convenience, or for economic or social reasons—as was still common among workers, peasants, and aristocrats—by the 1850s the middle-class couple was supposed to follow an idealized model: they met, courted, fell deeply in love, and joined for life because of a shared emotional bond. Of course, economic considerations in marriage by no means disappeared. But an entire culture of romantic love—popularized in advice manuals, novels and stories, and art, and practiced in courtship rituals, weddings, and married life—now surrounded the middle-class couple. The growing popularity among all classes toward the end of the nineteenth century of what historians call **companionate marriage** underscores the impact of historical change on human emotions and behaviors.

Strict guidelines for courtship and engagement enshrined in the concept of falling in love ensured that middle-class individuals would make an appropriate match. Young couples were seldom alone before they became engaged, and individuals rarely paired off with someone from an inappropriate class background. In the straight-laced "Victorian Era"—named for the long reign of the British queen Victoria (1837–1901)—premarital sex was taboo for women, though men might experiment, a double standard that revealed the value the middle classes placed on sexual morality and especially women's virginity before marriage.

Engagement also followed a complicated set of norms and rituals. Secret engagements led to public announcements, and then the couple could appear together, though with chaperones in potentially delicate situations. Couples might walk arm in arm, but custom placed strict limits on physical intimacy.

Marriage had its own set of informal rules. Usually a middle-class man could marry only if he could support a wife, children, and a servant, which meant he had to be well established in his career and fairly prosperous. Some middle-class men never married because they could not afford it. These customs created special difficulties for young middle-class women, who could rarely pursue an independent career or acquire a home without a husband. The system encouraged mixed-age marriages. A new husband was typically much older than his young wife, who usually had no career and entered marriage directly out of her parents' home or perhaps a girl's finishing school. She would have had little experience with the realities of adult life.

Cultural codes of the day insisted that love meant something different to men and women. Trained to fall passionately in love with "Mr. Right," young women equated marriage with emotional intensity. Men, on the other hand, were supposed to "find a wife": they took a more active but dispassionate role in courtship. Since women generally were quite young, the man was encouraged to see himself as the protector of a young and fragile creature, and the typical middle-class marriage was more similar to a child-parent relationship than a partnership of equals, a situation expertly portrayed in Henrik Ibsen's famous Realist play *A Doll's House* (1879). The inequality of marriage was codified in European legal systems that, with rare exceptions, placed property ownership in the hands of the husband.

Middle- and Working-Class Sexuality

A double standard in sexual relations paralleled the gender inequalities built into middle-class standards of love and marriage. Middle-class moralists of all stripes cast men as aggressively sexual creatures, while women—the "angels in the house"—were supposed to be pure and chaste and act as a brake on male desire. Contemporary science legitimized this double standard. According to late-nineteenth-century physicians, men, easily aroused by the sight of a wrist or ankle, fell prey to their raging biological drives, while respectable women were supposedly uninterested in sex by nature.

Middle-class moralists assumed that men would enter marriage with some sexual experience, though this was unthinkable for a middle-class woman. When middle-class men did seek premarital sex, middle-class women were off limits. Instead, bourgeois men took advantage of their class status and sought lower-class women, domestic servants, or prostitutes. If a young middle-class woman had experimented with or even was suspected of having had premarital sex, her chances for an acceptable marriage fell dramatically.

The sexual standards of the working classes stood in marked contrast to these norms in the early nineteenth century, but that changed over time. Premarital sex for both men and women was common and more acceptable among workers. In the first half of the nineteenth century, among the lower classes, about one-third of the births in many large European cities occurred outside of wedlock.

The second half of the century saw the reversal of this high rate of illegitimacy: in western, northern, and central Europe, more babies were born to married mothers. Young, unmarried workers were probably engaging in just as much sexual activity as their parents and grandparents, who had created the illegitimacy explosion of 1750 to 1850(see "New Patterns of Marriage and Illegitimacy" in Chapter 18). But in the later part of the nineteenth century, pregnancy for a young single woman, which a couple might see as the natural consequence of a serious relationship, led increasingly to marriage and the establishment of a two-parent household. Indeed, one in three working-class women was pregnant when she married.

This important development reflected the spread of middle-class ideals of family respectability among the working classes, as well as their gradual economic improvement. Romantic love held working-class families together, and marriage was less of an economic challenge. The urban working-class couple of the late nineteenth century thus became more stable, and that stability strengthened the family as an institution.

Separate Spheres and the Importance of Homemaking

After 1850 the work of wives became increasingly distinct and separate from that of their husbands in all classes. The preindustrial pattern among both peasants and cottage workers, in which husbands and wives both worked and shared basic household duties, became less and less common. In wealthier homes, this change was particularly dramatic. The good middle-class family man earned the wages to support the household; the public world of work, education, and politics was male space. Respectable middle-class women did not work outside the home and rarely even traveled alone in public. Working-class women, including servants and prostitutes, were more visible in public places, but if a middle-class woman went out

Christmas and the Sentimental Pleasures of the Middle-Class Home A prosperous and productive German couple celebrate Christmas with their many children around a tree decorated with lit candles, something of a new fad in wealthy households in 1875. As this print suggests, holiday rituals evoked the familial feelings of love and affection that grounded private life in the late nineteenth century. How do the children's gifts reflect the notions of separate spheres that organized family life? (bpk Bildagentur/Photo: Dietmar Katz/Art Resource, NY)

without a male escort, she might be accused of low morals or character. Thus many historians have stressed that the societal ideal in nineteenth-century Europe became a strict division of labor by gender within rigidly constructed **separate spheres**: the "private sphere," where the woman acted as wife, mother, and homemaker, and the "public sphere," where the "breadwinner" husband acted as wage earner and family provider.

For the middle classes, the private single-family home, a symbol of middle-class status and a sanctuary from the callous outside world of competitive capitalism, was central to the notion of separate spheres. At the heart of the middle-class home stood the woman: notions of femininity, motherhood, and family life came together in the ideal of domestic space. Middle-class homes grew to include separate sleeping rooms for parents and each family member—unheard of among the lower classes—as well as a special drawing room (or parlor), used to entertain guests. Plump sofas, bric-a-brac, and souvenirs graced domestic interiors; curtains of heavy red velvet and colorful silks draped doors and windows. Such ostentatious displays were far too expensive for the working classes.

Middle-class women were spared the masculine burdens of the outside working world, and lower-class servants ensured that they had free time to turn the private sphere into a domestic refuge of love and privacy. Numerous middle-class housekeeping manuals made the wife's responsibilities quite clear, as this Swedish handbook from 1889 suggests: "A man who spends most of his day away from the family, who has to work outside the home, counts on finding a restful and refreshing atmosphere when he returns home, and sometimes even a little merriment or a surprise. . . . It is his wife's duty to ensure that he is not disappointed in his expectation. She must do her utmost to make his stay at home as pleasant as possible; she can thus continue to keep her influence over him and retain his affection undiminished."[7]

By 1900 working-class families had adopted many middle-class values, but they did not have the means to fully realize the ideal of separate spheres. Women were the primary homemakers, and, as in the upper classes, men did little or no domestic labor. But as we have seen, many working-class women also worked, to contribute to family income. While middle-class family life centered on an ample daily meal, working-class women struggled to put sufficient food on the table. Working women could create a homelike environment that at least resembled that of the middle class — cleaning house, collecting trinkets, and decorating domestic interiors — but working men often preferred to spend time in the local pub with workmates, rather than come home for dinner. Indeed, alcoholism and domestic violence afflicted many working-class families, even as they struggled to build relationships based on romantic love.

Historians have often criticized the middle-class ideal of separate spheres because it restricted women's educational and employment opportunities, and the women's rights movement that emerged in the late nineteenth century certainly challenged the way that this social norm limited possibilities for women's self-expression and independence. In recent years, however, some scholars have been rethinking gender roles within the long-term development of consumer behavior and household economies. In the era of industrialization, these scholars suggest, the "breadwinner-homemaker" household that developed from about 1850 onward was rational consumer behavior that improved the lives of all family members, especially in the working classes.[8]

According to this view, the all-too-real limits on women's activity enforced by the notion of separate spheres had some benefits as well. When husbands specialized in earning an adequate cash income — the "family wage" that labor unions demanded — and wives specialized in managing the home, the working-class wife could produce desirable benefits that could not be bought in a market, such as improved health and better eating habits. For example, higher wages from the breadwinner could buy more raw food, but only the homemaker's careful selection, processing, and cooking would allow the family to benefit from increased spending on food. Although it was unpaid, running an urban household was a complicated, demanding, and valuable task. Twice-a-day food shopping, careful economizing, and fighting the growing crusade against dirt — not to mention child rearing — constituted a full-time occupation. Working yet another job for wages outside the home had limited appeal for most married women unless the earnings were essential for family survival. The homemaker's managerial skills, however, enabled the working-class couple to maximize their personal well-being.

The woman's guidance of the household went hand in hand with the increased pride in the home and family and the emotional importance attached to them in working- and middle-class families alike. According to one historian, by 1900 the English song "Home, Sweet Home" had become "almost a second national anthem."[9] Domesticity and family ties were now central to the lives of millions of people of all classes.

Child Rearing

Another striking sign of deepening emotional ties within the family was a growing emphasis on the love and concern that mothers gave their babies. Early emotional bonding and a willingness to make real sacrifices for the welfare of the infant became increasingly important among the comfortable classes by the end of the eighteenth century, though the ordinary mother of modest means adopted new attitudes only as the nineteenth century progressed.

The surge of maternal feeling was shaped by and reflected in a wave of specialized books on child rearing and infant hygiene, such as French family reformer Gustav Droz's phenomenally successful *Papa, Mama, and Baby*, which went through 121 editions between 1866 and 1884. Droz urged fathers to become affectionate toward their children and pitied those "who do not know how to roll around on the carpet, play at being a horse and a great wolf, and undress their baby."[10] Following expert advice, mothers increasingly breast-fed their infants, rather than paying wet nurses to do so. Another sign, from France, of increased parental affection is that fewer illegitimate babies were abandoned as foundlings after about 1850. Moreover, the practice of swaddling—wrapping babies in clothes or blankets so tightly they could not move—fell from favor. Instead, ordinary mothers allowed their babies freedom of movement and delighted in their spontaneity.

The loving care lavished on infants was matched by greater concern for older children and adolescents. They, too, were bound in the strong emotional ties of a more intimate and protective family. For one thing, European women began to limit the number of children they bore in order to care adequately for those they had (Figure 22.2). By the end of the nineteenth century, the birthrate was declining across Europe, and it continued to do so until after World War II. The Englishwoman who married in the 1860s, for example, had an average of about six children; her daughter marrying in the 1890s had only four; and her granddaughter marrying in the 1920s had only two or possibly three.

The most important reason for this revolutionary reduction in family size, in which the comfortable and well-educated classes took the lead, was parents' desire to improve their economic and social position and that of their children. Children were no longer an economic asset in the late nineteenth century. By having fewer youngsters, parents could give those they had valuable advantages, from music lessons and summer vacations to

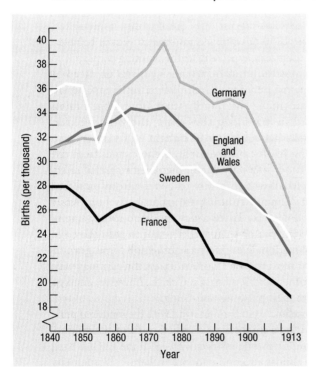

FIGURE 22.2 The Decline of Birthrates in England and Wales, France, Germany, and Sweden, 1840–1913 Women had fewer babies for a variety of reasons, including the fact that their children were increasingly less likely to die before reaching adulthood. How do these numbers compare with those in Figure 22.1? What does that comparison reveal about demographic trends in the nineteenth century?

long, expensive university educations. Thus the growing use in the late nineteenth century of a variety of contraceptive methods—the rhythm method, the withdrawal method, and mechanical devices, including after the 1840s condoms and diaphragms made of vulcanized rubber—reflected increased concern for children.

In middle-class households, parents expended considerable effort to ensure that they raised their children according to prevailing family values. Indeed, many parents, especially in the middle classes, probably became too concerned about their children, unwittingly subjecting them to an emotional pressure cooker. Professional family experts, including teachers, doctors, and reformers like Droz, produced a vast popular literature on child rearing that encouraged parents to focus on developing their children's self-control, self-fulfillment, and sense of Christian morality. Family specialists recommended against corporal punishment—still common in worker and peasant households—but even though they typically escaped beatings, the children of the wealthy grew up under constant observation and discipline, a style of parenting designed to teach the self-control necessary for adult success. Parents carefully monitored their children's sexual behavior, and masturbation—according to one expert "the most shameful and terrible of all vices"—was of particular concern.[11]

Attempts to repress the child's sexuality generated unhealthy tension, often made worse by the rigid division of gender roles within the family. At work all day, the father could be a stranger to his offspring; his world of business was far removed from the maternal world of spontaneous affection. Although fathers became more overtly loving during this period, the man of the house often set demanding rules, expecting the child to succeed where he himself had failed and making his approval conditional on achievement. This kind of distance was especially the case in the wealthiest families, in which domestic servants, nannies, and tutors did much of the work of child rearing. Many wealthy parents saw their children only over dinner, or on special occasions like birthdays or holidays.

The children of the working classes probably had more avenues of escape from such tensions than did those of the middle classes. Unlike their middle-class counterparts, who remained economically dependent on their families until a long education was finished or a proper marriage secured, working-class boys and girls went to work when they reached adolescence. Earning wages on their own, by the time they were sixteen or seventeen they could bargain with their parents for greater independence. If they were unsuccessful in these negotiations, they could and did leave home to live cheaply as paying lodgers in other working-class homes. Not until the twentieth century would middle-class youths be equally free to break away from the family when emotional ties became oppressive.

What were the most important changes in science and culture?

Major changes in Western intellectual life accompanied the emergence of urban society. Breakthroughs in the sciences, especially chemistry, physics, and electricity, profoundly influenced the Western worldview and spurred the creation of new products and whole industries. The natural and social sciences were also established as highly respected fields of study. In addition, between about the 1840s and the 1890s Western arts and literature underwent a shift from soaring Romanticism to tough-minded Realism, which reflected the joys and burdens of everyday life in the emerging urban society.

The Triumph of Science in Industry

As the pace of scientific advancements quickened and resulted in greater practical benefits, science exercised growing influence on human thought. The intellectual achievements of the Scientific Revolution had resulted in few such benefits, and theoretical knowledge had also played a relatively small role in the Industrial Revolution in England. But breakthroughs in industrial technology in the late eighteenth century enormously stimulated basic scientific inquiry, as researchers sought to explain how such things as steam engines and blast furnaces actually worked. The result was an explosive growth of fundamental scientific discoveries from the 1830s onward. In contrast to earlier periods, these theoretical discoveries were increasingly transformed into material improvements for the general population.

A perfect example of the translation of better scientific knowledge into practical human benefits was the work of Louis Pasteur and his followers in biology and the medical sciences (see "The Bacterial Revolution" in this chapter). Another was the development of the branch of physics known as **thermodynamics**. Building on Isaac Newton's laws of mechanics and on studies of steam engines, thermodynamics investigated the relationship between heat and mechanical energy. The law of conservation of energy held that different forms of energy — such as heat, electricity, and magnetism — could be converted but neither created nor destroyed. By mid-century, physicists had formulated the fundamental laws of thermodynamics, which were then applied to mechanical engineering, chemical processes, and many other fields.

The study and application of chemistry and electricity — fields in which science was put in the service of industry — likewise progressed rapidly. Chemists devised ways of measuring the atomic weight of different elements, and in 1869 the Russian chemist Dmitri Mendeleev (mehn-duh-LAY-uhf) (1834–1907) codified the rules of chemistry in the periodic law and the periodic table. Chemistry was subdivided into many specialized branches, including organic chemistry — the study of the compounds of carbon. Applying theoretical insights gleaned from this new field, researchers in large German chemical companies discovered ways of transforming the dirty, useless coal tar that accumulated in coke ovens into beautiful, expensive synthetic dyes for the world of fashion. German production of synthetic dyes soared, and by 1900 German chemical companies controlled 90 percent of world production.

Electricity, a scientific curiosity in 1800, was totally transformed by a century of technological advancement. It became a commercial form of energy, first used in communications (the telegraph, which spurred quick international communication with the laying of underwater cables), then in electrochemistry (refining aluminum, for example), and finally in central power generation (for lighting, transportation, and industrial motors). And by 1890 the internal combustion engine fueled by petroleum was an emerging competitor to steam and electricity alike.

The successful application of scientific research in the fast-growing electrical and organic chemical industries between 1880 and 1913 provided a model for other uses. Systematic "R&D"—research and development—was born in the late nineteenth century. Above all, the burst of industrial creativity and technological innovation, often called the **Second Industrial Revolution**, promoted the strong economic growth in the last third of the nineteenth century that drove the urban reforms and the rising standard of living considered in this chapter.

The triumph of science and technology had three other significant consequences. First, though ordinary citizens continued to lack detailed scientific knowledge, everyday experience and innumerable articles in newspapers and magazines impressed the importance of science on the popular mind. Second, as science became more prominent in popular thinking, the philosophical implications of science formulated in the Enlightenment spread to broad sections of the population. Natural processes appeared to be determined by rigid laws, leaving little room for either divine intervention or human will. Yet scientific and technical advances had also fed the Enlightenment's optimistic faith in human progress, which now appeared endless and automatic to growing numbers of people. Third, the methods of science acquired unrivaled prestige after 1850. For many, the union of practical experiment and abstract theory was the only reliable route to truth and objective reality. The "unscientific" intuitions of poets and the revelations of saints seemed hopelessly inferior.

Darwin and Natural Selection

Scientific research also progressed rapidly outside of the world of industry and technology, sometimes putting forth direct challenges to traditional religious beliefs. In geology, for example, Charles Lyell (1797–1875) effectively discredited the long-standing view that the earth's surface had been formed by short-lived cataclysms, such as biblical floods and earthquakes. Instead, according to Lyell's principle of uniformitarianism, the same geological processes that are at work today slowly formed the earth's surface over an immensely long time. Similarly, the evolutionary view of biological development, first proposed by the Greek Anaximander in the sixth century B.C.E., re-emerged in a more modern form in the work of French naturalist Jean-Baptiste Lamarck (1744–1829). Lamarck asserted that all forms of life had arisen through a long process of continuous adjustment to the environment, a dramatic challenge to the belief in divine creation of species.

Lamarck's work was flawed—he believed that the characteristics parents acquired in the course of their lives could be inherited by their children—and was not accepted, but it helped prepare the way for Charles Darwin (1809–1882), the most influential of all nineteenth-century evolutionary thinkers. As the official naturalist on a five-year scientific voyage to Latin America and the South Pacific beginning in 1831, Darwin carefully collected specimens of the different animal species he encountered on the voyage. Back in England, convinced by fossil evidence and by his friend Lyell that the earth and life on it were immensely ancient, Darwin came to doubt the general belief in a special divine creation of each species of animal. Instead, he concluded, all life had gradually evolved from a common ancestral origin in an unending "struggle for survival." After long hesitation, Darwin published his research, which immediately attracted wide attention.

Darwin's great originality lay in suggesting precisely how biological evolution might have occurred. His theory of **evolution** is summarized in the title of his work *On the Origin of Species by the Means of Natural Selection* (1859). Decisively influenced by the gloomy assertions of Thomas Malthus (MAL-thuhs) that populations naturally grow faster than their food supplies (see "Industry and Population" in Chapter 20), Darwin argued that chance differences among the individual members of a given species help some survive while others die. Thus the variations that prove useful in the struggle for survival are selected naturally, and they gradually spread to the entire species through reproduction.

Darwin's controversial theory had a powerful and many-sided influence on European thought and the European middle classes. Because his ideas seemed to suggest that evolution moved along without God's intervention, and that humans were simply one species among many others, some conservatives accused Darwin of anti-Christian beliefs and mocked him for suggesting that humans descended from apes. Others hailed Darwin as the great scientist par excellence, the "Newton of biology," who had revealed once again the powers of objective science.

Some thinkers went a step further and applied Darwin's theory of biological evolution to human affairs. English philosopher Herbert Spencer (1820–1903) saw the human race as driven forward to ever-greater specialization and progress by a brutal economic struggle that determined the "survival of the fittest." The poor were the ill-fated weak; the prosperous were the chosen strong. Spencer's **Social Darwinism** gained adherents among nationalists, who viewed global competition between countries as a grand struggle for survival, as well as among imperialists, who used Social Darwinist ideas to justify the "natural" rule of the supposedly more civilized West over its colonial subjects and territories.

The Modern University and the Social Sciences

By the 1880s major universities across Europe had been modernized, enlarged, and professionalized. Education now emphasized controlled research projects in newly established clinics and laboratories; advanced students conducted independent research in seminar settings. An increasingly diversified professoriate established many of the academic departments still found in today's universities, from anthropology to zoology.

Faculty devoted to the newly instituted human or social sciences took their place alongside the hard sciences. Using critical methods often borrowed from natural science, social scientists studied massive sets of numerical data that governments had begun to collect on everything from birthrates to crime and from population to prostitution. Like Karl Marx, they were fascinated by the rise of capitalism and modernity; unlike Marx, they preferred to understand rather than revolutionize society.

Sociology, the critical analysis of contemporary or historical social groups, emerged as a leading social science. Perhaps the most prominent and influential late-nineteenth-century sociologist was the German Max Weber (1864–1920). In his most famous book, *The Protestant Ethic and the Spirit of Capitalism* (1890), Weber argued that the rise of capitalism was directly linked to Protestantism in northern Europe. Pointing to the early and successful modernization of countries like the Netherlands and England, he concluded that Protestantism gave religious approval to hard work, saving, and investing—the foundations for capitalist development—because Protestant belief saw worldly success as a sign of God's approval.

This famous argument seriously challenged the basic ideas of Marxism: ideas, for Weber, were just as important as economics or class struggle in the rise of capitalism. Yet like Marx, Weber felt that people were alienated from their own humanity, trapped in what he called the "iron cage" of capitalist relations. Modern industrial society, according to Weber, had turned people into "specialists without spirit, hedonists without heart." An ambitious scholar, Weber wrote extensively on capitalist rationalization, modern bureaucracy, industrialization and agriculture, and the forms of political leadership.

In France, the prolific sociologist Émile Durkheim (1858–1917) earned an international reputation for his wide-ranging work. His study of the psychic and social basis of religion, *The Elementary Forms of Religious Life* (1912), remains a classic of social-scientific thought. In his pioneering work of quantitative sociology, *Suicide* (1897), Durkheim concluded that ever-higher suicide rates were caused by widespread feelings of what he called anomie, or rootlessness. Because modern society had stripped life of all sense of tradition, purpose, and belonging, Durkheim believed, anomie was inescapable; only an entirely new moral order might offer some relief.

Other sociologists contributed to the critique of modern society. The German Ferdinand Tönnies (1855–1936) argued that with industrialization Western civilization had undergone a fundamental transformation from "community" to "society." Rationalized self-interest had replaced traditional values, and selfish individualism had replaced generous communal support, leading to intensified alienation and a cold bureaucratic age. In *The Crowd* (1895), French sociologist Gustav Le Bon (1841–1931) wrote that alienated individuals were prone to gathering in mass crowds, where they lost control over their emotions and actions. According to the deeply conservative Le Bon, a strong, charismatic leader could easily manipulate the crowd's collective psyche and turn the servile mass into a violent and dangerous revolutionary mob.

The new sociologists cast a bleak light on urban industrial society. While they acknowledged some benefits of rationalization and modernization, they bemoaned the accompanying loss of community and tradition. In some ways, their diagnosis of the modern individual as an isolated atom suffering from anomie and desperately seeking human connection was chillingly prescient: the powerful Communist and Fascist movements that swept through Europe after World War I appeared to generate popular support precisely by offering ordinary people a renewed sense of social belonging.

Realism in Art and Literature

In art and literature, the key themes of **Realism** emerged around 1850 and continued to dominate Western culture until the 1890s. Deeply influenced by the social changes that had accompanied rapid industrialization, Realist artists and writers believed that artistic works should depict ordinary life exactly as it was. They forsook the grand historical subjects favored by academy artists as well as the personal, emotional viewpoint of the Romantics for strict, supposedly factual objectivity. The controversial and shocking Realists observed and recorded the world around them—often to expose the sordid reality of modern life.

Realism in the Arts   Realist depictions of gritty everyday life challenged the Romantic emphasis on nature and the emotions, as well as the Neoclassical focus on famous men and grand events. French painter Gustave Courbet's twenty-two-foot-long *Burial at Ornans* (1849) is a famous example of Realism in the arts. It portrays a bleak funeral in the artist's hometown. The painting's rejection of heroic subjects or grand themes shocked contemporary critics. When the organizers of a major exhibition in Paris in 1855 refused to show the work, claiming it was too large and too coarse, Courbet, already a leading figure in the Realist movement, withdrew all his paintings from the exhibition and staged a private exhibition that featured his own work. (Universal History Archive/Universal Images Group/Shutterstock)

Emphatically rejecting the Romantic search for the exotic and the sublime, Realism (or "Naturalism," as it was often called) energetically pursued the typical and the commonplace. Beginning with a dissection of the middle classes, from which most of them sprang, many Realists eventually focused on the working classes, especially the urban working classes, which had been largely ignored in imaginative literature before this time. The Realists exposed unexplored and taboo subjects, including labor strikes, violence, sexuality, and alcoholism, and portrayed slums and factories. Shocked middle-class critics denounced Realism as ugly sensationalism wrapped in pseudoscientific declarations and crude language—even as the movement attracted middle-class readers who were fascinated by the sensationalist view "from below."

The Realist movement began in France, where Romanticism had never been completely dominant. Artists like Gustave Courbet, Jean-François Millet, and Honoré Daumier painted scenes of laboring workers and peasants in somber colors and simple compositions, exemplified in Courbet's 1849 painting *Burial at Ornans*. Horrified critics rejected this painting because it depicted ordinary people in everyday life and entirely challenged established preferences for heroic compositions.

Literary Realism also began in France, where Honoré de Balzac, Gustave Flaubert, and Émile Zola became internationally famous novelists. Balzac (1799–1850) spent thirty years writing a vastly ambitious panorama of postrevolutionary French life. Known collectively as *The Human Comedy*, this series of nearly one hundred stories, novels, and essays vividly portrays more than two thousand characters from virtually all sectors of French society. Balzac pictured urban society as grasping, amoral, and brutal. In his novel *Father Goriot* (1835), the hero, a poor student from the provinces, eventually surrenders his idealistic integrity to feverish ambition and society's pervasive greed.

Madame Bovary (1857), the masterpiece of Gustave Flaubert (floh-BEHR) (1821–1880), is far narrower in scope than Balzac's work but is still famous for its psychological insight and critique of middle-class values. Unsuccessfully targeted by government censors as an outrage against public morality and religion, Flaubert's novel tells the story of Emma Bovary, a middle-class housewife who fantasizes about a life of romance and luxury. Her attempts to escape through love affairs and extravagant purchases destroy her family and herself. Without explicitly moralizing, Flaubert portrays the provincial middle class as materialistic and dull, while also taking aim at the influence of romantic novels and theater.

Novelist Émile Zola (1840–1902) was most famous for his seamy, animalistic view of working-class life, expressed in novels such as *Nana* (1880), about the triumphs and tragedy of a high-class prostitute, or *The Earth* (1887), about the brutal life of a family of downtrodden French peasants. But he also wrote gripping, carefully researched stories featuring the stock exchange, the big department store, and the army, as well as urban slums and bloody battles between police and striking coal miners. Like many later Realists, Zola sympathized with socialism, a view evident in his overpowering novel *Germinal* (1885).

Realism quickly spread beyond France. In England, Mary Ann Evans (1819–1880), who wrote under the pen name George Eliot, brilliantly achieved a deeply felt, less sensational kind of Realism in her great novel *Middlemarch: A Study of Provincial Life* (1871–1872). The novels of Thomas Hardy (1840–1928), such as *Tess of the D'Urbervilles* (1891) and *The Return of the Native* (1878), depict ordinary men and women frustrated and crushed by social prejudice, sexual puritanism, and bad luck. Russia's Count Leo Tolstoy (1828–1910) combined Realism in description and character development with an atypical moralizing, especially in his later work. In *War and Peace* (1864–1869), a monumental novel set against the background of Napoleon's invasion of Russia in 1812, Tolstoy developed his fatalistic theory of human history, which regards free will as an illusion and the achievements of even the greatest leaders as only the channeling of historical necessity. Yet Tolstoy's central message is one that most of the people discussed in this chapter would have readily accepted: human love, trust, and everyday family ties are life's enduring values.

NOTES

1. S. Marcus, "Reading the Illegible," in *The Victorian City: Images and Realities*, ed. H. J. Dyos and Michael Wolff, vol. 1 (London: Routledge & Kegan Paul, 1973), p. 266.

2. J. McKay, *Tramways and Trolleys: The Rise of Urban Mass Transport in Europe* (Princeton, N.J.: Princeton University Press, 1976), p. 81.

3. Bonnie S. Anderson and Judith P. Zinsser, *A History of Their Own: Women in Europe from Prehistory to the Present*, rev. ed., vol. 2 (New York: Oxford University Press, 2000), p. 195.

4. Quoted in R. P. Neuman, "The Sexual Question and Social Democracy in Imperial Germany," *Journal of Social History* 7 (Winter 1974): 276.

5. Quoted in J. A. Banks, "The Contagion of Numbers," in *The Victorian City: Images and Realities*, ed. H. J. Dyos and Michael Wolff, vol. 1 (London: Routledge & Kegan Paul, 1973), p. 112.

6. Quoted in R. Roberts, *The Classic Slum: Salford Life in the First Quarter of the Century* (Manchester, U.K.: University of Manchester Press, 1971), p. 95.

7. Quoted in J. Frykman and O. Löfgren, *Culture Builders: A Historical Anthropology of Middle-Class Life* (New Brunswick, N.J.: Rutgers University Press, 1987), p. 134.

8. See the pioneering work of J. de Vries, *The Industrious Revolution: Consumer Behavior and the Household Economy* (Cambridge: Cambridge University Press, 2008), especially pp. 186–237.

9. Roberts, *The Classic Slum*, p. 35.

10. Quoted in T. Zeldin, *France, 1848–1945*, vol. 1 (Oxford: Clarendon Press, 1973), p. 328.

11. Quoted in Frykman and Löfgren, *Culture Builders*, p. 114.

LOOKING BACK **LOOKING AHEAD**

When the peoples of northwestern Europe looked out at the economic and social landscape in the early twentieth century, they had good reason to feel that the promise of the Industrial Revolution was being realized. The dark days of urban squalor and brutal working hours had given way after 1850 to a gradual rise in the standard of living for all classes. Scientific discoveries were combined with the applied technology of public health and industrial production to save lives and drive continued economic growth.

Moreover, social and economic advances seemed to be matched by progress in the political sphere. The years following the dramatic failure of the revolutions of 1848 saw the creation of unified nation-states in Italy and Germany, and after 1870, as we shall see in the following chapter, nationalism and the nation-state reigned in Europe. Although the rise of nationalism created tensions among the European countries, these tensions would not explode until 1914 and the outbreak of the First World War. Instead, the most aggressive and destructive aspects of European nationalism found their initial outlet in the final and most powerful surge of Western overseas expansion. Thus Europe, transformed by industrialization and nationalism, rushed after 1875 to seize territory and build new or greatly expanded authoritarian empires in Asia and Africa.

MAKE CONNECTIONS

Think about the larger developments and continuities within and across chapters.

1. What were the most important changes in everyday life from the end of the eighteenth century (Chapter 18) to the end of the nineteenth century? What main causes or agents drove these changes?

2. Did the life of ordinary people improve, stay the same, or even deteriorate over the nineteenth century when compared to the previous century? What role did developments in science, medicine, and urban planning play in this process?

3. How did the emergence of a society divided into working and middle classes affect the workplace, homemaking, and family values and gender roles? Are the values and behaviors associated with the nineteenth-century lower, middle, and upper classes—in all their diversity—still around today? How have they changed?

Chapter 22 Review

IDENTIFY KEY TERMS

Identify and explain the significance of each item below.

utilitarianism (p. 649)

"Great Stink" (p. 649)

germ theory (p. 651)

professionalization (p. 656)

labor aristocracy (p. 658)

sweated industries (p. 659)

companionate marriage (p. 664)

separate spheres (p. 666)

thermodynamics (p. 670)

Second Industrial Revolution (p. 671)

evolution (p. 672)

Social Darwinism (p. 672)

Realism (p. 673)

REVIEW THE MAIN IDEAS

Answer the section heading questions from the chapter.

1. What were the main changes in urban life in the nineteenth century? (p. 646)

2. How did class and gender reinforce social difference in the nineteenth century? (p. 654)

3. How did urbanization affect family life and gender roles? (p. 663)

4. What were the most important changes in science and culture? (p. 669)

CHRONOLOGY

1848	• Cholera epidemic and first public health law in Britain
ca. 1850–1870	• Modernization of Paris
ca. 1850–1900	• Realism dominant in Western arts and literature
1850–1914	• Condition of working classes improves
1854	• Pasteur begins studying fermentation and in 1863 develops pasteurization
1858	• London's "Great Stink"
1859	• Darwin publishes *On the Origin of Species by the Means of Natural Selection*
1864–1886	• Contagious Diseases Act in force in Britain
1865	• Completion of London sewer system
1869	• Mendeleev creates periodic table
1880–1913	• Second Industrial Revolution; birthrate steadily declines in Europe
1885	• Zola publishes Realist novel *Germinal*
1890	• Max Weber publishes *The Protestant Ethic and the Spirit of Capitalism*
1890s	• Electric streetcars introduced in Europe

23

The Age of Nationalism

1850–1914

CHAPTER PREVIEW

- What were the main features of the authoritarian nation-state built by Napoleon III?

- How were strong nation-states forged in Italy, Germany, and the United States?

- How did Russian and Ottoman leaders modernize their states and societies?

- How did the relationship between government and the governed change after 1871?

- What were the costs and benefits of nationalism for ordinary people?

- How and why did revolutionary Marxism evolve in the late nineteenth century?

IN THE YEARS THAT FOLLOWED THE REVOLUTIONS OF 1848, nationalism— mass identification with the nation-state—emerged as an effective organizing principle capable of coping with the many-sided challenges of the unfinished industrial and political revolutions and the new urban society. Nationalism had been a powerful force since the early nineteenth century, but the goal of creating independent nation-states, inhabited by people sharing a common ethnicity, language, history, and territory, had repeatedly proved elusive, most spectacularly in the revolutions of 1848. By 1914, however, most Europeans lived in nation-states, and nationalism had become an almost universal faith in the Western world.

The governments of the new nation-states took various forms, from conservative authoritarianism to parliamentary monarchy to liberal republicanism. Whatever the political system, nationalism remade territorial boundaries and forged new relations between the nation-state and its citizens. In most cases the nation-state became increasingly responsive to the needs of its people, opening the political franchise and offering citizens at least rudimentary social and economic benefits. Yet the nation-state also demanded more from its citizens: rising income taxes, universal military service, and allegiance to the national idea. Nationalism, which before 1848 appealed primarily to liberals seeking political reform or national independence, became an ever more conservative ideology. At its worst, populists and fanatics manipulated and sometimes abused the patriotism of ordinary people to justify exclusionary policies against Jews and other ethnic minorities and to promote expansion in overseas colonies.

What were the main features of the authoritarian nation-state built by Napoleon III?

Early nationalism was generally liberal and idealistic and could be democratic and radical (see Chapter 21). Yet nationalism also flourished in authoritarian states, which imposed social and economic changes from above. Napoleon Bonaparte's France had already combined national feeling with authoritarian rule. Napoleon's nephew, Louis Napoleon (1808–1873), revived and extended this combination.

France's Second Republic

Although Louis Napoleon had played no part in French politics before 1848, he won three times as many votes as the four other presidential candidates combined in the French presidential election of December 1848. Louis Napoleon enjoyed popular support at a time of universal male suffrage for several reasons. First, he bore the famous name of his uncle, whom romantics had transformed into a demigod after 1820. Second, as Karl Marx stressed at the time, middle-class and peasant property owners feared the socialist challenge of urban workers and the chaos of the revolution of 1848, and they wanted a tough ruler to provide stability and protect their property. Third, Louis Napoleon advertised a positive social-economic program for the French people in pamphlets widely circulated before the election.

Above all, Louis Napoleon promoted a vision of national unity and social progress, in which the government represented all the people, rich and poor, and gave them economic and social benefits. But how, he asked, could these tasks be accomplished when corrupt French politicians supported the interests of special groups, particularly middle-class ones? Only a strong, even authoritarian leader, like the wildly popular first Napoleon, could solve this problem. Louis Napoleon cast himself as just such a leader. He promised that his rule would be linked to each citizen by direct democracy, his sovereignty uncorrupted by politicians and legislative bodies, his acts approved by mass plebiscites, referendums in which all citizens would cast votes to approve or disapprove of important questions of public policy. To his many enthusiastic supporters, Louis Napoleon was a strong and forward-looking champion of popular interests.

Elected to a four-year term by an overwhelming majority, Louis Napoleon was required by the constitution to share power with the National Assembly, which was overwhelmingly conservative. With some misgivings, he signed bills that increased the role of the Catholic Church in primary and secondary education and deprived many poor people of the right to vote, hoping that the Assembly would vote for funds to pay his personal debts and change the constitution so he could run for a second term.

But after the Assembly failed to cooperate with that last aim, Louis Napoleon conspired with key army officers to overthrow the government. On December 2, 1851, he illegally dismissed the legislature and seized power in a coup d'état. Acting in tandem with the coup, the national army crushed armed resistance in Paris and widespread insurrection in southern France. Louis Napoleon craftily wrapped himself in the mantel of his famous uncle. Claiming to be above political bickering, he restored universal male suffrage and proclaimed the arrival of the Second French Empire, a proud continuation of the mighty First Empire established by Bonaparte during the Napoleonic wars. As the first Napoleon had done, Louis Napoleon asked the French people to legalize his actions. They did: 92 percent voted to make him president for ten years. A year later, in a plebiscite, 97 percent voted to approve the Second French Empire and make Louis Napoleon its hereditary emperor.

Napoleon III's Second Empire

Louis Napoleon — now proclaimed Emperor Napoleon III — experienced both success and failure between 1852 and 1870, when he fell from power during the Franco-Prussian War. In the 1850s his policies brought economic growth. His government promoted the new investment banks and massive railroad construction that were at the heart of the Industrial Revolution on the continent. The French state fostered general economic expansion through an ambitious program of public works, which included rebuilding Paris to improve the urban environment. Business profits soared, rising wages of workers outpaced inflation, and unemployment declined greatly.

Initially, economic progress reduced social and political tensions as Louis Napoleon had hoped. Until the mid-1860s the emperor enjoyed support from France's most dissatisfied group, the urban workers. They appreciated the 1850s reforms, such as the regulation of pawnshops, support for credit unions, and better working-class housing. In the 1860s Louis Napoleon granted workers the right to form unions and the right to strike.

Although he repeatedly claimed that the Second Empire stood for peace, Louis Napoleon maintained an aggressive foreign policy. He was deeply committed to "the principle of nationalities," which meant redrawing European state borders on the basis of shared national characteristics. He led France to victory in the Crimean War (see "The 'Great Reforms' in Russia" later in this chapter) and then, in 1859, waged war against Austria for the cause of Italian unification (see "The Unification of Italy" ahead in this chapter). During the U.S. Civil War, he meddled unsuccessfully in internal Mexican politics, which drew intense criticism in France.

At first, political power remained in the hands of the emperor. Louis Napoleon alone chose his ministers, who had great freedom of action. Yet in order to win popular support, he retained the legislative Assembly and senate, although with reduced powers. Members were elected by universal male suffrage every six years, and the government took these elections seriously. It tried to entice notable people, even those who had opposed the regime, to stand as candidates to expand the base of support. Government officials and appointed mayors spread the word that election of mainstream candidates—and defeat of the opposition—would provide tax rebates, roads, and a range of other local benefits.

In elections in 1857 and again in 1863, Louis Napoleon's system produced overwhelming electoral victories for government-backed candidates. In the late 1860s, however, this electoral system gradually disintegrated. With increasing effectiveness, the middle-class liberals who had always wanted a less authoritarian regime denounced his rule. Napoleon was always sensitive to the public mood. Public opinion, he once said, always wins the last victory, and he responded to critics with ever-increasing liberalization. He granted freedom of the press and gave the Assembly greater powers and opposition candidates greater freedom, which they used to good advantage. In 1869 the opposition, consisting of republicans, monarchists, and liberals, polled almost 45 percent of the vote.

The next year, a sick and weary Louis Napoleon again granted France a new constitution, which combined a basic parliamentary regime with a hereditary emperor as chief of state. In a final plebiscite on the eve of the disastrous war with Prussia (see "The Franco-Prussian War and German Unification" ahead), 7.3 million Frenchmen approved the new constitution—only 1.5 million opposed it. Napoleon III's ability to rally voters' support for a strong central state and an emperor rather than a republic and an elected leader showed that popular nationalism was compatible with authoritarian government, even as France moved in an increasingly democratic direction.

How were strong nation-states forged in Italy, Germany, and the United States?

Napoleon III's authoritarian rule in the 1850s and 1860s provided the old ruling classes of Europe with a new model in politics, in which the expanding middle classes and even portions of the working classes supported a unified, conservative national state that promised economic growth and social benefits. Would this model work elsewhere? This was one of the great political questions in the 1850s and 1860s. In Europe, the national unification of Italy and Germany offered a resounding answer. In the United States, the increased power of the federal government after a costly civil war offered another. As these three examples suggest, it often took war and violence to nourish popular nationalism and forge a strong central state.

The Unification of Italy

The various nation-states on the Italian peninsula had never been united. Often a battleground for Europe's Great Powers, Italy was reorganized in 1815 at the Congress of Vienna into a hodgepodge of different states, each with its own government, and the wealthy northern Italian-speaking territories of Milan and Venice were incorporated into the Austrian Empire. Austrian foreign minister Prince Klemens von Metternich captured the essence of the situation when he dismissed the notion of "Italy" as "only a geographical expression" (Map 23.1).

Yet the struggle for a unified Italian nation — the **Risorgimento** — captured the imagination of many Italians. The appeal of Italian nationalism was exemplified in the Young Italy secret society founded by the radical and idealistic patriot Giuseppe Mazzini, who called for a centralized democratic republic based on universal male suffrage and the will of the people. In his best-known work, *Duties Towards Your County* (1858), Mazzini argued that language, historic traditions, and divine purpose defined a national people, and he called for the liberation of Italian territories from foreign governments (such as Austria) and unification based on "harmony and brotherhood."

Catholicism and the papacy offered another potential source of shared belonging and even a potential foundation for an Italian nation-state, but Pope Pius IX (pontificate

MAP 23.1   The Unification of Italy, 1859–1870
The leadership of Sardinia-Piedmont, nationalist fervor, and Garibaldi's attack on the Kingdom of the Two Sicilies were decisive factors in the unification of Italy.

1846–1878) opposed unification and most modern trends after the upheavals of 1848. In 1864 in the *Syllabus of Errors*, Pius IX denounced rationalism, socialism, separation of church and state, and religious liberty. The Catholic Church could not stop unification, but it resisted liberalism and progressive reform for the next two decades.

By the 1850s, many Italian nationalists focused on the promise of a national federation led by Victor Emmanuel II, the autocratic king of Sardinia-Piedmont. They looked to Piedmont for national leadership, much as German liberals looked to Prussia, because Piedmont boasted one of the most industrialized, wealthy, and socially advanced territories on the Italian peninsula. Victor Emmanuel, crowned in 1849, had retained the liberal constitution granted by his father under duress during the revolutions of 1848. This constitution combined a strong monarchy with a fair degree of civil liberties and parliamentary government, though deputies were elected by a limited franchise based on income. To some of the Italian middle classes, the Kingdom of Sardinia-Piedmont appeared to be a liberal, progressive state ideally suited to drive Austria out of northern Italy and lead the drive to Italian unification. By contrast, Mazzini's brand of democratic republicanism seemed idealistic and too radical.

The struggle for Italian unification under Emmanuel II was supported by Count Camillo Benso di Cavour (kuh-VOOR), a brilliant statesman who served as prime minister of Sardinia-Piedmont from 1852 until his death in 1861. A nobleman who had made a substantial fortune in business before entering politics, Cavour had limited and realistic national goals. Until 1859 he sought unity only with the states of northern and perhaps central Italy, which would nonetheless greatly expand the existing kingdom.

In the 1850s Cavour consolidated Sardinia-Piedmont as a liberal constitutional state capable of leading northern Italy. His program of building highways and railroads, expanding civil liberties, and opposing clerical privilege increased support for his efforts throughout northern Italy. Yet because Sardinia-Piedmont could not drive Austria out of the north without the help of a powerful ally, Cavour established a secret alliance with Napoleon III against Austria in July 1858.

Cavour then goaded Austria into attacking Piedmont in 1859, and Louis Napoleon came to Italy's defense. After defeating the Austrians at the Battles of Magenta and Solferino, however, Napoleon did a sudden about-face. Worried by criticism from French Catholics for supporting the pope's declared enemy, he abandoned Cavour and made a compromise peace with the Austrians in July 1859. The Kingdom of Sardinia-Piedmont received only Lombardy, the area around Milan, from Austria. The rest of Italy remained essentially unchanged.

Yet the skillful maneuvers of Cavour's allies in the moderate nationalist movement salvaged his plans for Italian unification. While the war against Austria raged in the north, pro-unification nationalists in Tuscany and elsewhere in central Italy led popular revolts that easily toppled their ruling princes. Encouraged by and appropriating these popular movements, middle-class nationalist leaders in central Italy called for fusion with Sardinia-Piedmont. In early 1860, Cavour regained Napoleon III's support by ceding Savoy and Nice to France. The people of central Italy then voted overwhelmingly to join a greatly enlarged kingdom under Victor Emmanuel. Cavour had achieved his original goal, a united northern Italian state (see Map 23.1).

For superpatriots such as Giuseppe Garibaldi (1807–1882), however, the unification of the north left the job half done. The son of a poor sailor, Garibaldi

Garibaldi and Victor Emmanuel II The historic 1860 meeting in Naples between the leader of Italy's revolutionary nationalists and the king of Sardinia sealed the unification of northern and southern Italy. With the sleeve of his red shirt showing, Garibaldi offers his hand — and his conquests — to the uniformed king and his moderate monarchical government. The idealized patriotism evident in this painting, completed in 1866, testifies to the growing appeal of popular nationalism. (Detail, fresco, 1886, by Pietro Aldi [1852–1888]/Palazzo Pubblico, Siena, Italy/Bridgeman Images)

personified the romantic, revolutionary nationalism and republicanism of Mazzini and 1848. Leading a corps of volunteers against Austria in 1859, Garibaldi emerged in 1860 as an independent force in Italian politics.

Partly to use him and partly to get rid of him, Cavour secretly supported Garibaldi's bold plan to "liberate" the Kingdom of the Two Sicilies. Landing in Sicily in May 1860, Garibaldi's guerrilla band of a thousand Red Shirts inspired the peasantry, who rose in bloody rebellion against their landlords. Outwitting the twenty-thousand-man royal army, the guerrilla leader won battles, gained volunteers, and took Palermo. Then Garibaldi and his men crossed to the mainland, marched triumphantly toward Naples, and prepared to attack Rome and the pope. The wily Cavour quickly sent Sardinian forces to occupy most of the Papal States (but not Rome) and to intercept Garibaldi.

Cavour realized that an attack on Rome would bring war with France, and he feared Garibaldi's radicalism and popular appeal. He immediately organized a plebiscite in the conquered territories. Despite the urging of some radical supporters, the patriotic Garibaldi did not oppose Cavour, and the people of the south voted to join the kingdom of Sardinia. When Garibaldi and Victor Emmanuel II rode together through Naples to cheering crowds in October 1860, they symbolically sealed the union of north and south, of monarch and nation-state.

Cavour had successfully controlled Garibaldi and turned popular nationalism in a conservative direction. The new kingdom of Italy, which expanded to include Venice in 1866 and Rome in 1870, was a parliamentary monarchy under Victor Emmanuel II. The new nation was hardly democratic or prosperous. Only a half million out of 22 million Italians had the right to vote, and great social inequalities divided the propertied classes and the common people. A deep and growing economic gap separated the progressive, industrializing north from the stagnant, agrarian south. Italy was united on paper, but profound divisions remained.

The Austro-Prussian War

In the aftermath of 1848 the German states were locked in a political stalemate. After Austria and Russia blocked Prussian king Friedrich Wilhelm IV's attempt in 1850 to unify Germany, tension grew between Austria and Prussia as they struggled to dominate the German Confederation (see "Prussia, the German Confederation, and the Frankfurt National Parliament" in Chapter 21).

Economic differences exacerbated this rivalry. Austria had not been included in the German Customs Union, or *Zollverein* (TZOLE-fur-ayne), when it was founded in 1834 to stimulate trade and increase state revenues. By the end of 1853 Austria was the only state in the German Confederation outside the union. As middle-class and business groups profited from participation in the *Zollverein*, Prussia's leading role within the customs union gave it a valuable advantage in its struggle against Austria.

Prussia had emerged from the upheavals of 1848 with a weak parliament that by 1859 was in the hands of the wealthy liberal middle class. Longing for national unification, these representatives wanted to establish that the parliament, not the king, held ultimate political power, including control of the army. At the same time, the national uprising in Italy in 1859 made a profound impression on Prussia's tough-minded Wilhelm I (r. 1861–1888). Convinced that great political change and war—perhaps with Austria, perhaps with France—were quite possible, Wilhelm I and his top military advisers pushed to raise taxes and increase the defense budget in order to double the size of the army. The Prussian parliament rejected the military budget in 1862, and the liberals triumphed completely in new elections, creating a deadlocked constitutional crisis. Wilhelm I then appointed Count Otto von Bismarck as Prussian prime minister and encouraged him to defy the parliament. This was a momentous choice.

Otto von Bismarck (1815–1898) was a master of **Realpolitik**, a German term referring to political practice based on a careful calculation of real-world conditions rather than ethical ideals or ideological assumptions. Bismarck had honed his political skills as a high-ranking diplomat for the Prussian government. Born into the landowning aristocracy and devoted to his sovereign, he had a strong personality and an unbounded desire for power. Yet in his drive to secure power for himself and for Prussia, Bismarck remained extraordinarily flexible and pragmatic. Keeping his options open, he moved with determination and cunning toward his goal.

When he took office as prime minister in 1862, in the midst of the constitutional crisis caused by the deadlock on the military budget, Bismarck made a strong but unfavorable impression. Declaring that Wilhelm's government would rule without parliamentary consent, he lashed out at the liberal middle-class opposition: "The great questions of the day will not be decided by speeches and resolutions—that was the blunder of 1848 and 1849—but by blood and iron."

Denounced by liberals for his view that "might makes right," Bismarck had the Prussian bureaucracy go right on collecting taxes, even though the parliament refused to approve the budget. Bismarck also reorganized the army. And for four years, from 1862 to 1866, voters continued to express their opposition by sending large liberal majorities to the parliament.

Opposition at home spurred Bismarck to search for success abroad. The extremely complicated question of Schleswig-Holstein—two provinces on the disputed border between Denmark and Germany, populated by a large majority of ethnic Germans—provided a welcome opportunity. In 1864 the Danish king tried, as he had in 1848, to bring these two provinces into a more centralized Danish state against the will of the German Confederation. In response, Prussia enlisted Austria in a short and successful war against Denmark (Map 23.2).

Bismarck, however, was convinced that Prussia had to control completely the northern, predominantly Protestant part of the confederation, which meant expelling Austria from German affairs. After the victory over Denmark, Bismarck's clever Realpolitik maneuvering left Prussia in a position to force Austria out by war. Recognizing that Russia, France, and Italy might come to Austria's defense, Bismarck persuaded them to remain neutral through a skillful blend of territorial promises and reminders of past Prussian support.

The Austro-Prussian War of 1866 that followed lasted only seven weeks. Using railroads to quickly mobilize troops, who were armed with new and more efficient breech-loading rifles, the Prussian army defeated Austria decisively at the Battle of Sadowa (SAH-daw-vah) in Bohemia on July 3. Anticipating Prussia's future needs, Bismarck offered Austria generous peace terms. Austria paid no reparations and lost no territory to Prussia, although Venetia was ceded to Italy. But the existing German Confederation was dissolved, and Austria agreed to withdraw from German affairs. Prussia conquered and annexed several small states north of the Main River and completely dominated the remaining principalities in the newly formed North German Confederation. The mainly Catholic states of the south remained independent but allied with Prussia. Bismarck's fundamental goal of Prussian expansion was partially realized (see Map 23.2).

Taming the German Parliament

Bismarck had long been convinced that the old order he so ardently defended would have to make peace with the liberal middle class and nationalists. Impressed with Napoleon III's example in France, he realized that nationalists were not necessarily hostile to conservative, authoritarian government. Moreover, the events of 1848 convinced Bismarck that the German middle class could be led to prefer national unity under conservative leadership rather than endure a long, uncertain battle for a truly liberal state. Thus during the Austrian war, he increasingly identified Prussia's fate with what he called the "national development of Germany."

To consolidate Prussian control, Bismarck fashioned a federal constitution for the new North German Confederation. Each state retained its own local government,

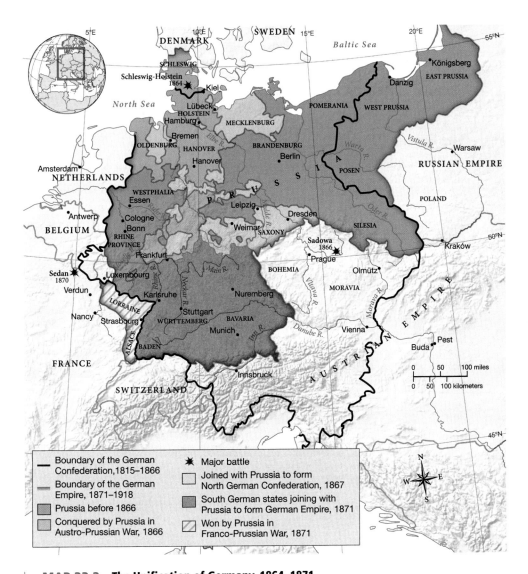

MAP 23.2 The Unification of Germany, 1864–1871

This map shows how Prussia expanded and a new German Empire was created through wars with Denmark (1864), Austria (1866), and France (1870–71).

but the king of Prussia became president of the confederation, and the new imperial chancellor — Bismarck — was responsible only to the president. The federal bureaucracy, under Wilhelm I and Bismarck, controlled the army and foreign affairs. A weak federal legislature, with members of the lower house elected by universal male suffrage, gave some voice to popular opinion. With this radical innovation, Bismarck opened the door to the possibility of going over the head of the middle class directly to the people, as Napoleon III had done in France. Ultimate power, however, still rested with the Prussian king and army.

In Prussia itself, Bismarck held out an olive branch to the parliamentary opposition. Marshalling all his diplomatic skill, he asked the parliament to pass a special indemnity bill to approve, after the fact, all the government's spending between 1862 and 1866. With German unity in sight, most of the liberals cooperated. The constitutional struggle in Prussia ended, and the German middle class came to accept the monarchical authority that Bismarck represented.

The Franco-Prussian War and German Unification

The final act in the drama of German unification followed quickly. Bismarck calculated that a patriotic war with France would drive the south German states into his arms. He manipulated a minor diplomatic issue — whether a distant relative of Prussia's Wilhelm I might become king of Spain, in defiance of French interests — to goad the leaders of the Second French Empire into a declaration of war on Prussia.

As soon as war began, Bismarck enlisted the support of the south German states. While other governments maintained their neutrality — Bismarck's generosity to Austria in 1866 paid big dividends — combined German forces under Prussian leadership decisively defeated the main French army at Sedan on September 1, 1870. Napoleon III was captured and humiliated. Three days later, French patriots in Paris proclaimed yet another French republic and vowed to continue fighting. But after five months, in January 1871, a besieged and starving Paris surrendered, and France accepted Bismarck's harsh peace terms.

By this time, the south German states had agreed to join a new German Empire. With Chancellor Bismarck by his side, Wilhelm I was proclaimed emperor of Germany in the Hall of Mirrors in the palace of Versailles. As in the 1866 constitution, the king of Prussia and his ministers had ultimate power in the new German Empire, and the lower house of the legislature was elected by universal male suffrage.

Bismarck imposed a severe penalty on France: payment of a colossal indemnity of 5 billion francs and loss of the rich eastern province of Alsace and part of Lorraine to Germany. French men and women of all classes viewed these territorial losses as a terrible crime (see Map 23.2). They could never forget and never forgive, and relations between France and Germany were poisoned after 1871.

The Franco-Prussian War, which many Europeans saw as a test of nations in a pitiless Darwinian struggle for existence, released a surge of patriotic feeling in the German Empire. United Germany had become the most powerful state in Europe in less than a decade, and most Germans were enormously proud of Bismarck's genius and the supposedly invincible Prussian army. Semi-authoritarian nationalism and a new conservatism, based on an alliance of the landed nobles and middle classes, had triumphed in Germany.

Civil War and Nation Building in the United States

The United States also experienced a process of bloody nation building. Although united under the U.S. federal Constitution, the country was divided by the slavery question, and economic development carried free and slaveholding states in very different directions. By 1850 an industrializing, urbanizing North was building canals and railroads and attracting large numbers of European immigrants. In sharp contrast, industry and cities developed more slowly in the South, and

European immigrants largely avoided the region. Even though three-quarters of all Southern white families were small farmers and owned no slaves, plantation owners holding twenty or more slaves dominated the economy and society. These profit-minded slave owners used enslaved Africans to establish a vast plantation economy across the Deep South, where cotton was king (Map 23.3). By 1850 the region produced 5 million bales a year, supplying textile mills in Europe and New England.

The rise of the cotton empire greatly expanded slave-based agriculture in the South, spurred exports, and ignited rapid U.S. economic growth. The large profits flowing from cotton led influential Southerners to defend slavery. Because Northern whites viewed their free-labor system as economically and morally superior to slavery, North-South antagonisms intensified.

Tensions reached a climax after 1848 when the United States won the Mexican-American War (1846–1848) and gained a vast area stretching from west Texas to the Pacific Ocean. Debate over the extension of slavery in this new territory hardened attitudes on both sides. Abraham Lincoln's election as president in 1860, on an anti-slavery, pro-Union party platform, gave Southern secessionists the chance they had been waiting for. Eleven states left the Union and formed the Confederate States of America.

The resulting Civil War (1861–1865), in which advanced weaponry brought the bloodiest conflict in American history, ended with the South decisively defeated and the Union preserved. In the aftermath, certain characteristics of American life and national culture took shape. Powerful business corporations emerged, steadfastly supported by the Republican Party during and after the war. The Homestead Act of 1862, which gave western land to settlers, and the Thirteenth Amendment of 1865, which ended slavery, reinforced the concept of free labor taking its chances in a market economy. Finally, the success of Lincoln and the North in holding the Union together seemed to confirm the notion of "**manifest destiny**": the idea that the United States was destined to straddle the continent as a great world power. Thus a revitalized American nation-state, grounded in economic and territorial expansion, grew out of a civil war.

How did Russian and Ottoman leaders modernize their states and societies?

The Russian and the Ottoman Empires experienced profound political crises in the mid-nineteenth century. These crises differed from those in Italy and Germany, for both empires were vast multinational states built on long traditions of military conquest and absolutist rule by the dominant Russians and Ottoman Turks. In the early nineteenth century the governing elites in both empires strongly opposed representative government and national independence for ethnic minorities, concentrating on absolutist rule and competition with other Great Powers. For both states, however, relentless power politics led to serious trouble. Their leaders recognized that they had to "modernize" and embrace the economic, military, and social-political reforms that might enable their countries to compete effectively with leading European nations such as Great Britain, Germany, and France.

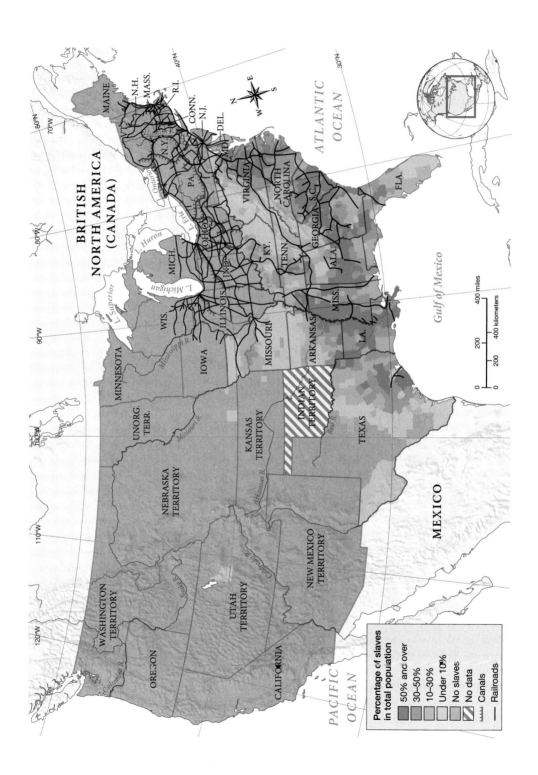

The "Great Reforms" in Russia

In the 1850s Russia was a poor agrarian society with a rapidly growing population. Almost 90 percent of the people lived off the land, and industrialization developed slowly. Bound to the lord from birth, the peasant serf was little more than a slave, and by the 1840s serfdom had become a central moral and political issue for the government. The slow pace of modernization encouraged the growth of protest movements, from radical Marxists clamoring for socialist revolution to middle-class intellectuals who sought a liberal constitutional state. Then a humiliating Russian defeat in the Crimean War underscored the need for modernizing reforms.

The **Crimean War** (1853–1856) grew out of general Great Power competition in the Middle East and Russian attempts to grab lands from the declining Ottoman Empire, which shared extensive and disputed borders with Russia. The initial cause was an apparently minor dispute between France and Russia over the protection of Christian shrines in Jerusalem, but the dispute escalated into a full-blown war in which France and Britain joined the Ottomans to halt Russian expansion into the Ottoman Empire's European territories.

Famous for incompetent leadership on all sides, the Crimean War revealed the awesome power of modern weaponry, particularly artillery, in ways that anticipated the U.S. Civil War. Massive naval engagements, doomed cavalry charges, and staggering casualties—Russia alone lost about 450,000 soldiers—captured the imagination of home-front audiences, who followed events in the national press. The Crimean War also brought professional women nurses to the front lines for the first time, exemplified most famously in the British volunteer nurse Florence Nightingale. Her advocacy of simple sanitary precautions, such as washing hands before medical procedures, helped reduce mortality rates among wounded soldiers.

By 1856 the French-led alliance had decisively defeated Russia. The conflict between Russia and the French and British helped break down the European balance of power established after the Napoleonic Wars at the Congress of Vienna. Austria had refused to come to Russia's aid in the war, so Russia turned its back on its former ally. Cooperation among the Great Powers was replaced by competition and hostility. The destruction of the old international system, the isolation of Austria, and conflict between Russia and France smoothed the way to Italian and German unification.

Defeat by superior armies and weaponry furthermore convinced Russia's leaders that they had fallen behind the nations of western Europe. Russia needed railroads, better armaments, and military reform to remain a Great Power. Military disaster thus forced liberal-leaning Tsar Alexander II (r. 1855–1881) and his ministers along the path of rapid social change and modernization.

In a bold move, Alexander II abolished serfdom in 1861. About 22 million emancipated peasants received citizenship rights and the chance to purchase, on

< **MAP 23.3   Slavery in the United States, 1860**
This map shows the United States on the eve of the Civil War. Although many conflicts contributed to the developing opposition between North and South, slavery was the fundamental, enduring issue that underlay all others. Lincoln's prediction, "I believe this government cannot endure permanently half slave and half free," proved correct.

average, about half of the land they cultivated. Yet they had to pay fairly high prices, and because the land was to be owned collectively, each peasant village was jointly responsible for the payments of all the families in the village. Collective ownership made it difficult for individual peasants to improve agricultural methods or leave their villages. Most peasant families continued to live in one-story log cabins with a single living room, a storage room (sometimes shared with animals), and a shallow cellar. Thus old patterns of behavior predominated, limiting the effects of reform.

Most of Alexander II's later reforms were also halfway measures. In 1864 the government established a new institution of local government, the zemstvo. Members were elected by a three-class system of townspeople, peasant villagers, and noble landowners, to manage local issues and concerns. Russian liberals hoped that this reform would lead to an elected national parliament, but it did not. The zemstvos remained subordinate to the traditional bureaucracy and the local nobility.

Street Scene from a Russian Village This portrayal of everyday life in a rural Russian village at the turn of the century, with dirt streets, idle peasants, and ramshackle wooden homes, seems to underscore Russian backwardness and the need for the modernizing reforms of the late nineteenth century. The photo here is from a card designed for a stereoscope, a device that gained immense popularity in the second half of the nineteenth century. With its dual-image cards viewed through a pair of lenses, the stereoscope gave the viewer the illusion that the scene portrayed came alive in three-dimensional space; companies marketed hundreds of thousands of cards with images of famous landmarks, epic landscapes, exotic foreigners, and natural wonders. Why, in your opinion, would a western European or American be interested in a scene from the Russian hinterland? (Universal History Archive/Getty Images)

In addition, changes to the legal system established independent courts and equality before the law. The government relaxed but did not remove censorship, and it somewhat liberalized policies toward Russian Jews.

Russian efforts to promote economic modernization proved more successful. Transportation and industry, both vital to the military, were transformed in two industrial surges. The first came after 1860, when the government subsidized private railway companies. The railroads linked important cities in the western territories of the empire and enabled Russia to export grain and thus earn money to finance further development. The jewel in the crown of the Russian rail system was the 5,700-mile-long Trans-Siberian Railway. Passing through seven time zones from Moscow to Vladivostok, this crucial rail line brought millions of immigrant peasants from western Russia into the lightly populated areas to the east. The grain they grew was moved west along the line, to help feed the growing cities in Russia's heartland (Map 23.4). Industrial suburbs grew up around Moscow and St. Petersburg, and a class of modern factory workers began to take shape. These workers helped spread Marxist thought, and a Russian revolutionary movement began to take shape after 1890.

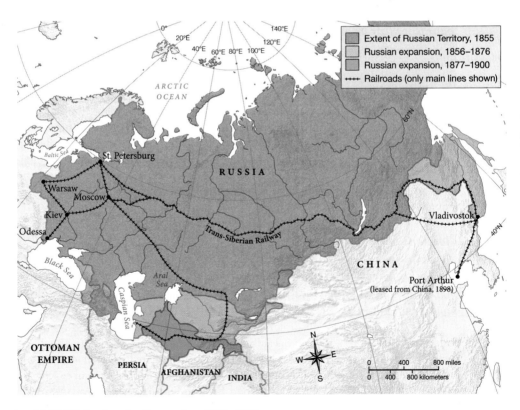

MAP 23.4   Russian Expansion, 1856–1900
The impressive expansion of the Russian railroad system in the second half of the nineteenth century, capped by the completion of the Trans-Siberian Railway around 1910, helped Russia integrate territories along its southern and eastern Asian borders into the imperial state.

Strengthened by industrial development, Russia began to expand by seizing lands on the borders. It took control of territory in far eastern Siberia, on the border with China, and in Central Asia, north of Afghanistan. It also encroached upon the Islamic lands of the Caucasus, along the northeast border of the Ottoman Empire. Russian peasants, offered the chance to escape the small plots of their ancestral homes, used the new rail systems to move to and settle in the newly colonized areas, at times displacing local residents (see Map 23.4). The rapid expansion of the Russian Empire to the south and east excited ardent Russian nationalists and superpatriots, who became some of the government's most enthusiastic supporters. Alexander II consolidated imperial control by suppressing nationalist movements among Poles, Ukrainians, and Baltic peoples in east-central Europe. By 1900 the Russian Empire commanded a vast and diverse array of peoples and places.

Alexander II's political reforms outraged conservatives but never went far enough for liberals and radicals. In 1881 a member of the "People's Will," a small anarchist group, assassinated the tsar, and the reform era came to an abrupt end. The new tsar, Alexander III (r. 1881–1894), was a determined reactionary. Nevertheless, from 1890 to 1900 economic modernization and industrialization again surged ahead, led by Sergei Witte (suhr-GAY VIH-tuh), finance minister from 1892 to 1903. The tough, competent Witte believed that industrial backwardness threatened Russia's greatness. Under his leadership, the government doubled the network of state-owned railways to thirty-five thousand miles. Witte established high protective tariffs to support industry, and he put the country on the gold standard to strengthen finances.

Witte's greatest innovation was to use Westerners to catch up with the West. He encouraged foreigners to build factories in Russia, believing that "the inflow of foreign capital is . . . the only way by which our industry will be able to supply our country quickly with abundant and cheap products."[1] His efforts were especially successful in southern Russia. There, in eastern Ukraine, foreign entrepreneurs and engineers built an enormous and up-to-date steel and coal industry. In 1900 peasants still constituted the great majority of the population, but Russia was catching up with the more industrialized West.

The Russian Revolution of 1905

Catching up in part meant further territorial expansion, for this was the age of Western imperialism. By 1903 Russia had established a sphere of influence in Chinese Manchuria and was eyeing northern Korea, which put Russia in conflict with an equally imperialistic Japan. When Tsar Nicholas II (r. 1894–1917), who replaced his father in 1894, ignored their diplomatic protests, the Japanese launched a surprise attack on Port Arthur, a Russian naval base in northern China, in February 1904. The resulting Russo-Japanese War lasted less than a year. Japan scored repeated victories and annihilated a Russian fleet, and a humiliated Russia surrendered in September 1905.

Once again military disaster abroad brought political upheaval at home. The business and professional classes had long wanted a liberal, representative government. Urban factory workers were organized in a radical and still-illegal labor movement. Peasants had gained little from the era of reforms and suffered from poverty and lack of land. The empire's minorities and subject nationalities, such as Poles, Ukrainians, and Latvians, continued to call for self-rule. With the army pinned down in Manchuria, these currents of discontent converged in the revolution of 1905.

On a Sunday in January 1905, a massive crowd of workers and their families marched peacefully on the Winter Palace in St. Petersburg to present a petition to Nicholas II. Suddenly troops opened fire, killing and wounding hundreds. The Bloody Sunday massacre produced a wave of general indignation that turned many Russians against the tsar.

By the summer of 1905 strikes and political rallies, peasant uprisings, revolts among minority nationalities, and mutinies by troops were sweeping the country. The **Russian Revolution of 1905** culminated in October that year in a paralyzing general strike that forced the government to capitulate. The tsar then issued the October Manifesto, which granted full civil rights and promised a popularly elected **Duma** (DO-mah, or parliament) with real legislative power. The manifesto helped split opposition to the tsarist government. Frightened middle-class leaders embraced the liberal reforms and turned their backs on the radical labor movement, which helped the government repress the popular uprising and survive as a constitutional monarchy.

On the eve of the first Duma in May 1906, the government issued the new constitution, the Fundamental Laws. The tsar retained great powers. The Duma, elected indirectly by universal male suffrage with a largely appointive upper house, could debate and pass laws, but the tsar had an absolute veto. As in Bismarck's Germany, the tsar appointed his ministers, who did not need to command a majority in the Duma.

The predominantly middle-class liberals, the largest group in the newly elected Duma, saw the Fundamental Laws as a step backward. Cooperation with Nicholas II's ministers soon broke down, and after months of deadlock the tsar dismissed the Duma. Thereupon he and his advisers, including the talented prime minister Pyotr Stolypin, unilaterally rewrote the electoral law to greatly increase the electoral weight of the conservative propertied classes. When new elections were held, the tsar could count on a legislative majority loyal to the monarchy. The government then pushed through important agrarian reforms designed to break down collective village ownership of land and encourage the more enterprising peasants — Stolypin's "wager on the strong and sober," meant to encourage economic growth. The government reformed the education and banking systems, but these acts were accompanied by harsh repression of dissidents and radicals. About three thousand suspected revolutionaries were executed by the state, and the hangman's noose became known as "Stolypin's necktie." In 1914, on the eve of the First World War, Russia was partially modernized, a repressive constitutional monarchy with a peasant-based but industrializing economy and significant pockets of discontent.

Reform and Readjustment in the Ottoman Empire

By the early nineteenth century the economic and political changes reshaping Europe were also at play in the Ottoman Empire, which stretched around the northeastern, eastern, and southern shores of the Mediterranean Sea. The borderlands of this vast empire experienced constant flux and conflict. Russia had occupied Ottoman provinces on the Danube River in the last decades of the eighteenth century and grabbed more during the Napoleonic Wars. In 1816 the Ottomans were forced to grant Serbia local autonomy. In 1830 the Greeks won independence, and French armies began their long and bloody takeover of Ottoman Algeria. Yet the Ottomans also achieved important victories. Forces under Muhammad Ali, the Ottoman governor in Egypt, restored order in the Islamic holy lands and conquered significant portions of Sudan, south of Egypt.

Muhammad Ali, a ruthless and intelligent soldier-politician, ruled Egypt in the name of the Ottoman sultan from 1805 to 1848. His modernizing reforms of agriculture, industry, and the military helped turn Egypt into the most powerful state in the eastern Mediterranean. In time, his growing strength directly challenged the Ottoman sultan and Istanbul's ruling elite. From 1831 to 1840 Egyptian troops under the leadership of Muhammad Ali's son Ibrahim occupied the Ottoman province of Syria and Palestine and threatened to depose the Ottoman sultan Mahmud II (r. 1808–1839).

This conflict forced the Ottomans to seek European support. Mahmud II's dynasty survived, but only because the European powers, led by Britain, allied with the Ottomans to discipline Muhammad Ali. The European powers preferred a weak and dependent Ottoman Empire to a strong, economically independent state under a dynamic leader such as Muhammad Ali.

Faced with growing European military and economic competition, liberal Ottoman statesmen in 1839 launched the **Tanzimat**, or "Reorganization." The radical Tanzimat reforms, borrowed from western European models, were designed to modernize the empire. The high point of reform came when the new liberal-minded sultan, Abdul Mejid (r. 1839–1861), issued the Imperial Rescript of 1856, just after the Ottoman victory in the Crimean War. Articles in the decree called for equality before the law regardless of religious faith, a modernized administration and army, and private ownership of land. As part of the reform policy, and under economic pressure from the European powers that had paid for the empire's war against Russia in Crimea, Ottoman leaders adopted free-trade policies. New commercial laws removed tariffs on foreign imports and permitted foreign merchants to operate freely throughout the empire.

The turn to nineteenth-century liberal capitalism had mixed effects. With the growth of Western-style banking and insurance systems, elite Christian and Jewish businessmen prospered. Yet most profits went to foreign investors rather than Ottoman subjects. In addition, the elimination of traditional state-controlled monopolies sharply cut imperial revenues. In 1851 Sultan Mejid was forced to borrow 55 million francs from British and French bankers to cover state deficits. Other loans followed, and intractable indebtedness led to the bankruptcy of the Ottoman state two decades later.

The Tanzimat reforms led to partial recovery but fell short of their goals. The Ottoman initiatives did not curtail the appetite of Western imperialists, who secured a stranglehold on the imperial economy by issuing loans. The reforms also failed to halt the growth of nationalism among some Christian subjects in the Balkans, which resulted in crises and increased pressure from neighboring Austria and Russia, eager to gain access to the Balkans and the eastern Mediterranean.

Finally, equality before the law for all citizens, regardless of religious affiliation, actually increased religious disputes, which were often encouraged and manipulated by the European powers eager to seize any pretext for intervention. This development embittered relations between religious conservatives and social liberals, a struggle that ultimately distracted the government from its reform mission. Religious conservatives in both the Muslim and Greek Orthodox communities detested the religious reforms, which they viewed as an impious departure from tradition. These conservatives became dependable supporters of Sultan Abdülhamid II (ahb-dool-hah-MEED)

(r. 1876–1909), who in 1876 halted the reform movement and turned away from European liberalism in his long and repressive reign.

Abdülhamid II's government failed to halt foreign efforts to fragment and ultimately take control over key Ottoman territories. Defeated in the Russo-Turkish War (1877–1878), the Ottomans ceded districts in the Caucasus to Russia; saw the Balkan territories of Romania, Montenegro, and Serbia declare independence; and granted the establishment of an autonomous Bulgaria, still nominally under the Ottoman sultan's control. By the 1890s the government's failures had encouraged a powerful resurgence of the modernizing impulse under the banner of the Committee of Union and Progress (CUP), an umbrella organization that united multiethnic reformist groups from across the empire. These fervent patriots, unofficially called the **Young Turks**, seized power in a 1908 coup and forced the sultan to implement new reforms. Although they failed to stop the rising tide of anti-Ottoman nationalism in the Balkans, the Young Turks helped prepare the way for the rise of modern secular Turkey after the defeat and collapse of the Ottoman Empire in World War I.

How did the relationship between government and the governed change after 1871?

The decades after 1870 brought rapid change to European politics. Despite some major differences among countries, European domestic politics had a new common framework, the nation-state. The nation-state made new demands on its citizens but also offered them a number of new benefits, embodied in growing state institutions and bureaucracies.

The Responsive National State

Common themes within the framework of the new nation-state were the emergence of mass politics and growing popular loyalty toward the nation. Traditional elites were forced into new arrangements in order to exercise power, and new, pragmatic politicians took leading roles. The major states of western Europe adopted constitutions of some sort, and universal male suffrage was granted in Britain, France, and Germany and elsewhere, at least in voting for the lower houses of parliament. New political parties representing a broad spectrum of interests and groups, from workers and liberals to Catholics and conservatives, engaged in hard-fought election campaigns.

Powerful bureaucracies also emerged to govern growing populations, manage modern economies, and administer social programs. The responsive national state offered its citizens free education and some welfare and public health benefits, and for good reason many ordinary people felt increasing loyalty to their governments.

Building support for nation-states also had a less positive side. Elite leaders only reluctantly extended the popular vote to their male citizens, and they dismissed women's demands for political equality. Many men were also forced to serve in the military. Although the British maintained an all-volunteer army until the First World War, most continental countries had established conscription systems by the 1870s. They also began to levy income taxes to pay for the expansion of national bureaucracies.

In addition, conservative and moderate leaders both found that workers who voted socialist—whose potential revolutionary power they feared—would rally around the flag in a diplomatic crisis or cheer when colonial interests seized a distant territory. Therefore, after 1871 governing elites frequently used antiliberal militarist and imperialist policies to unite national populations and overcome or mask intractable domestic conflicts. The failure to resolve internal conflicts and the tendency to manipulate foreign policy to win popular support inflamed the domestic and international tensions that erupted in the cataclysms of World War I and the Russian Revolution.

The German Empire

The history of Germany after 1871 exemplified many of the political developments associated with the formation of nation-states. Like the United States, the new German Empire adopted a federal system: a union of Prussia and twenty-four smaller states, each with separate legislatures. Much of the business of government was conducted at the state level, but there was a strong national government with a chancellor—until 1890, Bismarck—and a popularly elected parliament called the **Reichstag** (RIKES-tahg). Although Bismarck frequently ignored the wishes of the parliamentary majority, he preferred to win the support of the Reichstag to lend legitimacy to his policy goals. This situation gave the political parties opportunities to influence national policy. Until 1878 Bismarck relied mainly on the National Liberals, who supported legislation useful for economic growth and unification of the country.

Less wisely, the National Liberals backed Bismarck's attack on the Catholic Church, the so-called Kulturkampf (kool-TOOR-kahmpf), or "culture struggle." Like Bismarck, the middle-class National Liberals were alarmed by Pius IX's declaration of papal infallibility in 1870. That dogma seemed to ask German Catholics to put loyalty to their church, a foreign power, above their loyalty to their newly unified nation. Kulturkampf initiatives aimed at making the Catholic Church subject to government control. However, only in Protestant Prussia did the Kulturkampf have even limited success.

In 1878 Bismarck abandoned his attack on the church and instead courted the Catholic Center Party, whose supporters included many Catholic small farmers in western and southern Germany. By revoking free-trade policy and enacting high tariffs on cheap grain from the United States, Canada, and Russia, he won over both the Center Party and the conservative Protestant Junkers, nobles with large landholdings in East Prussia.

Other governments followed Bismarck's lead, and the 1880s and 1890s saw a widespread return to protectionism in Europe. France, in particular, established very high tariffs to protect agriculture and industry. European governments thus offered an effective response to foreign competition in a way that won popular loyalty. But the rise of protectionism exemplified the dangers of self-centered nationalism: new tariffs led to international name-calling and nasty trade wars.

After the failure of the Kulturkampf, Bismarck's government tried to stop the growth of the **German Social Democratic Party (SPD)**, Germany's Marxist, working-class political party that was established in the 1870s. Both conservative elites and middle-class liberals feared the SPD's revolutionary language and allegiance to a Marxist movement that transcended the nation-state. In 1878 Bismarck pushed through the Reichstag the Anti-Socialist Laws, which banned Social Democratic associations, meetings, and publications. The Social Democratic Party was driven underground, but it maintained substantial influence, and Bismarck decided to try another tack.

To win working-class support, Bismarck urged the Reichstag to enact state-supported social welfare measures. Big business and some conservatives accused him of creating "state socialism," but Bismarck ably pressed his program in many lively speeches. "Give the working-man the right to work as long as he is healthy," he said. "Assure him care when he is sick; assure him maintenance when he is old. If you do that," he added, "and do not fear the [financial] sacrifice, or cry out at State Socialism as soon as the words 'provision for old age' are uttered," then "working-men" would see that the German government, not the Social Democrats, had their best interests in mind.[2]

Bismarck carried the day, and his conservative nation-state was among the first to set up extensive social welfare programs. In 1883 he pushed through the Reichstag the first of several social security laws to help wage earners by providing national sickness insurance. Other laws established accident insurance, old-age pensions, and retirement benefits. Henceforth sick, injured, and retired workers could look forward to some regular benefits from the state. This national social security system, paid for through compulsory contributions by wage earners and employers as well as grants from the state, was the first of its kind anywhere. Bismarck's social security system did not wean workers from voting socialist, but it did give them a small stake in the system and protect them from some of the uncertainties of the competitive industrial economy. This enormously significant development was a product of political competition and conservative efforts to win popular support by defusing the SPD's radical appeal.

Increasingly, the key issue in German domestic politics was socialism and the rapid growth of the SPD. In 1890 the new emperor, the young, idealistic, and unstable Wilhelm II (r. 1888–1918), opposed Bismarck's attempt to renew the Anti-Socialist Laws. Eager to rule in his own right and to earn the support of the workers, Wilhelm II forced Bismarck to resign. Afterward, German foreign policy became far more aggressive — in part to distract the population from ongoing internal conflicts—but the government did pass new laws to aid workers and legalize socialist political activity.

Yet Wilhelm II was no more successful than Bismarck in getting workers to renounce socialism. Social Democrats won more and more seats in the Reichstag, becoming Germany's largest single party in 1912. Though this victory shocked aristocrats and their wealthy, conservative allies, who held exaggerated fears of an impending socialist upheaval, the revolutionary socialists had actually become less radical. In the years before World War I, the SPD broadened its base by adopting a more patriotic tone, allowing for greater military spending and imperialist expansion. German socialists abandoned revolutionary aims to concentrate instead on gradual social and political reform.

Republican France and the Third French Republic

Although Napoleon III's reign reduced some antagonisms between classes, the Franco-Prussian War undid these efforts. In 1871 France seemed hopelessly divided once again. The patriotic republicans who proclaimed the Third Republic in Paris after the military disaster at Sedan refused to admit defeat by the Germans. They defended Paris with great heroism for weeks, until they were starved into submission by German armies in January 1871.

The next national elections sent a large majority of conservatives and monarchists to the National Assembly, and France's new leaders decided they had no choice but to surrender Alsace (al-SAS) and Lorraine to Germany. The traumatized Parisians exploded in patriotic frustration and proclaimed the Paris Commune in March 1871. Its radical leaders wanted to establish a revolutionary government in Paris and rule without interference from the conservative French countryside. Their program included workplace reforms, the separation of church and state, press censorship, and radical feminism. The National Assembly, led by aging politician Adolphe Thiers (TEE-ehr), ordered the French army into Paris and brutally crushed the Commune. Twenty thousand people died in the fighting. As in June 1848, it was Paris against the provinces, French against French.

Out of this tragedy, France slowly formed a new national unity under the banner of the Third Republic, achieving considerable stability before 1914. How do we account for this? Luck played a part. Until 1875 the monarchists in the ostensibly republican National Assembly had a majority but could not agree on who should be king. The compromise Bourbon candidate refused to rule except under the white flag of his absolutist ancestors — a completely unacceptable condition for many supporters of a constitutional monarchy. In the meantime, Thiers's destruction of the Commune and his other firm measures showed the fearful provinces and the middle classes that the Third Republic could be politically moderate and socially conservative. Another stabilizing factor was the skill and determination of moderate republican leaders in the early years. France therefore reluctantly retained republican government, with a presidential system rather than a parliamentary monarchy. As President Thiers cautiously said, this was "the government which divides us least." By 1879 most members of both the upper and lower houses of the National Assembly were republicans, giving the Third Republic firm foundations.

The moderate republicans sought to preserve their creation by winning the allegiance of the next generation. The Assembly legalized trade unions, and France expanded its colonial empire. More important, a series of laws between 1879 and 1886 greatly broadened the state system of public, tax-supported schools and established free compulsory elementary education for both girls and boys. In the past, most elementary and much secondary education had occurred in Catholic schools, which had long been hostile to republicanism and secularism. Now free compulsory elementary education became secular republican education. Throughout the Western world, the expansion of public education was a critical nation-building tool in the late nineteenth century.

Although the educational reforms of the 1880s disturbed French Catholics, many of them rallied to the republic in the 1890s. The limited acceptance of the modern world by the more liberal Pope Leo XIII (pontificate 1878–1903) eased conflicts between church and state. Unfortunately, the **Dreyfus affair** renewed church-state tensions.

In 1894 Alfred Dreyfus, a Jewish captain in the French army, was falsely accused and convicted of treason. His case enlisted the support of prominent republicans and intellectuals, including novelist Émile Zola. In 1898 and 1899 the Dreyfus affair split France apart. On one side was the army, which had manufactured evidence against Dreyfus, joined by anti-Semites, conservative nationalists, and most of the Catholic establishment. On the other side stood liberals and most republicans.

Dreyfus was eventually declared innocent, but the battle revived republican animosity toward the Catholic Church. Between 1901 and 1905 the government severed all ties between the state and the church. It stopped paying priests' and bishops' salaries and placed committees of lay Catholics in control of all churches. Suddenly on their own financially, Catholic schools soon lost a third of their students, greatly increasing the state school system's reach and thus its power of indoctrination. In short, deep religious and political divisions, as well as a growing socialist movement, challenged the apparent stability of the Third Republic.

Great Britain and Ireland

Historians often cast late-nineteenth-century Britain as a shining example of peaceful and successful political evolution, where an effective two-party Parliament skillfully guided the country from classical liberalism to full-fledged democracy with hardly a misstep. This "Whig view" of British history is not so much wrong as it is incomplete. After the right to vote was granted to wealthy middle-class males in 1832, opinion leaders and politicians wrestled with further expansion of the franchise. In 1859 the Whig Party merged with other groups to form the Liberal Party, which advocated social reform and *laissez-faire* economics and would continue to challenge the opposing Conservative Party into the twentieth century. In the Second Reform Bill of 1867, Benjamin Disraeli and the Conservative Party extended the vote to all middle-class males and the best-paid workers to broaden their base of support beyond the landowning class. After 1867 English political parties and electoral campaigns became more modern, and the "lower orders" appeared to vote as responsibly as their "betters." Hence the Third Reform Bill of 1884, introduced by Liberal prime minister William Gladstone (1809–1898), gave the vote to almost every adult male. The long reign of Queen Victoria (r. 1837–1901), whose role in Britain's evolving constitutional monarchy became increasingly symbolic, offered the British a sense of pride and stability in an era of political change.

While the House of Commons drifted toward democracy, the House of Lords was content to slumber nobly. Between 1901 and 1910, however, the Lords tried to reassert themselves. Acting as supreme court of the land, they ruled against labor unions in two important decisions. And after the Liberal Party came to power in 1906, the Lords vetoed several measures passed by the Commons, including the so-called People's Budget, designed to increase spending on social welfare services. When the king threatened to create enough new peers to pass the bill, the Lords finally capitulated, as they had with the Reform Bill of 1832. Aristocratic conservatism yielded slowly to popular democracy.

Extensive social welfare measures, previously slow to come to Great Britain, were passed in a spectacular rush between 1906 and 1914. During those years the Liberal Party, inspired by the fiery Welshman David Lloyd George (1863–1945), enacted the People's Budget and substantially raised taxes on the rich. This income helped the government pay for national health insurance, unemployment benefits, old-age pensions, and a host of other social measures, although the refusal to grant women the right to vote encouraged a determined and increasingly militant women's suffrage movement.

This record of accomplishment was only part of the story, however. On the eve of World War I, the unanswered question of Ireland brought Great Britain to the brink of civil war. The terrible Irish famine of the 1840s and early 1850s had fueled an Irish revolutionary movement. The Irish Republican Brotherhood, established in 1858 and known as the "Fenians," engaged in violent campaigns against British rule. The British responded with repression and arrests. Seeking a way out, the English slowly granted concessions, such as rights for Irish peasants and abolition of Anglican Church privileges. Gladstone, who twenty years earlier had proclaimed, "My mission is to pacify Ireland," introduced bills to give Ireland self-government, or **home rule**, in 1886 and in 1893, though they failed to pass.

Ireland was on the brink of achieving self-government, but while the Catholic majority in the southern counties wanted home rule, the Protestants of the northern counties of Ulster opposed it. The Ulster Protestants (or Ulsterites) refused to submerge themselves in a majority-Catholic Ireland, just as Irish Catholics had refused to submit to a Protestant Britain.

Irish Home Rule In December 1867 members of the "Fenians," an underground group dedicated to Irish independence from British rule, detonated a bomb outside Clerkenwell Prison in London. Their attempt to liberate Irish Republican activists failed. Though the bomb blew a hole in the prison walls, damaged nearby buildings, and killed twelve innocent bystanders, no Fenians were freed. The British labeled the event the "Clerkenwell Outrage," and its violence evokes revealing parallels with the radical terrorist attacks of today. (From *Illustrierte Zeitung*, Leipzig, Germany, 4 January 1868/akg-images)

By December 1913 the Ulsterites had raised one hundred thousand armed volunteers, and much of English public opinion supported their cause. In 1914 the Liberals in the House of Lords introduced a compromise home-rule bill that did not apply to the northern counties. This bill, which openly betrayed promises made to Irish nationalists, was rejected in the Commons, and in September the original home-rule bill passed but with its implementation delayed. The Irish question had been overtaken by the world war that began in August 1914, and final resolution was suspended for the duration of the hostilities.

Irish developments illustrated once again the power of national feeling and national movements. Moreover, they demonstrated that central governments could not elicit greater loyalty unless they could capture and control that elemental current of national feeling. Though Great Britain had power, prosperity, and parliamentary rule, none of these availed in the face of the conflicting nationalisms created by Irish Catholics and Protestants. Similarly, progressive Sweden was powerless to stop a Norwegian national movement, which culminated in Norway's leaving Sweden and becoming fully independent in 1905. The Ottoman Empire also had similar difficulties in the Balkans in the late nineteenth century. It was only a matter of time before the Serbs, Bulgarians, and Romanians would break away.

The Austro-Hungarian Empire

The dilemma of conflicting nationalisms in Ireland or the Ottoman Empire helps one appreciate how desperate the situation in the Austro-Hungarian Empire had become by the early twentieth century. In 1848 Magyar nationalism had driven Hungarian patriots to declare an independent Hungarian republic, which Russian and Austrian armies savagely crushed in the summer of 1849. Throughout the 1850s Hungary was ruled as a conquered territory, and Emperor Franz Joseph and his bureaucracy tried hard to centralize the state and Germanize the language and culture of the different ethnic groups there.

Then, in the wake of its defeat by Prussia in 1866 and the loss of northern Italy, a weakened Austria agreed to a compromise and in 1867 established the so-called dual monarchy. The Austrian Empire was divided in two, and the Magyars gained virtual independence for Hungary. Henceforth each half of the empire dealt with its own ethnic minorities. The two states, now called the Austro-Hungarian Empire or Austria-Hungary, still shared the same monarch and common ministries for finance, defense, and foreign affairs.

In Austria, ethnic Germans were only one-third of the population, and many Germans saw their traditional dominance threatened by Czechs, Poles, and other Slavs. The language used in local government and elementary education became a particularly emotional issue in the Austrian parliament. From 1900 to 1914 the legislature was so divided that ministries generally could not obtain a majority and ruled instead by decree. Efforts by both conservatives and socialists to defuse national antagonisms by stressing economic issues that cut across ethnic lines were largely unsuccessful.

In Hungary, the Magyar nobility in 1867 restored the constitution of 1848 and used it to dominate both the Magyar peasantry and the minority populations until 1914. Only the wealthiest one-fourth of adult males had the right to vote, making the parliament the creature of the Magyar elite. Laws promoting the Magyar language in schools and government were bitterly resented, especially by Croatians and Romanians. While Magyar extremists campaigned for total separation from Austria, the radical leaders of their subject nationalities dreamed of independence from Hungary. Unlike most major countries that harnessed nationalism to strengthen the state after 1871, the Austro-Hungarian Empire was progressively weakened by it.

What were the costs and benefits of nationalism for ordinary people?

Although the familiar boundaries of Europe's nation-states were mostly in place by the 1870s, national leaders faced a unique problem: how could they encourage ordinary people to identify with the state? While shared languages and institutions and new national symbols helped build popular support, some people were marginalized, either excluded from political representation or turned into scapegoats.

Making National Citizens

Responding to national unification, an Italian statesman famously remarked, "We have made Italy. Now we must make Italians." His comment captured the dilemma faced by political leaders in the last third of the nineteenth century. As the nation-state extended voting rights and welfare benefits to more and more people, the question of national loyalty became increasingly important. How could the new nation-states win the people's heartfelt allegiance?

The issue was pressing. The recent unification of Italy and Germany, for example, had brought together a patchwork of previously independent states with different customs, loyalties, and in some cases languages. In Italy, only about 2 percent of the population spoke the language that would become official Italian. In Germany, regional and religious differences and strong traditions of local political autonomy undermined collective feeling. In Great Britain, deep class differences still dampened national unity, and across the territories of central and eastern Europe, overlapping ethnic groups with distinct languages and cultures challenged the logic of nation building. Even in France, where national boundaries had been fairly stable for several centuries, only about 50 percent of the people spoke proper French. The 60 percent of the population that still lived in rural areas often felt stronger allegiance to their village or region than to the distant nation headquartered in Paris.

Yet by the 1890s most ordinary people had accepted, if not embraced, the notion of national belonging, for various reasons. For one, centralized institutions imposed across entire territories reached even the lowliest citizen. Universal military conscription, introduced in most of Europe after the Franco-Prussian War (Britain was an exception), yanked peasants off their land and workers out of their factories and exposed young male conscripts to patriotic values. Free compulsory education leveled out language differences and taught children about glorious national traditions. In Italy and Germany, the introduction of a common currency, standard weights and measurements, and a national post office eroded regional differences. Boasting images of grand historical events or prominent leaders, even postage stamps and banknotes could impart a sense of national solidarity.

Improved transportation and communication networks broke down regional differences and reinforced the national idea as well. The extension of railroad service into hinterlands and the improvement of local roads shattered rural isolation, boosted the growth of national markets for commercial agriculture, and helped turn "peasants into Frenchmen."[3] Literacy rates and compulsory schooling advanced rapidly in the late nineteenth century, and more and more people read about national history or the latest political events in newspapers, magazines, and books.

Intellectuals, politicians, and ideologues of all stripes eagerly promoted national pride. At Humboldt University in Berlin, the prominent history professor Heinrich von Treitschke championed German superiority, especially over archrival Great Britain. Scholars like Treitschke uncovered the deep roots of national identity in ancient folk traditions; in shared language, customs, race, and religion; and in historic attachments to national territory. Such accounts, often based on flimsy historical evidence, were popularized in the classroom and the press. Few nationalist thinkers sympathized with French philosopher Ernest Renan, who suggested that national identity was based more on a people's current desire for a "common life" and an invented, idealized past than on actual, true-to-life historical experiences.

New symbols and rituals brought nationalism into the lives of ordinary people. Each nation had its own unique capital city, flag, military uniform, and national anthem. New symbols, such as Britain's doughty John Bull, France's republican Marianne, America's stern Uncle Sam, and Germany's stolid Michel, supposedly embodied shared national characteristics. All citizens could participate in newly invented national holidays, such as Bastille Day in France, first held in 1880 to commemorate the French Revolution, or Sedan Day in Germany, created to celebrate Germany's victory over France in 1871. Royal weddings, coronations, jubilees, and funerals brought citizens into the streets to celebrate the nation's leaders—British Queen Victoria's 1887 Golden Jubilee set a high standard. Public squares and parks received prominent commemorative statues and monuments, such as the grand memorial to Victor Emmanuel II in central Rome, or the ostentatious Monument to the Battle of Nations built in Leipzig to honor German victory in the Napoleonic Wars. Surrounded by these inescapable elements of everyday nationalism, most ordinary people grew to see themselves as members of their national communities.[4]

The Feminist Movement

Facing discrimination in education and employment and a lack of legal rights, some women began to demand that the nation-state guarantee the rights of women and the equality of the sexes. Women had much to fight for in the late nineteenth century. The ideal of separate spheres and the rigid gender division of labor meant that middle-class women faced great obstacles when they needed or wanted to move into the man's world of paid employment. Married women were subordinated to their husbands by law and lacked many basic legal rights. In England, a wife had no legal identity and hence no right to own property in her own name. Even the wages she might earn belonged to her husband. In France, the Napoleonic Code enshrined the principle of female subordination and gave the wife few legal rights regarding property, divorce, and custody of the children.

First-Wave Feminists in Action In July 1905 a woman campaigning for the right to vote is restrained by policemen at a suffragette demonstration in London. British suffragettes often engaged in provocative public acts of civil disobedience in their campaigns. The responsive national state offered benefits to its citizens, but only grudgingly offered women full political rights. (Manchester Daily Express/SSPL/Getty Images)

Following women such as Mary Wollstonecraft, middle-class feminists campaigned for equal legal rights for women as well as access to higher education, professional employment, and the vote. They argued that unmarried women and middle-class widows with inadequate incomes simply had to have more opportunities to support themselves. Feminists also argued that paid employment, as opposed to unpaid housework, could relieve the monotony that some women found in their sheltered middle-class existence.

In the late nineteenth century women's organizations scored some significant victories, such as the 1882 law giving English married women full property rights. In the decade before World War I, the British women's **suffrage movement** mounted a militant struggle for the right to vote. Inspired by the slogan "Deeds Not Words," women "suffragettes" marched in public demonstrations, heckled members of Parliament, and slashed paintings in London's National Gallery. Jailed for political activities, they went on highly publicized hunger strikes. Conservatives dismissed "the shrieking sisterhood," and British women received the vote only in 1919.

In Germany before 1900, women were not admitted as fully registered students at a single university. Determined pioneers had to fight to break through sexist barriers to advanced education and professional employment. By 1913 the Federation of German Women's Association, an umbrella organization for regional feminist groups, had some 470,000 members. Their protests had a direct impact on the revised German Civil Code of 1906, which granted women substantial gains in family law and property rights.

Women inspired by utopian and especially Marxist socialism blazed an alternative path. Often scorning the reform programs of middle-class feminists, socialist women leaders argued that the liberation of working-class women would come only with the liberation of the entire working class through Marxist revolution. In the meantime, they championed the cause of working women and won some practical improvements, especially in Germany, where the socialist movement was most effectively organized.

Progress toward women's rights was slow and hard-won, yet the state did respond with more gender-equitable property and family laws, workplace reforms, and civil rights. Women's right to vote, however, was typically only granted in the years after World War I.

Nationalism and Racism

Whereas nationalism in the first two-thirds of the nineteenth century had often promoted liberal reform and peaceful brotherhood, after the 1870s it took on more populist and exclusionary tones. The growing popularity of supposedly scientific understandings of racial difference fueled this animosity. Though we now understand that there is no genetic basis for distinct human races, most people in the late nineteenth century believed that race was a product of heredity or "blood." Many felt pride in their own national racial characteristics — French, English, German, Jewish, Polish, and many others — that were supposedly passed down from generation to generation. Unfortunately, pride in one's own heritage easily led to denigration of someone else's.

Modern attempts to use race to categorize distinct groups of people had their roots in Enlightenment thought (see Chapter 16). Now a new group of intellectuals, including race theorists such as Count Arthur de Gobineau, claimed that their ideas about racial difference were scientific, based on hard biological "facts" about bloodlines and heredity. In *On the Inequality of the Human Races* (1854), Gobineau divided humanity into the white, black, and yellow races based on geographical location and championed the white "Aryan race" for its supposedly superior qualities. Social Darwinist ideas about the "survival of the fittest" (see "Darwin and Natural Selection," in Chapter 22), when applied to the "contest" between nations and races, further popularized stereotypes about inferior and superior races.

The close links between nationalism and scientific racism helped justify imperial expansion, as we shall see in the next chapter. Nationalist racism also fostered domestic persecution and exclusion, as witnessed in Bismarck's Kulturkampf and the Dreyfus affair. According to race theorists, the nation was supposed to be racially pure, and ethnic minorities were viewed as outsiders and targets for reform, repression, and relocation. Thus ethnic Russian leaders targeted minority Poles and

Czechs for "Russification" so they might learn the Russian language and assimilate into Russian society. Germans likewise viewed the many ethnic Poles in East Prussia as a "national threat" that required "Germanization" before they could be seen as equals to the superior Germans. For many nationalists, driven by ugly currents of race hatred, Jews were the ultimate outsiders, the stereotypical "inferior race" that posed the greatest challenge to national purity.

Jewish Emancipation and Modern Anti-Semitism

Changing political principles and the triumph of the nation-state had revolutionized Jewish life in western and central Europe. By the 1870s, Jews across western and central Europe had won "emancipation," that is, legal and civic equality with other citizens. In 1871, for example, the constitution of the new German Empire abolished all restrictions on Jewish marriage, choice of occupation, place of residence, and property ownership. Many European Jewish families had improved their economic situation enough to enter the middle classes. They often identified strongly with their respective nation-states and, with good reason, saw themselves as patriotic citizens. Even with these changes, Jews faced discrimination in employment opportunities and social relations.

Vicious anti-Semitism reappeared with force in central and eastern Europe after the stock market crash of 1873. Drawing on long traditions of religious intolerance, segregation into ghettos, and periodic anti-Jewish riots (or pogroms), this anti-Semitism also

An Anti-Jewish Pogrom in the Pale of Settlement In April 1903 a violent anti-Semitic riot (or pogrom) broke out in Kishinev, a city in the Pale of Settlement that is the capital of current-day Moldova. In two days of rioting, a mob angered by specious anti-Semitic propaganda murdered at least forty-seven Jews and vandalized and looted hundreds of Jewish homes and businesses. As this cover page from an Italian illustrated magazine suggests, the pogrom focused international media coverage on the violent persecution of Jews in Russia. (By Achille Beltrame, from *La Domenica del Corriere*, 1903/Alfredo Dagli Orti/Shutterstock)

built on the exclusionary aspects of popular nationalism and the pseudoscience of race. Fanatic anti-Semites whipped up resentment against Jewish achievement and "financial control" and claimed that Jewish "blood" posed a biological threat to Christian peoples. Such ideas were popularized by the repeated publication of the notorious forgery "The Protocols of the Elders of Zion," a fake account of a secret meeting supposedly held at the First Zionist Congress in Basel in 1897 that suggested that Jewish elders planned to dominate the globe. Such anti-Semitic beliefs were particularly popular among conservatives, extreme nationalists, and people who felt threatened by Jewish competition, such as small shopkeepers, officeworkers, and professionals.

Anti-Semites created nationalist political parties that attacked and insulted Jews to win popular support. In one noted example, anti-Semitism combined with a large-scale public works program helped Austrian politician Karl Lueger (LOU-ger) and his Christian Socialist Party win striking electoral victories in Vienna in the 1890s. Lueger, mayor of Vienna from 1897 to 1910, tried to limit Jewish immigration from the Russian Empire and used fierce anti-Semitic rhetoric to appeal to the worst instincts of the electorate, especially the lower middle class. Future Nazi dictator Adolf Hitler lived in Vienna during this time, and his fervent hatred of Jews drew strength from Lueger's racist rhetoric.

Before 1914 anti-Semitism was most oppressive in eastern Europe, where Jews suffered from rampant poverty. Four of Europe's 7 million Jewish people lived with few legal rights in the western borderlands of the Russian Empire—the Pale of Settlement (see Chapter 16). In the Pale, officials used anti-Semitism to channel popular discontent away from the government and onto the Jewish minority. Jews were regularly denounced as foreign exploiters who corrupted national traditions, and between 1881 and 1884 a wave of violent pogroms (or popular anti-Jewish riots) commenced in southern Russia. The police and the army stood aside for days while peasants looted and destroyed Jewish property, and official harassment continued in the following decades. Another wave of pogroms broke out in 1903; mass anti-Semitic rioting in Odessa in 1905, which killed at least four hundred Jews, marked the worst event.

The growth of radical anti-Semitism spurred the emergence of **Zionism**, a Jewish political movement whose adherents believed that Christian Europeans would never overcome their anti-Semitic hatred. To escape anti-Semitism, Zionists such as Theodor Herzl advocated the creation of a Jewish state in Palestine—a homeland where European Jews could settle and live free of oppression. Zionism was particularly popular among Jews living in the Pale. While some embraced the vision of a Zionist settlement in Palestine, many more emigrated to western or central Europe and the United States. About 2.75 million Jews left central and eastern Europe between 1881 and 1914.

How and why did revolutionary Marxism evolve in the late nineteenth century?

Socialist parties, generally Marxist groups dedicated to international proletarian revolution, grew rapidly in the late nineteenth century. The radical rhetoric of socialist politicians continued to trouble the conservative upper classes. But behind the talk of revolution, Marxism was becoming more mainstream, particularly as the consolidation of labor unions and the turn to Marxist "revisionism" promised real practical improvements for workers.

The Socialist International

The growth of socialist parties after 1871 was phenomenal. In Germany, neither Bismarck's Anti-Socialist Laws nor his extensive social security system checked the growth of the German Social Democratic Party (SPD), which espoused revolutionary Marxism even though it sought reform through legal parliamentary politics. By 1912 the SPD had millions of working-class followers and was the largest party in the Reichstag. Socialist parties grew in other countries as well, though nowhere else with such success. In 1883 Russian exiles in Switzerland founded the Russian Social Democratic Party, and various socialist groups were unified in 1905 in the French Section of the Workers International. Belgium and Austria-Hungary also had strong socialist parties.

Marxist socialist parties strove to join together in an international organization, and in 1864 Marx himself helped found the socialist International Working Men's Association, also known as the First International. In the following years, Marx battled successfully to control the organization and used its annual international meetings to spread his doctrines of socialist revolution. He endorsed the radical patriotism of the Paris Commune and its terrible struggle against the French state as a giant step toward socialist revolution. Marx's fervent embrace of working-class violence frightened many of his early supporters, especially the more moderate British labor leaders. Internal tensions led to the collapse of the First International in 1876.

Yet even after Marx's death in 1884 international proletarian solidarity remained an important objective for Marxists. In 1889, as the individual parties in different countries grew stronger, socialist leaders came together to form the Second International, which lasted until 1914. Though only a federation of national socialist parties, the Second International had a powerful psychological impact. It had a permanent executive, and every three years delegates from the different parties met to interpret Marxist doctrines and plan coordinated action. May 1 (May Day) was declared an annual socialist holiday, a day for strikes, marches, and demonstrations. Prosperous elites and conservative middle-class citizens feared the growing power of socialism and the Second International, but many workers joined the cause.

Labor Unions and the Evolution of Working-Class Radicalism

Was socialism really radical and revolutionary in these years? On the whole, it was not. As socialist parties grew and attracted many members, they looked less and less toward revolution and more and more toward gradual change and steady improvement for the working class. The mainstream of European socialism became militantly moderate. Socialists still liked to alarm mainstream politicians with revolutionary rhetoric. But they increasingly worked within the system, often joining labor unions to win practical workplace reforms.

Workers were less inclined to follow radical programs for several reasons. As they gained the right to vote and won tangible benefits, they focused more on elections than on revolutions. And workers were not immune to patriotic education and indoctrination during military service. Many responded positively to drum-beating parades and aggressive foreign policy as they loyally voted for socialist parties. Nor were workers by any means a unified group with shared social and political interests—as we saw in Chapter 22.

Perhaps most important of all, workers' standard of living rose gradually but substantially after 1850. The quality of life in urban areas improved dramatically as well. For all these reasons, workers became more moderate: they demanded gains, but they were less likely to take to the barricades in pursuit of them.

The growth of labor unions reinforced the trend toward moderation. In the early stages of industrialization, unions were considered subversive bodies to be hounded and crushed, and were generally prohibited by law. Determined workers organized and fought back. In Great Britain in 1824 and 1825 unions won the legal right to exist—though generally not the right to strike. Limited primarily to highly skilled workers such as machinists and carpenters, these "new model unions" concentrated on winning better wages and hours through collective bargaining and compromise. This approach helped pave the way to the full acceptance of unions across Europe in the 1870s, and after 1890 unions for unskilled workers developed.

Marxist Revisionism

Germany, the most industrialized and unionized continental country by 1914, offers an instructive case study of the transformation of socialism around 1900. German unions did not receive basic rights until 1869, and until the Anti-Socialist Laws were repealed in 1890, they were frequently harassed by the government. As a result, in 1895 Germany had only about 270,000 union members in a male industrial work-force of nearly 8 million. Then, with almost all legal harassment eliminated, union membership skyrocketed, reaching roughly 3 million in 1912.

This great expansion both reflected and influenced the changing character of German unions. Increasingly, union activists focused on bread-and-butter issues—wages, hours, working conditions—rather than on fomenting revolution. Genuine collective bargaining, long opposed by socialist intellectuals as a sellout, was officially recognized as desirable by the German Trade Union Congress in 1899. When employers proved unwilling to bargain, strikes forced them to change their minds. In 1913 alone, over ten thousand collective bargaining agreements benefiting 1.25 million workers were signed.

The German trade unions and many of their leaders were in fact, if not in name, thoroughgoing revisionists. **Marxist revisionism** was an effort to update Marx's doctrines to reflect current realities. Thus the socialist Eduard Bernstein (1850–1932) argued in 1899 in his *Evolutionary Socialism* that many of Marx's predictions had been proven false. Socialists, according to thinkers like Bernstein, should reform their doctrines and tactics to meet these changed conditions. They should combine with other progressive forces to win continued steps forward for workers through legislation, unions, and further economic expansion; revolution might happen later, but the movement, not the final goal, was the point. These views were denounced as heresy by hard-core Marxists in the SPD and later by the leaders of the Second International. Yet the revisionist, gradualist approach continued to gain the tacit acceptance of many German socialists, particularly in the trade unions.

Moderation found followers elsewhere. In France, the famous socialist leader Jean Jaurès (1859–1914) formally repudiated revisionism in order to establish a unified socialist party, but he remained at heart a gradualist and optimistic secular humanist. Questions of revolution or revisionism also divided Russian Marxists on the eve of the Russian Revolution, as we shall see in Chapter 25.

By the early twentieth century socialist parties had clear-cut national characteristics. Russians and socialists in the Austro-Hungarian Empire tended to be the most radical. The German party talked revolution and practiced reformism, greatly influenced by its enormous trade-union movement. The French party talked revolution and tried to practice it, unrestrained by a trade-union movement that was both very weak and very radical. In Britain, the socialist but non-Marxist Labour Party, reflecting the well-established union movement, was formally committed to gradual reform. In Spain and Italy, Marxist socialism was very weak. There anarchism, seeking to smash the state rather than the bourgeoisie, dominated radical thought and action.

In short, socialist policies and doctrines varied from country to country. Although leaders liked to talk about "socialist internationalism," the notion of international unity was more myth than reality. This helps explain why when war came in 1914, almost all socialist parties and most workers supported their national governments and turned away from international solidarity.

NOTES

1. Quoted in J. McKay, *Pioneers for Profit: Foreign Entrepreneurship and Russian Industrialization, 1885–1913* (Chicago: University of Chicago Press, 1970), p. 11.
2. W. Dawson, *Bismarck and State Socialism* (London: Swan Sonnenschein & Co., 1890), pp. 63–64.
3. E. Weber, *Peasants into Frenchmen: The Modernization of Rural France, 1870–1914* (Stanford, Calif.: Stanford University Press, 1976).
4. See E. Hobsbawm, "Mass Producing Traditions: Europe, 1870–1914," in *The Invention of Tradition*, ed. E. Hobsbawm and T. Ranger (New York: Cambridge University Press, 1992), pp. 263–307.

LOOKING BACK LOOKING AHEAD

In 1900 the triumph of the national state in Europe seemed almost complete. In the aging Austro-Hungarian, Russian, and Ottoman Empires, ethnic minorities continued to fight for national independence. Class, religion, and ethnicity still divided people across the rest of Europe. But in most places, the politically unified nation-state governed with the consent and even the devotion of many citizens. Many men and women embraced patriotism and identified as members of a national group. This newfound sense of national identity could be ugly and exclusionary, but it could also erode traditional social differences.

Responsive and capable of tackling many practical problems, the European nation-state of 1900 was in part the realization of patriotic ideologues and the middle-class liberals active in the unsuccessful revolutions of 1848. Yet whereas early nationalists had envisioned a Europe of free peoples and international peace, the nationalists of 1900 had been nurtured in an atmosphere of competition between

European states and the wars of unification in the 1850s and 1860s. This new generation of nationalists reveled in the strength of their unity, and the nation-state became the foundation of a new system of global power.

Thus after 1870, even as the responsive nation-state brought some benefits and some burdens to ordinary people, Europe's leading countries extended their imperial control around the globe. In Asia and Africa, the European powers seized territory, fought brutal colonial wars, and built authoritarian empires. Moreover, in Europe itself the universal faith in nationalism, which usually reduced social tensions within states, promoted a bitter competition between states. In this way European nationalism threatened the very progress and unity it had helped to build. In 1914 the power of unified nation-states would turn on itself, unleashing the First World War and doling out self-inflicted wounds of enormous proportions to all of Europe's peoples.

MAKE CONNECTIONS

Think about the larger developments and continuities within and across chapters.

1. By 1900 most countries in Europe and North America had established modern nation-states, but the process of nation building varied dramatically. Which countries were most successful in building viable nation-states? What accounts for the variation?

2. The new nation-state made demands on its citizens but also offered them benefits and a new way to think about and experience social community. How would you evaluate the balance? Was the consolidation of the nation-state good for most people?

3. Liberalism, socialism, and nationalism first emerged as coherent ideologies in the decades around 1800 (Chapter 21). How had they changed by 1900?

Chapter 23 Review

IDENTIFY KEY TERMS

Identify and explain the significance of each item below.

Risorgimento (p. 682)

Realpolitik (p. 685)

manifest destiny (p. 689)

Crimean War (p. 691)

Russian Revolution of 1905 (p. 695)

Duma (p. 695)

Tanzimat (p. 696)

Young Turks (p. 697)

Reichstag (p. 698)

German Social Democratic Party (SPD) (p. 698)

Dreyfus affair (p. 700)

home rule (p. 702)

suffrage movement (p. 706)

Zionism (p. 709)

Marxist revisionism (p. 711)

REVIEW THE MAIN IDEAS

Answer the section heading questions from the chapter.

1. What were the main features of the authoritarian nation-state built by Napoleon III? (p. 679)

2. How were strong nation-states forged in Italy, Germany, and the United States? (p. 681)

3. How did Russian and Ottoman leaders modernize their states and societies? (p. 689)

4. How did the relationship between government and the governed change after 1871? (p. 697)

5. What were the costs and benefits of nationalism for ordinary people? (p. 704)

6. How and why did revolutionary Marxism evolve in the late nineteenth century? (p. 709)

CHRONOLOGY

1839–1876	• Western-style Tanzimat reforms in Ottoman Empire
1852	• Louis Napoleon proclaimed emperor of France
1853–1856	• Crimean War
1859–1870	• Unification of Italy
1861	• Tsar Alexander II abolishes Russian serfdom
1861–1865	• U.S. Civil War
1866	• Austro-Prussian War
1871	• Franco-Prussian War ends; unification of Germany; defeat of Paris Commune; establishment of Third Republic in France
1870–1878	• Kulturkampf, Bismarck's attack on Catholic Church
1880s	• Educational reforms in France create a secular public school system
1880s–1890s	• Widespread return to protectionism among European states
1881–1884; 1903–1906	• Waves of anti-Jewish pogroms in the Pale of Settlement
1890–1900	• Witte initiates second surge of Russian industrialization
1896	• Zionist leader Theodor Herzl publishes *The Jewish State*
1905	• Revolution in Russia; Norway wins independence from Sweden
1906–1914	• Social reform in Great Britain
1908	• Young Turks seize power in Ottoman Empire
1914	• Outbreak of World War I

24

The West and the World

1815–1914

CHAPTER PREVIEW

- What were the global consequences of European industrialization?

- How was massive migration an integral part of Western expansion?

- How did the New Imperialism change Western colonialism?

- How did non-Westerners respond to Western expansion?

WHILE INDUSTRIALIZATION AND NATIONALISM were transforming urban and rural life throughout Europe, western Europeans were reshaping the world. At the peak of its power and pride, the West entered the third and most dynamic phase of the aggressive expansion that had begun with the Crusades and continued with the rise of seaborne colonial empires. At the same time, millions of Europeans emigrated abroad, primarily to North and South America but also to Australia, North and South Africa, and Asiatic Russia. An ever-growing stream of people, products, and ideas flowed into and out of Europe in the nineteenth century. Hardly any corner of the globe was left untouched.

The most spectacular manifestations of Western expansion came in the late nineteenth century when the leading European nations established or enlarged their colonial empires. This political annexation of territory in the 1880s—the "New Imperialism"—was the capstone of Europe's underlying economic and technological transformation. Europe's New Imperialism rested on a formidable combination of superior military might and strong authoritarian rule, and it posed a brutal challenge to African and Asian peoples. Colonized peoples met this challenge in different ways. By 1914 non-Western elites in many lands were leading an anti-imperialist struggle for dignity and genuine independence that would eventually triumph after 1945.

What were the global consequences of European industrialization?

The Industrial Revolution created a tremendously dynamic economic system. In the nineteenth century, that system expanded across the face of the earth. Some of this extension into non-Western areas was peaceful and beneficial, for the West had many products and techniques the rest of the world desired. If peaceful methods failed, however, Europeans used their superior military power to force non-Western nations to open their doors to Western economic interests. In general, Europeans fashioned the global economic system so that the largest share of the ever-increasing gains from trade, technology, and migration flowed to the West and its propertied classes.

The Rise of Global Inequality

The Industrial Revolution in Europe marked a momentous turning point. Those regions that industrialized, mainly Europe and North America, increased their wealth and power enormously in comparison to those that did not. A gap between the core industrializing regions and the soon-to-be colonized or semi-colonized regions outside the European–North American core (Africa, Asia, the Middle East, and Latin America) emerged and widened throughout the nineteenth century. Moreover, this pattern of uneven global development became institutionalized, or built into the structure of the world economy. Thus a "lopsided world" evolved, a world with a rich north and a poor south — albeit with regional variations.

In recent years economic historians have charted the long-term evolution of this gap, and Figure 24.1 summarizes the findings of one important study. Three main points stand out. First, in 1750 the average standard of living was no higher in Europe as a whole than in the rest of the world. Second, it was industrialization that opened the gaps in average wealth and well-being among countries and regions. Third, income per person stagnated in the colonized

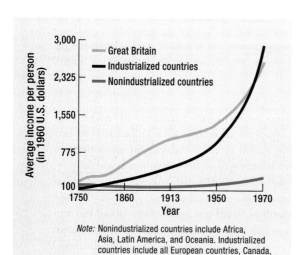

Note: Nonindustrialized countries include Africa, Asia, Latin America, and Oceania. Industrialized countries include all European countries, Canada, the United States, and Japan.

FIGURE 24.1 The Growth of Average Income per Person in Industrialized Countries, Nonindustrialized Countries, and Great Britain, 1750–1970
Growth is given in 1960 U.S. dollars and prices.

world before 1913, in striking contrast to the industrializing regions. Only after 1945, in the era of decolonization and political independence, did former colonies make real economic progress and begin the process of industrialization.

The rise of these enormous income disparities, which indicate striking disparities in food and clothing, health and education, and life expectancy and general material well-being, has generated a great deal of debate. One school stresses that the West used science, technology, capitalist organization, and even its rational world-view to create massive wealth and then used that wealth and power to its advantage. Another school argues that the West used its political and economic power to steal much of the world's riches, continuing in the nineteenth and twentieth centuries the rapacious colonialism born of the era of expansion. Because these issues are complex, it is helpful to consider them in the context of world trade in the nineteenth century.

The World Market

Commerce between nations typically stimulates economic development. In the nineteenth century European development brought an enormous increase in international trade. Great Britain took the lead in cultivating export markets for its booming industrial output, as British manufacturers looked first to Europe and then around the world, seeking consumers for their growing numbers of mass-produced goods.

Take the case of cotton textile markets in Great Britain and India. By 1820 Britain was exporting 50 percent of its production. Europe bought about one-half of these exports, while India bought only 6 percent and had its own well-established textile industry with international markets. Then after continental European nations and the United States erected tariff barriers on textiles to promote domestic industry, British cotton manufacturers aggressively sought other foreign markets in non-Western areas. By 1850 India was buying 25 percent and Europe only 16 percent of a much larger volume of production. As a British colony, India could not raise tariffs to protect its ancient cotton textile industry, which collapsed, leaving thousands of Indian weavers unemployed.

In addition to its dominance in the export market, Britain was also the world's largest importer of goods and the largest trader of agricultural products, raw materials, and manufactured goods. Under free-trade policies, open access to Britain's market stimulated the development of mines and plantations in many non-Western areas.

Improved transportation systems fostered international trade. Wherever railroads were built, they drastically reduced transportation costs, opened new economic opportunities, and called forth new skills and attitudes. European investors funded much of the railroad construction in Latin America, Asia, and Africa, where railroads typically connected seaports with resource-rich inland cities and regions, as opposed to linking and developing cities and regions within a given country. Thus railroads served Western economic interests by facilitating the inflow and sale of Western manufactured goods and the export and the development of local raw materials.

The power of steam revolutionized transportation by sea as well as by land. Steam power began to supplant sails in the late 1860s. Passenger and freight rates tumbled as ship design became more efficient and the intercontinental shipment of low-priced raw materials became feasible. The time needed to cross the Atlantic dropped from three weeks in 1870 to about ten days in 1900, and the opening of the Suez and Panama Canals (in 1869 and 1914, respectively) shortened transport time to other areas of the globe considerably. In addition, improved port facilities made loading and unloading cargo less expensive, faster, and more dependable.

The revolution in land and sea travel encouraged European entrepreneurs to open up and exploit vast new territories. Improved transportation enabled Asia, Africa, and Latin America to ship not only familiar agricultural products — spices, tea, sugar, coffee — but also new raw materials for industry, such as jute, rubber, cotton, and coconut oil. The export of raw materials supplied by these "primary producers" to Western manufacturers boosted economic growth in Europe and North America but did little to establish independent industry in the developing world.

New communication systems directed the flow of goods across global networks. Transoceanic telegraph cables, in place by the 1880s, enabled rapid communications among the financial centers of the world. While a British tramp freighter steamed from Calcutta to New York, a broker in London could arrange by telegram for it to carry American cargo to Australia. The same communications network conveyed world commodity prices instantaneously.

As their economies grew, Europeans began to make massive foreign investments, beginning in about 1840. By the outbreak of World War I, Europeans had invested more than $40 billion abroad. Great Britain, France, and Germany were the principal investing countries (Map 24.1). The great gap between rich and poor within Europe meant that the wealthy and moderately well-to-do could and did send great sums abroad in search of interest and dividends.

Most of the capital exported did not go to European colonies or protectorates in Asia and Africa. About three-quarters of total European investment went to other European countries, or to settler colonies — so-called **neo-Europes**, a term coined by historian Alfred Crosby to describe regions where the climate and topography resembled the European homeland, including the United States, Canada, Australia, New Zealand, Latin America, and parts of Siberia. In these relatively advanced regions, which had already attracted significant settler populations of ethnic Europeans, Europe found its most profitable opportunities for investment in construction of railroads, ports, and resource extraction of cheap food and raw materials.

Much of this investment was peaceful and mutually beneficial for lenders and borrowers. The extension of Western economic power and the construction of neo-Europes, however, were disastrous for indigenous peoples. Native Americans and Australian Aborigines especially were decimated by the diseases, liquor, and weapons of an aggressively expanding Western society.

Western Pressures on China

Europe's development of robust offshoots in sparsely populated North America, Australia, and much of Latin America absorbed huge quantities of goods, investments, and migrants. Yet Europe's economic and cultural penetration of old, densely populated civilizations was also significant. Interaction with such civilizations increased the Europeans' trade and profit, and they were prepared to use force to attain their desires. China provides a striking example of European intrusion into non-Western lands.

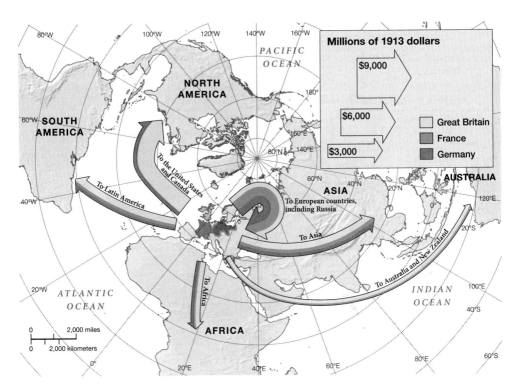

MAP 24.1   European Investment to 1914
Foreign investment grew rapidly after 1850, and Britain, France, and Germany were the major investing nations. As this map suggests, most European investment was not directed to the African and Asian areas seized in the New Imperialism after 1880.

For centuries China had sent more goods and inventions to Europe than it had received, and such was still the case in the early nineteenth century. Trade with Europe was carefully regulated by the Chinese imperial government, ruled by the Qing (ching), or Manchu, Dynasty in the nineteenth century. Qing officials required all foreign merchants to live in the southern port of Guangzhou (Canton) and to buy and sell only to licensed Chinese merchants. Practices considered harmful to Chinese interests were strictly forbidden.

For years the little community of foreign merchants in Guangzhou had to accept this system. By the 1820s, however, the dominant merchants, the British, were flexing their muscles. Moreover, in opium — that "destructive and ensnaring vice" denounced by Chinese decrees — the British found a means to break China's self-imposed isolation. British merchants smuggled opium grown legally in British-occupied India into China, where its use and sale were illegal. Huge profits and growing addiction led to a rapid increase in sales. By 1836 the British merchants in Guangzhou were demanding the creation of an independent British colony in China and "safe and unrestricted liberty" in their Chinese trade. Spurred on by economic motives, they pressured the British government to take decisive action and enlisted

Commissioner Lin Zexu Overseeing the Destruction of Opium at Guangzhou, 1839
A formidable Chinese bureaucrat known for his competence and high moral standards, Lin Zexu was sent to Guangzhou (Canton) as imperial commissioner in late 1838 to halt the illegal importation of opium by the British. He made a huge impact on the opium trade within a matter of months. As a result, British troops invaded China, and the ultimate British victory in the Opium Wars forced China to grant European merchants one-sided trade agreements. (Pictures from History/Bridgeman Images)

the support of British manufacturers with visions of vast Chinese markets to be opened to their goods.

At the same time, the Qing government decided that the opium trade had to be stamped out. It was ruining the people and stripping the empire of its silver, which went to British merchants to pay for the drug. The government began to vigorously prosecute Chinese drug dealers. In 1839 it sent special envoy Lin Zexu to Guangzhou to deal with the crisis. Lin Zexu punished Chinese who purchased opium and seized the opium supplies of the British merchants, who then withdrew to the barren island of Hong Kong. He sent a famous letter justifying his policy to Queen Victoria in London.

The wealthy, well-connected British merchants appealed to their allies in London for support, and the British government responded. It also wanted free, unregulated trade with China, as well as the establishment of diplomatic relations on the European model, complete with ambassadors, embassies, and published treaties. Using troops from India and taking advantage of its control of the seas, Britain occupied several coastal cities and in the first of two **Opium Wars** forced China to give in to British demands. In the Treaty of Nanking in 1842, the imperial government was required to permanently cede the island of Hong Kong to Britain, pay an indemnity of $100 million, and open up four large cities to unlimited foreign trade with low tariffs.

With Britain's new power over Chinese commerce, the opium trade flourished, and Hong Kong developed rapidly as an Anglo-Chinese enclave. But disputes over trade between China and the Western powers continued. Finally, the second Opium War (1856–1860) culminated in the occupation of Beijing by seventeen thousand British and French troops, who burned down the emperor's summer palace. Another round of one-sided treaties gave European merchants and missionaries greater privileges and protection and forced the Chinese to accept trade and investment on unfavorable terms in several more cities. Thus did Europeans use opium addiction and military aggression to blow a hole in the wall of Chinese seclusion and open the country to foreign ideas and uneven foreign trade.

Japan and the United States

China's neighbor Japan had its own highly distinctive civilization and even less use for Westerners. European traders and missionaries first arrived in Japan, an archipelago nation slightly smaller than California, in the sixteenth century. By 1640 Japanese leaders had decided to expel all foreigners and seal off the country from all European influences in order to preserve traditional Japanese culture and society. When American and British whaling ships began to appear off Japanese coasts almost two hundred years later, the policy of exclusion was still in effect. An order of 1825 commanded Japanese officials to "drive away foreign vessels without second thought."[1]

Japan's unbending isolation seemed hostile and barbaric to the West, particularly to the United States. It complicated the practical problems of ensuring the safety of shipwrecked American sailors and the provisioning of whaling ships and China traders sailing in the eastern Pacific. It also thwarted American business leaders' hope of trade and profit. Moreover, Americans shared the self-confidence and dynamism of expanding Western society, and they felt destined to play a great role in the Pacific. To Americans it seemed the duty of the United States to force the Japanese to open their ports and behave as a "civilized" nation.

After several unsuccessful American attempts to establish commercial relations with Japan, Commodore Matthew Perry steamed into Edo (now Tokyo) Bay in 1853. Relying on **gunboat diplomacy** by threatening to attack, Perry demanded diplomatic negotiations with the emperor. Some Japanese military leaders urged resistance, but senior officials realized how defenseless their cities were against naval bombardment. Shocked and humiliated, they reluctantly signed a treaty with the United States that opened two ports and permitted trade. Over the next five years, more treaties spelled out the rights and privileges of the Western nations and their merchants in Japan. The country was "opened." What the British had done in China with two wars, the Americans had achieved in Japan with the threat of one.

Western Intervention in Egypt

Egypt's experience illustrates not only the explosive power of the expanding European economy but also its seductive appeal for indigenous elites. Since 525 B.C.E. a succession of foreigners had ruled Egypt, most recently the Ottoman sultans. In 1798 French armies under Napoleon Bonaparte invaded the Egyptian part of the Ottoman Empire and occupied the territory for three years. Into the power vacuum left by the French withdrawal stepped an extraordinary Albanian-born, Turkish-speaking general, Muhammad Ali (1769–1849).

First appointed governor of Egypt in 1805 by the Ottoman sultan, Muhammad Ali set out to build his own state based on European models. He built a large army by drafting illiterate Egyptian peasants, and he hired French and Italian army officers to train these raw recruits and their Turkish officers in modern military methods. He reformed the government bureaucracy, cultivated new lands, and improved communication networks. By the end of his reign in 1848, Ali had established a strong and virtually independent Egyptian state, to be ruled by his family on a hereditary basis within the Ottoman Empire (see "Reform and Readjustment in the Ottoman Empire" in Chapter 23).

Europeans saw opportunities for work and profit in Ali's modernizing Egypt. By 1864 more than fifty thousand European lived in the port city of Alexandria; they worked as army officers, engineers, doctors, government officials, and police officers. Others turned to trade, finance, and shipping.

To pay for his ambitious plans, Ali encouraged the development of commercial agriculture. This move had profound implications. Egyptian peasants were poor but largely self-sufficient, growing food for their own consumption on state-owned lands allotted to them by tradition. When high-ranking officials and members of Muhammad Ali's family began carving large private landholdings out of the state domain, they forced peasants to grow cash crops such as cotton and rice geared to European markets. Egyptian landowners "modernized" agriculture, but to the detriment of peasant living standards.

These trends continued under Muhammad Ali's grandson Ismail (ihs-MAH-eel), who in 1863 began his sixteen-year rule as Egypt's khedive (kuh-DEEV), or prince. Educated at France's leading military academy, Ismail was a westernizing autocrat. The large irrigation networks he promoted boosted cotton production and exports to Europe, and with his support a French company completed the Suez Canal in 1869. The Arabic of the Egyptian masses replaced the Turkish spoken by Ottoman rulers as the official language. Young Egyptians educated in Europe spread new skills, and Cairo acquired modern boulevards and Western hotels. As Ismail proudly declared, "My country is no longer in Africa, we now form part of Europe."[2]

Yet Ismail's projects were enormously expensive, and by 1876 Egypt owed foreign bondholders a colossal debt that it could not pay. France and Great Britain intervened and forced Ismail to appoint French and British commissioners to oversee Egyptian finances. This decision marked a sharp break with the past. Throughout most of the nineteenth century, Europeans had used military might and political force primarily to make sure that non-Western lands would accept European trade and investment. Now Europeans were going to effectively rule Egypt.

Foreign financial control evoked a violent nationalistic reaction among Egyptian army officers, religious leaders, and young intellectuals. In 1879, under the leadership of Colonel Ahmed Arabi, they formed the Egyptian Nationalist Party. When the French and British forced Ismail to abdicate in favor of his ineffectual son, Mohamed Tewfik Pasha (r. 1879–1892), in 1882, riots broke out in Alexandria. A number of Europeans were killed, and Tewfik (TAW-fik) and his court had to flee to British ships for safety. When the British fleet bombarded Alexandria, more riots swept the country, and Colonel Arabi led a revolt. But a British expeditionary force put down the rebellion and occupied all of Egypt that year.

The British claimed their occupation was temporary, but British armies remained in Egypt until 1956. Before the First World War (1914–1918), they maintained the façade of Egypt as an autonomous province of the Ottoman Empire; the khedive, however, was a mere puppet who mostly carried out the bidding of the British colonial authorities. British rule did result in tax reforms and somewhat better conditions for peasants, and foreign bondholders received interest on their loans. But Egyptians saw the British as foreign occupiers, and anticolonial resistance grew during and after the First World War.

The British takeover in Egypt provided a new model for European expansion in densely populated lands. Such expansion was based on military force, political domination, and a self-justifying ideology of beneficial reform. This model predominated until at least 1914. In China, Japan, and Egypt, and across the globe, Europe's Industrial Revolution and subsequent expansion contributed to fundamental political changes as well as economic growth.

How was massive migration an integral part of Western expansion?

A poignant human drama accompanied European expansion: millions of people left their ancestral lands in history's greatest migration. To ordinary people for whom the opening of China and the interest on the Egyptian debt had not the slightest significance, this great movement was the central experience in the saga of Western expansion. It was, in part, because of this **global mass migration** that the West's impact on the world in the nineteenth century was so powerful and many-sided.

The Pressure of Population

In the early eighteenth century European population growth entered its third and decisive stage, which continued unabated until the early twentieth century. Birthrates eventually declined in the nineteenth century, but so did death rates, mainly because of the rising standard of living and the revolution in public health. During the hundred years before 1900 the population of Europe (including Asiatic Russia) more than doubled, from approximately 188 to roughly 432 million.

These figures actually understate Europe's population explosion, for between 1815 and 1932 more than 60 million Europeans left the subcontinent. These emigrants went primarily to the rapidly growing neo-Europes—North and South America, Australia, New Zealand, and Siberia. Since the population of native Africans, Asians, and Americans grew more slowly than that of Europeans, the number of Europeans and people of predominantly European origin jumped from about 24 percent of the world's total in 1800 to about 38 percent on the eve of World War I.

The growth of the European population drove more and more people to emigrate. As in the eighteenth century, the rapid increase in numbers in Europe proper led to relative overpopulation in area after area. In most countries, emigration increased twenty years after a rapid growth in population, as children grew up, saw little available land and few economic opportunities, and departed. This pattern was especially prevalent when rapid population increase predated extensive industrial development, which offered the best long-term hope of creating jobs and reducing poverty. Thus millions of country folk in industrialized parts of Europe moved to

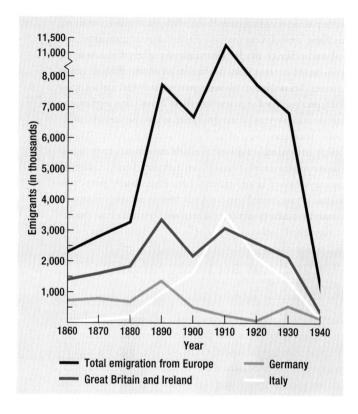

FIGURE 24.2
Emigration from Europe by Decade, 1860–1940
Emigration from Europe followed regional economic trends, as the comparison in this chart suggests. Overall, emigration from Europe grew quickly until the outbreak of World War I in 1914, after which it declined rapidly.

cities in search of work, while those in more slowly industrializing regions moved abroad.

Three facts about this emigration stand out. First, the number of men and women who left Europe increased rapidly at the end of the nineteenth century and leading up to World War I. As Figure 24.2 shows, more than 11 million left in the first decade of the twentieth century, over five times the number departing in the 1850s. Large-scale emigration was a defining characteristic of European society at the turn of the century.

Second, different countries had very different patterns of migration. People left Britain and Ireland in large numbers from the 1840s on. This outflow reflected not only rural poverty but also the movement of skilled industrial technicians and the preferences shown to British migrants in the overseas British Empire. Ultimately, about one-third of all European emigrants between 1840 and 1920 came from the British Isles. German emigration was quite different. It grew irregularly after about 1830, reaching a first peak in the early 1850s and another peak in the early 1880s. Then it declined rapidly, for at that point Germany's rapid industrialization provided adequate jobs at home. This pattern contrasted sharply with that of Italy. More and more Italians left the country right up to 1914, forced out by relatively slow industrial growth and poor living standards in Italian villages. In short, migration patterns mirrored social and economic conditions in the various European countries and provinces.

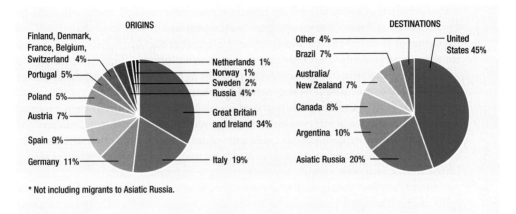

FIGURE 24.3 is shown above. ORIGINS pie chart labels: Finland, Denmark, France, Belgium, Switzerland 4%; Portugal 5%; Poland 5%; Austria 7%; Spain 9%; Germany 11%; Netherlands 1%; Norway 1%; Sweden 2%; Russia 4%*; Great Britain and Ireland 34%; Italy 19%. DESTINATIONS pie chart labels: Other 4%; Brazil 7%; Australia/New Zealand 7%; Canada 8%; Argentina 10%; Asiatic Russia 20%; United States 45%.

* Not including migrants to Asiatic Russia.

FIGURE 24.3   Origins and Destinations of European Emigrants, 1851–1960
European emigrants came from many countries; almost half of them went to the United States.

Third, although the United States did absorb the largest overall number of European emigrants, fewer than half of all these emigrants went to the United States. Asiatic Russia, Canada, Argentina, Brazil, Australia, and New Zealand also attracted large numbers, as Figure 24.3 shows. Moreover, immigrants accounted for a larger proportion of the total population in Argentina, Brazil, and Canada than in the United States. The common American assumption that European emigration meant immigration to the United States is quite inaccurate.

European Emigration

What kind of people left Europe, and what were their reasons for doing so? The European emigrant was generally an energetic small farmer or skilled artisan trying hard to stay ahead of poverty, not a desperately impoverished landless peasant or urban proletarian. Small peasant landowners and village craftsmen typically left Europe because of the lack of available land and the growing availability of inexpensive factory-made goods, which threatened their traditional livelihoods.

Immigrants brought great benefits to the countries that received them, largely because the vast majority were young, unmarried, and ready to work hard to improve their lives in the new land, at least for a time. Many Europeans moved but remained within Europe, settling temporarily or permanently in another European country. Jews from central Europe and peasants from Ireland moved to Great Britain; Russians and Poles sought work in Germany; and Spaniards, Portuguese, and Italians went to France. Many Europeans returned home after some time abroad. One in two immigrants to Argentina and probably one in three to the United States eventually returned to their native lands. Unlike the Irish or Russian Jews, these Europeans might be able to buy land and did not face persecution back at home.

The mass movement of Italians illustrates many of the characteristics of European emigration. As late as the 1880s, three of every four Italians worked in agriculture. With the influx of cheap North American wheat, many small landowning peasants whose standard of living was falling began to leave their country. Some called themselves "swallows." After harvesting their own wheat and flax in Italy, they "flew" to Argentina or Brazil to harvest wheat between December and April. Returning to Italy for the spring planting, they repeated this exhausting process. This was a very hard life, but a frugal worker could save $250 to $300 in the course of a season, at a time when an Italian agricultural worker earned less than $1 a day in Italy.

Ties of family and friendship played a crucial role in the emigration process. Many people from a given province or village settled together in rural enclaves or tightly knit urban neighborhoods thousands of miles away. Very often a prominent individual — a businessman, a religious leader, an ambitious family member — would blaze the way, and others would follow, forming a "migration chain."

Many landless young European men and women were spurred to leave by a spirit of revolt and independence. In Sweden, Norway, Jewish Russia, and Italy, these young people felt frustrated by the power of the small minority in the privileged classes, which often controlled both church and government and resisted demands for liberal reform and greater opportunity. For many, then, emigration was a radical way to gain basic human rights. Emigration rates slowed in countries where the people won political and social reforms, such as the right to vote, equality before the law, or social security benefits.

The Immigrant Experience in the United States

As we have seen, not all European immigrants moved to North America, but about one-half of the 60 million Europeans who left their homelands did come to the United States. Their work and lives had a major impact on Europe and the United States alike.

Between 1890 and 1925 over 20 million men, women, and children passed through the Ellis Island Immigration Station in New York City harbor. During these years, southern and eastern Europeans, such as Italians, Poles, and Russian Jews, far outnumbered the northern Europeans who had predominated in the mid-nineteenth-century wave of migration to the United States. Transporting migrants across the North Atlantic was big business. Well-established steamship companies such as Cunard, White Star, and Hamburg-America advertised inexpensive fares and good accommodations. The reality was usually different. For the vast majority who could afford only third-class passage in the steerage compartment, the eight- to fourteen-day journey from Naples, Hamburg, or Liverpool was cramped, cold, and unsanitary.

Once they arrived at Ellis Island, steerage passengers were subjected to a four- to five-hour examination in the Great Hall. Physicians checked their health. Customs officers inspected legal documents. Bureaucrats administered intelligence tests and evaluated the migrants' financial and moral status. The exams worried and sometimes insulted the new arrivals. As one Polish-Jewish immigrant remembered, "They asked us questions. 'How much is two and one? How much is two and two?' But the next young girl, also from our city, went and they asked her, 'How do you wash stairs, from the top or from the bottom?' She says, 'I don't come to America to wash stairs.'"[3]

Migrants with obvious illnesses were required to stay in the island's hospital as long as several weeks to see if they improved. Sick passengers whom officials judged

Migrants Crossing the Atlantic to Reach the United States Between 1800 and 1930, about 30 million Europeans left home to seek better lives in the United States, and today over 40 percent of Americans are descendants of people who went through immigration control on Ellis Island, the country's main immigration station in New York City harbor. Although advertising posters promised colorful and adventurous passage to South America as well as the United States, the many people who bought tickets in the least expensive "steerage" compartment faced a crowded and uncomfortable journey. Yet poor job prospects at home, political or ethnic persecution, and the lure of the booming U.S. economy led many to take the trip. (Granger/Granger – All rights reserved)

either a threat to public health or a likely drain on public finances were sent home. Suspected anarchists and, later, Bolsheviks were also deported.

By today's standards, it was remarkably easy to move to the United States—only about 2 percent of all migrants were denied entry. After they cleared processing, the new arrivals were ferried to New York City, where they either stayed or departed for other industrialized cities of the Northeast and Midwest. The migrants typically took unskilled jobs for low wages, but by keeping labor costs down, they fueled the rapid industrialization of late-nineteenth-century America. They also transformed the United States from a land of predominantly British and northern European settlers into a vibrant multiethnic society.

Asian Emigration

Not all emigration was from Europe. Many Chinese, Japanese, Indians, and Filipinos—to name only four key groups—also responded to rural hardship with temporary or permanent emigration. At least 3 million Asians moved abroad before 1920. Most went as indentured laborers to work under difficult conditions on the plantations or in the gold mines of Latin America, southern Asia, Africa, California, Hawaii, and Australia. In a new global trend, white estate owners often used Asian immigrants to replace or supplement black workers after the suppression of the slave trade.

In the 1840s, for example, the Spanish government recruited Chinese laborers to meet the strong demand for field hands in Cuba. Between 1853 and 1873, when such immigration was stopped, more than 130,000 Chinese laborers had moved to Cuba. The majority spent their lives as virtual slaves. Peruvian plantation and mine owners likewise brought in more than 100,000 workers from China in the nineteenth century, and there were similar movements of Asians elsewhere.

Emigration from Asia would undoubtedly have grown much more if planters and mine owners had been able to hire as many Asian workers as they wished. But the original European settlers, disturbed by the presence of Asians who had moved beyond the fields and mines into towns, demanded a halt to Asian immigration. In 1882, the American government instituted the Chinese Exclusion Act, and Australia followed suit in 1901 with the Immigrant Restriction Act — discriminatory laws designed to keep Asians from entering the country.

In fact, the explosion of mass mobility in the late nineteenth century, combined with the growing appeal of nationalism and scientific racism (see "Nationalism and Racism" in Chapter 23), encouraged a variety of attempts to control immigration flows and seal off national borders. National governments established strict rules for granting citizenship and asylum to foreigners. Passports and custom posts were created so state governments could monitor travelers across increasingly tight national boundaries. Such attempts were often inspired by **nativism**, beliefs that led to policies giving preferential treatment to native-born inhabitants above immigrants. Thus French nativists tried to limit the influx of Italian migrant workers, German nativists stopped Poles from crossing eastern borders, and American nativists (in the 1920s) restricted immigration from southern and eastern Europe and banned it outright from much of Asia.

A crucial factor in migration patterns before 1914 was, therefore, immigration policies that offered preferred status to "acceptable" racial and ethnic groups in the open lands of possible permanent settlement. This, too, was part of Western dominance in the increasingly lopsided world. Largely successful in monopolizing the best overseas opportunities, Europeans and people of European ancestry reaped the main benefits from the mass migration. By 1913 people in Australia, Canada, and the United States had joined the British in having the highest average incomes in the world, while incomes in Asia and Africa lagged far behind.

How did the New Imperialism change Western colonialism?

The expansion of Western society reached its apex between about 1880 and 1914. In those years, the leading European nations not only continued to send massive streams of migrants, money, and manufactured goods around the world, but also rushed to create or enlarge vast empires. This political empire building, under direct European rule, contrasted sharply with economic intervention in non-Western territories between 1816 and 1880, which had, for example, "opened" China and Japan to international trade on unequal terms but left these countries politically independent. By contrast, the direct political control of the empires of the late nineteenth century recalled the old European colonial empires of the sixteenth to eighteenth centuries. Because this renewed imperial push came after a long pause in European expansionism, contemporaries called it the **New Imperialism**.

Characterized by a frantic rush to plant the flag over as many people and as much territory as possible, the New Imperialism had momentous consequences.

By the early twentieth century almost 84 percent of the globe was dominated by European nations, and Britain alone controlled one-quarter of the earth's territory and one-third of its population. Aimed primarily at Africa and Asia, the New Imperialism created tensions among competing European states and led to wars and threats of war with non-European powers.

The European Presence in Africa Before 1880

Prior to 1880, European nations controlled only about 10 percent of Africa. The French had begun the conquest of Algeria in 1830, and by 1880 many French, Italian, and Spanish colonists had settled among the overwhelming Arab majority there. Yet the overall effect on Africa was minor.

At the southern tip of the continent, Britain had taken possession of the Dutch settlements in and around Cape Town during the wars with Napoleon Bonaparte. This takeover had led disgruntled Dutch cattle ranchers and farmers in 1835 to make their Great Trek into the interior, where they fought the Zulu and Xhosa (KO-sah) peoples for land. After 1853 the Boers, or **Afrikaners** (a-frih-KAH-nuhrz), as the descendants of the Dutch in the Cape Colony were beginning to call themselves, proclaimed their independence and defended it against British armies. By 1880 Afrikaner and British settlers, who detested each other and lived in separate areas, had wrested control of much of South Africa from the Zulu, Xhosa, and other African peoples.

In addition to the French in the north and the British and Afrikaners in the south, the Portuguese maintained a loose hold on their old possessions on the coast of West Africa in Angola and Mozambique. Elsewhere, over the great mass of the continent, Europeans did not rule.

The Berlin Conference and the Scramble for Africa

Between 1880 and 1900 the situation changed drastically. In a spectacular manifestation of the New Imperialism, Britain, France, Belgium, Germany, and Italy scrambled for African possessions as if their national livelihoods depended on it (Map 24.2). By 1900 nearly the whole continent had been carved up and placed under European rule: only Ethiopia, which fought off Italian invaders, and Liberia, which had been settled by freed slaves from the United States, remained independent.

In the complex story of the European seizure of Africa, certain events and individuals stand out. Of enormous importance was the British occupation of Egypt in 1882, which established a new model of formal political control. King Leopold II of Belgium (r. 1865–1909), an energetic, strong-willed monarch of a tiny country with a lust for distant territory, also played a crucial role. As early as 1861, he had laid out his vision of expansion: "The sea bathes our coast, the world lies before us. Steam and electricity have annihilated distance, and all the nonappropriated lands on the surface of the globe can become the field of our operations and of our success."[4]

By 1876 Leopold's expansionism focused on central Africa. He formed a financial syndicate under his personal control to send Henry M. Stanley, a sensation-seeking journalist and part-time explorer, to the Congo basin. Stanley established trading stations, signed unfair treaties with African chiefs, and planted the Belgian flag. Leopold's actions alarmed the French, who quickly sent out an expedition under

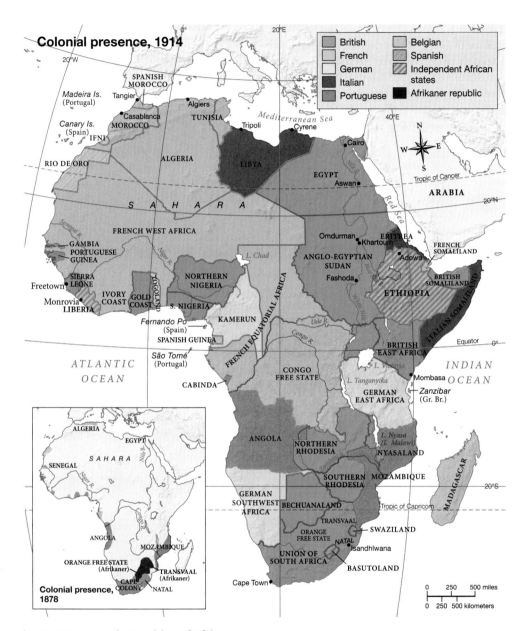

MAP 24.2 The Partition of Africa

The European powers carved up Africa after 1880 and built vast political empires. European states also seized territory in Asia in the nineteenth century, although some Asian states and peoples managed to maintain their political independence (see Map 24.3). Compare the patterns of European imperialism in Africa and Asia, using this map and Map 24.3.

Pierre de Brazza. In 1880 de Brazza signed a treaty of protection with the chief of the large Teke tribe and began to establish a French protectorate on the north bank of the Congo River.

By 1882 much of Europe had caught "African fever," and a gold-rush mentality threatened the balance of power in Europe. To lay down some basic rules for this new and dangerous global competition for territory in Africa, French statesman Jules Ferry, an ardent republican who also embraced imperialism, and German chancellor Otto von Bismarck arranged for the competitors to meet in Berlin in 1884 and 1885. The **Berlin Conference**, attended by over ten Western powers including the United States, established the principle that European claims to African territory had to rest on "effective occupation" (a strong presence on the ground) to be recognized by other states. The conference basically legitimized British claims in Egypt and southern Africa. With Bismarck's tacit approval, the French could now press southward from Algeria, eastward from their old forts on the Senegal coast, and northward from their protectorate on the Congo River to take control of parts of West and Central Africa.

At the conference, European statesmen also recognized King Leopold's personal rule over a supposedly neutral Congo Free State and agreed to work to stop slavery and the slave trade in Africa. In reality, conditions in Leopold's Congo Free State — a territory about the size of the United States east of the Mississippi River — exemplify some of the worst abuses perpetrated against native peoples by any European imperial power. Belgian colonial administrators sought to enrich themselves by harvesting Congo's ample supplies of elephant ivory and rubber, both in high demand in European markets. Africans in the Congo were coerced by the *Force Publique*, Leopold's private army, to labor in the jungle, where conditions were little better than slavery. The profits never materialized, and the *Force Publique* punished Congolese who resisted colonial demands or simply failed to meet the quotas for rubber collection by torturing, dismembering, and even murdering them.

As reports and photos of the atrocities — often collected by appalled white Christian missionaries — made their way back to Europe, a public scandal ensued. Widespread outrage and the determined efforts of the anticolonial Congo Reform Association (whose members included Mark Twain and Booker T. Washington) ultimately forced Leopold in 1908 to end his personal rule. The Congo Free State became a formal colony of the Belgian state, and the *Force Publique* was disbanded, but only after 5 to 10 million Africans had lost their lives to Leopold's mad pursuit of profit and power.

The Berlin Conference coincided with Germany's sudden emergence as an imperial power. Before about 1880, Bismarck, like many other European leaders, had seen little value in colonies. In 1884 and 1885, as nationalist agitation for colonial expansion increased, Bismarck did an abrupt about-face. Germany established protectorates over a number of small African kingdoms and tribes in Togo, the Cameroons region, southwest Africa, and, later, East Africa. Revolts against exploitative German rule in the colonies of German Southwest Africa (present-day Namibia) and German East Africa (present-day Burundi, Rwanda, and Tanzania) led to German military intervention and full-scale warfare. In German Southwest Africa, German troops massacred some 100,000 Herero and Nama Africans. Some historians see in this example of European imperialism at its worst a prelude to Nazi genocide of European Jews in the Second World War.

Atrocities on a Rubber Plantation in the Belgian Congo Native rubber workers display the severed hands of two of their countrymen murdered by plantation overseers in 1904. The white men are Baptist missionaries, who documented many such atrocities for publication by anti-imperialist critics in Europe. The "Congo Free State" controlled by the Belgians stands as one of the most violent and brutal examples of European imperialism. (Everett Collection Historical/Alamy)

The British in Africa After 1885

Meanwhile, the British began to enlarge their own African colonies, beginning at the southern tip of the African continent. Led by Cecil Rhodes (1853–1902), prime minister of Britain's Cape Colony, British colonists leapfrogged over the two Afrikaner states — the Orange Free State and the Transvaal (see Map 24.2) — in the early 1890s and established protectorates over Bechuanaland (bech-WAH-nuh-land; now Botswana) and Rhodesia (now Zimbabwe and Zambia), named in honor of its founder.

English-speaking capitalists like Rhodes developed fabulously rich gold mines in the Transvaal, and this unilateral territorial and economic expansion heightened tensions between the British and Afrikaner settlers (or Boers, descendants of Dutch colonialists). In 1899 the conflict erupted in the bloody **South African War**, or **Boer War** (1899–1902). After a series of defeats at the hands of the determined Afrikaners, the British shipped some 180,000 troops to southern Africa. Overwhelming British forces put the Afrikaners on the defensive, and they responded with an intensive guerrilla war that took two years to put down. During the fighting, both sides enlisted the support of indigenous African troops. The British forces resorted to "scorched earth" policies, burning crops and villages in Afrikaner regions, and, most notoriously, forced Afrikaners and some native Africans into concentration camps in an attempt to halt the guerrilla campaign. News of these tactics provoked liberal outrage at home in Britain.

The war ended with a British victory in 1902. In 1910 the Afrikaner-Boer territories were united with the old Cape Colony and the eastern province of Natal in a new Union of South Africa, established as a largely "self-governing" colony but still under British control. Gradually, however, the defeated Afrikaners used their numerical superiority over the British settlers to take political power, as even the most educated nonwhites lost the right to vote, except in the Cape Colony.

The British also fought to enlarge their colonies in West Africa, pushing northward from the Cape Colony, westward from Zanzibar, and southward from Egypt. In 1885 British troops stationed in the Sudanese city of Khartoum, an outpost on the Nile that protected imperial interests in Egypt, were massacred by fiercely independent Muslim Sudanese.

A decade later the British sought to establish permanent rule in Sudanese territory. Under the command of General Sir Herbert Kitchener (who would serve Britain as secretary of state for war during World War I), a well-armed force moved cautiously and more successfully up the Nile River, building a railroad to supply arms and reinforcements as it went. Finally, in 1898 these British troops confronted the poorly armed Sudanese army at the Battle of Omdurman (ahm-duhr-MAHN) (see Map 24.2). Sudanese soldiers charged the British lines time and time again, only to be cut down by the recently invented Maxim machine gun. In the solemn words of one English observer, "It was not a battle but an execution. The bodies were . . . spread evenly over acres and acres." In the end, about 10,000 Sudanese soldiers lay dead, while 28 Britons had been killed and 145 wounded.[5]

Continuing up the Nile after the battle, Kitchener's armies found that a small French force had already occupied the village of Fashoda (fuh-SHOH-duh). Locked in imperial competition with Britain ever since the British occupation of Egypt, France had tried to be first to reach one of Africa's last areas unclaimed by Europeans — the upper reaches of the Nile. The result was a serious diplomatic crisis known as the **Fashoda Incident**, which brought the threat of war between two major European powers. Wracked by the Dreyfus affair (see "Republican France and the Third French Republic" in Chapter 23) and unwilling to fight, France eventually backed down and withdrew its forces, allowing the British to take over.

The British conquest of Sudan exemplifies the general process of empire building in Africa. Like the Muslim-Sudanese force at Omdurman, or the Herero and Nama in German South West Africa, native peoples who openly resisted European control were blown away by vastly superior military force. But as the Fashoda Incident showed, however much the European powers squabbled for territory around the world, they stopped short of actually fighting one other. Imperial ambitions were not worth a great European war.

Imperialism in Asia

Although their sudden division of Africa was more spectacular, Europeans also exerted political control over much of Asia. Along with the British in India, the Dutch in present-day Indonesia were major players. In 1815 the Dutch ruled little more than the island of Java in the East Indies. Thereafter they gradually brought almost all of the three-thousand-mile Malay Archipelago under their political authority, though — in good imperialist fashion — they had to share some of the spoils with Britain and Germany. In the critical decade of the 1880s, the French under the leadership of Jules Ferry took Indochina (Map 24.3).

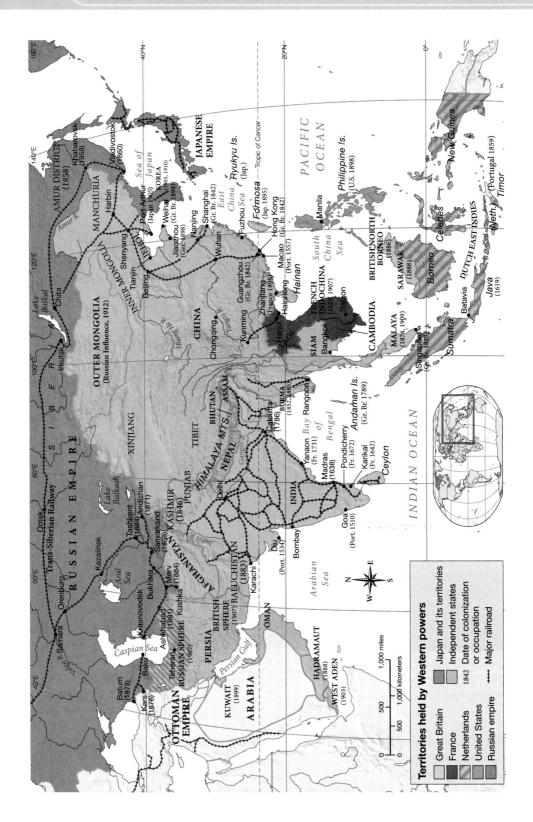

Territories held by Western powers

- Great Britain
- France
- Netherlands
- United States
- Russian empire

- Japan and its territories
- Independent states
- 1842 Date of colonization or occupation
- ⁺⁺⁺⁺ Major railroad

Russians also acquired territories in Asia, moving steadily forward on two fronts throughout the nineteenth century. To the south they conquered Muslim areas in the Caucasus and in Central Asia, reaching the border of Afghanistan in 1885. To the east they nibbled on China's outlying provinces, especially in the 1890s.

The United States likewise widened its imperialist sights, taking the Philippines from Spain in 1898 through the Spanish-American War. When it quickly became clear that the United States had no intention of granting the independence it had promised, Philippine patriots rose in revolt and were suppressed only after long, bitter fighting. Some Americans protested the taking of the Philippines, but to no avail. Thus another great Western power joined the imperialist ranks in Asia.

Causes of the New Imperialism

Many factors contributed to the late-nineteenth-century rush for empire. First, economic motives were important in the extension of political empires, especially in the British Empire. By the late 1870s France, Germany, and the United States were industrializing rapidly behind rising tariff barriers. Great Britain was losing its early economic lead and facing increasingly tough competition in foreign markets. In this changing economic climate, the seizure of Asian and African territory by continental powers in the 1880s raised alarms in Britain. Fearing that France and Germany would seal off their empires with high tariffs, resulting in the permanent loss of future economic opportunities, the British followed suit and began their own push to expand empire.

Actually, the overall economic gains of the New Imperialism proved quite limited before 1914. The new colonies were simply too poor to buy much, and they offered few immediately profitable investments. Nonetheless, even the poorest, most barren desert was jealously prized, and no territory was ever abandoned because each leading country saw colonies as crucial to national security and military power. For instance, safeguarding the Suez Canal played a key role in the British occupation of Egypt, and protecting Egypt in turn led to the bloody conquest of Sudan. Far-flung possessions guaranteed ever-growing navies the safe havens and the dependable coaling stations they needed in time of crisis or war.

Along with economic motives, many people were convinced that colonies were essential to great nations. "There has never been a great power without great colonies," concluded one French publicist. The influential nationalist historian of Germany, Heinrich von Treitschke, spoke for many when he wrote: "Every virile people has established colonial power. . . . All great nations in the fullness of their strength have desired to set their mark upon barbarian lands and those who fail to participate in this great rivalry will play a pitiable role in time to come."[6]

< **MAP 24.3 Asia in 1914**
India remained under British rule, while China preserved a precarious political independence. The Dutch Empire in modern-day Indonesia was old, but French control of Indochina was a product of the New Imperialism. Russia continued to expand to the south and to the east as well.

Treitschke's harsh statement reflects not only the increasing aggressiveness of European nationalism after Bismarck's wars of German unification, but also Social Darwinian theories of brutal competition among races and nations. The strongest nation, in this view, would always conquer the weaker in the grand race for national survival and domination. Thus European nations—in their imagined role as racially distinct representatives of the superior white race—had to seize colonies to show they were strong and powerful. Moreover, since victory of the fittest in the struggle for survival was nature's inescapable law, the conquest of "inferior" peoples was just. "The path of progress is strewn with the wreck . . . of inferior races," wrote one professor in 1900. "Yet these dead peoples are, in very truth, the stepping stones on which mankind has risen to the higher intellectual and deeper emotional life of today."[7] Social Darwinism and pseudoscientific racial doctrines fostered imperialist expansion.

So did the Western world's unprecedented technological and military superiority. Three aspects were particularly important. First, the rapidly firing Maxim machine gun, so lethal at Omdurman, was an ultimate weapon in many another unequal battle. Second, newly discovered quinine proved effective in controlling malaria, which had previously decimated whites in the tropics whenever they left breezy coastal enclaves and dared to venture into mosquito-infested interiors. Third, the steamship and the international telegraph permitted Western powers to quickly concentrate their firepower in a given area when it was needed. Never before—and never again after 1914—would the technological gap between the West and non-Western regions of the world be so great.

Attempts to manage social tensions and domestic political conflicts in Europe contributed to overseas expansion. In Germany and Russia, and in other countries to a lesser extent, conservative political leaders manipulated colonial issues to divert popular attention from the class struggle at home and to create a false sense of national unity. Thus imperial propagandists relentlessly stressed that colonies benefited workers as well as capitalists, providing jobs and cheap raw materials that raised workers' standard of living. Government leaders and their allies in the tabloid press successfully encouraged the masses to savor foreign triumphs and to glory in the supposed increase in national prestige. In short, conservative leaders defined imperialism as a national necessity, which they used to justify the status quo and their hold on power.

Finally, certain special-interest groups in each country were powerful agents of expansion. White settlers in the colonial areas demanded more land and greater state protection. Missionaries and humanitarians wanted to spread religion and stop the slave trade within Africa. Shipping companies wanted lucrative subsidies to protect rapidly growing global trade. Military men and colonial officials foresaw rapid advancement and highly paid positions in growing empires. The actions of such groups pushed the course of empire forward.

A "Civilizing Mission"

Western society did not rest the case for empire solely on naked conquest and a Darwinian racial struggle, or on power politics and the need for naval bases on every ocean. Imperialists developed additional arguments for imperialism to satisfy their consciences and answer their critics. A favorite idea was that Westerners could and should civilize more primitive nonwhite peoples. Supposedly "savage" Africans and

Asians would eventually receive the benefits of industrialization and urbanization, Western education, Christianity, advanced medicine, and finally higher standards of living. In time, they might be ready for self-government and Western democracy. Thus the French repeatedly spoke of their imperial endeavors as a sacred "civilizing mission." As one German missionary put it, prayer and hard work under German direction would lead "the work-shy native to work of his own free will" and thus lead him to "an existence fit for human beings."[8] Another argument was that imperial government protected natives from tribal warfare as well as from cruder forms of exploitation by white settlers and business people. In 1899 Rudyard Kipling (1865–1936), who wrote masterfully of Anglo-Indian life and was perhaps the most influential British author of the 1890s, summarized such ideas in his poem "The White Man's Burden."

Outside of Europe, many Americans also accepted the ideology of the **white man's burden**. It was an important factor in the decision to rule, rather than liberate, the Philippines after the Spanish-American War. Like their European counterparts, these Americans believed that their civilization had reached unprecedented heights and that they had unique benefits to bestow on supposedly less advanced peoples.

Though the colonial administrators and generals in charge of imperial endeavors were men, European women played a central role in the "civilizing mission." Europeans who embraced the "white man's burden" believed that the presence of white women in the colonies might help stop what they called "race mixing": the tendency of European men to establish relationships or cross-race marriages with indigenous women. Proponents of imperial expansion actively encouraged women to serve in the colonies, and many answered the call. Some women worked as colonial missionaries, teachers, and nurses; others accompanied their husbands overseas. If they stayed in the colonies long enough to establish a semipermanent household, European women might oversee native servants. Colonial encounters thus established complicated social hierarchies that entangled race, class, and gender.

European control also facilitated the spread of Christianity. Catholic and Protestant missionaries—both men and women—competed with Islam and native religions south of the Sahara, seeking converts and building schools. Many Africans' first real contact with whites was in mission schools. Some peoples, such as the Ibo in Nigeria, became highly Christianized.

Such occasional successes in sub-Saharan Africa contrasted with the general failure of missionary efforts in India, China, and the Islamic world. There Christians often preached in vain to peoples with ancient, complex religious beliefs. Yet the number of Christian believers around the world did increase substantially in the nineteenth century, and missionary groups kept trying.

Orientalism

Even though many Westerners felt superior to non-Western peoples, they were often fascinated by foreign cultures. In the late 1970s the literary scholar Edward Said (sigh-EED) (1935–2003) coined the term **Orientalism** to describe this fascination and the stereotypical and often racist Western understandings of non-Westerners. Said originally used "Orientalism" to refer to the way Europeans viewed Arab societies in

North Africa and the Middle East. The term caught on, however, and is often used more broadly to refer to Western views of non-Western peoples across the globe.

Said believed that it was almost impossible for people in the West to look at or understand non-Westerners without falling into an Orientalist stereotype. Politicians, scholarly experts, writers and artists, and ordinary people readily adopted "us versus them" views of foreign peoples. The West, they believed, was modern, while the non-West was primitive. The West was white, the non-West colored; the West was rational, the non-West emotional; the West was Christian, the non-West pagan or Islamic. As part of this view, Westerners imagined the Orient as a place of mystery and romance, populated with exotic, dark-skinned peoples, where Westerners might have exciting experiences of foreign societies and cultures.

Such views swept through North American and European scholarship, arts, and literature in the late nineteenth century. The emergence of ethnography and anthropology as academic disciplines in the 1880s was part of the process. Inspired by a new culture of collecting, scholars and adventurers went into the field, where they studied supposedly primitive cultures and traded for, bought, or stole artifacts from non-Western peoples. The results of their work were reported in scientific studies, articles, and books, and intriguing objects filled the display cases of new public museums of ethnography and natural history. A slew of novels published around 1900 portrayed romance and high adventure in the colonies. Artists followed suit, and dramatic paintings of ferocious Arab warriors, Eastern slave markets, and the sultan's harem adorned museum walls and wealthy middle-class parlors.

Scholars, authors, and artists were not necessarily racists or imperialists, but as Said explained, they found it difficult to escape Orientalist stereotypes. In the end they helped justify colonial expansion and spread notions of Western superiority.

European Critics of Imperialism

The expansion of empire aroused sharp, even bitter, critics. A forceful attack was made by radical English economist J. A. Hobson (1858–1940) in *Imperialism* (1902), a work that influenced Lenin and others. Deeply angered by British tactics during the unpopular South African (Boer) War, Hobson contended that the rush to acquire colonies was due to the economic needs of unregulated capitalism, particularly the need of the rich to find outlets for their surplus capital. Yet, Hobson argued, only unscrupulous special-interest groups profited from imperial possessions, at the expense of both European working-class taxpayers and indigenous peoples. Moreover, the quest for empire diverted popular attention away from domestic reform and the need to reduce the great gap between rich and poor.

Like Hobson, Marxist critics offered a thorough critique of Western imperialism. Rosa Luxemburg, a radical member of the German Social Democratic Party, argued that capitalism needed to expand into noncapitalist Asia and Africa to maintain high profits. The Russian Marxist and future revolutionary leader Vladimir Lenin concluded that imperialism represented the "highest stage" of advanced monopoly capitalism and predicted that its onset signaled the decay and coming collapse of capitalist society. These and similar arguments were not very persuasive, however. Most people then (and now) were sold on the idea that imperialism was profitable for the homeland and beneficial to the colonized.

Hobson and other critics struck home, however, with their moral condemnation of whites' imperious rule of nonwhites. They rebelled against crude Social Darwinian thought. "O Evolution, what crimes are committed in thy name!" cried one foe. Another sardonically coined a new beatitude: "Blessed are the strong, for they shall prey on the weak."[9] Kipling and his kind were lampooned as racist bullies whose rule rested on brutality, racial contempt, and the Maxim gun. Similarly, in 1902 in the novel *Heart of Darkness* — a demolishing critique of the Belgian exploitation of the Congo — Polish-born novelist Joseph Conrad (1857–1924) castigated the "pure selfishness" of Europeans in supposedly civilizing Africa. The main character, once a liberal scholar, turns into a savage brute.

Critics charged Europeans with applying a degrading double standard and failing to live up to their own noble ideals. At home, Europeans had won or were winning representative government, individual liberties, and a certain equality of opportunity. In their empires, Europeans imposed military dictatorships. Colonial administrators forced Africans and Asians to work involuntarily, almost like slaves, and subjected them to shameless discrimination. Only by renouncing imperialism, its critics insisted, and giving captive peoples the freedoms Western society had struggled for since the French Revolution would Europeans be worthy of their traditions.

How did non-Westerners respond to Western expansion?

To Africans and Asians, Western expansion was a profoundly disruptive assault on existing ruling classes, local economies, and long-standing ways of life. Christian missionaries and European secular ideologies challenged established beliefs and values. Non-Western peoples experienced imperialism as an invasion, one made all the more painful by the power and arrogance of the European intruders.

The Patterns of Response

Generally, the initial response of African and Asian rulers to aggressive Western expansion was to try to drive the unwelcome foreigners away. This was the case in China, Japan, and Sudan. Violent antiforeign reactions exploded elsewhere again and again, as in the lengthy U.S.-Indian wars, but the superior military technology of the industrialized West almost invariably prevailed. Beaten in battle, many Africans and Asians concentrated on preserving their cultural traditions at all costs. Others found themselves forced to reconsider their initial hostility. Some (such as Ismail of Egypt) concluded that the West was indeed superior in some ways and that it was therefore necessary to copy some European achievements, especially if they wished to escape full-blown Western political rule.

Thus one can think of responses to the Western impact as a spectrum, with "traditionalists" at one end, "westernizers" or "modernizers" at the other, and many shades of opinion in between. Both before and after European domination, the internal struggle among these groups was often intense. With time, however, the modernizers tended to gain the upper hand.

When the power of both the traditionalists and the modernizers was shattered by superior force, some Asians and Africans accepted imperial rule. Political participation in non-Western lands was historically limited to small elites, and ordinary people often did what their rulers told them to do. Europeans, clothed in power and convinced of their righteousness, tried to govern smoothly and effectively. At times they received considerable support from both traditionalists (local chiefs, landowners, religious leaders) and modernizers (Western-educated professional classes and civil servants).

Nevertheless, imperial rule was in many ways an imposing edifice built on sand. Support for European rule among subjugated peoples was shallow and weak. Colonized lands were primarily peasant societies, and much of the burden of colonization fell on small farmers who tenaciously fought for some measure of autonomy. When colonists demanded extra taxes or crops, peasants played dumb and hid the extent of their harvest; when colonists asked for increased labor, peasants dragged their feet. These everyday forms of evasion and resistance—termed "weapons of the weak" by one historian—stopped short of open defiance but nonetheless presented a real challenge to Western rule.[10] Moreover, leaders always arose to openly oppose the Europeans, for at least two basic reasons.

First, the nonconformists—the eventual anti-imperialist leaders—developed a burning desire for human dignity, economic emancipation, and political independence. Second, potential leaders ironically found in the Western world the ideologies underlying and justifying their protest. They discovered liberalism, with its credos of civil liberties and political self-determination. They echoed the demands of anti-imperialists in Europe and America that the West live up to its own ideals. Above all, they found themselves attracted to nationalism, which asserted that every people had the right to control its own destiny. After 1917 anti-imperialist revolt would find another European-made weapon in Lenin's version of Marxist socialism. Thus the anti-imperialist search for dignity drew strength from Western thought and culture, particularly in three major Asian countries—India, Japan, and China.

The British Empire in India

India was the jewel of the British Empire, and no colonial area experienced a more profound British impact. Unlike Japan and China, which maintained a real if precarious independence, and unlike African territories, which Europeans annexed only at the end of the nineteenth century, India was ruled more or less absolutely by Britain for a very long time.

Arriving in India on the heels of the Portuguese in the seventeenth century, the British East India Company had conquered the last independent native state by 1848. The last "traditional" response to British rule by the existing ruling groups—an attempt to drive the invaders out by military force—was broken in 1857 and 1858 in the **Great Rebellion** (which the British called a "mutiny"). This insurrection by Muslim and Hindu mercenaries in the British army spread throughout northern and central India before it was finally put down, primarily by loyal indigenous troops from southern India. Britain then established direct control until Indian independence was gained in 1947.

India was ruled by the British Parliament in London and administered by a tiny, all-white civil service in India. In 1900 this elite consisted of fewer than 3,500 top officials, who controlled a population of 300 million. The white elite, backed by white officers and indigenous troops, was competent and generally well disposed toward the welfare of the Indian population. Yet it practiced strict job discrimination and social segregation, and most of its members saw the jumble of Indian peoples and castes as racially inferior. Elite colonial administrators and military leaders like Lord Kitchener believed in the "inherent superiority of the European" in India. As Kitchener put it, "however well educated and clever a native may be, and however brave he may prove himself, I believe that no rank we can bestow on him would cause him to be considered an equal of the British officer."[11]

British women played an important part in the imperial enterprise, especially after the opening of the Suez Canal in 1869 made it much easier for civil servants and businessmen to bring their wives and children with them to India. British families tended to live in separate communities, where they occupied large houses with well-shaded porches, handsome lawns, and a multitude of servants. It was the wife's responsibility to manage this complex household. Many officials' wives learned to relish their duties, and they directed their households and servants with the same self-confident authoritarianism that characterized their husbands' political rule.

A small minority of British women—feminists, social reformers, or missionaries, both married and single—sought to go further and shoulder the "white women's burden" in India.[12] These women tried especially to improve the lives of Indian women, both Hindu and Muslim, promoting education and legislation to move them closer to the better conditions they believed Western women had attained. Their greatest success was educating some elite Hindu women who took up the cause of reform.

Inspired by the "civilizing mission" and strong feelings of racial superiority, British imperialists worked energetically to westernize Indian society. Realizing that they needed well-educated Indians to serve as skilled subordinates in both the government and the army, the British established a modern system of secondary education, with all instruction in English. Thus some Indians gained excellent opportunities for economic and social advancement. High-caste Hindus, particularly quick to respond, emerged as skillful intermediaries between the British rulers and the Indian people, and soon they formed a new elite profoundly influenced by Western thought and culture.

This new Indian elite joined British officials and businessmen to promote modern economic development, constructing irrigation projects for agriculture, building the world's third-largest railroad network, and forming large tea and jute plantations geared to the world economy. Unfortunately, the lot of the Indian masses improved little, for the profits went to indigenous and British elites.

Finally, the British created a unified, powerful state with a well-educated, English-speaking Indian bureaucracy. They placed under the same system of law and administration the different Hindu and Muslim peoples and the vanquished kingdoms of the entire subcontinent—groups that had fought each other for centuries and had been repeatedly conquered by Muslim and Mongol invaders. It was as if Europe, with its many states and varieties of Christianity, had been conquered and united in a single great empire.

The transformation of India engendered a decisive reaction to European rule: the rise of national resistance among the Indian elite. No matter how anglicized and necessary a member of the indigenous educated classes became, he or she could never become the white ruler's equal. The top jobs, the best clubs, the modern hotels, and even certain railroad compartments were off limits to Indians. Racial discrimination meant injured pride and bitter injustice. It flagrantly contradicted the cherished Western concepts of human rights and equality that the Indian elite had learned about in Western schools. Moreover, it was based on dictatorship, no matter how benign.

By 1885, when educated Indians came together to found the predominantly Hindu Indian National Congress, demands were increasing for the equality and self-government that Britain had already granted white-settler colonies, such as Canada and Australia. By 1907, emboldened in part by Japan's success (see the next section, "Reforming Japan"), a radical faction in the Indian National Congress called for Indian independence. Although Hindus and Muslims disagreed on what shape the Indian future should take, Indians were finding an answer to the foreign challenge. The experience of discriminatory British rule and exposure to liberal Western ideals, along with the revitalization of the Hindu religion and the determined resistance to colonial abuse, had created a genuine movement for national independence.

Reforming Japan

When Commodore Matthew Perry arrived in Tokyo in 1853 with his crude but effective gunboat diplomacy, Japan was a complex feudal society. At the top stood a figurehead emperor, but real power was in the hands of a hereditary military governor, the shogun. With the help of a warrior nobility known as samurai, the shogun governed a country of hard-working, productive peasants and city dwellers. The intensely proud samurai were deeply angered by the sudden American intrusion and the unequal treaties with Western countries that followed.

When foreign diplomats and merchants began to settle in Yokohama, radical samurai reacted with a wave of antiforeign terrorism and antigovernment assassinations that lasted from 1858 to 1863. In response, American, British, Dutch, and French warships demolished key forts, further weakening the power and prestige of the shogun's government. Then in 1867 a coalition led by patriotic samurai seized control of the government with hardly any bloodshed and restored the political power of the emperor in the **Meiji Restoration**, a great turning point in Japanese history.

The battle cry of the Meiji (MAY-jee) reformers was "Enrich the state and strengthen the armed forces," and their immediate goal was to meet the foreign threat. Yet how were these tasks to be accomplished? In a remarkable about-face, the leaders of Meiji Japan dropped their antiforeign attacks. Convinced that Western civilization was indeed superior in its military and industrial aspects, they initiated a series of measures to reform Japan along modern lines. In the broadest sense, the Meiji leaders tried to harness Western models of industrialization and political reform to protect their country and catch up with Europe.

In 1871 the new leaders abolished the old feudal structure of aristocratic, decentralized government and formed a strong unified state. Following the example of the French Revolution, they dismantled the four-class legal system and declared social equality. They decreed freedom of movement in a country where traveling abroad had been a serious crime. They created a free, competitive, government-stimulated economy. Japan began to build railroads and modern factories. In addition, Japan skillfully adapted the West's science and technology, particularly in industry, medicine, and education, and many Japanese studied abroad. The government paid large salaries to attract foreign experts, who were replaced by trained Japanese as soon as possible.

Yet the overriding concern of Japan's political leadership was always to maintain a powerful state and a strong military. State leaders created a powerful modern navy and completely reorganized the army along European lines, forming a professional officer corps and requiring three years of military service of all males. This army of draftees effectively put down disturbances in the countryside, and in 1877 it crushed a major rebellion by feudal elements protesting the loss of their privileges.

By 1890, when the new state was firmly established, the wholesale borrowing of the early restoration had given way to a more selective emphasis on those things foreign that were in keeping with Japanese tradition. Following the model of the German Empire, Japan established an authoritarian constitution and rejected democracy. The power of the emperor and his ministers was vast, that of the legislature limited.

Japan also successfully copied the imperialism of Western society. Expansion proved that Japan was strong and cemented the nation together in a great mission. Having "opened" Korea with its own gunboat diplomacy in 1876, Japan decisively defeated China in the Sino-Japanese War fought over Korean territory in 1894 and 1895 and took Formosa (modern-day Taiwan). In the next years, Japan competed aggressively with European powers for influence and territory in China, particularly in Manchuria, where Japanese and Russian imperialism collided. In 1904 Japan launched the Russo-Japanese War (1904–1905) by attacking Russia without a formal declaration of war. After a series of bloody battles, Japan took over Russia's former protectorate in Port Arthur and emerged with a valuable foothold in China (see Map 24.3). By 1910, with the annexation of Korea, Japan had become a major imperial power.

Japan became the first non-Western country to combine European-style economic and political reforms with its own long-standing values and traditions in order to meet the many-sided challenge of Western expansion. Moreover, Japan demonstrated that a modern Asian nation could defeat and humble Russia, a great Western power. Japan's achievement fascinated many Chinese and Vietnamese nationalists and provided patriots throughout Asia and Africa with an inspiring example of national recovery and liberation.

Toward Revolution in China

In 1860 the two-hundred-year-old Qing Dynasty in China appeared on the verge of collapse. Efforts to repel foreigners had failed, and rebellion and chaos wracked the country. Yet the government drew on its traditional strengths and made a surprising comeback that lasted more than thirty years.

Two factors were crucial in this reversal. First, the traditional ruling groups temporarily produced new and effective leadership. Loyal scholar-statesmen and generals quelled disturbances such as the great Tai Ping rebellion. The remarkable empress dowager Tzu Hsi (tsoo shee) governed in the name of her young son, combining shrewd insight with vigorous action to revitalize the bureaucracy.

Second, destructive foreign aggression lessened, for the Europeans had obtained their primary goal of establishing commercial and diplomatic relations. Indeed, some

Demonizing the Boxer Rebellion
The Sunday supplement to *Le Petit Parisien*, a popular French newspaper, ran a series of gruesome front-page pictures of ferocious Boxers burning buildings, murdering priests, and slaughtering Chinese Christians. In this 1910 illustration, Boxer rebels invade a church in Mukden, Manchuria, and massacre the Christian worshippers. Whipping up European outrage about Chinese atrocities was a prelude to harsh reprisals by the Western powers. (Print Collector/Getty Images)

Europeans contributed to the dynasty's recovery. A talented Irishman effectively reorganized China's customs office, increasing government tax receipts, and a sympathetic American diplomat represented China in foreign lands, helping to strengthen the Chinese government. Such efforts dovetailed with the dynasty's efforts to adopt some aspects of Western government and technology while maintaining traditional Chinese values and beliefs.

This parallel movement toward domestic reform and limited cooperation with the West collapsed under the blows of Japanese imperialism. Defeat in the Sino-Japanese War (1894–1895) and the subsequent harsh peace treaty revealed China's helplessness in the face of aggression, triggering a rush by foreign powers for concessions and protectorates. At the high point of this rush in 1898, it appeared that the European powers might actually divide China among themselves, as they had recently divided Africa. Probably only the jealousy each nation felt toward its imperialist competitors saved China from partition. In any event, the tempo of foreign encroachment greatly accelerated after 1894.

China's precarious position after the war with Japan led to a renewed drive for fundamental reforms. Like the leaders of the Meiji Restoration, some modernizers saw salvation in Western institutions. In 1898 they convinced the young emperor to launch a desperate **hundred days of reform** in an attempt to meet the foreign challenge. More radical reformers, such as the revolutionary Sun Yatsen (1866–1925), who came from the peasantry and was educated in Hawaii by Christian missionaries, sought to overthrow the dynasty altogether and establish a republic.

The efforts at radical reform by the young emperor and his allies threatened the Qing establishment and the empress dowager Tzu Hsi, who had dominated the court for a quarter of a century. In a palace coup, she and her supporters imprisoned the emperor, rejected the reform movement, and put reactionary officials in charge. Hope for reform from above was crushed.

A violent antiforeign reaction swept the country, encouraged by the Qing court and led by a secret society that foreigners called the Boxers. The patriotic Boxers blamed China's ills on foreigners, charging foreign missionaries with undermining reverence for ancestors and thereby threatening the Chinese family and the society as a whole. In the agony of defeat and unwanted reforms, the Boxers and other secret societies struck out at their enemies. In northeastern China, more than two hundred foreign missionaries and several thousand Chinese Christians were killed, prompting threats and demands from Western governments. The empress dowager answered by declaring war on the foreign powers, hoping that the Boxers might help limit European influence and control.

The imperialist response was swift and harsh. After the Boxers besieged the embassy quarter in Beijing, foreign governments (including Japan, Britain, France, Germany, and the United States) organized an international force of twenty thousand soldiers to rescue their diplomats and punish China. These troops defeated the Boxers and occupied and plundered Beijing. In 1901 China was forced to accept a long list of penalties, including a heavy financial indemnity payable over forty years.

The years after this heavy defeat were ever more troubled. Anarchy and foreign influence spread as the power and prestige of the Qing Dynasty declined still further. Antiforeign, antigovernment revolutionary groups agitated and plotted. Finally, in 1912 a spontaneous uprising toppled the Qing Dynasty. After thousands of years of emperors, a loose coalition of revolutionaries proclaimed a Western-style republic and called for an elected parliament. The transformation of China under the impact of expanding Western society entered a new phase, and the end was not in sight.

NOTES

1. Quoted in J. W. Hall, *Japan: From Prehistory to Modern Times* (New York: Delacorte Press, 1970), p. 250.
2. Quoted in Earl of Cromer, *Modern Egypt* (London, 1911), p. 48.
3. Quoted in Brooke Hauser, *The New Kids: Big Dreams and Brave Journeys at a High School for Immigrant Teens* (New York: Free Press, 2011), title page.
4. Quoted in W. L. Langer, *European Alliances and Alignments, 1871–1890* (New York: Vintage Books, 1931), p. 290.
5. Quoted in J. Ellis, *The Social History of the Machine Gun* (New York: Pantheon Books, 1975), pp. 86, 101. The numbers given for British casualties at the Battle of Omdurman vary; the total casualties quoted here come from an original British army report. See Lieutenant General H. M. L. Rundle, M.G., Chief of Staff, "Herewith Returns of Killed and Wounded of the Expeditionary Force at the Battle of Khartum, on September 2, 1898," Khartum, September 9, 1898, at North East Medals, http://www.britishmedals.us/kevin/other/lgomdurman.html.
6. Quoted in G. H. Nadel and P. Curtis, eds., *Imperialism and Colonialism* (New York: Macmillan, 1964), p. 94.
7. Quoted in W. L. Langer, *The Diplomacy of Imperialism*, 2d ed. (New York: Alfred A. Knopf, 1951), pp. 86, 88.
8. Quoted in S. Conrad, *Globalisation and the Nation in Imperial Germany* (New York: Cambridge University Press, 2010), p. 78.
9. Quoted in Langer, *The Diplomacy of Imperialism*, p. 88.
10. J. C. Scott, *Weapons of the Weak: Everyday Forms of Peasant Resistance* (New Haven, Conn.: Yale University Press, 1985), p. xvi.

11. Quoted in K. M. Panikkar, *Asia and Western Dominance: A Survey of the Vasco da Gama Epoch of Asian History* (London: George Allen & Unwin, 1959), p. 116.

12. A. Burton, "The White Women's Burden: British Feminists and 'The Indian Women,' 1865–1915," in *Western Women and Imperialism: Complicity and Resistance*, ed. N. Chaudri and M. Strobel (Bloomington: Indiana University Press, 1992), pp. 137–157.

LOOKING BACK **LOOKING AHEAD**

In the early twentieth century educated Europeans had good reason to believe that they were living in an age of progress. The largest wave of mass migration in human history had spread Europeans and their ideas around the world, even as it relieved social pressures at home. The ongoing triumphs of industry and science and the steady improvements in the standard of living beginning about 1850 were undeniable, and it was generally assumed that these favorable trends would continue. There had also been progress in the political realm. The bitter class conflicts that culminated in the bloody civil strife of 1848 had given way in most European countries to stable nation-states with elected legislative bodies that responded to real problems and enjoyed popular support. Moreover, there had been no general European war since Napoleon's defeat in 1815. Only the brief, limited wars connected with German and Italian unification at midcentury had broken the peace in the European heartland.

In the global arena, peace was much more elusive. In the name of imperialism, Europeans (and North Americans) used war and the threat of war to open markets and punish foreign governments around the world. Although criticized by some intellectuals and leftists such as J. A. Hobson, these foreign campaigns resonated with European citizens and stimulated popular nationalism. Like fans in a sports bar, the peoples of Europe followed their colonial teams and cheered them on to victories that were almost certain. Thus imperialism and nationalism reinforced and strengthened each other in Europe, especially after 1875.

This was a dangerous development. Easy imperialist victories over weak states and poorly armed non-Western peoples encouraged excessive pride and led Europeans to underestimate the fragility of their accomplishments as well as the murderous power of their weaponry. Imperialism also made nationalism more aggressive and militaristic. At the same time that European imperialism was dividing the world, the leading European states were also dividing themselves into two opposing military alliances. Thus when the two armed camps stumbled into war in 1914, there would be a superabundance of nationalistic fervor, patriotic sacrifice, and cataclysmic destruction.

MAKE CONNECTIONS

Think about the larger developments and continuities within and across chapters.

1. How did the expansion of European empires transform everyday life around the world?

2. Historians often use the term *New Imperialism* to describe the globalization of empire that began in the later nineteenth century. Was the New Imperialism really that different from earlier waves of European expansion (Chapters 14 and 17)?

3. In what ways does the global impact of European imperialism in the late nineteenth century continue to shape world relations and conflicts today?

Chapter 24 Review

IDENTIFY KEY TERMS

Identify and explain the significance of each item below.

neo-Europes (p. 718)

Opium Wars (p. 720)

gunboat diplomacy (p. 721)

global mass migration (p. 723)

nativism (p. 728)

New Imperialism (p. 728)

Afrikaners (p. 729)

Berlin Conference (p. 731)

South African (Boer) War (p. 732)

Fashoda Incident (p. 733)

white man's burden (p. 737)

Orientalism (p. 737)

Great Rebellion (p. 740)

Meiji Restoration (p. 742)

hundred days of reform (p. 744)

REVIEW THE MAIN IDEAS

Answer the section heading questions from the chapter.

1. What were the global consequences of European industrialization? (p. 716)

2. How was massive migration an integral part of Western expansion? (p. 723)

3. How did the New Imperialism change Western colonialism? (p. 728)

4. How did non-Westerners respond to Western expansion? (p. 739)

CHRONOLOGY

1805–1848	• Muhammad Ali modernizes Egypt
1839–1842	• First Opium War; Treaty of Nanking
1853	• U.S. Commodore Perry "opens" Japan for trade
1856–1860	• Second Opium War
1857–1858	• Britain crushes Great Rebellion in India
1867	• Meiji Restoration in Japan
1869	• Suez Canal opens
1880–1900	• Most of Africa falls under European rule
1884–1885	• Berlin Conference settles European imperial claims in Africa
1894–1895	• China defeated in Sino-Japanese War
1898	• United States takes over Philippines; hundred days of reform in China; Battle of Omdurman; Fashoda Incident
1899–1902	• South African (Boer) War
1900–1910	• High point of European immigration
1902	• Conrad publishes *Heart of Darkness*; Hobson publishes *Imperialism*
1904–1905	• Russo-Japanese War
1914	• Panama Canal opens; outbreak of World War I

25

War and Revolution

1914–1919

CHAPTER PREVIEW

- What caused the outbreak of the First World War?

- How did the First World War differ from previous wars?

- In what ways did the war transform life on the home front?

- Why did world war lead to a successful Communist revolution in Russia?

- What were the benefits and costs of the postwar peace settlement?

IN THE SUMMER OF 1914 the nations of Europe went willingly to war, confidently expecting a short war leading to a decisive victory after which life would return to normal. Instead, the First World War was long, indecisive, and tremendously destructive. To the shell-shocked generation of survivors, it was known simply as the Great War because of its unprecedented scope and intensity.

From today's perspective, it is clear that the First World War was closely connected to the ideals and developments of the previous century. Industrialization, which promised a rising standard of living, also produced horrendous weapons that killed and maimed millions. Imperialism, which promised to civilize those the Europeans considered savages, led to intractable international conflicts. Nationalism, which promised to bring compatriots together in a harmonious nation-state, encouraged hateful prejudice and chauvinism. The extraordinary violence of world war shook nineteenth-century idealism to its core.

The war would have an enormous impact on European society. The need to provide extensive supplies and countless soldiers created mass suffering, encouraged the rise of the bureaucratic state, and brought women in increasing numbers into the workplace. Millions were killed or wounded at the front, and millions more grieved these losses. Grand states collapsed: the Russian, Austro-Hungarian, and Ottoman Empires passed into history. The trauma of war also contributed to the rise of extremist politics that would ultimately lead to yet another world war.

What caused the outbreak of the First World War?

Historians have long debated why Europeans so readily pursued a war that was long and costly and failed to resolve the problems faced by the combatant nations. There was no single most important cause. Growing competition over colonies and world markets, a belligerent arms race, and a series of diplomatic crises sharpened international tensions. On the home front, new forms of populist nationalism strengthened people's unquestioning belief in "my country right or wrong" while ongoing domestic conflicts encouraged governments to pursue aggressive foreign policies in attempts to bolster national unity. All helped pave the road to war.

Growing International Conflict

The First World War began, in part, because European statesmen failed to resolve the diplomatic problems created by Germany's rise to Great Power status. The Franco-Prussian War and the unification of Germany opened a new era in international relations. By the war's end in 1871, France was defeated, and Bismarck had made Prussia-Germany the most powerful nation in Europe (see "The Franco-Prussian War and German Unification" in Chapter 23). After 1871 Bismarck declared that Germany was a "satisfied" power. Within Europe, he stated, Germany had no territorial ambitions and wanted only peace.

But how was peace to be preserved? Bismarck's first concern was to keep France—bitter over its defeat and the loss of Alsace and Lorraine—diplomatically isolated and without allies. His second concern was the threat to peace posed by the enormous multinational empires of Austria-Hungary and Russia, particularly in southeastern Europe, where the waning strength of the Ottoman Empire had created a threatening power vacuum in the disputed border territories of the Balkans.

Bismarck's accomplishments were effective, but only temporary. From 1871 to the late 1880s, he maintained German leadership in international affairs, and he signed a series of defensive alliances with Austria-Hungary and Russia designed to isolate France. Yet in 1890 the new emperor Wilhelm II dismissed Bismarck, in part because he disagreed with the chancellor's friendly policy toward Russia. Wilhelm II was an impulsive and bombastic leader, given to making bold and tactless statements on sensitive international affairs, and under his leadership Bismarck's carefully planned alliance system began to unravel. Germany refused to renew a nonaggression pact with Russia, the centerpiece of Bismarck's system, in spite of Russian willingness to do so. This fateful move prompted long-isolated republican France to court absolutist Russia, offering loans, arms, and diplomatic support. In early 1894 France and Russia became military allies. As a result, continental Europe was divided into two rival blocs. The **Triple Alliance** of Austria, Germany, and Italy faced an increasingly hostile Dual Alliance of Russia and France, and the German general staff began secret preparations for a war on two fronts (Map 25.1).

As rivalries deepened on the continent, Great Britain's foreign policy became increasingly crucial. After 1891 Britain was the only uncommitted Great Power. Many Germans and some Britons felt that the industrially advanced, ethnically related Germanic and Anglo-Saxon peoples were natural allies. However, the good relations that had prevailed between Prussia and Great Britain since the mid-eighteenth century gave way to a bitter Anglo-German rivalry.

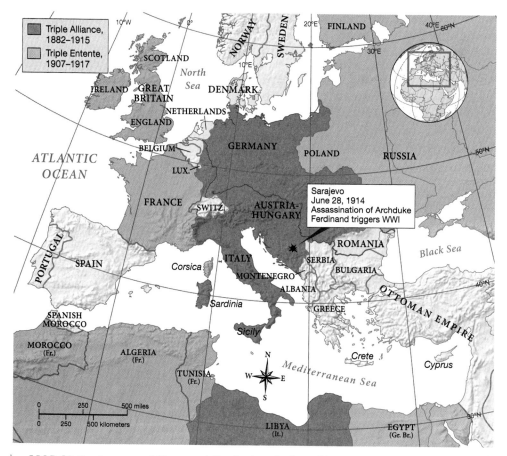

MAP 25.1   European Alliances at the Outbreak of World War I, 1914
At the start of World War I, Europe was divided into two hostile alliances: the Triple Entente of Britain, France, and Russia, and the Triple Alliance of Germany, Austria-Hungary, and Italy. Italy never fought with the Triple Alliance but instead joined the Entente in 1915.

There were several reasons for this ill-fated development. Commercial competition in world markets between Germany and Great Britain increased sharply in the 1890s, as Germany became a great industrial power. Germany's ambitious pursuit of colonies further threatened British interests. Above all, Germany's decision in 1900 to expand its battle fleet posed a challenge to Britain's long-standing naval supremacy. In response to German expansion, British leaders prudently shored up their exposed global position with alliances and agreements. Britain improved its often-strained relations with the United States, concluded an alliance with Japan in 1902, and allied with France in the Anglo-French Entente of 1904, which settled all outstanding colonial disputes between the two countries.

Alarmed by Britain's closer ties to France, Germany's leaders decided to test the strength of their alliance. In 1905 Wilhelm II declared that Morocco—where France had colonial interests—was an independent, sovereign state and demanded that Germany receive the same trading rights as France. In March the German emperor paid a surprise visit to Tangier on the Moroccan coast, toured the city on a white stallion, and declared his support for Moroccan independence. This rather awkward proclamation initiated an international crisis that almost led to war between Germany and France. Then Wilhelm II insisted on an international conference in hopes that his saber rattling would settle the Moroccan question to Germany's benefit. But his crude bullying only brought France and Britain closer together, and Germany left the conference empty-handed.

The result of the First Moroccan Crisis in 1905 was something of a diplomatic revolution. Britain, France, Russia, and even the United States began to see Germany as a potential threat. At the same time, German leaders began to see sinister plots to encircle Germany and block its development as a world power. In 1907 Russia, battered by its disastrous war with Japan and the revolution of 1905, agreed to settle its quarrels with Great Britain in Persia and Central Asia and signed the Anglo-Russian Agreement. This agreement laid the foundation of the **Triple Entente** (ahn-TAHNT), an alliance between Britain, Russia, and France.

Animosity between the German-led Triple Alliance and the Triple Entente sharpened in 1911, when French troops went into the Moroccan hinterland to put down an anticolonial rebellion and Germany sent a gunboat to a Moroccan port in response. International agreements to resolve this Second Moroccan Crisis allowed France to claim Morocco as a permanent protectorate and gave Germany some territorial concessions in the Congo, but the Triple Entente viewed Germany as a worrisome aggressor.

Germany's decision to expand its navy with a large, enormously expensive fleet of big-gun battleships, known as "dreadnoughts" because of their great size and power, heightened international tensions. German patriots saw a large navy as the legitimate right of a grand world power and as a source of national pride. But British leaders saw the German buildup as a military challenge that forced them to spend the "People's Budget" (see "Great Britain and Ireland" in Chapter 23) on battleships rather than social welfare. In 1909 the London *Daily Mail* hysterically informed its readers that "Germany is deliberately preparing to destroy the British Empire."[1] By then Britain had sided psychologically, if not officially, with France and Russia, and the leading nations of Europe were divided into two hostile camps, both ill-prepared to deal with growing international tensions (see Map 25.1).

The Mood of 1914

Diplomatic rivalries and international crises played key roles in the rush to war, but a complete understanding of the war's origins requires an account of the "mood of 1914"—the attitudes and convictions of Europeans around 1914.[2] Widespread militarism and nationalism encouraged leaders and citizens alike to see international relations as an arena for the testing of national power, with war if necessary.

Germany was especially famous for its powerful and aggressive army, but military institutions played a prominent role in affairs of state and in the lives of ordinary people across Europe. In a period marked by diplomatic tensions, politicians relied on generals and military experts to help shape public policy. All the Great Powers built up their armed forces and designed mobilization plans to rush men and weapons to the field of battle. Universal conscription in Germany, France, Italy, Austria-Hungary, and Russia—only Britain still relied on a volunteer army—exposed hundreds of thousands of young men each year to military culture and discipline.

The continent had not experienced a major conflict since the Franco-Prussian War (1870–1871), so Europeans vastly underestimated the destructive potential of modern weapons. Encouraged by the patriotic national press, many believed that war was glorious, manly, and heroic. If they expected another conflict, they thought it would be over quickly. Leading politicians and intellectuals likewise portrayed war as a test of strength that would lead to national unity and renewal. Such ideas permeated European society. As one German volunteer wrote in his diary as he left for the front in 1914, "this war is a challenge for our time and for each individual, a test by fire, that we may ripen into manhood, become men able to cope with the coming stupendous years and events."[3]

Support for military values was closely linked to a growing sense of popular nationalism, the notion that one's country was superior to all others. Since the 1850s the spread of the idea that members of an ethnic group should live together in a homogeneous, united nation-state had provoked all kinds of international conflicts over borders and citizenship rights. Nationalism drove the spiraling arms race and the struggle over colonies. Broad popular commitment to national interests above all else weakened groups that thought in terms of international communities and consequences. Expressions of antiwar sentiment by socialists, pacifists, and women's groups were seen as a betrayal of country in time of need. Inspired by nationalist beliefs, much of the population was ready for war.

Leading statesmen had practical reasons for promoting militarism and nationalism. Political leaders had long used foreign adventurism and diplomatic posturing to distract the people from domestic conflicts. In Great Britain, leaders faced civil war in Northern Ireland and a vocal and increasingly radical women's movement. In Russia, defeat in the Russo-Japanese War (1904–1905) and the revolution of 1905 had greatly weakened support for the tsarist regime. In Germany, the victory of the Marxist Social Democratic Party in the parliamentary elections of 1912 led government authorities to worry that the country was falling apart. The French likewise faced domestic labor and budget problems.

Determined to hold on to power and frightened by rising popular movements, ruling classes across Europe were willing to gamble on diplomatic brinksmanship and even war to postpone dealing with intractable social and political conflicts. Victory promised to preserve the privileged positions of elites and rally the masses behind the national cause. The patriotic nationalism bolstered by the outbreak of war did bring unity in the short run, but the wealthy governing classes underestimated the risk of war to themselves. They had forgotten that great wars and great social revolutions very often go hand in hand.

The July Crisis and the Outbreak of War

On June 28, 1914, Archduke Franz Ferdinand, heir to the Austro-Hungarian throne, was assassinated by a Serbian revolutionary during a state visit to the Bosnian capital of Sarajevo (sar-uh-YAY-voh). After failed attempts to bomb the archduke's motor-cade, Gavrilo Princip, a fanatical member of the radical group the Black Hand, shot the archduke and his wife, Sophie, in their automobile. After his capture, Princip remained defiant: "I am a Yugoslav nationalist, aiming for the unification of all Yugoslavs, and I do not care what form of state, but it must be free from Austria."[4]

Princip's deed, in the crisis-ridden borderlands between the weakened Ottoman and Austro-Hungarian Empires, led Europe into world war. In the early years of the twentieth century, war in the Balkans — "the powder keg of Europe" — seemed inevitable. Between 1900 and 1914 the Western powers had successfully forced the Ottoman rulers to give up their European territories. Serbs, Bulgarians, Albanians, and others now sought to consolidate their independent nation-states in the redrawn map of southeastern Europe, and the threat of wars loomed (Map 25.2).

Independent Serbia was eager to build a state that would include all ethnic Serbs and was thus openly hostile to Austria-Hungary and the Ottoman Empire, since both states included substantial Serbian minorities. To block Serbian expansion, Austria in 1908 annexed the territories of Bosnia and Herzegovina (hehrt-suh-goh-VEE-nuh). The southern part of the Austro-Hungarian Empire now included an even larger Serbian population. Serb leaders expressed rage but could do nothing without support from Russia, their traditional ally.

The tensions in the Balkans soon erupted into regional warfare. In the First Balkan War (1912), Serbia joined Greece and Bulgaria to attack the Ottoman Empire and then quarreled with Bulgaria over the spoils of victory. In the Second Balkan War (1913), Bulgaria attacked its former allies. Austria intervened and forced Serbia to give up Albania. After centuries, nationalism had finally destroyed the Ottoman Empire in Europe. Encouraged by their success against the Ottomans, Balkan nationalists increased their demands for freedom from Austria-Hungary. The leaders of that multinational empire viewed such demands as a serious threat.

Within this complex context, the assassination of Archduke Franz Ferdinand instigated a five-week period of intense diplomatic activity known as the July Crisis. The leaders of Austria-Hungary concluded that Serbia was implicated in the assassination and deserved severe punishment. On July 23 Austria-Hungary gave Serbia an unconditional ultimatum that would violate Serbian sovereignty. When Serbia replied moderately but evasively, Austria mobilized its armies and declared war on Serbia on July 28. In this way, multinational Austria-Hungary, desperate to save its empire, deliberately chose war to stem the rising tide of hostile nationalism within its borders.

Commitments made under the existing alliance system helped turn a little war into a world war. Bethmann-Hollweg, the German chancellor, promised Austria-Hungary that Germany would "faithfully stand by" its ally in case of war. This "blank check" of unconditional support encouraged the prowar faction in Vienna to take a

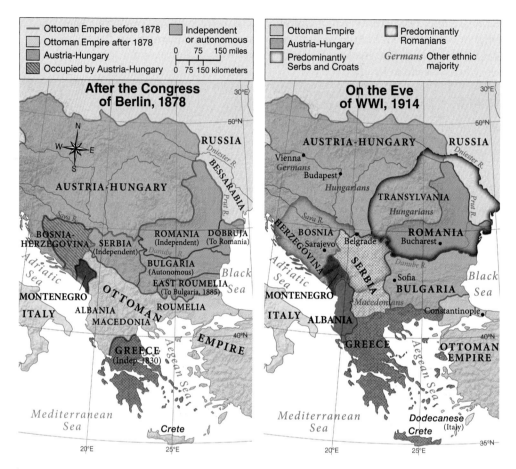

MAP 25.2 The Balkans, 1878–1914

After the Congress of Berlin in 1878, the Ottoman Empire suffered large territorial losses but remained a power in the Balkans. By 1914 Ottoman control had given way to ethnic population groups that flowed across political boundaries, and growing Serbian national aspirations threatened Austria-Hungary.

hard line against the Serbs, at a time when moderation might still have limited the crisis. At the same time, Serbia's traditional ally Russia—backed by France—encouraged the Serbs to refuse Austrian demands. Such decisions made the outbreak of war almost inevitable.

The complicated diplomatic situation spiraled out of control as military plans and timetables began to dictate policy. Vast Russia required much more time to mobilize its armies than did Germany and Austria-Hungary. And since the complicated mobilization plans of the Russian general staff assumed a two-front war with both Austria and Germany, Russia could not mobilize against one without mobilizing against the other. Therefore, on July 29 Tsar Nicholas II ordered full mobilization, which in effect declared war on both Austria-Hungary and Germany; formal declarations of war among the combatant nations followed over the next few days.

The German general staff had long thought in terms of a two-front war. Their misguided **Schlieffen Plan** called for a quick victory over France after a lightning attack through neutral Belgium—the quickest way to reach Paris—before turning on Russia. On August 3 German armies invaded Belgium. Great Britain, infuriated by the German violation of Belgian neutrality, declared war on Germany the following day.

The speed of the July Crisis created shock, panic, and excitement. In the final days of July and the first few days of August, massive crowds thronged the streets of Paris, London, St. Petersburg, Berlin, and Vienna, seeking news and shouting prowar slogans. Events proceeded rapidly, and those who opposed the war could do little to prevent its arrival. In a little over a month, a limited Austrian-Serbian war had become a European-wide conflict, and the First World War had begun.

How did the First World War differ from previous wars?

When the Germans invaded Belgium in August 1914, they and many others thought that the war would be short and relatively painless. Many sincerely believed that "the boys will be home by Christmas." They were wrong. On the western front in France and the eastern front in Russia, and on the borders of the Ottoman Empire, the belligerent armies bogged down in a new and extremely costly kind of war, later labeled **total war** by German general Erich Ludendorff. Total war meant new roles for soldiers and civilians alike. At the front, it meant lengthy, deadly battles fought with all the destructive weapons a highly industrialized society could produce. At home, national economies were geared toward the war effort. Governments revoked civil liberties, and many civilians lost lives or livelihoods as occupying armies moved through their towns and cities. The struggle expanded outside Europe, and the Middle East, Africa, East Asia, and the United States were all brought into the maelstrom.

Stalemate and Slaughter on the Western Front

In the face of the German invasion, the Belgian army defended its homeland and fell back in good order to join a rapidly landed British army corps near the Franco-Belgian border. At the same time, Russian armies attacked eastern Germany, forcing the Germans to transfer much-needed troops to the east. Instead of quickly capturing Paris as per the Schlieffen Plan, by the end of August dead-tired German soldiers were advancing slowly along an enormous front in the scorching summer heat. Afraid that armed Belgian partisans (called *francs-tireurs*) were attacking German troops behind the lines, the German occupiers dealt harshly with local resistance. German soldiers executed civilians suspected of joining the partisans and, in an out-of-control tragedy, burned the medieval core of the Belgian city of Louvain. Entente propaganda made the most of the German "Rape of Belgium" and the atrocities committed by German troops.

On September 6 the French attacked a gap in the German line in the Battle of the Marne. For three days, France threw everything into the attack. At one point, the French government desperately requisitioned all the taxis of Paris to rush reserves to the front. Finally, the Germans fell back. France had been miraculously saved (Map 25.3).

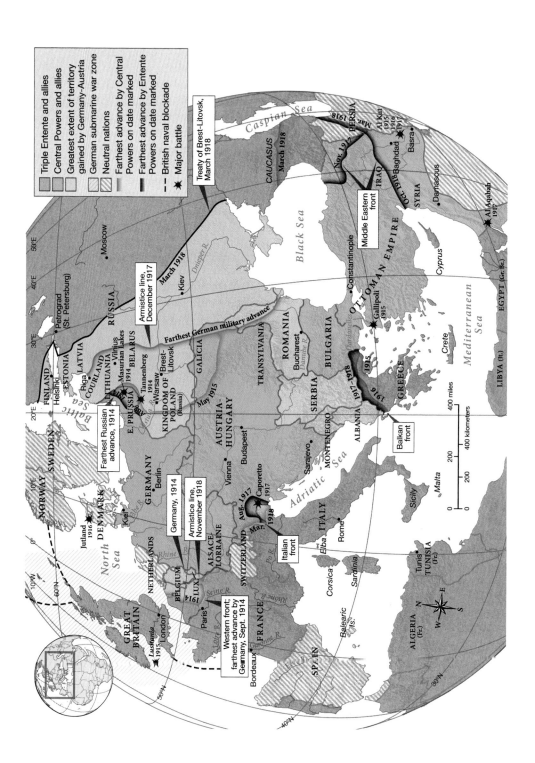

Triple Entente and allies

Central Powers and allies

Greatest extent of territory gained by Germany-Austria

German submarine war zone

Neutral nations

Farthest advance by Central Powers on date marked

Farthest advance by Entente Powers on date marked

British naval blockade

Major battle

Treaty of Brest-Litovsk, March 1918

"Greetings from the trenches." This German postcard shows three soldiers writing letters to their loved ones at home; the card was probably produced on a small, frontline printing press, for quick use by soldiers in the field. The post was typically the only connection between soldiers and their relatives, and over 28 billion pieces of mail passed between home and front on all sides during the war. (photo: Sammlung Sauer/picturealliance/ZB/akg-images)

Ein Gruss aus dem Schützengraben.

With the armies stalled, both sides began to dig trenches to protect themselves from machine-gun fire. By November 1914 an unbroken line of four hundred miles of defensive positions extended along the western front, from the Belgian coast through northern France and on to the Swiss frontier. Armies on both sides dug in behind rows of trenches, mines, and barbed wire.

The cost in lives of **trench warfare** was staggering, the gains in territory minuscule. Conditions in the trenches were atrocious. Enlisted men rotated in and out of position, at best spending two weeks at base, two weeks in reserve positions, and two weeks in the trenches. They had little leave time to visit loved ones at home, though they exchanged billions of letters and postcards with friends and family. At the front, mud and vermin, bad food, damp and cold, and wretched living quarters were the norm. Soldiers spent most of their time repairing rough trenches and dugouts and standing watch for an enemy they rarely saw.

During combat, recently invented weapons, the products of the industrial age, made battle impersonal, traumatic, and extremely deadly. The machine gun, hand grenades, poison gas, flamethrowers, long-range artillery, the airplane, and the tank were all used to murderous effect. Military units were often decimated in poorly planned frontal assaults, and comrades could rarely retrieve the wounded and dead

< MAP 25.3   **World War I in Europe and the Middle East, 1914–1918**
Trench warfare on the western front was concentrated in Belgium and northern France, while the war in the east and the Ottoman Empire encompassed an enormous territory.

from no-man's land between the lines. Bodies, mangled by high explosives, were ground into the mud and disappeared, or became part of the earthworks themselves.

The leading generals of the combatant nations, who had learned military tactics and strategy in the nineteenth century, struggled to understand trench warfare. For four years they mostly repeated the same mistakes, mounting massive offensives designed to achieve decisive breakthroughs. Brutal frontal assaults against highly fortified trenches might overrun the enemy's frontline, but because of the extent of the defensive trench system, attacking soldiers rarely captured any substantial territory. The French and British offensives of 1915 never gained more than three miles of territory. In 1916 the German campaign against Verdun left over 700,000 soldiers killed or wounded and ended with the combatants in their original positions. The results in 1917 were little better. In hard-fought battles on all fronts, millions of young men were wounded or died for no real gain.

The Battle of the Somme, a great British offensive undertaken in the summer of 1916 in northern France, exemplified the horrors of trench warfare. The battle began with a weeklong heavy artillery bombardment on the German lines, intended to cut the barbed wire fortifications, decimate the enemy trenches, and prevent the Germans from making an effective defense. For seven days and nights, the British artillery fired nonstop on the German lines, delivering about 1.5 million shells. On July 1 the British went "over the top," climbing out of the trenches and moving into no-man's land toward the German lines, dug into a series of ridges about half a mile away.

During the bombardment, the Germans had fled to their dugouts — underground shelters dug deep into the trenches — where they suffered from lack of water, food, and sleep. But they survived. As the British soldiers neared the German lines and the shelling stopped, the Germans emerged from their bunkers, set up their machine guns, and mowed down the approaching troops. Traversing the gently sloping farmland of the Somme River district, the attackers made easy targets. About 20,000 British men were killed and 40,000 more were wounded on just the first day, a crushing loss that shook troop morale and public opinion at home. The battle lasted until November, and in the end the British did push the Germans back — a whole seven miles. Some 420,000 British, 200,000 French, and 600,000 Germans were killed or wounded fighting over an insignificant scrap of land.

The Widening War

On the eastern front, the slaughter did not immediately degenerate into trench warfare, and the fighting was dominated by Germany. Repulsing the initial Russian attacks, the Germans won major victories at the Battles of Tannenberg and the Masurian Lakes in August and September 1914. Russia put real pressure on the relatively weak Austro-Hungarian army, but by 1915 the eastern front had stabilized in Germany's favor. A staggering 2.5 million Russian soldiers had been killed, wounded, or captured. German armies occupied huge swaths of the Russian Empire in central Europe, including ethnic Polish, Belorussian, and Baltic territories (see Map 25.3). Yet Russia continued to fight, marking another wrong assumption of the Schlieffen Plan.

To govern these occupied territories, the Germans installed a vast military bureaucracy, with some 15,000 army administrators and professional specialists. Anti-Slavic prejudice dominated the mind-set of the occupiers, who viewed the local Slavs as savages and ethnic "mongrels." German military administrators used prisoners of war and refugees as forced labor. They stole animals and crops from local farmers to supply the occupying army or send home to Germany. About one-third of the civilian population died or became refugees under this brutal occupation. In the long run, the German state hoped to turn these territories into German possessions, a chilling forerunner of Nazi policies in World War II.[5]

The changing tides of victory and hopes for territorial gains brought neutral countries into the war. Italy, a member of the Triple Alliance since 1882, had declared its neutrality in 1914 on the grounds that its ally Austria had violated the pact by launching a war of aggression. Then in May 1915 Italy switched sides to join the Triple Entente in return for promises of Austrian territory. The war along the Italian-Austrian front was bitter and deadly and cost some 600,000 Italian lives.

In October 1914 the Ottoman Empire joined Austria and Germany, by then known as the Central Powers. The following September Bulgaria followed the Ottoman Empire's lead in order to settle old scores with Serbia. The Balkans, with the exception of Greece, were occupied by the Central Powers. The Austro-Hungarian invasion and occupation of Serbia, aided by the Bulgarians, was particularly vicious and deadly.

The entry of the Ottomans carried the war into the Middle East. Heavy fighting between the Ottomans and the Russians in the Caucasus enveloped the Armenians, who lived on both sides of the border and had experienced brutal repression by the

Deportation of Ottoman Armenians When some Armenians welcomed Russian armies as liberators after years of persecution, the Ottoman government ordered a mass deportation of its Armenian citizens from their homeland in the empire's eastern provinces. This photo shows Armenian refugees forced by Turkish militias to cross the Anatolian hinterland in 1915, under conditions designed to lead to their deaths. About 1 million civilians perished from murder, starvation, and disease during the Armenian genocide, the deliberate and systematic destruction of the Armenian population of the Ottoman Empire during World War I. (Pictures from History/Bridgeman Images)

Ottomans in 1909. When in 1915 some Armenians welcomed Russian armies as liberators, the Ottoman government ordered a mass deportation of its Armenian citizens from their homeland. In this early example of modern ethnic cleansing, often labeled genocide, about 1 million Armenians died from murder, starvation, and disease.

In 1915, at the Battle of Gallipoli, British forces tried and failed to take the Dardanelles and Constantinople from the Ottoman Turks. The invasion force was pinned down on the beaches, and the ten-month-long battle cost the Ottomans 300,000 and the British 265,000 men killed, wounded, or missing.

The British were more successful at inciting the Arabs to revolt against their Ottoman rulers. They opened negotiations with the foremost Arab leader, Hussein ibn-Ali (1856–1931). In the name of the Ottoman sultan, Hussein ruled much of the Ottoman Empire's territory along the Red Sea, an area known as the Hejaz that included Mecca, the holiest city in the Muslim world. In 1915, Hussein managed to win vague British commitments for an independent postwar Arab kingdom. Fulfilling his promise to the British, in 1916 Hussein rebelled against the Turks, proclaiming himself king of the Arabs. He was aided by the British liaison officer T. E. Lawrence, who in 1917 helped lead Arab soldiers in a guerrilla war against the Turks on the Arabian peninsula.

The British, aided by colonial troops from India, enjoyed similar victories in the Ottoman province of Mesopotamia (today's Iraq). British troops quickly occupied the southern Iraqi city of Basra in 1914, securing access to the region's oil fields. After a series of setbacks at the hands of Ottoman troops, the British captured Baghdad in 1917. In September 1918 British armies and their Arab allies rolled into Syria, a large and diverse Ottoman territory that included the holy lands of Palestine and the present-day countries of Syria, Lebanon, Jordan, and Israel. This offensive culminated in the triumphal entry of Hussein's son Faisal into Damascus. Arab patriots in Syria and Iraq now expected a large, unified Arab nation-state to rise from the dust of the Ottoman collapse — though they would later be disappointed by the Western powers (see "The Peace Settlement in the Middle East" later in this chapter).

The war spread to East Asia and colonial Africa as well. Japan declared war on Germany in 1914, seized Germany's Pacific and East Asian colonies, and used the opportunity to expand its influence in China. In Africa, instead of rebelling as the Germans hoped, colonial subjects of the British and French generally supported the Allied powers and helped local British and French commanders take over German colonies.

As the European world war spilled out of European borders, it brought non-European peoples into the conflict. More than a million Africans and Asians served in the various armies of the warring powers; more than double that number served as porters to carry equipment and build defenses. The French, facing a shortage of young men, made especially heavy use of colonial troops from North Africa. Soldiers from India played a key role in Britain's campaigns against the Ottomans, though under the command of British officers. And large numbers of soldiers came from the British Commonwealth, a voluntary association of former British colonies. Canadians, Australians, and New Zealanders fought with the British; those from Australia and New Zealand (the ANZAC Army Corps) fought with particular distinction in the failed Allied assault on Gallipoli.

After three years of refusing to play a fighting role, the United States was finally drawn into the expanding conflict. American intervention grew out of the war at sea and general sympathy for the Triple Entente. At the beginning of the war, Britain and France established a naval blockade to strangle the Central Powers. No neutral cargo ship was permitted to sail to Germany. In early 1915 Germany retaliated with attacks on the Entente's supply ships from a murderously effective new weapon, the submarine.

In May 1915 a German submarine sank the British passenger liner *Lusitania*, claiming 1,198 lives, among them 128 U.S. citizens. President Woodrow Wilson protested vigorously, using the tragedy to incite American public opinion against the Germans. To avoid almost-certain war with the United States, Germany halted its unrestricted submarine campaign for almost two years.

Early in 1917 the German military command—hoping that improved submarines could starve Britain into submission before the United States could come to its rescue—resumed unrestricted submarine warfare. Instead of weakening the British, however, the move tipped the balance against the Central Powers by prompting the United States to declare war on Germany. The first U.S. troops reached France in June 1917.

In what ways did the war transform life on the home front?

The war's impact on civilians was no less massive than it was on the men crouched in the trenches. Total war encouraged the growth of state bureaucracies, transformed the lives of ordinary women and men, and by the end inspired mass antiwar protest movements.

Mobilizing for Total War

In August 1914 many people believed that their nation was right to defend itself from foreign aggression and so greeted the outbreak of hostilities enthusiastically. With the exception of those on the extreme left, even socialists supported the war. Yet by mid-October generals and politicians had begun to realize that they had underestimated the demands of total war. Heavy casualties and the stalemate meant that each combatant country experienced a desperate need for men and weapons. To keep the war machine moving, national leaders aggressively intervened in society and the economy.

By the late nineteenth century the responsive national state had already shown an eagerness to manage the welfare of its citizens (see "The Responsive National State" in Chapter 23). Now, confronted by the crisis of total war, the state intruded even further into people's daily lives. New government ministries mobilized soldiers and armaments, established rationing programs, and provided care for war widows and wounded veterans. Censorship offices controlled news about the course of the war. Government planning boards temporarily abandoned free-market capitalism and set mandatory production goals and limits on wages and prices. Government management of highly productive industrial economies worked: it yielded an effective and immensely destructive war effort on all sides.

Germany went furthest in developing a planned economy to wage total war. As soon as war began, the industrialist Walter Rathenau convinced the government to set up the War Raw Materials Board to ration and distribute raw materials. Under Rathenau's direction, every useful material from foreign oil to barnyard manure was inventoried and rationed. Moreover, the board launched successful attempts to produce substitutes, such as synthetic rubber and nitrates, for scarce war supplies. Food was rationed in accordance with physical need. Germany failed to tax the war profits of private firms heavily enough, however. This failure contributed to massive deficit financing, inflation, the growth of a black market, and the eventual re-emergence of class conflict.

Following the terrible Battles of Verdun and the Somme in 1916, German military leaders forced the Reichstag to accept the Auxiliary Service Law, which required all males between seventeen and sixty to work only at jobs considered critical to the war effort. Women also worked in war factories, mines, and steel mills, where they labored, like men, at heavy and dangerous jobs. While war production increased, people lived on little more than one thousand calories a day—about half the normal average.

After 1917 Germany's leaders ruled by decree. Generals Paul von Hindenburg and Erich Ludendorff—heroes of the Battle of Tannenberg—drove Chancellor Bethmann-Hollweg from office. With the support of the newly formed ultraconservative Fatherland Party, the generals established a military dictatorship. Hindenburg called for the ultimate mobilization for total war. Germany could win, he said, only "if all the treasures of our soil that agriculture and industry can produce are used exclusively for the conduct of War. . . . All other considerations must come second."[6] Thus in Germany total war led to attempts to establish history's first "totalitarian" society, a model for future National Socialists, or Nazis.

Although only Germany was directly ruled by a military government, leaders in all the belligerent nations took power from parliaments, suspended civil liberties, and ignored democratic procedures. After 1915 the British Ministry of Munitions organized private industry to produce for the war, allocated labor, set wage and price rates, and settled labor disputes. In France, a weakened parliament met without public oversight, and the courts jailed pacifists who dared criticize the state. Once the United States entered the war, new federal agencies such as the War Labor Board and the War Industries Board regulated industry, labor relations, and agricultural production, while the Espionage and Sedition Acts weakened civil liberties. The war may have been deadly for citizen armies, but it was certainly good for the growth of the bureaucratic nation-state.

The Social Impact of Total War

The social changes wrought by total war were no less profound than the economic impact, though again there were important national variations. National conscription sent millions of men to the front, exposing many to foreign lands for the first time in their lives. The insatiable needs of the military created a tremendous demand for workers, making jobs readily available. This situation—seldom, if ever, seen before 1914, when unemployment and poverty had been facts of urban life—brought momentous changes.

The need for workers meant greater power and prestige for labor unions. Unions cooperated with war governments on workplace rules, wages, and production schedules in return for real participation in important decisions. The entry of labor leaders and unions into policymaking councils paralleled the entry of socialist leaders into war governments. Both reflected a new government openness to the needs of those at the bottom of society.

The role of women changed dramatically. The production of vast amounts of arms and ammunition required huge numbers of laborers, and women moved into skilled industrial jobs long considered men's work. Women became highly visible in public — as munitions workers, bank tellers, and mail carriers, and even as police officers, firefighters, and farm laborers. Women also served as auxiliaries and nurses at the front.

The war expanded the range of women's activities and helped change attitudes about proper gender roles, but the long-term results were mixed. Women gained experience in jobs previously reserved for men, but at war's end millions of demobilized soldiers demanded their jobs back, and governments forced women out of

Women Workers Building a Truck in a London Workshop, 1917 Millions of men on all sides were drafted to fight in the war, creating a serious labor shortage on the home front. When women began to fill jobs formerly reserved for men, they challenged middle-class gender roles. (Hulton Deutsch/ Getty Images)

the workplace. Thus women's employment gains were mostly temporary, except in nursing and social work, already considered "women's work."

The dislocations of war loosened sexual morality, and some women defied convention and expressed their new-found freedom by bobbing their hair, shortening their skirts, and smoking in public. Yet supposedly "loose" women were often criticized for betraying their soldier-husbands away at the front. As a result of women's many-sided war effort, the United States, Britain, Germany, Poland, and other countries granted women the right to vote immediately after the war. Yet women's rights movements faded in the 1920s and 1930s, in large part because feminist leaders found it difficult to regain momentum after the wartime crisis.

To some extent, the war promoted greater social equality, blurring class distinctions and lessening the gap between rich and poor. In Great Britain, the bottom third of the population generally lived better than they ever had, for the poorest gained most from the severe shortage of labor. Elsewhere, greater equality was reflected in full employment, distribution of scarce rations according to physical needs, and a sharing of hardships. In general, despite some war profiteering, European society became more uniform and egalitarian.

Death itself had no respect for traditional social distinctions. It savagely decimated the young aristocratic officers who led the charge, and it fell heavily on the mass of drafted peasants and unskilled workers who followed, leading commentators to speak of a "lost generation." Yet death often spared highly skilled workers and foremen. Their lives were too valuable to squander at the front, for they were needed to train the newly recruited women and older unskilled men laboring in war plants at home.

Growing Political Tensions

During the first two years of war, many soldiers and civilians supported their governments. Patriotic nationalism and belief in a just cause united peoples behind their national leaders. Each government used rigorous censorship and crude propaganda to bolster popular support. German propaganda falsely pictured black soldiers from France's African empire abusing German women, while the French and British ceaselessly recounted and exaggerated German atrocities in Belgium and elsewhere. Patriotic posters and slogans, slanted news, and biased editorials inflamed national hatreds, helped control public opinion, and encouraged soldiers to keep fighting.

Political and social tensions re-emerged, however, and by the spring of 1916 ordinary people were beginning to crack under the strain of total war. Strikes and protest marches over war-related burdens and shortages flared up on every home front. On May 1, 1916, several thousand demonstrators in Berlin heard the radical socialist leader Karl Liebknecht (1871–1919) attack the costs of the war effort. Liebknecht was arrested and imprisoned, but his daring action electrified Europe's far left. In France, Georges Clemenceau (zhorzh kleh-muhn-SOH) (1841–1929) established a virtual dictatorship, arrested strikers, and jailed without trial journalists and politicians who dared to suggest a compromise peace with Germany.

In April 1916 Irish republican nationalists took advantage of the tense wartime conditions to step up their rebellion against British rule. During the great Easter Rising, armed republican militias took over parts of Dublin and proclaimed an independent Irish Republic. After a week of bitter fighting, British troops crushed the rebels and executed their leaders. Though the republicans were defeated, the punitive aftermath fueled anti-British sentiment in Ireland. The Rising set the stage for the success of the nationalist Sinn Fein Party and a full-scale civil war for Irish independence in the early 1920s.

On all sides, soldiers' morale began to decline. Numerous French units mutinied and refused to fight after the disastrous French offensive of May 1917. Only tough military justice, including death sentences for mutiny leaders, and a tacit agreement with the troops that there would be no more grand offensives, enabled the new general-in-chief, Henri-Philippe Pétain (pay-TAN), to restore order. Facing defeat, wretched conditions at the front, and growing hopelessness, Russian soldiers deserted in droves, providing fuel for the Russian Revolution of 1917. After the murderous Battle of Caporetto in northern Italy, which lasted from October to November in 1917, the Italian army collapsed in despair. In the massive battles of 1916 and 1917, the British armies had been "bled dry." Only the promised arrival of fresh troops from the United States stiffened the resolve of the Allies.

The strains were even worse for the Central Powers. In October 1916 a young socialist assassinated the chief minister of Austria-Hungary. The following month, when the aging emperor Franz Joseph died, a symbol of unity disappeared. In spite of absolute censorship, political dissatisfaction and conflicts among nationalities grew. Both Czech and Balkan leaders demanded independent states for their peoples. By April 1917 the Austro-Hungarian people and army were exhausted. Another winter of war would bring revolution and disintegration.

Germans likewise suffered immensely. The British naval blockade greatly limited food imports, and some 750,000 German civilians starved to death. The rest endured heavy rationing of everyday goods such as matches, bread, cooking oil, and meat. A growing minority of moderate socialists in the Reichstag gave voice to popular discontent when they called for a compromise "peace without annexations or reparations."

Such a peace was unthinkable for the Fatherland Party. Yet Germany's rulers faced growing unrest. When the bread ration was further reduced in April 1917, more than 200,000 workers and women struck and demonstrated for a week in Berlin, returning to work only under the threat of prison and military discipline. That same month, radicals left the Social Democratic Party to form the Independent Social Democratic Party; in 1918 they would found the German Communist Party. Thus Germany, like its ally Austria-Hungary (and its enemy France), was beginning to crack in 1917. Yet it was Russia that collapsed first and saved the Central Powers—for a time.

Why did world war lead to a successful Communist revolution in Russia?

Growing out of the crisis of the First World War, the Russian Revolution of 1917 was one of modern history's most momentous events. For some, the revolution was Marx's socialist vision come true; for others, it was the triumph of a despised Communist dictatorship. To all, it presented a radically new prototype of state and society.

The Fall of Imperial Russia

Like their allies and enemies, many Russians had embraced war with patriotic enthusiasm in 1914. At the Winter Palace, throngs of people knelt and sang "God Save the Tsar!" while Tsar Nicholas II (r. 1894–1917) repeated the oath Alexander I had sworn in 1812 during Napoleon's invasion of Russia, vowing never to make peace as long as the enemy stood on Russian soil. Russia's lower house of parliament, the Duma, voted to support the war. Conservatives anticipated expansion in the Balkans, while liberals and most socialists believed that alliance with Britain and France would bring democratic reforms. For a moment, Russia was united.

Enthusiasm for the war soon waned as better-equipped German armies inflicted terrible losses. By 1915 substantial numbers of Russian soldiers were being sent to the front without rifles; they were told to find their arms among the dead. Russia's battered peasant army nonetheless continued to fight, and Russia moved toward full mobilization on the home front. The government set up special committees to coordinate defense, industry, transportation, and agriculture. These efforts improved the military situation, but overall Russia mobilized less effectively than the other combatants.

One problem was weak leadership. Under the constitution resulting from the revolution of 1905 (see "The Russian Revolution of 1905" in Chapter 23), the tsar had retained complete control over the bureaucracy and the army, and he resisted popular involvement in government. Excluded from power, the Duma, the educated middle classes, and the masses became increasingly critical of the tsar's leadership. In September 1915 parties ranging from conservative to moderate socialists formed the Progressive bloc, which called for a completely new government responsible to the Duma instead of the tsar. In response, Nicholas temporarily adjourned the Duma. The tsar then announced that he was traveling to the front to lead and rally Russia's armies, leaving the government in the hands of his wife, the Tsarina Alexandra.

His departure was a fatal turning point. In his absence, Alexandra arbitrarily dismissed loyal political advisers. She turned to her court favorite, the disreputable and unpopular Rasputin, an uneducated Siberian preacher whose influence with the tsarina rested on his purported ability to heal Alexis—the royals' only son and heir to the throne—from his hemophilia. In a desperate attempt to right the situation, three members of the high aristocracy murdered Rasputin in December 1916. The ensuing scandal further undermined support for the tsarist government.

Imperial Russia had entered a terminal crisis that led to the **February Revolution** of 1917. (Though the events happened in March, the name of the revolution matches the traditional Russian calendar, which used a different dating system.) Tens of thousands of soldiers deserted, swelling the number of the disaffected at home. By early 1917 the cities were wracked by food shortages, heating fuel was in short supply, and the economy was breaking down. In March violent street demonstrations broke out in Petrograd (now named St. Petersburg), spread to the factories, and then engulfed the city. From the front, the tsar ordered the army to open fire on the protesters, but the soldiers refused to shoot and joined the revolutionary crowd instead. The Duma declared a provisional government on March 12, 1917. Three days later, Nicholas abdicated.

The Provisional Government

The February Revolution was the result of an unplanned uprising of hungry, angry people in the capital, but it was eagerly accepted throughout the country. The patriotic upper and middle classes embraced the prospect of a more determined war effort, while workers anticipated better wages and more food. After generations of autocracy, the provisional government established equality before the law, granting freedoms of religion, speech, and assembly, as well as the right of unions to organize and strike.

Yet the provisional government made a crucial mistake: though the Russian people were sick of fighting, the new leaders failed to take Russia out of the war. A government formed in May 1917 included the fiery agrarian socialist Alexander Kerensky, who became prime minister in July. For the patriotic Kerensky, as for other moderate socialists, the continuation of war was still a national duty. Kerensky refused to confiscate large landholdings and give them to peasants, fearing that such drastic action would complete the disintegration of Russia's peasant army. Human suffering and war-weariness grew, testing the limited strength of the provisional government.

From its first day, the provisional government had to share power with a formidable rival — the **Petrograd Soviet** (or council) of Workers' and Soldiers' Deputies. Modeled on the revolutionary soviets of 1905, the Petrograd Soviet comprised two to three thousand workers, soldiers, and socialist intellectuals. Seeing itself as a true grassroots product of revolutionary democracy, the Soviet acted as a parallel government. It issued its own radical orders, weakening the authority of the provisional government.

The most famous edict of the Petrograd Soviet was Army Order No. 1, which stripped officers of their authority and placed power in the hands of elected committees of common soldiers. Designed to protect the revolution from resistance by the aristocratic officer corps, the order led to a collapse of army discipline.

In July 1917 the provisional government mounted a poorly considered summer offensive against the Germans. The campaign was a miserable failure, and peasant soldiers deserted in droves, returning home to help their families get a share of the land that peasants were seizing in a grassroots agrarian revolt. By the summer of 1917 Russia was descending into anarchy.

Lenin and the Bolshevik Revolution

Vladimir Ilyich Lenin (1870–1924), one of Russia's many revolutionary leaders, rose to power as the provisional government faltered. Born into the middle class, Lenin turned against imperial Russia when his older brother was executed in 1887 for plotting to kill archconservative Tsar Alexander III. As a law student, Lenin eagerly studied Marxist socialism, which began to win converts among radical intellectuals during Russia's industrialization in the 1890s. A pragmatic and flexible thinker, Lenin updated Marx's revolutionary philosophy to address existing conditions in Russia.

Three interrelated concepts were central for Lenin. First, he stressed that only violent revolution could destroy capitalism. He tirelessly denounced all "revisionist" theories of a peaceful evolution to socialism (see "Marxist Revisionism" in Chapter 23) as a betrayal of Marx's message of violent class conflict. Second, Lenin argued that

Lenin Rallies the Masses Bolshevik leader Vladimir Lenin, known for his fiery speeches, addresses a crowd in Moscow's Red Square in October 1917. (Sovfoto/Getty Images)

under certain conditions a Communist revolution was possible even in a predominantly agrarian country like Russia. Peasants, who were numerous, poor, and exploited, could take the place of Marx's traditional working class in the coming revolutionary conflict. Third, Lenin believed that the possibility of revolution was determined more by human leadership than by historical laws. He called for a highly disciplined workers' party strictly controlled by a small, dedicated elite of intellectuals and professional revolutionaries that would not stop until revolution brought it to power. Lenin's version of Marxism had a major impact on events in Russia and ultimately changed the way future revolutionaries engaged in radical revolt around the world.

Other Russian Marxists challenged Lenin's ideas. At meetings of the Russian Social Democratic Labor Party in London in 1903, matters came to a head. Lenin demanded a small, disciplined, elitist party dedicated to Communist revolution, while his more revisionist opponents wanted a democratic, reformist party with mass membership (like the German Social Democratic Party). The Russian Marxists split into two rival factions. Lenin called his camp the **Bolsheviks**, or "majority group"; his opponents were Mensheviks, or "minority group." The Bolsheviks had only a tenuous majority of a single vote, but Lenin kept the name for propaganda reasons and they became the revolutionary party he wanted: tough, disciplined, and led from above.

Unlike other socialists, Lenin had not rallied around the national flag in 1914. Observing events from neutral Switzerland, where he had moved that year to avoid persecution by the tsar's police, Lenin viewed the war as a product of imperialist rivalries and an opportunity for socialist revolution. After the February Revolution of 1917, the German government provided Lenin with safe passage in a sealed train across Germany and back into Russia. The Germans hoped Lenin would undermine the sagging war effort of the provisional government. They were not disappointed.

Arriving triumphantly at Petrograd's Finland Station on April 3, Lenin attacked at once. He rejected all cooperation with what he called the "bourgeois" provisional government. His slogans were radical in the extreme: "All power to the soviets"; "All land to the peasants"; "Stop the war now." Lenin was a superb tactician. His promises of "Peace, Land, and Bread" spoke to the expectations of suffering soldiers, peasants, and workers and earned the Bolsheviks substantial popular support. The moment for revolution was at hand.

Yet Lenin and the Bolsheviks almost lost the struggle for Russia. A premature attempt to seize power in July collapsed, and Lenin went into hiding. However, this temporary setback made little difference in the long run. The army's commander in chief, General Lavr Kornilov, led a feeble coup against the provisional Kerensky government in September. In the face of this rightist counter-revolutionary threat, the Bolsheviks re-emerged. Kornilov's forces disintegrated, but Kerensky lost all credit with the army, the only force that might have saved democratic government in Russia.

Trotsky and the Seizure of Power

Throughout the summer, the Bolsheviks greatly increased their popular support. Party membership soared from 50,000 to 240,000, and in October the Bolsheviks gained a fragile majority in the Petrograd Soviet. Now Lenin's supporter Leon Trotsky (1879–1940), a spellbinding revolutionary orator and radical Marxist, brilliantly executed the Bolshevik seizure of power.

Painting a vivid but untruthful picture of German and counter-revolutionary plots, Trotsky convinced the Petrograd Soviet to form a special military-revolutionary committee in October and make him its leader. Thus military power in the capital passed into Bolshevik hands.

On the night of November 6, militants from Trotsky's committee joined with trusted Bolshevik soldiers to seize government buildings in Petrograd and arrest members of the provisional government. Then they went on to the Congress of Soviets, where a Bolshevik majority—roughly 390 of 650 excited delegates—declared that all power had passed to the soviets and named Lenin head of the new government. John Reed, a sympathetic American journalist, described the enthusiasm that greeted Lenin at the congress:

> Now Lenin, gripping the edge of the reading stand . . . stood there waiting, apparently oblivious to the long-rolling ovation, which lasted several minutes. When it finished, he said simply, "We shall now proceed to construct the Socialist order!" Again that overwhelming human roar.[7]

The Bolsheviks came to power for three key reasons. First, by late 1917 democracy had given way to anarchy: power was there for those who could take it. Second, in Lenin and Trotsky the Bolsheviks had an utterly determined and superior leadership, which both the tsarist and the provisional governments lacked. Third, as Reed's comment suggests, Bolshevik policies appealed to ordinary Russians. Exhausted by war and weary of tsarist autocracy, they were eager for radical changes. The Bolsheviks appealed to the hope for peace, better living conditions, and a more equitable society.

Dictatorship and Civil War

The Bolsheviks' truly monumental accomplishment was not taking power, but keeping it. Over the next four years, they conquered the chaos they had helped create and began to build a Communist society. How was this done?

Lenin made it seem that the Bolsheviks were directing events over which they actually had little control. Since summer, a peasant revolt had swept across Russia, as impoverished peasants had seized for themselves the estates of the landlords and the church. Thus when Lenin mandated land reform, he merely approved what peasants were already doing. Similarly, urban workers had established their own local soviets or committees and demanded direct control of individual factories. This, too, Lenin ratified with a decree in November 1917.

The Bolsheviks proclaimed their regime a "provisional workers' and peasants' government," promising that a freely elected Constituent Assembly would draw up a new constitution. But free elections in November produced a stunning setback: the Bolsheviks won only 23 percent of the elected delegates. The Socialist Revolutionary Party — the peasants' party — had a clear plurality with about 40 percent of the vote. After the Constituent Assembly met for one day, however, Bolshevik soldiers acting under Lenin's orders disbanded it. By January 1918 Lenin had moved to establish a one-party state.

Lenin acknowledged that Russia had effectively lost the war with Germany and that the only realistic goal was peace at any price. That price was very high. Germany demanded that the Soviet government give up all its western territories, areas inhabited primarily by Poles, Finns, Lithuanians, and other non-Russians — people who had been conquered by the tsars over three centuries and put into the "prisonhouse of nationalities," as Lenin had earlier called the Russian Empire.

At first, Lenin's fellow Bolsheviks refused to accept such great territorial losses. But when German armies resumed their unopposed march into Russia in February 1918, Lenin had his way in a very close vote. A third of old Russia's population was sliced away by the **Treaty of Brest-Litovsk**, signed with Germany in March 1918. With peace, Lenin escaped the disaster of continued war and could pursue his goal of absolute power for the Bolsheviks — now also called Communists — within Russia.

The peace treaty and the abolition of the Constituent Assembly inspired armed opposition to the Bolshevik regime. People who had supported self-rule in November saw that once again they were getting dictatorship. The officers of the old army organized the so-called White opposition to the Bolsheviks in southern Russia, Ukraine, Siberia, and the area west of Petrograd. The Whites came from many social groups and were united only by their hatred of communism and the Bolsheviks — the Reds.

By the summer of 1918 Russia was in a full-fledged civil war. Eighteen self-proclaimed regional governments — several of which represented minority nationalities — challenged Lenin's government in Moscow. By the end of the year White armies were on the attack. In October 1919 they closed in on central Russia from three sides, and it appeared they might triumph. They did not.

Lenin and the Red Army beat back the counter-revolutionary White armies for several reasons. Most important, the Bolsheviks had quickly developed a better army. Once again, Trotsky's leadership was decisive. At first, the Bolsheviks had preached democracy in the military and had even elected officers in 1917. But beginning in March 1918, Trotsky became war commissar of the newly formed Red Army. He re-established strict discipline and the draft. Soldiers deserting or disobeying an order were summarily shot. Moreover, Trotsky made effective use of former tsarist army officers, who were actively recruited and given unprecedented powers over their troops. Trotsky's disciplined and effective fighting force repeatedly defeated the Whites in the field.

Ironically, foreign military intervention helped the Bolsheviks. For a variety of reasons, but primarily to stop the spread of communism, the Western Allies (including the United States, Britain, France, and Japan) sent troops to support the White armies. Yet they never sent enough aid to tip the balance, and the Bolsheviks used the specter of foreign intervention to attract former tsarist army officers to their side.

Other conditions favored a Bolshevik victory as well. Strategically, the Reds controlled central Russia and the crucial cities of Moscow and Petrograd. The Whites attacked from the fringes and lacked coordination. Moreover, the poorly defined political program of the Whites was a mishmash of liberal republicanism and monarchism incapable of uniting the Bolsheviks' enemies. And while the Bolsheviks promised ethnic minorities in Russian-controlled territories substantial autonomy, the nationalist Whites sought to preserve the tsarist empire.

The Bolsheviks mobilized the home front for the war by establishing a harsh system of centralized controls called **War Communism**. The leadership nationalized banks and industries and outlawed private enterprise. Bolshevik commissars introduced rationing, seized grain from peasants to feed the cities, and maintained strict workplace discipline. Although normal economic activity broke down, these measures maintained labor discipline and kept the Red Army supplied with men and material.

Revolutionary terror also contributed to the Communist victory. Lenin and the Bolsheviks set up a fearsome secret police known as the Cheka, dedicated to suppressing counter-revolutionaries. During the civil war, the Cheka imprisoned and executed without trial tens of thousands of supposed "class enemies." Victims included clergymen, aristocrats, the wealthy Russian bourgeoisie, deserters from the Red Army, and political opponents of all kinds. Even Nicholas, Alexandra, and their children were secretly executed, their bodies disfigured and hidden in a forest to avoid public outrage. The "Red Terror" of 1918 to 1920 helped establish the secret police as a central tool of the emerging Communist government.

By the spring of 1920 the White armies were almost completely defeated, and the Bolsheviks had retaken much of the territory ceded to Germany under the Treaty of Brest-Litovsk. The Red Army reconquered Belarus and Ukraine, both of which had briefly gained independence. The Bolsheviks then moved westward into Polish territory, but they were halted on the outskirts of Warsaw in August 1920 by troops under the leadership of the Polish field marshal and chief of state Jozef Pilsudski. This defeat halted Bolshevik attempts to spread communism farther into central Europe, though in 1921 the Red Army overran the independent national governments of the Caucasus. The Russian civil war was over, and the Bolsheviks had won an impressive victory.

What were the benefits and costs of the postwar peace settlement?

Even as civil war raged in Russia and chaos engulfed much of central and eastern Europe, the war in the west came to an end in November 1918. Early in 1919 the victorious Western Allies came together in Paris, where they worked out terms for peace with Germany and created the peacekeeping League of Nations. Expectations were high; optimism was almost unlimited. Nevertheless, the peace settlement of 1919 turned out to be a disappointment for peoples and politicians alike. Rather than lasting peace, the immediate postwar years brought economic crisis and violent political conflict.

The End of the War

In early 1918 the German leadership decided that the time was ripe for a last-ditch, all-out attack on France. The defeat of Russia had released men and materials for the western front. The looming arrival of the first U.S. troops and the growth of dissent at home quickened German leaders' resolve. In the Spring Offensive of 1918, Ludendorff launched an extensive attack on the French lines. German armies came within thirty-five miles of Paris, but Ludendorff's exhausted, overextended forces never broke through. They were stopped in July at the second Battle of the Marne, where 140,000 American soldiers saw action. The late but massive American intervention bolstered the Allied victory.

By September British, French, and American armies were advancing steadily on all fronts. Hindenburg and Ludendorff realized that Germany had lost the war. Not wanting to shoulder the blame, they insisted that moderate politicians should take responsibility for the defeat. On October 4 the German emperor formed a new, more liberal civilian government to sue for peace.

As negotiations over an armistice dragged on, frustrated Germans rose up in revolt. On November 3 sailors in Kiel mutinied, and throughout northern Germany soldiers and workers established revolutionary councils modeled on the Russian soviets. The same day, Austria-Hungary surrendered to the Allies and began breaking apart. Revolution erupted in Germany, and masses of workers demonstrated for peace in Berlin. With army discipline collapsing, Wilhelm II abdicated and fled to Holland. Socialist leaders in Berlin proclaimed a German republic on November 9 and agreed to tough Allied terms of surrender. The armistice went into effect on November 11, 1918. The war was over.

Revolution in Austria-Hungary and Germany

Military defeat brought turmoil and revolution to Austria-Hungary and Germany, as it had to Russia. Having started the war to preserve an imperial state, the Austro-Hungarian Empire perished in the attempt. The independent states of Austria, Hungary, and Czechoslovakia, and a larger Romania, Italy, and Poland, were carved out of its territories (Map 25.4). For four months in 1919, until conservative nationalists seized power, Hungary became a Marxist republic along Bolshevik lines. The Serbs greatly expanded their territory by gaining control of the western Balkans; the enlarged state took the name Yugoslavia.

MAP 25.4   Territorial Changes After World War I
World War I brought tremendous changes to eastern Europe. New nations and new boundaries were established, and a dangerous power vacuum was created by the relatively weak states established between Germany and Soviet Russia.

In late 1918 Germany experienced a dramatic revolution that resembled the Russian Revolution of March 1917. In both cases, a genuine popular uprising welled up from below, toppled an authoritarian monarchy, and created a liberal provisional republic. In both countries, liberals and moderate socialist politicians struggled with more radical workers' and soldiers' councils (or soviets) for political dominance. In Germany, however, moderates from the Social Democratic Party and their liberal allies held on to power and established the Weimar Republic—a democratic government that would lead Germany for the next fifteen years. Their success was a deep disappointment for Russia's Bolsheviks, who had hoped that a more radical revolution in Germany would help spread communism across the European continent.

There were several reasons for the German outcome. The great majority of the Marxist politicians in the Social Democratic Party were moderate revisionists, not revolutionaries. They wanted political democracy and civil liberties and favored the gradual elimination of capitalism. They were also German nationalists, appalled by the prospect of civil war and revolutionary terror. Of crucial importance was the fact that the moderate Social Democrats quickly came to terms with the army and big business, which helped prevent total national collapse.

Yet the triumph of the Social Democrats brought violent chaos to Germany in early 1919. The new republic was attacked from both sides of the political spectrum. Radical Communists led by Karl Liebknecht and Rosa Luxemburg tried to seize control of the government in the Spartacist Uprising in Berlin in January 1919. The Social Democrats called in nationalist Free Corps militias, bands of demobilized soldiers who had kept their weapons, to crush the uprising. Liebknecht and Luxemburg were arrested and then brutally murdered by Free Corps soldiers. In Bavaria, a short-lived Bolshevik-style republic was violently overthrown on government orders by the Free Corps. Nationwide strikes by leftist workers and a short-lived, right-wing military takeover — the Kapp Putsch — were repressed by the central government.

By the summer of 1920 the situation in Germany had calmed down, but the new republican government faced deep discontent. Communists and radical socialists blamed the Social Democrats for the murders of Liebknecht and Luxemburg and the repression in Bavaria. Right-wing nationalists, including the new National Socialist German Workers (or Nazi) Party, founded in 1920, despised the government from the start. They spread the myth that the German army had never actually lost the war on the battlefield — instead, the nation had been "stabbed in the back" by socialists and pacifists at home. In Germany, the end of the war brought only a fragile sense of political stability.

The Treaty of Versailles

In January 1919 over seventy delegates from twenty-seven nations met in Paris to hammer out a peace accord. The conference produced several treaties, including the **Treaty of Versailles**, which laid out the terms of the postwar settlement with Germany. The peace negotiations inspired great expectations. A young British diplomat later wrote that the victors "were journeying to Paris . . . to found a new order in Europe. We were preparing not Peace only, but Eternal Peace."[8]

This idealism was greatly strengthened by U.S. president Wilson's January 1918 peace proposal, the **Fourteen Points**. The plan called for open diplomacy, a reduction in armaments, freedom of commerce and trade, and the establishment of a **League of Nations**, an international body designed to provide a place for peaceful resolution of international problems. Perhaps most important, Wilson demanded that peace be based on the principle of **national self-determination**, meaning that peoples should be able to choose their own national governments through democratic majority-rule elections and live free from outside interference in territories with clearly defined, permanent borders. Despite the general optimism inspired by these ideas, the conference and the treaty itself quickly generated disagreement.

The "Big Three"—the United States, Great Britain, and France—controlled the conference. Germany, Austria-Hungary, and Russia were excluded, though their lands were placed on the negotiating table. Italy took part, but its role was quite limited. Representatives from the Middle East, Africa, and East Asia attended as well, but their concerns were largely ignored.

Almost immediately, the Big Three began to quarrel. Wilson, who was wildly cheered by European crowds as the champion of democratic international cooperation, insisted that the matter of the League of Nations should come first, for he passionately believed that only a permanent international organization could avert future wars. Wilson had his way—the delegates agreed to create the League, though the details would be worked out later and the final structure was too weak to achieve its grand purpose. Prime Ministers Lloyd George of Great Britain and Georges Clemenceau of France were unenthusiastic about the League. They were primarily concerned with punishing Germany.

The question of what to do with Germany in fact dominated discussions among the Big Three. Clemenceau wanted Germany to pay for its aggression. The war in the west had been fought largely on French soil, and like most French people, Clemenceau wanted revenge, economic retribution, and lasting security for France. This, he believed, required the creation of a buffer state between France and Germany, the permanent demilitarization of Germany, and vast reparation payments. Lloyd George supported Clemenceau, but was less harsh. Wilson disagreed. Clemenceau's demands seemed vindictive, and they violated Wilson's sense of Christian morality and the principle of national self-determination. By April the conference was deadlocked. Wilson packed his bags to go home.

In the end, Clemenceau agreed to a compromise. He gave up the French demand for a Rhineland buffer state in return for French military occupation of the region for fifteen years and a formal defensive alliance with the United States and Great Britain. Both Wilson and Lloyd George promised that their countries would come to France's aid in the event of a German attack. The Allies moved quickly to finish the settlement, believing that further adjustments would be possible within the dual framework of a strong Western alliance and the League of Nations.

The various agreements signed at Versailles redrew the map of Europe, and the war's losers paid the price. The new independent nations of Poland, Czechoslovakia, Finland, the Baltic States, and Yugoslavia were carved out of the Austro-Hungarian and Russian Empires. The Ottoman Empire was also split apart, or "partitioned," its territories placed under the control of the victors.

The Treaty of Versailles, signed by the Allies and Germany, was key to the settlement. Germany's African and Asian colonies were given to France, Britain, and Japan as League of Nations mandates or administered territories, though Germany's losses within Europe were relatively minor, thanks to Wilson. Alsace-Lorraine was returned to France. Ethnic Polish territories seized by Prussia during the eighteenth-century partition of Poland (see "Catherine the Great of Russia" in Chapter 16) were returned to a new independent Polish state. Predominantly German Danzig was also placed within the Polish border but as a self-governing city under League of Nations protection. Germany had to limit its army to 100,000 men, agree to build no military fortifications in the Rhineland, and accept temporary French occupation of that region.

More harshly, in Article 231, the **war guilt clause**, the Allies declared that Germany (with Austria) was entirely responsible for the war and thus had to pay reparations equal to all civilian damages caused by the fighting. This much-criticized clause expressed French and to some extent British demands for revenge. For the Germans, reparations were a crippling financial burden and a cutting insult to German national pride. Many Germans believed wartime propaganda that had repeatedly claimed that Germany was an innocent victim, forced into war by a circle of barbaric enemies. When presented with these terms, the new German government protested vigorously but to no avail. On June 28, 1919, representatives of the German Social Democrats signed the treaty in Louis XIV's Hall of Mirrors at Versailles, where Bismarck's empire had been joyously proclaimed almost fifty years before (see "The Franco-Prussian War and German Unification" in Chapter 23).

The rapidly concluded Versailles treaties were far from perfect, but within the context of war-shattered Europe they were a beginning. Germany had been punished but not dismembered. A new world organization complemented a traditional defensive alliance of satisfied powers: Britain, France, and the United States. The remaining serious problems, the Allies hoped, could be worked out in the future. Allied leaders had seen speed as essential because they feared that the Bolshevik Revolution might spread. The best answer to Lenin's unending calls for worldwide upheaval, they believed, was peace and tranquility.

Yet the great hopes of early 1919 had turned to ashes by the end of the year. The Western alliance had collapsed, and a grandiose plan for permanent peace had given way to a fragile truce, for several reasons. First, the U.S. Senate and, to a lesser extent, the American people rejected Wilson's handiwork. Republican senators led by Henry Cabot Lodge believed that the treaty gave away Congress's constitutional right to declare war and demanded changes in the articles. In failing health after extensive travel to drum up popular support for the treaty, Wilson rejected all compromise. In doing so, he ensured that the Senate would never ratify the treaty and that the United States would never join the League of Nations. Moreover, the Senate refused to ratify treaties forming a defensive alliance with France and Great Britain. America had turned its back on Europe; the new gospel of isolationism represented a tragic renunciation of international responsibility. Using U.S. actions as an excuse, Great Britain too refused to ratify its defensive alliance with France. Bitterly betrayed by its allies, France stood alone.

A second cause for the failure of the peace was that the principle of national self-determination, which had engendered such enthusiasm, was good in theory but flawed in practice. In Europe, the borders of new states such as Poland, Czechoslovakia, and Yugoslavia cut through a jumble of ethnic and religious groups that often despised each other. The new central European nations — relatively small and powerless countries trapped between a resurgent Germany and the Soviet Union — would prove to be economically weak and politically unstable, the source of conflict in the years to come. In the colonies, desires for self-determination were simply ignored, leading to problems particularly in the Middle East.

The Peace Settlement in the Middle East

Although Allied leaders at Versailles focused mainly on European issues, they also imposed a political settlement on what had been the Ottoman Empire. Their decisions, made in Paris and at other international conferences, brought radical and controversial changes to the region. The Allies dismantled or partitioned the Ottoman Empire, Britain and France expanded their influence in the region, Jewish peoples were promised a "national homeland" in British-controlled Palestine, and Arab nationalists felt cheated and betrayed.

The British government had encouraged the wartime Arab revolt against the Ottoman Turks and had even made vague promises of an independent Arab kingdom, but when the fighting stopped, the British and the French chose instead to honor their own secret wartime agreements to divide and rule the Ottoman lands. Most important was the Sykes-Picot Agreement of 1916, named after the British and French diplomats who negotiated the deal.

In the secret accord, Britain and France agreed that the lands of the Ottoman Empire would be administered by the European powers under what they called the **mandate system**. Under the terms of the mandates, granted to individual European powers by the League of Nations, former Ottoman territories (and former German colonies) would be placed under the "tutelage" of European authorities until they could "stand alone." France would receive a mandate to govern modern-day Lebanon and Syria and much of southern Turkey, and Britain would control Palestine, Transjordan, and Iraq. Though the official goal of the mandate system was to eventually grant these regions national independence, it quickly became clear that the Allies hardly intended to do so. Critics labeled the system colonialism under another name, and when Britain and France set about implementing their agreements after the armistice, Arab nationalists reacted with understandable surprise and resentment.

British plans for the former Ottoman lands that would become Palestine (and later Israel) further angered Arab nationalists. The **Balfour Declaration** of November 1917, written by British foreign secretary Arthur Balfour, had announced that Britain favored a "National Home for the Jewish People" in Palestine, but without discriminating against the civil and religious rights of the non-Jewish communities already living in the region. Some members of the British cabinet believed the declaration would appeal to German, Austrian, and American Jews and thus help the British war effort. Others sincerely supported the Zionist vision of a Jewish homeland (see "Jewish Emancipation and Modern Anti-Semitism" in Chapter 23), which they hoped would also help Britain maintain control of the Suez Canal. Whatever the motives, the declaration enraged the region's Arabs.

In 1914 Jews accounted for about 11 percent of the population in the three Ottoman districts that the British would lump together to form Palestine; the rest of the population was predominantly Arab. Both groups understood that Balfour's "National Home" implied the establishment of some kind of Jewish state that would violate majority rule. Moreover, a state founded on religious and ethnic exclusivity was out of keeping with Islamic and Ottoman tradition, which had historically been more tolerant of religious diversity and minorities than Christian Europe had been.

Though Arab leaders attended the Paris Peace Conference, their efforts to secure autonomy in the Middle East came to nothing. Only the kingdom of Hejaz—today part of Saudi Arabia—was granted independence. In response, Arab nationalists came together in Damascus as the General Syrian Congress in 1919 and unsuccessfully called again for political independence. The congress proclaimed Syria an independent kingdom; a similar congress declared Iraqi independence.

The Western reaction was swift and decisive. A French army stationed in Lebanon attacked Syria, taking Damascus in July 1920. The Arab government fled, and the French took over. Meanwhile, the British bloodily put down an uprising in Iraq and established control there. Brushing aside Arab opposition, the British mandate in Palestine formally incorporated the Balfour Declaration and its commitment to a Jewish national home. Western imperialism, in the form of the mandate system authorized by the League of Nations, appeared to have replaced Ottoman rule in the Middle East. In the following decades, deadly anti-imperial riots and violent conflicts between Arabs and Jews would repeatedly undermine the region's stability.

The Allies sought to impose even harsher terms on the defeated Turks than on the "liberated" Arabs. A treaty forced on the Ottoman sultan dismembered the Turkish heartland. Great Britain and France occupied parts of modern-day Turkey, and Italy and Greece claimed shares. There was a sizable Greek minority in western Turkey, and Greek nationalists wanted to build a modern Greek empire modeled on long-dead Byzantium. In 1919 Greek armies carried by British ships landed on the Turkish coast at Smyrna (SMUHR-nuh; today's Izmir) and advanced unopposed into the interior, while French troops moved in from the south. Turkey seemed finished.

Yet Turkey survived the postwar invasions. A Turkish National Movement emerged, led by Mustafa Kemal (1881–1938), a prominent general in the successful Turkish defeat of the British at the Battle of Gallipoli. The leaders of the movement overthrew the sultan and refused to acknowledge the Allied dismemberment of their country. Under Kemal's direction, a revived Turkish army gradually mounted a forceful resistance, and despite staggering losses, his troops repulsed the invaders. The Greeks and British sued for peace. In 1923, after long negotiations, the resulting Treaty of Lausanne (loh-ZAN) recognized the territorial integrity of Turkey. The treaty abolished the hated capitulations that the European powers had imposed over the centuries to give their citizens special privileges in the Ottoman Empire.

The peace accords included an agreement for a shattering example of what we would now call "ethnic cleansing," under which Greeks were forced to leave Turkish-majority lands for Greece, while Turks moved from Greece and former Balkan territories to the Turkish mainland. The result, driven by ideals of national self-determination and racial purity, was a humanitarian disaster. Ethnic Greeks constituted about 16 percent of the Turkish population, and now between 1.5 and 2 million people had to pick up and move west. At the same time, 500,000 to 600,000 ethnic Turks moved out of Greece and Bulgaria to the Anatolian peninsula (modern-day Turkey). Very few wanted to leave their homes, and though the authorities set up transit camps, refugees faced harsh conditions, rampant looting, and physical abuse. In this case, race trumped religion: Muslim Greeks were forced west, and Christian Turks forced east, and the population exchange destroyed a vital, multicultural ethnic patchwork. The agreements at Lausanne became a model for future examples of ethnic cleansing, most notably the exchange of Germans and Slavs in central Europe after the Second World War, as well as the exchange of Hindus and Muslims that followed Indian independence in 1947.

Kemal, a secular nationalist, believed that Turkey should modernize and secularize along Western lines. He established a republic, was elected president, and created a one-party system — partly inspired by the Bolshevik example — to transform his country. The most radical reforms pertained to religion and culture. For centuries, Islamic religious authorities had regulated most of the intellectual, political, and social activities of Ottoman citizens. Profoundly influenced by the example of western Europe, Kemal set out to limit the place of religion and religious leaders in daily affairs. He decreed a controversial separation of church and state, promulgated law codes inspired by European models, and established a secular public school system. Women received rights that they never had before. By the time of his death in 1938, Kemal had implemented much of his revolutionary program and had moved the former Ottoman heartland much closer to Europe, foretelling later Turkish efforts to join the European Union as a full-fledged member.

The Human Costs of the War

World War I broke empires, inspired revolutions, and changed national borders on a world scale. It also had immense human costs, and men and women in the combatant nations struggled to deal with its legacy in the years that followed. The raw numbers are astonishing: estimates vary, but total deaths on the battlefield numbered about 8 million soldiers. Russia had the highest number of military casualties, followed by Germany. France had the highest proportionate number of losses; about one out of every ten adult males died in the war. The other belligerents paid a high price as well (Figure 25.1). Between 7 and 10 million civilians died because of the war and war-related hardships, and another 20 million people died in the worldwide influenza epidemic that followed the war in 1918.

The number of dead, the violence of their deaths, and the nature of trench warfare made proper burials difficult, if not impossible. When remains were gathered after or during the fighting, the chaos and danger of the battlefield limited accurate identification. Soldiers were typically interred where they fell, and by 1918 thousands of ad hoc military cemeteries were scattered across northern France and Flanders. After the war, the bodies were moved to more formal cemeteries, but hundreds of thousands remained unidentified. British and German soldiers ultimately remained in foreign soil, in graveyards managed by national commissions. After some delay, the bodies of most of the French combatants were brought home to local cemeteries.

Millions of ordinary people grieved, turning to family, friends, neighbors, and the church for comfort. Towns and villages across Europe raised public memorials to honor the dead and held ceremonies on important anniversaries: on November 11, the day the war ended, and in Britain on July 1, to commemorate the Battle of the Somme. These were poignant and often tearful moments for participants. For the first time, many nations built a Tomb of the Unknown Soldier as a site for national mourning. Memorials were also built on the main battlefields of the war. All expressed the general need to recognize the great sorrow and suffering caused by so much death.

The victims of the First World War included millions of widows and orphans and huge numbers of emotionally scarred and disabled veterans. Countless soldiers suffered from what the British called "shell shock" — now termed post-traumatic stress disorder (PTSD). Contemporary physicians and policymakers poorly understood this complex mental health issue. Although some soldiers suffering from PTSD

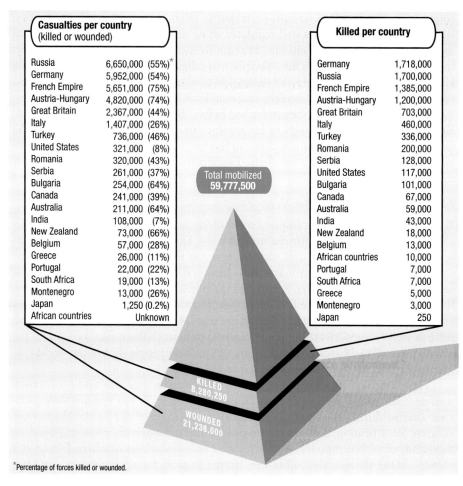

Casualties per country (killed or wounded)			
Russia	6,650,000	(55%)*	
Germany	5,952,000	(54%)	
French Empire	5,651,000	(75%)	
Austria-Hungary	4,820,000	(74%)	
Great Britain	2,367,000	(44%)	
Italy	1,407,000	(26%)	
Turkey	736,000	(46%)	
United States	321,000	(8%)	
Romania	320,000	(43%)	
Serbia	261,000	(37%)	
Bulgaria	254,000	(64%)	
Canada	241,000	(39%)	
Australia	211,000	(64%)	
India	108,000	(7%)	
New Zealand	73,000	(66%)	
Belgium	57,000	(28%)	
Greece	26,000	(11%)	
Portugal	22,000	(22%)	
South Africa	19,000	(13%)	
Montenegro	13,000	(26%)	
Japan	1,250	(0.2%)	
African countries	Unknown		

Killed per country	
Germany	1,718,000
Russia	1,700,000
French Empire	1,385,000
Austria-Hungary	1,200,000
Great Britain	703,000
Italy	460,000
Turkey	336,000
Romania	200,000
Serbia	128,000
United States	117,000
Bulgaria	101,000
Canada	67,000
Australia	59,000
India	43,000
New Zealand	18,000
Belgium	13,000
African countries	10,000
Portugal	7,000
South Africa	7,000
Greece	5,000
Montenegro	3,000
Japan	250

Total mobilized
59,777,500

KILLED
8,280,250

WOUNDED
21,238,000

*Percentage of forces killed or wounded.

FIGURE 25.1   Casualties of World War I
The losses of World War I were the highest ever for a war in Europe. These numbers are approximate because of problems with record keeping caused by the destructive nature of total war.

received medical treatment, others were accused of cowardice and shirking and were denied veterans' benefits.

Some 10 million soldiers came home physically disfigured or mutilated. Governments tried to take care of the disabled and the survivor families, but there was rarely enough money to adequately fund pensions and job-training programs. Artificial limbs were expensive, uncomfortable, and awkward, and some employers refused to hire disabled workers. Crippled veterans were often forced to beg on the streets, a common sight for the next decade.

The German case is illustrative. Nearly 10 percent of German civilians were direct victims of the war in one way or another, and the new German government struggled to take care of them. Veterans' groups organized to lobby for state support, and fully one-third of the federal budget of the Weimar Republic was tied up in war-related pensions and benefits. With the onset of the Great Depression in 1929, benefits were cut, leaving bitter veterans vulnerable to Nazi propagandists who paid homage to the sacrifices of the war while calling for the overthrow of the republican government. The human cost of the war thus had another steep price. Across Europe, newly formed radical right-wing parties, including the German Nazis and the Italian Fascists, successfully manipulated popular feelings of loss and resentment to undermine fragile parliamentary governments.

NOTES

1. Quoted in J. Remak, *The Origins of World War I* (New York: Holt, Rinehart & Winston, 1967), p. 84.
2. On the mood of 1914, see J. Joll, *The Origins of the First World War* (New York: Longman, 1992), pp. 199–233.
3. Quoted in G. L. Mosse, *Fallen Soldiers: Reshaping the Memory of the World Wars* (New York: Oxford University Press, 1990), p. 64.
4. Quoted in N. Malcolm, *Bosnia: A Short History* (New York: New York University Press, 1996), p. 153.
5. V. G. Liulevicius, *War Land on the Eastern Front: Culture, National Identity, and German Occupation in World War I* (New York: Cambridge University Press, 2000), pp. 54–89.
6. Quoted in F. P. Chambers, *The War Behind the War, 1914–1918* (London: Faber & Faber, 1939), p. 168.
7. J. Reed, *Ten Days That Shook the World* (New York: International Publishers, 1967), p. 126.
8. Quoted in H. Nicolson, *Peacemaking 1919* (New York: Grosset & Dunlap Universal Library, 1965), pp. 8, 31–32.
9. Quoted in C. Barnett, *The Swordbearers: Supreme Command in the First World War* (New York: Morrow, 1964), p. 40.

LOOKING BACK **LOOKING AHEAD**

When chief of the German general staff Count Helmuth von Moltke imagined the war of the future in a letter to his wife in 1905, his comments were surprisingly accurate. "It will become a war between peoples which will not be concluded with a single battle," the general wrote, "but which will be a long, weary struggle with a country that will not acknowledge defeat until the whole strength of its people is broken."[9] As von Moltke predicted, World War I broke peoples and nations. The trials of total war increased the power of the centralized state and brought down the Austro-Hungarian, Ottoman, and Russian Empires. The brutal violence shocked and horrified observers across the world; ordinary citizens were left to mourn their losses.

Despite high hopes for Wilson's Fourteen Points, the Treaty of Versailles hardly brought lasting peace. The war's disruptions encouraged radical political conflict in the 1920s and 1930s and the rise of fascist and Communist totalitarian regimes across Europe, which led to the even more extreme violence of the Second World War. Indeed, some historians believe that the years from 1914 to 1945 might most accurately be labeled a modern Thirty Years' War, since the problems unleashed in August 1914 were only really resolved in the 1950s. This strong assertion contains a great deal of truth. For all of Europe, World War I was a revolutionary conflict of gigantic proportions with lasting traumatic effects.

MAKE CONNECTIONS

Think about the larger developments and continuities within and across chapters.

1. While the war was being fought, peoples on all sides of the fighting often referred to the First World War as "the Great War." Why would they find this label appropriate?

2. How did long-standing political rivalries and tensions among the European powers contribute to the outbreak of the First World War (Chapters 19, 23, and 24)?

3. In what ways are current conflicts in the Middle East related to the peace treaties of the First World War and the partition of the Ottoman Empire?

Chapter 25 Review

IDENTIFY KEY TERMS

Identify and explain the significance of each item below.

Triple Alliance (p. 750)	War Communism (p. 771)
Triple Entente (p. 751)	Treaty of Versailles (p. 774)
Schlieffen Plan (p. 755)	Fourteen Points (p. 774)
total war (p. 755)	League of Nations (p. 774)
trench warfare (p. 757)	national self-determination (p. 774)
February Revolution (p. 766)	war guilt clause (p. 776)
Petrograd Soviet (p. 767)	mandate system (p. 777)
Bolsheviks (p. 768)	Balfour Declaration (p. 777)
Treaty of Brest-Litovsk (p. 770)	

REVIEW THE MAIN IDEAS

Answer the section heading questions from the chapter.

1. What caused the outbreak of the First World War? (p. 749)
2. How did the First World War differ from previous wars? (p. 755)
3. In what ways did the war transform life on the home front? (p. 761)
4. Why did world war lead to a successful Communist revolution in Russia? (p. 765)
5. What were the benefits and costs of the postwar peace settlement? (p. 772)

CHRONOLOGY

1914–1918	• World War I
June 28, 1914	• Serbian nationalist assassinates Archduke Franz Ferdinand
August 1914	• War begins
September 1914	• Battle of the Marne; German victories on the eastern front
October 1914	• Ottoman Empire joins the Central Powers
1915	• Italy joins the Triple Entente; German submarine sinks the *Lusitania*; Germany halts unrestricted submarine warfare; Battle of Gallipoli
1915–1918	• Armenian genocide; German armies occupy large parts of east-central Europe
April 1916	• Easter Rebellion in Ireland
1916	• Battles of Verdun and the Somme; Arab rebellion against Ottoman Empire begins
1917	• Germany resumes unrestricted submarine warfare
March 1917	• February Revolution in Russia
April 1917	• United States enters the war
November 1917	• Bolshevik Revolution in Russia; Balfour Declaration on Jewish homeland in Palestine
March 1918	• Treaty of Brest-Litovsk signed between German and Russia, taking Russia out of the war
March–July 1918	• German Spring Offensive on the western front
November 11, 1918	• End of First World War; revolution in Germany
1918–1920	• Civil war in Russia
1919	• Treaty of Versailles; Allies invade Turkey
1923	• Treaty of Lausanne recognizes Turkish independence

26

Opportunity and Crisis in the Age of Modernity

1880–1940

CHAPTER PREVIEW

- How did intellectual developments reflect the ambiguities of modernity?

- How did modernism revolutionize Western culture?

- How did consumer society change everyday life?

- What obstacles to lasting peace did European leaders face?

- What were the causes and consequences of the Great Depression?

WHEN ALLIED DIPLOMATS MET IN PARIS IN EARLY 1919 with their optimistic plans for building a lasting peace, many people looked forward to happier times. After the terrible trauma of total war, they hoped that life would return to normal and would make sense in the familiar prewar terms of peace, progress, and prosperity. Yet life would never be the same. World War I and the Russian Revolution had changed too many things. Instead of a return to past certainties, Europeans faced the ambiguities and contradictions of the modern age.

While faith in science and progress remained strong, late-nineteenth-century thinkers had already called attention to the uncertainty and irrationalism that accompanied modern life. By 1900 developments in philosophy and the sciences had substantiated and popularized such ideas. The modernist movement had begun its sweep through literature, music, and the arts, as avant-garde innovators rejected old cultural forms and began to experiment with new ones. Radical innovations in the arts and sciences dominated Western culture in the 1920s and 1930s and remained influential after World War II. An emerging consumer society, and the new media of radio and film, transformed the habits of everyday life and leisure.

As modern science, art, and culture challenged received wisdom of all kinds, the system of international relations established under the Treaty of Versailles began to unravel. Despite some progress in the mid-1920s, political stability was short-lived, and the Great Depression that began in 1929 shocked the status quo. Democratic liberalism was besieged by the rise of authoritarian and Fascist governments, and another world conflict seemed imminent.

How did intellectual developments reflect the ambiguities of modernity?

The decades surrounding the First World War — from the 1880s to the 1930s — brought intense cultural and intellectual experimentation. As people grappled with the costs of the war and the challenges of postwar recovery, philosophers and scientists questioned and even abandoned many of the cherished values and beliefs that had guided Western society since the eighteenth-century Enlightenment and the nineteenth-century triumph of industry and science.

Modern Philosophy

In the 1920s many people still embraced Enlightenment ideals of progress, reason, and scientific rationalism. At the turn of the century supporters of these philosophies had some cause for optimism. Women and workers were gradually gaining support in their struggles for political and social recognition, and the rising standard of living, the taming of the city, and the growth of state-supported social programs suggested that life was indeed improving. The bloodbath of the First World War had shaken faith in progress, but the notion that the rational human mind could discover the laws of society and then wisely act on them remained strong.

Nevertheless, as Western society entered the age of modernity, people faced growing uncertainties and contradictions. They discovered that modernity — generally defined by historians as the highly industrialized, urbanized class society that had arrived in most of Europe and North America by 1900 — brought pessimism and crisis as well as opportunity and promise. Modernity, they realized, was in essence "Janus faced." Janus, a Roman god, is typically depicted as a single head with two opposing faces — one happy, one sad. Modernity also had at least two sides, a positive one embodied in the developments associated with science and the spread of reason, and a negative one embodied in persistent irrationalism and pessimism and the violence and destruction of modern war.

Modern philosophy echoed the Janus face of modernity. By the late nineteenth century a small group of serious thinkers had mounted a determined attack on the optimism of Enlightenment rationality. These critics rejected the general faith in progress and the rational human mind. The German philosopher Friedrich Nietzsche (NEE-chuh) (1844–1900) was particularly influential, though not until after his death. Never a systematic philosopher, Nietzsche wrote more as a prophet in a provocative and poetic style. In the first of his *Untimely Meditations* (1873), he argued that ever since classical Athens, the West had overemphasized rationality and stifled the authentic passions and animal instincts that drive human activity and true creativity.

Nietzsche questioned the conventional values of Western society. He believed that reason, progress, and respectability were outworn social and psychological constructs that suffocated self-realization and excellence. Though he was the son of a Lutheran minister, Nietzsche famously rejected religion. In his 1887 book, *On the Genealogy of Morals*, he claimed that Christianity embodied a "slave morality" that glorified weakness, envy, and mediocrity. In one of his most famous lines, an apparent madman proclaims that "God is dead," metaphorically murdered by lackadaisical modern Christians who no longer really believed in him.

Nietzsche painted a dark world, perhaps foreshadowing his own loss of sanity in 1889. He warned that Western society was entering a period of nihilism — the grim idea that human life is entirely without meaning, truth, or purpose. Nietzsche asserted that all moral systems were invented lies and that liberalism, democracy, and socialism were corrupt systems designed to promote the weak at the expense of the strong. The West was in decline; false values had triumphed; the death of God left people disoriented and depressed. According to Nietzsche, the only hope for the individual was to accept the meaninglessness of human existence and then make that very meaninglessness a source of self-defined personal integrity and hence liberation. In this way, at least a few superior individuals could free themselves from the humdrum thinking of the masses and become true heroes.

Little read during his active years, Nietzsche's works attracted growing attention in the early twentieth century. Artists and writers experimented with his ideas, which were fundamental to the rise of the philosophy of existentialism in the 1920s. Subsequent generations remade Nietzsche to suit their own needs, and his influence remains enormous to this day.

The growing dissatisfaction with established ideas before 1914 was apparent in other important thinkers as well. In the 1890s French philosophy professor Henri Bergson (1859–1941), for one, argued that immediate experience and intuition were as important as rational and scientific thinking for understanding reality. According to Bergson, a religious experience or mystical poem was often more accessible to human comprehension than a scientific law or a mathematical equation.

The First World War accelerated the revolt against established certainties in philosophy, but that revolt went in two very different directions. In English-speaking countries, the main development was the acceptance of logical positivism in university circles. In the continental countries, the primary development in philosophy was existentialism.

Logical positivism was truly revolutionary. Adherents of this worldview argued that what we know about human life must be based on rational facts and direct observation. They concluded that theology and most traditional philosophy were meaningless because even the most cherished ideas about God, eternal truth, and ethics were impossible to prove using logic. This outlook is often associated with the

Austrian philosopher Ludwig Wittgenstein (VIHT-guhn-shtine) (1889–1951), who later immigrated to England, where he trained numerous disciples.

In his pugnacious *Tractatus Logico-Philosophicus* (*Essay on Logical Philosophy*), published in 1922, Wittgenstein argued that philosophy is only the logical clarification of thoughts and that therefore it should concentrate on the study of language, which expresses thoughts. In his view, the great philosophical issues of the ages—God, freedom, morality, and so on—were quite literally senseless, a great waste of time, for neither scientific experiments nor mathematical logic could demonstrate their validity. Statements about such matters reflected only the personal preferences of a given individual. As Wittgenstein put it in the famous last sentence of this work, "Of what one cannot speak, of that one must keep silent." Logical positivism, which has remained dominant in England and the United States to this day, drastically reduced the scope of philosophical inquiry and offered little solace to ordinary people.

On the continent, others looked for answers in **existentialism**. This new philosophy loosely united highly diverse and even contradictory thinkers in a search for usable moral values in a world of anxiety and uncertainty. Modern existentialism had many nineteenth-century forerunners, including Nietzsche, the Danish religious philosopher Søren Kierkegaard (1813–1855), and the Russian novelist Fyodor Dostoyevsky (1821–1881). The philosophy gained recognition in Germany in the 1920s when philosophers Martin Heidegger (1889–1976) and Karl Jaspers (1883–1969) found a sympathetic audience among disillusioned postwar university students. These writers placed great emphasis on the loneliness and meaninglessness of human existence and the need to come to terms with the fear caused by this situation.

Most existential thinkers in the twentieth century were atheists. Often inspired by Nietzsche, they did not believe that a supreme being had established humanity's fundamental nature and given life its meaning. In the words of French existentialist Jean-Paul Sartre (SAHR-truh) (1905–1980), "existence precedes essence." By that, Sartre meant that there are no God-given, timeless truths outside or independent of individual existence. Only after they are born do people struggle to define their essence, entirely on their own. According to thinkers like Sartre and his lifelong intellectual partner Simone de Beauvoir (1908–1986), existence itself is absurd. Human beings are terribly alone, for there is no God to help them. They are left to confront the inevitable arrival of death and so are hounded by despair. The crisis of the existential thinker epitomized the modern intellectual crisis—the shattering of beliefs in God, reason, and progress.

At the same time, existentialists recognized that human beings must act in the world. Indeed, in the words of Sartre, "man is condemned to be free." Because life is meaningless, existentialists believe that individuals are forced to create their own meaning and define themselves through their actions. Such radical freedom is frightening, and Sartre concluded that most people try to escape it by structuring their lives around conventional social norms. According to Sartre, to escape is to live in "bad faith," to hide from the hard truths of existence. To live authentically, individuals must become "engaged" and choose their own actions in full awareness of their responsibility for their own behavior. Existentialism thus had a powerful ethical component. It placed great stress on individual responsibility and choice, on "being in the world" in the right way.

Existentialism had important precedents in the late nineteenth and early twentieth centuries, but the philosophy really came of age in France during and immediately after World War II. The terrible conditions of that war, discussed in the next chapter, reinforced the existential view of and approach to life. After World War II, French existentialists such as Sartre and Albert Camus (1913–1960) became enormously influential. They offered powerful but unsettling answers to the profound moral issues and the crises of the first half of the twentieth century.

The Revival of Christianity

Although philosophers such as Nietzsche, Wittgenstein, and Sartre believed that religion had little to teach people in the modern age, the decades after the First World War witnessed a tenacious revival of Christian thought. Christianity—and religion in general—had been on the defensive in intellectual circles since the Enlightenment. In the years before 1914 some theologians, especially Protestant ones, had felt the need to interpret Christian doctrine and the Bible so that they did not seem to contradict science, evolution, and common sense. They saw Christ primarily as a great moral teacher and downplayed the mysterious, spiritual aspects of his divinity. Indeed, some modern theologians were embarrassed by the miraculous, unscientific aspects of Christianity and rejected them.

Especially after World War I, a number of thinkers and theologians began to revitalize the fundamental beliefs of Christianity. Sometimes called Christian existentialists because they shared the loneliness and despair of atheistic existentialists, they stressed human beings' sinful nature, their need for faith, and the mystery of God's forgiveness. The revival of Christian belief after World War I was fed by the rediscovery of the work of the nineteenth-century Danish theologian Søren Kierkegaard (KIHR-kuh-gahrd), whose ideas became extremely influential. Kierkegaard believed it was impossible for ordinary people to prove the existence of God, but he rejected the notion that Christianity was an empty practice. In his classic *Sickness unto Death* (1849), Kierkegaard mastered his religious doubts by suggesting that people must take a "leap of faith" and accept the existence of an objectively unknowable but nonetheless awesome and majestic God.

In the 1920s the Swiss Protestant theologian Karl Barth (1886–1968) propounded similar ideas. In brilliant and influential writings, Barth argued that human beings were imperfect, sinful creatures whose reason and will are hopelessly flawed. Religious truth is therefore made known to human beings only through God's grace, not through reason. People have to accept God's word and the supernatural revelation of Jesus Christ with awe, trust, and obedience, not reason or logic.

Among Catholics, the leading existential Christian was Gabriel Marcel (1889–1973). Born into a cultivated French family, Marcel found in the Catholic Church an answer to what he called the postwar "broken world." Catholicism and religious belief provided the hope, humanity, honesty, and piety for which he hungered. Marcel denounced anti-Semitism and supported closer ties with non-Catholics.

After 1914 religion became much more meaningful to intellectuals than it had been before the war. Between about 1920 and 1950, poets T. S. Eliot and W. H. Auden, novelists Evelyn Waugh and Aldous Huxley, historian Arnold Toynbee, writer C. S. Lewis, psychoanalyst Karl Stern, and physicist Max Planck all either converted to a faith or became attracted to religion for the first time. Religion, often of an existential variety, offered one meaningful answer to the horrific costs of the First and Second World Wars and the ambiguities of the age of modernity. In the words of English novelist Graham Greene, a Roman Catholic convert, "One began to believe in heaven because one believed in hell."[1]

The New Physics

Ever since the Scientific Revolution of the seventeenth century, scientific advances and their implications had greatly influenced the beliefs of thinking people. By the late nineteenth century science was one of the main pillars supporting Western society's optimistic and rationalistic worldview. Progressive minds believed that science, unlike religion or philosophical speculation, was based on hard facts and controlled experiments. Unchanging natural laws seemed to determine physical processes and permit useful solutions to more and more problems. All this marked the upside of the modern age, especially for people no longer committed to traditional religious beliefs.

By the 1920s, developments in the science of physics had begun to cast doubt on the unchanging, factual basis of natural law. An important first step came at the

Unlocking the Power of the Atom Many of the fanciful visions of science fiction came true in the twentieth century, although not exactly as first imagined. This 1927 Swedish reprint of a drawing by American cartoonist Robert Fuller satirizes a pair of professors who have split the atom and unwittingly destroyed their building and neighborhood in the process. In the Second World War, professors indeed harnessed the atom in bombs and decimated faraway cities and foreign civilians. (© Mary Evans Picture Library/The Image Works)

end of the nineteenth century with the discovery that atoms were not like hard, permanent little billiard balls. They were actually composed of many far-smaller, fast-moving, unstable particles, such as electrons and protons. Polish-born physicist Marie Curie (1867–1934) and her French husband, Pierre, for example, discovered that radium constantly emits subatomic particles and thus does not have a constant atomic weight. Building on this and other work in radiation, German physicist Max Planck (1858–1947) showed in 1900 that subatomic energy is emitted in uneven little spurts, which Planck called "quanta," and not in a steady stream, as previously believed. Planck's discovery called into question the old sharp distinction between matter and energy: the implication was that matter and energy might be different forms of the same thing. The view of atoms as the stable basic building blocks of nature, with a different kind of unbreakable atom for each of the ninety-two chemical elements, was badly shaken.

In 1905 the German-Jewish genius Albert Einstein (1879–1955) further challenged the mathematical laws at the base of Newtonian physics. Einstein's **theory of special relativity** postulated that time and space are relative to the viewpoint of the observer and that only the speed of light is constant for all frames of reference in the universe. In order to make his revolutionary and paradoxical idea somewhat comprehensible to the nonmathematical layperson, Einstein used analogies involving moving trains: if a woman in the middle of a moving car got up and walked forward to the door, she had gone, relative to the train, a half car length. But relative to an observer on the embankment, she had gone farther. To Einstein, this meant that time and distance were not natural universals but depended on the position and motion of the observer.

In addition, Einstein's theory stated that matter and energy were interchangeable and that even a particle of matter contains enormous levels of potential energy. These ideas unified an apparently infinite universe with the incredibly small, fast-moving subatomic world. In comparison, the closed framework of the Newtonian physics developed during the Scientific Revolution, exemplified by Newton's supposedly immutable laws of motion and mechanics, was quite limited (see "Newton's Synthesis," Chapter 16).

The 1920s opened the "heroic age of physics," in the apt words of Ernest Rutherford (1871–1937), one of its leading pioneers. Breakthrough followed breakthrough. In 1919 Rutherford showed that the atom could be split. By 1944 seven subatomic particles had been identified, the most important of which was the neutron. Physicists realized that the neutron's capacity to shatter the nucleus of another atom could lead to chain reactions of shattered atoms that would release unbelievable force. This discovery was fundamental to the subsequent development of the nuclear bomb.

Although few nonscientists truly understood the revolution in physics, its implications, as presented by newspapers and popular science fiction writers, fascinated millions of men and women in the 1920s and 1930s. As radical as Einstein's ideas was a notion popularized by German physicist Werner Heisenberg (HIGH-zuhn-buhrg) (1901–1976). In 1927 Heisenberg formulated the "uncertainty principle," which postulates that nature itself is ultimately unknowable and unpredictable. He suggested that the universe lacked any absolute objective reality. Everything was "relative," that is, dependent on the observer's frame of reference. Such ideas challenged familiar certainties: instead of Newton's dependable, rational laws, there seemed to be only tendencies and probabilities in an extraordinarily complex and uncertain universe. Like modern philosophy, physics no longer provided comforting truths about natural laws or optimistic answers about humanity's place in an understandable world.

Freudian Psychology

With physics presenting an uncertain universe so unrelated to ordinary human experience, questions regarding the power and potential of the rational human mind assumed special significance. The findings and speculations of Sigmund Freud were particularly influential, yet also deeply provoking.

Before Freud, poets and mystics had probed the unconscious and irrational aspects of human behavior. But most scientists assumed that the conscious mind processed sense experiences in a rational and logical way. Human behavior in turn was the result of rational calculation—of "thinking." Beginning in the late 1880s Freud developed a very different view of the human psyche. Basing his insights on the analysis of dreams and of "hysteria," a sort of nervous breakdown, Freud concluded that human behavior was basically irrational, governed by the unconscious, a mental reservoir that contained vital instinctual drives and powerful memories. Though the unconscious profoundly influenced people's behavior, it was unknowable to the conscious mind, leaving people unaware of the source or meaning of their actions. Freud explained these ideas in his magisterial book *The Interpretation of Dreams*, first published in 1900.

Freud eventually described three structures of the self—the **id**, the **ego**, and the **superego**—that were basically at war with one another. The primitive, irrational id was entirely unconscious. The source of sexual, aggressive, and pleasure-seeking instincts, the id sought immediate fulfillment of all desires and was totally amoral. Keeping the id in check was the superego, the conscience or internalized voice of parental or social control. For Freud, the superego was also irrational. Overly strict and puritanical, it was constantly in conflict with the pleasure-seeking id. The third component was the ego, the rational self that was mostly conscious and worked to negotiate between the demands of the id and the superego.

For Freud, the healthy individual possessed a strong ego that effectively balanced the id and superego. Neurosis, or mental illness, resulted when the three structures were out of balance. Since the id's instinctual drives were extremely powerful, the danger for individuals and indeed whole societies was that unacknowledged drives might overwhelm the control mechanisms of the ego in a violent, distorted way. Freud's "talking cure"—in which neurotic patients lay back on a couch and shared their innermost thoughts with the psychoanalyst—was an attempt to resolve such unconscious tensions and restore the rational ego to its predominant role.

Freudian psychology and clinical psychiatry had become an international medical movement by 1910, but only after 1919 did they receive more public attention, especially in northern Europe. In the United States, Freud's ideas attained immense popularity after the Second World War. Many opponents and even some enthusiasts interpreted Freud as saying that the first requirement for mental health was an uninhibited sex life; popular understandings of Freud thus reflected and encouraged growing sexual experimentation, particularly among middle-class women. For more serious students, the psychology of Freud and his followers weakened the old easy optimism about the rational and progressive nature of the human mind.

How did modernism revolutionize Western culture?

Like the scientists and intellectuals who were part of an increasingly unsettled modern culture, creative artists rejected old forms and values. **Modernism** in architecture, art, literature, and music meant constant experimentation and a search for new kinds of expression. Many artists produced critical, challenging works that called attention to the irrational aspects of Western society. Their work was strikingly original, and the era of early-twentieth-century modernism is widely viewed as one of the greatest in Western art.

Architecture and Design

Already in the late nineteenth century, architects inspired by modernism had begun to transform the physical framework of urban society. The United States, with its rapid urban growth and lack of rigid building traditions, pioneered the new architecture. In the 1890s the Chicago School of architects, led by Louis H. Sullivan (1856–1924), used inexpensive steel, reinforced concrete, and electric elevators to build skyscrapers and office buildings lacking almost any exterior ornamentation. In the first decade of the twentieth century, Sullivan's student Frank Lloyd Wright (1867–1959) built a series of radically modern houses featuring low lines, open interiors, and mass-produced building materials. European architects were inspired by these and other American examples of modern construction.

Modern architects believed that buildings and living spaces in general should be ordered according to a new principle: **functionalism**. Buildings, like industrial products, should be "functional" — that is, they should serve, as well as possible, the purpose for which they were made. According to the Franco-Swiss architect Le Corbusier (luh cowr-booz-YAY) (1887–1965), one of the great champions of modernism, "a house is a machine for living in."[2] Corbusier's polemical work *Towards a New Architecture*, published in 1923, laid out guidelines meant to revolutionize building design. Corbusier argued that architects should affirm and adopt the latest scientific technologies. Rejecting fancy ornamentation, they should find beauty in the clean, straight lines of practical construction and efficient machinery. The resulting buildings, fashioned according to what was soon called the "International Style," were typically symmetrical rectangles made of concrete, glass, and steel.

In Europe, architectural leadership centered in German-speaking countries until Hitler took power in 1933. In 1911 twenty-eight-year-old Walter Gropius (1883–1969) broke sharply with the past in his design of the Fagus shoe factory at Alfeld, Germany — a clean, light, elegant building of glass and iron. In 1919 Gropius merged the schools of fine and applied arts at Weimar into a single interdisciplinary school, the **Bauhaus**. The Bauhaus brought together many leading modern architects, designers, and theatrical innovators.

The impact of the Bauhaus on everyday life, from architecture to interior design, was immense. Working as an effective, inspired team, Bauhaus instructors and students sought to revolutionize product design by unifying art, craft, and technology. They combined the study of fine art, including painting and sculpture, with the study of applied art in the crafts of printing, weaving, and furniture making. Bauhaus adherents argued that everyday objects should reflect the highly rationalized, industrialized, and modern society in which — and for which — they were made. No object was too insignificant to be treated as an object of high design, and the industrial ethos of the Bauhaus was brought to bear on textiles, typography, dishware, and furniture. Such goods were mass-produced and marketed at affordable prices, bringing high-concept design into the lives of ordinary Europeans. Bauhaus architects applied the same principles in designing buildings, from factories to working-class housing projects and private homes.

Another leading modern architect, Ludwig Mies van der Rohe (1886–1969), followed Gropius as director of the Bauhaus in 1930. Like many modernist intellectuals, after 1933 he moved to the United States to escape the repressive Nazi regime. His classic steel-frame and glass-wall Lake Shore Apartments in Chicago, built between 1948 and 1951, epitomized the spread and triumph of the modernist International Style in the great building boom that followed the Second World War.

New Artistic Movements

In the decades surrounding the First World War, the visual arts also entered a phase of radical experimentation. For the previous several centuries, artists had tried to produce accurate representations of reality. Now a committed avant-garde emerged to challenge that practice. From Impressionism and Expressionism to Dadaism and Surrealism, a sometimes-bewildering array of artistic movements followed one after another. Modern painting and sculpture became increasingly abstract as artists turned their backs on figurative representation and began to break down form into its constituent parts: lines, shapes, and colors.

Berlin, Munich, Moscow, Vienna, New York, and especially Paris became famous for their radical artistic undergrounds. Commercial art galleries and exhibition halls promoted the new work, and schools and institutions, such as the Bauhaus, emerged to train a generation in modern techniques. Young artists flocked to these cultural centers to participate in the new movements, earn a living making art, and perhaps change the world with their revolutionary ideas.

One of the earliest modernist movements was Impressionism, which blossomed in Paris in the 1870s. French artists such as Claude Monet (1840–1926) and Edgar Degas (1834–1917), and the American Mary Cassatt (1844–1926), who settled in Paris in 1875, tried to portray their sensory "impressions" in their work. Impressionists looked to the world around them for subject matter, turning their backs on traditional themes such as battles, religious scenes, and wealthy elites. Monet's colorful and atmospheric paintings of farmland haystacks and Degas's many pastel drawings of ballerinas exemplify the way Impressionists moved toward abstraction. Capturing a fleeting moment of color and light, in often blurry and quickly painted images, was far more important than making a heavily detailed, precise rendering of an actual object.

An astonishing array of art movements followed Impressionism. Postimpressionists and Expressionists, such as Vincent van Gogh (1853–1890), built

A Cubist-Constructivist Set Design for *Romeo and Juliet* This 1920 set design for a Moscow production of Shakespeare's famous play is by the noted female avant-garde artist Liubov Popova. Her set is deeply influenced by Cubism and Constructivism, a Russian art movement that often used familiar mechanical forms in abstract works of art. The watercolor testifies to the cross-fertilization of modern art movements, in this case theater, painting, and design. It also exemplifies the artistic experimentation popular in the Soviet Union before Stalin began to force artists to follow the dictates of Socialist Realism. (Private Collection/Moscow, Russia/ Scala/Art Resource, NY)

on Impressionist motifs of color and light but added a deep psychological element to their pictures, reflecting the attempt to search within the self and express inner feelings on the canvas.

After 1900 a generation of artists overturned the art world status quo. In Paris in 1907 painter Pablo Picasso (1881–1973), along with others, established Cubism—a highly analytical approach that concentrated on a complex geometry of zigzagging lines and sharply angled overlapping planes. Cubism exemplified the ongoing trend toward abstract, nonrepresentational art. In 1909 Italian Filippo Tommaso Marinetti (1876–1944) announced the arrival of Futurism, a movement in art and literature determined to glorify modernity and destroy the burdens of the past. According to Marinetti, traditional culture could not adequately deal with the advances of modern technology—automobiles, radios, telephones, phonographs, ocean liners, airplanes, the cinema, the newspaper—and the way these had changed human consciousness. Marinetti embraced the future, championing the speed and confusion of modernity and calling for new art forms that could express the modern condition.

The shock of World War I encouraged further radicalization. In 1916 a group of international artists and intellectuals in exile in Zurich, Switzerland, championed a new movement they called **Dadaism**, which attacked all the familiar standards of art and delighted in outrageous behavior. The war had shown once and for all that life was meaningless, the Dadaists argued, so art should be meaningless as well. Dadaists tried to shock their audiences with what they called "anti-art," works and public performances that were insulting and entirely nonsensical. A well-known example is a reproduction of Leonardo da Vinci's *Mona Lisa* in which the masterpiece is ridiculed with the addition of a hand-drawn mustache and an obscene inscription. After the war, Dadaism became an international movement, spreading to Paris, New York, and particularly Berlin in the early 1920s.

During the mid-1920s some Dadaists turned to Surrealism, a movement deeply influenced by the Freudian idea of the unconscious. Surrealists painted fantastic worlds of wild dreams and uncomfortable symbols, where watches melted and giant metronomes beat time in precisely drawn but impossibly alien landscapes.

Many modern artists sincerely believed that art had a transformative mission. By calling attention to the bankruptcy of mainstream society, they thought art had the power to change the world. The sometimes-nonsensical manifestos written by members of the Dadaist, Futurist, and Surrealist movements were meant to spread their ideas, challenge conventional assumptions of all kinds, and foment social change.

By the 1920s art and culture had become increasingly politicized. Many avant-garde artists sided with the far left; some became committed Communists. Such artists and modern art movements in general had a difficult time surviving the political crises of the 1930s. Between 1933 and 1945, the National Socialist (Nazi) Party came to power in Germany and brought a second world war to the European continent. The Nazis despised the abstract ambiguities of modernism, and hundreds of artists and intellectuals — often Jews and leftists — fled to the United States to escape Nazi repression. After World War II, New York greatly benefited from this transfusion of talent and replaced Paris and Berlin as the world capital of modern art.

Twentieth-Century Literature

In the decades that followed the First World War, Western literature was deeply influenced by the turn toward radical experimentation that swept through the other arts. The great nineteenth-century novelists had typically written as all-knowing narrators, describing realistic characters and their relationships to an understandable, if sometimes harsh, society. Modernist writers developed new techniques to express new realities. In the twentieth century many authors adopted the limited, often confused viewpoint of a single individual. Like Freud, they focused on the complexity and irrationality of the human mind, where feelings, memories, and desires were forever scrambled. French novelist Marcel Proust (PROOST) (1871–1922), in his semi-autobiographical, multivolume *Remembrance of Things Past*, published in 1927, recalled bittersweet memories of childhood and youthful love and tried to discover their innermost meaning. To do so, Proust lived like a hermit in a soundproof Paris apartment for ten years, withdrawing from the present to dwell on the past.

Some novelists used the **stream-of-consciousness technique**, relying on internal monologues to explore the human psyche. In *Jacob's Room* (1922), the English author Virginia Woolf (1882–1941) created a novel made up of a series of such monologues in which she tried to capture the inner voice in prose. In this and other stories, Woolf portrayed characters whose ideas and emotions from different periods of their lives bubble up as randomly as from a patient on a psychoanalyst's couch. William Faulkner (1897–1962), one of America's great novelists, used the same technique in *The Sound and the Fury* (1929), with much of its intense drama confusedly seen through the eyes of a man who is mentally disabled.

The most famous and perhaps most experimental stream-of-consciousness novel was *Ulysses* (1922) by Irish novelist James Joyce (1882–1941). Into an account of a single day in the life of an ordinary man, Joyce weaves an extended ironic parallel between the aimless wanderings of his hero through the streets and pubs of Dublin and the adventures of Homer's hero Ulysses on his way home from Troy. *Ulysses* was surely one of the most disturbing novels of its generation. Abandoning any sense of a conventional plot, breaking rules of grammar, and blending foreign words, puns, bits of knowledge, and scraps of memory together in bewildering confusion, *Ulysses* is intended to mirror modern life: a gigantic riddle impossible to unravel. Since Joyce included frank descriptions of the main character's sexual thoughts and encounters, the novel was considered obscene in Great Britain and the United States and was banned there until the early 1930s.

As creative writers turned their attention from society to the individual and from realism to psychological relativity, they rejected the idea of progress. Some described "anti-utopias," nightmare visions of things to come, as in the T. S. Eliot poem *The Waste Land* (1922), which depicts a world of growing desolation:

> April is the cruelest month, breeding
> Lilacs out of the dead land, mixing
> Memory and desire, stirring
> Dull roots with spring rain.
> . . .
> What are the roots that clutch, what branches grow
> Out of this stony rubbish? Son of man,
> You cannot say, or guess, for you know only
> A heap of broken images, where the sun beats,
> And the dead tree gives no shelter, the cricket no relief,
> And the dry stone no sound of water.[3]

With its biblical references, images of a ruined and wasted natural world, and general human incomprehension, Eliot (1888–1965) expressed the crisis of confidence that followed the First World War. The Czech writer Franz Kafka (1883–1924) likewise portrayed an incomprehensible, alienating world. Kafka's novels *The Trial* (1925) and *The Castle* (1926) are stories about helpless people crushed by inexplicably hostile forces, as is his famous novella *The Metamorphosis* (1915), in which the main character turns into a giant insect. The German-Jewish Kafka died young, at forty-one, and was spared the horror of seeing the world of his nightmares materialize in the Nazi state. In these and many other works, authors between the wars used new literary techniques and dark imagery to capture the anxiety of the modern age.

Modern Music

Developments in modern music paralleled those in painting and fiction. Composers and performers captured the emotional intensity and shock of modernism in radically experimental forms. The ballet *The Rite of Spring* by Russian composer Igor Stravinsky (1882–1971), for example, practically caused a riot when it was first performed in Paris in 1913. The combination of pulsating rhythms and dissonant sounds from the orchestra pit with earthy representations of lovemaking by the strangely dressed dancers on the stage shocked audiences accustomed to traditional ballet.

After the First World War, when irrationality and violence had seemed to pervade human experience, modernism flourished in opera and ballet. One of the most powerful examples was the opera *Wozzeck*, by Alban Berg (1885–1935), first performed in Berlin in 1925. Blending a half-sung, half-spoken kind of dialogue with harsh, atonal music, *Wozzeck* is a gruesome tale of a soldier driven by inner terrors and vague suspicions of infidelity to murder his mistress.

Some composers turned their backs on long-established musical conventions. Just as abstract painters arranged lines and color but did not draw identifiable objects, so modern composers arranged sounds without creating recognizable harmonies. Led by Viennese composer Arnold Schönberg (SHURN-buhrg) (1874–1951), they abandoned traditional harmony and tonality. The musical notes in a given piece were no longer united and organized by a key; instead they were independent and unrelated. Schönberg's twelve-tone music of the 1920s arranged all twelve notes of the scale in an abstract mathematical pattern, or "tone row." This pattern sounded like no pattern at all to the ordinary listener and could be detected only by a highly trained eye studying the musical score. Accustomed to the harmonies of classical and romantic music, audiences generally resisted atonal music. Only after the Second World War did it begin to win acceptance.

How did consumer society change everyday life?

Fundamental innovations in the basic provision and consumption of goods and services accompanied the radical transformation of artistic and intellectual life. A range of new mass-produced goods, from telephones to vacuum cleaners, and the arrival of cinema and radio, heralded the first steps toward a consumer revolution that would be fully consolidated in the 1950s and 1960s.

Modern Mass Culture

The emerging consumer society of the 1920s is a good example of the way technological developments can lead to widespread social change. The arrival of a highly industrialized manufacturing system dedicated to mass-producing inexpensive goods, the establishment of efficient transportation systems that could bring these goods to national markets, and the rise of professional advertising experts to sell them were all part of a revolution in the way consumer goods were made, marketed, and used by ordinary people.

Contemporaries viewed the new mass culture as a distinctly modern aspect of everyday life. It seemed that consumer goods themselves were modernizing society by changing so many ingrained habits. Some people embraced the new ways; others worried that these changes threatened familiar values and precious traditions.

Critics had good reason to worry. Mass-produced goods had a profound impact on the lives of ordinary people. Housework and private life were increasingly organized around an array of modern appliances, from electric ovens, washing machines, and refrigerators to telephones and radios. The aggressive marketing of fashionable clothing and personal care products, such as shampoo, perfume, and makeup, encouraged a cult of youthful "sex appeal." Advertisements increasingly linked individual attractiveness to the use of brand-name products. The mass production and marketing of automobiles and the rise of tourist agencies opened roads to increased mobility and travel.

Commercialized mass entertainment likewise prospered and began to dominate the way people spent their leisure time. Movies and radio thrilled millions. Professional sporting events drew throngs of fans. Thriving print media brought readers an astounding variety of newspapers, inexpensive books, and glossy illustrated magazines. Flashy restaurants, theatrical revues, and nightclubs competed for evening customers.

Department stores epitomized the emergence of consumer society. Already well established across Europe and the United States by the 1890s, they had become veritable temples of commerce by the 1920s. The typical store sold an enticing variety of goods, including clothing, housewares, food, and spirits. Larger stores included travel bureaus, movie theaters, and refreshment stands. Aggressive advertising campaigns, youthful and attractive salespeople, and easy credit and return policies helped attract customers in droves.

The emergence of modern consumer culture both undermined and reinforced existing social differences. On one hand, consumerism helped democratize Western society. Since anyone with the means could purchase any item, consumer culture helped break down old social barriers based on class, region, and religion. Yet it also reinforced social differences. Manufacturers soon realized they could profit by marketing goods to specific groups. Catholics, for example, could purchase their own popular literature and inexpensive devotional items; young people eagerly bought the latest fashions marketed directly to them. In addition, the expense of many items meant that only the wealthy could purchase them. Automobiles and, in the 1920s, even vacuum cleaners cost so much that ownership became a status symbol.

The changes in women's lives were particularly striking. The new household items transformed how women performed housework. Advice literature of all kinds encouraged housewives to rush out and buy the latest appliances so they could "modernize" the home. Consumer culture brought growing public visibility to women, especially the young. Girls and young women worked behind the counters and shopped in the aisles of department stores, and they went out on the street alone in ways unthinkable in the nineteenth century.

Contemporaries spoke repeatedly about the new **"modern girl,"** an independent young woman who could vote and held a job, spent her salary on the latest fashions, applied makeup and smoked cigarettes, and used her sex appeal to charm any number of modern men. "The woman of yesterday" yearned for marriage and children and "honor[ed] the achievements of the 'good old days,'" wrote one

German feminist in 1929. The "woman of today," she continued, "refuses to be regarded as a physically weak being . . . and seeks to support herself through gainful employment. . . . Her task is to clear the way for equal rights for women in all areas of life."[4]

Despite such enthusiasm, the modern girl was in some ways a stereotype, a product of marketing campaigns dedicated to selling goods. Few young women could afford to live up to this image, even if they did have jobs. Yet the changes in women's roles associated with the First World War and the emergence of consumer society did loosen traditional limits on women's behavior.

The emerging consumer culture generated a chorus of complaint from cultural critics of all stripes. On the left, socialist writers worried that its appeal undermined working-class radicalism, because mass culture created passive consumers rather than active, class-conscious revolutionaries. On the right, conservatives complained that money spent on frivolous consumer goods sapped the livelihood of industrious artisans and undermined proud national traditions. Religious leaders protested that modern consumerism encouraged rampant individualism and that greedy materialism was replacing spirituality. Many bemoaned the supposedly loose morals of the modern girl and fretted over the decline of traditional family values.

Despite such criticism—which continued after World War II—consumer society was here to stay. Ordinary people enjoyed the pleasures of mass consumption, and individual identities were tied ever more closely to modern mass-produced goods. Yet the Great Depression of 1929 soon made actual participation in the new world of goods elusive. The promise of prosperity would only truly be realized during the economic boom that followed the Second World War.

The Appeal of Cinema

Nowhere was the influence of mass culture more evident than in the rapid growth of commercial entertainment, especially cinema and radio. Both became major industries in the interwar years, and an eager public enthusiastically embraced them, spending their hard-earned money and their leisure hours watching movies or listening to radio broadcasts. These mass media overshadowed and began to replace the traditional amusements of people in cities, and then in small towns and villages, changing familiar ways of life.

Cinema first emerged in the United States around 1880, driven in part by the inventions of Thomas Edison. By 1910 American directors and business people had set up "movie factories," at first in the New York area and then in Los Angeles. Europeans were quick to follow. By 1914 small production companies had formed in Great Britain, France, Germany, and Italy, among others. World War I quickened the pace. National leaders realized that movies offered distraction to troops and citizens and served as an effective means of spreading propaganda. Audiences lined up to see *The Battle of the Somme*, a British film released in August 1916 that was frankly intended to encourage popular support for the war. For the audience, watching this early example of cinematic propaganda (which now seems quite primitive) could be heart wrenching: "The tears in many people's eyes and the silence that prevailed when I saw the film showed that every heart was full of love and sympathy for our soldiers," wrote one viewer to the *London Times* that September.[5]

Cinema became a true mass medium in the 1920s, the golden age of silent film. The United States was again a world leader, but European nations also established important national studios. Germany's Universal Film Company (or UFA) was particularly renowned. In the massive Babelsberg Studios just outside Berlin, talented UFA directors produced classic Expressionist films such as *Nosferatu* (1922), a creepy vampire story, and *Metropolis* (1927), about a future society in the midst of a working-class revolt. Such films made use of cutting-edge production techniques, thrilling audiences with fast and slow motion, montage sequences, unsettling close-ups, and unusual dissolves.

Film making became big business on an international scale. Studios competed to place their movies on foreign screens, and European theater owners were sometimes forced to book whole blocks of American films to get the few pictures they really wanted. In response, European governments set quotas on the number of U.S. films they imported. By 1926 U.S. money was drawing German directors and stars to Hollywood and consolidating America's international domination. These practices put European producers at a disadvantage until "talkies" permitted a revival of national film industries in the 1930s, particularly in France.

Motion pictures would remain the central entertainment of the masses until after the Second World War and the rise of television. People flocked to the gigantic movie palaces built across Europe in the mid-1920s, splendid theaters that could seat thousands. There they viewed the latest features, which were reviewed by critics in newspapers and flashy illustrated magazines. Cinema audiences grew rapidly in the 1930s. In Great Britain in the late 1930s, one in every four adults went to the movies twice a week, and two in five went at least once a week. Audience numbers were similar in other countries.

As these numbers suggest, motion pictures could be powerful tools of indoctrination, especially in countries with dictatorial regimes. In the Soviet Union, Lenin encouraged the development of the movie industry, believing that the new medium was essential to the social and ideological transformation of the country. Beginning in the mid-1920s, a series of epic films, the most famous of which were directed by Sergei Eisenstein (1898–1948), brilliantly dramatized the Communist view of Russian history. In Nazi Germany, the film maker Leni Riefenstahl (REE-fuhn-shtahl) (1902–2003) directed a masterpiece of documentary propaganda, *Triumph of the Will*, based on the 1934 Nazi Party rally at Nuremberg. Riefenstahl combined stunning aerial photography with mass processions of young Nazi fanatics and images of joyful crowds welcoming Adolf Hitler. Her film, released in 1935, was a brilliant yet chilling documentary of the rise of Nazism.

The Arrival of Radio

Like film, radio became a full-blown mass medium in the 1920s. Experimental radio sets were first available in the 1880s; the work of Italian inventor Guglielmo Marconi (1874–1937) around 1900 and the development of the vacuum tube in 1904 made possible primitive transmissions of speech and music. But the first major public broadcasts of news and special events occurred only in the early 1920s, in Great Britain and the United States.

Every major country quickly established national broadcasting networks. In the United States such networks were privately owned and were financed by advertising, but in Europe the typical pattern was direct control by the government. In Great Britain, Parliament set up an independent public corporation, the British Broadcasting Corporation (BBC), supported by licensing fees. Whatever the institutional framework, radio enjoyed a meteoric growth in popularity. By the late 1930s more than three out of every four households in both democratic Great Britain and dictatorial Germany had at least one radio.

Like the movies, radio was well suited for political propaganda. Dictators such as Hitler and Italy's Benito Mussolini could reach enormous national audiences with their dramatic speeches. In democratic countries, politicians such as American president Franklin Roosevelt and British prime minister Stanley Baldwin effectively used informal "fireside chats" to bolster their popularity.

What obstacles to lasting peace did European leaders face?

The Versailles settlement had established a shaky truce to end World War I, not a solid postwar peace. In the 1920s, leaders faced a gigantic task as they sought to create a stable international order within the general context of social crisis, halting economic growth, and political turmoil.

Germany and the Western Powers

Germany was the key to lasting stability. Yet to Germans of all political parties, the Treaty of Versailles represented a harsh dictated peace, to be revised or repudiated as soon as possible. Germany still had the potential to become the strongest country in Europe, but its future remained uncertain. Moreover, with ominous implications, France and Great Britain did not see eye to eye on Germany.

Immediately after the war, the French wanted to stress the harsh elements in the Treaty of Versailles. Most of the war in the west had been fought on French soil, and the expected costs of reconstruction, as well as of repaying war debts to the United States, were staggering. Thus French politicians believed that massive reparations from Germany were vital for economic recovery. After having compromised with President Wilson only to be betrayed by America's failure to ratify the treaty, many French leaders saw strict implementation of all provisions of the Treaty of Versailles as France's last best hope. Large reparation payments could hold Germany down indefinitely, ensuring French security.

The British soon felt differently. Before the war Germany had been Great Britain's second-best market in the world; after the war a healthy, prosperous Germany appeared to be essential to the British economy. Many British agreed with the analysis of the English economist John Maynard Keynes (1883–1946), who eloquently denounced the Treaty of Versailles in his book *The Economic Consequences of the Peace* (1919). According to Keynes, astronomical reparations

Jugend Nr. 36

**Ihr Mütter der Welt,
starben d a f ü r Eure Söhne?**

"**Mothers of the World, Did Your Sons Die _For This_?**" In 1923 the French army occupied the industrial district of the Ruhr in Germany in an effort to force reparation payments. The occupying forces included colonial troops from West Africa, and Germans responded with a racist propaganda campaign that cast the West African soldiers as uncivilized savages intent on ravaging German women. (Kharbine-Tapabor/Shutterstock)

and harsh economic measures would impoverish Germany, encourage Bolshevism, and increase economic hardship in all countries. Only a complete revision of the treaty could save Germany — and Europe. Keynes's influential critique engendered much public discussion and helped create sympathy for Germany in the English-speaking world.

In addition, British politicians were suspicious of both France's army — the largest in Europe, and authorized at Versailles to occupy the German Rhineland until 1935 — and France's expansive foreign policy. Since 1890 France had looked to Russia as a powerful ally against Germany. But with Russia hostile and Communist, and with Britain and the United States unwilling to make any firm commitments, France turned to the newly formed states of central Europe for diplomatic support. In 1921 France signed a mutual defense pact with Poland and associated itself closely with the so-called Little Entente, an alliance that joined Czechoslovakia, Romania, and Yugoslavia against defeated and bitter Hungary.

While French and British leaders drifted in different directions, the Allied commission created to determine German reparations completed its work. In April 1921 it announced that Germany had to pay the enormous sum of 132 billion gold marks ($33 billion) in annual installments of 2.5 billion gold marks. Facing possible occupation of more of its territory, the young German republic — generally known as the Weimar Republic — made its first payment in 1921. Then in 1922, wracked by rapid inflation and political assassinations and motivated by hostility and arrogance as well, German leaders announced their inability to pay more. They proposed a moratorium on reparations for three years, with the clear implication that thereafter the payments would be either drastically reduced or eliminated entirely.

The British were willing to accept a moratorium, but the French were not. Led by their tough-minded prime minister, Raymond Poincaré (1860–1934), they decided they had to either call Germany's bluff or see the entire peace settlement dissolve to France's great disadvantage. If the Germans refused to pay reparations, France would use military occupation to paralyze Germany and force it to accept the Treaty of Versailles. So, despite strong British protests, in early January 1923 French and Belgian armies moved out of the Rhineland and began to occupy the Ruhr district, the heartland of industrial Germany, creating the most serious international crisis of the 1920s.

Strengthened by a wave of German patriotism, the German government ordered the people of the Ruhr to stop working, a way to passively resist the French occupation. The coal mines and steel mills of the Ruhr fell silent, leaving 10 percent of Germany's population out of work. The French responded by sealing off the Ruhr and the Rhineland from the rest of Germany, letting in only enough food to prevent starvation. German public opinion was incensed when the French sent over forty thousand colonial troops from North and West Africa to control the territory. German propagandists labeled these troops the "black shame," warning that the African soldiers were savages, eager to brutalize civilians and assault German women. These racist attacks, though entirely unfounded, nonetheless intensified tensions.

By the summer of 1923 France and Germany were engaged in a great test of wills. French armies could not collect reparations from striking workers at gunpoint, but the occupation was paralyzing Germany and its economy. To support the workers and their employers, the German government began to print money to pay its bills, causing runaway inflation. Prices soared as German money rapidly lost all value. People went to the store with bags of banknotes; they returned home with handfuls of groceries. Catastrophic inflation cruelly mocked the old middle-class virtues of thrift, caution, and self-reliance as savings were wiped out. Many Germans felt betrayed. They hated and blamed the Western governments, their own government, big business, the Jews, and the Communists for their misfortune. Right-wing nationalists—including Adolf Hitler and the newly established Nazi Party—eagerly capitalized on the widespread discontent.

In August 1923, as the mark lost value and unrest spread throughout Germany, Gustav Stresemann (SHTRAY-zuh-mahn) (1878–1929) assumed leadership of the government. Stresemann tried compromise. He called off passive resistance in the Ruhr and in October agreed in principle to pay reparations, but asked for a re-examination of Germany's ability to pay. Poincaré accepted. His hard line had become unpopular in France, and it was hated in Britain and the United States. In addition, power in both Germany and France was passing to more moderate leaders who realized that continued confrontation was a destructive, no-win situation. Thus, after five long years of hostility and tension, culminating in a kind of undeclared war in the Ruhr in 1923, Germany and France both decided to try compromise. The British, and even the Americans, were willing to help. The first step was to reach an agreement on the reparations question.

Hope in Foreign Affairs

In 1924 an international committee of financial experts headed by American banker Charles G. Dawes met to re-examine German reparation payments from a broad perspective. The resulting **Dawes Plan** (1924) was accepted by France, Germany, and Britain. Germany's yearly reparation payments were reduced and linked to the level of German economic output. Germany would also receive large loans from the

United States to promote economic recovery. In short, Germany would get private loans from the United States in order to pay reparations to France and Britain, thus enabling those countries to repay the large war debts they owed the United States.

This circular flow of international payments was complicated and risky, but for a while it worked. With continual inflows of American capital, the German republic experienced a shaky economic recovery. Germany paid about $1.3 billion in reparations in 1927 and 1928, enabling France and Britain to repay the United States. In this way the Americans belatedly played a part in the general settlement that, though far from ideal, facilitated precarious economic growth in the mid 1920s.

A political settlement accompanied the economic accords. In 1925 the leaders of Europe signed a number of agreements at Locarno, Switzerland. Germany and France solemnly pledged to accept their common border, and both Britain and Italy agreed to fight either France or Germany if one invaded the other. Stresemann reluctantly agreed to settle boundary disputes with Poland and Czechoslovakia by peaceful means, although he did not agree on permanent borders to Germany's east. In response, France reaffirmed its pledge of military aid to those countries if Germany attacked them. The refusal to settle Germany's eastern borders angered the Poles, and though the "spirit of Locarno" lent some hope to those seeking international stability, political tensions deepened in central Europe.

Other developments suggested possibilities for international peace. In 1926 Germany joined the League of Nations, and in 1928 fifteen countries signed the Kellogg-Briand Pact, initiated by French prime minister Aristide Briand and U.S. secretary of state Frank B. Kellogg. The signing states agreed to "renounce [war] as an instrument of international policy" and to settle international disputes peacefully. The pact made no provisions for disciplinary action in case war actually broke out and would not prevent the arrival of the Second World War in 1939. In the late 1920s, however, it fostered a cautious optimism and encouraged the hope that the United States would accept its responsibilities as a great world power by contributing to European stability.

Hope in Democratic Government

Domestic politics also offered reason to hope. During the occupation of the Ruhr and the great inflation, republican government in Germany had appeared on the verge of collapse. In 1923 Communists momentarily entered provincial governments, and in November an obscure politician named Adolf Hitler leaped onto a table in a beer hall in Munich and proclaimed a "national socialist revolution." But the young republican government easily crushed Hitler's Beer Hall Putsch (a violent attempt to overthrow a government), and he was sentenced to a short term in prison. In the late 1920s liberal democracy seemed to take root in Weimar Germany. Elections were held regularly, and republican democracy appeared to have growing support among a majority of Germans. A new currency was established, and the economy stabilized. The moderate businessmen who tended to dominate the various German coalition governments were convinced that economic prosperity demanded good relations with the Western powers, and they supported parliamentary government at home.

Sharp political divisions remained, however. Throughout the 1920s Hitler's Nazi Party attracted support from fanatical anti-Semites, ultranationalists, and disgruntled ex-servicemen. Many unrepentant nationalists and monarchists supported the far right. On the left, members of Germany's recently formed Communist Party were noisy and active. The Communists, directed from Moscow, reserved their greatest hatred and sharpest barbs for their cousins the Social Democrats, whom they accused of betraying the revolution. Though the working class was divided, a majority supported the nonrevolutionary Social Democrats.

The situation in France was similar to that in Germany. Communists and Socialists battled for workers' support. After 1924 the democratically elected government rested mainly in the hands of coalitions of moderates, with business interests well represented. France's great accomplishment was the rapid rebuilding of its war-torn northeastern region. The expense of this undertaking led, however, to a large deficit and substantial inflation. By early 1926 the franc had fallen to 10 percent of its prewar value, causing a severe crisis. Poincaré was recalled to office, while Briand remained minister for foreign affairs. Poincaré slashed spending and raised taxes, restoring confidence in the economy. The franc was stabilized at about one-fifth of its prewar value, and the economy remained fairly stable until 1930.

Britain, too, faced challenges after 1920. The great problem was unemployment. In June 1921 almost 2.2 million people—or 23 percent of the labor force—were out of work, and throughout the 1920s unemployment hovered around 12 percent, leading to a massive general strike in 1926. Yet the state provided unemployment benefits and supplemented the payments with subsidized housing, medical aid, and increased old-age pensions. These and other measures kept living standards from seriously declining, helped moderate class tensions, and pointed the way toward the welfare state Britain would establish after World War II.

Relative social harmony was accompanied by the rise of the Labour Party, founded in 1900 as a determined champion of greater social equality and the working class. Committed to the kind of moderate revisionist socialism that had emerged before World War I, the Labour Party replaced the Liberal Party as the main opposition to the Conservatives. This shift reflected the decline of old liberal ideals of competitive capitalism, limited government control, and individual responsibility. In 1924 and from 1929 to 1931, the Labour Party under Ramsay MacDonald (1866–1937) governed the country with the support of the smaller Liberal Party. Yet Labour moved toward socialism gradually and democratically, so as not to antagonize the middle classes.

The British Conservatives showed the same compromising spirit on social issues. In 1922 Britain granted southern, Catholic, Ireland full autonomy after a bitter guerrilla war, thereby removing a key source of prewar friction. Despite conflicts such as the 1926 strike by hard-pressed coal miners, which led to an unsuccessful general strike, social unrest in Britain was limited in the 1920s and 1930s. Developments in both international relations and the domestic politics of the leading democracies across western Europe gave some cause for optimism in the late 1920s.

What were the causes and consequences of the Great Depression?

This fragile optimism was short-lived. Beginning in 1929, a massive economic downturn struck the entire world with ever-greater intensity. Recovery was slow and uneven, and contemporaries labeled the economic crisis the **Great Depression**, to emphasize its severity and duration. Only with the Second World War did the depression disappear in much of the world. The prolonged economic collapse shattered the fragile political stability of the mid-1920s and encouraged the growth of extremists on both ends of the political spectrum.

The Economic Crisis

Though economic activity was already declining moderately in many countries by early 1929, the crash of the stock market in the United States in October of that year initiated a worldwide crisis. The American economy had prospered in the late 1920s, but there were large inequalities in income and a serious imbalance between actual business investment and stock market speculation. Thus net investment—in factories, farms, equipment, and the like—actually fell from $3.5 billion in 1925 to $3.2 billion in 1929. In the same years, as money flooded into stocks, the value of shares traded on the exchanges soared from $27 billion to $87 billion. Such inflated prices should have raised serious concerns about economic solvency, but even experts failed to predict the looming collapse.

This stock market boom—or "bubble" in today's language—was built on borrowed money. Many wealthy investors, speculators, and people of modest means bought stocks by paying only a small fraction of the total purchase price and borrowing the remainder from their stockbrokers. Such buying "on margin" was extremely risky. When prices started falling in 1929, the hard-pressed margin buyers had to either put up more money, which was often impossible, or sell their shares to pay off their brokers. Thousands of people started selling all at once. The result was a financial panic. Countless investors and speculators were wiped out in a matter of days or weeks.

The consequences were swift and severe. Stripped of wealth and confidence, battered investors and their fellow citizens started buying fewer goods. Prices fell, production began to slow down, and unemployment began to rise. Soon the entire American economy was caught in a spiraling decline.

The financial panic triggered an international financial crisis. Throughout the 1920s American bankers and investors had lent large amounts of capital to many countries. Once the panic broke, U.S. bankers began recalling the loans they had made to foreign businesses. Gold reserves began to flow rapidly out of European countries, particularly Germany and Austria, toward the United States. It became very hard for European businesses to borrow money, and panicky Europeans began to withdraw their savings from banks. These banking problems eventually led to the crash of the largest bank in Austria in 1931 and then to general financial chaos. The recall of loans by American bankers also accelerated a collapse in world prices when businesses dumped industrial goods and agricultural commodities in a frantic attempt to get cash to pay their loans.

The financial crisis led to a general crisis of production: between 1929 and 1933 world output of goods fell by an estimated 38 percent. As this happened, each country turned inward and tried to manage the crisis alone. In 1931, for example, Britain went off the gold standard, refusing to convert banknotes into gold, and reduced the value of its money. Britain's goal was to make its goods cheaper and therefore more salable in the world market. But more than twenty other nations, including the United States in 1934, also went off the gold standard, so few countries gained a real advantage from this step—though Britain was an exception. Similarly, country after country followed the example of the United States when in 1930 it raised protective tariffs to their highest levels ever and tried to seal off shrinking national markets for domestic producers. Such actions further limited international trade. Within this context of fragmented and destructive economic nationalism, a recovery did not begin until 1933 and it was a halting one at that.

Although opinions differ, two factors probably best explain the relentless slide to the bottom from 1929 to early 1933. First, the international economy lacked leadership able to maintain stability when the crisis came. Neither Britain nor the United States—the world's economic leaders at the time—successfully stabilized the international economic system in 1929. The American decisions to cut back on international lending and erect high tariffs, as we have seen, had damaging ripple effects.

The second factor was poor national economic policy in almost every country. Governments generally cut their budgets when they should have raised spending and accepted large deficits in order to stimulate their economies. After World War II, this "counter-cyclical policy," advocated by John Maynard Keynes, became a well-established weapon against downturn and depression. But in the 1930s orthodox economists who believed balanced budgets to be the key to economic growth generally regarded Keynes's prescription with horror.

Mass Unemployment

The lack of large-scale government spending contributed to the rise of mass unemployment. As the financial crisis led to production cuts, workers lost their jobs and had little money to buy goods. In Britain, where unemployment had averaged 12 percent in the 1920s, it averaged more than 18 percent between 1930 and 1935. Far worse was the case of Germany, where in 1932 one in every three workers was jobless. In the United States, unemployment had averaged only 5 percent in the 1920s. In 1933 it soared to about 30 percent: almost 13 million people were out of work (Map 26.1).

Mass unemployment created great social problems. Poverty increased dramatically, although in most countries unemployed workers generally received some kind of meager unemployment benefits or public aid that prevented starvation. Millions of people lost their spirit, condemned to an apparently hopeless search for work. Homes and ways of life were disrupted in millions of personal tragedies. Young people postponed marriages, and birthrates fell sharply. As poverty or the threat of poverty became a grinding reality, cases of suicide and mental illness increased. In 1932 a union official in Manchester, England, called on city officials to do more to provide work and warned that "hungry men are angry men."[6] Only strong government action could deal with mass unemployment, a social powder keg preparing to explode.

The New Deal in the United States

The Great Depression and the government response to it marked a major turning point in American history. President Herbert Hoover (U.S. pres. 1929–1933) and his administration initially reacted to the stock market crash and economic decline

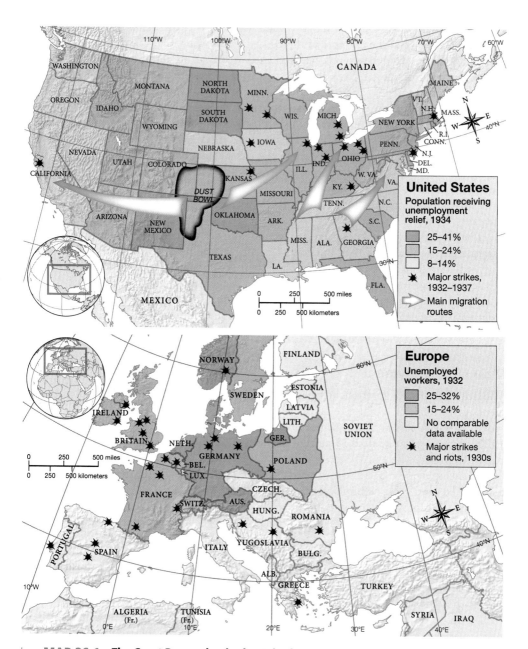

MAP 26.1   The Great Depression in the United States and Europe, 1929–1939
These maps show that unemployment was high almost everywhere but that national and regional differences were also substantial.

with dogged optimism but limited action. When the full force of the financial crisis struck Europe in the summer of 1931 and boomeranged back to the United States, people's worst fears became reality. Banks failed; unemployment soared. Between 1929 and 1932 industrial production fell by about 50 percent.

In these dire circumstances, Franklin Delano Roosevelt (U.S. pres. 1933–1945) won a landslide presidential victory in 1932 with grand but vague promises of a "New Deal for the forgotten man." Roosevelt's goal was to reform capitalism in order to save it. Though Roosevelt rejected socialism and government ownership of industry, he advocated forceful government intervention in the economy and instituted a broad range of government-supported social programs designed to stimulate the economy and provide jobs.

In the United States, innovative federal programs promoted agricultural recovery, a top priority. Almost half of the American population still lived in rural areas, and the depression hit farmers hard. Roosevelt took the United States off the gold standard and devalued the dollar in an effort to raise American prices and rescue farmers. The Agricultural Adjustment Act of 1933 also aimed at raising prices—and thus farm income—by limiting agricultural production. These measures worked for a while, and in 1936 farmers repaid Roosevelt with overwhelming support in his re-election campaign.

The most ambitious attempt to control and plan the economy was the National Recovery Administration (NRA). Intended to reduce competition among industries by setting minimum prices and wages, the NRA broke with the cherished American tradition of free competition. Though participation was voluntary, the NRA aroused conflicts among business people, consumers, and bureaucrats and never worked well. The program was abandoned when declared unconstitutional by the Supreme Court in 1935.

Roosevelt and his advisers then attacked the key problem of mass unemployment. The federal government accepted the responsibility of employing as many people as financially possible. New agencies like the **Works Progress Administration (WPA)**, set up in 1935, were created to undertake a vast range of projects. One-fifth of the entire U.S. labor force worked for the WPA at some point in the 1930s, constructing public buildings, bridges, and highways. The WPA was enormously popular, and the opportunity of taking a government job helped check the threat of social revolution in the United States.

In 1935 the U.S. government also established a national social security system with old-age pensions and unemployment benefits. The National Labor Relations Act of 1935 gave union organizers the green light by guaranteeing rights of collective bargaining. Union membership more than doubled from 4 million in 1935 to 9 million in 1940. In general, between 1935 and 1938 government rulings and social reforms tried to help ordinary people and chipped away at the privileges of the wealthy.

Programs like the WPA were part of the New Deal's fundamental commitment to use the federal government to provide relief welfare for all Americans. This commitment marked a profound shift from the traditional stress on family support and community responsibility. Embraced by a large majority in the 1930s, this shift in attitudes proved to be one of the New Deal's most enduring legacies.

Despite undeniable accomplishments in social reform, the New Deal was only partly successful in responding to the Great Depression. At the height of the recovery in May 1937, 7 million workers were still unemployed—better than the high of about 13 million in 1933 but way beyond the numbers from the 1920s. The economic situation then worsened seriously in the recession of 1937 and 1938, and unemployment had risen to a staggering 10 million when war broke out in Europe in September 1939. The New Deal never pulled the United States out of the depression; it took the government spending associated with the Second World War to do that.

The Scandinavian Response to the Depression

Of all the Western democracies, the Scandinavian countries under Social Democratic leadership responded most successfully to the challenge of the Great Depression. Having grown steadily in the late nineteenth century, the Social Democrats had become the largest political party in Sweden and then in Norway after the First World War. In the 1920s they passed important social reform legislation that benefited both farmers and workers and developed a unique kind of socialism. Flexible and nonrevolutionary, Scandinavian socialism grew out of a strong tradition of cooperative community action. Even before 1900 Scandinavian agricultural cooperatives had shown how individual peasant families could join together for everyone's benefit. Labor leaders and capitalists were also inclined to cooperate with one another.

When the economic crisis struck in 1929, socialist governments in Scandinavia built on this pattern of cooperative social action. Sweden in particular pioneered in the use of large-scale deficits to finance public works and thereby maintain production and employment. In ways that paralleled some aspects of Roosevelt's New Deal, Scandinavian governments also increased public benefit programs such as old-age pensions, unemployment insurance, subsidized housing, and maternity allowances. All this spending required a large bureaucracy and high taxes, first on the rich and then on practically everyone. Yet both private and cooperative enterprise thrived, as did democracy. Some observers saw Scandinavia's welfare socialism as an appealing middle way between sick capitalism and cruel communism or fascism.

Recovery and Reform in Britain and France

In Britain, MacDonald's Labour government and then, after 1931, the Conservative-dominated coalition government followed orthodox economic theory. The budget was balanced, spending was tightly controlled, and unemployed workers received barely enough welfare to live. Nevertheless, the economy recovered considerably after 1932. By 1937 total production was about 20 percent higher than in 1929. In fact, for Britain the years after 1932 were actually somewhat better than the 1920s had been, the opposite of the situation in the United States and France.

This good but by no means brilliant performance reflected the gradual reorientation of the British economy. After going off the gold standard in 1931 and establishing protective tariffs in 1932, Britain concentrated increasingly on the national, rather than the international, market. The old export industries of the Industrial Revolution, such as textiles and coal, continued to decline, but new industries, such as automobiles and electrical appliances, grew in response to demand at home. Moreover, low interest rates encouraged a housing boom. By the end of the decade,

Oslo Breakfast Scandinavian Social Democrats championed cooperation and practical welfare measures, playing down strident rhetoric and theories of class conflict. The "Oslo Breakfast" program portrayed in this pamphlet from the mid-1930s exemplified the Scandinavian approach. It provided every schoolchild in the Norwegian capital with a good breakfast free of charge. (Courtesy, Directorate for Health and Social Affairs, Oslo)

there were highly visible differences between the old, depressed industrial areas of the north and the new, growing areas of the south.

Because France was relatively less industrialized and thus more isolated from the world economy, the Great Depression came to it late. But once the depression hit France, it persisted. Decline was steady until 1935, and a short-lived recovery never brought production or employment back up to predepression levels.

Economic stagnation both reflected and heightened an ongoing political crisis. The French parliament was made up of many political parties that could never cooperate for long. While divisions between the Socialist and Communist Parties undermined any successful leadership from the left, French Fascist organizations agitated against parliamentary democracy and turned to Mussolini's Italy and Hitler's Germany for inspiration. In 1933 alone, for example, five coalition cabinets formed and fell in rapid succession. In February 1934 a loose coalition of right-wing groups rioted in Paris and threatened to take over the republic. Moderate republicanism was weakened by attacks from both sides.

The February riot encouraged politicians on the left to join forces in defense of a democratic reform program. Frightened by the growing strength of the Fascists at home and abroad, and encouraged by a new line from Moscow that encouraged Socialists and Communists to join together to face the fascist threat, the French Communist and Socialist parties formed an alliance—the **Popular Front**—for the national elections of May 1936. Their clear victory reflected the trend toward polarization. The number of Communists in the parliament jumped dramatically from 10 to 72, while the Socialists, led by Léon Blum, became the strongest party in France, with 146 seats. The Radicals—who were actually quite moderate—slipped badly, and the conservatives lost ground to the far right.

In the next few months, Blum's Popular Front government made the first and only real attempt to deal with the social and economic problems of the 1930s in France. Inspired by Roosevelt's New Deal, it encouraged the union movement and launched a far-reaching program of social reform, complete with paid vacations and a forty-hour workweek. Supported by workers and the lower middle class, these measures were quickly sabotaged by rapid inflation and accusations of revolution from Fascists and frightened conservatives. Wealthy people sneaked their money out of the country, labor unrest grew, and France entered a severe financial crisis. Blum was forced to announce a "breathing spell" in social reform.

Political dissent in France was encouraged by the Spanish Civil War (1936–1939), during which authoritarian Fascist rebels overthrew the democratically elected republican government. French Communists demanded that the government support the Spanish republicans, while many French conservatives would gladly have joined Hitler and Mussolini in aiding the Spanish Fascists. Extremism grew, and France itself was within sight of civil war. Blum was forced to resign in June 1937, and the Popular Front quickly collapsed. An anxious and divided France drifted aimlessly once again, preoccupied by Hitler and German rearmament.

NOTES

1. G. Greene, *Another Mexico* (New York: Viking Press, 1939), p. 3.
2. C. E. Jeanneret-Gris (Le Corbusier), *Towards a New Architecture* (London: J. Rodker, 1931), p. 15.
3. From *The Waste Land* by T. S. Eliot. Used by permission of Faber and Faber Ltd.
4. E. Herrmann, *This Is the New Woman* (1929), quoted in *The Weimar Republic Sourcebook*, ed. A. Kaes, M. Jay, and E. Dimendberg (Berkeley: University of California Press, 1994), pp. 206–208.
5. Quoted in R. Smither, ed., *The Battles of the Somme and Ancre* (London: Imperial War Museum, 1993), p. 67.
6. Quoted in S. B. Clough et al., eds., *Economic History of Europe: Twentieth Century* (New York: Harper & Row, 1968), pp. 243–245.
7. S. Freud, *Civilization and Its Discontents* (New York: W. W. Norton, 1961), p. 112.

LOOKING BACK LOOKING AHEAD

The decades before and especially after World War I brought intense intellectual and cultural innovation. The results were both richly productive and deeply troubling. From T. S. Eliot's poem *The Waste Land* to Einstein's theory of special relativity to the sleek glass and steel buildings of the Bauhaus, the intellectual products of the time stand among the highest achievements of Western arts and sciences. At the same time, mass culture, embodied in cinema, radio, and an emerging consumer society, transformed everyday life. Yet the modern vision was often bleak and cold. Modern art and consumer society alike challenged traditional values, contributing to feelings of disorientation and pessimism that had begun late in the nineteenth century and were exacerbated by the searing events of the war.

The situation was worsened by ongoing political and economic turmoil. The Treaty of Versailles had failed to create a lasting peace or resolve the question of Germany's role in Europe. The Great Depression revealed the fragility of the world economic system and cast millions out of work. In the end, perhaps, the era's intellectual achievements and the overall sense of crisis were closely related.

Sigmund Freud captured the general mood of gloom and foreboding in 1930. "Men have gained control over the forces of nature to such an extent that . . . they would have no difficulty in exterminating one another to the last man," he wrote. "They know this, and hence comes a large part of their current unrest, their unhappiness and their mood of anxiety."[7] Freud's dark words reflected the extraordinary human costs of World War I and the horrific power of modern weaponry. They also expressed his despair over the growing popularity of repressive dictatorial regimes. During the interwar years, many European nations—including Italy, Germany, Spain, Poland, Portugal, Austria, and Hungary—would fall one by one to authoritarian or Fascist dictatorships, succumbing to the temptations of totalitarianism. Liberal democracy was severely weakened. European stability was threatened by the radical programs of Soviet Communists on the left and Fascists on the right, and Freud uncannily predicted the great conflict to come.

MAKE CONNECTIONS

Think about the larger developments and continuities within and across chapters.

1. How did trends in politics, economics, culture, and the arts and sciences come together to create a general sense of crisis but also opportunity in the 1920s and 1930s?

2. To what extent did the problems of the 1920s and 1930s have roots in the First World War (Chapter 25)?

3. What made modern art and intellectual thought "modern"?

Chapter 26 Review

IDENTIFY KEY TERMS

Identify and explain the significance of each item below.

logical positivism (p. 786)

existentialism (p. 787)

theory of special relativity (p. 790)

id, ego, and superego (p. 791)

modernism (p. 792)

functionalism (p. 792)

Bauhaus (p. 792)

Dadaism (p. 795)

stream-of-consciousness technique (p. 796)

"modern girl" (p. 798)

Dawes Plan (p. 803)

Great Depression (p. 805)

Works Progress Administration (WPA) (p. 809)

Popular Front (p. 811)

REVIEW THE MAIN IDEAS

Answer the section heading questions from the chapter.

1. How did intellectual developments reflect the ambiguities of modernity? (p. 785)

2. How did modernism revolutionize Western culture? (p. 792)

3. How did consumer society change everyday life? (p. 797)

4. What obstacles to lasting peace did European leaders face? (p. 801)

5. What were the causes and consequences of the Great Depression? (p. 805)

CHRONOLOGY

1887	• Nietzsche publishes *On the Genealogy of Morals*
1900	• Freud publishes *The Interpretation of Dreams*
1913	• Stravinsky's *The Rite of Spring* premieres in Paris
1919	• Treaty of Versailles; Freudian psychology gains popularity; Keynes publishes *The Economic Consequences of the Peace*; Rutherford splits the atom; Bauhaus school founded
1920s	• Existentialism, Dadaism, and Surrealism gain prominence
1922	• Eliot publishes *The Waste Land*; Joyce publishes *Ulysses*; Woolf publishes *Jacob's Room*; Wittgenstein writes on logical positivism
1922	• First radio broadcast by British Broadcasting Corporation (BBC)
1923	• French and Belgian armies occupy the Ruhr; Corbusier publishes *Towards a New Architecture*
1924	• Dawes Plan
1925	• Berg's opera *Wozzeck* first performed; Kafka publishes *The Trial*
1926	• Germany joins the League of Nations
1927	• Heisenberg formulates the "uncertainty principle"
1928	• Kellogg-Briand Pact
1929–1939	• Great Depression
1932	• Franklin Roosevelt announces "New Deal for the forgotten man"
1933	• The National Socialist Party takes power in Germany
1935	• Release of Riefenstahl's documentary film *Triumph of the Will*
1936	• Formation of Popular Front in France
1939	• Start of World War II

27

Dictatorships and the Second World War

1919–1945

CHAPTER PREVIEW

- What were the most important characteristics of Communist and Fascist ideologies?

- How did Stalinism transform state and society in the Soviet Union?

- What kind of government did Mussolini establish in Italy?

- What policies did Nazi Germany pursue, and why did they appeal to ordinary Germans?

- What explains the success and then defeat of Germany and Japan during World War II?

THE INTENSE WAVE OF ARTISTIC AND CULTURAL INNOVATION in the 1920s and 1930s, which shook the foundations of Western thought, was paralleled by radical developments in the realm of politics, as Communist and Fascist states undertook determined assaults on democratic government and individual rights across Europe. On the eve of the Second World War, popularly elected governments survived only in Great Britain, France, Czechoslovakia, the Low Countries, Scandinavia, and Switzerland.

Totalitarian regimes in the Communist Soviet Union, Fascist Italy, and Nazi Germany practiced a dynamic but ruthless tyranny. Their attempts to revolutionize state and society went far beyond traditional forms of conservative authoritarianism. Communist and Fascist states promised to greatly improve the lives of ordinary citizens and intervened radically in those lives in pursuit of utopian schemes of social engineering. Their drive for territorial expansion threatened neighboring nations. The human costs of these policies were appalling. Millions died as Stalin forced communism on the Soviet Union in the 1930s. Attempts to build a "racially pure" New Order in Europe by Hitler's Nazi Germany led to the deaths of tens of millions more in World War II and the Holocaust, a scale of destruction far beyond that of World War I.

What were the most important characteristics of Communist and Fascist ideologies?

Both conservative and radical dictatorships took power in Europe in the 1920s and 1930s. Although these two types of dictatorship shared some characteristics, in essence they were quite different. Conservative authoritarian regimes, which had a long history in Europe, were limited in scope. Radical totalitarian dictatorships, based on the ideologies of communism and fascism, were a new and frightening development aimed at the radical reconstruction of society.

Conservative Authoritarianism and Radical Totalitarian Dictatorships

The traditional form of antidemocratic government in European history was conservative authoritarianism. Like Catherine the Great in Russia and Metternich in Austria, the leaders of such governments relied on obedient state bureaucracies in their efforts to control society. Though political opponents were often jailed or exiled, these older authoritarian governments were limited in both power and objectives. They had neither the ability nor the desire to control many aspects of their subjects' lives. As long as the people did not try to change the system, they were typically allowed considerable personal independence.

After the First World War, authoritarianism revived, especially in eastern Europe. What emerged, however, were new kinds of radical dictatorship that went much further than conservative authoritarianism, particularly in the Soviet Union, Italy, and Germany. In addition, Communist and Fascist political parties were established in all major European nations and mounted challenges to democratic rule.

Some scholars use the term **totalitarianism** to describe these radical dictatorships, which made unprecedented "total claims" on the beliefs and behavior of their citizens. The totalitarian model emphasizes the characteristics that Fascist and Communist dictatorships had in common. One-party totalitarian states used violent political repression and intense propaganda to gain complete power. In addition, the state tried to dominate the economic, social, intellectual, and cultural aspects of people's lives.

Most historians agree that totalitarianism owed much to the experience of total war in 1914 to 1918 (see Chapter 25). World War I required state governments to limit individual liberties and intervene in the economy in order to achieve one supreme objective: victory. Totalitarian leaders were inspired by the example of the modern state at war. They showed a callous disregard for human life and greatly expanded the power of the state in pursuit of social control.

Communist and Fascist dictatorships shared other characteristics. Both rejected parliamentary government and liberal values. Classical liberals (see "Liberalism and the Middle Class" in Chapter 21) sought to limit the power of the state and protect the rights of the individual. Totalitarians, on the other hand, believed that individualism undermined equality and unity, and they rejected democracy in favor of one-party political systems.

A charismatic leader typically dominated the totalitarian state — Joseph Stalin in the Soviet Union, Benito Mussolini in Italy, Adolf Hitler in Germany. All three created political parties of a new kind, dedicated to promoting idealized visions of collective harmony. They used force and terror to intimidate and destroy political opponents and pursued policies of imperial expansion to exploit other lands. They censored the mass media and instituted propaganda campaigns to advance their goals. Finally, and perhaps most important, totalitarian governments engaged in massive projects of state-controlled social engineering dedicated to replacing individualism with a unified "people" capable of exercising the collective will.

Communism and Fascism

Communism and fascism clearly shared a desire to revolutionize state and society. Yet some scholars have argued that the differences between the two systems are more important than the similarities. To understand those differences, it is important to consider the way ideology, or a guiding political philosophy, was linked to radical experiments in social engineering.

Following Marx, Soviet Communists strove to create an international brotherhood of workers. In the Communist utopia ruled by the revolutionary working class, economic exploitation would supposedly disappear and society would be based on fundamental social equality. Under **Stalinism** — the name given to the Communist system in the Soviet Union during Stalin's rule — the state aggressively intervened in all walks of life to pursue this social leveling. Using brute force to destroy the upper and middle classes, the Stalinist state nationalized private property, pushed rapid industrialization, and collectivized agriculture.

The Fascist vision of a new society was quite different. Leaders who embraced **fascism**, such as Mussolini and Hitler, claimed that they were striving to build a new community on a national — not an international — level. Extreme nationalists, and often racists, Fascists glorified war and the military. For them, the nation was the highest embodiment of the people, and the powerful leader was the materialization of the people's collective will.

Like Communists, Fascists promised to improve the lives of ordinary workers. Fascist governments intervened in the economy, but unlike Communist regimes they did not try to level class differences and nationalize private property. Instead, they presented a vision of a community bound together by nationalism. In the ideal Fascist state, all social strata and classes would work together to build a harmonious national community.

Communists and Fascists differed in another crucial respect: the question of race. Where Communists sought to build a new world around the destruction of class differences, Fascists typically sought to build a new national community grounded in racial homogeneity. Fascists embraced the doctrine of **eugenics**, a pseudoscience that maintained that the selective breeding of human beings could improve the

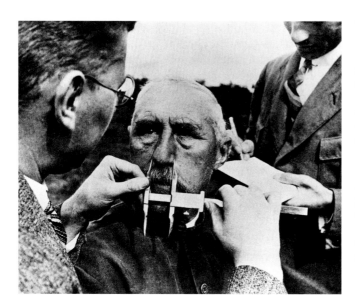

Eugenics in Nazi Germany Nazi "race scientists" believed they could use the eugenic methods of social engineering to build a powerful Aryan race. In this photograph, published in a popular magazine in 1933, a clinician measures a man's nose. Such pseudoscientific methods were used to determine an individual's supposed "racial value." (Hulton Deutsch/Getty Images)

general characteristics of a national population. Eugenics was popular throughout the Western world in the 1920s and 1930s and was viewed by many as a legitimate social policy. But Fascists, especially the German National Socialists, or Nazis, pushed these ideas to the extreme.

Adopting a radicalized view of eugenics, the Nazis maintained that the German nation had to be "purified" of groups of people deemed "unfit" by the regime. Following state policies intended to support what they called "racial hygiene," Nazi authorities attempted to control, segregate, or eliminate those of "lesser value," including Jews, Sinti and Roma (often called Gypsies, a term that can have pejorative connotations) and other ethnic minorities, homosexuals, and people suffering from chronic mental or physical disabilities. The pursuit of "racial hygiene" ultimately led to the Holocaust, the attempt to purge Germany and Europe of all Jews and other undesirable groups by mass killing during World War II. Though the Soviets readily persecuted specific ethnic groups they believed were disloyal to the Communist state, in general they justified these attacks using ideologies of class rather than race or biology.

Perhaps because both championed the overthrow of existing society, Communists and Fascists were sworn enemies. The result was a clash of ideologies, which was in large part responsible for the horrific destruction and loss of life in the middle of the twentieth century. Explaining the nature of totalitarian dictatorships thus remains a crucial project for historians, even as they look more closely at the ideological differences between communism and fascism.

One important set of questions explores the way dictatorial regimes earned the support of the people they governed. Neither Hitler nor Stalin ever achieved the total control each sought. Nor did they rule alone; modern dictators need the help of large state bureaucracies and the cooperation of large numbers of ordinary people. Which was more important for creating popular support: terror and coercion or material rewards? Under what circumstances did people resist or perpetrate totalitarian tyranny? These questions lead us toward what Holocaust survivor Primo Levi called the "gray zone" of moral compromise, which defined everyday life in totalitarian societies.

How did Stalinism transform state and society in the Soviet Union?

Lenin's harshest critics claim that he established the basic outlines of a modern totalitarian dictatorship after the Bolshevik Revolution and during the Russian civil war. If so, Joseph Stalin (1879–1953) certainly finished the job. After he consolidated his power in the mid-1920s, Stalin and his government undertook a radical attempt to transform Soviet society into a Communist state.

From Lenin to Stalin

By spring 1921 Lenin and the Bolsheviks had won the civil war, but they ruled a shattered and devastated land. Many farms were in ruins, and food supplies were exhausted. In southern Russia, drought combined with the ravages of war to produce the worst famine in generations. Industrial production had broken down completely. In the face of economic disintegration, riots by peasants and workers, and an open rebellion by previously pro-Bolshevik sailors at Kronstadt, Lenin was tough but, as ever, flexible. He repressed the Kronstadt rebels, and in March 1921 he replaced War Communism with the **New Economic Policy (NEP)**, which re-established limited economic freedom in an attempt to rebuild agriculture and industry. During the civil war, the Bolsheviks had simply seized grain without payment. Now peasant producers were permitted to sell their surpluses in free markets, and private traders and small handicraft manufacturers were allowed to reappear. Heavy industry, railroads, and banks, however, remained wholly nationalized.

The NEP was a political and economic success. Politically, it was a necessary but temporary compromise with the Soviet Union's overwhelming peasant majority. Realizing that his government was not strong enough to take land from the peasants and turn them into state workers, Lenin made concessions to the only force capable of overturning his government. The NEP brought rapid economic recovery, and by 1926 industrial output surpassed, and agricultural production almost equaled, prewar levels.

In 1924, as the economy recovered and the government partially relaxed its censorship and repression, Lenin died without a chosen successor, creating an intense struggle for power in the inner circles of the Communist Party. The principal contenders were Stalin and Trotsky. Joseph Dzhugashvili (joo-guhsh-VEEL-yih) — later known as Stalin (from the Russian for "steel") — was a good organizer but a poor speaker and writer, and he had no experience outside of Russia. Trotsky, an inspiring leader who had planned the 1917 Bolshevik takeover and then created the victorious Red Army, appeared to have all the advantages in the power struggle. Yet Stalin won because he was more effective at gaining the all-important support of the party. Having risen to general secretary of the party's Central Committee in 1922, he used his office to win friends and allies with jobs and promises.

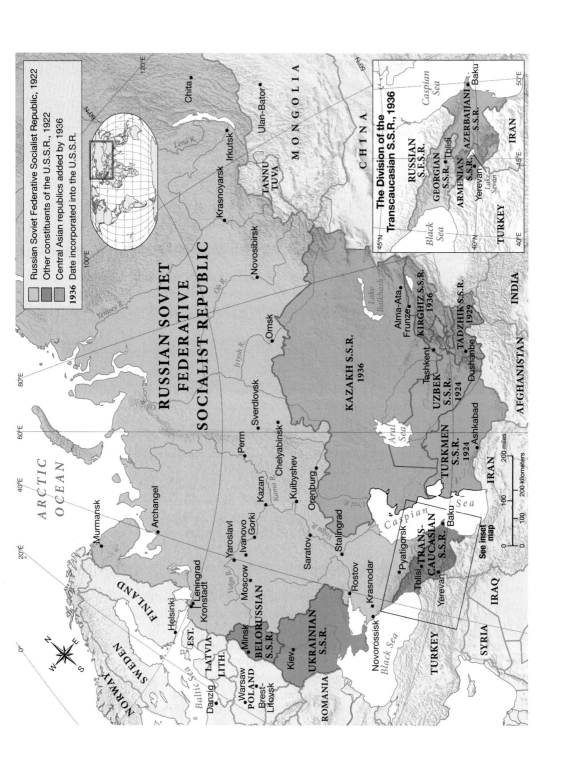

Russian Soviet Federative Socialist Republic, 1922

Other constituents of the U.S.S.R., 1922

Central Asian republics added by 1936

1936 Date incorporated into the U.S.S.R.

RUSSIAN SOVIET FEDERATIVE SOCIALIST REPUBLIC

ARCTIC OCEAN

MONGOLIA

CHINA

KAZAKH S.S.R. 1936

KIRGHIZ S.S.R. 1936

TADZHIK S.S.R. 1929

UZBEK S.S.R. 1924

TURKMEN S.S.R. 1924

AFGHANISTAN

INDIA

IRAN

IRAQ

SYRIA

TURKEY

UKRAINIAN S.S.R.

BELORUSSIAN S.S.R.

TRANS-CAUCASIAN S.S.R.

ROMANIA

POLAND

FINLAND

SWEDEN

NORWAY

Black Sea

Caspian Sea

Aral Sea

Lake Balkhash

The Division of the Transcaucasian S.S.R., 1936

RUSSIAN S.F.S.R.

GEORGIAN S.S.R.

ARMENIAN S.S.R.

AZERBAIJAN S.S.R.

Baku

Tbilisi

Yerevan

Lake Sevan

Caspian Sea

Black Sea

TURKEY

IRAN

Cities: Chita, Irkutsk, Ulan-Bator, Krasnoyarsk, Novosibirsk, Omsk, Sverdlovsk, Perm, Chelyabinsk, Kazan, Kuibyshev, Orenburg, Saratov, Stalingrad, Rostov, Krasnodar, Novorossisk, Moscow, Ivanovo, Gorki, Yaroslavl, Leningrad, Kronstadt, Helsinki, Murmansk, Archangel, Minsk, Kiev, Warsaw, Brest-Litovsk, Danzig, Alma-Ata, Frunze, Tashkent, Dushanbe, Ashkabad, Pyatigorsk, Tbilisi, Baku, Yerevan

Rivers: Lena R., Yenisey R., Ob R., Irtysh R., Ural R., Volga R., Kama R., Don R.

Seas: Baltic Sea

See inset map

200 miles
200 kilometers
100
0

EST. LATVIA LITH.

Stalin also won because he was better able to relate Marxist teaching to Soviet realities in the 1920s. Stalin developed a theory of "socialism in one country," which was more appealing to the majority of party members than Trotsky's doctrine of "permanent revolution." Stalin argued that the Russian-dominated Soviet Union had the ability to build socialism on its own. Trotsky maintained that socialism in the Soviet Union could succeed only if a socialist revolution swept throughout Europe. To many Russian Communists, this view sold their country short and promised risky conflicts with capitalist countries. Stalin's willingness to revoke NEP reforms furthermore appealed to young party militants, who detested the NEP's reliance on capitalist free markets.

With cunning skill, Stalin achieved supreme power between 1922 and 1927. First he allied with Trotsky's personal enemies to crush his rival, and then he moved against all who might challenge his ascendancy, including former allies. Stalin's final triumph came at the party congress of December 1927, which condemned all "deviation from the general party line" that he had formulated. The dictator and his followers were ready to launch "the revolution from above," radically changing the lives of millions of people.

Stalin and the Nationalities Question

Stalin's ascendancy had a momentous impact on the policy of the new Soviet state toward non-Russians. The Communists had inherited the vast multiethnic territories of the former Russian Empire. Lenin initially argued that these ethnic groups should have the right to self-determination even if they claimed independence from the Soviet state. In 1922, reflecting such ideas, the Union of Soviet Socialist Republics (or U.S.S.R.) was organized as a federation of four Soviet republics: the Russian Soviet Federative Socialist Republic, Ukraine, Belorussia, and a Transcaucasian republic. The last was later split into Armenia, Azerbaijan, and Georgia, and five Central Asian republics were established in the 1920s and 1930s (Map 27.1).

In contrast to Lenin, Stalin argued for more centralized Russian control of these ethnic regions. His view would dominate state policy until the breakup of the Soviet Union in the early 1990s. The Soviet republics were granted some cultural independence but no true political autonomy. Party leaders allowed the use of non-Russian languages in regional schools and government institutions, but the right to secede was a fiction, and real authority remained in Moscow, in the hands of the Russian Communist Party. The Stalinists thus established a far-flung Communist empire on the imperial holdings of the former tsars.

< **MAP 27.1   The Formation of the U.S.S.R.**
When the Bolsheviks successfully overthrew the tsarist government and won the civil war that followed, they inherited the vast territories of the former Russian Empire. Following policies instituted by Stalin, they established a Union of Soviet Socialist Republics (U.S.S.R.) that gave limited cultural autonomy but no real political independence to the Soviet republics now under Communist control.

The Five-Year Plans

The party congress of 1927, which ratified Stalin's consolidation of power, marked the end of the NEP. The following year marked the start of the era of the Communist five-year plans. The first **five-year plan** had staggering economic objectives. In just five years, total industrial output was to increase by 250 percent, with heavy industry, the preferred sector, growing even faster. Agricultural production was slated to increase by 150 percent, and one-fifth of the peasants in the Soviet Union were to give up their private plots and join collective farms.

Stalin unleashed this "second revolution" for interrelated reasons. There were, first of all, ideological considerations. Stalin and his militant supporters were deeply committed to communism as they understood it. They feared a gradual restoration of capitalism and wished to promote the working classes. Moreover, Communist leaders were eager to abolish the NEP's private traders, independent artisans, and property-owning peasants. Economic motivations were also important. A fragile economic recovery stalled in 1927 and 1928, and a new offensive seemed necessary to ensure industrial and agricultural growth. Such economic development would allow the U.S.S.R. to catch up with the West and so overcome traditional Russian "backwardness," and the Soviet Union began to train a new class of Communist engineers and technicians to manage the transition.

The independent peasantry remained a major problem as well. For centuries the peasants had wanted to own their own land, and finally they had it. Sooner or later, Stalinists reasoned, landowning peasants would embrace conservative capitalism and pose a threat to the regime. At the same time, the Communists — mainly urban dwellers — believed that the feared and despised "class enemy" in the villages could be squeezed to provide the enormous sums needed for all-out industrialization.

To resolve these issues, in 1929 Stalin ordered the **collectivization of agriculture** — the forced consolidation of individual peasant farms into large, state-controlled enterprises that served as agricultural factories. Peasants across the Soviet Union were compelled to move off their small plots onto large state-run farms, where their tools, livestock, and produce would be held in common and central planners could control all work.

The increasingly repressive measures instituted by the state first focused on the **kulaks**, the class of well-off peasants who had benefited the most from the NEP. The kulaks were small in number, but propagandists cast them as the great enemy of progress. Stalin called for their "liquidation" and seizure of their property. Stripped of land and livestock, many starved or were deported to forced-labor camps for "re-education."

Forced collectivization led to disaster. Large numbers of peasants opposed to the change slaughtered their animals and burned their crops rather than turn them over to state commissars. Between 1929 and 1933 the number of horses, cattle, sheep, and goats in the Soviet Union fell by at least half. Nor were the state-controlled collective farms more productive. During the first five-year plan, the output of grain barely increased, and collectivized agriculture was unable to make any substantial financial contribution to Soviet industrial development.

Collectivization in the fertile farmlands of the Ukraine was more rapid and violent than in other Soviet territories. The drive against peasants snowballed into an assault on Ukrainians in general, who had sought independence from Soviet rule after the First World War. Stalin and his associates viewed this peasant resistance as an expression of unacceptable anti-Soviet nationalism. In 1932, as collectivization and deportations continued, party leaders set levels of grain deliveries for the Ukrainian collectives at excessively high levels and refused to relax those quotas or allow food relief when Ukrainian Communist leaders reported that starvation was occurring. The result was a terrible man-made famine in Ukraine in 1932 and 1933, which claimed 3 to 3.5 million lives.

Collectivization was a cruel but real victory for Stalinist ideologues. Though millions died, by the end of 1938 government representatives had moved 93 percent of peasant households onto collective farms, neutralizing them as a political threat. Nonetheless, peasant resistance had forced the supposedly all-powerful state to make modest concessions. Peasants secured the right to limit a family's labor on the state-run farms and to cultivate tiny family plots, which provided them with much of their food. In 1938 these family plots produced 22 percent of all Soviet agricultural produce on only 4 percent of all cultivated land.

The rapid industrialization mandated by the five-year plans was more successful — indeed, quite spectacular. A huge State Planning Commission, the "Gosplan," was created to set production goals and control deliveries of raw and finished materials. This was a complex and difficult task, and production bottlenecks and slowdowns often resulted. In addition, Stalinist planning favored heavy industry over the production of consumer goods, which led to shortages of basic necessities. Despite such problems, Soviet industry produced about four times as much in 1937 as it had in 1928. No other major country had ever achieved such rapid industrial growth.

Steel was the idol of the Stalinist age. The Soviet state needed heavy machinery for rapid development, and an industrial labor force was created almost overnight as peasant men and women began working in the huge steel mills built across the country. Independent trade unions lost most of their power. The government could assign workers to any job anywhere in the U.S.S.R., and an internal passport system ensured that individuals could move only with permission. When factory managers needed more hands, they called on their counterparts on the collective farms, who sent them millions of "unneeded" peasants over the years. Rapid industrial growth led to urban development: more than 25 million people, mostly peasants, migrated to cities during the 1930s.

The new workers often lived in deplorable conditions in hastily built industrial cities such as Magnitogorsk (Magnetic Mountain City) in the Ural Mountains. Yet they also experienced some benefits of upward mobility. In a letter published in the Magnitogorsk newspaper, an ordinary electrician described the opportunities created by rapid industrialization:

> In old tsarist Russia, we weren't even considered people. We couldn't dream about education, or getting a job in a state enterprise. And now I'm a citizen of the U.S.S.R. Like all citizens I have the right to a job, to education, to leisure. . . .
> In 1931, I came to Magnitogorsk. From a common laborer I have turned into a skilled worker. . . . I live in a country where one feels like living and learning. And if the enemy should attack this country, I will sacrifice my life in order to destroy the enemy and save my country.[1]

We should read such words with care, since they appeared in a state-censored publication. Yet the enthusiasm was at least partly authentic. The great industrialization drive of 1928 to 1937 was an awe-inspiring achievement, purchased at enormous sacrifice on the part of ordinary Soviet citizens.

Life and Culture in Soviet Society

Daily life was difficult in Stalin's Soviet Union. The lack of housing was a particularly serious problem. Millions were moving into the cities, but the government built few new apartments. A relatively lucky family received one room for all its members and shared both a kitchen and a toilet with others living on the same floor.

There were constant shortages of goods as well. Because consumption was reduced to pay for investment, there was little improvement in the average standard of living in the years before World War II. The average nonfarm wage purchased only about half as many goods in 1932 as it had in 1928. After 1932 real wages rose slowly, but by 1937 workers could still buy only about 60 percent of what they had bought in 1928 and less than they could purchase in 1913. Collectivized peasants experienced greater hardships.

Life was by no means hopeless, however. Idealism and ideology had real appeal for many Communists and ordinary citizens, who saw themselves heroically building the world's first socialist society while capitalism crumbled in a worldwide depression and degenerated into fascism in the West. This optimistic belief in the future of the Soviet Union attracted many disillusioned Westerners to communism in the 1930s. On a more practical level, Soviet workers received important social benefits, such as old-age pensions, free medical services, free education, and day-care centers for children. Unemployment was almost unknown.

Stalinism also opened possibilities for personal advancement. Rapid industrialization required massive numbers of skilled workers, engineers, and plant managers. In the 1930s the Stalinist state broke with the egalitarian policies of the 1920s and offered tremendous incentives to those who could serve its needs. It paid the mass of unskilled workers and collective farmers very low wages but provided high salaries and special privileges to its growing technical and managerial elite. This group joined with the political and artistic elites in a new upper class, whose members grew rich and powerful.

The radical transformation of Soviet society had a profound impact on women's lives. Marxists had traditionally believed that both capitalism and middle-class husbands exploited women, and the Russian Revolution of 1917 immediately proclaimed complete equality for women. In the 1920s divorce and abortion were made easily available, and women were urged to work outside the home. After Stalin came to power, he reversed this trend. The government revoked many laws supporting women's emancipation in order to strengthen the traditional family and build up the state's population.

The massive mobilization of women was a striking characteristic of the Stalinist state. The Soviets opened higher education to women, who could now enter the ranks of the better-paid specialists in industry and science. Medicine practically became a woman's profession. By 1950, 75 percent of all doctors in the Soviet Union were female. Alongside such advances, however, Soviet society demanded great sacrifices from women. The vast majority had no choice but to work outside the home. Wages were so low that it was almost impossible for a family or couple to live only on the husband's earnings. Peasant women continued to work on farms, and millions of women toiled in factories and in heavy construction, building dams, roads, and steel mills in summer heat and winter frost. Men continued to dominate the very best jobs. Finally, rapid change and economic hardship led to many broken families, creating further physical and emotional strains for women.

In the U.S.S.R. culture was thoroughly politicized. Party activists lectured workers in factories and peasants on collective farms, while newspapers, films, and radio broadcasts endlessly revealed capitalist plots and recounted socialist achievements. Whereas the 1920s had seen considerable modernist experimentation in theater and the arts, in the 1930s intellectuals were ordered by Stalin to become "engineers of human minds." Following the dictates of "Socialist Realism," they were instructed to exalt the lives of ordinary workers and glorify Russian nationalism. Russian history was rewritten so that early tsars such as Ivan the Terrible and Peter the Great became worthy forerunners of the greatest Russian leader of all—Stalin. Writers and artists who could effectively combine genuine creativity and political propaganda became the darlings of the regime.

Stalin seldom appeared in public, but his presence was everywhere—in portraits, statues, books, and quotations from his writings. Although the government persecuted those who practiced religion and turned churches into "museums of atheism," the state had both an earthly religion and a high priest—Marxism-Leninism and Joseph Stalin.

Stalinist Terror and the Great Purges

In the mid-1930s the great offensive to build socialism and a new society culminated in ruthless police terror and a massive purging of the Communist Party. First used by the Bolsheviks in the civil war to maintain their power, terror as state policy was revived in the collectivization drive against the peasants. Top members of the party and government publicly supported Stalin's initiatives, but there was internal dissent. In late 1934 a top Soviet official, Sergei Kirov, was mysteriously killed. Stalin—who probably ordered Kirov's murder—blamed the assassination on "Fascist agents" within the party. He used the incident to launch a reign of terror that purged the Communist Party of supposed traitors and solidified his own control.

Murderous repression picked up steam over the next two years. It culminated in the "great purge" of 1936 to 1938, which opened with a series of spectacular public show trials in which false evidence, often gathered using torture, was used to incriminate party administrators and Red Army leaders. In August 1936 sixteen "Old Bolsheviks"—prominent leaders who had been in the party since the Russian Revolution—confessed to all manner of contrived plots against Stalin. All were executed. In 1937 the secret police arrested a mass of lesser party officials and newer members, using torture to extract confessions. In addition to the party faithful, army officers, union officials, managers, intellectuals, and numerous average citizens were accused of counter-revolutionary activities. At least 6 million people were arrested. Probably 1 to 2 million were executed or never returned from prisons and forced-labor camps.

Stalin's mass purges remain baffling, for most historians believe that the victims posed no threat and were innocent of their supposed crimes. Some scholars have argued that the terror was a defining characteristic of the totalitarian state, which must always fight real or imaginary enemies. Certainly the highly publicized purges sent a warning: no one was secure; everyone had to serve the party and its leader with redoubled devotion.

The long-standing interpretation that puts most of the blame for the purges on Stalin has been confirmed by recent research in newly opened Soviet archives. Apparently fearful of active resistance, Stalin and his allies used the harshest measures against their political enemies, real or imagined. Moreover, many in the general population shared such fears. Bombarded with ideology and political slogans, numerous people responded energetically to Stalin's directives. Investigations and trials snowballed into mass hysteria, resulting in a modern witch-hunt that claimed millions of victims. In this view of the 1930s, a deluded Stalin found large numbers of willing collaborators.[2]

The purges seriously weakened the Soviet Union in military, economic, and intellectual terms. But they left Stalin in command of a vast new state apparatus, staffed by the 1.5 million new party members enlisted to replace the purge victims. Thus more than half of all Communist Party members in 1941 had joined since the purges. Taking the place of those forced out by the regime, they experienced rapid social advance. Often the children of workers, they had usually studied in the new technical schools, and they soon proved capable of managing the government and large-scale production. Despite the human costs, the great purges thus brought substantial practical rewards to a new generation of committed Communists. They would serve Stalin effectively until his death in 1953, and they would govern the Soviet Union until the early 1980s.

What kind of government did Mussolini establish in Italy?

Mussolini's Fascist movement and his seizure of power in 1922 were important steps in the rise of dictatorships in Europe between the two world wars. Mussolini and his supporters were the first to call themselves "Fascists" — revolutionaries determined to create a new totalitarian state based on extreme nationalism and militarism.

The Seizure of Power

In the early twentieth century, Italy was a liberal constitutional monarchy that recognized the civil rights of Italians. On the eve of World War I, the parliament granted universal male suffrage, and Italy appeared to be moving toward democracy. But there were serious problems. Much of the Italian population was still poor, and many peasants were more attached to their villages and local interests than to the national state. Moreover, the papacy, many devout Catholics, conservatives, and landowners remained strongly opposed to liberal institutions, and relations between church and state were often tense. Class differences were also extreme, leading to the development of a powerful revolutionary socialist movement.

World War I worsened the political situation. To win support for the war effort, the Italian government had promised territorial expansion as well as social and land reform, which it could not deliver. Instead, the Versailles treaty denied Italy any territorial gains, and soaring unemployment and inflation after the war created mass hardship. In response, the Italian Socialist Party followed the Bolshevik example, and radical workers and peasants began occupying factories and seizing land in 1920. These actions mobilized the property-owning classes. Moreover, after the war the pope lifted his ban on participation by Catholics in Italian politics, and a strong Catholic party emerged. Thus by 1921 revolutionary socialists, conservatives, Catholics, and property owners were all opposed—though for different reasons—to the liberal government.

Into these crosscurrents of unrest and fear stepped bullying, blustering Benito Mussolini (1883–1945). Mussolini began his political career before World War I as a Socialist Party leader and radical newspaper editor. In 1914 he had urged that Italy join the Allies, a stand for which he was expelled from the Socialist Party. Returning home after being wounded at the front in 1917, Mussolini began organizing bitter war veterans like himself into a band of Fascists—from the Italian word for "a union of forces."

At first Mussolini's program was a radical combination of nationalist and socialist demands. As such, it competed directly with the well-organized Socialist Party and failed to get off the ground. When Mussolini saw that his violent verbal assaults on rival Socialists won him growing support from conservatives and the middle classes, he shifted gears in 1920 and became a sworn enemy of socialism. Mussolini and his private militia of **Black Shirts** grew increasingly violent. Few people were killed, but Socialist Party newspapers, union halls, and local headquarters were destroyed, and the Black Shirts managed to push Socialists out of city governments in northern Italy.

Fascism soon became a mass movement, one which Mussolini claimed would help the little people against the established interests. In 1922, in the midst of chaos largely created by his Black Shirt militias, Mussolini stepped forward as the savior of order and property. Striking a conservative, anticommunist note in his speeches and gaining the support of army leaders, Mussolini demanded the resignation of the existing government. In October 1922 a band of armed Fascists marched on Rome to threaten the king and force him to appoint Mussolini prime minister of Italy. The threat worked. Victor Emmanuel III (r. 1900–1946)—who himself had no love for the liberal regime—asked Mussolini to take over the government and form a new cabinet. Thus, after widespread violence and a threat of armed uprising, Mussolini seized power using the legal framework of the Italian constitution.

The Fascist Regime in Action

Mussolini became prime minister in 1922 and moved cautiously in his first two years in office to establish control of the government. At first, he promised a "return to order" and consolidated his support among Italian elites. Fooled by Mussolini's apparent moderation, the Italian parliament passed an electoral law that gave two-thirds of the representatives in the parliament to the party that won the most votes. This change allowed the Fascist Party and its allies to win an overwhelming majority in April 1924. Shortly thereafter, a group of Fascist extremists kidnapped and murdered the leading Socialist politician Giacomo Matteotti (JAHK-oh-moh mat-tee-OH-tee). Alarmed, a group of prominent parliamentary leaders demanded that Mussolini's armed squads be dissolved and all violence be banned.

Mussolini and Hitler
In September 1937 Italian dictator Benito Mussolini traveled to Germany to cement the Rome-Berlin Axis alliance. In this photo, Mussolini (left), Nazi leader Adolf Hitler (center), and the Italian foreign minister (right) review maps on a train specially outfitted for the Italians' visit. (ullstein bild/ Getty Images)

Mussolini may not have ordered Matteotti's murder, but he took advantage of the resulting political crisis. Declaring his desire to "make the nation Fascist," he imposed a series of repressive measures. The government ruled by decree, abolished freedom of the press, and organized fixed elections. Mussolini arrested his political opponents, disbanded all independent labor unions, and put dedicated Fascists in control of Italy's schools. Mussolini trumpeted his goal in a famous slogan: "Everything in the state, nothing outside the state, nothing against the state." By the end of 1926 Italy was a one-party dictatorship under Mussolini's unquestioned leadership.

Mussolini's Fascist Party drew support from broad sectors of the population, in large part because he was willing to compromise with the traditional elites that controlled the army, the economy, and the state. He left big business to regulate itself, and there was no land reform. Mussolini also drew increasing support from the Catholic Church. In the **Lateran Agreement** of 1929, he recognized the Vatican as an independent state, and he agreed to give the church significant financial support in return for the pope's support. Because he was forced to compromise with these conservative elites, Mussolini never established complete totalitarian control.

Mussolini's government nonetheless proceeded with attempts to bring fascism to Italy. The state engineered popular consent by staging massive rallies and sporting events, creating Fascist youth and women's movements, and providing new social welfare benefits. Newspapers, radio, and film promoted a "cult of the Duce" (leader), portraying Mussolini as a powerful strongman who embodied the best qualities of the Italian people. Like other Fascist regimes, his government was vehemently opposed to liberal feminism and promoted traditional gender roles. Mussolini also gained support by manipulating popular pride in the grand history of the ancient Roman Empire—as one propagandist put it, "Fascism, in its entirety, is the resurrection of Roman-ness."[3]

Mussolini matched his aggressive rhetoric with military action: Italian armies invaded the African nation of Ethiopia in October 1935. After surprising setbacks at the hands of the poorly armed Ethiopian army, the Italians won in 1936, and Mussolini could proudly declare that Italy again had its empire. Although it shocked international opinion, the war resulted in close ties between Italy and Nazi Germany.

After a visit to Berlin in the fall of 1937, the Italian dictator pledged support for Hitler and promised that Italy and Germany would "march together right to the end."[4]

Deeply influenced by Hitler's example (see the next section), Mussolini's government passed a series of anti-Jewish racial laws in 1938. Though the laws were unpopular, Jews were forced out of public schools and dismissed from professional careers. Nevertheless, extreme anti-Semitic persecution did not occur in Italy until late in World War II, when Italy was under Nazi control. Though Mussolini's repressive tactics were never as ruthless as those in Nazi Germany, his government did much to establish a Fascist state in Italy before the war.

What policies did Nazi Germany pursue, and why did they appeal to ordinary Germans?

German National Socialism (or Nazism) shared some characteristics with Italian fascism, but Nazism was far more interventionist. Under Hitler, the Nazi dictatorship smashed or took over most independent organizations, established firm control over the German state and society, and violently persecuted Jews and other non-German peoples. Truly totalitarian in aspiration, Nazi Germany's policies of racial aggression and territorial expansion led to history's most destructive war.

Fascist Youth on Parade Totalitarian governments in Italy and Nazi Germany established mass youth organizations to instill the values of national unity and train young soldiers for the state. These members of the Balilla, Italy's Fascist youth organization, raise their rifles in salute at a mass rally in 1939. (Hulton Deutsch/Getty Images)

The Roots of National Socialism

National Socialism grew out of many complex developments, of which the most influential were nationalism and racism. These two ideas captured the mind of the young Adolf Hitler (1889–1945), and he dominated Nazism until the end of World War II.

The son of an Austrian customs official, Hitler spent his childhood in small towns in Austria. A mediocre student, he dropped out of high school at age fourteen. He then moved to Vienna, where he developed an unshakable belief in the crudest distortions of Social Darwinism, the superiority of Germanic races, and the inevitability of racial conflict. Exposure to poor eastern European Jews contributed to his anti-Semitic prejudice. Jews, Hitler now claimed, directed an international conspiracy of finance capitalism and Marxist socialism against German culture, German unity, and the German people.

Hitler was not alone. As we have seen, racist anti-Semitism became wildly popular on the far-right wing of European politics in the decades surrounding the First World War. Such irrational beliefs, rooted in centuries of Christian anti-Semitism, were given pseudoscientific legitimacy by nineteenth-century developments in biology and eugenics. These ideas came to define Hitler's worldview and would play an immense role in the ideology and actions of National Socialism.

Hitler greeted the outbreak of the First World War as a salvation. The struggle and discipline of war gave life meaning, and Hitler served bravely as a dispatch carrier on the western front. Germany's defeat shattered his world. Convinced that Jews and Marxists had "stabbed Germany in the back," he vowed to fight on.

In late 1919 Hitler joined a tiny extremist group in Munich called the German Workers' Party. In addition to denouncing Jews, Marxists, and democrats, the party promised a uniquely German National Socialism that would abolish the injustices of capitalism and create a mighty "people's community." By 1921 Hitler had gained control of this small but growing party, renamed the National Socialist German Workers' Party, or Nazis for short. Hitler became a master of mass propaganda and political showmanship. His wild, histrionic speeches, filled with demagogic attacks on the Versailles treaty, Jews, war profiteers, and the Weimar Republic, thrilled audiences eager to escape the crises that followed German defeat in World War I.

In late 1923, when the Weimar Republic seemed on the verge of collapse, Hitler organized an armed uprising in Munich — the so-called Beer Hall Putsch. Despite the failure of the poorly planned coup and Hitler's arrest, National Socialism had been born.

Hitler's Road to Power

At his trial, Hitler gained enormous publicity by denouncing the Weimar Republic. He used his brief prison term to dictate his book *Mein Kampf* (My Struggle), where he laid out his basic ideas on "racial purification" and territorial expansion that would define National Socialism.

In *Mein Kampf,* Hitler claimed that Germans were a "master race" that needed to defend its "pure blood" from groups he labeled "racial degenerates," including Jews, Slavs, and others. The German race was destined to triumph and grow, and, according to Hitler, it needed *Lebensraum* (living space). The future dictator outlined a sweeping vision of war and conquest in which the German master race would colonize east and central Europe and ultimately replace the "subhuman" Jews and Slavs living there. Hitler championed the idea of the leader-dictator, or *Führer* (FYOUR-uhr), whose unlimited power would embody the people's will and lead the German nation to victory. These ideas would ultimately propel the world into the Second World War.

In the years of relative prosperity and stability between 1924 and 1929, Hitler built up the Nazi Party. From the failed beer hall revolt, he had concluded that the Nazis had to come to power through electoral competition rather than armed rebellion. To appeal to middle-class voters, Hitler de-emphasized the anticapitalist elements of National Socialism and vowed to fight communism. The Nazis still remained a small splinter group in 1928, when they received only 2.6 percent of the vote in the general elections.

The Great Depression of 1929 brought the ascent of National Socialism. Now Hitler promised German voters economic as well as political salvation. His appeals for "national rebirth" appealed to a broad spectrum of voters, including middle- and lower-class groups — small business owners, officeworkers, artisans, peasants, and skilled workers. Seized by panic as bankruptcies increased, unemployment soared, and the Communists made dramatic election gains, voters deserted conservative and moderate parties for the Nazis. In the election of 1930 the Nazis won 6.5 million votes and 107 seats, and in July 1932 they gained 14.5 million votes — 38 percent of the total. They were now the largest party in the Reichstag, where Nazi deputies pursued the legal strategy of using democracy to destroy democracy.

The breakdown of democratic government helped the Nazis seize power. Chancellor Heinrich Brüning (BROU-nihng) tried to overcome the economic crisis by cutting back government spending and ruthlessly forcing down prices and wages. His conservative economic policies intensified Germany's economic collapse and convinced many voters that the country's republican leaders were stupid and corrupt, adding to Hitler's appeal.

Division on the left also contributed to Nazi success. Even though the two left-wing parties together outnumbered the Nazis in the Reichstag, the Communists refused to cooperate with the Social Democrats. Failing to resolve their differences, these parties could not mount an effective opposition to the Nazi takeover.

Finally, Hitler excelled in the dirty backroom politics of the decaying Weimar Republic. In 1932 Hitler cleverly gained the support of the conservative politicians in power, who thought they could use Hitler for their own advantage, to resolve the political crisis, but also to clamp down on leftists. They accepted Hitler's demand to be appointed chancellor in a coalition government, believing that he could be used and controlled. On January 30, 1933, Adolf Hitler, leader of the most popular political party in Germany, was appointed chancellor by President Hindenburg.

State and Society in Nazi Germany

Hitler moved rapidly and skillfully to establish an unshakable dictatorship that would pursue the Nazi program of racial segregation and spatial expansion. First, Hitler and the Nazi Party worked to consolidate their power. To maintain appearances, Hitler called for new elections. In February 1933, in the midst of an electoral campaign plagued by violence—much of it caused by Nazi toughs—the Reichstag building was partly destroyed by fire. Hitler blamed the Communists and convinced Hindenburg to sign emergency acts that abolished freedom of speech and assembly as well as most personal liberties.

The façade of democratic government was soon torn asunder. When the Nazis won only 44 percent of the vote in the elections, Hitler outlawed the Communist Party and arrested its parliamentary representatives. Then on March 23, 1933, the Nazis pushed through the Reichstag the **Enabling Act**, which gave Hitler dictatorial power for four years. The Nazis' deceitful stress on legality, coupled with divide-and-conquer techniques, disarmed the opposition until it was too late for effective resistance.

Germany became a one-party Nazi state. Elections were farces. The new regime took over the government bureaucracy intact, installing Nazis in top positions. At the same time, it created a series of overlapping Nazi Party organizations responsible solely to Hitler. As recent research has shown, the resulting system of dual government was riddled with rivalries, contradictions, and inefficiencies. The Nazi state was often disorganized and lacked the all-encompassing unity that its propagandists claimed. Yet this fractured system suited Hitler and his purposes. The lack of unity encouraged competition among state personnel, who worked to outdo each other to fulfill Hitler's vaguely expressed goals. The Führer thus played the established bureaucracy against his personal party government and maintained dictatorial control.

Once the Nazis were firmly in command, Hitler and the party turned their attention to constructing a National Socialist society defined by national unity and racial exclusion. First they eliminated political enemies. Communists, Social Democrats, and trade-union leaders were forced out of their jobs or arrested and taken to hastily built concentration camps. The Nazis outlawed strikes and abolished independent labor unions, which were replaced by the Nazi-controlled German Labor Front.

Hitler then purged the Nazi Party itself of its more extremist elements. The Nazi storm troopers (the SA), the quasi-military band of 3 million toughs in brown shirts who had fought Communists and beaten up Jews before the Nazis took power, now expected top positions in the army. Some SA radicals even talked of a "second revolution" that would create equality among all Germans by sweeping away capitalism. Now that he was in power, however, Hitler was eager to win the support of the traditional military and maintain social order. He decided that the leadership of the SA had to be eliminated. On the night of June 30, 1934, Hitler's elite personal guard—the SS—arrested and executed about one hundred SA leaders and other political enemies. Afterward, the SS grew rapidly. Under its methodical, ruthless leader Heinrich Himmler (1900–1945), the SS took over the political police and the concentration camp system.

The Nazis instituted a policy called "coordination" that forced existing institutions to conform to National Socialist ideology. Professionals—doctors and lawyers, teachers and engineers—saw their previously independent organizations swallowed up by Nazi associations. Charity and civic organizations were also put under Nazi control, and universities, publishers, and writers were quickly brought into line. Democratic, socialist, and Jewish literature was put on ever-growing blacklists. Passionate students and radicalized professors burned forbidden books in public squares. Modern art and architecture—which the Nazis considered "degenerate"—were prohibited.

By 1934 the Nazi dictatorship was largely in place. Acting on its vision of racial eugenics, the party began a many-faceted campaign against those deemed incapable of making positive biological contributions to the "master race." The Nazis persecuted a number of groups. Jews headed the list, but Slavic peoples, Sinti and Roma, homosexuals, and Jehovah's Witnesses were also considered social "deviants." Nazi bureaucrats furthermore invented two categories targeted for "racial hygiene": the "hereditarily ill" and "asocials." The "hereditarily ill" included people with chronic mental or physical disabilities, such as schizophrenics, manic depressives, epileptics, and people suffering from what Nazi physicians called "congenital feeblemindedness." The catchall category of "asocials" included common criminals, alcoholics, prostitutes, the "work shy" (or chronically unemployed), beggars and vagrants, and others on the margins of German society.

Nazi leaders used a variety of measures to convince Germans that "racial hygiene" was justified and necessary. In what some historians term the Nazi "racial state," barbarism and race hatred were institutionalized with the force of science and law.[5] New university academies, such as the German Society for Racial Research, wrote studies that measured and defined racial differences; prejudice was thus presented in the guise of enlightened medical science, a means for creating a strong national race. Schoolroom lessons, articles in the popular press, feature films, traveling exhibitions, and even children's board games touted the benefits of racist eugenic practice.

The results were monstrous, a barbaric violation of the ethical norms most of us take for granted. Thousands of innocent people faced social ostracism and then brutal repression, simply because the Nazis deemed them racial outsiders. Convinced by their own racial ideology, Nazi authorities denied outsiders welfare benefits and put them out of work, forced people with disabilities into special hospitals where they could be segregated from "healthy" Germans, and imprisoned homosexuals and "asocials" in concentration camps for "re-education." Under a series of sterilization laws, Nazi medical workers forcibly sterilized some 400,000 German citizens, mainly "asocials" or the "hereditarily ill," so their "degenerate blood" would not pollute the "Aryan race." The eugenics campaign reached a crescendo in 1938, when the authorities initiated a coldhearted euthanasia program—dubbed "mercy killing" by Nazi physicians and administrators—and systematically murdered about 70,000 Germans with chronic disabilities.

From the beginning, German Jews were a special target of Nazi racial persecution. Anti-Jewish propaganda was ever present in Nazi Germany. Ugly posters of stereotypical Jews; feature films and documentaries about the Jewish "menace"; signs in shop windows, banks, and parks forbidding Jewish entry—all and more were used to stigmatize German Jews. Such means were backed up with harsh legal oppression. Shortly after they took power, Nazi authorities issued the Professional Civil Service Restoration Act, which banned Jews from working in government jobs; by 1934 many Jewish lawyers, doctors, professors, civil servants, and musicians had been summarily dismissed from their jobs. In 1935 the infamous Nuremberg Laws classified as Jewish anyone having three or more Jewish grandparents, outlawed marriage and sexual relations between Jews and those defined as German, and deprived Jews of all rights of citizenship. Conversion to Christianity and abandonment of the Jewish faith made no difference.

In late 1938 the assault on the Jews accelerated. During a well-organized wave of violence known as Kristallnacht (or the Night of Broken Glass pogrom), Nazi gangs smashed windows and looted over 7,000 Jewish-owned shops, destroyed many homes, burned down over 200 synagogues, and killed dozens of Jews. German Jews were then rounded up and made to pay for the damage. By 1939 some 300,000 of Germany's 500,000 Jews had emigrated, sacrificing almost all their property to escape persecution. Some Germans privately opposed these outrages, but most went along or looked the other way. Historians still debate the degree to which this lack of opposition expressed popular anti-Semitism. In any case, it revealed widespread support for Hitler's government.

Popular Support for National Socialism

Why did millions of ordinary Germans back a brutally repressive, racist regime? A combination of coercion and reward enlisted popular support for the racial state. Using the secret police and the growing concentration camp system in a reign of ruthless terror, the regime persecuted its political and "racial" enemies. Yet for the large majority of ordinary German citizens who were not Jews, Communists, or members of other targeted groups, Hitler's government brought new opportunities. The German "master race" clearly benefited from Nazi policies and programs. Even the creation of demonized outsider groups probably contributed to feelings of national unity and support for the Hitler regime.

Moreover, Hitler had promised the masses economic recovery, and he delivered. The Nazi state launched a large public works program to help pull Germany out of the depression. Work began on superhighways, offices, gigantic sports stadiums, and public housing, which created jobs and instilled pride in national recovery. By 1938 unemployment had fallen to 2 percent, and there was a shortage of workers. Between 1932 and 1938 the standard of living for the average worker increased moderately. Business profits rose sharply.

The persecution of Jews brought substantial benefits to ordinary Germans as well. As Jews were forced out of their jobs and compelled to sell their homes and businesses, Germans stepped in to take their place in a process known as Aryanization (named after the "Aryan master race" prized by the Nazis for their supposedly pure German blood). For millions of so-called Aryans, a rising standard of living—at whatever ethical price—was tangible evidence that Nazi promises were more than show and propaganda.

Economic recovery was accompanied by a wave of social and cultural innovation intended to construct what Nazi propagandists called the *Volksgemeinschaft* (FOLKS-ge-MINE-shaft)—a "people's community" for racially pure Germans. The party set up mass organizations to spread Nazi ideology and enlist volunteers for the Nazi cause. Millions of Germans joined the Hitler Youth, the League of German Women, and the German Labor Front. Mass rallies, such as annual May Day celebrations and Nazi Party conventions in Nuremberg, brought together thousands of participants. Glowing reports on such events in the Nazi-controlled press brought the message home to millions more.

As the economy recovered, the government also proudly touted a glittering array of inexpensive and enticing people's products. Items such as the Volkswagen (the "People's Car") were intended to link individuals' desire for consumer goods to the collective ideology of the "people's community." Though such programs faltered as the state increasingly focused on rearmament for the approaching war, they suggested to all that the regime was working hard to improve German living standards.

Women played a special role in the Nazi state. Promising to "liberate women from women's liberation," Nazi ideologues championed a return to traditional family values. They outlawed abortion, discouraged women from holding jobs or obtaining higher education, and glorified domesticity and motherhood. Women were cast as protectors of the hearth and home and were instructed to raise young boys and girls in accordance with Nazi ideals. In the later 1930s, facing labor shortages, the Nazis had to reluctantly reverse course and encourage women to enter the labor force. Whatever the employment situation, the millions of women enrolled in Nazi mass organizations, which organized charity drives and other social programs, experienced a sense of freedom and community in these public activities.

Nazi propagandists continually played up the supposed accomplishments of the regime. Economic growth, the vision of the *Volksgemeinschaft*, national pride in recovery, and feelings of belonging created by acts of racial exclusion led many Germans to support the regime. Hitler himself remained popular with broad sections of the population well into the war.

Not all Germans supported Hitler, however, and a number of groups actively resisted him after 1933. But opponents of the Nazis were never unified, which helps explain their lack of success. Furthermore, the regime harshly clamped down on dissidents: tens of thousands of political enemies were imprisoned, and thousands were executed. After Communists and socialists were smashed by the SS system, a second group of opponents arose in the Catholic and Protestant churches. Their efforts, however, were directed primarily at preserving religious life, not at overthrowing Hitler. In 1938 and again during the war, a few high-ranking army officers, who feared the consequences of Hitler's reckless aggression, plotted against him, but their plans were unsuccessful.

Aggression and Appeasement

The Nazification of German society fulfilled only part of the Nazi agenda. While building the "people's community," the regime aggressively pursued territorial expansion for the supposedly superior German race. Although Germany withdrew from the League of Nations in 1933, at first Hitler carefully camouflaged his expansionist goals. Germany was still militarily weak, and the Nazi leader loudly proclaimed his peaceful intentions. Then in March 1935 Hitler declared that Germany would no longer abide by the disarmament clauses of the Treaty of Versailles. He established a military draft and began to build up the German army. France and Great Britain protested strongly and warned against future aggressive actions.

Any hope of a united front against Hitler quickly collapsed. Britain adopted a policy of **appeasement**, granting Hitler what he demanded to avoid war. British appeasement, which practically dictated French policy, was largely motivated by the pacifism of a population still horrified by the memory of the First World War. As in Germany, many powerful conservatives in Britain underestimated Hitler. They believed that Soviet communism was the real danger and that Hitler could be used to stop it. Such strong anticommunist feelings made an alliance between the Western powers and Stalin against Hitler highly unlikely.

When Hitler suddenly marched his armies into the demilitarized Rhineland in March 1936, brazenly violating the treaties of Versailles and Locarno (Map 27.2), Britain refused to act. France could do little without British support. Emboldened, Hitler moved ever more aggressively, enlisting powerful allies in international affairs. Italy and Germany established the Rome-Berlin Axis in 1936. Japan, also under the rule of a Fascist dictatorship, joined the Axis alliance that same year.

MAP 27.2   The Growth of Nazi Germany, 1933–1939
Until March 1939 Hitler's conquests brought ethnic Germans into the Nazi state; then he turned on the Slavic and Jewish peoples he had always hated. He stripped Czechoslovakia of its independence and attacked Poland in September 1939.

A Republican Militia in the Spanish Civil War The enthusiasm of the republican forces of the democratically elected government of Spain could not overcome the rebel Fascist armies of Francisco Franco during the Spanish Civil War (1936–1939). Once in power, Franco ruled over a repressive dictatorial state in Spain until his death in 1975. Women combatants like the *milicianas* pictured here, carrying rifles with their male comrades, made a significant contribution to the republican cause. (Universal History Archive/Getty Images)

At the same time, Germany and Italy intervened in the Spanish Civil War (1936–1939), where their military aid helped General Francisco Franco's revolutionary Fascist movement defeat the democratically elected republican government. Republican Spain's only official aid in the fight against Franco came from the Soviet Union, for public opinion in Britain and especially in France was hopelessly divided on whether to intervene.

In late 1937 Hitler moved forward with plans to seize Austria and Czechoslovakia as the first step in his long-contemplated drive for living space in the east. By threatening Austria with invasion, Hitler forced the Austrian chancellor to put local Nazis in control of the government in March 1938. The next day, in the Anschluss (annexation), German armies moved in unopposed, and Austria became part of Greater Germany (see Map 27.2).

Simultaneously, Hitler demanded that territories inhabited mostly by ethnic Germans in western Czechoslovakia — the Sudetenland — be ceded to Nazi Germany. Though democratic Czechoslovakia was allied with France and the Soviet Union and prepared to defend itself, appeasement triumphed again. In negotiations British prime minister Neville Chamberlain and the French agreed with Hitler that Germany should immediately take over the Sudetenland. Returning to London from the Munich Conference in September 1938, Chamberlain told cheering crowds that he had secured "peace with honor [and] peace for our time." Sold out by the Western powers, Czechoslovakia gave in.

Chamberlain's peace was short-lived. In March 1939 Hitler's armies invaded and occupied the rest of Czechoslovakia. The effect on Western public opinion was electrifying. This time, there was no possible ethnic rationale for Nazi aggression, since Hitler was seizing ethnic Czechs and Slovaks — not Germans — as captive peoples. When Hitler next used the question of German minorities in Danzig as a pretext to confront Poland, a suddenly militant Chamberlain declared that Britain and France would fight if Hitler attacked his eastern neighbor. Hitler did not take these warnings seriously.

In August 1939, in an about-face that stunned the world, sworn enemies Hitler and Stalin signed a nonaggression pact that paved the road to war. Each dictator promised to remain neutral if the other became involved in open hostilities. An attached secret protocol ruthlessly divided Poland, the Baltic nations, Finland, and a part of Romania into German and Soviet spheres of influence. Stalin agreed to the pact because he remained distrustful of Western intentions and because Hitler offered immediate territorial gain.

For Hitler, everything was now set. On September 1, 1939, German armies and warplanes smashed into Poland from three sides. Two days later, Britain and France, finally true to their word, declared war on Germany. The Second World War had begun.

What explains the success and then defeat of Germany and Japan during World War II?

Nazi Germany's unlimited ambition unleashed an apocalyptic cataclysm. German armies quickly conquered much of western and eastern Europe, while the Japanese overran much of Southeast Asia. This reckless aggression brought together a coalition of unlikely but powerful allies determined to halt the Fascist advance: Britain, the United States, and the Soviet Union. After years of slaughter and genocide that decimated much of Europe and East Asia, this "Grand Alliance" decisively defeated the Axis powers.

German Victories in Europe

Using planes, tanks, and trucks in the first example of a blitzkrieg, or "lightning war," Hitler's armies crushed Poland in four weeks. While the Soviet Union took its part of the booty — the eastern half of Poland and the independent Baltic states of Lithuania, Estonia, and Latvia — French and British armies prepared their defenses in the west.

In spring 1940 the Nazi lightning war struck again. After Germany occupied Denmark, Norway, and Holland, motorized columns broke into France through southern Belgium, split the Franco-British forces, and trapped the entire British army on the French beaches of Dunkirk. By heroic efforts, the British withdrew their troops — although equipment could not be saved. Soon after, France was taken by the Nazis. By July 1940 Hitler ruled practically all of continental Europe. Italy was a German ally. Romania, Hungary, and Bulgaria joined the Axis powers, and the Soviet Union, Spain, and Sweden were friendly neutrals. Only the Balkans and Britain, the nation led by the uncompromising Winston Churchill (1874–1965), remained unconquered.

To prepare for an amphibious invasion of Britain, Germany sought to gain control of the air. In the Battle of Britain, which began in July 1940, up to a thousand German planes a day attacked British airfields and key factories, dueling with British defenders high in the skies. Losses were heavy on both sides. In September 1940 Hitler turned from military objectives to indiscriminate bombing of British cities in an attempt to break British morale. British aircraft factories increased production, and, encouraged by the words of the ever-determined Churchill, the heavily bombed people of London defiantly dug in. By October Britain was beating Germany three to one in the air war, and the Battle of Britain was over. Stymied there, the Nazi war machine invaded and occupied Greece and the Balkans.

Hitler now allowed his lifetime obsession of creating a vast eastern European empire ruled by the master race to dictate policy. In June 1941 he broke his pact with Stalin and launched German armies into the Soviet Union (Map 27.3). By October most of Ukraine had been conquered, Leningrad was surrounded, and Moscow was besieged. But the Soviets did not collapse, and when a severe winter struck German armies outfitted only in summer uniforms, the invaders retreated. Nevertheless, Hitler and his allies now ruled over a European empire stretching from eastern Europe to the English Channel. Hitler, the Nazi leadership, and the loyal German army were positioned to accelerate the construction of their so-called New Order in Europe.

Europe Under Nazi Occupation

Hitler's **New Order** was based firmly on the guiding principle of National Socialism: racial imperialism. Occupied peoples were treated according to their place in the Nazi racial hierarchy. All were subject to harsh policies dedicated to ethnic cleansing and the plunder of resources for the Nazi war effort.

Within the New Order, the "Nordic" peoples — the Dutch, Danes, and Norwegians — received preferential treatment, for the Germans believed they were related to the Aryan master race. In Holland, Denmark, and Norway, the Nazis established puppet governments of various kinds. Though many people hated the conquerors, the Nazis found willing collaborators who ruled in accord with German needs. France was divided into two parts. The German army occupied the north, including Paris. The southeast remained nominally independent. There the aging First World War general Marshal Henri-Philippe Pétain formed a new French government — the Vichy (VIH-shee) regime — that adopted many aspects of National Socialist ideology and willingly placed French Jews in the hands of the Nazis.

In all conquered territories, the Nazis used a variety of techniques to enrich Germany and support the war effort. Occupied nations were forced to pay for the costs of the war and for the occupation itself, and the price was high. Nazi administrators stole goods and money from local Jews, set currency exchanges at favorable

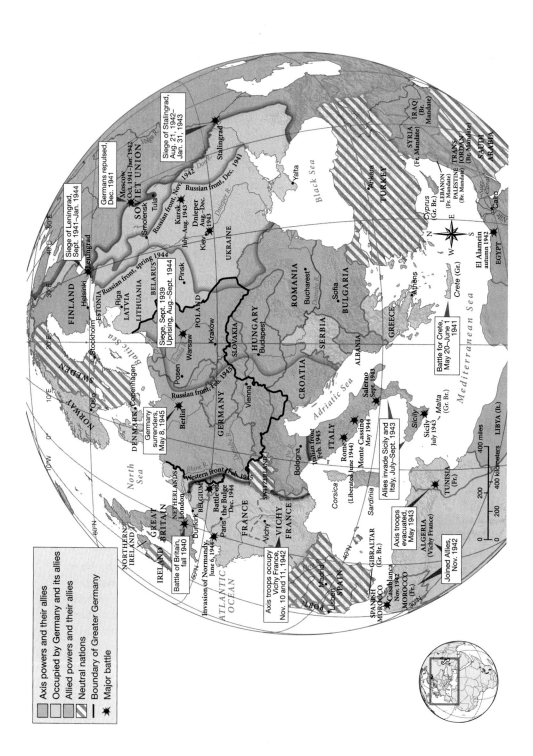

Siege of Stalingrad,
Aug. 21, 1942–
Jan. 31, 1943

Germans repulsed,
Dec. 1941

Siege of Leningrad,
Sept. 1941–Jan. 1944

Moscow
Oct. 1941–Jan. 1942

SOVIET UNION

Russian front, Dec. 1941

Stalingrad

Smolensk

Tula

Kursk
July–Aug. 1943

Dnieper
Aug.–Dec.
1943

Kiev

Yalta

Black Sea

TURKEY

Ankara

Cyprus
(Gr. Br.)

SYRIA
(Fr. Mandate)

LEBANON
(Fr. Mandate)

PALESTINE
(Br. Mandate)

IRAQ
(Br.
Mandate)

TRANS-
JORDAN
(Br. Mandate)

SAUDI
ARABIA

Cairo

Suez Canal

EGYPT

El Alamein
autumn 1942

Mediterranean Sea

Crete (Gr.)

Athens

GREECE

Battle for Crete,
May 20–June 1
1941

Russian front, spring 1944

BELARUS

Pinsk

Siege of Leningrad,
Sept. 1941–Jan. 1944

Helsinki

FINLAND

Riga

LATVIA

LITHUANIA

ESTONIA

Siege, Sept. 1939
Uprising, Aug.–Sept. 1944

Warsaw

POLAND

UKRAINE

ROMANIA

Bucharest

Sofia

BULGARIA

SERBIA

Stockholm

SWEDEN

Baltic Sea

Kraków

Posen

HUNGARY

Budapest

SLOVAKIA

CROATIA

ALBANIA

Adriatic Sea

Salerno
Sept. 1943

Malta
(Gr. Br.)

Sicily
July 1943

Sicily

Allies invade Sicily and
Italy, July–Sept. 1943

LIBYA (It.)

400 miles

400 kilometers

200

200

Germany
surrenders,
May 8, 1945

Berlin

GERMANY

Russian front, Feb. 1945

Vienna

SWITZERLAND

Italian front
Feb. 1945

Bologna

ITALY

Rome
(Liberated June 1944)

Monte Cassino
May 1944

Corsica

Sardinia

TUNISIA
(Fr.)

Axis troops
evacuated,
May 1943

ALGERIA
(Vichy France)

Joined Allies,
Nov. 1942

Copenhagen

DENMARK

Rhine R.

Western front, Feb. 1945

Paris

NETHERLANDS

BELGIUM

Dunkirk

London

GREAT
BRITAIN

NORTHERN
IRELAND

IRELAND

Battle of Britain,
fall 1940

Invasion of Normandy,
June 6, 1944

Battle of
the Bulge
Dec. 1944

FRANCE

Vichy

VICHY
FRANCE

Axis troops occupy
Vichy France,
Nov. 10 and 11, 1942

North
Sea

ATLANTIC
OCEAN

Oslo

NORWAY

Madrid

SPAIN

Lisbon

PORT.

GIBRALTAR
(Gr. Br.)

SPANISH
MOROCCO

Casablanca
Nov. 1942

MOROCCO
(Fr.)

N
E
S
W

Volga R.
Don R.
Dnieper R.
Danube R.
Vistula R.
Danube R.

50°E
40°E
30°E
20°E
10°E
0°
10°W

60°N
50°N
40°N
30°N

Axis powers and their allies

Occupied by Germany and its allies

Allied powers and their allies

Neutral nations

Boundary of Greater Germany

Major battle

rates, and forced occupied peoples to accept worthless wartime scrip. Soldiers were encouraged not only to steal but also to purchase goods at cheap exchange rates and send them home. A flood of plunder reached Germany, helping maintain high living standards and preserving home-front morale well into the war. Nazi victory, furthermore, placed national Jewish populations across Europe under German control, allowing the mass murder of Europe's Jews.

In central and eastern Europe, the war and German rule were far more ruthless and deadly than in the west. From the start, the Nazi leadership had cast the war in the east as one of annihilation. The Nazis now set out to build a vast colonial empire where Jews would be exterminated and Poles, Ukrainians, and Russians would be enslaved and forced to die out. According to the plans, ethnic German peasants would resettle the resulting abandoned lands. In pursuit of such goals, large parts of western Poland were incorporated into Germany. Another part of Poland was placed under the rule of a merciless civilian administration.

With the support of military commanders, Himmler's elite SS corps now implemented a program of destruction and annihilation to create a "mass settlement space" for racially pure Germans. Across the east, the Nazi armies destroyed cities and factories, stole crops and farm animals, and subjected conquered peoples to forced starvation and mass murder. Nazi occupation in the east destroyed the lives of millions.[6]

Small but determined underground resistance groups fought back against these atrocities. They were hardly unified. Communists and socialists often disagreed with more centrist or nationalist groups on long-term goals and short-term tactics. In Yugoslavia, for example, Communist and royalist military resistance groups attacked the Germans, but also each other. Poland, under German occupation longer than any other nation, had the most determined and well-organized resistance. The Nazis had closed all Polish universities and outlawed national newspapers, but the Poles organized secret classes and maintained a thriving underground press. Underground members of the Polish Home Army, led by the government in exile in London, passed intelligence about German operations to the Allies and committed sabotage. The famous French resistance undertook similar actions, as did groups in Italy, Greece, Russia, and the Netherlands.

The resistance presented a real challenge to the Nazi New Order, and the German response was swift and deadly. The Nazi army and the SS tortured captured resistance members and executed hostages in reprisal for attacks. Responding to actions undertaken by resistance groups, the German army murdered the male populations of Lidice (Czechoslovakia) and Oradour (France) and leveled the entire towns. Despite such reprisals, Nazi occupiers were never able to eradicate popular resistance to their rule.

< MAP 27.3   **World War II in Europe and Africa, 1939–1945**
This map shows the extent of Hitler's empire before the Battle of Stalingrad in late 1942 and the subsequent advances of the Allies until Germany surrendered on May 8, 1945. Compare this map with Map 27.2 to trace the rise and fall of the Nazi empire over time.

The Holocaust

The ultimate abomination of Nazi racism was the condemnation of all European Jews and other peoples considered racially inferior to extreme racial persecution and then annihilation in the **Holocaust**, a great spasm of racially inspired mass murder.

As already described, the Nazis began to use social, legal, and economic means to persecute Jews and other "undesirable" groups immediately after taking power. Between 1938 and 1940 persecution turned deadly in the Nazi euthanasia (mercy killing) campaign, an important step toward genocide. Just as Germany began the war, as already mentioned, some 70,000 people with physical and mental disabilities were forced into special hospitals, barracks, and camps. Deemed by Nazi administrators to be "unworthy lives" who might "pollute" the German race, they were murdered in cold blood. The victims were mostly ethnic Germans, and the euthanasia campaign was stopped after church leaders and ordinary families spoke out. The staff involved took what they learned in this program to the extermination camps the Nazis would soon build in the east (Map 27.4).

The German victory over Poland in 1939 brought some 3 million Jews under Nazi control. Jews in German-occupied territories were soon forced to move into urban districts termed "ghettos." In walled-off ghettos in cities large and small—two of the most important were in Warsaw and Lodz—hundreds of thousands of Polish Jews lived in crowded and unsanitary conditions, without real work or adequate sustenance. Over 500,000 people died under these conditions.

The racial violence reached new extremes when Germany invaded the Soviet Union in 1941. Three military death squads known as Special Task Forces (*Einsatzgruppen*) and other military units followed the advancing German armies. They moved systematically from town to town, shooting Jews and other target populations. The victims of these mobile killing units were often forced to dig their own graves in local woods or fields before they were shot. In this way the German armed forces murdered some 2 million civilians.

In late 1941 Hitler and the Nazi leadership, in some still-debated combination, ordered the SS to implement the mass murder of all Jews in Europe. What the Nazi leadership called the "final solution of the Jewish question" had begun. The Germans set up an industrialized killing machine that remains unparalleled, with an extensive network of concentration camps, factory complexes, and railroad transport lines to imprison and murder Jews and other so-called undesirables and to exploit their labor before they died. In the occupied east, the surviving residents of the ghettos were loaded onto trains and taken to camps such as Auschwitz-Birkenau, the best known of the Nazi killing centers, where over 1 million people—the vast majority of them Jews—were murdered in gas chambers. Some few were put to work as expendable laborers. The Jews of Germany and occupied western and central Europe were rounded up, put on trains, and sent to the camps. Even after it was quite clear that Germany would lose the war, the killing continued.

Given the scope and organization of Nazi persecution, there was little opportunity for successful Jewish resistance, yet some Jews did evade or challenge the killing machine. Some brave Jews went underground or masqueraded as Christian to escape Nazi roundups; others fled to rural areas and joined bands of anti-Nazi partisans. Jews also organized secret resistance groups in ghettos and concentration camps.

MAP 27.4 **The Holocaust, 1941–1945**
The leaders of Nazi Germany established an extensive network of ghettos and concentration and extermination camps to persecute their political opponents and those people deemed "racially undesirable" by the regime. The death camps, where the Nazi SS systematically murdered millions of European Jews, Soviet prisoners of war, and others, were located primarily in Nazi-occupied territories in eastern Europe, but the conditions in the concentration camps within Germany's borders were almost as brutal.

When news of pending deportation to the Treblinka killing center reached the Jews still living in the Warsaw Ghetto in January 1943, poorly armed underground resistance groups opened fire on German troops. The Ghetto Uprising, with sporadic fighting dominated by the vastly superior German forces, lasted until May, when the last Jews were taken to extermination camps and the ghetto was razed to the ground. In Auschwitz itself, in October 1944, a group of Jewish prisoners revolted

A "Transport" Arrives at Auschwitz Upon arrival at Auschwitz in May 1944, Jews from Subcarpathian Rus, a rural district on the border of Czechoslovakia and Ukraine, undergo a "selection" managed by Nazi officers and prisoners in striped uniforms. Camp guards will send the fittest people to the barracks, where they will probably soon die from forced labor under the most atrocious conditions. The aged, ill, very young, or otherwise infirm will be murdered immediately in the Auschwitz gas chambers. The tower over the main gate to the camp, which today opens onto a vast museum complex, is visible in the background. (Galerie Bilderwelt/ Getty Images)

and burned down one of the camp's crematoriums before all were captured and summarily executed.

The murderous attack on European Jews was the ultimate monstrosity of Nazi "racial hygiene" and racial imperialism. By 1945 the Nazis had killed about 6 million Jews and some 5 million other Europeans, including millions of ethnic Poles and Russian POWs. Who was responsible for this terrible crime? Historians continue to debate this critical question. Some lay the guilt on Hitler and the Nazi leadership, arguing that ordinary Germans had little knowledge of the extermination camps or were forced to participate by Nazi terror and totalitarian control. Other scholars conclude that far more Germans knew about and were at best indifferent to the fate of "racial inferiors." The question remains: what inspired those who actually worked in the killing machine—the "desk murderers" in Berlin who sent trains to the east, the soldiers who shot Jews in the Polish forests, the guards at Auschwitz? Some historians believe that widely shared anti-Semitism led "ordinary Germans" to become Hitler's "willing executioners." Others argue that heightened peer pressure, the desire to advance in the ranks, and the need to prove one's strength under the most brutalizing wartime violence turned average Germans into reluctant killers.

The conditioning of racist Nazi propaganda clearly played a role. Whatever the motivation, numerous Germans were somehow prepared to join the SS ideologues and perpetrate ever-greater crimes, from mistreatment to arrest to mass murder.[7]

Japanese Empire and the War in the Pacific

The racist war of annihilation in Europe was matched by racially inspired warfare in East Asia. In response to political divisions and economic crisis, a Fascist government had taken control of Japan in the 1930s. As in Germany and Italy, the Japanese government was highly nationalistic and militaristic, and it was deeply committed to imperial expansion. According to Japanese race theory, the Asian races were far superior to Western ones. In speeches, schools, and newspapers, ultranationalists eagerly voiced the extreme anti-Western views that had risen in the 1920s and 1930s. They glorified the warrior virtues of honor and sacrifice and proclaimed that Japan would liberate East Asia from Western colonialists.

Japan soon acted on its racial-imperial ambitions. In 1931 Japanese armies invaded and occupied Manchuria, a vast territory bordering northeastern China. In 1937 Japan brutally invaded China itself. Seeking to cement ties with the Fascist regimes of Europe, in 1940 the Japanese entered into a formal alliance with Italy and Germany, and in summer 1941 Japanese armies occupied southern portions of the French colony of Indochina (now Vietnam and Cambodia).

The goal was to establish what the Japanese called the Greater East Asia Co-Prosperity Sphere. Under the slogan "Asia for Asians," Japanese propagandists maintained that this expansion would free Asians from hated Western imperialists. By promising to create a mutually advantageous union for long-term development, the Japanese tapped currents of nationalist sentiment, and most local populations were glad to see the Westerners go.

But the Co-Prosperity Sphere was a sham. Real power remained in the hands of the Japanese. They exhibited great cruelty toward civilian populations and prisoners of war, and they exploited local peoples for Japan's wartime needs, arousing local populations against them. Nonetheless, the ability of the Japanese to defeat the Western colonial powers set a powerful example for national liberation groups in Asia, which would become important in the decolonization movement that followed World War II.

Japanese expansion from 1937 to 1941 evoked a sharp response from U.S. president Franklin Roosevelt, and Japan's leaders came to believe that war with the United States was inevitable. After much debate, they decided to launch a surprise attack on the U.S. fleet based at Pearl Harbor in the Hawaiian Islands. On December 7, 1941, the Japanese sank or crippled every American battleship, but by chance all the American aircraft carriers were at sea and escaped unharmed. Pearl Harbor brought the Americans into the war in a spirit of anger and revenge.

As the Americans mobilized for war, Japanese armies overran more European and American colonies in Southeast Asia. By May 1942 Japan controlled a vast empire (Map 27.5) and was threatening Australia. The Americans pushed back and engaged the Japanese in a series of hard-fought naval battles. In July 1943 the Americans and their Australian allies opened a successful island-hopping campaign that slowly forced Japan out of its conquered territories. The war in the Pacific was extremely

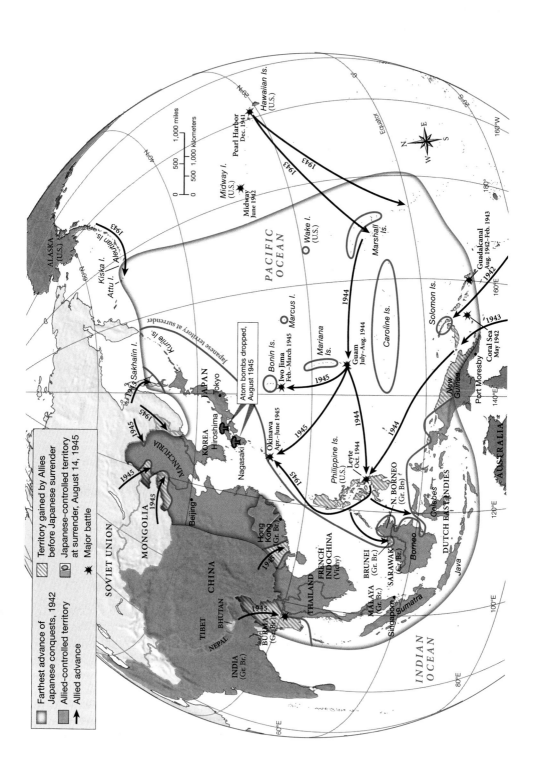

brutal—a "war without mercy," in the words of a leading American scholar—and soldiers on both sides committed atrocities. A product of spiraling violence, mutual hatred, and dehumanizing racial stereotypes, the fighting intensified as the United States moved toward Japan.[8]

The Grand Alliance and the "Hinge of Fate"

While the Nazis and the Japanese built their savage empires, Great Britain, the United States, and the Soviet Union joined together in a military pact Churchill termed the Grand Alliance. This was a matter of circumstance more than of choice. It had taken the Japanese surprise attack to bring the isolationist United States into the war. Moreover, the British and Americans were determined opponents of Soviet communism, and disagreements between the Soviets and the capitalist powers during the course of the war sowed mutual distrust. Stalin repeatedly urged Britain and the United States to open a second front in France to relieve pressure on Soviet forces, but Churchill and Roosevelt refused until the summer of 1944. Despite such tensions, the overriding goal of defeating the Axis powers brought together these reluctant allies.

In one area of agreement, the Grand Alliance concurred on a policy of "Europe first." Only after Hitler was defeated would the Allies mount an all-out attack on Japan, the lesser threat. The Allies also agreed to concentrate on immediate military needs, postponing tough political questions about the eventual peace settlement that might have divided them. To further encourage mutual trust, the Allies adopted the principle of the unconditional surrender of Germany and Japan. This policy cemented the Grand Alliance because it denied Hitler any hope of dividing his foes. It also meant that Soviet and Anglo-American armies would almost certainly be forced to invade and occupy all of Germany, and that Japan would fight to the bitter end.

The military resources of the Grand Alliance were awesome. The United States harnessed its vast industrial base to wage global war and in 1943 outproduced not only Germany, Italy, and Japan, but all the rest of the world combined. Great Britain became an impregnable floating fortress, a gigantic frontline staging area for a decisive blow to the heart of Germany. After a determined push, the Soviet Union's military strength was so great that it might well have defeated Germany without Western help. Stalin drew heavily on the heroic resolve of the Soviet people, especially those in the central Russian heartland. Broad-based Russian nationalism, as opposed to narrow communist ideology, became a powerful unifying force in what the Soviet state called the Great Patriotic War of the Fatherland.

The combined might of the Allies forced back the Nazi armies on all fronts (see Map 27.3). At the Second Battle of El Alamein (el al-uh-MAYN) in October–November 1942, British forces decisively defeated combined German and Italian

< **MAP 27.5 World War II in the Pacific**
In 1942 Japanese forces overran an enormous amount of territory, which the Allies slowly recaptured in a long, bitter struggle. As this map shows, Japan still held a large Asian empire in August 1945, when the unprecedented devastation of atomic warfare suddenly forced it to surrender.

armies and halted the Axis penetration of North Africa. Winston Churchill called the battle the "hinge of fate" that opened the door to Allied victory. Shortly thereafter, an Anglo-American force landed in Morocco and Algeria. These French possessions, which were under the control of Pétain's Vichy government, went over to the Allies. Fearful of an Allied invasion across the Mediterranean, German forces occupied Vichy France in November 1942, and the collaborationist French government effectively ceased to exist.

After driving the Axis powers out of North Africa, U.S. and British forces invaded Sicily in the summer of 1943 and mainland Italy that autumn. Mussolini was overthrown by a coup d'état, and the new Italian government publicly accepted unconditional surrender. In response, Nazi armies invaded and seized control of northern and central Italy, and German paratroopers rescued Mussolini in a daring raid and put him at the head of a puppet government. Facing stiff German resistance, the Allies battled their way slowly up the Italian peninsula. The Germans were clearly on the defensive.

The spring of 1943 brought crucial Allied victories at sea and in the air. In the first years of the war, German submarines had successfully attacked North Atlantic shipping, severely hampering the British war effort. Later new antisubmarine technologies favored the Allies. Soon massive convoys of hundreds of ships were streaming across the Atlantic, bringing much-needed troops and supplies from the United States to Britain.

The German air force had never really recovered from its defeat in the Battle of Britain. With almost unchallenged air superiority, the United States and Britain now mounted massive bombing raids on German cities to maim industrial production and break civilian morale. By the war's end, hardly a German city of any size remained untouched, and many—including Dresden, Hamburg, and Cologne—lay in ruins.

Great Britain and the United States had made critical advances in the western theater, but the worst German defeats came at the hands of the Red Army on the eastern front. Although the Germans had almost captured the major cities of Moscow and Leningrad in early winter 1941, they were forced back by determined Soviet counterattacks. The Germans mounted a second and initially successful invasion of the Soviet Union in the summer of 1942, but the campaign turned into a disaster. The downfall came at the **Battle of Stalingrad**, when in November 1942 the Soviets surrounded and systematically destroyed the entire German Sixth Army of 300,000 men. In January 1943 only 123,000 soldiers were left to surrender. Hitler, who had refused to allow a retreat, suffered a catastrophic defeat. For the first time, German public opinion turned decisively against the war. In summer 1943 the larger, better-equipped Soviet armies took the offensive and began to push the Germans back along the entire eastern front (see Map 27.3).

Allied Victory

The balance of power was now clearly in Allied hands, yet bitter fighting continued in Europe for almost two years. Germany, less fully mobilized for war in 1941 than Britain, stepped up its efforts. The German war industry, under the Nazi minister of armaments Albert Speer, put to work millions of prisoners of war and slave laborers from across occupied Europe. Between early 1942 and July 1944, German war production tripled despite heavy Anglo-American bombing.

Soviet Troops After the Battle of Stalingrad Triumphant Soviet soldiers march through the center of bomb-damaged Stalingrad after the end of the battle on February 2, 1943. In the background stands the destroyed department store that housed the headquarters of German Field Marshal von Paulus before his Sixth Army was surrounded and forced to surrender. Hundreds of thousands of soldiers on both sides lost their lives, and of the approximately 100,000 German prisoners taken by the Red Army, only about 5,000 returned home after the war.   (Emmanuel Yevzerikhin/Getty Images)

German resistance against Hitler also failed to halt the fighting. An unsuccessful attempt by conservative army leaders to assassinate Hitler in July 1944 only brought increased repression by the fanatic Nazis who had taken over the government. Closely disciplined by the regime, frightened by the prospect of unconditional surrender, and terrorized by Nazi propaganda that portrayed the advancing Russian armies as rapacious Slavic beasts, the Germans fought on with suicidal resolve.

On June 6, 1944, American and British forces under General Dwight Eisenhower landed on the beaches of Normandy, France, in history's greatest naval invasion. In a hundred dramatic days, more than 2 million men and almost half a million vehicles broke through the German lines and pushed inland. Rejecting proposals to strike straight at Berlin in a massive attack, Eisenhower moved forward cautiously on a broad front. Not until March 1945 did American troops cross the Rhine and enter Germany. By spring of 1945 the Allies had finally forced the Germans out of the Italian peninsula. That April, Mussolini was captured in northern Italy by Communist partisans and executed, along with his mistress and other Fascist leaders.

The Soviets, who had been advancing steadily since July 1943, reached the outskirts of Warsaw by August 1944. Anticipating German defeat, the Polish

Nuclear Wasteland at Hiroshima Only a handful of buildings remain standing in the ruins of Hiroshima in September 1945. Fearing the costs of a prolonged ground and naval campaign against the Japanese mainland, the United States dropped atomic bombs on Hiroshima and Nagasaki in August 1945. The bombings ended the war and opened the nuclear age. (AP Images)

underground Home Army ordered an uprising, so that the Poles might take the city on their own and establish independence from the Soviets. The Warsaw Uprising was a tragic miscalculation. Citing military pressure, the Red Army refused to enter the city. Stalin and Soviet leaders thus allowed the Germans to destroy the Polish insurgents, a cynical move that paved the way for the establishment of a postwar Communist regime. Only after the decimated Home Army surrendered did the Red Army continue its advance. Warsaw lay in ruins, and between 150,000 and 200,000 Poles—mostly civilians—had lost their lives.

Over the next six months, the Soviets moved southward into Romania, Hungary, and Yugoslavia. In January 1945 the Red Army crossed Poland into Germany, and on April 26 it met American forces on the Elbe River. The Allies had overrun Europe and closed their vise on Nazi Germany. As Soviet forces fought their way into Berlin, Hitler committed suicide, and on May 8 the remaining German commanders capitulated.

The war in the Pacific also drew to a close. Despite repeated U.S. victories through the summer of 1945, Japanese troops had continued to fight with enormous courage and determination. American commanders believed the invasion and conquest of Japan itself might cost 1 million American casualties and claim 10 to 20 million Japanese lives. In fact, Japan was almost helpless, its industry and dense, fragile wooden cities largely destroyed by intense American bombing. Yet the Japanese seemed determined to fight on, ready to die for a hopeless cause.

After much discussion at the upper levels of the U.S. government, American planes dropped atomic bombs on Hiroshima and Nagasaki in Japan on August 6 and 9, 1945. The mass bombing of cities and civilians, one of the terrible new practices of World War II, now ended in the final nightmare—unprecedented human destruction in a single blinding flash. On August 14, 1945, the Japanese announced their surrender. The Second World War, which had claimed the lives of more than 50 million soldiers and civilians, was over.

NOTES

1. Quoted in S. Kotkin, *Magnetic Mountain: Stalinism as a Civilization* (Berkeley: University of California Press, 1997), pp. 221–222.
2. R. Thurston, *Life and Terror in Stalin's Russia, 1934–1941* (New Haven, Conn.: Yale University Press, 1996), esp. pp. 16–106; also M. Malia, *The Soviet Tragedy: A History of Socialism in Russia, 1917–1991* (New York: Free Press, 1995), pp. 227–270.
3. Quoted in C. Duggan, *A Concise History of Italy* (New York: Cambridge University Press, 1994), p. 227.
4. Quoted in Duggan, *A Concise History of Italy*, p. 234.
5. M. Burleigh and W. Wippermann, *The Racial State: Germany, 1933–1945* (New York: Cambridge University Press, 1991).
6. See, for example, the population statistics on the German occupation of Belarus in C. Gerlach, "German Economic Interests, Occupation Policy, and the Murder of the Jews in Belorussia, 1941–43," in *National Socialist Extermination Policies: Contemporary German Perspectives and Controversies*, ed. U. Herbert (New York: Berghan Books, 2000), pp. 210–239. See also M. Allen, *The Business of Genocide: The SS, Slave Labor, and the Concentration Camps* (Chapel Hill: University of North Carolina Press, 2002), pp. 270–285.
7. D. Goldhagen, *Hitler's Willing Executioners: Ordinary Germans and the Holocaust* (New York: Vintage Books, 1997); for an alternate explanation, see C. Browning, *Ordinary Men: Reserve Police Battalion 101 and the Final Solution in Poland* (New York: Harper, 1992).
8. J. Dower, *War Without Mercy: Race and Power in the Pacific War* (New York: Pantheon, 1986).
9. E. Hobsbawm, *The Age of Extremes: A History of the World, 1914–1991* (New York: Vintage, 1996), p. 21.

LOOKING BACK **LOOKING AHEAD**

The first half of the twentieth century brought almost unimaginable violence and destruction, leading historian Eric Hobsbawm to label the era the "age of catastrophe."[9] Shaken by the rapid cultural change and economic collapse that followed the tragedy of World War I, many Europeans embraced the radical politics of communism and fascism. Some found appeal in visions of a classless society or a racially pure national community, and totalitarian leaders like Stalin and Hitler capitalized on these desires for social order, building dictatorial regimes that demanded total allegiance to an ideological vision. Even as these regimes rewarded supporters and promised ordinary people a new age, they violently repressed their enemies, real and imagined. The vision proved fatal: the great clash of ideologies that emerged in the 1920s and 1930s led to history's most deadly war, killing millions and devastating large swaths of Europe and East Asia.

Only the reluctant Grand Alliance of the liberal United States and Great Britain with the Communist Soviet Union was able to defeat the Axis powers. After 1945 fascism was finished, discredited by total defeat and the postwar revelation of the Holocaust. To make sure, the Allies would occupy the lands of their former enemies. Rebuilding a devastated Europe proved a challenging but in the end manageable task: once recovery took off, the postwar decades brought an economic boom that led to levels of prosperity unimaginable in the interwar years. Maintaining an alliance between the capitalist West and the Communist East was something else. Trust quickly broke down. Europe would be divided into two hostile camps, and Cold War tensions between East and West would dominate European and world politics for the next forty years.

MAKE CONNECTIONS

Think about the larger developments and continuities within and across chapters.

1. Historians continue to disagree on whether "totalitarianism" is an appropriate way to describe Communist and Fascist dictatorships in Europe. How would you define this term? Is it a useful label to describe state and society under Stalin, Mussolini, and Hitler? Why is the debate over totalitarianism still important today?

2. Why would ordinary people support dictatorships that trampled on democracy, political freedoms, and civil rights?

3. Summarize the key issues in the origins of World War II and the key turning points in the war itself. Was political ideology the main driving force behind these events, or were other factors at play?

Chapter 27 Review

IDENTIFY KEY TERMS

Identify and explain the significance of each item below.

totalitarianism (p. 816)

Stalinism (p. 817)

fascism (p. 817)

eugenics (p. 817)

New Economic Policy (NEP) (p. 819)

five-year plan (p. 822)

collectivization of agriculture (p. 822)

kulaks (p. 822)

Black Shirts (p. 827)

Lateran Agreement (p. 828)

National Socialism (p. 830)

Enabling Act (p. 832)

appeasement (p. 835)

New Order (p. 839)

Holocaust (p. 842)

Battle of Stalingrad (p. 848)

REVIEW THE MAIN IDEAS

Answer the section heading questions from the chapter.

1. What were the most important characteristics of Communist and Fascist ideologies? (p. 816)
2. How did Stalinism transform state and society in the Soviet Union? (p. 819)
3. What kind of government did Mussolini establish in Italy? (p. 826)
4. What policies did Nazi Germany pursue, and why did they appeal to ordinary Germans? (p. 829)
5. What explains the success and then defeat of Germany and Japan during World War II? (p. 838)

CHRONOLOGY

1921	• New Economic Policy (NEP) in U.S.S.R.
1922	• Mussolini gains power in Italy; growth of Nazi Party in Germany
1927	• Stalin comes to power in U.S.S.R.
1928	• Stalin's first five-year plan
1929	• Lateran Agreement; start of collectivization in Soviet Union
1932–1933	• Famine in Ukraine
1933	• Hitler appointed chancellor in Germany; Reichstag passes the Enabling Act, granting Hitler absolute dictatorial power
1935	• Nuremberg Laws deprive Jews of citizenship rights
1936	• Start of great purges under Stalin; Spanish Civil War begins
1937	• Japanese army invades China
1938	• Kristallnacht marks beginning of more aggressive anti-Jewish policy in Germany
1939	• Germany occupies Czech lands and invades western Poland; Britain and France declare war on Germany, starting World War II; Soviet Union occupies eastern Poland
1940	• Germany defeats and occupies France; Battle of Britain begins
1941	• Germany invades U.S.S.R.; Japan attacks Pearl Harbor; United States enters war
1941–1945	• The Holocaust
1942–1943	• Battle of Stalingrad
1944	• Allied invasion at Normandy
1945	• Soviet and U.S. forces enter Germany; United States drops atomic bombs on Japan; World War II ends

28

Cold War Conflict and Consensus

1945–1965

CHAPTER PREVIEW

- Why was World War II followed so quickly by the Cold War?

- What were the sources of postwar recovery and stability in western Europe?

- What was the pattern of postwar development in the Soviet bloc?

- How did decolonization proceed in the Cold War era?

- What were the key changes in social relations in postwar Europe?

THE DEFEAT OF THE NAZIS AND THEIR ALLIES in 1945 left Europe in ruins. In the immediate postwar years, as Europeans struggled to overcome the effects of rampant death and destruction, the victorious Allies worked to shape an effective peace accord. Disagreements between the Soviet Union and the Western allies emerged during this process and quickly led to an apparently endless Cold War between the two new superpowers: the United States and the Soviet Union. This conflict split much of Europe and then the world into a Soviet-aligned Communist bloc and a U.S.-aligned capitalist bloc and spurred military, economic, and technological competition.

Amid these tensions, battered western European countries fashioned a remarkable recovery, building stable democratic institutions and vibrant economies. In the Soviet Union and the East Bloc—the label applied to central and eastern European countries governed by Soviet-backed Communist regimes—Communist leaders repressed challenges to one-party rule but also offered limited reforms, leading to stability there as well.

The postwar decades also brought fundamental change on a global scale, as people living in Europe's colonies won liberation from imperialist rule. Cold War hostilities had an immense impact on this process of decolonization. At the same time, evolving class structures, new migration patterns, and new roles for women and youths remade European society, laying the groundwork for major transformation in the decades to come.

Why was World War II followed so quickly by the Cold War?

In 1945 the Allies faced the momentous challenges of rebuilding a shattered Europe, dealing with Nazi criminals, and creating a lasting peace. The Allies found it difficult to cooperate in peacemaking, and Great Britain and the United States were soon at loggerheads with the Soviet Union (U.S.S.R.). By 1949 most of Europe was divided into East and West Blocs allied with the U.S.S.R. and the United States, respectively. For the next forty years, the competing superpowers engaged in the **Cold War**, a determined competition for political and military superiority around the world.

The Legacies of the Second World War

In the summer of 1945 Europe lay in ruins. Across the continent, the fighting had destroyed cities and landscapes and obliterated buildings, factories, farms, rail tracks, roads, and bridges. Many cities—including Leningrad, Warsaw, Vienna, Budapest, Rotterdam, and Coventry—were completely devastated. Postwar observers compared the remaining piles of rubble to moonscapes. Surviving cities such as Prague and Paris were left relatively unscathed, mostly by chance.

The human costs of the Second World War are almost incalculable (Map 28.1). The death toll far exceeded the mortality figures for World War I. At least 20 million Soviets, including soldiers and civilians, died in the war. Between 9 and 11 million noncombatants lost their lives in Nazi concentration camps, including approximately 6 million Jews. One out of every five Poles died in the war, including 3 million of Poland's 3.25 million Jews. German deaths numbered 5 million, 2 million of them civilians. France and Britain both lost fewer soldiers than in World War I, but about 350,000 French civilians were killed in the fighting. Over 400,000 U.S. soldiers died in the European and Pacific campaigns, and other nations across Europe and the globe also lost staggering numbers. In total, about 50 million human beings perished in the conflict.

The destruction of war also left tens of millions homeless—25 million in the U.S.S.R. and 20 million in Germany alone. The wartime policies of Hitler and Stalin had forced some 30 million people from their homes in the hardest-hit war zones of central and eastern Europe. The end of the war and the start of the peace increased their numbers. Some 13 million ethnic Germans fled west before the advancing Soviet troops or were expelled from eastern Europe under the terms

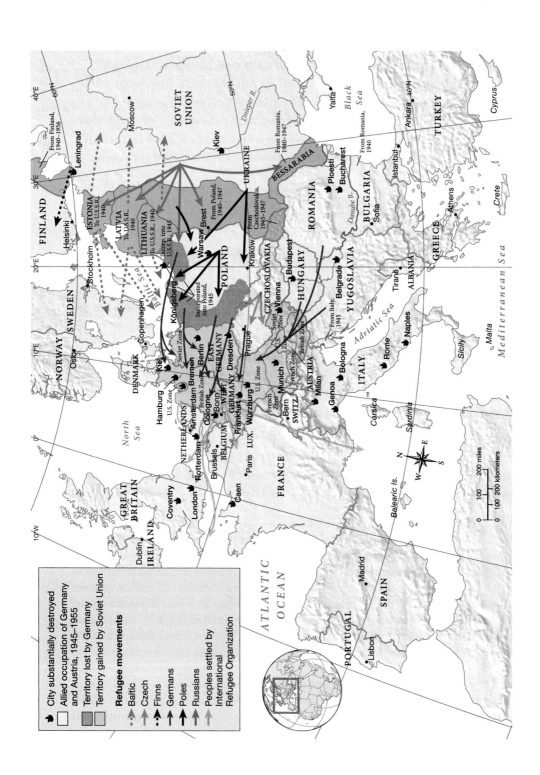

Legend:

City substantially destroyed

Allied occupation of Germany and Austria, 1945–1955

Territory lost by Germany

Territory gained by Soviet Union

Refugee movements

Baltic

Czech

Finns

Germans

Poles

Russians

Peoples settled by International Refugee Organization

Displaced Persons in the Ruins of Berlin The end of the war in 1945 stopped the fighting but not the suffering. For the next two years, millions of displaced persons wandered across Europe searching for sustenance, lost family members, and a place to call home. (Fred Rampage/ Getty Images)

of Allied agreements. Forced laborers from Poland, France, the Balkans, and other nations, brought to Germany by the Nazis, now sought to go home. A woman in Berlin described the "small, tired caravans of people" passing through the city in spring 1945 pushing "pitiful handcarts piled high with sacks, crates, and trunks." The elderly refugees were particularly wretched, "pale, dilapidated, apathetic. Half-dead sacks of bones."[1]

These **displaced persons** or DPs — their numbers increased by concentration camp survivors and freed prisoners of war, and hundreds of thousands of orphaned children — searched for food and shelter. From 1945 to 1947 the newly established United Nations Relief and Rehabilitation Administration (UNRRA) opened over 760 DP camps and spent $10 billion to house, feed, clothe, and repatriate the refugees.

< MAP 28.1   The Aftermath of World War II in Europe, ca. 1945–1950
By 1945 millions of people displaced by war and territorial changes were on the move. The Soviet Union and Poland took land from Germany, which the Allies partitioned into occupation zones. Those zones subsequently formed the basis of the East and West German states. Austria was detached from Germany and similarly divided, but the Soviets later permitted Austria to reunify as a neutral state.

For DPs, going home was not always the best option. Soviet citizens who had spent time in the West were seen as politically unreliable by political leaders in the U.S.S.R. Many DPs faced prison terms, exile to labor camps in the Siberian gulag, and even execution upon their return to Soviet territories. Jewish DPs faced unique problems. Their families and communities had been destroyed, and persistent anti-Semitism often made them unwelcome in their former homelands. Many stayed in special Jewish DP camps in Germany for years. After the creation of Israel in 1948, over 330,000 European Jews left for the new Jewish state. By 1952 about 100,000 Jews had also immigrated to the United States. When the last DP camp closed in 1957, the UNRRA had cared for and resettled many millions of refugees, Jews and non-Jews alike.

When the fighting stopped, Germany and Austria had been divided into four occupation zones, each governed by one of the Allies — the United States, the Soviet Union, Great Britain, and France. The Soviets collected substantial reparations from their zone in eastern Germany and from former German allies Hungary and Romania. In Soviet-occupied Germany, administrators seized factories and equipment, even tearing up railroad tracks and sending the rails to the U.S.S.R.

The authorities in each zone tried to punish those guilty of Nazi atrocities. Across Europe, almost 100,000 Germans and Austrians were convicted of war crimes. Many more were investigated or indicted. In Soviet-dominated central and eastern Europe — where the worst crimes had taken place — retribution was particularly intense. There and in other parts of Europe, collaborators, non-Germans who had assisted the German occupiers during the war, were also punished. In the days and months immediately after the war, spontaneous acts of retribution brought some collaborators to account. In both France and Italy, unofficial groups seeking revenge summarily executed some 25,000 persons. French women accused of "horizontal collaboration" — having sexual relations with German soldiers during the occupation — were publicly humiliated by angry mobs. Newly established postwar governments also formed official courts to sanction collaborators or send them to prison. A small number received the death sentence.

In Germany and Austria, occupation authorities set up "denazification" procedures meant to identify and punish former Nazi Party members responsible for the worst crimes and eradicate National Socialist ideology from social and political institutions. At the Nuremberg trials (1945–1946), an international military tribunal organized by the four Allied powers tried the highest-ranking Nazi military and civilian leaders who had survived the war, charging them with war crimes and crimes against humanity. After chilling testimony from victims of the regime, which revealed the full systematic horror of Nazi atrocities, twelve were sentenced to death and ten more to lengthy prison terms.

The Nuremberg trials marked the last time the four Allies worked closely together to punish former Nazis. As the Cold War developed and the Soviets and the Western Allies drew increasingly apart, each carried out separate denazification programs in their own zones of occupation. In the Western zones, military courts at first actively prosecuted leading Nazis. But the huge numbers implicated in Nazi crimes, German opposition to the proceedings, and the need for stability in the looming Cold War made thorough denazification impractical. Except for the worst offenders, the Western authorities had quietly shelved denazification by 1948. The process was similar in the

Soviet zone. At first, punishment was swift and harsh. About 45,000 former party officials, upper-class industrialists, and large landowners identified as Nazis were sentenced to prison or death. As in the West, however, former Nazis who cooperated with the Soviet authorities could avoid prosecution. Thus many former Nazis found positions in government and industry in both the Soviet and Western zones.

The Peace Settlement and Cold War Origins

In the years immediately after the war, as ordinary people across Europe struggled to come to terms with the war and recover from the ruin, the victorious Allies—the U.S.S.R., the United States, and Great Britain—tried to shape a reasonable and lasting peace. Yet the Allies began to quarrel almost as soon as the unifying threat of Nazi Germany disappeared, and the interests of the Communist Soviet Union and the capitalist Britain and United States increasingly diverged. The hostility between the Eastern and Western superpowers was the sad but logical outgrowth of military developments, wartime agreements, and long-standing political and ideological differences that stretched back to the Russian Revolution.

Once the United States entered the war in late 1941, the Americans and the British had made military victory their highest priority. They did not try to take advantage of the Soviet Union's precarious position in 1942 because they feared that hard bargaining would encourage Stalin to consider making a separate peace with Hitler. Together, the Allies avoided discussion of postwar aims and the shape of the eventual peace settlement and focused instead on pursuing a policy of German unconditional surrender to solidify the alliance. By late 1943 negotiations about the postwar settlement could no longer be postponed. The conference that the "Big Three"—Stalin, Roosevelt, and Churchill—held in the Iranian capital of Teheran in November 1943 proved crucial for determining the shape of the postwar world.

The Big Three In 1945 a triumphant Winston Churchill, an ailing Franklin Roosevelt, and a determined Stalin met at Yalta in southern Russia to plan for peace. Cooperation soon gave way to bitter hostility, and the decisions made by these leaders transformed the map of Europe. (Franklin D. Roosevelt Presidential Library and Museum of the National Archives and Records Administration/U.S. National Archives/photo CT53-70:5)

At Teheran, the Big Three jovially reaffirmed their determination to crush Germany, and this was followed by tense discussions of Poland's postwar borders and a strategy to win the war. Stalin, concerned that the U.S.S.R. was bearing the brunt of the fighting, asked his allies to relieve his armies by opening a second front in German-occupied France. Churchill, fearing the military dangers of a direct attack, argued that American and British forces should follow up their Italian campaign with an indirect attack on Germany through the Balkans. Roosevelt, however, agreed with Stalin that an American-British assault through France would be better, though the date for the invasion was set later than the Soviet leader desired.

The decision to invade France had momentous implications for the Cold War. While the delay in opening a second front fanned Stalin's distrust of the Allies, the agreement on a British-U.S. invasion of France ensured that the American-British and Soviet armies would come together in defeated Germany along a north-south line and that Soviet troops would play the predominant role in pushing the Germans out of eastern and central Europe. Thus the basic shape of postwar Europe was cast even as the fighting continued.

When the Big Three met again in February 1945 at Yalta, on the Black Sea in southern Russia, advancing Soviet armies had already occupied Poland, Bulgaria, Romania, Hungary, part of Yugoslavia, and much of Czechoslovakia and were within a hundred miles of Berlin. The stalled American-British forces had yet to cross the Rhine into Germany. Moreover, the United States was far from defeating Japan. In short, the U.S.S.R.'s position on the ground was far stronger than that of the United States and Britain, which played to Stalin's advantage.

The Allies agreed at Yalta that each of the four victorious powers would occupy a separate zone of Germany and that the Germans would pay heavy reparations to the Soviet Union. At American insistence, Stalin agreed to declare war on Japan after Germany's defeat. As for Poland, the Big Three agreed that the U.S.S.R. would permanently incorporate the eastern Polish territories its army had occupied in 1939 and that Poland would be compensated with German lands to the west. They also agreed in an ambiguous compromise that the new governments in Soviet-occupied Europe would be freely elected but "friendly" to the Soviet Union.

The Yalta compromise over elections in these countries broke down almost immediately. Even before the conference, Communist parties were taking control in Bulgaria and Poland. Elsewhere, the Soviets formed coalition governments that included Social Democrats and other leftist parties but reserved key government posts for Moscow-trained Communists. At the Potsdam Conference of July 1945, the differences over elections in Soviet-occupied Europe surged to the fore. Roosevelt had died and had been succeeded by Harry Truman (U.S. pres. 1945–1953), who demanded immediate free elections throughout central and eastern Europe. Stalin refused point-blank. "A freely elected government in any of these East European countries would be anti-Soviet," he admitted simply, "and that we cannot allow."[2]

Here, then, were the keys to the much-debated origins of the Cold War. While fighting Germany, the Allies could maintain an alliance of necessity. As the war drew to a close, long-standing hostility between East and West re-emerged. Mutual distrust, security concerns, and antagonistic desires for economic, political, and territorial control began to destroy the former partnership.

Stalin, who had lived through two enormously destructive German invasions, was determined to establish a buffer zone of sympathetic states around the U.S.S.R. and at the same time expand the reach of communism and the Soviet state. Stalin believed that only Communists could be dependable allies and that free elections would result in independent and possibly hostile governments on his western border. With Soviet armies in central and eastern Europe, there was no way short of war for the United States to control the region's political future, and war was out of the question. The United States, for its part, pushed to maintain democratic capitalism in western Europe. The Americans quickly showed that they, too, were willing to use their vast political, economic, and military power to maintain predominance in their sphere of influence.

West Versus East

The Cold War took shape over the next five years, as both sides hardened their positions. After Japan's surrender in September 1945, Truman cut off aid to the ailing U.S.S.R. In October he declared that the United States would never recognize any government established by force against the will of its people. In March 1946 former British prime minister Churchill ominously informed an American audience that an "iron curtain" had fallen across the continent, dividing Europe into two antagonistic camps (Map 28.2).

The Soviet Union was indeed consolidating its hold on central and eastern Europe. In fact, the Soviets enjoyed some popular support in the region, though this varied from country to country. After all, the Red Army had thrown out the German invaders, and after the abuses of fascism the ideals of Communist equality retained some appeal. Yet the Communist parties in these areas quickly recognized that they lacked enough support to take power in free elections. In Romania, Bulgaria, Poland, and Hungary, Communist politicians, backed by Moscow, repressed their liberal opponents and engineered phony elections that established Communist-led regimes. They purged the last remaining noncommunists from the coalition governments set up after the war and by 1948 had established Soviet-style, one-party Communist dictatorships.

The pattern was somewhat different in Czechoslovakia, where Communists enjoyed success in open elections and initially formed a coalition government with other parties. When the noncommunist ministers resigned in February 1948, the Communists took over the government and began Stalinizing the country. This seizure of power in Czechoslovakia contributed to Western fears of limitless Communist expansion.

In western Europe, communism also enjoyed some support. In Italy, which boasted the largest Communist Party outside of the Soviet bloc, Communists won 19 percent of the vote in 1946; French Communists earned 28 percent of the vote the same year. These large, well-organized parties criticized the growing role of the United States in western Europe and challenged their own governments with violent rhetoric and large strikes. At the same time, bitter civil wars in Greece and China pitted Communist revolutionaries against authoritarian leaders backed by the United States.

By early 1947 it appeared to many Americans that the U.S.S.R. was determined to export communism by subversion throughout Europe and around the world. The

MAP 28.2   Cold War Europe in the 1950s
The Cold War divided Europe into two hostile military alliances that formed to the east and west of an "iron curtain."

United States responded with the **Truman Doctrine**, aimed at "containing" communism to areas already under Communist governments. The United States, President Truman promised, would use diplomatic, economic, and even military means to resist the expansion of communism anywhere on the globe. In the first examples of containment policies in action, Truman asked Congress to provide military aid to anticommunist forces in the Greek Civil War (1944–1949) and counter the threat of Soviet expansion in Turkey. With American support, both countries remained in the Western bloc.

The American determination to enforce containment hardened when the Soviets exploded their own atomic bomb in 1949, raising popular fears of a looming nuclear holocaust. At home and abroad, the United States engaged in an anticommunist crusade. Emotional, moralistic denunciations of Stalin and Communist regimes became part of American public life. By the early 1950s the U.S. government was restructuring its military to meet the Soviet threat, pouring money into defense spending and testing nuclear weapons that dwarfed the destructive power of atomic bombs.

Military aid and a defense buildup were only one aspect of Truman's policy of containment. In 1947 western Europe was still on the verge of economic collapse. Food was scarce, inflation was high, and black markets flourished. Recognizing that an economically and politically stable western Europe would be an effective block against the popular appeal of communism, U.S. secretary of state George C. Marshall offered Europe economic aid — the **Marshall Plan** — to help it rebuild. As Marshall wrote in a State Department bulletin, "Its purpose should be the revival of a working economy in the world so as to permit the emergence of political and social conditions in which free institutions can exist."[3]

The Marshall Plan was one of the most successful foreign aid programs in history. When it ended in 1951, the United States had given about $13 billion in aid (equivalent to over $200 billion in 2019 dollars) to fifteen western European nations, and Europe's economy was on the way to recovery. Marshall Plan funding was initially offered to East Bloc countries as well, but fearing Western interference in the Soviet sphere, they rejected the offer. In 1949 the Soviets established the **Council for Mutual Economic Assistance (COMECON)**, an economic organization of Communist states intended to rebuild the East Bloc independently of the West. Thus the generous aid of the Marshall Plan was limited to countries in the Western bloc, which further increased Cold War divisions.

In the late 1940s Berlin, the capital city of Germany, was on the frontline of the Cold War. Like the rest of Germany and Austria, Berlin had been divided into four zones of occupation. In June 1948 the Western allies replaced the currency in the western zones of Germany and Berlin, an early move in plans to establish a separate West German state sympathetic to U.S. interests. The currency reform violated the peace settlement and raised Stalin's fears of the American presence in Europe. In addition, growing ties among Britain, France, Belgium, and the Netherlands convinced Stalin that a Western bloc was forming against the Soviet Union. In response, the Soviet dictator used the one card he had to play — access to Berlin — to force the allies to the bargaining table. Stalin blocked all traffic through the Soviet zone of Germany to Berlin in an attempt to win concessions and perhaps reunify the city under Soviet control. Acting firmly, the Western allies coordinated around-the-clock flights of hundreds of planes over the Soviet roadblocks, supplying provisions to West Berliners and thwarting Soviet efforts to swallow up the western half of the city. After 324 days, the Berlin airlift succeeded, and the Soviets reopened the roads.

Success in breaking the Berlin blockade had several lasting results. First, it paved the way for the creation of two separate German states in 1949: the Federal Republic of Germany (West Germany), aligned with the United States, and the German Democratic Republic (East Germany), aligned with the U.S.S.R. Germany would remain divided for the next forty-one years, a radical solution to the "German problem" that satisfied people fearful of the nation's possible military resurgence.

The Berlin crisis also seemed to show that containment worked, and thus strengthened U.S. resolve to maintain a strong European and U.S. military presence in western Europe. In 1949 the United States formed **NATO** (the North Atlantic Treaty Organization), an anti-Soviet military alliance of Western governments. As one British diplomat put it, NATO was designed "to keep the Russians out, the Americans in, and the Germans down."[4] With U.S. backing, West Germany joined NATO in 1955 and was allowed to rebuild its military to help defend western Europe against possible Soviet attack. That same year, the Soviets countered by organizing the **Warsaw Pact**, a military alliance among the U.S.S.R. and its Communist satellites. In both political and military terms, most of Europe was divided into two hostile blocs.

The superpower confrontation that emerged from the ruins of World War II took shape in Europe, but it quickly spread around the globe. The Cold War turned hot in East Asia. When Soviet-backed Communist North Korea invaded South Korea in 1950, President Truman swiftly sent U.S. troops. In the end, the Korean War was indecisive: the fragile truce agreed to in 1953 left Korea divided between a Communist north and a capitalist south. The war nonetheless showed that though the superpowers might maintain a fragile peace in Europe, they were perfectly willing to engage in open conflict in non-Western territories. By the early 1950s the confrontation between the Soviet Union and its satellite states and the United States and its European allies had become an apparently permanent feature of world affairs.

Big Science in the Nuclear Age

Cold War hostilities helped foster a nuclear arms race, a space race, and the computer revolution, all made possible by stunning advances in science and technology. During the Second World War, theoretical science lost its innocence when it was joined with practical technology (applied science) on a massive scale. Many leading university scientists went to work on top-secret projects to help their governments fight the war. The development by British scientists of radar to detect enemy aircraft was a particularly important outcome of this new kind of sharply focused research. The air war also stimulated the development of rocketry and jet aircraft. The most spectacular and deadly result of directed scientific research during the war was the atomic bomb, which showed the world both the awesome power and the heavy moral responsibilities of modern science.

The impressive results of this directed research inspired a new model for science — Big Science. By combining theoretical work with sophisticated engineering in a large bureaucratic organization, Big Science could tackle extremely difficult problems, from new and improved weapons for the military to better products for consumers. Big Science was extremely expensive, requiring large-scale financing from governments and large corporations.

After the war, scientists continued to contribute to advances in military technologies, and a large portion of postwar research supported the expanding arms race. New weapons such as missiles, nuclear submarines, and spy satellites demanded breakthroughs no less remarkable than those responsible for radar and the first atomic bomb. After 1945 roughly one-quarter of all men and women trained in science and engineering in the West — and perhaps more in the Soviet Union — were employed full-time in the production of weapons to kill other humans. By the 1960s both sides had enough nuclear firepower to destroy each other and the rest of the world many times over.

Sophisticated science, lavish government spending, and military needs came together in the space race of the 1960s. In 1957 the Soviets used long-range rockets developed in their nuclear weapons program to launch Sputnik, the first man-made satellite to orbit the earth. In 1961 they sent the world's first cosmonaut circling the globe. Embarrassed by Soviet triumphs, the United States caught "Sputnikitis" and made an all-out commitment to catch up with the Soviets. The U.S. National Aeronautics and Space Administration (NASA), founded in 1958, won a symbolic victory by landing a manned spacecraft on the moon in 1969. Four more moon landings followed by 1972.

Advanced nuclear weapons and the space race were made possible by the concurrent revolution in computer technology. The search for better weaponry in World War II boosted the development of sophisticated data-processing machines, including the electronic Colossus computer used by the British to break German military codes. The massive mainframe ENIAC (Electronic Numerical Integrator and Computer), built for the U.S. Army at the University of Pennsylvania, went into operation in 1945. The invention of the transistor in 1947 further advanced computer design. From the mid-1950s on, this small, efficient electronic switching device increasingly replaced bulky vacuum tubes as the key computer components. By the 1960s sophisticated computers were indispensable tools for a variety of military, commercial, and scientific uses, foreshadowing the rise of personal computers in the decades to come.

Big Science had tangible benefits for ordinary people. During the postwar green revolution, directed agricultural research greatly increased the world's food supplies. Farming was industrialized and became more and more productive per acre, resulting in far fewer people being needed to grow food. The application of scientific advances to industrial processes made consumer goods less expensive and more available to larger numbers of people. The transistor, for example, was used in computers but also in portable radios, kitchen appliances, and many other consumer products. In sum, in the nuclear age, Big Science created new sources of material well-being and entertainment as well as destruction.

What were the sources of postwar recovery and stability in western Europe?

In the late 1940s the outlook for Europe appeared bleak. Yet the continent recovered, with the nations of western Europe in the lead. In less than a generation, many western European countries constructed democratic political institutions, while a period of unprecedented economic growth and a consumer revolution brought a sense of prosperity to ever-larger numbers of people. Politicians entered collective economic agreements and established the European Economic Community, the first steps toward broader European unity.

The Search for Political and Social Consensus

In the first years after the war, economic conditions in western Europe were terrible. Infrastructure of all kinds barely functioned, and runaway inflation and a thriving black market testified to severe shortages and hardships. In 1948, as Marshall

Plan dollars poured in, the battered economies of western Europe began to improve. The outbreak of the Korean War in 1950 further stimulated economic activity, and Europe entered a period of rapid economic progress that lasted into the late 1960s. Never before had the European economy grown so fast. By the late 1950s contemporaries were talking about a widespread **economic miracle** that had brought robust growth to most western European countries.

There were many reasons for this stunning economic performance. American aid got the process off to a fast start. Moreover, economic growth became a basic objective of all western European governments, for leaders and voters alike were determined to avoid a return to the dangerous and demoralizing stagnation of the 1930s.

The postwar governments in western Europe thus embraced new political and economic policies that led to a remarkably lasting social consensus. They turned to liberal democracy and generally adopted Keynesian economics (see "Germany and the Western Powers" in Chapter 26) in successful attempts to stimulate their economies. In addition, whether they leaned to the left or to the right, national leaders in the core European states applied an imaginative mixture of government planning and free-market capitalism to promote economic growth. They nationalized — or established government ownership of — significant sectors of the economy, used economic regulation to encourage growth, and established generous social benefits programs, paid for with high taxes, for all citizens. This consensual framework for good government lasted until the middle of the 1970s.

In politics, a new team of European politicians emerged to guide the postwar recovery. Across the West, newly formed Christian Democratic parties became important power brokers. Rooted in the Catholic parties of the prewar decades, the **Christian Democrats** offered voters tired of radical politics a center-right vision of reconciliation and recovery. Socialists and Communists, active in the resistance against Hitler, also increased their power and prestige, especially in France and Italy. They, too, provided fresh leadership as they pushed for social change and economic reform.

Across much of continental Europe, the centrist Christian Democrats defeated their left-wing competition. In Italy, the Christian Democrats were the leading party in the first postwar elections in 1946, and in early 1948 they won an absolute majority in the parliament in a landslide victory. In France, the Popular Republican Movement, a Christian Democratic party, provided some of the best postwar leaders after General Charles de Gaulle (duh GOHL) resigned from his position as head of the provisional government in January 1946. West Germans, too, elected a Christian Democratic government from 1949 until 1969.

As they provided effective leadership for their respective countries, Christian Democrats drew inspiration from a common Christian and European heritage. They firmly rejected authoritarianism and narrow nationalism and placed their faith in democracy and liberalism. At the same time, the anticommunist rhetoric of these steadfast cold warriors was unrelenting. Rejecting the class-based politics of the left, they championed a return to traditional family values, a vision with great appeal after a war that left many broken families and destitute households; the Christian Democrats often received a majority of women's votes.

Following their U.S. allies, Christian Democrats advocated free-market economics and promised voters prosperity and ample supplies of consumer goods.

They established education subsidies, family and housing allowances, public transportation, and public health insurance throughout continental Europe. When necessary, Christian Democratic leaders accepted the need for limited government planning. In France, the government established modernization commissions for key industries, and state-controlled banks funneled money into industrial development. In West Germany, the Christian Democrats broke decisively with the straitjacketed Nazi economy and promoted a "social-market economy" based on a combination of free-market liberalism, limited state intervention, and an extensive social benefits network.

Though Portugal, Spain, and Greece generally supported NATO and the United States in the Cold War, they proved exceptions to the rule of democratic transformation outside the Soviet bloc. In Portugal and Spain, nationalist authoritarian regimes had taken power in the 1930s. Portugal's authoritarian state was overthrown in a left-wing military coup only in 1974, while Spain's dictator Francisco Franco remained in power until his death in 1975. The authoritarian monarchy established in Greece when the civil war ended in 1949, bolstered by military support and kept in power in a series of army coups, was likewise replaced by a democratic government only in 1975.

By contrast, the Scandinavian countries and Great Britain took decisive turns to the left. Norway, Denmark, and especially Sweden earned a global reputation for long-term Social Democratic governance, generous state-sponsored benefit programs, tolerant lifestyles, and independent attitudes toward Cold War conflicts.

Even though wartime austerity and rationing programs were in place until the mid-1950s, Britain offered the most comprehensive state benefit programs outside Scandinavia. The social-democratic Labour Party took power after the war and ambitiously established a "cradle-to-grave" welfare state. Many British industries were nationalized, including banks, iron and steel industries, and utilities and public transportation networks. The government provided free medical services and hospital care, generous retirement pensions, and unemployment benefits, all subsidized by progressive taxation that pegged tax payments to income levels, with the wealthy paying significantly more than those below them. Although the Labour Party suffered defeats throughout much of the 1950s and early 1960s, its Conservative opponents maintained much of the welfare state when they came to power. Across western Europe, economic growth and state-sponsored benefits systems raised living standards higher than ever before.

Toward European Unity

Though there were important regional differences across much of western Europe, politicians and citizens supported policies that brought together limited state planning, strong economic growth, and democratic government, and this political and social consensus accompanied the first tentative steps on the long road toward a more unified Europe.

A number of new financial arrangements and institutions encouraged slow but steady moves toward European integration, as did cooperation with the United States. To receive Marshall Plan aid, the European states were required by the Americans to cooperate with one another, leading to the creation of the Organization for European Economic Cooperation and the Council of Europe in 1948, both of which promoted commerce and cooperation among European countries.

European federalists hoped that the Council of Europe would evolve into a European parliament with sovereign rights, but this did not happen. Britain, with its still-vast empire and its close relationship with the United States, consistently opposed conceding sovereignty to the council. On the continent, many prominent nationalists and Communists agreed with the British view.

Frustrated in political consolidation, European federalists turned to economics as a way of working toward genuine unity. Christian Democratic governments in West Germany, Italy, Belgium, the Netherlands, and Luxembourg founded the European Coal and Steel Community in 1951 (the British steadfastly refused to join). The founding states quickly attained their immediate economic goal—a single, transnational market for steel and coal without national tariffs or quotas. Close economic ties, advocates hoped, would eventually bind the six member nations so closely together that war among them would become unthinkable.

In 1957, the six countries of the Coal and Steel Community signed the Treaty of Rome, which created the European Economic Community, or **Common Market**. The first goal of the treaty was a gradual reduction of all tariffs among the six in order to create a single market. Other goals included the free movement of capital and labor and common economic policies and institutions. The Common Market encouraged trade among European states, promoted global exports, and helped build shared resources for the modernization of national industries. European integration thus meant not only increased transnational cooperation but also economic growth on the national level.

In the 1960s, hopes for rapid progress toward political as well as economic union were frustrated by a resurgence of nationalism. French president Charles de Gaulle, re-elected to office in 1958, viewed the United States as the main threat to genuine French (and European) independence. He withdrew all French military forces from what he called an "American-controlled" NATO, developed France's own nuclear weapons, and vetoed the scheduled advent of majority rule within the Common Market. Thus, the 1950s and 1960s established a lasting pattern: Europeans would establish ever-closer economic ties, but the Common Market remained a union of independent, sovereign states.

The Consumer Revolution

In the late 1950s western Europe's rapidly expanding economy led to a rising standard of living and remarkable growth in the number and availability of standardized consumer goods. Modern consumer society had precedents in the decades before the Second World War, but the years of the "economic miracle" saw the arrival of a veritable consumer revolution: as the percentage of income spent on necessities such as housing and food declined dramatically, nearly full employment and high wages meant that more Europeans could buy more things than ever before. Shaken by war and eager to rebuild their homes and families, western Europeans embraced the new products of consumer society. Like North Americans, they filled their houses and apartments with modern appliances such as washing machines, and they eagerly purchased the latest entertainment devices of the day: radios, record players, and televisions.

The consumer market became an increasingly important engine for general economic growth. For example, the European automobile industry expanded phenomenally after lagging far behind that of the United States since the 1920s. In 1948 there were only 5 million cars in western Europe; by 1965 there were 44 million. No longer reserved for the elites, car ownership became possible for better-paid workers. With the expansion of social security safeguards reducing the need to accumulate savings for hard times and old age, ordinary people were increasingly willing to take on debt, and new banks and credit unions and even retail outlets increasingly offered loans—or "credit"—for consumer purchases on easy terms.

Visions of consumer abundance became a powerful weapon in an era of Cold War competition. Politicians in both East and West claimed that their respective systems could best provide citizens with ample consumer goods. In the competition over consumption, Western capitalism clearly surpassed Eastern planned economies in the production and distribution of inexpensive products. Western leaders boasted about the abundance of goods on store shelves and promised new forms of social equality in which all citizens would have equal access to consumer items—rather than encouraging equality through state-enforced social leveling, as in the East Bloc. The race to provide ordinary people with higher living standards would be a central aspect of the Cold War, and the Communist East Bloc consistently struggled to catch up to Western standards of prosperity.

What was the pattern of postwar development in the Soviet bloc?

In the counties of the East Bloc, the Soviet Union established firm control over the peoples it had supposedly "liberated" during the Second World War. Although reforms after Stalin's death in 1953 led to economic improvement and limited gains in civil rights, postwar recovery in Communist central and eastern Europe was deeply influenced by developments in the U.S.S.R.

Postwar Life in the East Bloc

The "Great Patriotic War of the Fatherland" had fostered Russian nationalism and a relaxation of dictatorial terror. Even before the war ended, however, Stalin was moving the U.S.S.R. back toward rigid dictatorship, disappointing citizens who hoped for greater freedoms and perhaps a turn to democracy. By early 1946 Stalin maintained that another war with the West was inevitable as long as capitalism existed. Working to extend Communist influence across the globe, the Soviets established the Cominform, or Communist Information Bureau, an international organization dedicated to maintaining Russian control over Communist parties abroad, in western Europe and the East Bloc. Stalin's new superpower foe, the United States, served as an excuse for re-establishing a harsh dictatorship in the U.S.S.R. itself. Stalin reasserted the Communist Party's control of the government and his absolute mastery of the party. Rigid ideological indoctrination, attacks on religion, and the absence of civil liberties were soon facts of life for citizens of the Soviet empire. Millions of supposed political enemies were sent to prison, exile, or forced-labor camps.

As discussed earlier, in the satellite states of central and eastern Europe—including East Germany, Poland, Hungary, Czechoslovakia, Romania, Albania, and Bulgaria—national Communist parties remade state and society on the Soviet model. Though there were significant differences in these East Bloc countries, postwar developments followed a similar pattern. Popular Communist leaders who had led the resistance against Germany were ousted and replaced by politicians who supported Stalinist policies. With Soviet backing, national Communist parties absorbed their Social Democratic rivals and established one-party dictatorships subservient to the Communist Party in Moscow. State security services arrested, imprisoned, and sometimes executed dissenters. Show trials of supposedly disloyal Communist Party leaders took place across the East Bloc from the late 1940s into the 1950s, but were particularly prominent in Bulgaria, Czechoslovakia, Hungary, and Romania. The trials testified to the influence of Soviet advisers and the unrestrained power of the domestic secret police in the satellite states, as well as Stalin's urge to establish complete control—and his increasing paranoia.

Yugoslavia was an exception to the general rule of Communist takeover. There Josip Broz Tito (TEE-toh) (1892–1980), a Communist leader active in the anti-Nazi resistance, successfully resisted Soviet domination and established an independent Communist state. Because there was no Russian army in Yugoslavia, the country remained outside of the Soviet bloc and prospered as a multiethnic state until it began to break apart in 1991.

Within the East Bloc, the newly installed Communist governments moved quickly to restructure national economies along Soviet lines, introducing five-year plans to cope with the enormous task of economic reconstruction. Most industries and businesses were nationalized. These efforts transformed prewar patterns of everyday life, even as they laid the groundwork for industrial development later in the decade.

In their attempts to revive the economy, Communist planners gave top priority to heavy industry and the military. At the same time, East Bloc planners neglected consumer goods and housing, in part because they were generally suspicious of Western-style consumer culture. A glut of consumer goods, they believed, created waste, encouraged rampant individualism, and led to social inequality. Thus, for practical and ideological reasons, the provision of consumer goods lagged in the East Bloc, leading to complaints and widespread disillusionment with the constantly deferred promise of socialist prosperity.

Communist regimes also moved aggressively to collectivize agriculture, as the Soviets had done in the 1930s (see "The Five Year Plans" in Chapter 27). By the early 1960s independent farmers had virtually disappeared in most of the East Bloc. Poland was the exception: there the Stalinist regime tolerated the existence of private agriculture, hoping to maintain stability in the large and potentially rebellious country.

For many people in the East Bloc, everyday life was hard throughout the 1950s. Socialist planned economies often led to production problems and persistent shortages of basic household items. Party leaders encouraged workers to perform almost superhuman labor to "build socialism," often for low pay and under poor conditions. In East Germany, popular discontent with this situation led to open revolt in June 1953. A strike by Berlin construction workers protesting poor wages and increased work quotas led to nationwide demonstrations that were put down with Soviet troops and tanks. At least fifty-five protesters were killed and about five thousand

Rebellion in East Germany In June 1953 disgruntled construction workers in East Berlin walked off the job to protest low pay and high work quotas, setting off a nationwide rebellion against the Communist regime. The protesters could do little against the Soviet tanks and troops that put down the revolt. (Deutsches Historisches Museum, Berlin, Germany/© DHM/Bridgeman Images)

were arrested during the uprising. When the revolt ended, the authorities rescinded the increased work quotas, but hardliner Stalinists within the East German government used the conflict to strengthen their position.

Communist censors purged culture and art of independent voices in aggressive campaigns that imposed rigid anti-Western ideological conformity. In the 1950s and 1960s the Communist states required artists and writers to conform to the dictates of **Socialist Realism**, which idealized the working classes and the Soviet Union. Party propagandists denounced artists who strayed from the party line and forced many talented writers, composers, and film directors to produce works that conformed to the state's political goals. In short, the postwar East Bloc resembled the U.S.S.R. in the 1930s, although police terror was far less intense.

Reform and De-Stalinization

In 1953 the aging Stalin finally died, and the dictatorship that he had built began to change. Even as Stalin's heirs struggled for power, they realized that reforms were necessary because of the widespread hardship created by Stalinist repression. The new leadership curbed the power of the secret police, gradually closed many forced-labor camps, and tried to spur economic growth, which had sputtered in the postwar years. Moreover, Stalin's belligerent foreign policy had led directly to a strong Western alliance, which had taken steps to isolate the Soviet Union.

The Soviet leadership was badly split on the question of just how much change could be permitted while still preserving the system. Conservatives wanted to move slowly. Reformers, led by the remarkable Nikita Khrushchev (1894–1971), argued for major innovations. Khrushchev (kroush-CHAWF), who had joined the party as a coal miner in 1918 and risen to a high-level position in Ukraine in the 1930s, emerged as the new Soviet premier in 1955.

To strengthen his position and that of his fellow reformers, Khrushchev launched a surprising attack on Stalin and his crimes at a closed session of the Twentieth Party Congress in 1956. In his famous "secret speech," Khrushchev told Communist delegates startled by his open admission of errors that Stalin had "supported the glorification of his own person with all conceivable methods" to build a propagandistic "cult of personality." The delegates applauded when Khrushchev reported that Stalin had bungled the country's defense in World War II and unjustly imprisoned and tortured thousands of loyal Communists.

The U.S.S.R. now entered a period of genuine liberalization — or **de-Stalinization**, as it was called in the West. Khrushchev's speech was read at Communist Party meetings held throughout the country, and it strengthened the reform movement. The party maintained its monopoly on political power, but Khrushchev enlisted younger, reform-minded members. Calling for a relaxation of tensions with the West, the new premier announced a policy of "peaceful coexistence." In domestic policies, state planners shifted resources from heavy industry and the military toward consumer goods and agriculture, and they relaxed Stalinist workplace controls. Leaders in other Communist countries grudgingly adopted similar reforms, and the East Bloc's generally low standard of living began to improve.

Khrushchev was proud of Soviet achievements and liked to boast that East Bloc living standards and access to consumer goods would soon surpass those of the West. Soviet and East Bloc reforms did spark a limited consumer revolution. Consumers' options were more modest than those in the West, but people in Communist countries also purchased automobiles, televisions, and other consumer goods in increasing numbers in the 1960s.

Writers and intellectuals saw de-Stalinization as a chance to push against the constraints of Socialist Realism. Russian author Boris Pasternak (1890–1960), for example, published his classic novel *Doctor Zhivago* in 1957, which appeared in the West but not in the Soviet Union until 1988. *Doctor Zhivago* was both a literary masterpiece and a powerful challenge to communism. It tells the story of a poet who rejects the violence and brutality of the October Revolution of 1917 and the Stalinist years. Mainstream Communist critics denounced Pasternak, whose book was circulated in secret — but in an era of liberalization he was neither arrested nor shot. Other talented writers followed Pasternak's lead, and courageous editors let the sparks fly. Aleksandr Solzhenitsyn (sohl-zhuh-NEET-suhn) (1918–2008) created a sensation when his *One Day in the Life of Ivan Denisovich* was published in the U.S.S.R. in 1962. Solzhenitsyn's novel, a damning indictment of the Stalinist past, portrays in grim detail life in a Soviet labor camp — a life to which Solzhenitsyn himself had been unjustly condemned.

Foreign Policy and Domestic Rebellion

Khrushchev also de-Stalinized Soviet foreign policy. "Peaceful coexistence" with capitalism was possible, he argued, and war was not inevitable. As a result, Cold War tensions relaxed considerably between 1955 and 1957. At the same time, Khrushchev began wooing the new nations of Asia and Africa — even those that were not Communist — with promises of support and economic aid.

In the East Bloc states, Communist leaders responded in complex ways to de-Stalinization. In East Germany the regime stubbornly resisted reform, but in Poland and Hungary de-Stalinization stimulated rebelliousness. Poland took the lead in 1956, when extensive popular demonstrations brought a new government to power. The new First Secretary of the Polish Communist Party proclaimed that there were "many roads to socialism," and by promising to remain loyal to the Warsaw Pact, Poland managed to win greater autonomy from Soviet control. The new leadership maintained the Communist system even as it tolerated a free peasantry and an independent Catholic Church.

Hungary experienced an ultimately tragic revolution the same year. In October 1956, the people of Budapest installed Imre Nagy (im-rey nadge), a liberal Communist reformer, as the new prime minister. Encouraged by extensive popular protests and joined by other Communist reformers, Nagy proposed to democratize Hungary. Though never renouncing communism, he demanded open, multiparty elections, the relaxation of political repression, and other reforms. Bold moves in Hungary raised widespread hopes that Communist states could undergo substantial but peaceful change, driven from within.

At first, it seemed that the Soviets might negotiate, but the breathing space was short-lived. When Nagy announced that Hungary would leave the Warsaw Pact and asked the United Nations to protect the country's neutrality, the Soviets grew alarmed about the possibility that Hungary's independent course would affect other East Bloc countries. On November 4 Soviet troops moved in on the capital city of Budapest and crushed the revolution. Around 2,700 Hungarians died in the crackdown. Fighting was bitter until the end, for the Hungarians hoped that the United Nations would come to their aid. This did not occur—in part because the Western powers were involved in the Suez crisis (see "Independence and Conflict in the Middle East" ahead) and were, in general, reluctant to directly confront the Soviets in Europe with military force. When a newly installed Communist regime executed Nagy and other protest leaders and sent thousands more to prison, many people in the East Bloc concluded that their best hope was to strive for internal reform without openly challenging Soviet control.

The outcome of the Hungarian uprising weakened support for Soviet-style communism in western Europe—the brutal repression deeply discouraged those who still believed in the possibility of an equitable socialist society, and tens of thousands of Communist Party members in the West resigned in disgust. At the same time, Western politicians recognized that the U.S.S.R. would use military force to defend its control of the East Bloc, and that only open war between East and West had the potential to overturn Communist rule there. This price was too high, and it seemed that Communist domination of the satellite states was there to stay.

The Limits of Reform

By late 1962 Khrushchev's Communist colleagues began to see de-Stalinization as a dangerous threat to the authority of the party, and opposition to Khrushchev's reformist policies gained momentum in party circles. Moreover, Khrushchev's policy toward the West was erratic and ultimately unsuccessful. In 1958, in a failed attempt to staunch the flow of hundreds of thousands of disgruntled East German residents who used the open border between East and West Berlin to move permanently to the West, Khrushchev tightened border controls and ordered the Western allies to evacuate the city within six months. In response, the allies reaffirmed their unity in West Berlin, and Khrushchev backed down. Then, with Khrushchev's backing, in 1961 the East German authorities built a wall between East and West Berlin, sealing off West Berlin, in clear violation of existing access agreements between the Great Powers. The

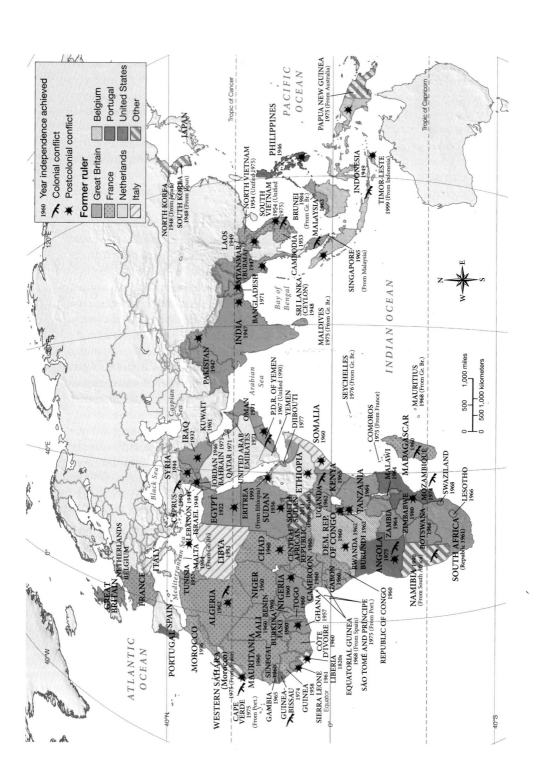

recently elected U.S. president, John F. Kennedy (U.S. pres. 1961–1963), insisted publicly that the United States would never abandon Berlin. Privately hoping that the wall would lessen Cold War tensions by easing hostilities in Berlin, Kennedy did little to prevent its construction.

Emboldened by American acceptance of the Berlin Wall and seeing a chance to change the balance of military power decisively, Premier Khrushchev secretly ordered missiles with nuclear warheads installed in Fidel Castro's Communist Cuba in 1962. When U.S. intelligence discovered missile sites under construction, Kennedy ordered a naval blockade of Cuba. After a tense diplomatic crisis, Khrushchev agreed to remove the Soviet missiles in return for American pledges not to disturb Castro's regime. In a secret agreement, Kennedy also promised to remove U.S. nuclear missiles from Turkey.

Khrushchev's influence in the party, already slipping, declined rapidly after the Cuban missile crisis. In 1964 the reformist premier was displaced in a bloodless coup, and he spent the rest of his life under house arrest. Under his successor, Leonid Brezhnev (1906–1982), the U.S.S.R. began a period of limited re-Stalinization and economic stagnation. Almost immediately, Brezhnev (BREHZH-nehf) and his supporters started talking quietly of Stalin's achievements and downplaying his crimes, disappointing people eager for further liberalization. Soviet leaders, determined never to suffer Khrushchev's humiliation in the face of American nuclear superiority, launched a massive arms buildup in the mid-1960s. Even so, the Soviets cautiously avoided direct confrontation with the United States.

Despite popular protests and changes in leadership, the U.S.S.R. and its satellite countries had achieved some stability by the late 1950s. Communist regimes addressed dissent and uprisings with an effective combination of military force, political repression, and limited economic reform. East and West traded propaganda threats, but both sides basically accepted the division of Europe into spheres of influence. Violent conflicts now took place in the developing world, where decolonization was opening new paths for Cold War confrontation.

How did decolonization proceed in the Cold War era?

In one of world history's great turning points during the Cold War era, Europe's long-standing overseas expansion was dramatically reversed. The retreat from imperial control—a process Europeans called **decolonization**—was profoundly influenced by Cold War conflicts and remade the world map. In just two decades, over fifty new nations joined the global community (Map 28.3). In some cases, decolonization proceeded relatively smoothly. In others, colonized peoples won independence only after long and bloody struggles.

< **MAP 28.3 Decolonization in Africa and Asia, 1947 to the Present**
Divided primarily along religious lines into two states, British India led the way to political independence in 1947. Most African territories achieved statehood by the mid-1960s as European empires passed away, unlamented.

Decolonization and the Global Cold War

The most basic cause of imperial collapse was the rising demand of non-Western peoples for national self-determination, racial equality, and personal dignity. This demand spread from intellectuals to ordinary people in nearly every colonial territory after the First World War. By 1939 the colonial powers were already on the defensive; the Second World War prepared the way for the eventual triumph of independence movements.

European empires had been based on an enormous power differential between the rulers and the ruled, a difference that had greatly declined by 1945. Western Europe was economically devastated and militarily weak immediately after the war. Moreover, the Japanese had driven imperial rulers from large parts of East Asia during the war in the Pacific, shattering the myth of European superiority and invincibility. In Southeast Asia, European imperialists confronted strong anticolonial nationalist movements that re-emerged with new enthusiasm after the defeat of the Japanese.

To some degree, the Great Powers regarded their empires very differently after 1945. Empire had rested on self-confidence and self-righteousness; Europeans had believed their superiority to be not only technical and military but also spiritual, racial, and moral. The horrors of the First and Second World Wars undermined such complacent arrogance and gave opponents of imperialism much greater influence in Europe. Increasing pressure from the United States, which had long presented itself as an enemy of empire despite its own imperialist actions in the Philippines and the Americas, encouraged Europeans to let go. Indeed, Americans were eager to extend their own influence in Europe's former colonies. Economically weakened, and with their political power and moral authority in tatters, the imperial powers preferred to avoid bloody colonial wars and generally turned to rebuilding at home.

Furthermore, the imperial powers faced dedicated anticolonial resistance. Popular politicians, including China's Mao Zedong, India's Mohandas Gandhi, Egypt's Gamal Abdel Nasser, and many others provided determined leadership in the struggle against European imperialism. A new generation of intellectuals, such as Jomo Kenyatta of Kenya and Aimé Césaire and Frantz Fanon, both from Martinique, wrote trenchant critiques of imperial power, often rooted in Marxist ideas. Anticolonial politicians and intellectuals alike helped inspire colonized peoples to resist and overturn imperial rule.

Around the globe, the Cold War had an inescapable impact on decolonization. Liberation from colonial rule had long been a central goal for proponents of Communist world revolution. The Soviets and, after 1949, the Communist Chinese advocated rebellion in the developing world and promised to help end colonial exploitation and bring freedom and equality in a socialist state. They supported Communist independence movements with economic and military aid, and the guerrilla insurgent armed with a Soviet-made AK-47 machine gun became the new symbol of Marxist revolution.

Western Europe and particularly the United States offered a competing vision of independence, based on free-market economics and, ostensibly, liberal democracy — though the United States was often willing to support authoritarian regimes that voiced staunch anticommunism. Like the U.S.S.R., the United States extended economic aid and weaponry to decolonizing nations. The Americans promoted cautious moves toward self-determination in the context of containment, attempting to limit the influence of communism in newly liberated states.

After they had won independence, the leaders of the new nations often found themselves trapped between the superpowers, compelled to voice support for one bloc or the other. Many new leaders followed a third way and adopted a policy of **nonalignment**, remaining neutral in the Cold War and playing both sides for what they could get.

The Struggle for Power in Asia

The first major fight for independence that followed World War II, between the Netherlands and anticolonial insurgents in Indonesia, in many ways exemplified decolonization in the rest of the Cold War world. The Dutch had been involved in Indonesia since the early seventeenth century (see "The Birth of the Global Economy" in Chapter 14) and had extended their colonial power over the centuries. During World War II, however, the Japanese had overrun the archipelago, encouraging hopes among the locals for independence from Western control. Following the Japanese defeat in 1945, the Dutch returned, hoping to use Indonesia's raw materials, particularly rubber, to support economic recovery at home. But Dutch imperialists faced a determined group of rebels inspired by a powerful combination of nationalism, Marxism, and Islam. Four years of deadly guerrilla war followed, and in 1949 the Netherlands reluctantly accepted Indonesian independence. The new Indonesian president became an effective advocate of nonalignment. He had close ties to the Indonesian Communist Party but received foreign aid from the United States as well as the Soviet Union.

A similar combination of communism and anticolonialism inspired the independence movement in parts of French Indochina (now Vietnam, Cambodia, and Laos), though noncommunist nationalists were also involved. France desperately wished to maintain control over these prized colonies and tried its best to re-establish colonial rule after the Japanese occupation collapsed. Despite substantial American aid, the French army fighting in Vietnam was defeated in 1954 by forces under the guerrilla leader Ho Chi Minh (hoh chee mihn) (1890–1969), who was supported by the U.S.S.R. and China. Vietnam was divided. As in Korea, a shaky truce established a Communist North and a pro-Western South Vietnam, which led to civil war and subsequent intervention by the United States. Cambodia and Laos also gained independence under noncommunist regimes, though Communist rebels remained active in both countries.

India—Britain's oldest, largest, and most lucrative imperial possession—played a key role in the decolonization process. Nationalist opposition to British rule coalesced after the First World War under the leadership of British-educated lawyer Mohandas (sometimes called "Mahatma," or "Great-Souled") Gandhi (1869–1948), one of the twentieth century's most influential figures. In the 1920s and 1930s Gandhi (GAHN-dee) built a mass movement preaching nonviolent "noncooperation" with the British. In 1935 he wrested from the frustrated and unnerved British a new, liberal constitution that was practically a blueprint for independence. The Second World War interrupted progress toward Indian self-rule, but when the Labour Party came to power in Great Britain in 1945, it was ready to relinquish sovereignty. British socialists had long been critics of imperialism, and the heavy cost of governing India had become a large financial burden to the war-wracked country.

A Refugee Camp During the Partition of India A young Muslim man, facing an uncertain future, sits above a refugee camp established on the grounds of a medieval fortress in the northern Indian city of Delhi. In the camp, Muslim refugees wait to cross the border to the newly founded Pakistan. The chaos that accompanied the mass migration of Muslims and Hindus during the partition of India in 1947 cost the lives of up to 1 million migrants and disrupted the livelihoods of millions more. (Margaret-Bourke White/The LIFE Picture Collection/Getty Images)

Britain withdrew peacefully, but conflict between India's Hindu and Muslim populations posed a lasting dilemma for South Asia. As independence neared, the Muslim minority grew increasingly anxious about their status in an India dominated by the Hindu majority. Muslim leaders called for partition—the division of India into separate Hindu and Muslim states—and the British agreed. When independence was made official on August 15, 1947, predominantly Muslim territories on India's eastern and western borders became Pakistan (the eastern section is today's Bangladesh). Seeking relief from the ethnic conflict that erupted, millions of Muslim and Hindu refugees fled both ways across the new borders, a massive population exchange that left mayhem and death in its wake. In just a few summer weeks, up to 1 million people lost their lives (estimates vary widely). Then in January 1948 a radical Hindu nationalist opposed to partition assassinated Gandhi, and Jawaharlal Nehru became Indian prime minister.

As the Cold War heated up in the early 1950s, Pakistan, an Islamic republic, developed close ties with the United States. Under the leadership of Nehru, India successfully maintained a policy of nonalignment. India became a liberal, if social-ist-friendly, democratic state that dealt with both the United States and the U.S.S.R.

Pakistan and India both joined the British Commonwealth, a voluntary and cooperative association of former British colonies that already included Canada, Australia, and New Zealand.

Where Indian nationalism drew on Western parliamentary liberalism, Chinese nationalism developed and triumphed in the framework of Marxist-Leninist ideology. After the withdrawal of the occupying Japanese army in 1945, China erupted again in open civil war. The authoritarian Guomindang (National People's Party), led by Jiang Jieshi (traditionally called Chiang Kai-shek; 1887–1975), fought to repress the Chinese Communists, led by Mao Zedong (MA-OW zuh-DOUNG) and supported by a popular grassroots uprising.

During the revolutionary war that ensued, the Soviets gave Mao aid, and the Americans gave Jiang much more. Winning the support of the peasantry by promising to expropriate the holdings of the big landowners, the Communists forced the Guomindang to withdraw to the island of Taiwan in 1949. Mao and the Communists united China's 550 million inhabitants in a strong centralized state, and the "Red Chinese" began building a new society that adapted Marxism to Chinese conditions. The new government promoted land reform, extended education and health-care programs to the peasantry, and introduced Soviet-style five-year plans that boosted industrial production. It also brought Stalinist-style repression—mass arrests, forced-labor camps, and ceaseless propaganda campaigns—to the Chinese people.

Independence and Conflict in the Middle East

In some areas of the Middle East, the movement toward political independence went relatively smoothly. The French League of Nations mandates in Syria and Lebanon had collapsed during the Second World War, and Saudi Arabia and Transjordan had already achieved independence from Britain. But events in the British mandate of Palestine and in Egypt showed that decolonization in the Middle East could lead to violence and lasting conflict.

As part of the peace accords that followed the First World War, the British government had advocated a Jewish homeland alongside the Arab population (see "The Peace Settlement in the Middle East" in Chapter 25). This tenuous compromise unraveled after World War II. Neither Jews nor Arabs were happy with British rule, and violence and terrorism mounted on both sides. In 1947 the British decided to leave Palestine, and the United Nations voted in a nonbinding resolution to divide the territory into two states—one Arab and one Jewish. The Jews accepted the plan and founded the state of Israel in 1948.

The Palestinians and the surrounding Arab nations viewed Jewish independence as a betrayal of their own interests, and they attacked the Jewish state as soon as it was proclaimed. The Israelis drove off the invaders and conquered more territory. Roughly 900,000 Arab Palestinians fled or were expelled from their homes, creating an ongoing refugee problem. Holocaust survivors from Europe streamed into Israel, as Theodor Herzl's Zionist dream came true (see "Jewish Emancipation and Modern Anti-Semitism" in Chapter 23). The next fifty years saw four more Arab-Israeli wars and innumerable clashes between Israelis and Palestinians.

The 1948 Arab defeat triggered a nationalist revolution in Egypt in 1952, led by the young army officer Gamal Abdel Nasser (1918–1970). The revolutionaries drove

Egyptian President Abdul Nasser Greets a Crowd The charismatic president was immensely popular with ordinary Egyptians and enjoyed mingling with his supporters. Here, on July 28, 1956, Nasser stretches his arms to greet a cheering crowd at a train station on the route from Alexandria to Cairo. The previous day, ignoring French and British protests, Nasser announced that Egypt would nationalize the all-important Suez Canal, a crucial event in the history of postwar decolonization. (AP Images)

out the pro-Western king, and in 1954 Nasser became president of an Egyptian republic. A crafty politician, Nasser advocated nonalignment and expertly played the superpowers against each other, securing loans from the United States and purchasing Soviet arms.

In July 1956 Nasser abruptly nationalized the foreign-owned Suez Canal Company, a major remnant of Western power in the Middle East. Infuriated, the British and the French, along with the Israelis, planned a secret military operation. The Israeli army invaded the Sinai Peninsula bordering the canal, and British and French bombers attacked Egyptian airfields. World opinion was outraged, and the United States feared that such a blatant show of imperialism would encourage the Arab states to join the Soviet bloc. The Americans joined with the Soviets to force the British, French, and Israelis to back down. Egyptian nationalism triumphed: Nasser got his canal, and Israel left the Sinai. The Suez crisis, a watershed in the history of European imperialism, showed that the European powers could no longer maintain their global empires.

Decolonization in Africa

In less than a decade, most of Africa won independence from European imperialism, a remarkable movement of world historical importance. The new African states were quickly caught up in the struggles between the Cold War superpowers, and decolonization all too often left a lasting legacy of economic decline and political struggle (see Map 28.3).

Starting in 1957, most of Britain's African colonies achieved independence with relatively little bloodshed and then entered a very loose association with Britain as members of the British Commonwealth. Ghana, Nigeria, Tanzania, and other countries gained independence in this way, but there were exceptions. In Kenya, British forces brutally crushed the nationalist Mau Mau rebellion in the early 1950s, but nonetheless recognized Kenyan independence in 1963. In South Africa, the white-dominated government left the Commonwealth in 1961 and declared an independent republic in order to preserve apartheid — an exploitative system of racial segregation enforced by law.

The decolonization of the Belgian Congo was one of the great tragedies of the Cold War. Belgian leaders, profiting from the colony's wealth of natural resources and proud of their small nation's imperial status, maintained a system of apartheid there and dragged their feet in granting independence. These conditions sparked an anticolonial movement that grew increasingly aggressive in the late 1950s under the able leadership of the charismatic Patrice Lumumba. In January 1960 the Belgians gave in and hastily announced that the Congo would be independent six months later, a schedule that was irresponsibly fast. Lumumba was chosen prime minister in democratic elections, but when the Belgians pulled out on schedule, the new government was entirely unprepared. Chaos broke out when the Congolese army attacked Belgian military officers who remained in the country.

With substantial financial investments in the Congo, the United States and western Europe worried that the new nation might fall into Soviet hands. U.S. leaders cast Lumumba as a Soviet proxy, an oversimplification of his nonalignment policies, and American anxiety increased when Lumumba asked the U.S.S.R. for aid and protection. In a troubling example of containment in action, the CIA helped implement a military coup against Lumumba, who was taken prisoner by Congolese army officers and then assassinated. The military set up a U.S.-backed dictatorship under the corrupt general Joseph Mobutu. Mobutu ruled until 1997 and became one of the world's wealthiest men, while the Congo remained one of the poorest, most violent, and most politically torn countries in the world.

French colonies in Africa followed several roads to independence. Like the British, the French offered most of their African colonies, including Tunisia, Morocco, and Senegal, the choice of a total break or independence within a kind of French commonwealth. All but one of the new states chose the latter option, largely because they identified with French culture and wanted aid from their former colonizer. The French were eager to help — provided the former colonies accepted close economic ties on French terms. As in the past, the French and their Common Market partners, who helped foot the bill, saw themselves as continuing their civilizing mission in sub-Saharan Africa. More important, they saw in Africa raw materials for their factories, markets for their industrial goods, outlets for profitable investment, and good temporary jobs for their engineers and teachers.

Things were far more difficult in the French colony of Algeria, a large Muslim state on the Mediterranean Sea where some 1.2 million white European settlers, including some 800,000 French, had taken up permanent residency by the 1950s. Nicknamed pieds-noirs (literally "black feet"), many of these Europeans had raised families in Algeria for three or four generations, and they enforced a two-tiered system of citizenship, dominating politics and the economy. When Algerian rebels, inspired by Islamic fundamentalism and Communist ideals, established the National Liberation Front (FLN) and revolted against French colonialism in the early 1950s, the presence of the pieds-noirs complicated matters. Worried about their position in the colony, the pieds-noirs pressured the French government to help them. In response, France sent some 400,000 troops to crush the FLN and put down the revolt.

The resulting Algerian War—long, bloody, and marred by atrocities committed on both sides—lasted from 1954 to 1962. FLN radicals repeatedly attacked pied-noir civilians in savage terrorist attacks, while the French army engaged in systematic torture, mass arrests (often of innocent suspects), and the forced relocation and internment of millions of Muslim civilians suspected of supporting the insurgents.

By 1958 French forces had successfully limited FLN military actions, but their disproportionate use of force encouraged many Muslims to support or join the FLN. News reports about torture and abuse of civilians turned significant elements of French public opinion against the war, and international outrage further pressured French leaders to end the conflict. Efforts to open peace talks led to a revolt by the Algerian French and threats of a coup d'état by the French army. In 1958 the immensely popular General Charles de Gaulle was reinstated as French prime minister as part of the movement to keep Algeria French. His appointment at first calmed the army, the pieds-noirs, and the French public.

Yet to the dismay of the pieds-noirs and army hardliners, de Gaulle pragmatically moved toward Algerian self-determination. In 1961 furious pieds-noirs and army leaders formed the OAS (Secret Army Organization) and began a terrorist revolt against Muslim Algerians and the French government. In April of that year the OAS mounted an all-out but short-lived putsch, taking over Algiers and threatening the government in Paris. Loyal army units defeated the rebellion, the leading generals were purged, and negotiations between the French government and FLN leaders continued. In April 1962, after more than a century of exploitative French rule and a decade of brutal anticolonial warfare, Algeria became independent under the FLN. Then in a massive exodus, over 1 million pieds-noirs fled to France and the Americas.

By the mid-1960s most African states had won independence, some through bloody insurrections. There were exceptions: Portugal, for one, waged war against independence movements in Angola and Mozambique until the 1970s. Even in liberated countries, the colonial legacy had long-term negative effects. South African blacks still longed for liberation from apartheid, and white rulers in Rhodesia continued a bloody civil war against African insurgents until 1979. Elsewhere African leaders may have expressed support for socialist or democratic principles in order to win aid from the superpowers. In practice, however, corrupt and authoritarian African leaders like Mobutu in the Congo often established lasting authoritarian dictatorships and enriched themselves at the expense of their populations.

Even after decolonization, in the 1960s and 1970s western European countries managed to increase their economic and cultural ties with their former African colonies. Above all, they used the lure of special trading privileges and provided heavy investment in French- and English-language education to enhance a powerful Western presence in the new African states. This situation led a variety of leaders and scholars to charge that western Europe (and the United States) had imposed a system of **neocolonialism** on the former colonies. According to this view, neocolonialism was a system designed to perpetuate Western economic domination and undermine the promise of political independence, thereby extending to Africa (and much of Asia) the kind of economic subordination that the United States had imposed on Latin America in the nineteenth century.

What were the key changes in social relations in postwar Europe?

While Europe staged its astonishing recovery from the Nazi nightmare and colonized peoples won independence, the basic structures of Western society were also in transition. A changing class structure, new patterns of global migration, and new roles for women and youths had dramatic impacts on everyday life, albeit with different effects in the East Bloc and western Europe.

Changing Class Structures

The combination of rapid economic growth, growing prosperity and mass consumption, and the provision of generous, state-sponsored social benefit programs went a long way toward creating a new society in Europe after the Second World War. Old class barriers relaxed, and class distinctions became fuzzier.

Changes in the structure of the middle class were particularly important. In the nineteenth and early twentieth centuries, the model for the middle class had been the independent, self-employed individual who owned a business or practiced a liberal profession such as law or medicine. Ownership of property — frequently inherited property — and strong family ties had often been the keys to wealth and standing within the middle class. After 1945 this pattern changed drastically in western Europe. A new breed of managers and experts — so-called white-collar workers — replaced property owners as the leaders of the middle class. The ability to earn an ample income largely replaced inherited property and family connections in determining an individual's social position in the middle and upper-middle classes. At the same time, the middle class grew massively and became harder to define.

There were several reasons for these developments. Rapid industrial and technological expansion and the consolidation of businesses created a powerful demand for technologists and managers in large corporations and government agencies. Moreover, the old propertied middle class lost control of many family-owned businesses. Numerous small businesses (including family farms) could no longer turn a profit, so their former owners regretfully joined the ranks of salaried employees.

Similar processes were at work in the East Bloc, where class leveling was an avowed goal of the authoritarian socialist state. The nationalization of industry, expropriation of property, and aggressive attempts to open employment opportunities to workers and equalize wage structures effectively reduced class differences. Communist Party members typically received better jobs and more pay than non-members, but by the 1960s the income differential between the top and bottom strata of East Bloc societies was far smaller than in the West.

In both East and West, managers and civil servants represented the model for a new middle class. Well paid and highly trained, often with professional degrees, these pragmatic experts were primarily concerned with efficiency and practical solutions to concrete problems.

The structure of the lower classes also became more flexible and open. Continuing trends that began in the nineteenth century, large numbers of people left the countryside for the city. The population of one of the most traditional and least mobile groups in European society — farmers — drastically declined. Meanwhile, the number of industrial workers in western Europe began to fall, as new jobs for white-collar and service employees grew rapidly. This change marked a significant transition in the world of labor. The social benefits extended by postwar governments also helped promote greater equality because they raised lower-class living standards and were paid for in part by higher taxes on the wealthy. In general, European workers were better educated and more specialized than before, and the new workforce bore a greater resemblance to the growing middle class of salaried specialists than to traditional industrial workers.

Patterns of Postwar Migration

The 1850s to the 1930s had been an age of global migration, as countless Europeans moved around the continent and the world seeking economic opportunity or freedom from political or religious persecution (see "European Emigration" in Chapter 24). The 1950s and 1960s witnessed new waves of migration that had a significant impact on European society.

Some postwar migration took place within countries. Declining job prospects in Europe's rural areas encouraged small farmers to seek better prospects in cities. In the poorer countries of Spain, Portugal, and Italy, millions moved to more developed regions of their own countries. The process was similar in the East Bloc, where the forced collectivization of agriculture and state subsidies for heavy industry opened opportunities in urban areas. And before the erection of the Berlin Wall in 1961, some 3.5 million East Germans moved to the Federal Republic of Germany, seeking higher pay and a better life.

Many other Europeans moved across national borders seeking work. The general pattern was from south to north. Workers from less developed countries like Italy, Spain, and socialist Yugoslavia moved to the industrialized north, particularly to West Germany, which — having lost 5 million people during the war — was in desperate need of able-bodied workers. In the 1950s and 1960s West Germany and other prosperous countries implemented **guest worker programs** designed to recruit much-needed labor for the booming economy. West Germany signed labor agreements with Italy, Greece, Spain, Portugal, Yugoslavia, Turkey, and the North African countries of Tunisia and Morocco. By the early 1970s there were 2.8 million foreign workers in Germany and another 2.3 million in France, where they made up 11 percent of the workforce.

Most guest workers were young, unskilled single men who labored for low wages in entry-level jobs and sent much of their pay to their families at home. According to government plans, these guest workers were supposed to return to their home countries after a specified period. Many built new lives, however, and, to the dismay of the authorities and conservative nationalists, chose to live permanently in their adoptive countries.

Europe was also changed by **postcolonial migration**, the movement of people from the former colonies and the developing world into prosperous Europe. In contrast to guest workers, who enlisted in formal recruitment programs, postcolonial migrants could often claim citizenship rights from their former colonizers and moved spontaneously. Immigrants from the Caribbean, India, Africa, and Asia went to Britain; people from North Africa, especially Algeria, and from sub-Saharan countries such as Cameroon and the Ivory Coast moved to France; Indonesians migrated to the Netherlands. Postcolonial immigrants also moved to eastern Europe, though in far fewer numbers.

These new migration patterns had dramatic results. Immigrant labor helped fuel economic recovery, while growing ethnic diversity changed the face of Europe and enriched the cultural life of the continent. The new residents were not always welcome, however. Adaptation to European lifestyles could be difficult, and immigrants often lived in separate communities where they spoke their own languages. They faced employment and housing discrimination, as well as the harsh anti-immigrant rhetoric and policies of xenophobic politicians. Even prominent European intellectuals worried aloud that Muslim migrants from North Africa and Turkey would never adopt European values and customs. The tensions that surrounded changed migration patterns would pose significant challenges to social integration in the decades to come.

New Roles for Women

The postwar culmination of a one-hundred-year-long trend toward early marriage, early childbearing, and small family size in wealthy urban societies had revolutionary implications for women. Above all, pregnancy and child care occupied a much smaller portion of a woman's life than in earlier times. The postwar baby boom did make for larger families and fairly rapid population growth of 1 to 1.5 percent per year in many European countries, but the long-term decline in birthrates resumed by the 1960s. By the early 1970s about half of Western women were having their last baby by the age of twenty-six or twenty-seven. When the youngest child trooped off to kindergarten, the average mother had more than forty years of life in front of her.

This was a momentous transition. Throughout history male-dominated society insisted on defining most women as mothers or potential mothers, and motherhood was very demanding. In the postwar years, however, motherhood no longer absorbed the energies of a lifetime, and more and more married women looked for new roles in the world of work outside the family.

Three major forces helped women searching for jobs in the changing post–World War II workplace. First, the economic boom created strong demand for labor. Second, the economy continued its gradual shift away from the old male-dominated heavy industries, such as coal, steel, and shipbuilding, and toward the white-collar service industries in which some women already worked, such as government, education, sales, and health care. Third, young women shared fully in the postwar education revolution and so were positioned to take advantage of the growing need for officeworkers and well-trained professionals. Thus more and more married women became full-time and part-time wage earners.

In the East Bloc, Communist leaders opened up numerous jobs to women, who accounted for almost half of all employed persons. Many women made their way into previously male professions, including factory work but also medicine and engineering. In western Europe and North America, the percentage of married women in the workforce rose from a range of roughly 20 to 25 percent in 1950 to anywhere from 30 to 60 percent in the 1970s.

All was not easy for women entering paid employment. Married women workers faced widespread discrimination in pay, advancement, and occupational choice in comparison to men. Moreover, many women could find only part-time work. As the divorce rate rose in the 1960s, part-time work, with its low pay and scanty benefits, often meant poverty for many women with children. Finally, married women who held jobs in both the East and West still carried most of the child-rearing and house-keeping responsibilities and were left with an exhausting "double burden." Trying to live up to society's seemingly contradictory ideals was one reason that many women accepted part-time employment.

The injustices that married women encountered as wage earners contributed greatly to the movement for women's equality and emancipation that arose in the 1960s. Sexism and discrimination in the workplace—and in the home—grew loathsome and evoked the sense of injustice that drives revolutions and reforms.

Youth Culture and the Generation Gap

The bulging cohort of so-called baby boomers born after World War II created a distinctive and very international youth culture that brought remarkable changes to postwar youth roles and lifestyles. That subculture, found across Europe and the United States, was rooted in fashions and musical tastes that set its members off from their elders and fueled anxious comments about a growing "generation gap."

Youth styles in the United States often provided inspiration for movements in Europe. Groups like the British Teddy boys, the West German *Halbstarken* (half-strongs), and the French *blousons noirs* (black jackets) modeled their rebellious clothing and cynical attitudes on the bad-boy characters played by U.S. film stars such as James Dean and Marlon Brando. American jazz and rock 'n' roll spread rapidly in western Europe, aided by the invention of the long-playing record album (or LP) and the 45-rpm "single" in the late 1940s, as well as the growth of the corporate music industry. American musicians such as Elvis Presley, Bill Haley and His Comets, and Gene Vincent thrilled European youths and worried parents, teachers, and politicians.

Youths played a key role in the consumer revolution. Marketing experts and manufacturers quickly recognized that the young people they now called "teenagers" had money to spend due to postwar prosperity. An array of advertisements and products consciously targeted the youth market. In France, for example, magazine advertising aimed at adolescents grew by 400 percent between 1959 and 1962. As the baby boomers entered their late teens, they eagerly purchased trendy clothing and the latest pop music hits, as well as record players, transistor radios, magazines, hair products, and makeup, all marketed for the "young generation."

The new youth culture became an inescapable part of Western society. One clear sign of this new presence was the rapid growth in the number of universities and college students. Before the 1960s, in North America and Europe, only a small elite received a university education. In 1950 only 3 to 4 percent of western European youths went on to higher education; numbers in the United States were only slightly higher. Then, as government subsidies made education more affordable to ordinary people, enrollments skyrocketed. By 1960 at least three times more European students attended some kind of university than they had before World War II, and the number continued to rise sharply until the 1970s.

The rapid expansion of higher education opened new opportunities for the middle and lower classes, but it also made for overcrowded classrooms. Many students felt that they were not getting the kind of education they needed for jobs in the modern world. At the same time, some reflective students feared that universities were doing nothing but turning out docile technocrats both to stock and to serve "the establishment." Thus it was no coincidence that students became leaders in a counterculture that attacked the ideals of the affluent society of the postwar world and rocked the West in the late 1960s.

NOTES

1. Anonymous, *A Woman in Berlin: Eight Weeks in the Conquered City: A Diary* (New York: Metropolitan Books, 2005), pp. 239–240.
2. Quoted in N. Graebner, *Cold War Diplomacy, 1945–1960* (Princeton, N.J.: Van Nostrand, 1962), p. 17.
3. From a speech delivered by G. Marshall at Harvard University on June 5, 1947, reprinted in *Department of State Bulletin* (June 15, 1947), pp. 1159–1160.
4. Quoted in T. Judt, *Postwar: A History of Europe Since 1945* (New York: Penguin, 2005), p. 150.

LOOKING BACK **LOOKING AHEAD**

The unprecedented human and physical destruction of World War II left Europeans shaken, searching in the ruins for new livelihoods and a workable political order. A tension-filled peace settlement left the continent divided into two hostile political-military blocs, and the resulting Cold War, complete with the possibility of atomic annihilation, threatened to explode into open confrontation. Albert Einstein voiced a common anxiety when he said, "I do not know with what weapons World War III will be fought, but World War IV will be fought with sticks and stones."

Despite such fears, the division of Europe led to the emergence of a stable world system. In the West Bloc, economic growth, state provision of social benefits, and the strong NATO alliance engendered social and political consensus. In the East Bloc, a combination of political repression and partial reform likewise limited dissent and encouraged stability. During the height of the Cold War, Europe's former colonies won liberation in a process that was often flawed but that nonetheless resulted in political independence for millions of people. And large-scale transformations, including the rise of Big Science and rapid economic growth, opened new opportunities for women and immigrants and contributed to stability on both sides of the iron curtain.

By the early 1960s Europeans had entered a remarkable age of affluence that almost eliminated real poverty on most of the continent. Superpower confrontations had led not to European war but to peaceful coexistence. The following decades, however, would see substantial challenges to this postwar consensus. Youth revolts and a determined feminist movement, an oil crisis and a deep economic recession, and political dissent and revolution in the East Bloc would shake and remake the foundations of Western society.

MAKE CONNECTIONS

Think about the larger developments and continuities within and across chapters.

1. How did the Cold War shape politics and everyday life in the United States and western Europe, the U.S.S.R. and the East Bloc, and the decolonizing world? Why was its influence so pervasive?

2. How were the postwar social transformations in class structures, patterns of migration, and the lives of women and youths related to the broad political and economic changes that followed World War II? How did they differ on either side of the iron curtain?

3. Compare and contrast the treaties and agreements that ended the First and Second World Wars (Chapter 25). Did the participants who shaped the peace accords face similar problems? Which set of agreements did a better job of resolving outstanding issues, and why?

Chapter 28 Review

IDENTIFY KEY TERMS

Identify and explain the significance of each item below.

Cold War (p. 855)
displaced persons (p. 857)
Truman Doctrine (p. 862)
Marshall Plan (p. 863)
Council for Mutual Economic
    Assistance (COMECON) (p. 863)
NATO (p. 864)
Warsaw Pact (p. 864)
economic miracle (p. 866)

Christian Democrats (p. 866)
Common Market (p. 868)
Socialist Realism (p. 871)
de-Stalinization (p. 872)
decolonization (p. 875)
nonalignment (p. 877)
neocolonialism (p. 882)
guest worker programs (p. 884)
postcolonial migration (p. 884)

REVIEW THE MAIN IDEAS

Answer the section heading questions from the chapter.

1. Why was World War II followed so quickly by the Cold War? (p. 855)
2. What were the sources of postwar recovery and stability in western Europe? (p. 865)
3. What was the pattern of postwar development in the Soviet bloc? (p. 869)
4. How did decolonization proceed in the Cold War era? (p. 875)
5. What were the key changes in social relations in postwar Europe? (p. 883)

CHRONOLOGY

1945	• Yalta Conference; end of World War II in Europe; Potsdam Conference; Nuremberg trials begin
1945–1960s	• Decolonization of Asia and Africa
1945–1965	• United States takes lead in Big Science
1947	• Truman Doctrine; Marshall Plan
1948	• Foundation of Israel
1948–1949	• Berlin airlift
1949	• Creation of East and West Germany; formation of NATO; establishment of COMECON
1950–1953	• Korean War
1953	• Death of Stalin
1954–1962	• Algerian War of Independence
1955	• Warsaw Pact founded
1955–1964	• Khrushchev in power; de-Stalinization of Soviet Union
1956	• Suez crisis
1957	• Formation of Common Market; Pasternak publishes *Doctor Zhivago*
1961	• Building of Berlin Wall
1962	• Cuban missile crisis; Solzhenitsyn publishes *One Day in the Life of Ivan Denisovich*
1964	• Brezhnev replaces Khrushchev as Soviet leader

29

Challenging the Postwar Order

1960–1991

CHAPTER PREVIEW

- Why did the postwar consensus of the 1950s break down?

- What were the consequences of economic stagnation in the 1970s?

- What led to the decline of "developed socialism" in the East Bloc?

- What were the causes and consequences of the 1989 revolutions in the East Bloc?

AS EUROPE ENTERED THE 1960S, the political and social systems forged in the postwar era appeared sound. Centrist politicians in western Europe agreed that managed economic expansion, abundant jobs, and state-sponsored benefit programs would continue to improve living standards and forge social consensus. In the Soviet Union and the East Bloc, although conditions varied by country, modest economic growth and limited reforms amid continued political repression likewise contributed to a sense of stability. Cold War tensions diminished, and it seemed that a remarkable age of affluence would ease political differences and lead to social harmony.

By the mid-1960s, however, this hard-won sense of stability had begun to disappear as popular protest movements in East and West arose to challenge dominant certainties. In the early 1970s the astonishing postwar economic advance ground to a halt, with serious consequences. In western Europe, a new generation of conservative political leaders advanced new policies to deal with economic decline and the growth of global competition. New political groups across the political spectrum, from feminists and environmentalists to national separatists and right-wing populists, added to the atmosphere of crisis and conflict.

In the East Bloc, leaders vacillated between central economic control and liberalization and left in place tight controls on social freedom, leading to stagnation and frustration. In the 1980s popular dissident movements emerged in Poland and other satellite states, and efforts to reform the Communist system in the Soviet Union from the top down snowballed out of control. In 1989, as revolutions swept away Communist rule throughout the entire Soviet bloc, the Cold War reached a dramatic conclusion.

Why did the postwar consensus of the 1950s break down?

In the early 1960s politics and society in prosperous western Europe remained relatively stable. East Bloc governments, bolstered by modest economic growth and state-enforced political conformity, and committed to generous welfare benefits for their citizens, maintained control. As the 1960s progressed, politics in the West shifted noticeably to the left, and amid this more liberalized society, a youthful counterculture emerged to critique the status quo. In the East Bloc, Khrushchev's limited reforms also inspired rebellions. Thus activists around the world rose in protest against the perceived inequalities of both capitalism and communism, leading to dramatic events in 1968, exemplified in Paris and Prague.

Cold War Tensions Thaw

In western Europe, the first two decades of postwar reconstruction had been overseen for the most part by center-right Christian Democrats, who successfully maintained postwar stability around Cold War politics, free-market economics with limited state intervention, and welfare provisions. In the mid- to late 1960s, buoyed by the rapidly expanding economy, much of western Europe moved politically to the left. Socialists entered the Italian government in 1963. In Britain, the Labour Party returned to power in 1964, after thirteen years in opposition. In West Germany, the aging postwar chancellor Konrad Adenauer (1876–1967) retired in 1963, and in 1969 Willy Brandt (1913–1992) became the first Social Democratic West German chancellor; his party would govern Germany until 1982. There were important exceptions to this general trend. Though the tough-minded, independent French president Charles de Gaulle resigned in 1969, the centrist Gaullists remained in power in France until 1981. And in Spain, Portugal, and Greece, authoritarian regimes remained in power until the mid-1970s.

Despite these exceptions, the general leftward drift eased Cold War tensions. Western European leaders took major steps to normalize relations with the East Bloc. Willy Brandt took the lead. In December 1970 he flew to Poland for the signing of a historic treaty of reconciliation. In a dramatic moment, Brandt laid a wreath at the tomb of the Polish unknown soldier and another at the monument commemorating the armed uprising of Warsaw's Jewish ghetto against occupying Nazi armies.

A West German Leader Apologizes for the Holocaust In 1970 West German chancellor Willy Brandt knelt before the Jewish Heroes' Monument in Warsaw, Poland, to ask forgiveness for the German mass murder of European Jews and other groups during the Second World War. Brandt's action, captured in photo and film by the onlooking press, symbolized the chancellor's policy of Ostpolitik, the normalization of relations between the East and West Blocs. (bpk, Bildagentur/ Hanns Hubmann/Art Resource, NY)

Standing before the ghetto memorial, a somber Brandt fell to his knees as if in prayer. "I wanted," Brandt said later, "to ask pardon in the name of our people for a million-fold crime which was committed in the misused name of the Germans."[1]

Brandt's gesture at the Warsaw Ghetto memorial and the treaty with Poland were part of his broader, conciliatory foreign policy termed **Ostpolitik** (German for "Eastern policy"). Brandt sought a comprehensive peace settlement for central Europe and the two postwar German states. Rejecting West Germany's official hard line toward the East Bloc, the chancellor negotiated new treaties with the Soviet Union and Czechoslovakia, as well as Poland, that formally accepted existing state boundaries — rejected by West Germany's government since 1945 — in return for a mutual renunciation of force or the threat of force. Using the imaginative formula of "two German states within one German nation," he broke decisively with past policy and opened direct relations with East Germany.

Brandt's Ostpolitik was part of a general relaxation of East-West tensions, termed **détente** (day-TAHNT), that began in the early 1970s. Though Cold War hostilities continued in the developing world, diplomatic relations between the United States and the Soviet Union grew less strained. The superpowers agreed to limit the testing and proliferation of nuclear weapons and in 1975 mounted a joint U.S.-U.S.S.R. space mission.

The move toward détente reached a high point in 1975 when the United States, Canada, the Soviet Union, and all European nations (except isolationist Albania and tiny Andorra) met in Helsinki to sign the Final Act of the Conference on Security and Cooperation in Europe. Under what came to be called the Helsinki Accords, the thirty-five participating nations agreed that Europe's existing political frontiers could not be changed by force. They accepted numerous provisions guaranteeing the civil rights and political freedoms of their citizens, and the agreement helped diminish Cold War conflict. Although Communist regimes would continue to curtail domestic freedoms and violate human rights guarantees, the accords encouraged East Bloc dissidents, who could now demand that their governments respect international declarations on human rights.

Newly empowered center-left leaders in western Europe also pushed through reforms at home. Building on the benefit programs established in the 1950s, they increased state spending on public services even further. Center-left politicians did not advocate "socialism" as practiced in the Soviet bloc, where strict economic planning, the nationalization of key economic sectors, and one-party dictatorships ensured state control. To the contrary, they maintained a firm commitment to capitalist free markets and democracy. At the same time, they viewed state-sponsored benefits as a way to ameliorate the inequalities of a competitive market economy. As a result, western European democracies spent more and more state funds on health care, education, old-age insurance, and public housing, all paid for with high taxes.

By the early 1970s state spending on such programs hovered around 40 percent of the gross domestic product in France, West Germany, and Great Britain, and even more in Scandinavia and the Netherlands. Center-right politicians generally supported increased spending on entitlements—as long as the economy prospered. The economic downturn in the mid-1970s, however, undermined support for the welfare state consensus (see ahead).

The Affluent Society

While politics shifted to the left in the 1960s, Europe entered a decade of economic growth and high wages, which meant that an expanding middle class could increasingly enjoy the benefits of the consumer revolution that began in the 1950s. Yet this so-called age of affluence had clear limits. The living standards of workers and immigrants did not rise as fast as those of the educated middle classes, and the expanding economy did not always reach underdeveloped regions, such as southern Italy. The 1960s nonetheless brought general prosperity to millions, and the consolidation of a full-blown consumer society had a profound impact on daily life.

Many Europeans now had more money to spend on leisure time and recreational pursuits, which encouraged the growth of the tourist industry. With month-long paid vacations required by law in most western European countries and widespread automobile ownership, travel to beaches and ski resorts came within the reach of the middle class and much of the working class. By the late 1960s packaged tours with cheap group airfares and bargain hotel accommodations had made even distant lands easily accessible.

Consumerism also changed life at home. Household appliances that were still luxuries in the 1950s were now commonplace; televisions overtook radio as a popular form of domestic entertainment while vacuum cleaners, refrigerators, and washing machines transformed women's housework. Studies later showed that these new "laborsaving devices" caused women to spend even more time cleaning and cooking to new exacting standards, but at the time electric appliances were considered indispensable to what contemporaries called a "modern lifestyle." The establishment of U.S.-style self-service supermarkets across western Europe changed the way food was produced, purchased, and prepared and threatened to force independent bakers, butchers, and neighborhood grocers out of business.

Intellectuals and cultural critics greeted the age of affluence with a chorus of criticism. Some worried that rampant consumerism created a bland conformity that wiped out regional and national traditions. The great majority of ordinary people, they argued, now ate the same foods, wore the same clothes, and watched the same programs on television, sapping creativity and individualism. Others complained bitterly that these changes threatened to Americanize Europe. Neither group could do much to stop the spread of consumer culture.

Worries about the Americanization of Europe were overstated. European nations preserved distinctive national cultures even during the consumer revolution, but social change nonetheless occurred. The moral authority of religious doctrine lost ground before the growing materialism of consumer society. In predominantly Protestant lands—Great Britain, Scandinavia, and parts of West Germany—church membership and regular attendance both declined significantly. Even in traditionally Catholic countries, such as Italy, Ireland, and France, outward signs of popular belief seemed to falter. At the **Second Vatican Council**, convened from 1962 to 1965, Catholic leaders agreed on a number of reforms meant to democratize and renew the church and broaden its appeal. They called for new openness in Catholic theology and declared that masses would henceforth be held in local languages rather than in Latin, which few could understand. These resolutions, however, did little to halt the slide toward secularization.

Family ties also weakened in the age of affluence. The number of adults living alone reached new highs, men and women married later, the nuclear family became smaller and more mobile, and divorce rates rose rapidly. By the 1970s the baby boom of the postwar decades was over, and population growth leveled out across Europe and even began to decline in prosperous northwestern Europe.

The Counterculture Movement

The dramatic emergence of a youthful counterculture accompanied growing economic prosperity. The "sixties generation" angrily criticized the comforts of the affluent society and challenged the social and political status quo.

Simple demographics played an important role in the emergence of the counterculture. Young soldiers returning home after World War II in 1945 eagerly established families, and the next two decades brought a dramatic increase in the number of births per year in Europe and North America. The children born during the postwar baby boom grew up in an era of political liberalism and unprecedented material abundance, yet many came to challenge the growing conformity that seemed to be a part of consumer society and the unequal distribution of wealth that arose from market economics.

Counterculture movements in both Europe and the United States drew inspiration from the American civil rights movement. In the late 1950s and early 1960s African Americans effectively challenged institutionalized inequality, using the courts, public demonstrations, sit-ins, and boycotts to throw off a deeply entrenched system of segregation and repression. If dedicated African Americans and their white supporters could successfully reform entrenched power structures, student leaders reasoned, so could they. In 1964 and 1965, at the University of California–Berkeley, students consciously adapted the tactics of the civil rights movement, including demonstrations and sit-ins, to challenge limits on free speech and academic freedom at the university. Soon students across the United States and western Europe, where rigid rules controlled student activities at overcrowded universities, were engaged in active protests. The youth movement had come of age, and it mounted a determined challenge to the Western consensus.

Eager for economic justice and more tolerant societies, student activists in western Europe and the United States embraced new forms of Marxism, creating a multidimensional movement that came to be known as the **New Left**. In general, adherents of the various strands of the New Left believed that Marxism in the Soviet Union had been perverted to serve the needs of a repressive totalitarian state but that Western capitalism, with its cold disregard for social equality, was little better. What was needed was a more humanitarian style of socialism that could avoid the worst excesses of both capitalism and Soviet-style communism. New Left critics further attacked what they saw as the conformity of consumer society.

New Left ideas inspired student intellectuals, but much counterculture activity revolved around a lifestyle rebellion that had broad appeal. Politics and daily life merged, a process captured in the popular 1960s slogan "the personal is political." Nowhere was this more obvious than in the so-called sexual revolution. The 1960s brought frank discussion about sexuality, a new willingness to engage in premarital sex, and a growing acceptance of homosexuality. Sexual experimentation was facilitated by the development of the birth control pill, which helped eliminate the risk of unwanted pregnancy for millions of women after it went on the market in most Western countries in the 1960s. Much of the new openness about sex crossed generational lines, but for the young the idea of sexual emancipation was closely linked to radical politics. Sexual openness and "free love," the sixties generation claimed, moved people beyond traditional norms and might also shape a more humane society.

The revolutionary aspects of the sexual revolution are easily exaggerated. According to a poll of West German college students taken in 1968, for example, the overwhelming majority wished to establish permanent families on traditional middle-class models. Yet the sexual behavior of young people did change in the 1960s and 1970s. More young people engaged in premarital sex, and they did so at an earlier age than ever before. A 1973 study reported that only 4.5 percent of West German youths born in 1945 and 1946 had experienced sexual relations before their seventeenth birthday, but that 32 percent of those born in 1953 and 1954 had done so.[2] Such trends were found in other Western countries and continued in the following decades.

Along with sexual freedom, drug use and rock music encouraged lifestyle rebellion. Taking drugs challenged conventional morals; in the infamous words of the

U.S. cult figure Timothy Leary, users could "turn on, tune in, and drop out." The popular music of the 1960s championed these alternative lifestyles. Rock bands like the Beatles, the Rolling Stones, and many others sang songs about drugs and casual sex. Counterculture "scenes" developed in cities such as San Francisco, Paris, and West Berlin. Carnaby Street, the center of "swinging London" in the 1960s, was world famous for its clothing boutiques and record stores, underscoring the connections between generational revolt and consumer culture.

The United States and Vietnam

The growth of the counterculture movement was closely linked to the escalation of the Vietnam War. Although many student radicals at the time argued that imperialism was the main cause, American involvement in Vietnam was more clearly a product of the Cold War policy of containment. After Vietnam won independence from France in 1954, U.S. president Dwight D. Eisenhower (U.S. pres. 1953–1961) refused to sign the Geneva Accords that temporarily divided the country into a Communist north and an anticommunist south. When the South Vietnamese government declined to hold free elections that would unify the two zones, Eisenhower provided the south with military aid to combat guerrilla insurgents in South Vietnam who were supported by the Communist north.

President John F. Kennedy (U.S. pres. 1961–1963) increased the number of American "military advisers" to 16,000, and in 1964 President Lyndon B. Johnson (U.S. pres. 1963–1969) greatly expanded America's role in the conflict, providing South Vietnam with massive military aid and eventually some 500,000 American troops. Though the United States bombed North Vietnam with ever-greater intensity, it did not invade the north or set up a naval blockade.

In the end, American intervention backfired. The undeclared war in Vietnam, fought nightly on American television, eventually divided the nation. Initial support was strong. The politicians, the media, and the population as a whole saw the war as part of a legitimate defense against the spread of Communist totalitarianism. But an antiwar movement that believed that the United States was fighting an immoral and imperialistic war against a small country and a heroic people quickly emerged on college campuses. In October 1965 student protesters joined forces with old-line socialists, New Left intellectuals, and pacifists in antiwar demonstrations in fifty American cities. The protests spread to western Europe. By 1967 a growing number of U.S. and European critics denounced the American presence in Vietnam as a criminal intrusion into another people's civil war.

Criticism reached a crescendo after the Vietcong staged the Tet Offensive in January 1968, the Communists' first comprehensive attack on major South Vietnamese cities. The Vietcong, an army of Communist insurgents and guerrilla fighters located in South Vietnam, suffered heavy losses, but the Tet Offensive signaled that the war was not close to ending, as Washington had claimed. The American people grew increasingly weary of the war and pressured their leaders to stop the fighting. Within months of Tet, President Johnson announced that he would not stand for re-election and called for negotiations with North Vietnam.

President Richard M. Nixon (U.S. pres. 1969–1974) sought to gradually disengage America from Vietnam once he took office. Nixon intensified the bombing campaign against the north, opened peace talks, and pursued a policy of "Vietnamization" designed to give the South Vietnamese responsibility for the war and reduce the U.S. presence. He suspended the draft and cut American forces in Vietnam from 550,000 to 24,000 in four years. In 1973 Nixon finally reached a peace agreement with North Vietnam and the Vietcong that allowed the remaining American forces to complete their withdrawal and gave the United States the right to resume bombing if the accords were broken. Fighting declined markedly in South Vietnam, where the South Vietnamese army appeared to hold its own against the Vietcong.

Although the storm of criticism in the United States passed with the peace settlement, America's disillusionment with the war had far-reaching repercussions. In late 1974, when North Vietnam launched a successful invasion against South Vietnamese armies, the U.S. Congress refused to permit any American military response. In April 1975 the last U.S. troops were evacuated from Saigon, the South Vietnamese capital, and in July 1976 North and South Vietnam were unified under a Communist regime, ending a conflict that had begun with the anticolonial struggle against the French at the end of World War II.

Student Revolts and 1968

While the Vietnam War raged, American escalation engendered worldwide opposition, and the counterculture became increasingly radical. In western European and North American cities, students and sympathetic followers organized massive antiwar demonstrations and then extended their protests to support colonial independence movements, to demand an end to the nuclear arms race, and to call for world peace and liberation from social conventions of all kinds.

Political activism erupted in 1968 in a series of protests and riots that circled the globe. African Americans rioted across the United States after the assassination of civil rights leader Martin Luther King, Jr., and antiwar demonstrators battled police at the Democratic National Convention in Chicago. Young protesters marched for political reform in Mexico City, where police responded by shooting and killing several hundred. Students in Tokyo rioted against the war and for university reforms. Protesters clashed with police in the West and East Blocs as well. Berlin and London witnessed massive, sometimes-violent demonstrations, students in Warsaw protested government censorship, and youths in Prague were in the forefront of the attempt to radically reform communism from within.

One of the most famous and perhaps most far-reaching of these revolts occurred in France in May 1968, when massive student protests coincided with a general strike that brought the French economy to a standstill. The "May Events" began when a group of students dismayed by conservative university policies and inspired by New Left ideals occupied buildings at the University of Paris. Violent clashes with police followed. When police tried to clear the area around the university on the night of May 10, a pitched street battle took place. At the end of the night, 460 arrests had been made by police, 367 people were wounded, and about 200 cars had been burned by protesters.

The "May Events" might have been a typically short-lived student protest against overcrowded universities, U.S. involvement in Vietnam, and the abuses of capitalism, but the demonstrations triggered a national revolt. By May 18 some 10 million workers were out on strike, and protesters occupied factories across France. For a brief moment, it seemed as if counterculture hopes for a revolution from below would come to pass. The French Fifth Republic was on the verge of collapse, and a shaken President de Gaulle surrounded Paris with troops.

In the end, however, the New Left goals of the radical students contradicted the bread-and-butter demands of the striking workers. When the government promised workplace reforms, including immediate pay raises, the strikers returned to work. President de Gaulle dissolved the French parliament and called for new elections. His conservative party won almost 75 percent of the seats, showing that the majority of the French people supported neither general strikes nor student-led revolutions. The universities shut down for the summer, administrators enacted educational reforms, and the protests had dissipated by the time the fall semester began. The May Events marked the high point of counterculture activism in Europe; in the early 1970s the movement declined.

As the political enthusiasm of the counterculture waned, committed activists disagreed about the best way to continue to fight for social change. Some followed what West German student leader Rudi Dutschke called "the long march through the institutions" and began to work for change from within the system. They ran for office and joined the emerging feminist, antinuclear, and environmental groups that would gain increasing prominence in the following decades.

Others followed a more radical path. Across Europe, but particularly in Italy and West Germany, fringe New Left groups tried to bring radical change by turning to violence and terrorism. Like the American Weather Underground, the Italian Red Brigades and the West German Red Army Faction robbed banks, bombed public buildings, and kidnapped and killed business leaders and conservative politicians. After spasms of violence in the late 1970s — in Italy, for example, the Red Brigades murdered former prime minister Aldo Moro in 1978 — security forces succeeded in incarcerating most of the terrorist leaders, and the movement fizzled out.

Counterculture protests generated a great deal of excitement and trained a generation of activists. In the end, however, the protests of the sixties generation resulted in short-term and mostly limited political change. Lifestyle rebellions involving sex, drugs, and rock music certainly expanded the boundaries of acceptable personal behavior, but they hardly overturned the existing system.

The 1960s in the East Bloc

The building of the Berlin Wall in 1961 suggested that communism was there to stay, and NATO's refusal to intervene showed that the United States and western Europe basically accepted this premise. In the West, the wall became a symbol of the repressive nature of communism in the East Bloc, where halting experiments with economic and cultural liberalization brought only limited reform.

East Bloc economies clearly lagged behind those of the West, exposing the weaknesses of central planning. To address these problems, in the 1960s Communist governments implemented cautious forms of decentralization and limited market policies. The results were mixed. Hungary's so-called New Economic Mechanism, which broke up state monopolies, allowed some private retail stores, and encouraged private agriculture, was perhaps most successful. East Germany's New Economic System, inaugurated in 1963, also brought moderate success, though it was reversed when the government returned to centralization in the late 1960s. In other East Bloc countries, however, economic growth flagged; in Poland the economy stagnated in the 1960s.

Recognizing that ordinary people in the East Bloc were growing tired of the shortages of basic consumer goods caused by the overwhelming emphasis on heavy industry, Communist planning commissions began to redirect resources to the consumer sector. Again, the results varied. By 1970, for example, ownership of televisions in the more developed nations of East Germany, Czechoslovakia, and Hungary approached that of the affluent nations of western Europe, and other consumer goods were also more available. In the more conservative Albania and Romania, where leaders held fast to Stalinist practices, provision of consumer goods faltered.

In the 1960s Communist regimes cautiously granted cultural freedoms. In the Soviet Union, the cultural thaw allowed dissidents like Aleksandr Solzhenitsyn to publish critical works of fiction (see "Reform and De-Stalinization" in Chapter 28), and this relative tolerance spread to other East Bloc countries as well. In East Germany, for example, during the Bitterfeld Movement — named after a conference of writers, officials, and workers held at Bitterfeld, an industrial city south of Berlin — the regime encouraged intellectuals to take a more critical view of life in the East Bloc, as long as they did not directly oppose communism.

Cultural openness only went so far, however. The most outspoken dissidents were harassed and often forced to emigrate to the West; others went underground, creating books, periodicals, newspapers, and pamphlets that were printed secretly and passed hand to hand by dissident readers. This *samizdat* ("self-published") literature emerged in Russia, Poland, and other countries in the mid-1950s and blossomed in the 1960s. These unofficial networks of communication kept critical thought alive and built contacts among dissidents, creating the foundation for the reform movements of the 1970s and 1980s.

The citizens of East Bloc countries sought political liberty as well, and the limits on reform were sharply revealed in Czechoslovakia during the 1968 "Prague Spring" (named for the country's capital

The Invasion of Czechoslovakia Armed with Czechoslovakian flags and Molotov cocktails, courageous Czechs in downtown Prague in August 1968 try to stop a Soviet tank and repel the invasion and occupation of their country by the Soviet Union and its Warsaw Pact allies. Realizing that military resistance would be suicidal, the Czechs capitulated to Soviet control. (Libor Hajsky/AP Images)

city). In January 1968 reform elements in the Czechoslovak Communist Party gained a majority and voted out the long-time Stalinist leader in favor of Alexander Dubček (1921–1992), whose new government launched dramatic reforms. Educated in Moscow, Dubček (DOOB-chehk) was a dedicated Communist, but he and his allies believed that they could reconcile genuine socialism with personal freedom and party democracy. They called for relaxed state censorship and replaced rigid bureaucratic planning with local decision making by trade unions, workers' councils, and consumers. The reform program—labeled "Socialism with a Human Face"—proved enormously popular.

Remembering that the Hungarian revolution had revealed the difficulty of reforming communism from within, Dubček constantly proclaimed his loyalty to the Soviet Union and the Warsaw Pact. But his reforms nevertheless threatened hard-line Communists, particularly in Poland and East Germany, where leaders knew full well that they lacked popular support. Moreover, Soviet authorities feared that a liberalized Czechoslovakia would eventually be drawn to neutrality or even to NATO. Thus the East Bloc leadership launched a concerted campaign of intimidation against the reformers. Finally, in August 1968, five hundred thousand Soviet and East Bloc troops occupied Czechoslovakia. The Czechoslovaks made no attempt to resist militarily, and the arrested leaders surrendered to Soviet demands. The Czechoslovak experiment in humanizing communism from within came to an end.

Shortly after the invasion of Czechoslovakia, Soviet premier Leonid Brezhnev (1906–1982) announced that the U.S.S.R. would now follow the so-called **Brezhnev Doctrine**, under which the Soviet Union and its allies had the right to intervene militarily in any East Bloc country whenever they thought doing so was necessary to preserve Communist rule. The 1968 invasion of Czechoslovakia was the crucial event of the Brezhnev era: it demonstrated the determination of the Communist elite to maintain the status quo throughout the Soviet bloc, which would last for another twenty years. At the same time, the Soviet crackdown encouraged dissidents to change their focus from "reforming" Communist regimes from within to building a civil society that might bring internal freedoms independent of Communist repression.

What were the consequences of economic stagnation in the 1970s?

The great postwar economic boom came to a close in the early 1970s, opening a long period of economic stagnation, widespread unemployment, and social dislocation. By the end of the 1980s the postwar consensus based on prosperity, full employment, modest regulation, and generous welfare provisions had been deeply shaken. Led by a new generation of conservative politicians, the West restructured its economy and entered the information age.

Economic Crisis and Hardship

Starting in the early 1970s the West entered into a long period of economic decline. One of the early causes of the downturn was the collapse of the international monetary system, which since 1945 had been based on the American dollar, valued in gold at $35 an ounce. In the postwar decades the United States spent billions of dollars on foreign aid and foreign wars, weakening the value of American currency. In 1971 President Nixon attempted to reverse this trend by abruptly stopping the exchange of U.S. currency for gold. The value of the dollar fell sharply, and inflation accelerated worldwide. Countries abandoned fixed rates of currency exchange, and great uncertainty replaced postwar predictability in international trade and finance.

Even more damaging to the global economy was the dramatic increase in the price of energy and a decrease in its availability. The great postwar boom had been fueled in large part by cheap and plentiful oil from the Middle East, and the main energy supplies of the developed world were thus increasingly linked to this turbulent region. In 1967, in the Six-Day War, Israel quickly defeated Egypt, Jordan, and Syria and occupied more of the former territories of Palestine, angering Arab leaders and exacerbating anti-Western feeling in the Arab states. Tension between Arab states and the West was also fueled by economics. Over the years **OPEC**, the Organization of Petroleum Exporting Countries, had watched the price of crude oil decline compared with the rising price of Western manufactured goods. OPEC decided to reverse that trend by presenting a united front against Western oil companies.

The stage was thus already set for a revolution in energy prices when Egypt and Syria launched a surprise attack on Israel in October 1973, setting off the fourth Arab-Israeli war. With the help of U.S. weapons, Israel again achieved a quick victory. In response, the Arab members of OPEC declared an embargo on oil shipments to the United States and other industrialized nations that supported Israel in the war, and they simultaneously raised oil prices. Within a year, crude oil prices quadrupled. Western nations realized that the rapid price increase was economically destructive, but together they did nothing. Thus governments, industry, and individuals dealt piecemeal with the so-called oil shock—a "shock" that turned out to be an earthquake.

Coming on the heels of the upheaval in the international monetary system, the revolution in energy prices plunged the world into its worst economic decline since the 1930s. Energy-intensive industries that had driven the economy up in the 1950s and 1960s now dragged it down. Unemployment rose, productivity and living standards declined, and inflation soared. Economists coined a new term—**stagflation**—to describe the combination of low growth and high inflation that drove the worldwide recession. By 1976 a modest recovery was in progress, but in 1979 a fundamentalist Islamic revolution overthrew the shah of Iran. When oil production in that country collapsed, the price of crude oil doubled again, and the world economy succumbed to its second oil shock. Unemployment and inflation rose dramatically before another uneven recovery began in 1982.

Anxious observers, recalling the disastrous consequences of the Great Depression, worried that the European Common Market would disintegrate in the face of severe economic dislocation and that economic nationalism would halt steps toward European unity. Yet the Common Market continued to attract new members. In 1973 Britain finally joined, as did Denmark and Ireland. After replacing authoritarian regimes with democratic governments in the 1970s, Greece joined in 1981, and Portugal and Spain entered in 1986. The nations of the Common Market cooperated more closely in international undertakings, and the movement toward western European unity stayed alive.

The developing world was hit hard by slow growth, and the global economic downturn widened the gap between rich and poor countries. Governments across South America, sub-Saharan Africa, and South Asia borrowed heavily from the United States and western Europe in attempts to restructure their economies, setting the stage for a serious international debt crisis. At the same time, the East Asian countries of Japan and then Singapore, South Korea, and Taiwan started exporting high-tech consumer goods to the West. Competition from these East Asian "tiger economies," whose labor costs were comparatively low, shifted manufacturing jobs away from the highly industrialized countries of northern Europe and North America. Even though the world economy slowly began to recover in the 1980s, western Europe could no longer create enough jobs to replace those that were lost.

By the end of the 1970s, the foundations of economic growth in the industrialized West had begun shifting to high-tech information industries, such as computing and biotechnology, and to services, including medicine, banking, and finance. Scholars spoke of the shift as the arrival of "the information age" or **postindustrial society**. Technological advances streamlined the production of many goods, making many industrial jobs superfluous. In western Europe, heavy industry, such as steel, mining, automobile manufacture, and shipbuilding, lost ground. Factory closings led to the emergence of "rust belts"—formerly prosperous industrialized areas that were now ghost lands, with vacant lots, idle machinery, and empty inner cities. The highly industrialized Ruhr district in northwest West Germany and the once-extensive factory regions around Birmingham (Great Britain) and Detroit, Michigan, were classic examples. By 1985 the unemployment rate in western Europe had risen to its highest level since the Great Depression. Nineteen million people were jobless.

The crisis struck countless ordinary people, upending lives and causing real hardship. The punk rock songs of the late 1970s captured the mood of hostility and cynicism among young people. Yet on the whole, the welfare system fashioned in the postwar era prevented mass suffering and degradation. The responsive, socially concerned national state undoubtedly contributed to the preservation of political stability and democracy in the face of economic difficulties that might have brought revolution and dictatorship in earlier times.

With the commitment of governments to supporting social needs, government spending in most European countries continued to rise sharply during the 1970s and early 1980s. In 1982 western European governments spent an average of more than 50 percent of all national income on social programs, as compared to only 37 percent fifteen years earlier. Across western Europe, people were willing to see their governments increase spending, but they resisted higher taxes. This imbalance contributed to the rapid growth of budget deficits, national debts, and inflation. While increased spending was generally popular, a powerful reaction against government's ever-increasing role had set in by the late 1970s that would transform governance in the 1980s.

The New Conservatism

The transition to a postindustrial society was led to a great extent by a new generation of conservative political leaders, who believed they had viable solutions for restructuring the relations between the state and the economy. During the thirty years following World War II, both Social Democrats and the more conservative Christian Democrats had usually agreed that economic growth and social stability were best achieved through full employment and high wages, some government regulation, and generous social benefit programs. In the late 1970s, however, with a weakened economy and increased global competition, this consensus began to unravel. Whether politics turned to the right, as in Great Britain, the United States, and West Germany, or to the left, as in France and Spain, leaders moved to cut government spending and regulation in attempts to improve economic performance.

The new conservatives of the 1980s followed a philosophy that came to be known as **neoliberalism** because of its roots in the free market, laissez-faire policies favored by eighteenth-century liberal economists such as Adam Smith (see "Adam Smith and Economic Liberalism" in Chapter 17). Neoliberal theorists like U.S. economist Milton Friedman argued that governments should cut support for social services, including housing, education, and health insurance; limit business subsidies; and retreat from regulation of all kinds. (Neoliberalism should be distinguished from modern American liberalism, which generally supports social programs and some state regulation of the economy.) Neoliberals also called for **privatization**—the sale of state-managed industries to private owners. Placing government-owned industries such as transportation and communication networks and heavy industry in private hands, they argued, would both reduce government spending and lead to greater workplace efficiency. A central goal was to increase private profits, which neoliberals believed were the real engine of economic growth.

The effects of neoliberal policies are best illustrated by events in Great Britain. The broad shift toward greater conservatism, coupled with growing voter dissatisfaction with high taxes and runaway state budgets, helped elect Margaret Thatcher (1925–2013) prime minister in 1979. A member of the Conservative Party and a convinced neoliberal, Thatcher was determined to scale back the role of government, and in the 1980s—the "Thatcher years"—she pushed through a series of controversial free-market policies that transformed Britain. Thatcher's government cut spending on health care, education, and public housing; reduced taxes; and privatized or sold off government-run enterprises. In one of her most popular actions, Thatcher encouraged low- and moderate-income renters in state-owned housing projects to buy their apartments at rock-bottom prices. This initiative, part of Thatcher's broader privatization campaign, created a whole new class of property owners, thereby eroding the electoral base of Britain's socialist Labour Party.

Though Thatcher never eliminated all social programs, her policies helped replace the interventionist ethos of the welfare state with a greater reliance on private enterprise and the free market. This transition involved significant human costs. In the first three years of her government, heavy industries such as steel, coal mining, and textiles shut down, and unemployment rates in Britain doubled to over 12 percent. The gap between rich and poor widened, and increasing poverty led to discontent and crime. Strikes and working-class protests sometimes led to violent riots. Street violence often had racial overtones: immigrants from former British colonies in Africa, India, and the Caribbean, dismayed with poor jobs and racial discrimination, clashed repeatedly with police. Thatcher successfully rallied support by leading a British victory over Argentina in the brief Falklands War (1982), but over time her position weakened. By 1990 Thatcher's popularity had fallen to record lows, and she was replaced by Conservative Party leader John Major.

In the United States, two-term president Ronald Reagan (U.S. pres. 1981–1989) followed a similar path, though his success in cutting government was more limited. Reagan's campaign slogan — "government is not the solution to our problem, government is the problem" — summed up a movement in line with Thatcher's ideas, which was labeled the conservative movement in the United States. With widespread popular support and the agreement of most congressional Democrats as well as Republicans, Reagan pushed through major across-the-board cuts in income taxes in 1981. But Reagan and Congress failed to limit government spending, which increased as a percentage of national income in the course of his presidency. A massive military buildup was partly responsible, but spending on social programs — despite Reagan's pledges to rein it in — also grew rapidly. The harsh recession of the early 1980s required the government to spend more on unemployment benefits, welfare benefits, and medical treatment for the poor. Moreover, Reagan's antiwelfare rhetoric mobilized the liberal opposition and eventually turned many moderates against him. The budget deficit soared, and U.S. government debt tripled in a decade.

West Germany also turned to the right. After more than a decade in power, the Social Democrats foundered, and in 1982 Christian Democrat Helmut Kohl (1930–2017) became the new chancellor. Like Thatcher, Kohl cut taxes and government spending. His policies led to increasing unemployment in heavy industry but also to solid economic growth. By the mid-1980s West Germany was one of the most prosperous countries in the world. In foreign policy, Kohl drew close to President Reagan. The chancellor agreed to deploy U.S. cruise missiles and nuclear-armed Pershing missiles on West German territory, a decision that contributed to renewed superpower tensions. In power for sixteen years, Kohl and the Christian Democrats governed during the opening of the Berlin Wall in 1989, the reunification of East and West Germany in 1990, and the end of the Cold War.

The most striking temporary exception to the general drift to the right in European politics was François Mitterrand (1916–1996) of France. After his election as president in 1981, Mitterrand and his Socialist Party led France on a lurch to the left. This marked a significant change in French politics, which had been dominated by center-right parties for some twenty-five years. Working at first in a coalition that included the French Communist Party, Mitterrand launched a vast program of nationalization and public investment designed to spend the country out of economic stagnation. By 1983 this attempt had clearly failed, and Mitterrand's Socialist government made a dramatic about-face. The Socialists were compelled to reprivatize industries they had just nationalized. They imposed a wide variety of austerity measures and maintained those policies for the rest of the decade.

Despite persistent economic crises and high social costs, by 1990 the developed nations of western Europe and North America were far more productive than they had been in the early 1970s. Western Europe was at the center of the emerging global economy, and its citizens were far richer than those in Soviet bloc countries. Even so, the collapse of the postwar consensus and the remaking of Europe in the transitional decades of the 1970s and 1980s helped generate new forms of protest and dissent across the political spectrum.

Challenges and Victories for Women

The 1970s marked the arrival of a diverse and widespread feminist movement devoted to securing genuine gender equality and promoting the general interests of women. Three basic reasons accounted for this dramatic development. First, ongoing changes in underlying patterns of motherhood and paid work created novel conditions and new demands. Second, a vanguard of feminist intellectuals articulated a powerful critique of gender relations that stimulated many women to rethink their assumptions and challenge the status quo. Third, taking a lesson from the civil rights movement in the United States and protests against the Vietnam War, dissatisfied women recognized that they had to organize if they were to influence politics and secure fundamental reforms.

Feminists could draw on a long heritage of protest, stretching back to the French Revolution and the women's movements of the late nineteenth century. They were also inspired by recent writings, such as the foundational book *The Second Sex* (1949) by the French writer and philosopher Simone de Beauvoir (1908–1986). Beauvoir, who worked closely with the existentialist philosopher Jean-Paul Sartre, analyzed the position of women within the framework of existential thought. Drawing on history, philosophy, psychology, biology, and literature, Beauvoir argued that women had almost always been trapped by particularly inflexible and limiting conditions. Only through courageous action and self-assertive creativity could a woman become a completely free person and escape the role of the inferior "other" that men had constructed for her gender.

The Second Sex inspired a generation of women intellectuals, and by the late 1960s and the 1970s **second-wave feminism** had spread through North America and Europe. In the United States, writer and organizer Betty Friedan's (1921–2006) pathbreaking study *The Feminine Mystique* (1963) pointed the way. Friedan called attention to the stifling aspects of women's domestic life, devoted to the service of husbands and children. Housewives lived in a "gilded cage," she concluded, because they

Feminist Protest in Amsterdam, ca. 1970 Members of the Dutch branch of the Women's Liberation Movement burn brassieres in front of a statue of Dutch feminist Wilhelmina Drucker. In the 1970s and 1980s, women's groups across western Europe and North America repeatedly organized public protests for women's rights, including an end to sexism, equal pay, and access to abortion. (Central Press/Getty Images)

were usually not allowed to hold professional jobs or become mature adults and genuine human beings. In 1966 Friedan helped found the National Organization for Women (NOW) to press for women's rights. NOW flourished, growing from seven hundred members in 1967 to forty thousand in 1974.

Many other women's organizations rose in Europe and North America. The diverse groups drew inspiration from Marx, Freud, or political liberalism, but in general feminists attacked patriarchy (the domination of society by men) and sexism (the inequalities faced by women simply because they were female). Throughout the 1970s publications, conferences, and institutions devoted to women's issues reinforced the emerging international movement. Advocates of women's rights pushed for new statutes governing the workplace: laws against discrimination, acts requiring equal pay for equal work, and measures such as maternal leave and affordable day care designed to help women combine careers and family responsibilities.

The movement also addressed women's rights beyond the workplace, including the right to divorce (in some Catholic countries), legalized abortion, the needs of single mothers, and protection from rape and physical violence. In almost every country, the effort to decriminalize abortion served as a catalyst in mobilizing an effective, self-conscious women's movement—and an opposition to it.

In countries that had long placed women in a subordinate position, the legal changes were little less than revolutionary. In Italy, for example, new laws abolished restrictions on divorce and abortion that had been strengthened by Mussolini and defended energetically by the Catholic Church in the postwar era. Yet while the women's movement of the 1970s won new rights for women, subsequently it became more diffuse, a victim of both its successes and the resurgence of an antifeminist opposition.

The Rise of the Environmental Movement

Like feminism, environmentalism had roots in the 1960s counterculture. Early environmentalists drew inspiration from writers like U.S. biologist Rachel Carson, whose book *Silent Spring*, published in 1962, was quickly translated into twelve European languages. Carson's chilling title referred to a future in which people in developed society would wake up one spring morning and hear no birds singing because they had all been killed by the rampant use of pesticides. The book had a striking impact on the growth of environmental movements in Europe and North America.

By the 1970s the destructive environmental costs of industrial development in western Europe and the East Bloc were everywhere apparent. The mighty Rhine River, which flows from Switzerland, past France, and through Germany and the Netherlands, was an industrial sewer. The forests of southwestern Germany were dying from acid rain, a result of smokestack emissions. The pristine coast of Brittany, in northwest France, was fouled by oil spills from massive tanker ships. Rapid industrialization in the East Bloc, undertaken with little regard for environmental impact, severely polluted waterways, contaminated farmlands and forests, and degraded air quality. Nuclear power plants across Europe were generating toxic waste that would last for centuries; serious accidents at nuclear plants—at Three Mile Island in Pennsylvania (1979) and at Chernobyl in Soviet Ukraine (1986)—revealed nuclear power's potential to create human and environmental disaster (Map 29.1). These were just some examples of the environmental threats that inspired a growing environmental movement to challenge government and industry to clean up their acts.

Environmentalists had two main agendas. First, they worked to lessen the ill effects of unbridled industrial development on the natural environment. Second, they argued that local environmental problems often increased human poverty, inequality, and violence around the globe, and they sought ways to ameliorate the impact of environmental decline on human well-being. Environmental groups pursued their goals in various ways. Some used the mass media to reach potential supporters; some worked closely with politicians and public officials to change government policies. Others took a more confrontational stance.

In North America and western Europe, environmentalists also built new institutions. In 1971 Canadian activists established Greenpeace, a nongovernmental organization ded-

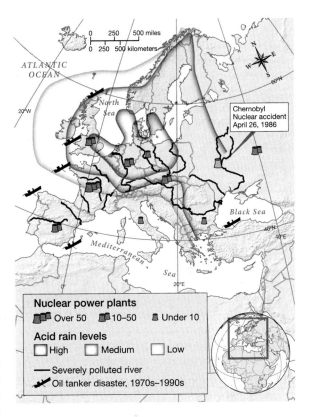

MAP 29.1   Pollution in Europe, ca. 1990
Despite attempts to remedy the negative consequences of the human impact on the environment, pollution remains a significant challenge for Europeans in the twenty-first century.

icated to environmental conservation and protection. Greenpeace quickly grew into an international organization, with strong support in Europe and the United States. In West Germany the environmentalist Green Party, founded in 1979, met with astounding success when it elected members to parliament in 1983, the first time in sixty years that a new political party had been seated in Germany. Its success was a model for likeminded activists in Europe and North America, and Green Party members were later elected to parliaments in Belgium, Italy, and Sweden. In the East Bloc, government planners increasingly recognized and tried to ameliorate environmental problems in the 1980s, but official censorship meant that groups like the Greens would not emerge there until after the end of Communist rule.

Separatism and Right-Wing Extremism

The 1970s also saw the rise of determined separatist movements across Europe. In Ireland, Spain, Belgium, and Switzerland—and in Yugoslavia and Czechoslovakia in the East Bloc—regional ethnic groups struggled for special rights, political autonomy, and even national independence. This separatism was most violent in Spain and Northern Ireland, where well-established insurgent groups used terrorist attacks to win government concessions. In the ethnic Basque region of northern Spain, the ETA (short, in the Basque language, for Basque Homeland and Freedom) tried to use bombings and assassinations to force the government to grant independence. After the death in 1975 of Fascist dictator Francisco Franco, who had ruled Spain for almost forty years, a new constitution granted the Basque region special autonomy, but it was not enough. The ETA stepped up its terrorist campaigns, killing over four hundred people in the 1980s.

The Provisional Irish Republican Army (IRA), a paramilitary organization in Northern Ireland, used similar tactics. Though Ireland had won autonomy in 1922, Great Britain retained control of six primarily Protestant counties in the north of the island. In the late 1960s violence re-emerged as the IRA, hoping to unite these counties with Ireland, attacked British security forces, which it saw as an occupying army. On "Bloody Sunday" in January 1972, British soldiers shot and killed thirteen demonstrators who had been protesting anti-Catholic discrimination in the town of Derry, and the violence escalated. For the next thirty years the IRA attacked soldiers and civilians in Northern Ireland and in Britain itself. Over three thousand British soldiers, civilians, and IRA members were killed during the "Time of Troubles" before negotiations between the IRA and the British government opened in the late 1990s; a settlement was finally reached in 1998.

In the 1970s and 1980s mainstream European politicians also faced challenges from newly assertive political forces on the far right, including the National Front in France, the Northern League in Italy, the Austrian Freedom Party, and the National Democratic Party in West Germany. Populist leaders such as Jean-Marie Le Pen, the founder of the French National Front, opposed European integration and called for an embrace of nationalism, often at the expense of the non-European immigrants who were a growing proportion of western Europe's working-class population. New right-wing politicians promoted themselves as the champions of ordinary (white) workers, complaining that immigrants swelled welfare rolls and stole jobs from native-born Europeans. Though their programs at times veered close to open racism, in the 1980s they began to win seats in national parliaments.

What led to the decline of "developed socialism" in the East Bloc?

In the postwar decades the Communist states of the East Bloc had achieved a shaky social consensus based on a rising standard of living, an extensive welfare system, and political repression. In the long run, leaders promised, "developed socialism" would prove better than capitalism. But such claims were an attempt to paper over serious tensions in socialist society. When Mikhail Gorbachev burst on the scene in 1985, the new Soviet leader opened an era of reform that was as sweeping as it was unexpected.

State and Society in the East Bloc

By the 1970s many of the professed goals of communism had been achieved. Communist leaders in central and eastern Europe and the Soviet Union adopted the term **developed socialism** (sometimes called "real existing socialism") to describe the accomplishments of their societies. Agriculture had been thoroughly collectivized, and although Poland was an exception, 80 to 90 percent of Soviet and East Bloc farmers worked on huge collective farms. Industry and business had been nationalized, and only a small portion of the economy remained in private hands in most East Bloc countries. The state had also done much to level class differences. Though some people — particularly party members — clearly had greater access to opportunities and resources, the gap between rich and poor was far smaller than in the West. An extensive system of government-supported social benefits included free medical care, guaranteed employment, inexpensive public transportation, and large subsidies for entertainment, rent, and food.

Everyday life under developed socialism was often an uneasy mixture of outward conformity and private disengagement — or apathy. The Communist Party dominated public life. Party-led mass organizations for youth, women, workers, and sports groups staged huge rallies, colorful festivals, and new holidays that exposed citizens to the values of the socialist state. But while East Bloc citizens might participate in public events, at home, and in private, they often grumbled about and sidestepped the Communist authorities.

East Bloc living standards were well above those in the developing world, but below those in the West. Centralized economic planning continued to result in shortages, and people complained about the poor quality and lack of choice of the most basic goods. Under these conditions, informal networks of family and friends helped people find hard-to-get goods and offered support beyond party organizations. Though the secret police persecuted those who openly challenged the system and generated mountains of files on ordinary people, they generally left alone those who demonstrated the required conformity.

Women in particular experienced the contradictions of the socialist system. Official state policy guaranteed equal rights for women and encouraged them to join the workforce in positions formerly reserved for men, and an extensive system of state-supported child care freed women to accept these employment opportunities and eased the work of parenting. Yet women rarely made it into the upper ranks of business or politics, and they faced the same double burden as those in the West. In addition, government control of the public sphere meant that the independent groups dedicated to feminist reform that emerged in the West in the 1970s developed more slowly in the East Bloc and the Soviet Union. Women could complain to the Communist authorities about unequal or sexist conditions at work or at home, but until the 1980s they could not build private, nongovernmental organizations to lobby for change.

Though everyday life was fairly comfortable in the East Bloc, a number of deeply rooted structural problems undermined popular support for Soviet-style communism. These fundamental problems would contribute to the re-emergence of civic dissent and ultimately to the revolutions of 1989. East Bloc countries — like those in the West — were hard hit by the energy crisis and stagflation of the 1970s. For a time, access to inexpensive oil from the Soviet Union, which had huge resources, helped prop up faltering economies, but this cushion began to fall apart in the 1980s.

For a number of reasons, East Bloc leaders refused to make the economic reforms that might have made developed socialism more effective. First, a move toward Western-style postindustrial society would have required fundamental changes to the Communist system. As in the West, it would have hurt the already weakened living standard of industrial workers. But Communist East Bloc states were publicly committed to supporting the working classes, including coal miners, shipbuilders, and factory and construction workers. To pursue the neoliberal reforms undertaken in the West would have destroyed support for the government among these important constituencies, which was already tenuous at best. In addition, East Bloc regimes refused to cut spending on social benefits because that was, after all, one of the proudest achievements of socialism.

Second, East Bloc economies faltered. High-tech industries failed to take off in Communist Europe, in part because the West maintained embargoes on technology exports. The state continued to provide subsidies to heavy industries such as steel and mining, even though the industrial goods produced in the East Bloc were increasingly uncompetitive in the new global system. To stave off total collapse, governments borrowed massive amounts of hard currency from Western banks and governments, helping to convince ordinary people that communism was bankrupt and setting up a cycle of indebtedness that helped bring down the entire system in 1989.

Economic decline was hardly the only reason people increasingly questioned one-party Communist rule. The best career and educational opportunities were reserved for party members or handed out as political favors, leaving many talented people underemployed and resentful. Tight controls on travel continually called attention to the burdens of daily life in a repressive society. The one-party state had repeatedly quashed popular reform movements, retreated from economic liberalization, and jailed or exiled dissidents, even those who wished to reform communism from within. Though many East Bloc citizens still found the promise of Marxist egalitarian socialism appealing, they increasingly doubted the legitimacy of Soviet-style communism: the dream of distributing goods "from each according to his means, to each according to his needs" (as Marx had once put it) hardly made up for the deficiencies of developed socialism.

Dissent in Czechoslovakia and Poland

Stagnation in the East Bloc encouraged small numbers of dedicated people to try to change society from below. Developments in Czechoslovakia and Poland were the most striking and significant, and determined protest movements re-emerged in both countries in the mid-1970s. Remembering a history of violent repression and Soviet invasion, dissenters carefully avoided direct challenges to government leaders. Nor did they try to reform the Communist Party from within, as Dubček and his followers had attempted in Prague in 1968. Instead, they worked to build a civil society from below—to create a realm of freedom beyond formal politics, where civil liberties and human rights could be exercised independently of the Communist system.

In Czechoslovakia in 1977 a small group of citizens, including future Czechoslovak president Václav Havel (VAH-slahf HAH-vuhl) (1936–2011), signed a manifesto that came to be known as Charter 77. The group criticized the government for ignoring the human rights provision of the Helsinki Accords and called on Communist leaders to respect civil and political liberties. They also criticized censorship and argued for improved environmental policies. Despite immediate state repression, the group challenged passive acceptance of Communist authority and voiced public dissatisfaction with developed socialism.

In Poland, an unruly satellite from the beginning, the Communists had failed to dominate society to the extent seen elsewhere in the East Bloc. Most agricultural land remained in private hands, and the Catholic Church thrived. The Communists also failed to manage the economy effectively. The 1960s brought stagnation, and in 1970 Poland's working class rose again in angry protest. A new Communist leader came to power, and he wagered that massive inflows of Western capital and technology, especially from rich and now-friendly West Germany, could produce a Polish economic miracle. Instead, bureaucratic incompetence and the first oil shock in 1973 sent the economy into a nosedive. Workers, intellectuals, and the church became increasingly restive. Then the real Polish miracle occurred: Cardinal Karol Wojtyła (voy-TIH-wah), archbishop of Kraków, was elected pope in 1978 as John Paul II. In June 1979 he returned to Poland from Rome, preaching love of Christ and country and the "inalienable rights of man." The pope drew enormous crowds and electrified the Polish nation.

In August 1980 strikes broke out across Poland; at the gigantic Lenin Shipyards in Gdansk (formerly known as Danzig) sixteen thousand workers laid down their tools and occupied the plant. As other workers joined "in solidarity," the strikers advanced the ideals of civil society, including the right to form trade unions free from state control, freedom of speech, release of political prisoners, and economic reforms. After the strikers occupied the shipyard for eighteen days, the government gave in and accepted the workers' demands in the Gdansk Agreement. In a state in which the Communist Party claimed to rule on behalf of the proletariat, a working-class revolt had won an unprecedented, even revolutionary, victory.

Led by feisty Lenin Shipyards electrician and devout Catholic Lech Wałęsa (lehk vah-WEHN-suh) (b. 1943), the workers organized a free and democratic trade union called **Solidarity**. As in Czechoslovakia, Solidarity worked cautiously to shape an active civil society. Joined by intellectuals and supported by the Catholic Church, it became a national union with a full-time staff of 40,000 and 9.5 million members. Cultural and intellectual freedom blossomed in Poland, and Solidarity enjoyed tremendous public support. But Solidarity's leaders pursued a self-limiting revolution, meant only to defend the concessions won in the Gdansk Agreement. Solidarity thus practiced moderation, refusing to challenge directly the Communist monopoly on political power. At the same time, the ever-present threat of calling a nationwide strike gave it real leverage in negotiations with the Communist bosses.

Solidarity's combination of strength and moderation postponed a showdown, as the Soviet

Lech Wałęsa and Solidarity An inspiration for fellow workers at the Lenin Shipyards in the dramatic and successful strike against the Communist leaders in August 1980, Wałęsa played a key role in Solidarity before and after it was outlawed. Here he speaks at a protest rally in the port city of Gdansk during the strike. Wałęsa personified the enduring opposition to Communist rule in eastern Europe. (STR/Reuters/Forum/Erazm Ciolek/Newscom)

Union played a waiting game of threats and pressure. After a confrontation in March 1981, Wałęsa settled for minor government concessions, and Solidarity dropped plans for a massive general strike. Criticism of Wałęsa's moderate leadership gradually grew, and Solidarity lost its cohesiveness. The worsening economic crisis also encouraged radical actions among disgruntled Solidarity members, and the Polish Communist leadership shrewdly denounced the union for promoting economic collapse and provoking a possible Soviet invasion. In December 1981 Wojciech Jaruzelski (VOY-chehk yahr-oo-ZEHL-skee), the general who led Poland's Communist government, suddenly proclaimed martial law and arrested Solidarity's leaders.

Outlawed and driven underground, Solidarity survived in part because of the government's unwillingness (and probably its inability) to impose full-scale terror. Moreover, millions of Poles decided to continue acting as if they were free — the hallmark of civil society — even though they were not. Cultural and intellectual life remained extremely vigorous as the Polish economy continued to deteriorate. Thus popular support for outlawed Solidarity remained strong under martial law in the 1980s, preparing the way for the union's political rebirth toward the end of the decade.

The rise and survival of Solidarity showed that ordinary Poles would stubbornly struggle for greater political and religious liberty, cultural freedom, trade-union rights, patriotic nationalism, and a more humane socialism. Not least, Solidarity's challenge encouraged fresh thinking in the Soviet Union, ever the key to lasting change in the East Bloc.

From Détente Back to Cold War

Soviet and East Bloc leaders faced challenges from abroad as optimistic hopes for détente in international relations faded in the late 1970s. Brezhnev's Soviet Union ignored the human rights provisions of the Helsinki agreement, and East-West political competition remained very much alive outside Europe. Many Americans became convinced that the Soviet Union was taking advantage of détente, steadily building up its military might and pushing for political gains and revolutions in Africa, Asia, and Latin America. The Soviet invasion of Afghanistan in December 1979, designed to save an increasingly unpopular Marxist regime, alarmed the West. Many Americans feared that the oil-rich states of the Persian Gulf would be next, and once again they looked to the NATO alliance and military might to thwart Communist expansion.

President Jimmy Carter (U.S. pres. 1977–1981) tried to lead NATO beyond verbal condemnation of the Soviet Union and urged economic sanctions against it, but only Great Britain among the European allies supported the American initiative. The alliance showed the same lack of concerted action when the Solidarity movement rose in Poland. Some observers concluded that NATO had lost the will to act decisively in dealing with the Soviet bloc.

The Atlantic alliance endured, however, and the U.S. military buildup launched by Carter in his last years in office was greatly accelerated by President Reagan, who was swept into office in 1980 by a wave of patriotism and economic discontent. The new American leadership acted as if the military balance had tipped in favor of the Soviet Union, which Reagan anathematized as the "evil empire." Increasing defense spending enormously, the Reagan administration deployed short-range nuclear missiles in western Europe and built up the navy to preserve American power in the post-Vietnam age. The broad shift toward greater conservatism in the 1980s gave Reagan invaluable allies in western Europe. Margaret Thatcher worked well with Reagan and was a forceful advocate for a revitalized Atlantic alliance, and under Helmut Kohl West Germany likewise worked with the United States to coordinate military and political policy toward the Soviet bloc.

Gorbachev's Reforms in the Soviet Union

Cold War tensions aside, the Soviet Union's Communist elite seemed safe from any challenge from below in the early 1980s. A well-established system of administrative controls stretched downward from the central ministries and state committees to provincial cities and from there to factories, neighborhoods, and villages. At each level of this massive state bureaucracy, the overlapping hierarchy of the 17.5-million-member Communist Party maintained tight state control. Organized opposition was impossible, and average people left politics to the bosses.

Although the massive state and party bureaucracy safeguarded the elite, it promoted widespread apathy and stagnation. When the ailing Brezhnev finally died in 1982, his successor, the long-time chief of the secret police, Yuri Andropov (1914–1984), tried to invigorate the system. Relatively little came of his efforts, but they combined with a sharply worsening economic situation to set the stage for the emergence in 1985 of Mikhail Gorbachev (b. 1931), the most vigorous Soviet leader in a generation.

A lawyer and experienced Communist Party official, Gorbachev believed in communism but realized that the Soviet Union was failing to keep up with the West and was losing its superpower status. Thus he tried to revitalize the Soviet system with fundamental reforms. An idealist who wanted to improve conditions for ordinary citizens, Gorbachev understood that the enormous expense of the Cold War arms race had had a disastrous impact on living conditions in the Soviet Union; improvement at home, he realized, required better relations with the West.

In his first year in office, Gorbachev consolidated his power, attacked corruption and incompetence in the bureaucracy, and tried to reduce alcoholism, which was widespread and lethal in Soviet society. He worked out an ambitious reform program designed to restructure the economy to provide for the real needs of the Soviet population. To accomplish this economic restructuring, or **perestroika** (pehr-uh-STROY-kuh), Gorbachev and his supporters eased government price controls on some goods, gave more independence to state enterprises, and created profit-seeking private cooperatives to provide personal services. These small-scale reforms initially produced improvements, but shortages grew as the economy stalled at an intermediate point between central planning and free-market mechanisms. By late 1988 widespread consumer dissatisfaction posed a serious threat to Gorbachev's leadership and the entire reform program.

Gorbachev's bold and far-reaching campaign for greater freedom of expression was much more successful. Very popular in a country where censorship, dull uniformity, and outright lies had long characterized public discourse, the newfound openness, or **glasnost** (GLAZ-nohst), of the government and the media marked an astonishing break with the past. Long-banned émigré writers sold millions of copies of their works in new editions, while denunciations of Stalin and his terror became standard fare in plays and movies. In another example of glasnost in action, after several days of hesitation the usually secretive Soviet government issued daily reports on the 1986 nuclear plant accident at Chernobyl, one of the worst environmental disasters in history. Indeed, the initial openness in government pronouncements quickly went much further than Gorbachev intended and led to something approaching free speech, a veritable cultural revolution.

Democratization was another element of reform. Beginning as an attack on corruption in the Communist Party, it led to the expansion of the ballot, with candidates outside the Communist Party for the first time in the Soviet Union since 1917. Gorbachev and the party remained in control, but a minority of critical independents was elected in April 1989 to a revitalized Congress of People's Deputies. Millions of Soviets then watched the new congress for hours on television as Gorbachev and his ministers saw their proposals debated and even rejected. An active civil society was emerging—a new political culture at odds with the Communist Party's monopoly of power and control.

Democratization also ignited demands for greater political and cultural autonomy and even national independence among non-Russian minorities living in the fifteen Soviet republics. The Soviet population numbered about 145 million ethnic Russians and 140.6 million non-Russians, including 55 million Muslims in the Central Asian republics and over 44 million Ukrainians. Once Gorbachev opened the doors to greater public expression, tensions flared between central Soviet control and national separatist movements. Independence groups were particularly active in the Baltic Soviet socialist republics of Lithuania, Latvia, and Estonia; in western Ukraine; and in the Transcaucasian republics of Armenia, Azerbaijan, and Georgia.

Finally, Gorbachev brought reforms to the field of foreign affairs. He withdrew Soviet troops from Afghanistan in February 1989 and sought to reduce East-West tensions. Of enormous importance, the Soviet leader sought to halt the arms race with the United States and convinced President Reagan of his sincerity. In a Washington summit in December 1987, the two leaders agreed to eliminate all land-based intermediate-range missiles in Europe, setting the stage for more arms reductions. Gorbachev pledged to respect the political choices of the peoples of East Bloc countries, repudiating the Brezhnev Doctrine and giving encouragement to reform movements in Poland, Czechoslovakia, and Hungary. By early 1989 it seemed that if Gorbachev held to his word, the tragic Soviet occupation of eastern Europe might wither away, taking the long Cold War with it once and for all.

What were the causes and consequences of the 1989 revolutions in the East Bloc?

In 1989 Gorbachev's plan to reform communism from within snowballed out of control. A series of largely peaceful revolutions swept across eastern Europe, overturning existing Communist regimes (Map 29.2). The peoples of the East Bloc gained political freedom, West Germany absorbed its East German rival, and as Gorbachev's reforms boomeranged, a complicated anticommunist revolution swept through the Soviet Union. The Cold War came to an end, and the United States suddenly stood as the world's only superpower.

MAP 29.2 Democratic Movements in Eastern Europe, 1989
Countries that had been satellites in the orbit of the Soviet Union began to set themselves free in 1989.

The Collapse of Communism in the East Bloc

The collapse of Communist rule in the Soviet satellite states surprised many Western commentators, who had expected Cold War divisions to persist for many years. Yet while the revolutions of 1989 appeared to erupt quite suddenly, long-standing structural weaknesses in the Communist system had prepared the way. East Bloc economies never really recovered from the economic catastrophe of the 1970s. State spending on outdated industries and extensive social benefits led to massive indebtedness to Western banks and undermined economic growth, while limits on personal and political freedoms fueled a growing sense of injustice.

In this general climate of economic stagnation and popular anger, Solidarity and the Polish people led the way to revolution. In 1988 widespread strikes, raging inflation, and the outlawed Solidarity's refusal to cooperate with the military government had brought Poland to the brink of economic collapse. Poland's frustrated Communist leaders offered to negotiate with Solidarity if the outlawed union's leaders could get the strikers back to work and resolve the political crisis. The subsequent agreement in April 1989 legalized Solidarity and declared that a large minority of representatives to the Polish parliament would be chosen by free elections that June. Still guaranteed a parliamentary majority and expecting to win many of the contested seats, the Communists believed that their rule was guaranteed for four years and that Solidarity would keep the workers in line.

Lacking access to the state-run media, Solidarity succeeded nonetheless in mobilizing the country and winning all but one of the contested seats in an overwhelming victory. Moreover, many angry voters crossed off the names of unopposed party candidates, so that the Communist Party failed to win the majority its leaders had anticipated. Solidarity members jubilantly entered the Polish parliament, and a dangerous stalemate quickly developed. But Lech Wałęsa, a gifted politician who always repudiated violence, adroitly obtained a majority by securing the allegiance of two minor procommunist parties that had been part of the coalition government after World War II. In August 1989 Tadeusz Mazowiecki (ta-DAY-ush MAH-zoe-vee-ETS-key) (1927–2013), the editor of one of Solidarity's weekly newspapers, was sworn in as Poland's new noncommunist prime minister.

In its first year and a half, the new Solidarity government cautiously introduced revolutionary political changes. It eliminated the hated secret police, the Communist ministers in the government, and finally Communist Party leader Jaruzelski himself, but it did so step-by-step to avoid confrontation with the army or the Soviet Union. In economics, however, the Solidarity government was radical from the beginning. It applied economic shock therapy, an intense dose of neoliberal policy designed to make a clean break with state planning and move quickly to market mechanisms and private property. Thus the government abolished controls on many prices on January 1, 1990, and drastically reformed the monetary system.

Hungary followed Poland. Hungary's moderate Communist Party leader János Kádár (KAH-dahr) had permitted liberalization of the rigid planned economy after the 1956 uprising in exchange for political loyalty and continued Communist control. In May 1988, in an effort to retain power by granting modest political concessions, the party replaced the ill and aging Kádár with a reform-minded Communist. But liberal opposition groups rejected piecemeal progress, and in the summer of 1989 the Hungarian Communist Party agreed to hold free elections the following March. Welcoming Western investment and moving rapidly toward multiparty democracy, Hungary's Communists now enjoyed considerable popular support, and they believed, quite mistakenly, that they could defeat the opposition in the upcoming elections.

In an effort to strengthen their support at home, the Hungarians opened their border to East Germans and tore down the barbed wire curtain separating Hungary from Austria. Tens of thousands of dissatisfied East German "vacationers" then poured into Hungary, crossed into Austria as refugees, and continued on to immediate resettlement in thriving West Germany.

The flight of East Germans fed the rapid growth of a home-grown, spontaneous protest movement in East Germany. Workers joined intellectuals, environmentalists, and Protestant ministers in huge candlelight demonstrations. While some activists insisted that a democratic but still socialist East Germany was both possible and desirable, numerous East German citizens continued to depart en masse. In a desperate attempt to stabilize the situation, the East German government opened the Berlin Wall in November 1989, allowing free travel across the former border. A new, reformist government took power and scheduled free elections.

In Czechoslovakia, Communist rule began to dissolve peacefully in November to December 1989. This so-called **Velvet Revolution** grew out of popular demonstrations led by students and joined by intellectuals and a dissident playwright-turned-moral-revolutionary named Václav Havel (1936–2011). When the protesters took control of the streets, the Communist government resigned, leading to

The Opening of the Berlin Wall The sudden and unanticipated opening of the Berlin Wall on November 10, 1989, dramatized the spectacular fall of communism throughout east-central Europe. West Berliners welcomed the East Germans who piled into their "Trabi" automobiles to cross the border. Millions of East German citizens traveled into West Berlin and the Federal Republic of Germany in the first few days after the surprise relaxation of inter-German travel controls. (© DPA/ Courtesy Everett Collection)

a power-sharing arrangement termed the "Government of National Understanding." As 1989 ended, the Czechoslovakian assembly elected Havel president.

In Romania, popular revolution turned violent and bloody. There the dictator Nicolae Ceaușescu (chow-SHESS-koo) (1918–1989) had long combined tight party control with stubborn independence from Moscow. Faced with mass protests in December 1989, Ceaușescu ordered his ruthless security forces to quell unrest, sparking an armed uprising. Perhaps 750 people were killed in the fighting; the numbers were often exaggerated. After the dictator and his wife were captured and executed by a military court, Ceaușescu's forces were defeated. A coalition government emerged, although the legacy of Ceaușescu's long and oppressive rule left a troubled country.

German Unification and the End of the Cold War

The dissolution of communism in East Germany that began in 1989 reopened the "German question" and raised the threat of renewed Cold War conflict over Germany. Taking power in October 1989, East German reform Communists, enthusiastically supported by leading intellectuals and former dissidents, wanted to preserve socialism by making it genuinely democratic and responsive to the needs of the people. They argued for a "third way" that would go beyond the failed Stalinism they had experienced and the ruthless capitalism they saw in the West. These reformers supported closer ties with West Germany but feared unification, hoping to preserve a distinct East German identity with a socialist system.

Over the next year, however, East Germany was absorbed into an enlarged West Germany, much as a faltering company is swallowed by a stronger rival and ceases to exist. Three factors were particularly important in this outcome. First, in the first week after the Berlin Wall was opened, almost 9 million East Germans — roughly half of the total population — poured across the border into West Germany. Almost all returned to their homes in the east, but the exhilaration of crossing a long-closed border aroused long-dormant hopes of unity among ordinary citizens.

Second, West German chancellor Helmut Kohl and his closest advisers skillfully exploited the historic opportunity handed them. Sure of support from the United States, whose leadership he had steadfastly followed, in November 1989 Kohl presented a ten-point plan for step-by-step unification in cooperation with both East Germany and the international community. Kohl then promised the struggling citizens of East Germany an immediate economic bonanza — a generous though limited exchange of East German marks in savings accounts and pensions into much more valuable West German marks. This offer helped popularize the Alliance for Germany, a well-financed political party established in East Germany with the support of Kohl's West German Christian Democrats. In March 1990 the Alliance won almost 50 percent of the votes in an East German parliamentary election, outdistancing the Party of Democratic Socialism (the renamed East German Communist Party) (16 percent) and the revived Social Democratic Party (22 percent). The Alliance for Germany quickly negotiated an economic and political union on favorable terms with Kohl. The rapid pace of reunification quickly overwhelmed those who argued for the preservation of an independent socialist society in East Germany.

Third, in the summer of 1990 the crucial international aspect of German unification was successfully resolved. Unification would once again make Germany the strongest state in central Europe and would directly affect the security of the Soviet Union. But Gorbachev swallowed hard — Western cartoonists showed Stalin turning over in his grave — and negotiated the best deal he could. In a historic agreement signed by Gorbachev and Kohl in July 1990, Kohl solemnly affirmed Germany's peaceful intentions and pledged never to develop nuclear, biological, or chemical weapons. The Germans sweetened the deal by promising enormous loans to the hard-pressed Soviet Union. In October 1990 East Germany merged into West Germany, forming a single nation under the West German laws and constitution.

The peaceful reunification of Germany accelerated the pace of agreements to liquidate the Cold War. In November 1990 delegates from twenty-two European countries joined those from the United States and the Soviet Union in Paris and agreed to a scaling down of all their armed forces. The delegates also solemnly affirmed that all existing borders in Europe, including those of unified Germany and the emerging Baltic States, were legal and valid. The Paris Accord was for all practical purposes a general peace treaty bringing an end to both World War II and the Cold War.

Peace in Europe encouraged the United States and the Soviet Union to scrap a significant portion of their nuclear weapons. In September 1991 a confident President George H. W. Bush canceled the around-the-clock alert status for American bombers outfitted with atomic bombs, and Gorbachev quickly followed suit with his own forces. For the first time in four decades, Soviet and American nuclear weapons were not standing ready for mutual destruction.

The Disintegration of the Soviet Union

As 1990 began, the tough work of dismantling some forty-five years of Communist rule had begun in all but two East Bloc states—tiny Albania and the vast Soviet Union. The great question now became whether the Soviet Union would follow its former satellites.

In February 1990, as competing Russian politicians noisily presented their programs and nationalists in the non-Russian republics demanded autonomy or independence from the Soviet Union, the Communist Party suffered a stunning defeat in local elections throughout the country. As in East Bloc countries, democrats and anticommunists won clear majorities in the leading cities of the Russian Soviet Republic, by far the largest republic in the Soviet Union. Moreover, in Lithuania the people elected an uncompromising nationalist as president, and the newly chosen parliament declared Lithuania an independent state.

Gorbachev responded by placing an economic embargo on Lithuania, but he refused to use the army to crush the separatist government. The result was a tense political standoff that undermined popular support for Gorbachev. Separating himself further from Communist hardliners, Gorbachev asked Soviet citizens to ratify a new constitution that formally abolished the Communist Party's monopoly of political power and expanded the power of the Congress of People's Deputies. While retaining his post as party secretary, Gorbachev then convinced a majority of deputies to elect him president of the Soviet Union.

Despite his victory, Gorbachev's power continued to erode, and his unwillingness to risk a universal suffrage election for the presidency strengthened his archrival, Boris Yeltsin (1931–2007). A radical reform Communist, Yeltsin embraced the democratic movement, and in May 1990 he was elected parliamentary leader of the Russian Soviet Republic. He boldly announced that Russia would put its interests first and declare its independence from the Soviet Union, broadening the base of the anticommunist movement by joining the patriotism of ordinary Russians with the democratic aspirations of big-city intellectuals. Gorbachev tried to save the Soviet Union with a new treaty that would link the member republics in a looser, freely accepted confederation, but six of the fifteen Soviet republics rejected his plan.

Opposed by democrats and nationalists, Gorbachev was also challenged by the Communist old guard. In August 1991 a gang of hardliners kidnapped him and his family in the Caucasus and tried to seize the Soviet government. The attempted coup collapsed in the face of massive popular resistance that rallied around Yeltsin. As a spellbound world watched on television, Yeltsin defiantly denounced the rebels from atop a stalled tank in central Moscow and declared the "rebirth of Russia." The army supported Yeltsin, and Gorbachev was rescued and returned to power as head of the Soviet Union.

The leaders of the coup had wanted to preserve Communist power, state ownership, and the multinational Soviet Union; they succeeded in destroying all three. An anticommunist revolution swept Russia as Yeltsin and his supporters outlawed the Communist Party and confiscated its property. Locked in a personal and political duel with Gorbachev, Yeltsin and his democratic allies declared Russia independent, withdrew from the Soviet Union, and changed the country's name from the Russian Soviet Republic to the Russian Federation. All the other Soviet republics also withdrew. Gorbachev resigned on December 25, 1991, and the next day the Supreme Soviet dissolved itself, marking the end of the Soviet Union. The independent republics of the old Soviet Union then established a loose confederation, the Commonwealth of Independent States, which played only a minor role in the 1990s.

NOTES

1. Quoted in Kessing's Research Report, *Germany and East Europe Since 1945: From the Potsdam Agreement to Chancellor Brandt's "Ostpolitik"* (New York: Charles Scribner's Sons, 1973), pp. 284–285.
2. M. Mitterauer, *The History of Youth* (Oxford: Basil Blackwell, 1992), p. 40.

LOOKING BACK LOOKING AHEAD

The unexpected collapse of Communist Europe capped three decades of turbulent change. In the 1960s the consensus established after the Second World War was challenged by protest movements in the East and West Blocs alike. In the 1970s a global recession had devastating effects across the globe. In the 1980s conservative Western leaders pushed neoliberal plans to revive growth and meet growing global competition. In the East Bloc, structural problems and spontaneous revolt brought down communism, dissolved the Soviet Union, and ended the Cold War.

With the world economy on the road to recovery and new free-market systems in place across the former East Bloc, all of Europe would now have the opportunity to enter the information age. After forty years of Cold War division, the continent regained an underlying unity as faith in democratic government and market economics became the common European creed. In 1991 hopes for peaceful democratic progress were almost universal. According to philosopher Francis Fukuyama, the world had reached "the end of history"—the end of the Cold War, he argued, would lead to peaceful development based on growing tolerance, free-market economics, and liberal democracy.

The post–Cold War years saw the realization of some of these hopes, but the new era brought its own problems and tragedies. In the former Yugoslavia, ethnic and nationalist tensions flared, leading to a disastrous civil war. The struggle to rebuild the shattered societies of the former East Bloc countries was far more difficult than the people living in them had hoped. Poor economic growth continued to complicate attempts to deal with the wide-open global economy. New conflicts with Islamic nations in the Middle East involved some European nations in war. The European Union expanded, but political disagreements, environmental issues, increased anxiety about non-Western immigrants, and a host of other problems undermined moves toward true European unity. History was far from over—the realities of a post–Cold War world continued to yield difficult challenges as Europe entered the twenty-first century.

MAKE CONNECTIONS

Think about the larger developments and continuities within and across chapters.

1. How did the revolts that shook western European countries and the East Bloc develop out of issues left unresolved in the 1950s era of postwar reconstruction (Chapter 28)?
2. Both East and West Blocs faced similar economic problems in the 1970s, yet communism collapsed in the East and capitalism recovered. How do you account for the difference? Were economic problems the main basis for popular opposition to communism?
3. What were some of the basic ideas behind the neoliberal economic policies that emerged in the West in the 1970s and 1980s? Why are they still popular today?

Chapter 29 Review

IDENTIFY KEY TERMS

Identify and explain the significance of each item below.

Ostpolitik (p. 892)

détente (p. 892)

Second Vatican Council (p. 894)

New Left (p. 895)

Brezhnev Doctrine (p. 900)

OPEC (p. 901)

stagflation (p. 901)

postindustrial society (p. 902)

neoliberalism (p. 903)

privatization (p. 903)

second-wave feminism (p. 905)

developed socialism (p. 908)

Solidarity (p. 911)

perestroika (p. 913)

glasnost (p. 913)

Velvet Revolution (p. 917)

REVIEW THE MAIN IDEAS

Answer the section heading questions from the chapter.

1. Why did the postwar consensus of the 1950s break down? (p. 891)
2. What were the consequences of economic stagnation in the 1970s? (p. 900)
3. What led to the decline of "developed socialism" in the East Bloc? (p. 908)
4. What were the causes and consequences of the 1989 revolutions in the East Bloc? (p. 914)

CHRONOLOGY

1961	• Building of Berlin Wall suggests permanence of the East Bloc
1962–1965	• Second Vatican Council
1963	• Wolf publishes *Divided Heaven*; Friedan publishes *The Feminine Mystique*
1964	• Civil Rights Act in the United States
1964–1973	• Peak of U.S. involvement in Vietnam War
1966	• Formation of National Organization for Women (NOW)
1968	• Soviet invasion of Czechoslovakia; "May Events" protests in France
1971	• Founding of Greenpeace
1973	• OPEC oil embargo
1975	• Helsinki Accords
1979	• Margaret Thatcher becomes British prime minister; founding of West German Green Party; Soviet invasion of Afghanistan
1985	• Mikhail Gorbachev named Soviet premier
1987	• United States and Soviet Union sign arms reduction treaty
1989	• Soviet withdrawal from Afghanistan
1989–1991	• Fall of communism in eastern Europe
December 1991	• Dissolution of the Soviet Union

30

Life in an Age of Globalization

1990 TO THE PRESENT

CHAPTER PREVIEW

- How did life change in Russia and the former East Bloc countries after 1989?

- How did globalization affect European life and society?

- How is growing ethnic diversity changing contemporary Europe?

- What challenges will Europeans face in the coming decades?

ON NOVEMBER 9, 2009, THE TWENTIETH ANNIVERSARY of the opening of the Berlin Wall, jubilant crowds filled the streets around the Brandenburg Gate at the former border between East and West Berlin. World leaders and tens of thousands of onlookers applauded as former Polish president Lech Wałęsa pushed over a line of one thousand eight-foot-tall foam dominos, symbolizing the collapse of communism.

The crowd had reason to celebrate. The revolutions of 1989 had opened a new chapter in European and world history. Capitalism spread across the former East Bloc and Soviet Union (now the Russian Federation and fourteen other republics), along with the potential for political reform. Some of these hopes were realized, but the new era also brought problems and tragedies. The process of remaking formerly Communist societies was more difficult than expected. At the same time, across the West and around the world, globalization, the digital revolution, and the ongoing flow of immigrants into western Europe had impacts both positive and negative.

As Europeans faced serious tensions and complex changes in the twenty-first century, they also came together to form a strong new

923

European Union (EU) that would prove a formidable economic competitor to the United States. Ties between western Europe and the United States began to loosen, but Europe and North America—as well as the rest of the world—confronted common challenges. Finding solutions to problems in the Middle East and addressing the growth of authoritarian populism, environmental degradation, energy needs, and human rights would require not only innovation but also creative cooperation.

How did life change in Russia and the former East Bloc countries after 1989?

Establishing stable democratic governments in the former East Bloc countries and the fifteen diverse republics of the former Soviet Union was not easy. While Russia initially moved toward economic reform and political openness, by 2010 it had returned to its authoritarian traditions. The transformation of the Communist East Bloc was also difficult. After a period of tense reform, some countries, such as Poland and the Czech Republic, established relatively prosperous democracies and joined NATO and then the European Union (see "The New European Union" later in the chapter). Others lagged behind. In multiethnic Yugoslavia, the collapse of communism and the onset of a disastrous civil war broke the country apart.

Economic Shock Therapy in Russia

Politics and economics were closely intertwined in Russia after the dissolution of the Soviet Union. President Boris Yeltsin (r. 1991–1999), his democratic supporters, and his economic ministers wanted to create conditions that would prevent a return to communism and right the faltering economy. Adopting the model of economic reform already implemented in Poland in 1990 (see "Economic and Political Transformations in the Former East Bloc" ahead), and agreeing with neoliberal Western advisers who argued that a quick turn to free markets would speed economic growth, Russian reformers opted in January 1992 for liberalization at breakneck speed—so-called **shock therapy**, a set of economic policies also adopted by other former Communist countries.

To implement the plan, the Russians abolished price controls on most consumer goods, with the exception of bread, vodka, oil, and public transportation. The government also launched a rapid privatization program, selling formerly state-owned industries and agricultural concerns to private investors. Thousands of factories and mines were turned over to new private companies. In an attempt to share the wealth privatization was expected to generate, each citizen received a voucher worth 10,000 rubles (about $22) to buy stock in these private companies. Ownership of these assets, however, usually remained in the hands of the old bosses—the managers and government officials from the Communist era—undermining the reformers' goal of worker participation.

Instead of reviving production and bringing widespread prosperity through shock therapy, prices immediately soared, increasing by a factor of twenty-six in the course of 1992. At the same time, production fell a staggering 20 percent. Nor did the situation stabilize quickly. After 1995 inflation still raged, though at slower rates, and output continued to fall. According to most estimates, Russia produced from one-third to one-half less in 1996 than it had in 1991. The Russian economy crashed again in 1998 in the wake of Asia's financial crisis.

Shock therapy worked poorly for several reasons. Soviet industry had been highly monopolized and strongly tilted toward military goods. Production of many items had been concentrated in one or two gigantic factories or in interconnected combines. With privatization, these powerful state monopolies became powerful private monopolies that cut production and raised prices in order to maximize profits. Moreover, Yeltsin's government handed out enormous subsidies to corporate managers and bureaucrats, ostensibly to reinforce faltering firms and avoid bankruptcies, but also to buy political allegiance. New corporate leaders included criminals who intimidated would-be rivals in attempts to prevent the formation of competing businesses.

Runaway inflation and poorly executed privatization brought a profound social revolution to Russia. The new capitalist elite — the so-called Oligarchs — acquired great wealth and power, while large numbers of people struggled to make ends meet. The Oligarchs, Yeltsin's main supporters, maintained control with corrupt business practices and rampant cronyism.

At the other extreme, the vast majority of people saw their savings become practically worthless. Pensions lost much of their value, living standards drastically declined, and many people sold their personal goods to survive. Under these conditions, effective representative government failed to develop, and many Russians came to equate democracy with the corruption, poverty, and national decline they experienced throughout the 1990s. Yeltsin became increasingly unpopular; only the backing of the Oligarchs kept him in power.

Russian Revival Under Vladimir Putin

This widespread disillusionment set the stage for the rise of Vladimir Putin (POO-tihn) (b. 1952), who was elected president as Yeltsin's chosen successor in 2000 and re-elected in a landslide in March 2004. A colonel in the secret police during the Communist era, Putin maintained relatively liberal economic policies but re-established semi-authoritarian political rule. Critics labeled Putin's system an "imitation democracy," and indeed a façade of democratic institutions masked authoritarian rule.[1] Putin's government maintained control with rigged elections, a weak parliament, the intimidation of political opponents, and the distribution of state-owned public assets to win support of the new elite. In addition, the Russian president increased military spending and expanded the secret police.

Putin's government combined authoritarian politics with economic reform. The regime clamped down on the excesses of the Oligarchs, lowered corporate and business taxes, and re-established some government control over key industries. Such reforms — aided greatly by high world prices for oil and natural gas, Russia's most important exports — led to a decade of economic expansion, encouraging the growth of a new middle class. In 2008, however, the global financial crisis and a rapid drop in the price of oil caused a downturn, and the Russian stock market collapsed. The government initiated a $200 billion rescue plan, and the economy stabilized and returned to modest growth in 2010.

Vladimir Putin on Vacation in 2009 After two terms as Russian president (2000–2008), Putin served as prime minister for four years before returning to the presidency in 2012. Putin's high approval ratings were due in part to his carefully crafted image of strength and manliness. (AFP/Getty Images)

Putin stepped down when his term limits expired in 2008 but was re-elected president in 2012 and then won 76 percent of the vote in the elections of 2018. International observers agreed that the election itself was open and democratic, but critics called attention to a number of suspected irregularities during the vote.

Throughout his rule Putin's government decisively limited political opposition. The 2003 arrest and imprisonment of the corrupt oil billionaire Mikhail Khodorkovsky, an Oligarch who had openly supported opposition parties, on charges of tax evasion and fraud showed early on that Putin and his United Russia Party would use state powers to stifle dissent. Though the Russian constitution guaranteed freedom of the press, the government cracked down on the independent media. Using a variety of tactics, officials and pro-government businessmen influenced news reports and intimidated critical journalists. The suspicious murder in 2006 of journalist Anna Politkovskaya, a prominent critic of the government's human rights abuses and its war in Chechnya, reinforced Western worries that the country was returning to Soviet-style press censorship. Other attacks on critics of Putin's Russia outraged Western public opinion, but faced with blanket denials there was little the West could do to rein in Russian tactics.

In foreign relations, Putin's Russia has taken an ambitious and at times interventionist stance toward the Commonwealth of Independent States, a loose confederation of most of the former Soviet republics (see ahead). Further abroad, Putin generally championed assertive anti-Western policies in an attempt to bolster Russia's status as a great Eurasian power and world player. He forcefully opposed the expansion of NATO into the former East Bloc and regularly challenged U.S. and NATO foreign policy goals. In the Syrian civil war that broke out in 2011, for example, Russian backing of Syrian president Bashar al-Assad flew in the face of U.S. attempts to depose him. In a dramatic turn of events, western security services accused Russia of using social media, fake websites, and stolen e-mails to interfere in the 2016 U.S. presidential elections, Great Britain's 2016 "Brexit" referendum on leaving the European Union, and the 2017 presidential elections in France.

Putin's domestic and foreign policies proved quite popular with a majority of Russians. His housing, education, and health-care reforms significantly improved living standards. Capitalizing on Russian patriotism, Putin repeatedly evoked the glories of Russian history, expressed pride in the accomplishments of the Soviet Union, and downplayed the abuses of the Stalinist system. Putin's carefully crafted manly image and his aggressive international diplomacy soothed the country's injured pride and symbolized its national revival.

Political Instability in the Former Soviet Republics

The collapse of the Soviet Union led to the establishment of the Russian Federation and fourteen other newly independent republics and brought major changes to east-central Europe and south-central Asia (Map 30.1). In some ways, the transformation of this vast and diverse region paralleled the experience of the former East Bloc countries and Russia itself. Though most of the fourteen new republics, which included almost one-half of the former Soviet Union's total population, adopted some sort of liberal market capitalism, political reforms varied broadly. In the Baltic republics, where Gorbachev's perestroika had quickly encouraged powerful separatist movements, reformers established working democratic government. While Ukrainians struggled to construct a working democratic system, elsewhere — in Belarus, Kazakhstan, and the other Central Asian republics, and the new republics in the Caucasus — systems of "imitation democracy" and outright authoritarian rule took hold.

Though Putin encouraged the former Soviet republics to join the Commonwealth of Independent States, a loose confederation dominated by Russia that supposedly represented regional common interests, stability and agreement proved elusive. Popular protests and revolts challenged local politicians and Russian interests alike. In the country of Georgia, the so-called Rose Revolution (November 2003) brought a pro-Western, pro-NATO leader to power. In Ukraine, the Orange Revolution (November 2004–January 2005) challenged the results of a national election and expressed popular nationalist desires for more distance from Russia. Similar **Color Revolutions** in Belarus, Kyrgyzstan, and Moldova exemplified the unpredictable path toward democratization in the new republics that bordered the powerful Russian Federation.

Putin took an aggressive and at times interventionist stance toward anti-Russian revolt in the Commonwealth of Independent States and the Russian borderlands. Conflict was particularly intense in the oil-rich Caucasus, where an unstable combination of nationalist separatism and ethnic and religious tensions challenged Russian dominance. Since the breakup of the Soviet Union, Russian troops have repeatedly invaded Chechnya (CHEHCH-nyuh), a tiny Muslim republic with

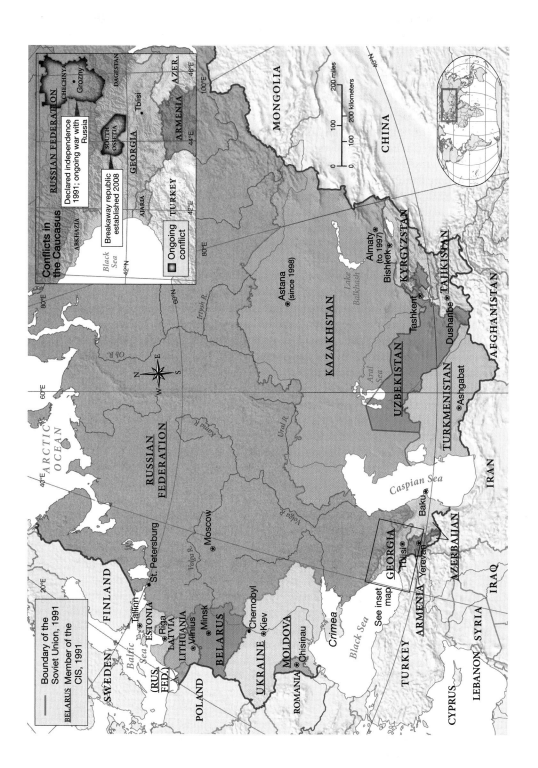

Conflicts in the Caucasus

RUSSIAN FEDERATION

Declared independence 1991; ongoing war with Russia

Breakaway republic established 2008

☐ Ongoing conflict

CHECHNYA · Grozny
DAGESTAN
AZER.
ARMENIA
46°E
Tbilisi
SOUTH OSSETIA
GEORGIA
44°E
ABKHAZIA
AJARIA
TURKEY
42°E

Black Sea
42°N

Boundary of the Soviet Union, 1991

BELARUS Member of the CIS, 1991

ARCTIC OCEAN
40°E
20°E
60°E
80°E
100°E
60°N

MONGOLIA
CHINA

200 miles
100   200 kilometers
0   100   200

Astana ⊛ (since 1998)

Almaty ⊛ (to 1997)
Bishkek ⊛
KYRGYZSTAN
TAJIKISTAN
Dushanbe ⊛
Tashkent ⊛
KAZAKHSTAN
Lake Balkhash
Aral Sea
UZBEKISTAN
TURKMENISTAN
Ashgabat ⊛
AFGHANISTAN

Irtysh R.
Ob R.
Kama R.
Ural R.

RUSSIAN FEDERATION

Volga R.
Moscow ⊛
Volga R.

Caspian Sea
Baku ⊛
IRAN

St. Petersburg
FINLAND
SWEDEN
Baltic Sea
ESTONIA
Tallinn
Riga
LATVIA
LITHUANIA
Vilnius
(RUS. FED.)
Minsk ⊛
BELARUS
Chernobyl · Kiev ⊛
UKRAINE
POLAND
MOLDOVA
Chisinau ⊛
ROMANIA
Crimea
Black Sea
See inset map
GEORGIA
Tbilisi ⊛
Yerevan ⊛
ARMENIA
AZERBAIJAN
TURKEY
CYPRUS
LEBANON SYRIA
IRAQ

1 million inhabitants on Russia's southern border that declared its independence in 1991. Despite ultimate Russian victory in the Chechen wars, the cost of the conflict was high. Thousands lost their lives, and both sides committed serious human rights abuses. Moscow declared an end to military operations in April 2009, but Chechen radicals, inspired by nationalism and Islamic radicalism, continued to fight an underground, terroristic campaign against Russia.

Russia also intervened in the independent state of Georgia, which won independence when the Soviet Union collapsed in 1991. Russian troops invaded Georgia in 2008 to support a separatist movement in South Ossetia (oh-SEE-shuh or oh-SET-tia), which eventually established a breakaway independent republic recognized only by Russia and a handful of small states.

Revolution broke out again in Ukraine in February 2014. When popular protests brought down the pro-Russian government, Putin sent Russian troops into Crimea, Ukraine's strategically valuable peninsula on the Black Sea where pro-Russian sentiment ran high. The territory, with a major naval base in the city of Sevastopol and large reserves of oil and natural gas, was incorporated into the Russian Federation. Then, in response to the anti-Russian policies of the new Ukrainian government, in April 2014 a group of armed rebels took over the regional capital Donetsk and other cities in eastern Ukraine and declared the establishment of the separatist, pro-Russian Donetsk and Luhansk "People's Republics" (see Map 30.1).

A full-scale military assault by Ukrainian government troops failed to push back or defeat the separatist forces. According to Ukrainian and U.S. sources, the Russians prevented the defeat of the insurrection by supplying substantial numbers of weapons and troops. In response, the United States and the European Union placed economic sanctions on Russia, and since February 2015 a shaky ceasefire has dampened hostilities in eastern Ukraine. Yet the outcome of the conflict remains uncertain, a revealing example of the way great power interests continue to create instability in the former Soviet republics.

Economic and Political Transformations in the Former East Bloc

Developments in the former East Bloc paralleled those in Russia in numerous ways. The former satellites worked to replace state-controlled production and distribution of goods of Soviet-style communism with market-based economic systems, and industries, businesses, and farms formerly managed by the state would now be privatized. In addition, these countries established systems of Western-style electoral politics.

< MAP 30.1   Russia and the Successor States, 1991–2019
After the failure of an attempt in August 1991 to depose Gorbachev, an anticommunist revolution swept the Soviet Union. The republics that formed the Soviet Union each declared their sovereignty and independence, with Russia, under President Boris Yeltsin, being the largest. Eleven of the fourteen republics then joined with Russia to form a loose confederation called the Commonwealth of Independent States, but the integrated economy of the Soviet Union dissolved into separate national economies, each with its own goals and policies. Conflict continued to simmer over these goals and policies, as evidenced by the ongoing civil war in Chechnya, the struggle between Russia and Georgia over South Ossetia, the Russian annexation of the Crimea, and the Ukrainian separatist movement.

The methods of restructuring and privatization varied from country to country. Encouraged by Western institutions such as the International Monetary Fund and the World Bank, Poland's new leaders were the first in eastern Europe to adopt shock therapy policies. Starting in 1990, the Poles liberalized prices and trade policies, raised taxes, cut state spending to reduce budget deficits, and quickly sold state-owned industries to private investors. As they would in Russia a few years later, these radical moves at first brought high inflation and a rapid decline in living standards, which generated public protests and strikes. But because the plan had the West's approval, Poland received Western financial support that eased the pain of transition. By the end of the decade, the country had one of the strongest economies in the former East Bloc. Other countries followed alternate paths. Czechoslovakia and the Baltic republic of Estonia, for example, slowed down privatization, continued more practices from the Communist past, and in general experienced less social disruption.

Economic growth in the former Communist countries was varied, but most observers agreed that Poland, the Czech Republic, and Hungary were the most successful. Each met the critical challenge of economic reconstruction more successfully than Russia. The reasons for these successes included considerable experience with limited market reforms before 1989, flexibility and lack of dogmatism in government policy, and an enthusiastic embrace of capitalism by a new entrepreneurial class. In its first five years of reform, Poland created twice as many new businesses as did Russia in a comparable period, despite having only a quarter of Russia's population.

In the years that followed 1989, Poland, the Czech Republic, and Hungary also did far better than Russia in creating new civic institutions, legal systems, and independent media outlets that reinforced political moderation and national revival. Lech Wałęsa in Poland and Václav Havel in Czechoslovakia were elected presidents of their countries and proved as remarkable in power as in opposition. After Czechoslovakia's Velvet Revolution in 1989, the Czechoslovak parliament accepted a "velvet divorce" in 1993, when Slovakian nationalists wanted to break off and form their own state, creating the separate Czech and Slovak Republics. In 1999 Poland, Hungary, and the Czech Republic were accepted into NATO, and in 2004 they and Slovakia gained admission to the European Union. Yet, as we shall see ahead, after the global recession of 2008, conservative populist parties took over in these key postcommunist countries and began to attack liberal institutions such as freedom of the press and independent judicial systems.

Romania and Bulgaria lagged behind in the postcommunist transition. Western traditions were weaker there, and both countries were poorer than their more successful neighbors. Romania and Bulgaria did make progress after 2000, however, and joined NATO in 2004 and the EU in 2007.

The social consequences of rebuilding the former East Bloc were similar to those in Russia, though people were generally spared the widespread shortages and misery that characterized Russia in the 1990s. Ordinary citizens and the elderly were once again the big losers, while the young and former Communist Party members were the big winners. Inequalities between richer and poorer regions also increased. Capital cities such as Warsaw, Prague, and Budapest concentrated wealth, power, and opportunity, while provincial centers stagnated and old industrial areas declined. Crime, corruption, and gangsterism increased in both the streets and the executive suites.

Though few former East Bloc residents wanted to return to communism, some expressed longings for the stability of the old system. They missed the guaranteed jobs and generous social benefits provided by the Communist state, and they found the individualism and competitiveness of capitalism cold and difficult. One Russian woman living on a pension of $448 a month in 2003 summed up the dilemma: "What we want is for our life to be as easy as it was in the Soviet Union, with the guarantee of a good, stable future and low prices—and at the same time this freedom that did not exist before."[2]

The question of whether or how to punish former Communist leaders who had committed political crimes or abused human rights emerged as a pressing issue in the former East Bloc. Germany tried major offenders and opened the records of the East German secret police (the Stasi) to the public, and by 1996 more than a million former residents had asked to see their files.[3] Other countries designed various means to deal with former Communist elites who might have committed crimes, with right-wing leaders generally taking a more punitive stand. The search for fair solutions proceeded slowly and with much controversy, a reminder of the troubling legacies of communism and the Cold War.

Civil War in Yugoslavia

Postcommunism turned tragic in Yugoslavia, which under Josip Broz Tito had been a federation of republics under centralized Communist rule. After Tito's death in 1980, power passed increasingly to the sister republics. This process encouraged a revival of regional, religious, and ethnic conflicts that were exacerbated by charges of ethnically inspired massacres during World War II and a dramatic economic decline in the mid-1980s.

The revolutions of 1989 accelerated the breakup of Yugoslavia. Serbian president Slobodan Milošević (1941–2006), a former Communist bureaucrat, wished to strengthen the federation's centralized government under Serbian control. In 1989 Milošević (mee-LOH-sheh-veech) severely limited the right of self-rule in the territory of Kosovo, an Autonomous Province established in the Republic of Serbia after the Second World War. In Kosovo ethnic Albanians constituted the overwhelming majority of residents, but the province included a medieval battleground that nationalists like Milošević claimed was sacred to Serbian identity. Religious differences reinforced ethnic and regional tensions: most Albanians were Muslims, while the vast majority of Serbs were Eastern Orthodox Christians.

In 1990 Milošević called for the unification of all Serbs in a "Greater Serbia," regardless of where they lived in the weakening Yugoslavian federation. This aggressive move strengthened the cause of national separatism, and in June 1991 the relatively wealthy federal republics of Slovenia and Croatia declared their independence. Milošević ordered the Yugoslavian federal army to invade both areas to assert Serbian control. The Serbs were quickly repulsed in Slovenia, but they managed to conquer about 30 percent of Croatia.

In 1992 the civil war spread to Bosnia-Herzegovina, which had also declared its independence. Serbs—about 30 percent of that region's population—refused to live under the more numerous Bosnian Muslims, or Bosniaks (Map 30.2). Yugoslavia had once been a tolerant and largely successful multiethnic state with different

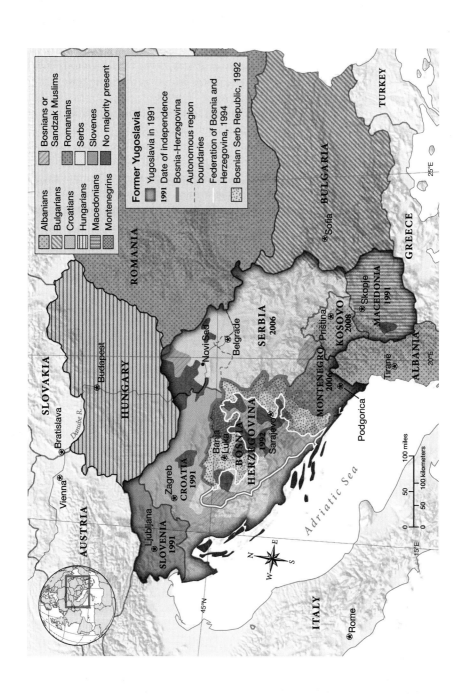

groups living side by side and often intermarrying. But the new goal of the armed factions in the Bosnian civil war was **ethnic cleansing**: the attempt to establish ethnically homogeneous territories by intimidation, forced deportation, and killing. The Yugoslavian army and irregular militias attempted to "cleanse" the territory of its non-Serb residents, unleashing ruthless brutality, with murder, rape, destruction, and the herding of refugees into concentration camps. Before the fighting in Bosnia ended, some three hundred thousand people were dead, and millions had been forced to flee their homes.

While appalling scenes of horror not seen in Europe since the Holocaust shocked the world, the Western nations had difficulty formulating an effective, unified response. The turning point came in July 1995 when Bosnian Serbs overran Srebrenica (sreb-reh-NEET-suh) — a Muslim city previously declared a United Nations safe area. Serb forces killed about eight thousand of the city's Bosniak civilians, primarily men and boys. Public outrage prompted NATO to bomb Bosnian Serb military targets intensively, and the Croatian army drove all the Serbs from Croatia. In November 1995 President Bill Clinton helped the warring sides hammer out a complicated accord that gave Bosnian Serbs about 49 percent of Bosnia and gave Bosniaks and the Roman Catholic Bosnian Croats the rest. About seven thousand troops from NATO and then after 2004 from the European Union were stationed in Bosnia to keep the peace; by 2012 only about six hundred remained, suggesting that while ethnic and religious tensions remained, the situation had improved.

The Kosovo Albanians, who hoped to establish self-rule, gained nothing from the Bosnian agreement. Frustrated Kosovar militants formed the Kosovo Liberation Army (KLA) and began to fight for independence. Serbian repression of the Kosovars increased, and in 1998 Serbian forces attacked both KLA guerrillas and unarmed villagers, displacing 250,000 people.

When Milošević refused to withdraw Serbian militias from Kosovo and accept self-government (but not independence) for Kosovo, NATO began bombing Serbia in March 1999. Serbian paramilitary forces responded by driving about 865,000 Albanian Kosovars into exile. NATO redoubled its destructive bombing campaign, which eventually forced Milošević to withdraw and allowed the Kosovars to regain their homeland. A United Nations and NATO peacekeeping force occupied Kosovo, ending ten years of Yugoslavian civil wars. Although U.S.-led NATO intervention finally brought an end to the conflict, the failure to take a stronger stand in the early years led to widespread and unnecessary suffering in the former Yugoslavia.

The war-weary and impoverished Serbs eventually voted the still-defiant Milošević out of office, and in July 2001 a new pro-Western Serbian government turned him over to a war crimes tribunal in the Netherlands to stand trial for crimes

< **MAP 30.2 The Breakup of Yugoslavia, 1991–2006**
Yugoslavia had the most ethnically diverse population in eastern Europe. The Republic of Croatia had substantial Serbian and Muslim minorities, while Bosnia-Herzegovina had large Muslim, Serbian, and Croatian populations, none of which had a majority. In June 1991 Serbia's brutal effort to seize territory and unite all Serbs in a single state brought a tragic civil war.

against humanity. After blustering his way through the initial stages of his trial, Milošević died in 2006 before the proceedings were complete. In 2008, after eight years of administration by the United Nations and NATO peacekeeping forces, the Republic of Kosovo declared its independence from Serbia. The United States and most states of the European Union recognized the declaration. Serbia and Russia did not, and the long-term status of this troubled emerging state remained uncertain.

How did globalization affect European life and society?

The new era of **globalization** that emerged in the last decades of the twentieth century brought new international economic, cultural, and political connections. Multinational corporations restructured national economies on a global scale, and an array of international governing bodies, such as the European Union, the United Nations, and the World Trade Organization, increasingly set policies that challenged the autonomy of traditional nation-states. At the same time the expansion and ready availability of highly efficient computer and media technologies led to ever-faster exchanges of goods, information, and entertainment around the world.

The Global Economy

Though large business interests had long profited from international trade and investment, multinational corporations grew and flourished in a world economy increasingly organized around free-market neoliberalism, which relaxed barriers to international trade. Multinational corporations built global systems of production and distribution that generated unprecedented wealth and generally escaped the control of regulators and politicians acting on the national level.

Conglomerates such as Siemens and Vivendi exemplified this business model. Siemens, with international headquarters in Berlin and Munich and offices around the globe, is one of the world's largest engineering companies, with vast holdings in energy, construction, health care, financial services, and industrial production. Vivendi, an extensive media and telecommunications company headquartered in Paris, controls a vast international network of producers and products, including music and film, publishing, television broadcasting, pay-TV, Internet services, and video games.

The development of sophisticated personal computer technologies and the Internet at the end of the twentieth century, coupled with the deregulation of national and international financial systems, further encouraged the growth of international trade. The ability to rapidly exchange information and capital meant that economic activity was no longer centered on national banks or stock exchanges, but rather flowed quickly across international borders. Large cities like London, Moscow, New York, and Hong Kong became global centers of banking, trade, and financial services. The influence of financial and insurance companies, communications conglomerates, and energy and legal firms headquartered in these global cities extended far beyond the borders of the traditional nation-state.

At the same time, the close connections between national economies also made the entire world vulnerable to economic panics and downturns. In 1997 a banking crisis in Thailand spread to Indonesia, South Korea, and Japan and then echoed around the world. The resulting slump in oil and gas prices hit Russia especially hard, leading to high inflation, bank failures, and the collapse of the Russian stock market. The crisis then spread to Latin America, plunging most countries there into a severe economic downturn. A decade later, a global recession triggered by a crisis in the U.S. housing market and financial system created the worst worldwide economic crisis since the Great Depression of the 1930s (see "The Global Recession and the Viability of the European Union" ahead).

The New European Union

Global economic pressures encouraged the expansion and consolidation of the European Common Market, which in 1993 proudly rechristened itself the **European Union (EU)** (Map 30.3). The EU added the free movement of capital and services and eventually individuals across national borders to the existing free trade in goods. In addition, member states sought to create a monetary union in which all EU countries would share a single currency. Membership in the monetary union required states to meet strict financial criteria defined in the 1991 **Maastricht Treaty**, which also set legal standards and anticipated the development of common policies on defense and foreign affairs.

Western European elites and opinion makers generally supported the economic integration embodied in the Maastricht Treaty. They felt that membership requirements, which imposed financial discipline on national governments, would combat Europe's ongoing economic problems and viewed the establishment of a single European currency as an irreversible historic step toward basic political unity. This unity would allow Europe as a whole to regain its place in world politics and to deal with the United States as an equal.

Support for the Maastricht Treaty, however, was hardly universal. Ordinary people, leftist political parties, and right-wing nationalists expressed considerable opposition to the new rules. Many people resented the EU's ever-growing bureaucracy in Brussels, which imposed common standards on everything from cheese production to day care, supposedly undermining national customs and local traditions. Moreover, increased unity meant yielding still more power to distant "Eurocrats" and political insiders, which limited national sovereignty and democratic control.

Above all, many citizens feared that the European Union would operate at their expense. Joining the monetary union required national governments to meet stringent fiscal standards, impose budget cuts, and contribute to the EU operating budget. The resulting reductions in health care and social benefits hit ordinary citizens and did little to reduce high unemployment. When put to the public for a vote, ratification of the Maastricht Treaty was usually very close. In France, for example, the treaty passed with just 50.1 percent of the vote. Even after the treaty was ratified, battles over budgets, benefits, and high unemployment continued throughout the EU in the 1990s.

Then in 2002, brand-new euros finally replaced the national currencies of all Eurozone countries. The establishment of the European monetary union built confidence in member nations and increased their willingness to accept new members. On May 1, 2004, the European Union began admitting its former East Bloc

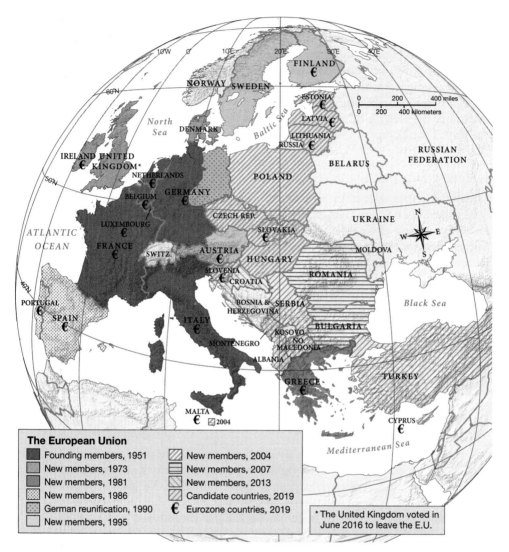

MAP 30.3   The European Union, 2019
No longer divided by ideological competition and the Cold War, much of today's Europe has banded together in a European Union that facilitates the open movement of people, jobs, and currency across national borders.

neighbors. This rapid expansion underscored the need to reform the EU's unwieldy governing structure, and in 2007 the member nations signed the Treaty of Lisbon, which streamlined the EU bureaucracy and reformed its political structure. When the Treaty of Lisbon went into effect on December 1, 2009, it capped a remarkable fifty-year effort to unify what had been a deeply divided and war-torn continent. By 2019, with the recent admission of Croatia in 2013, the EU was home to about 500 million citizens in twenty-eight countries. It included most of the former East

Bloc and, with the Baltic nations, three republics of the former Soviet Union. Yet profound questions about the meaning of European unity and identity remained. How would the European Union deal with disruptive membership issues, maintain its democratic ethos in the face of growing right-wing populism, and manage general economic and political crises? We return to these issues later in the chapter.

Supranational Organizations

Beyond the European Union, the trend toward globalization empowered a variety of other supranational organizations that had tremendous reach. National governments still played the leading role in defining and implementing policy, but they increasingly had to take the policies of institutions such as the United Nations and the World Trade Organization into consideration.

The United Nations (UN), established in 1945 after World War II, remains an important player on the world stage. Representatives from all independent countries meet in the UN General Assembly in New York City to try to forge international agreements. UN agencies deal with issues such as world hunger and poverty, and the International Court of Justice in The Hague, Netherlands, hears cases that violate international law. The UN also sends troops in attempts to preserve peace between warring parties—as in Yugoslavia in the 1990s or more recently in Ukraine. While the smaller UN Security Council has broad powers, including the ability to impose sanctions to punish uncooperative states and even to endorse military action, its five permanent members—the United States, Russia, France, Great Britain, and China—can each veto resolutions introduced in that body. The predominance of the United States and western European powers on the Security Council has led some critics to accuse the UN of implementing Western neocolonial policies. Others, including U.S. president Donald Trump, argue that UN policies should never take precedence over national needs, and UN resolutions are at times ignored or downplayed.

Nonprofit international financial institutions have also gained power. Like the United Nations, the World Bank and the International Monetary Fund (IMF) were established in the years following World War II to help rebuild war-torn Europe, and these organizations now provide loans to the developing world. Their funding comes primarily from donations from the United States and western Europe, and they typically extend loans on the condition that recipient countries adopt neoliberal economic reforms, including budget reduction, deregulation, and privatization. In the 1990s the World Bank and the IMF played especially active roles in shaping economic and social policy in the former East Bloc.

The **World Trade Organization (WTO)** is one of the most powerful supranational financial institutions. It sets trade and tariff agreements for over 150 member countries, thus helping manage a large percentage of the world's import-export policies. Like the IMF and the World Bank, the WTO generally promotes neoliberal policies.

Life in the Digital Age

The growing sophistication of rapidly proliferating information technologies has had a profound and rapidly evolving effect on patterns of communications, commerce, and politics. As tiny digital microchips replaced bulky transistors and the Internet grew in scope and popularity, more and more people organized their everyday lives around the use of ever-more-powerful high-tech devices.

Leisure-time pursuits were a case in point. Digital media changed popular forms of entertainment and replaced many physical products. The arrival of cable television, followed swiftly by DVDs and then online video streaming, let individuals watch movies or popular television shows on their personal computers or smartphones at any time. Europe's once-powerful public broadcasting systems, such as the BBC, were forced to compete with a variety of private enterprises, including Netflix, a U.S. online video provider that entered the European media market in 2014. Music downloads and streaming audio files replaced compact discs, vinyl records, and cassettes; digital cameras eliminated the need for expensive film; e-book readers and tablets offered a handheld portable library; and smartphone apps provided an endless variety of conveniences and distractions.

Digitalization and the Internet, which began its rapid expansion in the 1980s, transformed familiar forms of communication in a few short decades. Early in the twenty-first century, the evolution of the cell phone into the smartphone, with its multimedia telecommunications features, hastened the change. The growing popularity of communication tools such as e-mail, text messaging, Facebook, Twitter, Instagram, and other social media changed the way friends, families, and businesses kept in touch. Letters sent on paper became a relic of the past. A variety of chat platforms offered personal computer and smartphone users the ability to engage in virtual face-to-face meetings from any location across the globe. The old-fashioned "landline," connected to a stationary telephone, seemed ready to join the vinyl LP and the handwritten letter in the junk bin of history.

Entire industries were dramatically changed by the emergence of the Internet and the giant tech companies Apple, Google, Facebook, Amazon, and Microsoft. With faster speeds and better online security, people increasingly purchased goods from clothes to computers to groceries on the Web. Online file sharing of books and popular music transformed the publishing and music industries, while massive online retailers such as Amazon and eBay, which sell millions of goods across the globe without physical storefronts, transformed familiar retail systems.

The rapid growth of the Internet and social media raised complex questions related to politics and personal privacy. Individuals and groups could use smartphones and social media sites to organize protest campaigns for social justice. Facebook and Twitter, for example, helped mobilize demonstrators in Egypt during the Arab Spring (see "Turmoil in the Muslim World" later in this chapter). Online platforms also provided a ready means for the spread of hate speech and disinformation of all kinds. A number of authoritarian states from North Korea to Iran to Cuba, recognizing the disruptive powers of the Internet, strictly limited online access.

Governments and Web businesses, such as Facebook and Google, regularly used online tracking systems to amass an extraordinary amount of information on individuals, including political and personal activities; this information could be used in political campaigns or sold for targeted advertising. Hackers also attacked large databases, exposing the private information of millions of people to criminal use. Such abuses of data did not go unchecked. The revelation, for example, that the British consulting firm Cambridge Analytica had acquired the personal data of millions of

Facebook users for use in the U.S. 2016 presidential campaign led to a political scandal and calls for tighter regulation of data collection.

In general, online privacy rules developed along with the Internet and were more stringent in Europe than in the United States, as exemplified by the General Data Protection Regulation instituted by the EU in May 2018. According to this broad mandate, tech companies had to clearly describe their information-gathering practices and their use of private data; the new regulations required Internet users to specifically "opt in" before companies could collect their personal data. In the United States, to the contrary, simply clicking on a link generally exposed personal information to website managers.

The vast amount of information circulating on the Internet also led to the exposure of government and business secrets, with mixed results. The classified U.S. National Security Agency information leaked in 2013 by former CIA contractor Edward Snowden embarrassed U.S. diplomats and fueled debates about Internet surveillance, national security, and privacy protection. The materials posted online by the nonprofit organization WikiLeaks, dedicated to the publication of secret information and news leaks, documented numerous examples of government and corporate misconduct. In the U.S. presidential election of 2016, however, WikiLeaks published e-mails hacked from Hillary Clinton's campaign chairman, leading to accusations of election meddling and ongoing congressional investigations.

The Costs and Consequences of Globalization

Globalization transformed the lives of millions of people, as the technological changes associated with postindustrial society remade workplaces and lifestyles around the world. Widespread adoption of neoliberal free-trade policies and low labor costs in developing countries, including the former East Bloc, Latin America, and East Asia, made it less expensive to manufacture steel, automotive parts, computer components, and all manner of consumer goods in developing countries and then import them for sale in the West.

In the 1990s China, with its low wages and rapidly growing industrial infrastructure, emerged as an economic powerhouse that supplied goods across the world — even as the West's industrial heartlands continued to decline. Under these conditions, a car made by Volkswagen could still be sold as a product of high-quality German engineering despite being assembled in Chattanooga, Tennessee, using steel imported from South Korea and computer chips made in Taiwan.

The outsourcing of manufacturing jobs also dramatically changed the nature of work in western Europe and North America. In France in 1973, for example, some 40 percent of the employed population worked in industry — in mining, construction, manufacturing, and utilities. About 49 percent worked in services, including retail, hotels and restaurants, transportation, communications, financial and business services, and social and personal services. In 2004 only 24 percent of the French worked in industry, and a whopping 72 percent worked in services. The numbers varied country by country, yet across Europe the general trend was clear: by 2016 only about 15 percent of employed workers were still working in the once-booming manufacturing sector; in the United States, less than 9 percent of workers held such jobs.[4]

The deindustrialization of the West established a multitiered society with winners and losers. At the top was a small, affluent group of experts, executives, and professionals—about one-quarter of the total population—who managed the new global enterprises. In the second, larger tier, the middle class struggled with stagnating incomes and a declining standard of living as once-well-paid industrial workers faced stubborn unemployment and cuts in both welfare and workplace benefits. Many were forced to take low-paying jobs in the retail service sector.

In the bottom tier—in some areas as much as a quarter of the population—a poorly paid underclass performed the unskilled jobs of a postindustrial economy or were chronically unemployed. In western Europe and North America, inclusion in this lowest segment of society was often linked to race, ethnicity, and a lack of educational opportunity. Recently arrived immigrants had trouble finding jobs and often lived in unpleasant, hastily built housing, teetering on the edge of poverty. In London, unemployment rates among youths and particularly young black men soared above those of their white compatriots. Frustration over these conditions, coupled with anger at a police shooting, boiled over in immigrant neighborhoods across the city in August 2011, when angry youths rioted in the streets, burning buildings and looting stores.

Antiglobalization Activism French protesters carry the figure of Ronald McDonald through the streets to protest the trial of José Bové, a prominent leader in campaigns against the human and environmental costs associated with globalization. Bové was accused of demolishing a McDonald's franchise in a small town in southern France. With its worldwide fast-food restaurants that pay little attention to local traditions, McDonald's has often been the target of antiglobalization protests. (Witt/Haley/Sipa)

A similar wave of riots broke out in the multiethnic immigrant suburbs of Stockholm, Sweden, in May 2013, spurred by growing economic inequality and discrimination, and in late 2018 protests by so-called Yellow Vests brought street violence to cities across France over economic problems facing the working and middle classes. Police powers generally brought such unrest under control, and while parliamentarians recognized that poverty, unemployment, and perceived racism inspired unrest, they struggled to find solutions to problems generated by large-scale economic trends.

Geographic contrasts further revealed the unequal aspects of globalization. Urban redevelopment turned the downtown cores of major Western cities into consumerist playgrounds and work centers that only the wealthy could afford to live in, while poorer residents were pushed far out into the suburbs. Regions in the United States and Europe that had successfully shifted to a postindustrial economy, such as Silicon Valley or northern Italy and southern Germany and Austria, enjoyed prosperity. Lagging behind were regions historically dependent on heavy industry, such as the former East Bloc countries and the factory districts north of London, or underdeveloped areas, such as rural sections of southern Italy, Spain, and Greece. In addition, a global north-south divide increasingly separated Europe and North America—both still affluent despite their economic problems—from the industrializing nations of Africa and Latin America. Though India, China, and other East Asian nations experienced solid growth, other industrializing nations struggled to overcome decades of underdevelopment.

How is growing ethnic diversity changing contemporary Europe?

The ethnic makeup of European communities shifted dramatically in the early twenty-first century. Western Europe's remarkable decline in birthrates seemed to predict a shrinking and aging population in the future, yet the peaceful, wealthy European Union attracted rapidly growing numbers of refugees and immigrants from the former Soviet Union and East Bloc, North Africa, and the Middle East. The unexpected arrival of so many newcomers raised perplexing questions about ethnic diversity and the costs and benefits of multiculturalism.

The Prospect of Population Decline

In 2019 population rates were still growing rapidly in many poor countries but not in the world's industrialized nations. In 2000 families in developed countries had only 1.6 children on average; only in the United States did families have, almost exactly, the 2.1 children necessary to maintain a stable population. In Europe, where birthrates had been falling since the 1950s, national fertility rates ranged from 1.2 to 1.8 children per woman of childbearing age. By 2013 Italy and Ireland, once known for large Catholic families, had each achieved one of Europe's lowest birthrates—a mere 1.3 babies per woman. None of the twenty-eight countries in the EU had birthrates above 2.0; the average fertility rate was about 1.55 children per woman.[5]

If the current baby bust continues, the long-term consequences could be dramatic, though hardly predictable. At the least, Europe's population would decline and age. For example, total German population, barring much greater immigration, would gradually decline from about 83 million in 2019 to about 66 million around 2050.[6] The number of people of working age would fall, and because of longer life spans, nearly a third of the population would be over sixty. Social security taxes paid by the shrinking labor force would need to soar to meet the skyrocketing costs of pensions and health care for seniors—a recipe for generational conflict. As the premier of Bavaria, Germany's biggest state, has warned, the prospect of demographic decline is a "ticking time bomb under our social welfare system and entire economy."[7]

Why, in times of peace, did Europeans fail to reproduce? Studies showed that European women and men in their twenties, thirties, and early forties still wanted two or even three children—like their parents. But unlike their parents, young couples did not achieve their ideal family size. Many women postponed the birth of their first child into their thirties in order to finish their education and establish careers. Then, finding that balancing a child and a career was more difficult than anticipated, new mothers tended to postpone and eventually forgo having a second child. The better educated and the more economically successful a woman was, the more likely she was to have just one child or no children at all. The uneven, uninspiring European economic conditions since the mid-1970s also played a role. High unemployment fell heavily on young people, especially after the recession of 2008, convincing youths to delay settling down and having children.

By 2013 some population experts concluded that European birthrates had stabilized, though women continued to postpone having children. Moreover, the frightening economic implications of dramatic population decline emerged as a major public issue. Opinion leaders, politicians, and the media started to advocate for larger families and propose policies to provide more support for families with children. Europeans may yet respond with enough vigor to reverse their population decline and avoid societal crisis.

Changing Immigration Flows

As European demographic vitality waned in the 1990s, a new surge of migrants from the former Soviet bloc, Africa, and most recently the Middle East headed for western Europe. Some migrants entered the European Union legally, with proper documentation, but undocumented or irregular immigration into the European Union also exploded, as increasing numbers of people were smuggled in despite beefed-up border patrols. Large-scale immigration, both documented and undocumented, emerged as a critical and controversial issue.

The collapse of communism in the East Bloc and savage civil wars in Yugoslavia drove hundreds of thousands of refugees westward in the 1990s, as did equally brutal conflicts in Somalia and Rwanda. More recently, immigration flows have shifted to reflect the dislocation that emerged in North Africa and the Middle East in the wake of the U.S.-led invasions of Afghanistan and Iraq, the "Arab Spring" of 2011, and the war against the Islamic State (see "Turmoil in the Muslim World" later in the chapter). Smugglers with a callous disregard for the well-being of their charges demanded thousands of euros to bring undocumented migrants from these troubled regions across the Mediterranean to Greece, Spain, and Italy.

In the summer of 2015, during the height of the Syrian civil war, the migration issue reached crisis proportions. Counting irregular migrants is always difficult, but estimates suggest that in 2015–2016 more than 2.3 million people, mostly from Syria and Iraq, illegally entered the European Union. Many traveled across Turkey and crossed the Mediterranean Sea to the relatively accessible Greek islands. From there they passed through Serbia into Hungary and then struggled to travel north into more hospitable Austria, Germany, and northern Europe. Others continued to enter the EU from North Africa into Italy or Spain (Map 30.4).

When in 2015 Germany's first woman chancellor Angela Merkel (r. 2005–) responded to the crisis by promising homes for 800,000 migrants and encouraged other EU nations to take a share, tens of thousands of migrants trying to reach Germany choked train and bus stations on the Hungarian-Austrian border. Others languished in quickly established refugee camps built in northern Greece and the Hungarian countryside, and Hungary's anti-immigrant government quickly built a 108-mile razor-wire fence along the border with Serbia to squelch further movement.

The discovery of seventy-one dead migrants locked in an abandoned truck on an Austrian highway — and the deaths of thousands more who in the last several years attempted to cross the Mediterranean in rudimentary rubber rafts and leaky boats — underscored the venality of the smugglers and the human costs of uncontrolled immigration. However, EU experts estimate that in 2017 the number of irregular migrants entering the EU dropped to 204,719 and would continue to drop. Stricter border controls, the growth of popular anti-immigration sentiment across western Europe, and the election of far-right anti-immigrant governments in Hungary and Italy, which moved to close their national borders, accounted for much of the decline. Nonetheless, European leaders were still struggling to contain the humanitarian crisis and the political fallout caused by the largest movement of peoples across Europe since the end of World War II.[8]

Why was Europe such an attractive destination for non-European migrants? First, economic opportunity in relatively prosperous western Europe undoubtedly was one attraction. Germans, for example, earned on average three and a half times more than neighboring Poles, who in turn earned much more than people farther east and in North Africa. In 1998 most European Union states abolished all border controls; entrance into one country allowed for unimpeded travel almost anywhere (though Ireland and the United Kingdom opted out of this agreement). This meant that irregular migrants could enter across the relatively lax borders of Greece and south-central Europe and then move north across the continent in search of refuge and jobs. And because Europe was simply closer to the troubled regions of North Africa and the Middle East than other wealthy countries such as the United States or Japan, it was an "easier" and more accessible destination for desperate migrants.

Second, EU immigration policy offered migrants the possibility of acquiring asylum status if they could demonstrate that they faced severe persecution based on race, nationality, religion, political belief, or membership in a specific social group in their home countries. Many migrants turned to Europe as they fled civil wars in North Africa and the Middle East, as well as poverty and political repression in other parts of Africa. The rules for attaining asylum status varied by nation, though Germany and Sweden offered relatively liberal policies, housing for applicants, and relatively high benefit payments — about $425 per month per adult.

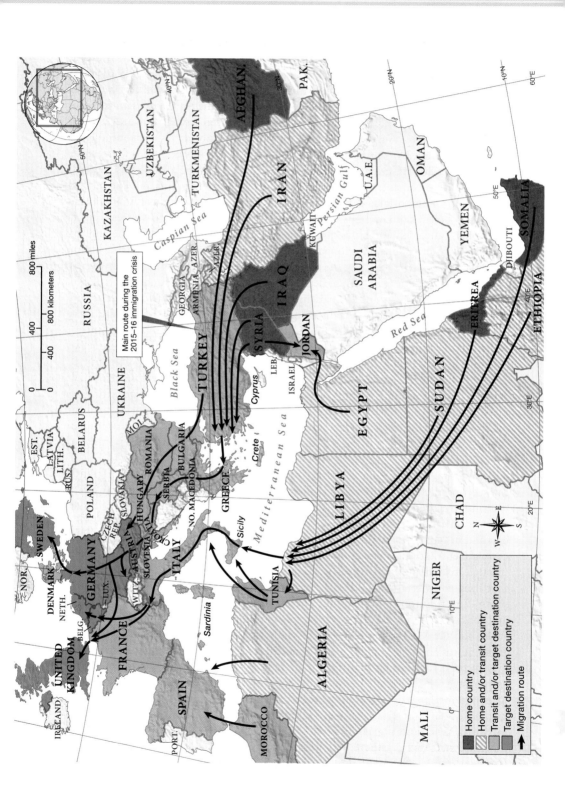

Main route during the 2015–16 immigration crisis

800 miles

800 kilometers

Legend:
- Home country
- Home and/or transit country
- Transit and/or target destination country
- Target destination country
- Migration route

Across Europe asylum regulations were nonetheless restrictive. Though numerous migrants applied, after an average fifteen-month wait many were rejected, classified as illegal job seekers, and deported to their home countries. The acceptance rate varied broadly across the different countries in the EU, but the total numbers for 2017 offer some insight into the general plight of the refugees. That year EU countries evaluated about 1 million asylum applications and granted about 538,000 people protected residency status. These numbers reflected a downward trend from the peak crisis in 2015, but were still far above the approximately 200,000 people who sought asylum in the EU in 2006.[9]

Toward a Multicultural Continent

By 2019 immigration had profoundly changed the ethnic makeup of the European continent, though the effects were unevenly distributed. One way to measure the effect of these new immigrants is to consider the rapid rise of their numbers. Since the 1960s the foreign population of western European nations has grown by two to ten times. In the Netherlands in 1960, only 1 percent of the population was foreign-born. In 2017 the foreign born made up 12 percent. Over the same years the proportion of foreign-born residents grew from 1.2 percent to almost 15 percent in Germany and from 4.7 percent to 12.2 percent in France. In 2017 non-natives constituted about 10 percent of the population, on average, across Europe — though they typically constituted a far smaller share of the former East Bloc nations.[10] For centuries the number of foreigners living in Europe had been relatively small. Now, permanently displaced ethnic groups, or diasporas, brought ethnic diversity to the continent.

The new immigrants were divided into two main groups. A small number of highly trained specialists found work in the upper ranks of education, business, and high-tech industries. Engineers from English-speaking India, for example, could land jobs in international computer companies. Most immigrants, however, had little access to high-quality education or language training, which limited their employment opportunities and made integration more difficult. They often lived in separate city districts marked by poor housing and crowded conditions, which set them apart from more established residents. Districts of London were home to tens of thousands of immigrants from the former colonies, and in Paris North Africans dominated some working-class suburbs.

< MAP 30.4 **Major Migration Routes into Contemporary Europe**
In the wake of wars and the collapse of the Arab Spring, migration from northern Africa and the Middle East into Europe reached crisis proportions. Aided by smugglers, thousands of migrants traveled two main routes: through Libya and across the Mediterranean Sea into southern Italy, and across Turkey to close-by Greek islands and then north through the Balkans. Countries with relatively lenient refugee regulations, such as Sweden and Germany, were favorite destinations. Under the Schengen Agreement, the EU's open-border policy made travel through Europe fairly easy. As the number of migrants increased in the fall of 2015 and the spring of 2016, however, European politicians began to close national borders, and many migrants were stranded in quickly built refugee camps.

Europe's Refugee Crisis   A Kurdish refugee family from northern Iraq seeks shelter in May 2018 in a refugee camp in Thessaloniki, Greece. People in the camp complained about lack of food, water, and a secure place to sleep. At the height of the refugee crisis in the fall and early winter of 2015–2016, about five thousand refugees reached Europe each day. While the number of migrants has declined, the crisis stoked anti-immigrant tensions across Europe and called into question the internal open-border system. (NurPhoto/Getty Images)

The **multiculturalism** associated with ethnic diversity inspired a variety of new cultural forms, as native and foreign traditions transformed European life-styles. Recipes and cooks from former colonies in North Africa enlivened French cooking, while the döner kebab — the Turkish version of a gyro sandwich — became Germany's "native" fast food. Indian restaurants proliferated across Britain, and controversy raged when the British foreign minister announced in 2001 that chicken tikka masala — a spicy Indian stew — was Great Britain's new national dish.[11] Multiculturalism also inspired a rich variety of works in literature, film, and the fine arts; from rap to reggae to rai, it had a profound effect on popular music, a medium with a huge audience.

The growth of immigration and ethnic diversity created vital social and cultural interactions and goods but also generated controversy and conflict. In most EU nations, immigrants can become full citizens if they meet certain legal qualifications; adopting the culture of the host country is not a requirement. This legal process has raised questions about who, exactly, could or should be European and about the way these new citizens might change European society. The idea that cultural and ethnic diversity could be a force for vitality and creativity has run counter to deep-seated beliefs about national homogeneity and unity, particularly among political conservatives. Some commentators accused the newcomers of taking jobs and welfare benefits from unemployed native Europeans, especially in times of economic decline.

Europe and Its Muslim Population

General concerns with migration often fused with concerns about Muslim migrants and Muslim residents who have grown up in Europe. Islam is now the largest minority religion in Europe. The EU's 15 to 20 million Muslims outnumber Catholics in Europe's mainly Protestant north, and they outnumber Protestants in Europe's Catholic south. Major cities have substantial Muslim minorities, who make up about 25 percent of the population in Marseilles and Rotterdam, 15 percent in Brussels, and 10 percent in Paris, Copenhagen, and London.[12]

Worries increased after the September 11, 2001, al-Qaeda attack on New York's World Trade Center and the subsequent war in Iraq. A string of terrorist attacks in Europe organized by Islamist extremists heightened anxieties. In March 2004, radical Moroccan Muslims living in Spain exploded bombs planted on trains bound for Madrid, killing 191 commuters and wounding 1,800 more. A year later, an attack on the London transit system carried out by British citizens of Pakistani descent killed over 50 people. Since then, a number of attacks have kept Islamist terrorism in the public eye—including the murderous January 2015 assault on the staff of the satiric French magazine *Charlie Hebdo*, which had published cartoons critical of the Prophet Muhammad, and the even more deadly attacks in Paris in November 2015, when extremists motivated by the ideologies of the Islamic State killed 130 people.

The vast majority of Europe's Muslims supported democracy and rejected violent extremism, but these spectacular attacks and other assaults by Islamist militants nonetheless sharpened the debate over immigration. Security was not the only issue. Critics across the political spectrum warned that Europe's rapidly growing Muslim population posed a dire threat to the West's liberal tradition, which embraced freedom of thought, representative government, toleration, separation of church and state, and, more recently, equal rights for women and gays. Islamist extremists and radical clerics living in Europe, critics proclaimed, rejected these fundamental Western values and preached the supremacy of Islamic laws for Europe's Muslims. Secular Europeans struggled to understand the depths of Muslim spirituality. French attempts to enforce a ban on wearing the hijab (the headscarf worn by many faithful Muslim women) in public schools expressed the tension between Western secularism and Islamic religiosity on a most personal level and evoked outrage and protests in the Muslim community.

As busy mosques came to outnumber dying churches in European cities, anti-immigrant, nationalist politicians exploited widespread doubts that immigrant populations from Muslim countries would ever assimilate into Western culture. Time was on the side of Euro-Islam, far-right critics warned. Europe's Muslim population, estimated at about 26 million in 2016, appeared likely to increase rapidly in the next several decades. Population rates are difficult to predict, but one recent account suggests that in 2050 the share of Muslims in Europe's total population could range from 11 to 14 percent, with the highest percentages in Sweden, Germany, France, and the United Kingdom and much smaller numbers in Spain and east-central Europe.[13]

Liberal pundits and politicians admitted that Islamist extremism could pose problems, but they emphasized the potential benefits of long-term integration of non-Western, Muslim residents. They argued that Europe badly needed newcomers to limit the impending population decline, boost social benefit budgets, and provide valuable technical skills. Some asserted that Europe should recognize that Islam has for centuries been a vital part of European life and culture and that mutual respect might help head off the resentment that can drive a tiny minority to separatism and acts of terror.

Liberal commentators also emphasized the role of economics and cultural discrimination as the root cause of terrorist activity. Although the first generation of Muslim migrants had found jobs as unskilled workers in Europe's great postwar boom, they and their children had been hard hit after 1973 by the general economic downturn and the decline of manufacturing. Offered only modest welfare benefits and limited access to education or housing, many second- and third-generation Muslim immigrants felt like outcasts in their adopted countries. To liberal observers, economics and discrimination had more influence on immigrants' attitudes about their host communities than did religion and extremist teachings. Liberals thus criticized anti-immigrant, anti-Muslim discrimination and its racist overtones.

What challenges will Europeans face in the coming decades?

Beyond Russia's interference in former Soviet territories, uncontrolled immigration, and radical Islamic terrorism, European societies faced a number of other interconnected challenges that posed long-term challenges, including growing differences between the United States and Europe, turmoil in the Muslim world, economic recession, the unity of the Eurozone, and environmental degradation. At the same time, the relative wealth of European societies provoked serious thinking about European identity and Europe's humanitarian mission in the community of nations.

Growing Strains in U.S.-European Relations

In the fifty years after World War II, the United States and western Europe generally maintained close diplomatic relations. Although they were never in total agreement, they usually worked together to promote international consensus, typically under U.S. guidance, as in the NATO alliance. For example, a U.S.-led coalition that included thousands of troops from France and the United Kingdom and smaller contributions from other NATO allies attacked Iraqi forces in Kuwait in the 1990–1991 Persian Gulf War, freeing the small nation from attempted annexation by Iraqi dictator Saddam Hussein. Over time, however, the growing power of the European Union and the new unilateral thrust of Washington's foreign policy created strains in traditional transatlantic relations.

The growing gap between the United States and Europe had several causes. For one, the European Union was now the world's largest trading block, challenging the predominance of the United States. Prosperous European businesses invested heavily in the United States, reversing a decades-long economic relationship in which investment dollars had flowed the other way.

A values gap between the United States and Europe likewise contributed to cooler relations. Ever more secular Europeans had a hard time understanding the intense religiosity of many Americans; in a 2017 survey 76 percent of people identifying as Christians in the United States "believe[d] in God with absolute certainty," compared to 23 percent in western Europe.[14] Relatively lax gun control laws and the use of capital punishment in the United States were viewed with dismay in Europe, where most countries had outlawed private handgun ownership and abolished the death penalty. Despite U.S. president Barack Obama's health-care reforms—which evoked controversy among Americans—U.S. reluctance to establish a single-payer, state-funded program surprised Europeans, who saw their own programs as highly advantageous.

In addition, under Presidents George W. Bush (U.S. pres. 2001–2009), Barack Obama (U.S. pres. 2009–2017), and Donald Trump (U.S. pres. 2017–), the United States often ignored international opinion and policy in pursuit of its own interests. This trend had been escalating at least since 1997, when, citing the economic impact, Washington refused to ratify the Kyoto Protocol intended to limit global warming; nearly two hundred countries had already signed off. Nor did the United States join the International Criminal Court, a global tribunal founded in 2002 that prosecutes individuals accused of crimes against humanity, and which nearly 140 states agreed to join. These positions troubled EU leaders, as did unflagging U.S. support for Israel in the ongoing Palestinian-Israeli crisis.

President Trump's policies of "America First" opened further rifts in U.S.-European relations. Trump announced in June 2017 that the United States would withdraw from the Paris Agreement, intended to control climate change, and his willingness to set tariffs on European imports upset familiar patterns of international trade. When criticized, the American president tweeted blistering attacks on European politicians, including German chancellor Angela Merkel and French president Emmanuel Macron (r. 2017–), which only served to further widen the rift.

Military considerations also undermined the close relationship between the United States and Europe. American-led wars in Afghanistan and Iraq, undertaken in response to the September 11 terrorist attacks against the United States, were a source of strain. On the morning of September 11, 2001, passenger planes hijacked by terrorists destroyed the World Trade Center towers in New York City and crashed into the Pentagon. Perpetrated by the radical Islamist group al-Qaeda, the attacks took the lives of more than three thousand people from many countries and put the personal safety of ordinary citizens at the top of the West's agenda.

Immediately after the September 11 attacks, the peoples and governments of Europe and the world joined Americans in heartfelt solidarity. Over time, however, tensions between Europe and the United States re-emerged and deepened markedly, particularly after President Bush declared a unilateral U.S. **war on terror**—a determined effort to fight terrorism in all its forms around the world. The main acts in Bush's war on terror were a U.S.-led war in Afghanistan, which started in 2001 and continues today, and another in Iraq, which lasted from 2003 to 2011. Both succeeded in quickly bringing down dictatorial regimes, but the wars fomented anti-Western sentiment in the Muslim world and failed to stop regional violence driven by ethnic and religious differences.

The U.S. invasion of Iraq and subsequent events caused some European leaders, notably in France and Germany, to question the rationale for and indeed the very effectiveness of a "war" on terror. Military victory, even over rogue states, would hardly end terrorism, since terrorist groups easily moved across national borders. Terrorism, they concluded, was better fought through police and intelligence measures. Europeans certainly shared U.S. worries about stability in the Middle East, and they faced their own problems with Islamist terrorist attacks. But European leaders worried that the tactics used in the Iraq War, exemplified by Washington's readiness to use its military without international agreements or UN backing, violated international law.

The presidency of Barack Obama brought some improvement to U.S.-European foreign relations. Upon election, Obama announced that he would halt deployment of missiles in central Europe and reduce nuclear arms, easing tensions with Russia. He pulled U.S. troops out of Iraq in 2011 and quietly shelved the language of the "war on terror."

Tensions over military issues renewed under President Trump, however, as he repeatedly derided NATO as an obsolete alliance and pressured European members to do more to support NATO budgets. As the EU expanded and U.S. support appeared increasingly tentative, some argued that Europe should determine its own military and defense policy without U.S. or NATO guidance. Although transatlantic ties remained firm, the United States and Europe seemed poised to move further apart, especially during the Trump presidency.

Turmoil in the Muslim World

Over the past decade, civil wars, sectarian terrorist attacks, civilian dislocation and misery, and flagging political and economic stability have shaken much of the Muslim world in North Africa and the Middle East. In many ways, these problems were the results of recent historical events. Yet the turmoil in North Africa and the Middle East had a deeper history that included the legacies of European colonialism, Cold War power plays, and the ongoing Palestinian-Israeli conflict.

Radical political Islam, a mixture of traditional religious beliefs and innovative social and political reform ideas, emerged in the 1920s, in part as an expression of resentment against the foreign control associated with the mandate system established in the Middle East after World War I (see Chapter 25). Islamist groups like the Muslim Brotherhood, founded in Egypt in 1928, gained support in the following decades. While the broad spectrum of Islamist ideas is difficult to summarize, adherents tended to fall into two main groups: a moderate or centrist group that worked peacefully to reform society within existing institutions, and a much smaller, more militant minority willing to use violence to achieve its goals.

Decolonization, the Cold War, and the ongoing Palestinian-Israeli conflict sharpened anti-Western and particularly anti-U.S. sentiments among radical Islamists. As the western European powers loosened their ties to the Middle East, the Americans stepped in. Applying containment policy to limit the spread of communism and eager to preserve steady supplies of oil, the United States supported secular, authoritarian regimes friendly to U.S. interests in Egypt, Saudi Arabia, Iran, and elsewhere. Such regimes were generally unpopular with faithful Muslims.

U.S. policies in the Middle East produced "blowback," or unforeseen and unintended consequences. One example was the Iranian revolution of 1979, when Islamist radicals antagonized by Western intervention, state corruption, and secularization overthrew the U.S.-supported shah and established an Islamic republic. The successful revolution encouraged militant Islamists elsewhere, as did the example of the mujahideen, the Muslim guerrilla fighters in Afghanistan who successfully fought off the Soviet army from 1979 to 1989. During that conflict, the United States supplied the mujahideen with military aid as part of Cold War containment policies, but this support also generated blowback. Many of the U.S.-armed mujahideen would go on to support the Taliban, a militant Islamist faction that came to rule Afghanistan in 1996. The Taliban established a strict Islamist state based on shari'a law. They denied women's right to education, banned Western movies and music, and provided a safe haven for the Saudi-born millionaire Osama bin Laden and the al-Qaeda terrorist network.

During the 1990s the United States, along with western Europe, became the main target for Islamist militants angered by Western intervention in the Middle East; al-Qaeda's attack on the World Trade Center was one tragic result. Afterwards President Bush declared with some justification that bin Laden and the terrorists "hate our freedoms: our freedom of religion, our freedom of speech, our freedom to vote."[15] In public calls for jihad (or struggle) against the United States and the West, however, bin Laden offered a more pragmatic list of grievances, including U.S. support for Israel in the Israeli-Palestinian crisis, the sanctions on Iraq that followed the Persian Gulf War, and the presence of U.S. military bases in Saudi Arabia — seen as an insult to the Muslim holy sites in Mecca and Medina.[16]

The Bush administration hoped that the invasions of Afghanistan and Iraq would end the terrorist attacks and bring peace and democracy to the Middle East, but both brought chaos instead. The military campaign in Afghanistan quickly achieved one of its goals, bringing down the Taliban, and the United States installed a friendly government. But U.S. troops failed to disable al-Qaeda, and Taliban insurgents mounted a determined and lasting guerrilla war. Although U.S. commandos killed Osama bin Laden in Pakistan in May 2011, the apparently unwinnable guerrilla war in Afghanistan became increasingly unpopular in the United States and among NATO allies in Europe.

With heavy fighting still under way in Afghanistan in late 2001, the Bush administration turned its attention to Saddam Hussein's Iraq, arguing that it was necessary to expand the war on terror to other hostile regimes in the Middle East. U.S. leaders justified their attack with charges that Saddam Hussein was still developing weapons of mass destruction in flagrant disregard of his 1991 promise to end all such programs. Some Americans shared the widespread doubts held by Europeans about the legality — and wisdom — of an American attack on Iraq, especially after UN inspectors found no weapons of mass destruction in the country. Even though they failed to win UN approval, in March 2003 the United States and Britain, with token support from a handful of other European states, invaded Iraq.

The invasion quickly overwhelmed the Iraqi army, and Saddam's dictatorship collapsed in April. Yet America's subsequent efforts to establish a stable pro-American Iraq proved difficult. Poor postwar planning and management by administration officials was one factor, but there were others. Iraq, a creation of Western imperialism after the First World War, was a fragile state with three distinct groups: non-Arab Kurds, Arab Sunni Muslims, and Arab Shi'ite Muslims. Sectarian conflicts among these groups led to a protracted civil war. Although the Obama administration felt confident enough to withdraw U.S. forces in 2011, the shaky Iraqi government continued to struggle with ethnic divisions and terrorist violence.

In early 2011 an unexpected chain of events that came to be called the **Arab Spring** further destabilized the Middle East and North Africa. In a provincial town in Tunisia, a poor fruit vendor set himself on fire to protest official harassment. His death eighteen days later unleashed a series of spontaneous mass protests that brought violence and regime change; six weeks later, Tunisia's authoritarian president fled the country, opening the way for reform. Massive popular demonstrations calling for democratic government and social tolerance broke out across the Middle East. In Egypt, demonstrators forced the resignation of President Hosni Mubarak, a U.S.-friendly leader who had ruled for thirty years. An armed uprising in Libya, supported by NATO air strikes, brought down the dictatorial government of Muammar Gaddafi that October. A civil war broke out in Syria in July 2011 as Libyan president Bashar al-Assad (elected 2000), with Russian support, hurled his army at the rebels and Western powers disagreed about what to do. Protests arose in other countries in the region as well, evoking a mixed response of repression and piecemeal reform.

As the popular movements inspired by the Arab Spring faltered, the emergence of the **Islamic State** (sometimes called IS or ISIS) brought insurgent violence to new heights. The Islamic State, an extremist Islamist militia dedicated to the establishment of a new caliphate to unify Muslims around the world, grew out of al-Qaeda and the various other insurgent groups fighting in Iraq and the Syrian civil war. By summer 2015 IS soldiers had taken control of substantial parts of central Syria and Iraq. Over 4 million Syrians and Iraqis lost their homes during the fighting, and hundreds of thousands streamed north in attempts to find asylum in Europe.

In the territories under their control, IS militants set up a terroristic government based on an extremist reading of shari'a law. Islamic State terror tactics included the violent persecution of sectarian religious groups; mass executions and beheadings of military, political, or sectarian enemies; and the "cultural cleansing" (destruction and looting) of ancient cultural monuments and shrines that failed to meet its stringent religious ideals. All these actions were documented in widespread Internet propaganda campaigns intended to demonstrate IS power and entice recruits.

By early 2019, as this was being written, the U.S. military and its allies had defeated the Islamic State in the field, yet the militant group could still mount isolated terrorist attacks across the globe, and much of the Middle East was still struggling to find peace and stability. The Arab Spring seemed, for the most part, a dismal failure. The young activists who sought greater political and social liberties from authoritarian regimes quickly lost control of the changes they unleashed. Multiple players now vied for power: military leaders and old elites, local chieftains representing ethnic or sectarian interests, and moderate and radical Islamists. In Egypt, the first open elections in decades brought to power representatives of the moderate wing of the Muslim Brotherhood; a year later, military leaders overthrew this elected government. In Libya, Syria, and especially Yemen, persistent civil wars undermined the search for stability. Western policymakers grappled in vain for clear and effective ways to help bring order to the region. Their efforts were especially freighted because problems in the Muslim world were at the center of many of Europe's problems. These included the immigration emergency of 2015–2016, ongoing Islamist terrorist attacks, and the disastrous human rights crisis faced by millions of Middle East residents.

The Global Recession and the Viability of the European Union

While chaos in the Muslim world caused great concern in the West, economic crisis shattered growth and political unity in Europe and North America. In 2008 the United States entered a deep recession, caused by the burst of the housing boom, bank failures, and an overheated financial securities market. The U.S. government spent massive sums to recharge the economy, giving banks, insurance agencies, auto companies, and financial services conglomerates billions of dollars in federal aid. By 2012 the economy had improved and much of the housing market had recovered, though some critics claimed that income inequality was higher than ever.

The 2008 recession swept into other parts of the world and across Europe, where a housing bubble, high national deficits, and a weak bond market made the crisis particularly acute. One of the first countries affected, and one of the hardest hit, was Iceland, where the currency and banking system collapsed outright. Other countries followed — Ireland and Latvia made deep and painful cuts in government spending to balance national budgets. By 2010 Britain was deeply in debt, and Spain, Portugal, and especially Greece were close to bankruptcy.

This sudden "euro crisis" put the very existence of the Eurozone in question. The common currency grouped together countries with vastly divergent economies. Germany and France, the zone's two strongest economies, felt pressure to provide financial support to ensure the stability of far weaker countries, including Greece and Portugal. They did so with strings attached: recipients of EU support were required to reduce deficits through austerity measures. Even so, the transfer of monies within the Eurozone angered the citizens of wealthier countries, who felt they were being asked to subsidize countries in financial difficulties of their own making. Such feelings were particularly powerful in Germany, encouraging Chancellor Merkel to move cautiously in providing financial stimulus to troubled Eurozone economies.

The difficulty dealing with the stubborn Greek debt crisis prompted debates about the viability of a single currency for nations with vastly different economies as well as widespread speculation that the Eurozone might fall apart. In 2010 and 2012 Greece received substantial bailouts from the IMF, the European Common Bank, and the European Union (the so-called Troika). In return for loans and some debt relief, Greek leaders were required to implement a painful austerity plan — which meant raising taxes, privatizing state-owned businesses, reforming labor markets, and drastically reducing government spending on employee wages, pensions, and other popular social benefits. Greek unemployment hit a record 25 percent in 2012, and more than half of young adults lacked jobs. Rampant joblessness meant declining tax revenues, and the Greek economy continued to weaken. As the government cut popular social programs, demonstrators took to the streets to protest declining living standards and the lack of work; in Athens, protests large and small were almost a daily occurrence.

The 2015 Greek elections brought the left-wing, populist Syriza Party to power. Syriza promised voters a tough stand against the Troika's fiscal demands and an end to austerity, yet Troika negotiators, led by Germany, maintained an uncompromising line: if Greece failed to meet its debt payments, it would be forced into a "Grexit" (a Greek exit from the Eurozone). Syriza backtracked and accepted further auster-ity measures in return for yet another bailout loan. Among other conditions, Greek leaders promised to sell off about 50 billion euros' worth of government-owned property, including airports, power plants and energy assets, roads and railroads, and the national post office.

Even as the Greek crisis shook European unity, in June 2016 residents of the United Kingdom narrowly voted to leave the EU altogether. The campaign for the referendum on **Brexit** (the informal name for the British exit from the EU) was intense, with populists on the right promising "Leavers" autonomy from the EU's economic and trade ties and freedom from the EU's relatively open immigration policies. The victory of those wanting out showed that many Brits did not want "Eurocrats" in Brussels intruding on national policy. Prime Minister David Cameron (r. 2010–2016) resigned and was replaced by Prime Minister Theresa May, who struggled with divisions in her own Tory (Conservative) Party over the best way to leave the EU. Standout issues included the right of EU residents to freely cross into the United Kingdom, the ability to preserve existing or make new trade deals, and the open border between Ireland and Northern Ireland. Although May and

"Stop Tory Brexit" Anti-Brexit campaigners unfurled a banner in front of the British Houses of Parliament in November 2018, protesting the Brexit deal negotiated by Tory (or Conservative Party) prime minister Theresa May and European Union leaders earlier that month. The protesters insisted that "Another Europe Is Possible" and demanded "Free Movement for All," a key EU policy that allows anyone in twenty-six EU countries (the so-called Schengen Area) to cross national borders without passports or other controls. Under the terms of Brexit, residents of the United Kingdom would be cut off from the EU free-trade zone and would no longer enjoy the right to open borders, among other changes. (Adrian Dennis/Getty Images)

EU representatives negotiated a tentative agreement on these and other issues in November 2018, the British Parliament voted overwhelmingly to reject the deal in January 2019. May was allowed to delay the U.K.'s departure, but the outcome of Brexit and its effects on the EU remained hard to predict.

The New Populism

As the material presented throughout this chapter suggests, one of the most significant aspects of Western politics after the turn of the century was the emergence of new forms of political populism in Europe and the United States. Populism, currently identified in the United States with President Donald Trump, is typically based on an appeal to the needs and virtues of ordinary people, who stand in determined opposition to a corrupt or exploitative elite and the broad effects of globalization.

In the 2000s powerful populist voices and political parties emerged on both sides of the political spectrum. On the left, the Greek Syriza Party, with its challenge to EU austerity policies, calls for increased public investment, and celebration of the ordinary worker, exemplified left-populism in Europe. In the United States leftist populism found expression in the Occupy movement, which began in the United States in 2011 and quickly spread to over eighty countries. Although the Occupy movement fizzled out, its condemnation of a tiny wealthy elite (the "1 percent") who supposedly exploited the vast majority of ordinary people inspired the surprisingly successful 2016 U.S. presidential campaign of Senator Bernie Sanders.

The new populism has had a greater impact on the politics of the far right. In the United States, New York businessman Donald Trump rode a wave of populist sentiment to win the presidency in 2016, surprising pollsters and complacent Democrats alike. Drawing on themes articulated by the Tea Party, which emerged in 2009, Trump's winning platform called for an end to oppressive taxation, strong immigration controls, the relaxation of government regulation of the economy and environment, support for fading rustbelt industries and jobs, and a foreign policy that put "America First."

In Europe, although far-right populist parties, including the French Popular Front and the Austrian Freedom Party, had already enjoyed electoral success in the 1990s, right-wing populism has grown dramatically in recent decades. European populists typically oppose membership in the European Union and the Eurozone. They champion nationalism, demand an end to immigration and tolerant refugee policies, and decry the growth of Islam in Europe. Whatever the cause, the number of Europeans voting for populists on the left and the right swelled from 7 percent in 2000 to over 25 percent in 2018.[17]

In Germany, for example, tens of thousands of people joined the anti-immigrant movement called Pegida (Patriotic Europeans Against the Islamization of the West) or the Alternative for Germany, a far-right political party that won impressive electoral gains in 2018. In Britain, an upstart populist movement including far-right members of the Tory Party successfully campaigned for Brexit. In both Italy and Austria, government coalitions in 2019 included populist parties. In the former East Bloc, right-wing populism has been especially strong: in 2018, populist, authoritarian governments ruled Poland and Hungary, where they worked to undermine freedom of the press and judicial independence.

Far-right populist success has been aided by bigotry and widespread misconceptions about immigration and the nature of Muslim faith. For example, recent polls show that Europeans routinely overestimate the number of Muslims in Europe. In France the public believes that 31 percent of the population is Muslim, when the actual number is about 8 percent; the British believe that 21 percent of the population is Muslim, when the actual number is only 5 percent.[18] Immigration and the supposed "Islamization" of Europe, along with fundamentalist terrorism, have become highly charged political issues, and conservative and far-right pundits and politicians across Europe offer a variety of diagnoses and solutions to these perceived problems.

As the political fringe grows in power, support for traditional centrist parties has shrunk, remaking the political structures that emerged in the post–World War II decade. Center-right parties certainly suffered, but the real losers have been Europe's social democratic parties. In fall 2018, center-left social democrats were included in only six governments in the twenty-eight EU member states. In 2017 the center-left French Socialist Party received just 7.4 percent in national elections, and the Dutch Labour Party won 5.7 percent. That same year Germany's once-mighty Social Democrats received just over 20 percent of the vote in the national elections, only one-half of what they won in 1998.[19] The outcome of these trends remains unclear. Yet the consensus politics shaped around neoliberal socioeconomic policies, state-sponsored benefits, multiculturalism and (relatively) open borders, and the EU project itself—embraced by center-left and center-right parties alike—no longer had much appeal to voters shaken by sweeping social change, economic stagnation, and mass migration.

Dependence on Fossil Fuels, Climate Change, and Environmental Degradation

One of the most significant long-term challenges facing Europe and the world in the early twenty-first century was the need for adequate energy resources. Maintaining standards of living in industrialized countries and modernizing the developing world required extremely high levels of energy use, and supplies were heavily dependent on fossil fuels: oil, coal, and natural gas. In 2011 Europe and Russia combined had about 12 percent of the world's population but annually consumed about 34 percent of the world's natural gas production, 22 percent of oil production, and 13 percent of coal output. Scientists warned that such high levels of usage were unsustainable over the long run and predicted that fossil fuel supplies will eventually run out, especially as the countries of the developing world—including giants such as India and China—increased their own rates of consumption.[20]

Struggles to control and profit from these shrinking resources often resulted in tense geopolitical conflicts. The need to preserve access to oil, for example, has led to a transformation in military power in the post–Cold War world. Between 1945 and 1990 the largest areas of military buildup were along the iron curtain in Europe and in East Asia, as U.S. forces formed a bulwark against the spread of communism. Today military power is increasingly concentrated in oil-producing areas such as the Middle East, which holds about 65 percent of the world's oil reserves. One scholar labeled conflicts in the Persian Gulf and Central Asia "resource wars" because they are fought, in large part, to preserve the West's access to the region's energy supplies.[21]

Beyond questions of supply, dependence on fossil fuels has led to serious environmental problems. Burning oil and coal releases massive amounts of carbon dioxide (CO_2) into the atmosphere, the leading cause of **climate change**, or global warming. While the future effects of climate change are difficult to predict, the vast majority of climatologists agree that global warming is proceeding far more quickly than previously predicted and that some climatic disruption is now unavoidable. Rising average temperatures already play havoc with familiar weather patterns, melting glaciers and polar ice packs and drying up freshwater resources. Moreover, in the next fifty years rising sea levels may well flood low-lying coastal areas around the world.

Since the 1990s the EU has spearheaded efforts to control energy consumption and contain climate change. EU leaders have imposed tight restrictions on CO_2 emissions, and Germany, the Netherlands, and Denmark have become world leaders in harnessing alternative energy sources such as solar and wind power. Some countries, hoping to combat the future effects of global warming, have also taken pre-emptive measures. The Dutch government, for example, has spent billions of dollars constructing new dikes, levees, and floodgates. These efforts provided models for U.S. urban planners after floodwaters churned up by Hurricane Sandy swamped low-lying swaths of New York City in October 2012.

Environmental degradation encompasses a number of problems beyond climate change. Overfishing and toxic waste threaten the world's oceans and freshwater lakes, which once seemed to be inexhaustible sources of food and drinking water. The disaster that resulted when an offshore oil rig exploded in the Gulf of Mexico in April 2010, spewing millions of gallons of oil into the gulf waters, underscored the close connections between energy consumption and water pollution. Deforestation, land degradation, soil erosion, and overfertilization; species extinction related to habitat loss; the accumulation of toxins in the air, land, and water; the disposal of poisonous nuclear waste—all will continue to pose serious problems in the twenty-first century.

Though North American and European governments, NGOs, and citizens have taken a number of steps to limit environmental degradation and regulate energy use, the overall effort to control energy consumption has been an especially difficult endeavor, underscoring the interconnectedness of the contemporary world. Rapidly industrializing countries such as India and China—the latter surpassed the United States in 2008 as the largest emitter of CO_2—have had a difficult time balancing environmental concerns and the energy use necessary for economic growth. Because of growing demand for electricity, for example, China currently accounts for about 47 percent of the world's coal consumption, causing hazardous air pollution in Chinese cities and contributing to climate change.[22]

Can international agreements and good intentions make a difference? In December 2015 representatives of almost two hundred nations met at the annual United Nations Climate Change Conference in Paris, France. The resulting Paris Agreement set ambitious goals for the reduction of CO_2 emissions by 2020 and promised to help developing countries manage the effects of climate change. President Trump's rejection of the agreement in 2017 marked a setback for environmentalists, but even before withdrawal of U.S. support the ultimate success of ambitious plans to limit human energy consumption was uncertain.

Promoting Human Rights

Though regional differences persisted in the twenty-eight EU member states, Europeans entering the twenty-first century enjoyed some of the highest living standards in the world, the sweet fruit of more than fifty years of peace, security, and overall economic growth. Nevertheless, the recent agonies of barbarism and war in the former Yugoslavia, as well as the memories of the horrors of World War II and the Holocaust, were reminders of the ever-present possibility of collective violence. For some Europeans, the realization that they had so much and so many others had so little kindled a desire to help. European intellectuals and opinion makers began to envision a new historic mission for Europe: the promotion of domestic peace and human rights in lands plagued by instability, violence, and oppression.

European leaders and humanitarians believed that more global agreements and new international institutions were needed to set moral standards and to regulate countries, leaders, armies, corporations, and individuals. In practice, this meant more curbs on the sovereign rights of the world's states, just as the states of the European Union had imposed increasingly strict standards of behavior on themselves to secure the rights and welfare of EU citizens. As one EU official concluded, the European Union has a "historical responsibility" to make morality "a basis of policy" because "human rights are more important than states' rights."[23]

In practical terms, this mission raised questions. Europe's evolving human rights policies would require military intervention to stop civil wars and to prevent tyrannical governments from slaughtering their own people. Thus the EU joined the United States to intervene militarily to stop the killing and protect minority rights in Bosnia, Croatia, and Kosovo. The EU states vigorously supported UN initiatives to verify compliance with anti–germ warfare conventions, outlaw the use of land mines, and establish a new international court to prosecute war criminals.

Europeans also broadened definitions of individual rights. Having abolished the death penalty in the EU, they condemned its continued use in China, the United States, and other countries. At home, Europe expanded personal rights. The pace-setting Netherlands gave pensions and workers' rights to prostitutes and provided assisted suicide (euthanasia) for the terminally ill. The Dutch recognized same-sex marriage in 2001. By the time France followed suit in 2013, nine western European countries had legalized same-sex marriage and twelve others had recognized alternative forms of civil union. (The U.S. Supreme Court guaranteed the right to same-sex marriage in June 2015.) The countries of the former East Bloc, where people were generally less supportive of gay rights, lagged behind in this regard.

Europeans extended their broad-based concept of human rights to the world's poorer countries, often criticizing globalization and unrestrained neoliberal capitalism. For example, Europe's moderate Social Democrats joined human rights campaigners in 2001 to secure drastic price cuts from international pharmaceutical corporations selling drugs to combat Africa's AIDS crisis. Advocating greater social equality and state-funded health care, European socialists embraced morality as a basis for the global expansion of human rights.

The record was inconsistent. Critics accused the European Union (and the United States) of selectively promoting human rights in their differential responses to the Arab Spring — the West was willing to act in some cases, as in Libya, but dragged its feet in others, as in Egypt and Syria. The conflicted response to the immigration emergency of 2015 underscored the difficulties of shaping unified human rights policies that would satisfy competing political and national interests. Attempts to extend rights to women, indigenous peoples, and immigrants remained controversial, especially on the far right. Even so, the general trend suggested that most of Europe's leaders and peoples took very seriously the ideals articulated in the 1948 UN Universal Declaration of Human Rights. In an era defined by sharp political conflicts, riven by growing social inequality, and troubled by environmental decline, this commitment to basic human rights offered some hope for meeting ongoing and future challenges.

NOTES

1. P. Anderson, "Managed Democracy," *London Review of Books*, August 27, 2015, pp. 19–27.
2. Quoted in T. Judt, *Postwar: A History of Europe Since 1945* (New York: Penguin, 2005), p. 691.
3. Judt, *Postwar*, pp. 698–699.
4. *Quarterly Labor Force Statistics*, vol. 2004/4 (Paris: OECD Publications, 2004), p. 64; "Which Sector Is the Main Employer in the EU Member States?" *Eurostat: Your Key to European Statistics*, October 24, 2017, https://ec.europa.eu/eurostat/web/products-eurostat-news/-/DDN-20171024-1; Robert E. Scott, "The Manufacturing Footprint and the Importance of U.S. Manufacturing Jobs," *Economic Policy Institute Briefing Paper No. 338*, January 22, 2015, https://www.epi.org/publication/the-manufacturing-footprint-and-the-importance-of-u-s-manufacturing-jobs/.
5. "Fertility Statistics," *Eurostat: Statistics Explained*, accessed August 7, 2015, http://ec.europa.eu/eurostat/statistics-explained/index.php/Fertility_statistics.
6. "Germany: More Babies?" *The Economist*, January 6, 2001, p. 6.
7. Quoted in "Germany: More Babies?" p. 6.
8. European Commission, *Annual Report on Migration and Asylum 2017* (European Migration Network, 2018), p. 47; "EU Migrant Crisis: Facts and Figures," News/European Parliament, June 30, 2017, http://www.europarl.europa.eu/news/en/headlines/society/20170629STO78630/eu-migrant-crisis-facts-and-figures.
9. "Asylum Statistics," *Eurostat*, April 2018, https://ec.europa.eu/eurostat/statistics-explained/index.php/Asylum_statistics#Final_decisions_taken_in_appeal.
10. Mark Mazower, *Dark Continent: Europe's Twentieth Century* (New York: Vintage, 2000), p. 415; United Nations, *International Migration Report 2017* (New York: UN Department of Economic and Social Affairs, 2017), pp. 28–29.
11. L. Collingham, *Curry: A Tale of Cooks and Conquerors* (London: Oxford University Press, 2006), pp. 2, 9.
12. J. Klausen, *The Islamic Challenge: Politics and Religion in Western Europe* (New York: Oxford University Press, 2006), p. 16; Malise Ruthven, "The Big Muslim Problem!" *New York Review*, December 17, 2009, p. 62.
13. "Europe's Growing Muslim Population," Pew Research Center, November 29, 2017, http://www.pewforum.org/2017/11/29/europes-growing-muslim-population/.
14. Jonathan Evans, "U.S. Adults Are More Religious Than Western Europeans," Pew Research Center, September 5, 2018, http://www.pewresearch.org/fact-tank/2018/09/05/u-s-adults-are-more-religious-than-western-europeans/.
15. Quoted in "Text: President Bush Addresses the Nation," *Washington Post Online*, September 20, 2001, http://www.washingtonpost.com/wp-srv/nation/specials/attacked/transcripts/bushaddress_092001.html.
16. See M. H. Hunt, ed., *The World Transformed, 1945 to the Present: A Documentary Reader* (Boston: Bedford/St. Martin's), pp. 410–411.
17. Jon Henley, "How Populism Emerged as an Electoral Force in Europe," *theguardian.com*, November 20, 2018, https://www.theguardian.com/world/ng-interactive/2018/nov/20/how-populism-emerged-as-electoral-force-in-europe.
18. "Islam in Europe," *The Economist*, January 7, 2015, http://www.economist.com/blogs/graphicdetail/2015/01/daily-chart-2.
19. Henley, "How Populism Emerged," p. 12.

20. Statistics in *BP Statistical Review of World Energy June 2012*, http://www.bp.com/en_no/norway/media/press-releases-and-news/2012/bp-statistical-review-of-world-energy-2012.html.

21. M. T. Klare, *Resource Wars: The New Landscape of Global Conflict* (New York: Henry Holt, 2001), pp. 25–40.

22. Edward Wong, "Beijing Takes Steps to Fight Pollution as Problem Worsens," *New York Times*, January 31, 2013, p. A4.

23. Quoted in *International Herald Tribune*, June 15, 2001, p. 6.

LOOKING BACK **LOOKING AHEAD**

The twenty-first century opened with changes and new challenges for the Western world. The collapse of the East Bloc brought more representative government to central and eastern Europe, but it left millions struggling to adapt to a different way of life in market economies. Digital technology and information systems that quickened the pace of communications and the global reach of new supranational institutions made the world a smaller place, yet globalization left some struggling to maintain their livelihoods. New contacts between peoples, made possible by increased migration, revitalized European society, but the massive influx of refugees in 2015–2016 raised concerns about cultural tolerance and the EU's open internal borders policy.

Despite the success of European democracy and liberalism, and despite the high living standards enjoyed by most Europeans, the challenges won't go away. The search for solutions to environmental degradation and conflicts between ethnic and religious groups, as well as the promotion of human rights across the globe, will clearly occupy European and world leaders for some time to come.

However these issues play out, the study of the past puts the present and the future in perspective. Others before us have trodden the paths of uncertainty and crisis, and the historian's ability to analyze and explain the choices they made helps us understand our current situation and helps save us from exaggerated self-pity in the face of our own predicaments. Perhaps our Western heritage may rightly inspire us with measured pride and self-confidence. We stand, momentarily, at the head of the long procession of Western civilization. Sometimes the procession has wandered, or backtracked, or done terrible things. But it has also carried the efforts and sacrifices of generations of toiling, struggling ancestors. Through no effort of our own, we are the beneficiaries of those sacrifices and achievements. Now that it is our turn to carry the torch onward, we may remember these ties with our forebears.

To change the metaphor, Westerners are like card players who have been dealt many good cards. Some of them are obvious, such as their technical and scientific heritage, their environmental resources, and their commitment to human rights and individual freedoms. Others are not so obvious, sometimes half-forgotten or even hidden up the sleeve. We can consider, for example, the almost-miraculous victory of peaceful revolution in the East Bloc in 1989 — an expression of what Václav Havel called "the power of the powerless." That revolution showed the regenerative strength of the Western ideals of individual rights and democratic government.

The study of history, of mighty struggles and fearsome challenges, of shining achievements and tragic failures, gives a sense of the essence of life itself: the process of change over time. Again and again we have seen how peoples and societies evolve, influenced by ideas, human passions, and material conditions. This process of change will continue as the future becomes the present and then the past. Students of history are well prepared to make sense of this unfolding process because they have closely observed it. They understand that change is rooted in existing historical forces, and they have tools to explore the intricate web of activity that propels life forward. Students of history can anticipate the new and unexpected in human development, for they have already seen great breakthroughs and revolutions. They have an understanding of how things really happen.

MAKE CONNECTIONS

Think about the larger developments and continuities within and across chapters.

1. Did people's lives really change dramatically during the wave of globalization that emerged in the late twentieth century? How have they stayed the same?

2. The globalization of today's world seems inseparable from advances in digital technology. How are the two connected? Were there other times in the history of Western society during which technological developments drove social, political, or cultural change?

3. How are the challenges that confront Europeans in the twenty-first century rooted in events and trends that came before?

Chapter 30 Review

IDENTIFY KEY TERMS

Identify and explain the significance of each item below.

shock therapy (p. 924)
Color Revolutions (p. 927)
ethnic cleansing (p. 933)
globalization (p. 934)
European Union (EU) (p. 935)
Maastricht Treaty (p. 935)
World Trade Organization (WTO)
   (p. 937)

multiculturalism (p. 946)
war on terror (p. 949)
Arab Spring (p. 952)
Islamic State (p. 952)
Brexit (p. 954)
climate change
   (p. 957)

REVIEW THE MAIN IDEAS

Answer the section heading questions from the chapter.

1. How did life change in Russia and the former East Bloc countries after 1989? (p. 924)

2. How did globalization affect European life and society? (p. 934)

3. How is growing ethnic diversity changing contemporary Europe? (p. 941)

4. What challenges will Europeans face in the coming decades? (p. 948)

CHRONOLOGY

1990s–2010s	• New waves of legal and illegal immigration to Europe
1991	• Maastricht Treaty
1991–2001	• Civil war in Yugoslavia
1993	• Creation of the European Union
2000–2008	• Resurgence of Russian economy under Putin
2001	• September 11 terrorist attack on the United States; war in Afghanistan begins
2002	• Euro replaces national currencies in Eurozone
2003–2011	• Iraq War
2004	• Train bombings in Madrid by Islamic extremists
2005	• Subway bombing in London by Islamic extremists
2008	• Worldwide financial crisis begins
2009	• Ratification of Treaty of Lisbon
2011	• Start of the Arab Spring in the Middle East and North Africa
2012–2013	• Mass protests against government austerity plans in Greece and Spain
2013	• France legalizes same-sex marriage
2014	• Russian Federation annexes Crimea; pro-Russian insurrection in eastern Ukraine
2014–2015	• Rise of the Islamic State
2015–2016	• Greek debt crisis; EU immigration crisis
2016	• Brexit referendum
2017–	• U.S. Pres. Trump takes hard line against NATO and European allies
2018	• UN Climate Control conference updates Paris Agreement

Glossary

Afrikaners: Descendants of the Dutch settlers in the Cape Colony in southern Africa. (Ch. 24)

appeasement: The British policy toward Germany prior to World War II that aimed at granting Hitler's territorial demands, including western Czechoslovakia, in order to avoid war. (Ch. 27)

Arab Spring: A series of popular revolts in several countries in the Middle East and North Africa that sought an end to authoritarian, often Western-supported regimes. (Ch. 30)

Aztec Empire: A large and complex Native American civilization in modern Mexico and Central America that possessed advanced mathematical, astronomical, and engineering technology. (Ch. 14)

Balfour Declaration: A 1917 British statement that declared British support of a National Home for the Jewish People in Palestine. (Ch. 25)

baroque style: A style in art and music lasting from roughly 1600 to 1750 characterized by the use of drama and motion to create heightened emotion, especially prevalent in Catholic countries. (Ch. 15)

Battle of Stalingrad: A Russian victory over Germany in winter 1942–1943 and a major turning point in the war, which led to the ultimate defeat of the Germans in May 1945. (Ch. 27)

Bauhaus: A German interdisciplinary school of fine and applied arts that brought together many leading modern architects, designers, and theatrical innovators. (Ch. 26)

Berlin Conference: A meeting of European leaders held in 1884 and 1885 in order to lay down some basic rules for imperialist competition in sub-Saharan Africa. (Ch. 24)

Black Shirts: Mussolini's private militia, which destroyed Socialist newspapers, union halls, and Socialist Party headquarters, eventually pushing Socialists out of the city governments of northern Italy. (Ch. 27)

blood sports: Events such as bullbaiting and cockfighting that involved inflicting violence and bloodshed on animals and that were popular with the eighteenth-century European masses. (Ch. 18)

Bolsheviks: Lenin's radical, revolutionary arm of the Russian party of Marxist socialism, which successfully installed a dictatorial socialist regime in Russia. (Ch. 25)

bourgeoisie: The upper-class minority who owned the means of production and, according to Marx, exploited the working-class proletariat. (Ch. 21)

boyars: The highest-ranking members of the Russian nobility. (Ch. 15)

Brexit: The informal name for Great Britain's exit from the European Union. (Ch. 30)

Brezhnev Doctrine: Doctrine created by Leonid Brezhnev that held that the Soviet Union had the right to intervene in any East Bloc country when necessary to preserve Communist rule. (Ch. 29)

cameralism: View that monarchy was the best form of government, that all elements of society should serve the monarch, and that, in turn, the state should use its resources and authority to increase the public good. (Ch. 16)

caravel: A small, maneuverable, two- or three-masted sailing ship developed by the Portuguese in the fifteenth century that gave them a distinct advantage in exploration and trade. (Ch. 14)

carnival: The few days of revelry in Catholic countries that preceded Lent and that included drinking, masquerading, dancing, and rowdy spectacles that upset the established order. (Ch. 18)

Cartesian dualism: Descartes's view that all of reality could ultimately be reduced to mind and matter. (Ch. 16)

charivari: Degrading public rituals used by village communities to police personal behavior and maintain moral standards. (Ch. 18)

Christian Democrats: Center-right political parties that rose to power in western Europe after the Second World War. (Ch. 28)

class-consciousness: Awareness of belonging to a distinct social and economic class whose interests might conflict with those of other classes. (Ch. 20)

climate change: Changes in long-standing weather patterns caused primarily by carbon dioxide emissions from the burning of fossil fuels. (Ch. 30)

Cold War: The rivalry between the Soviet Union and the United States that divided much of Europe into a Soviet-aligned Communist bloc and a U.S.-aligned capitalist bloc between 1945 and 1989. (Ch. 28)

collectivization of agriculture: The forcible consolidation of individual peasant farms into large state-controlled enterprises in the Soviet Union under Stalin. (Ch. 27)

Color Revolutions: A series of popular revolts and insurrections that challenged regional politicians and Russian interests in the former Soviet republics during the first decade of the twenty-first century. (Ch. 30)

Columbian exchange: The exchange of animals, plants, and diseases between the Old and the New Worlds. (Ch. 14)

Combination Acts: British laws passed in 1799 that outlawed unions and strikes, favoring capitalist business people over skilled artisans. Bitterly resented and widely disregarded by many craft guilds, the acts were repealed by Parliament in 1824. (Ch. 20)

Common Market: The European Economic Community, created by six western and central European countries in the West Bloc in 1957 as part of a larger search for European unity. (Ch. 28)

community controls: A pattern of cooperation and common action in a traditional village that sought to uphold the economic, social, and moral stability of the closely knit community. (Ch. 18)

companionate marriage: Marriage based on romantic love and middle-class family values that became increasingly dominant in the second half of the nineteenth century. (Ch. 22)

Congress of Vienna: A meeting of the Quadruple Alliance (Russia, Prussia, Austria, and Great Britain), restoration France, and smaller European states to fashion a general peace settlement that began after the defeat of Napoleon's France in 1814. (Ch. 21)

conquistadors: Spanish for "conquerors"; armed Spaniards such as Hernán Cortés and Francisco Pizarro, who sought to conquer people and territories in the New World for the Spanish crown. (Ch. 14)

constitutionalism: A form of government in which power is limited by law and balanced between the authority and power of the government, on the one hand, and the rights and liberties of the subjects or citizens on the other hand; could include constitutional monarchies or republics. (Ch. 15)

consumer revolution: The wide-ranging growth in consumption and new attitudes toward consumer goods that emerged in the cities of northwestern Europe in the second half of the eighteenth century. (Ch. 18)

Continental System: A blockade imposed by Napoleon to halt all trade between continental Europe and Britain, thereby weakening the British economy and military. (Ch. 19)

Copernican hypothesis: The idea that the sun, not the earth, was the center of the universe. (Ch. 16)

Corn Laws: British laws governing the import and export of grain, which were revised in 1815 to place high tariffs on imported grain, thus benefiting the aristocracy but making food prices high for working people. (Ch. 21)

Cossacks: Free groups and outlaw armies originally comprising runaway peasants living on the borders of Russian territory from the fourteenth century onward. By the end of the sixteenth century they had formed an alliance with the Russian state. (Ch. 15)

cottage industry: A stage of industrial development in which rural workers used hand tools in their homes to manufacture goods on a large scale for sale in a market. (Ch. 17)

Council for Mutual Economic Assistance (COMECON): An economic organization of Communist states meant to help rebuild East Bloc countries under Soviet auspices. (Ch. 28)

Crimean War: A conflict fought between 1853 and 1856 over Russian desires to expand into Ottoman territory; Russia was defeated by France, Britain, and the Ottomans, underscoring the need for reform in the Russian Empire. (Ch. 23)

Crystal Palace: The location of the Great Exhibition in 1851 in London; an architectural masterpiece made entirely of glass and iron. (Ch. 20)

Dadaism: An artistic movement of the 1910s and 1920s that attacked all accepted standards of art and behavior and delighted in outrageous conduct. (Ch. 26)

Dawes Plan: War reparations agreement that reduced Germany's yearly payments, made payments dependent on economic growth, and granted large U.S. loans to promote recovery. (Ch. 26)

debt peonage: A form of serfdom that allowed a planter or rancher to keep his workers or slaves in perpetual debt bondage by periodically advancing food, shelter, and a little money. (Ch. 17)

decolonization: The postwar reversal of Europe's overseas expansion caused by the rising demand of the colonized peoples themselves, the declining power of European nations, and the freedoms promised by U.S. and Soviet ideals. (Ch. 28)

deism: Belief in a distant, noninterventionist deity; common among Enlightenment thinkers. (Ch. 16)

de-Stalinization: The liberalization of the post-Stalin Soviet Union led by reformer Nikita Khrushchev. (Ch. 28)

détente: The progressive relaxation of Cold War tensions that emerged in the early 1970s. (Ch. 29)

developed socialism: A term used by Communist leaders to describe the socialist accomplishments of their societies, such as nationalized industry, collective agriculture, and extensive social welfare programs. (Ch. 29)

displaced persons: Postwar refugees, including 13 million Germans, former Nazi prisoners and forced laborers, and orphaned children. (Ch. 28)

Dreyfus affair: A divisive case in which Alfred Dreyfus, a Jewish captain in the French army, was falsely accused and convicted of treason. The Catholic Church sided with the anti-Semites against Dreyfus; after Dreyfus was declared innocent, the French government severed all ties between the state and the church. (Ch. 23)

Duma: The Russian parliament that opened in 1906, elected indirectly by universal male suffrage but controlled after 1907 by the tsar and the conservative classes. (Ch. 23)

economic liberalism: A belief in free trade and competition based on Adam Smith's argument that the invisible hand of free competition would benefit all individuals, rich and poor. (Ch. 17)

economic miracle: Term contemporaries used to describe rapid economic growth, often based on the consumer sector, in post–World War II western Europe. (Ch. 28)

Enabling Act: An act pushed through the Reichstag by the Nazis that gave Hitler absolute dictatorial power for four years. (Ch. 27)

enclosure: The movement to fence in fields in order to farm more effectively, at the expense of poor peasants, who relied on common fields for farming and pasture. (Ch. 17)

encomienda system: A system whereby the Spanish crown granted the conquerors the right to forcibly employ groups of Indians in exchange for providing food, shelter, and Christian teaching. (Ch. 14)

enlightened absolutism: Term coined by historians to describe the rule of eighteenth-century monarchs who, without renouncing their own absolute authority, adopted Enlightenment ideals of rationalism, progress, and tolerance. (Ch. 16)

Enlightenment: The influential intellectual and cultural movement of the late seventeenth and eighteenth centuries that introduced a new worldview based on the use of reason, the scientific method, and progress. (Ch. 16)

estates: The three legal categories, or orders, of France's inhabitants: the clergy, the nobility, and everyone else. (Ch. 19)

Estates General: A legislative body in prerevolutionary France made up of representatives of each of the three classes, or estates. It was called into session in 1789 for the first time since 1614. (Ch. 19)

ethnic cleansing: The attempt to establish ethnically homogeneous territories by intimidation, forced deportation, and killing. (Ch. 30)

eugenics: A pseudoscientific doctrine saying the selective breeding of human beings can improve the general characteristics of a national population, which helped inspire Nazi ideas about national unity and racial exclusion and ultimately contributed to the Holocaust. (Ch. 27)

European Union (EU): The economic, cultural, and political alliance of twenty-eight European nations. (Ch. 30)

evolution: Darwin's theory that chance differences among the individual members of a given species that prove useful in the struggle for survival are selected naturally, and they gradually spread to the entire species through reproduction. (Ch. 22)

existentialism: A philosophy that stresses the meaninglessness of existence and the importance of the individual in searching for moral values in an uncertain world. (Ch. 26)

Factory Acts: English laws passed from 1802 to 1833 that limited the workday of child laborers and set minimum hygiene and safety requirements. (Ch. 20)

fascism: A movement characterized by extreme, often expansionist nationalism; anti-socialism; a dynamic and violent leader; and glorification of war and the military. (Ch. 27)

Fashoda Incident: French colonial troops backed down in this 1898 diplomatic crisis caused by British-French competition over African territory in present-day South Sudan, preventing a European Great Power war over imperialist ambitions. (Ch. 24)

February Revolution: Unplanned uprisings accompanied by violent street demonstrations begun in March 1917 (old calendar February) in Petrograd, Russia, that led to the abdication of the tsar and the establishment of a provisional government. (Ch. 25)

five-year plan: A plan launched by Stalin in 1928 and termed the "revolution from above," aimed at modernizing the Soviet Union and creating a new Communist society with new attitudes, new loyalties, and a new socialist humanity. (Ch. 27)

Fourteen Points: Wilson's 1918 peace proposal calling for open diplomacy, a reduction in armaments, freedom of commerce and trade, the establishment of the League of Nations, and national self-determination. (Ch. 25)

Fronde: A series of violent uprisings during the early reign of Louis XIV triggered by growing royal control and increased taxation. (Ch. 15)

functionalism: The principle that buildings, like industrial products, should serve as well as possible the purpose for which they were made, without excessive ornamentation. (Ch. 26)

German Social Democratic Party (SPD): A German working-class political party founded in the 1870s, the SPD championed Marxism but in practice turned away from Marxist revolution and worked instead in the German parliament for social benefits and workplace reforms. (Ch. 23)

germ theory: The idea that disease was caused by the spread of living organisms that could be controlled. (Ch. 22)

Girondists: A moderate group that fought for control of the French National Convention in 1793. (Ch. 19)

glasnost: Soviet premier Mikhail Gorbachev's popular campaign for openness in government and the media. (Ch. 29)

globalization: A label for the new international economic, cultural, and political connections that emerged in the last decades of the twentieth century. (Ch. 30)

global mass migration: The mass movement of people from Europe in the nineteenth century; one reason that the West's impact on the world was so powerful and many-sided. (Ch. 24)

Grand Empire: The empire over which Napoleon and his allies ruled, encompassing virtually all of Europe except Great Britain and Russia. (Ch. 19)

Great Depression: A worldwide economic depression from 1929 through 1939, unique in its severity and duration and with slow and uneven recovery. (Ch. 26)

Greater Germany: A liberal plan for German national unification that included the German-speaking parts of the Austrian Empire, put forth at the national parliament in 1848 but rejected by Austrian rulers. (Ch. 21)

Great Famine: The result of four years of potato crop failure in the late 1840s in Ireland, a country that had grown dependent on potatoes as a dietary staple. (Ch. 21)

Great Fear: The fear of noble reprisals against peasant uprisings that seized the French countryside and led to further revolt. (Ch. 19)

Great Rebellion: The 1857 and 1858 insurrection by Muslim and Hindu mercenaries in the British army that spread throughout northern and central India before finally being crushed. (Ch. 24)

"Great Stink": In the summer of 1858 appalling fumes from the polluted River Thames threatened to shut down London, providing a boost to the emerging public health movement. (Ch. 22)

guest worker programs: Government-run programs in western Europe designed to recruit labor for the booming postwar economy. (Ch. 28)

guild system: The organization of artisanal production into trade-based associations, or guilds, each of which received a monopoly over its trade and the right to train apprentices and hire workers. (Ch. 17)

gunboat diplomacy: The use or threat of military force to coerce a government into economic or political agreements. (Ch. 24)

Haskalah: The Jewish Enlightenment of the second half of the eighteenth century, led by the Prussian philosopher Moses Mendelssohn. (Ch. 16)

Holocaust: The systematic effort of the Nazi state to exterminate all European Jews and other groups deemed racially inferior during the Second World War. (Ch. 27)

Holy Alliance: An alliance formed by the conservative rulers of Austria, Prussia, and Russia in September 1815 that became a symbol of the repression of liberal and revolutionary movements all over Europe. (Ch. 21)

home rule: The late-nineteenth-century movement to give Ireland a government independent from Great Britain; it was supported by Irish Catholics and resisted by Irish Protestants. (Ch. 23)

hundred days of reform: A series of Western-style reforms launched in 1898 by the Chinese government in an attempt to meet the foreign challenge. (Ch. 24)

id, ego, and superego: Freudian terms to describe the three parts of the self and the basis of human behavior, which Freud saw as basically irrational. (Ch. 26)

illegitimacy explosion: The sharp increase in out-of-wedlock births that occurred in Europe between 1750 and 1850, caused by low wages and the breakdown of community controls. (Ch. 18)

Inca Empire: The vast and sophisticated Peruvian empire centered at the capital city of Cuzco that was at its peak from 1438 until 1533. (Ch. 14)

Industrial Revolution: A term first coined in 1799 to describe the burst of major inventions and economic expansion that began in Britain in the late eighteenth century. (Ch. 20)

industrious revolution: The shift that occurred as families in northwestern Europe focused on earning wages instead of producing goods for household consumption; this reduced their economic self-sufficiency but increased their ability to purchase consumer goods. (Ch. 17)

iron law of wages: Theory proposed by English economist David Ricardo suggesting that the pressure of population growth prevents wages from rising above the subsistence level. (Ch. 20)

Islamic State: A radical Islamist militia in control of substantial parts of central Syria and Iraq, where it applies an extremist version of shari'a law. (Ch. 30)

Jacobin Club: A political club in revolutionary France whose members were well-educated radical republicans. (Ch. 19)

janissary corps: The core of the sultan's army, composed of slave conscripts from non-Muslim parts of the empire; after 1683 it became a volunteer force. (Ch. 15)

Jansenism: A sect of Catholicism originating with Cornelius Jansen that emphasized the heavy weight of original sin and accepted the doctrine of predestination; it was outlawed as heresy by the pope. (Ch. 18)

Junkers: The nobility of Brandenburg and Prussia, who were reluctant allies of Frederick William in his consolidation of the Prussian state. (Ch. 15)

just price: The idea that prices should be fair, protecting both consumers and producers, and that they should be imposed by government decree if necessary. (Ch. 18)

Karlsbad Decrees: Issued in 1819, these repressive regulations were designed to uphold Metternich's conservatism, requiring the German states to root out subversive ideas and squelch any liberal organizations. (Ch. 21)

kulaks: The better-off peasants who were stripped of land and livestock under Stalin and were generally not permitted to join collective farms; many of them starved or were deported to forced-labor camps for "re-education." (Ch. 27)

labor aristocracy: The highly skilled workers, such as factory foremen and construction bosses, who made up about 15 percent of the working classes from about 1850 to 1914. (Ch. 22)

laissez faire: A doctrine of economic liberalism that calls for unrestricted private enterprise and no government interference in the economy. (Ch. 21)

Lateran Agreement: A 1929 agreement that recognized the Vatican as an independent state, with Mussolini agreeing to give the church heavy financial support in return for public support from the pope. (Ch. 27)

law of inertia: A law hypothesized by Galileo that states that motion, not rest, is the natural state of an object, and that an object continues in motion forever unless stopped by some external force. (Ch. 16)

law of universal gravitation: Newton's law that all objects are attracted to one another and that the force of attraction is proportional to the objects' quantity of matter and inversely proportional to the square of the distance between them. (Ch. 16)

League of Nations: A permanent international organization, established during the 1919 Paris Peace Conference, designed to protect member states from aggression and avert future wars. (Ch. 25)

liberalism: The principal ideas of this movement were equality and liberty; liberals demanded representative government and equality before the law as well as individual freedoms such as freedom of the press, freedom of speech, freedom of assembly, freedom of worship, and freedom from arbitrary arrest. (Ch. 21)

logical positivism: A philosophy that sees meaning in only those beliefs that can be empirically proven and that therefore rejects most of the concerns of traditional philosophy, from the existence of God to the meaning of happiness, as nonsense. (Ch. 26)

Luddites: Group of handicraft workers who attacked factories in northern England in 1811 and later, smashing the new machines that they believed were putting them out of work. (Ch. 20)

Maastricht Treaty: The basis for the formation of the European Union, which set financial and cultural standards for potential member states and defined criteria for membership in the monetary union. (Ch. 30)

mandate system: The plan to allow Britain and France to administer former Ottoman territories, put into place after the end of the First World War. (Ch. 25)

manifest destiny: The idea that the United States was destined to expand across the North American continent and become a great world power. (Ch. 23)

Marshall Plan: American plan for providing economic aid to western Europe to help it rebuild. (Ch. 28)

Marxism: An influential political program based on the socialist ideas of German radical Karl Marx, which called for a working-class revolution to overthrow capitalist society and establish a Communist state. (Ch. 21)

Marxist revisionism: An effort by moderate socialists to update Marxist doctrines to reflect the realities of the late nineteenth century. (Ch. 23)

Meiji Restoration: The restoration of the Japanese emperor to power in 1867, leading to the subsequent modernization of Japan. (Ch. 24)

mercantilism: A system of economic regulations aimed at increasing the power of the state based on the belief that a nation's international power was based on its wealth, specifically its supply of gold and silver. (Ch. 15)

Methodists: Members of a Protestant revival movement started by John Wesley, so called because they were so methodical in their devotion. (Ch. 18)

millet system: A system used by the Ottomans whereby subjects were divided into religious communities, with each millet (nation) enjoying autonomous self-government under its religious leaders. (Ch. 15)

Mines Act of 1842: English law prohibiting underground work for all women and girls as well as for boys under ten. (Ch. 20)

"modern girl": The somewhat stereotypical image of the modern and independent working woman popular in the 1920s. (Ch. 26)

modernism: A label given to the artistic and cultural movements of the late nineteenth and early twentieth centuries, which were typified by radical experimentation that challenged traditional forms of artistic expression. (Ch. 26)

Mountain, the: Led by Robespierre, the French National Convention's radical faction, which seized legislative power in 1793. (Ch. 19)

multiculturalism: The mixing of ethnic styles in daily life and in cultural works such as film, music, art, and literature. (Ch. 30)

Napoleonic Code: French civil code promulgated in 1804 that reasserted the 1789 principles of the equality of all male citizens before the law and the absolute security of wealth and private property, as well as restricting rights accorded to women by previous revolutionary laws. (Ch. 19)

National Assembly: The first French revolutionary legislature, made up primarily of representatives of the third estate and a few from the nobility and clergy, in session from 1789 to 1791. (Ch. 19)

nationalism: The idea that each people had its own genius and specific identity that manifested itself especially in a common language and history, which often led to the desire for an independent political state. (Ch. 21)

national self-determination: The notion that peoples should be able to choose their own national governments through democratic majority rule elections and live free from outside interference in nation-states with clearly defined borders. (Ch. 25)

National Socialism: A movement and political party driven by extreme nationalism and racism, led by Adolf Hitler; its adherents ruled Germany from 1933 to 1945 and forced Europe into World War II. (Ch. 27)

nativism: Policies and beliefs, often influenced by nationalism, scientific racism, and mass migration, that give preferential treatment to established inhabitants over immigrants. (Ch. 24)

NATO: The North Atlantic Treaty Organization, an anti-Soviet military alliance of Western governments. (Ch. 28)

natural philosophy: An early modern term for the study of the nature of the universe, its purpose, and how it functioned; it encompassed what we would call "science" today. (Ch. 16)

Navigation Acts: A series of English laws that controlled the import of goods to Britain and British colonies. (Ch. 17)

neocolonialism: A postcolonial system that perpetuates Western economic exploitation in former colonial territories. (Ch. 28)

neo-Europes: Settler colonies with established populations of Europeans, such as North America, Australia, New Zealand, and Latin America, where Europe found outlets for population growth and its most profitable investment opportunities in the nineteenth century. (Ch. 24)

neoliberalism: Philosophy of 1980s conservatives who argued for privatization of state-run industries and decreased government spending on social services. (Ch. 29)

New Economic Policy (NEP): Lenin's 1921 policy to re-establish limited economic freedom in an attempt to rebuild agriculture and industry in the face of economic disintegration. (Ch. 27)

New Imperialism: The late-nineteenth-century drive by European countries to create vast political empires abroad. (Ch. 24)

New Left: A 1960s counterculture movement that embraced updated forms of Marxism to challenge both Western capitalism and Soviet-style communism. (Ch. 29)

New Order: Hitler's program based on racial imperialism, which gave preferential treatment to the "Nordic" peoples; the French, an "inferior" Latin people, occupied a middle position; and Slavs and Jews were treated harshly as "subhumans." (Ch. 27)

nonalignment: Policy of postcolonial governments to remain neutral in the Cold War and play both the United States and the Soviet Union for what they could get. (Ch. 28)

OPEC: The Organization of Petroleum Exporting Countries. (Ch. 29)

Opium Wars: Two mid-nineteenth-century conflicts between China and Great Britain over the British trade in opium, which were designed to "open" China to European free trade. In defeat, China gave European traders and missionaries increased protection and concessions. (Ch. 24)

Orientalism: A term coined by literary scholar Edward Said to describe the way Westerners described and misunderstood colonial subjects and cultures. (Ch. 24)

Ostpolitik: German for Chancellor Willy Brandt's new "Eastern policy"; West Germany's attempt in the 1970s to ease diplomatic tensions with East Germany, exemplifying the policies of détente. (Ch. 29)

Peace of Utrecht: A series of treaties, from 1713 to 1715, that ended the War of the Spanish Succession, ended French expansion in Europe, and marked the rise of the British Empire. (Ch. 15)

Peace of Westphalia: The name of a series of treaties that concluded the Thirty Years' War in 1648 and marked the end of large-scale religious violence in Europe. (Ch. 15)

perestroika: Economic restructuring and reform implemented by Premier Mikhail Gorbachev in the Soviet Union in 1985. (Ch. 29)

Peterloo Massacre: The army's violent suppression in 1819 of a protest that took place at Saint Peter's Fields in Manchester in reaction to the revision of the Corn Laws. (Ch. 21)

Petrograd Soviet: A huge, fluctuating mass meeting of two to three thousand workers, soldiers, and socialist intellectuals modeled on the revolutionary soviets (or councils) of 1905. (Ch. 25)

philosophes: A group of French intellectuals who proclaimed that they were bringing the light of knowledge to their fellow humans in the Age of Enlightenment. (Ch. 16)

Pietism: A Protestant revival movement in early-eighteenth-century Germany and Scandinavia that emphasized a warm and emotional religion, the priesthood of all believers, and the power of Christian rebirth in everyday affairs. (Ch. 18)

Popular Front: A short-lived New Deal–inspired alliance in France led by Léon Blum that encouraged the union movement and launched a far-reaching program of social reform. (Ch. 26)

postcolonial migration: The postwar movement of people from former colonies and the developing world into Europe. (Ch. 28)

postindustrial society: A society that relies on high-tech and service-oriented jobs for economic growth rather than heavy industry and manufacturing jobs. (Ch. 29)

privatization: The sale of state-managed industries such as transportation and communication networks to private owners; a key aspect of broader neoliberal economic reforms meant to control government spending, increase private profits, and foster economic growth, which were implemented in western Europe in response to the economic crisis of the 1970s. (Ch. 29)

professionalization: The process in which members of skilled trades and occupations established criteria for training and certification and banded together in professional organizations to defend their interests. (Ch. 22)

proletarianization: The transformation of large numbers of small peasant farmers into landless rural wage earners. (Ch. 17)

proletariat: The industrial working class who, according to Marx, were unfairly exploited by the profit-seeking bourgeoisie. (Ch. 21)

Protectorate: The English military dictatorship (1653–1658) established by Oliver Cromwell following the execution of Charles I. (Ch. 15)

Ptolemy's *Geography*: A second-century-c.e. work that synthesized the classical knowledge of geography and introduced the concepts of longitude and latitude. Reintroduced to Europeans about 1410 by Arab scholars, its ideas allowed cartographers to create more accurate maps. (Ch. 14)

public sphere: An idealized intellectual space that emerged in Europe during the Enlightenment, where the public came together to discuss important issues relating to society, economics, and politics. (Ch. 16)

Puritans: Members of a sixteenth- and seventeenth-century reform movement within the Church of England that advocated purifying it of Roman Catholic elements such as bishops, elaborate ceremonials, and wedding rings. (Ch. 15)

putting-out system: The eighteenth-century system of rural industry in which a merchant loaned raw materials to cottage workers, who processed them and returned the finished products to the merchant. (Ch. 17)

rationalism: A secular, critical way of thinking in which nothing was to be accepted on faith and everything was to be submitted to reason. (Ch. 16)

Realism: A literary movement that, in contrast to Romanticism, stressed the depiction of life as it actually was. (Ch. 22)

Realpolitik: A German term referring to political practice based on a careful calculation of real-world conditions rather than ethical ideals or ideological assumptions, employed by Bismarck and other nineteenth-century politicians. (Ch. 23)

Reform Bill of 1832: A major British political reform that increased the number of male voters by about 50 percent and gave political representation to new industrial areas. (Ch. 21)

Reichstag: The popularly elected lower house of government of the new German Empire after 1871. (Ch. 23)

Reign of Terror: The period from 1793 to 1794 during which Robespierre's Committee of Public Safety tried and executed thousands suspected of treason and a new revolutionary culture was imposed. (Ch. 19)

republicanism: A form of government in which there is no monarch and power rests in the hands of the people as exercised through elected representatives. (Ch. 15)

Risorgimento: The nineteenth-century struggle for Italian independence and unification. (Ch. 23)

Rocket: The name given to George Stephenson's effective locomotive that was first tested in 1829 on the Liverpool and Manchester Railway at 35 miles per hour. (Ch. 20)

rococo: A popular style in Europe in the eighteenth century, known for its soft pastels, ornate interiors, sentimental portraits, and starry-eyed lovers protected by hovering cupids. (Ch. 16)

Romanticism: An artistic movement at its height from about 1790 to the 1840s that was in part a revolt against classicism and the Enlightenment, characterized by a belief in emotional exuberance, unrestrained imagination, and spontaneity in both art and personal life. (Ch. 21)

Russian Revolution of 1905: A series of popular revolts and mass strikes that forced the tsarist government to grant moderate liberal reforms, including civil rights and a popularly elected parliament. (Ch. 23)

salon: Regular social gathering held by talented and rich Parisians in their homes, where philosophes and their followers met to discuss literature, science, and philosophy. (Ch. 16)

sans-culottes: The laboring poor of Paris, so called because the men wore trousers instead of the knee breeches of the aristocracy and middle class; the word came to refer to the militant radicals of the city. (Ch. 19)

Schlieffen Plan: Failed German plan calling for a lightning attack through neutral Belgium and a quick defeat of France before turning on Russia. (Ch. 25)

Second Industrial Revolution: The burst of technological innovation and science-driven industrialization that promoted strong economic growth in the last third of the nineteenth century. (Ch. 22)

second revolution: From 1792 to 1795, the second phase of the French Revolution, during which the fall of the French monarchy introduced a rapid radicalization of politics. (Ch. 19)

Second Vatican Council: A meeting of Catholic leaders convened from 1962 to 1965 that initiated a number of reforms, including the replacement of Latin with local languages in church services, designed to democratize the church and renew its appeal. (Ch. 29)

second-wave feminism: Label given to the revitalized feminist movement that emerged in the United States and western Europe in the late 1960s and 1970s. (Ch. 29)

sensationalism: The idea that all human ideas and thoughts are produced as a result of sensory impressions. (Ch. 16)

separate spheres: A gender division of labor with the wife at home as mother and homemaker and the husband as wage earner. (Chs. 20, 22)

shock therapy: Economic policies set in place in Russia and some former East Bloc countries after the collapse of communism, through which a quick turn to free markets was meant to speed economic growth. (Ch. 30)

Social Darwinism: A body of thought drawn from the ideas of Charles Darwin that applied the theory of biological evolution to human affairs and saw the human race as driven by an unending economic struggle that would determine the survival of the fittest. (Ch. 22)

socialism: A backlash against the emergence of individualism and the fragmentation of industrial society, and a move toward cooperation and a sense of community; the key ideas were economic planning, greater social equality, and state regulation of property. (Ch. 21)

Socialist Realism: Artistic movement that followed the dictates of Communist ideals, enforced by state control in the Soviet Union and East Bloc countries in the 1950s and 1960s. (Ch. 28)

Solidarity: Independent Polish trade union that worked for workers' rights and political reform throughout the 1980s. (Ch. 29)

South African (Boer) War: Conflict in 1899–1902 in which British troops defeated rebellious Afrikaners, ancestors of Dutch colonialists, leading to consolidation of South African territories. (Ch. 24)

spinning jenny: A simple, inexpensive, hand-powered spinning machine created by James Hargreaves in 1765. (Ch. 20)

stadholder: The executive officer in each of the United Provinces of the Netherlands, a position often held by the princes of Orange. (Ch. 15)

stagflation: Term coined in the early 1980s to describe the combination of low growth and high inflation that led to a worldwide recession. (Ch. 29)

Stalinism: The name given to the Communist system in the Soviet Union during the rule of Joseph Stalin. (Ch. 27)

steam engines: A breakthrough invention by Thomas Savery in 1698 and Thomas Newcomen in 1705 that burned coal to produce steam, which was then used to operate a pump; the early models were superseded by James Watt's more efficient steam engine, patented in 1769. (Ch. 20)

stream-of-consciousness technique: A literary technique, found in works by Virginia Woolf, James Joyce, and others, that uses interior monologue — a character's thoughts and feelings as they occur — to explore the human psyche. (Ch. 26)

suffrage movement: A militant movement for women's right to vote led by middle-class British women, which exemplified broader international campaigns for women's political rights around 1900. (Ch. 23)

sultan: The ruler of the Ottoman Empire; he owned all the agricultural land of the empire and was served by an army and bureaucracy composed of highly trained slaves. (Ch. 15)

sweated industries: Poorly paid handicraft production, often carried out by married women paid by the piece and working at home. (Ch. 22)

Tanzimat: A set of reforms designed to remake the Ottoman Empire on a western European model. (Ch. 23)

tariff protection: A government's way of supporting and aiding its own economy by laying high taxes on imported goods from other countries, as when the French responded to cheaper British goods flooding their country by imposing high tariffs on some imported products. (Ch. 20)

Test Act: Legislation passed by the English Parliament in 1673 to secure the position of the Anglican Church by stripping Puritans, Catholics, and other dissenters of the right to vote, preach, assemble, hold public office, and teach at or attend the universities. (Ch. 15)

theory of special relativity: Albert Einstein's theory that time and space are relative to the observer and that only the speed of light remains constant. (Ch. 26)

Thermidorian reaction: A reaction to the violence of the Reign of Terror in 1794, resulting in the execution of Robespierre and the loosening of economic controls. (Ch. 19)

thermodynamics: A branch of physics built on Newton's laws of mechanics that investigated the relationship between heat and mechanical energy. (Ch. 22)

total war: A war in which distinctions between the soldiers on the battlefield and civilians at home are blurred, and where massive government intervention in society and the economy ensures support for the war effort. (Ch. 25)

totalitarianism: A radical dictatorship that exercises "total claims" over the beliefs and behavior of its citizens by taking control of the economic, social, intellectual, and cultural aspects of society. (Ch. 27)

transatlantic slave trade: The forced migration of Africans across the Atlantic for slave labor on plantations and in other industries; the trade reached its peak in the eighteenth century and ultimately involved more than 12 million Africans. (Ch. 17)

Treaty of Brest-Litovsk: Peace treaty signed in March 1918 between the Central Powers and Russia that ended Russian participation in World War I and ceded territories containing a third of the Russian Empire's population to the Central Powers. (Ch. 25)

Treaty of Paris: The treaty that ended the Seven Years' War in Europe and the colonies in 1763, and ratified British victory on all colonial fronts. (Ch. 17)

Treaty of Tordesillas: A 1494 treaty that settled competing claims to newly discovered Atlantic territories by giving Spain everything to the west of an imaginary line drawn down the Atlantic and giving Portugal everything to the east. (Ch. 14)

Treaty of Versailles: The 1919 peace settlement that ended war between Germany and the Allied powers. (Ch. 25)

trench warfare: A type of fighting used in World War I behind rows of trenches, mines, and barbed wire; the cost in lives was staggering and the gains in territory minimal. (Ch. 25)

Triple Alliance: The alliance of Austria, Germany, and Italy. Italy left the alliance when war broke out in 1914 on the grounds that Austria had launched a war of aggression. (Ch. 25)

Triple Entente: The alliance of Great Britain, France, and Russia prior to and during the First World War. (Ch. 25)

Truman Doctrine: America's policy geared to containing communism to those countries already under Soviet control. (Ch. 28)

utilitarianism: The idea of Jeremy Bentham that social policies should promote the "greatest good for the greatest number." (Ch. 22)

Velvet Revolution: The term given to the relatively peaceful overthrow of communism in Czechoslovakia; the label came to signify the collapse of the East Bloc in general in 1989 to 1990. (Ch. 29)

viceroyalties: The name for the four administrative units of Spanish possessions in the Americas: New Spain, Peru, New Granada, and La Plata. (Ch. 14)

War Communism: The application of centralized state control during the Russian civil war, in which the Bolsheviks seized grain from peasants, introduced rationing, nationalized all banks and industry, and required strict workplace discipline. (Ch. 25)

war guilt clause: An article in the Treaty of Versailles that declared that Germany (with Austria) was solely responsible for the war and had to pay reparations equal to all civilian damages caused by the fighting. (Ch. 25)

war on terror: American policy under President George W. Bush to fight global terrorism in all its forms. (Ch. 30)

Warsaw Pact: Soviet-backed military alliance of East Bloc Communist countries in Europe. (Ch. 28)

water frame: A spinning machine created by Richard Arkwright that had a capacity of several hundred spindles and used waterpower; it therefore required a larger and more specialized mill—a factory. (Ch. 20)

wet-nursing: A widespread and flourishing business in the eighteenth century in which women were paid to breast-feed other women's babies. (Ch. 18)

white man's burden: The idea that Europeans could and should civilize more primitive nonwhite peoples and that imperialism would eventually provide nonwhites with modern achievements and higher standards of living. (Ch. 24)

Works Progress Administration (WPA): An American government agency, designed as a massive public jobs program, established in 1935 as part of Roosevelt's New Deal. (Ch. 26)

World Trade Organization (WTO): A powerful supranational financial institution that sets trade and tariff agreements for over 150 member countries and so helps manage a large percentage of the world's import-export policies. Like the IMF and the World Bank, the WTO promotes neoliberal policies around the world. (Ch. 30)

Young Turks: Fervent patriots who seized power in a 1908 coup in the Ottoman Empire, forcing the conservative sultan to implement reforms. (Ch. 23)

Zionism: A movement dedicated to combatting anti-Semitism in Europe by building a Jewish national homeland in Palestine, started by Theodor Herzl. (Ch. 23)

Index

A Note about the Index: Names of individuals appear in boldface. Letters in parentheses following pages refer to the following: *(i)* illustrations, including photographs and charts; *(m)* maps

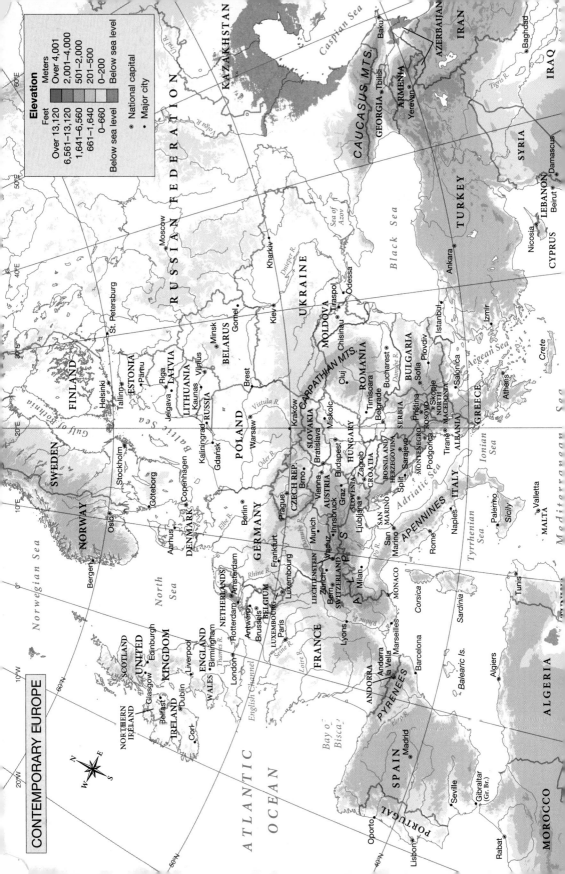

CONTEMPORARY EUROPE

Elevation

Feet	Meters
Over 13,120	Over 4,001
6,561–13,120	2,001–4,000
1,641–6,560	501–2,000
661–1,640	201–500
0–660	0–200
Below sea level	Below sea level

⊛ National capital
• Major city

ATLANTIC OCEAN

Norwegian Sea

North Sea

English Channel

Bay of Biscay

Mediterranean Sea

Tyrrhenian Sea

Adriatic Sea

Ionian Sea

Aegean Sea

Black Sea

Caspian Sea

Sea of Azov

Gulf of Bothnia

Baltic Sea

NORWAY — Bergen, Oslo

SWEDEN — Göteborg, Stockholm

FINLAND — Helsinki

RUSSIAN FEDERATION — Moscow, St. Petersburg

ESTONIA — Tallinn, Pärnu

LATVIA — Riga, Jelgava

LITHUANIA — Vilnius, Kaunas

RUSSIA — Kaliningrad

BELARUS — Minsk, Gomel, Brest

UKRAINE — Kiev, Kharkiv, Odessa

MOLDOVA — Chisinau, Tiraspol

POLAND — Warsaw, Gdańsk, Kraków

DENMARK — Copenhagen, Aarhus

UNITED KINGDOM — London, Birmingham, Liverpool, Edinburgh, Glasgow

SCOTLAND

ENGLAND

WALES

NORTHERN IRELAND — Belfast

IRELAND — Dublin, Cork

NETHERLANDS — Amsterdam, Rotterdam

BELGIUM — Brussels, Antwerp

LUXEMBOURG — Luxembourg

GERMANY — Berlin, Frankfurt, Munich

FRANCE — Paris, Lyons, Marseilles

SWITZERLAND — Bern, Zürich

LIECHTENSTEIN — Vaduz

AUSTRIA — Vienna, Graz, Innsbruck

CZECH REP. — Prague, Brno

SLOVAKIA — Bratislava

HUNGARY — Budapest

SLOVENIA — Ljubljana

CROATIA — Zagreb, Split

BOSNIA AND HERZEGOVINA — Sarajevo

SERBIA — Belgrade

MONTENEGRO — Podgorica

KOSOVO — Pristina

NORTH MACEDONIA — Skopje

ALBANIA — Tirana

ROMANIA — Bucharest, Cluj, Timisoara

BULGARIA — Sofia, Plovdiv

GREECE — Athens, Salonica

ITALY — Rome, Naples, Milan

SAN MARINO — San Marino

MONACO

ANDORRA — Andorra la Vella

SPAIN — Madrid, Barcelona, Seville

PORTUGAL — Lisbon, Oporto

MALTA — Valletta

TURKEY — Ankara, Istanbul, Izmir

GEORGIA — Tbilisi

ARMENIA — Yerevan

AZERBAIJAN — Baku

CYPRUS — Nicosia

LEBANON — Beirut

SYRIA — Damascus

IRAQ — Baghdad

IRAN

KAZAKHSTAN

MOROCCO — Rabat

ALGERIA — Algiers

Tunis

Gibraltar (Gr. Br.)

ALPS

PYRENEES

APENNINES

CARPATHIAN MTS.

CAUCASUS MTS.

Corsica

Sardinia

Sicily

Crete

Balearic Is.

Volga R.

Ural R.

Dnieper R.

Danube R.

Vistula R.

Oder R.

Elbe R.

Rhine R.

Seine R.

Loire R.

Rhône R.

Po R.

Thames R.

Tigris R.

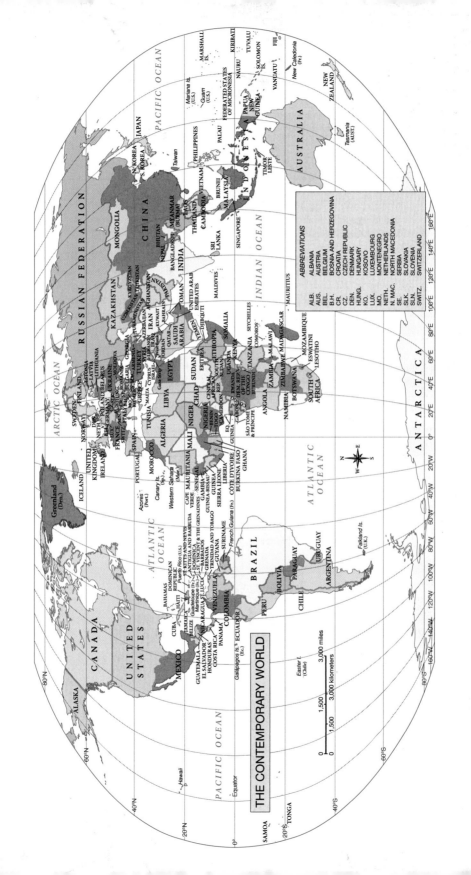

THE CONTEMPORARY WORLD

About the Authors

Merry E. Wiesner-Hanks (Ph.D., University of Wisconsin–Madison) taught first at Augustana College in Illinois, and from 1985 to 2018 at the University of Wisconsin–Milwaukee, where she is now Distinguished Professor of History emerita. She is the Senior Editor of the *Sixteenth Century Journal,* one of the editors of the *Journal of Global History,* and the author or editor of more than thirty books, including *A Concise History of the World.* From 2017 to 2019 she served as the president of the World History Association.

Clare Haru Crowston (Ph.D., Cornell University) teaches at the University of Illinois, where she is currently Professor of history and department chair. She is the author of *Credit, Fashion, Sex: Economies of Regard in Old Regime France* and *Fabricating Women: The Seamstresses of Old Regime France, 1675–1791,* which won the Berkshire and Hagley Prizes. She edited two special issues of the *Journal of Women's History,* has published numerous journal articles and reviews, and is a past president of the Society for French Historical Studies.

Joe Perry (Ph.D., University of Illinois at Urbana-Champaign) is Associate Professor of modern German and European history at Georgia State University. He has published numerous articles and is the author of *Christmas in Germany: A Cultural History* (2010). His current research interests focus on issues of consumption, gender, and popular culture in West Germany and Western Europe after World War II.

John P. McKay (Ph.D., University of California, Berkeley) is professor emeritus at the University of Illinois. He has written or edited numerous works, including the Herbert Baxter Adams Prize–winning book *Pioneers for Profit: Foreign Entrepreneurship and Russian Industrialization, 1885–1913.*